◆◆◆◆◆◆

ORGANIZATIONAL BEHAVIOR

A Management Challenge

Second Edition

◆◆◆◆◆◆

ORGANIZATIONAL BEHAVIOR

A Management Challenge

Second Edition

Gregory B. Northcraft
University of Arizona

Margaret A. Neale
Northwestern University

The Dryden Press
Harcourt Brace College Publishers

Fort Worth Philadelphia San Diego New York
Orlando Austin San Antonio Toronto Montreal
London Sydney Tokyo

Publisher	Liz Widdicombe
Acquisitions Editor	Ruth Rominger
Marketing Manager	Lise Johnson
Developmental Editor	Lisa Toftemark Rittby
Text Designer	Brian Salisbury
Copy Editor	Karen Carriere
Indexer	Joyce Teague
Compositor	GTS Graphics, Inc., Los Angeles
Production Services	Seaside Publishing Services, San Diego
Text Type	Janson and Stone Sans
Cover Image	Vasily Kandinsky, *Graceful Ascent*, March 1934, Solomon R. Guggenheim Museum, New York, Photo: David Heald copyright The Solomon R. Guggenheim Foundation, New York FN45.970.

Address for Editorial Correspondence
The Dryden Press, 301 Commerce Street, Suite 3700, Fort Worth, TX 76102

Address for Orders
The Dryden Press, 627 Sea Harbor Drive, Orlando, FL 32887
1-800-782-4479, or 1-800-433-0001 (in Florida)

ISBN: 0-03-074611-6

Library of Congress Catalog Number: 97-072827

Printed in the United States of America

3 4 5 6 7 8 0 1 2   048   9 8 7 6 5 4 3 2 1

The Dryden Press
Harcourt Brace College Publishers

◆◆◆◆◆◆

To our parents, for their critical contributions
in helping us become what we are today; and
to Al, Terri, C.J., Galen, and Natasha,
for their continuing, consistent, and enthusiastic
support of our efforts and us.

The Dryden Press Series in Management

Anthony, Perrewe, and Kacmar
Strategic Human Resource Management

Bartlett
*Cases in Strategic Management
for Business*

Bedeian
Management
Third Edition

Bedeian and Zammuto
Organizations: Theory and Design

Bereman and Lengnick-Hall
*Compensation Decision Making:
A Computer-Based Approach*

Boone and Kurtz
Contemporary Business
Seventh Edition

Bowman and Branchaw
Business Report Writing
Second Edition

Bracker, Montanari, and Morgan
Cases in Strategic Management

Calvasina and Barton
*Chopstick Company: A Business
Simulation*

Costin
Readings in Total Quality Management

Czinkota, Ronkainen, and Moffett
International Business
Third Edition

Daft
Management
Third Edition

Eckert, Ryan, and Ray
Small Business: An Entrepreneur's Plan
Third Edition

Etienne-Hamilton
*Operations Strategies for Competitive
Advantage: Text and Cases*

Foegen
Business Planning Guide
Second Edition

Gaither
Production and Operations Management
Sixth Edition

Gatewood and Harris
Human Resource Selection
Third Edition

Gold
*Exploring Organizational Behavior:
Readings, Cases, Experiences*

Greenhaus
Career Management
Second Edition

Harris and DeSimone
Human Resource Development

Higgins and Vincze
Strategic Management: Text and Cases
Fifth Edition

Hills, Bergman and Scarpello
Compensation Decision Making
Second Edition

Hodgetts
*Management: Theory, Process,
and Practice*

Hodgetts
Modern Human Relations at Work
Fifth Edition

Hodgetts and Kroeck
*Personnel and Human Resource
Management*

Hodgetts and Kuratko
Effective Small Business Management
Fourth Edition

Hodgetts and Kuratko
Management
Third Edition

Holley and Jennings
The Labor Relations Process
Fifth Edition

Huseman, Lahiff, and Penrose
*Business Communication:
Strategies and Skills*
Fourth Edition

Jauch and Coltrin
*The Managerial Experience:
Cases and Exercises*
Sixth Edition

Kemper
Experiencing Strategic Management

Kuehl and Lambing
*Small Business: Planning and
Management*
Third Edition

Kuratko and Hodgetts
*Entrepreneurship:
A Contemporary Approach*
Second Edition

Kuratko and Welch
Entrepreneurial Strategies: Text and Cases

Lewis
Io Enterprises Simulation

Luthans and Hodgetts
Business
Second Edition

McMullen and Long
*Developing New Ventures:
The Entrepreneurial Option*

Matsuura
International Business: A New Era

Mauser
American Business: An Introduction
Sixth Edition

Montanari, Morgan, and Bracker
*Strategic Management:
A Choice Approach*

Northcraft and Neale
*Organizational Behavior:
A Management Challenge*
Second Edition

Penderghast
Entrepreneurial Simulation Program

Sandburg
Career Design Software

Sawyer
*Business Policy and Strategic Manage-
ment: Planning, Strategy, and Action*

Schoderbek
Management
Second Edition

Schwartz
*Introduction to Management: Principles,
Practices, and Processes*
Second Edition

Varner
Contemporary Business Report Writing

Vecchio
Organizational Behavior
Second Edition

Walton
Corporate Encounters: Law, Ethics, and the Business Environment

Wolford and Vanneman
Business Communication

Wolters and Holley
Labor Relations: An Experiential and Case Approach

Zikmund
Business Research Methods
Third Edition

The Harcourt Brace College Outline Series

Pentico
Management Science

Pierson
Introduction to Business Information Systems

Sigband
Business Communication

◆◆◆◆◆◆

PREFACE

A book, like a large corporation, can't just be thrown together—it must be *organized*. And as with the organization of a large corporation, the organization of a book says something about the people who created it, what they believe is important, and what they are trying to accomplish. This book is organized around two themes: a subtle undercurrent and an explicit focus.

The subtle undercurrent of this book is its emphasis on understanding organizational behavior by understanding what goes on in the minds of managers and employees when they interact in organizations. Organization is, after all, in the eye of the beholder, and the real challenge of organizational behavior lies in managing the uncertainty, conflict, and complexities of organizational life that we each experience. This undercurrent probably reflects the rise of social cognition in the 1970s and 1980s as a central intellectual force in our parent fields of social psychology and organizational behavior.

The explicit focus of this book is making the wisdom and insights of organizational behavior research not just available but *accessible*—easy to learn and easy to apply—for students. Accessibility of material is important because it's what makes education both a rewarding activity for students and a manageable task for instructors. Naturally, this means that this book includes many special features that help both the student and the instructor. But accessibility, like quality, cannot be added on; it must be built in. So the text of this book has been written with accessibility in mind.

To that end, this book (while certainly comprehensive in coverage) is not an encyclopedia of organizational behavior. The table of contents is not a laundry list of what's out there in the field, nor are the individual chapters laundry lists within major topics. Instead, we have made a conscious attempt to build a book with a conceptual "flow." Instead of eighteen distinct mini-books on organizational behavior, chapters and topics are carefully sequenced and integrated to build on each other. Further, there are no "special topics" that end up as stand-alone chapters; instead, the presentation of this material has been integrated into the mainstream of organizational behavior theory. Stress, for instance, is presented in the context of organizational conflict. And culture and socialization are presented as part and parcel of organizational entry. A particularly good example of this integration is the handling of international issues; they are integrated within each chapter of the book.

An important issue in making the wisdom and insights or organizational behavior accessible to students is the delicate marriage of scholarly explication and concrete application. Alone, neither is particularly useful. We have merged these tasks by continually interweaving the presentation of concepts and theory with both formal and informal examples. The formal examples are drawn from traditional work organizations; the informal examples are taken from non-work organizations such as clubs, study groups, and even families, with which students are particularly familiar. The book's many annotated color photographs capture slices of organizational life to enhance the balance of theory and practice.

ORGANIZATION OF THE TEXT ◆◆◆◆◆◆

The five parts of the book also have a structure and logic. Part One defines the challenge of managing behavior in organizations and reviews past attempts to meet this challenge. Part One represents both the core of the book and the core of the field. It frames in the mind of the student an answer to the question, "Why study organizational behavior?" Parts Two and Three provide foundation knowledge for meeting the challenge of organizational behavior. For most employees, the individuals and small groups they interact with each day *are* their organization, so the foundation knowledge of organizational behavior is Part Two, "Individual Behavior," and Part Three, "Behavior in Groups." Part Four provides explicit integrated applications of this foundation knowledge to three primary issues in managing behavior in organizations: getting employees into organizations (Organizational Entry), putting them to work (Job Design), and helping them succeed (Managing for Performance). Finally, Part Five examines the larger context of organizational behavior. We all know that somewhere beyond these day-to-day interactions of everyday work life is a larger sense of organizations, including the environment, the structure of organizations, and the changes that organizations must endure. These are the focus of Part Five.

SPECIAL FEATURES ◆◆◆◆◆◆

Our goal of making the wisdom and insights of organizational behavior more accessible to students has been aided by the full-color photos and artwork provided in the text. The captions that accompany both the photos and the figures create a parallel text—a second chance for the book to teach and the student to learn. The photos and figures also provide vivid and concrete reference for the major concepts presented in the text.

"Focus On" Boxed Items

Formal examples of organizational behavior are presented in "FOCUS ON" boxed features sprinkled throughout the text and the brief cases that begin each chapter. These examples are drawn from a broad spectrum of both international and U.S. firms, the private and public sectors, and large and small organizations. The variety of examples provided encourages the student to see and understand the pervasiveness of organizational behavior in everyday life. Every chapter contains an "INTERNATIONAL FOCUS ON" boxed item, which should help ingrain in students an appreciation for the global marketplace in which they will be working.

| **End-of-Chapter Learning Aids** | "On Your Own" experiential exercises appear at the end of each chapter. These exercises are designed to be completed individually by students and can also be used as the basis for class discussion. The exercises allow students to gain knowledge while reflecting on their own aptitudes and abilities. |

"The Manager's Memo" represents a different slant on the typical end-of-chapter case and is another example of the book's integration. Each memo presents a management problem that the student must solve by applying concepts learned in the chapter. The cases are designed to be used either as discussion material or as assignments in which students respond to the memo in writing.

Under the heading "If You Want to Know More," each chapter contains a list of classic and contemporary readings on chapter topics. This list of readings can provide extra stimulation for ambitious students, or supplementary paper assignments, or even a way to get a better handle on "The Manager's Memo" closing case.

The **Discussion Questions** can be used as a basis for discussion or as a chance for students to test their learning. An extensive glossary of **Key Terms** is located at the end of the book.

Again, in keeping with the explicit focus of the book, each part ends with both a group exercise and a comprehensive case. The part-closing exercises have been chosen for their appropriateness regardless of class size. These part-closing cases and exercises further encourage students to integrate their understanding and application of material across the chapters of each part.

| **Special Chapters** | There are several unique chapters in this book. Chapter 2, "Facing the Challenge: Historical Perspectives," and Chapter 15, "Technology," represent the old and the new in organizational behavior. The history of organizational behavior is useful for understanding what has happened. Understanding technology in organizational behavior will be useful for understanding the future. Because of the book's emphasis on the importance of cognitions, expanded coverage has been provided on decision-making processes: Chapter 5, "Individual Decision Making," and Chapter 9, "Group Decision Making." |

Many chapters have undergone extensive revision for this second edition. Chapter 3 is now a "foundations of individual behavior" chapter and includes coverage of attitudes and personality, as well as processes of perception. The coverage of ethics as an issue in individual decision making has been enhanced in Chapter 5 to reflect its growing relevance to the practice of everyday business. Chapter 6 now features more material on stress in organizations. The coverage of communication processes in organizations has been dramatically increased and moved to Chapter 7, where it becomes one of the foundations for understanding behavior in groups. Chapter 8 now brings together the book's material on power, politics, and influence all in the same chapter. The focus of Chapter 12 has been modified to provide a greater emphasis on the use of teams in job design. Finally, Chapter 18 for this edition has been entirely devoted to examining issues concerning disabilities, sexual preference, and culture, gender, and ethnic diversity in the workplace.

ANCILLARY PACKAGE

A comprehensive set of ancillaries for students and instructors has been prepared to accompany *Organizational Behavior: A Management Challenge*, Second Edition.

For the Student

A *Study Guide/Exercise Manual*, prepared and revised by Barry A. Gold of Pace University, includes a detailed summary, key-terms quiz, and a self-help test of multiple choice and true/false questions for each chapter. Additionally, each chapter concludes with two individual experiential exercises.

For the Instructor

The following items are available for adopters.

Instructor's Manual   The *Instructor's Manual*, revised and reorganized by Terri L. Griffith of the University of Arizona, contains detailed chapter outlines, suggested answers to the discussion questions and "The Manager's Memo" cases, and instructions for using the "On Your Own" exercises. The manual includes one additional case and group exercise for each part of the book. A special topic also has been identified for each chapter and supplementary lecture material developed by Debra Arvanites at Villanova University, Dennis Duchon at the University of Texas at San Antonio and Bruce Kemelgor at the University of Louisville. A special feature of the manual is the inclusion of teaching notes and suggested class discussion questions for each of the transparency acetates.

Teaching Tools and Video Teaching Notes   In response to instructors' requests for opportunities to share new teaching tips with colleagues, Dryden is publishing numerous contributions of proven teaching techniques and ideas from instructors around the country. This new supplement includes exercises, cases, role plays, group and individual assignments, and additional lecture topics to enhance the teaching and learning experience. In addition, teaching notes on how to use the videos with the text and cases are provided for the instructor.

Test Bank   The *Test Bank*, written by Calvin Kellogg of The University of Mississippi and Rebecca J. Oatsvall of Meredith College, contains multiple choice questions, true/false items, and essay questions for each chapter. Each question is identified as either factual or application, its level of difficulty is indicated, and text page where the material is covered is given. A computerized version of the *Test Bank* is available in both IBM and Macintosh formats.

Video Package   A series of videos demonstrating individual and group organizational behavior concepts in simulated work environments is available to adopters of this text. Video teaching notes for the instructor can be found in *Teaching Tools*. These include teaching notes on how to use the videos with the text and cases.

Transparency Acetates   A total of more than 90 original color acetates that further enhance the text material in a visual format have been developed. Teaching notes for each of the acetates are included in the *Instructor's Manual*.

Optional Supplements	There is now a computer-assisted simulation for practicing people skills. *Io Enterprises: A Microcomputer Simulation*, by Chad T. Lewis and Philip C. Lewis of Gemini Innovations, Joseph E. Garcia of Western Washington University, and Robert A. Boudreau of the University of Lethbridge, is an optional part of the *Organizational Behavior: A Management Challenge* package. In this user-friendly simulation, students serve as members of a management team overseeing titanium mining operations on Io, the fifth moon of Jupiter, in the year 2086. During a simulated year on Io, management teams contend with various challenges and opportunities requiring the use of people skills. Increasing the productivity and profits of the mine requires making correct human resources decisions.

Io Enterprises allows professors to tailor scenarios involving application of people skills to the contents of a specific course or seminar. Information from team decision forms is entered into the Io Enterprises computer program by the instructor or his or her designate and management reports and scenarios are then generated for the next round of decisions. Students practice people skills as they make decisions for their mine and as they participate as part of a twenty-first century management team. The team with the highest profit at the end of the simulation year is declared the winner.

Exploring Organizational Behavior, by Barry A. Gold of Pace University, is a new supplemental readings, cases and exercises book, with thirty-six cutting-edge readings by leading scholars in organizational behavior and management, twelve contemporary cases and twelve classroom experiences. It may be used in conjunction with this text to provide students with additional sources and experiences for further exploring topics introduced throughout the second edition.

ACKNOWLEDGMENTS

We subtitled this book "A Management Challenge" because we believe that uncertainty, conflict, and complexity make managing behavior in organizations a difficult—even potentially hazardous—enterpirse. The same could be said for writing a book on this topic.

Not surprisingly, we have been reminded many times in the past two years that a major undertaking on this scale requires the coordination and cooperation of a great many people. We would like to acknowledge their efforts and thank them for their contributions. We owe a great debt to our project team at The Dryden Press for their hard work on this second edition. We are also indebted to our colleagues, students, and administrators in the Department of Management and Policy at the University of Arizona, and in the Department of Organization Behavior at the J. L. Kellogg Graduate School of Management at Northwestern University for gamely indulging our efforts.

We also are indebted to those active participants in this project whose thoughtful feedback provided through focus groups and manuscript reviews helped raise our own understanding of organizational behavior to new heights, including:

Royce Abrahamson
Southwest Texas State University

Aaron Andreasan
University of Montana

William P. Bottom
Washington University

Brian Boyd
University of Southern California

Jack W. Brittain
University of Texas at Dallas

Gene E. Burton
California State University, Fresno

Jennifer A. Chatman
Northwestern University

Faye Crosby
Smith College

Arthur L. Darrow
Bowling Green State University

Dennis L. Dossett
University of Missouri, St. Louis

Dennis Duchon
University of Texas, San Antonio

Dail Fields
Georgia Institute of Technology

Robert Fisher
Henderson State University

Cynthia V. Fukami
University of Denver

Bruce Garrison
Houston Baptist University

Barry A. Gold
Pace University

David B. Greenberger
Ohio State University

Terri L. Griffith
University of Arizona

Steven L. Grover
Indiana University

Scott Hammond
Brigham Young University

Eileen A. Hogan
George Mason University

John Hollenbeck
Michigan State University

Ralph Katerberg
University of Cincinnati

Calvin Kellogg
The University of Mississippi

Bruce Kemelgor
University of Louisville

Mary Kernan
Kent State University

David L. Luechauer
Miami University

Jeff Mello
Northeastern University

Herff Moore
University of Central Arkansas

Edward J. Morrison
University of Colorado, Boulder

Brian Neihoff
Kansas State University

Suzyn Ornstein
Suffolk University

Dennis Patzig
James Madison University

Karen Paul
Bowling Green State University

Bob Renn
Georgia State University

Peter Richardson
Southwest Missouri State University

Janice Rouiller
University of Maryland

Shiori Sakamoto
California State Polytechnic University

Sue Schafer
North Texas State University

Jane Siebler
Oregon State University

Ronald R. Sims
College of William and Mary

Sim B. Sitkin
University of Texas at Austin

Chester S. Spell
Georgia Institute of Technology

Linda K. Trevino
Pennsylvania State University

Robert J. Vandenberg
Georgia State University

Kelly A. Vaverek
Texas Christian University

There is an old saying that "Life is a great adventure—or nothing." For us, this book has been a great adventure in writing. We trust it also proves to be a great adventure in learning for students and instructors.

Gregory B. Northcraft
Margaret A. Neale

September 1993

◆◆◆◆◆◆

ABOUT THE AUTHORS

Gregory B. Northcraft is Professor of Management and Policy at the Karl Eller Graduate School of Management at the University of Arizona. He received bachelor's degrees in psychology and Russian language and literature from Dartmouth College, and in psychology and philosophy from Oxford University. Professor Northcraft received his master's degree and Ph.D. in social psychology from Stanford University. His major research interests include behavioral decision theory, conflict management, employee motivation, and job design, particularly in high-technology manufacturing settings. Professor Northcraft has authored or coauthored more than 40 articles and book chapters on these topics and has conducted management development programs in conflict management, human resource management, negotiation, and the management of change. Professor Northcraft also has interned for several major federal agencies and has held visiting professorships at the Amos Tuck School of Business Administration (Dartmouth College), the Guangzhou Institute of Foreign Trade (People's Republic of China), the J. L. Kellogg Graduate School of Management (Northwestern University), the Sasin Graduate Institute of Business Administration (Thailand), the University of National and World Economics (Bulgaria), and Janus Pannonius University (Hungary).

Margaret A. Neale is J. L. Kellogg Distinguished Professor of Dispute Resolution and Organization, Professor of Organization Behavior at the J. L. Kellogg Graduate School of Management at Northwestern University. She received her bachelor's degree in pharmacy from Northeast Louisiana University, her master's degrees from the Medical College of Virginia and Virginia Commonwealth University, and her Ph.D. in business administration from the University of Texas. Prior to her joining the faculty at Northwestern University, Professor Neale was on the faculty of the Karl Eller Graduate School of Management at the University of Arizona. Professor Neale's major research interests include bargaining and negotiation, third-party dispute intervention, behavioral decision theory, performance appraisal, and organizational justice. She is the author of more than 30 articles on these topics and is a coauthor with Max H. Bazerman of two books on negotiation, *Negotiating Rationally* and *Cognition and Rationality in Negotiation*. She has conducted executive seminars and management development programs throughout the United States and abroad for public agencies, trade associations, small businesses, and *Fortune* 500 corporations in the areas of negotiating skills, performance appraisal systems, employee commitment, work force demographics, and employee participation.

Brief Contents

◆◆◆◆◆◆

CONTENTS

Part Two   INDIVIDUAL BEHAVIOR   63

Part Three BEHAVIOR IN GROUPS 229

Chapter 7 ▶ Groups and Communication 230

Part Four   MANAGING FOR PERFORMANCE   387

Chapter 11   ▶ Organizational Entry and Socialization   388

Part Five THE LARGER CONTEXT OF ORGANIZATIONAL BEHAVIOR   497

Chapter 14 ▶ The Environment   498

1

◆◆◆◆◆◆

ORGANIZATIONAL BEHAVIOR: A MANAGEMENT CHALLENGE

Taking American Management by Storm

◆◆◆◆◆◆

The victory in the Persian Gulf War was marvelous for the United States and its allies, but it has turned out to be a bit of a disappointment for America's corporate bosses. Every morning during the Gulf War, you could practically hear corporate executives, managers, and supervisors looking in the mirror and moaning, "Why can't *I* be more like General Schwarzkopf?" Schwarzkopf, the U.S. commander of Operation Desert Storm, was tough but caring, decisive, upfront, willing to give credit to subordinates, and a genius at marshaling resources to attack a goal.

American executives could learn lots of lessons from the general's style of management. At the University of Texas, management professor James Fredrickson makes his students review a tape of Schwarzkopf's victory briefing as an example of boss as symbol.

Already, some civilian managers are embracing the model. Managers won't miss a chance to remind their bosses how Schwarzkopf was given a mission by then President Bush and the Joint Chiefs and then left relatively free to carry it out. While the military remains hierarchical, experts say, it has given greater decision-making power to the lower ranks. The corporate world has long talked about granting "empowerment" to members of the rank and file, but often such promises amount to nothing more than lip service.

Although most military types aren't renowned for being open and caring, Schwarzkopf built enormous loyalty by using such techniques as giving generous credit to subordinates, displaying concern for the safety of his troops, and mingling with them. (When was the last time you saw a CEO eat lunch in the company cafeteria?) "You never got the feeling that he was with the troops simply for a photo opportunity," says Wess Roberts, author of the 1989 management best-seller, *The Leadership Secrets of Attila the Hun.*

Source: Adapted from L. Reibstein, "The Gulf School of Management," *Newsweek*, April 1, 1991, 34–38. © 1991 Newsweek, Inc. All rights reserved. Reprinted with permission.

INTRODUCTION   ◆◆◆◆◆◆

This book is about organizational behavior. **Organizational behavior** is the description and explanation of how people behave in organizations.

Any book about organizational behavior is necessarily a book about people. People think and plan. Some people work hard and succeed, while others get discouraged, give up, and fail. And people dream. People have built monuments to civilization, including the tall buildings that dominate our cities' skylines, the factories that supply our daily needs and desires, and the libraries that house civilization's accumulated knowledge for future generations. People even have built the spaceships that carried astronauts to the moon and have successfully waged wars in faraway lands.

None of these achievements, however, is the product of one person. In fact, none of these achievements would have been possible if only one person had worked toward their completion. Instead, these achievements are made possible because people work together.

When people come together to combine their talents and efforts, they form **organizations.** A good working definition for the word *organization* is provided by J. D. Mooney in his book, *The Principles of Organization:*

> Organization is the form of every human association for the attainment of a common purpose . . . the framework of every group moving toward a common objective . . . It refers to the complete body, with all its correlated functions . . . It refers to the coordination of all these [functions] as they cooperate for the common purpose.[1]

Mooney emphasized that organizations are "pure process," not buildings or machines or anything tangible. Organizations instead are practices, procedures, and relationships entered into to coordinate human talents and efforts toward common goals. This book is also about organizations.

Our lives are taken up participating in an endless series of organizations including families, schools, clubs, and the firms and corporations for which we work. Some organizations (like Schwarzkopf's army) succeed in combining the talents and efforts of their members to produce major accomplishments (like defeating Iraq's invasion of Kuwait) while other organizations never produce much of anything. A quick scan of the daily newspaper reveals both the latest discoveries and breakthroughs achieved by organizations *and* the latest fiascoes and bankruptcies. Some workers are fiercely loyal to and proud of the organizations to which they belong. Some organizations are plagued by high absenteeism, turnover, and even sabotage from within. Why are some organizations successful while others fail? This is the challenge of understanding how and why people work together in organizations. This is the challenge of organizational behavior.

Before discussing the specifics of how and why people behave the ways they do in organizations, it is important to have an overall sense of behavior in organizations. In this opening chapter, we will contrast two approaches to understanding behavior in organizations. Our first approach comes from the field of management. **Management** is a *prescriptive* view of behavior in organizations. The field of management prescribes what organizations are supposed to accom-

---

[1]J. D. Mooney, *The Principles of Organization* (New York: Harper and Brothers, 1939), 3.

plish and how they are supposed to accomplish it. Our second approach to understanding behavior in organizations is a *descriptive* view; it describes how people actually behave in organizations. This descriptive view provides an introduction to the field of organizational behavior.

Management and organizational behavior are not alternative views of behavior in organizations. Rather, they are *complementary*. In order for an organization to accomplish its objectives, its managers must understand how and why people behave the way they do in organizations. Organizational behavior provides the foundation for good management.

MANAGEMENT: A PRESCRIPTIVE VIEW ◆◆◆◆◆◆◆

From the viewpoint of someone joining an organization for the first time, perhaps a newly graduated business major, the importance of organizations probably seems straightforward. Everyone knows that people come together and form organizations because organizations can accomplish things that are beyond the reach of individuals. People come together to accomplish what none of them could accomplish alone. The meaning of behavior in organizations, therefore, revolves around managing behavior to take advantage of the performance benefits of groups over individuals.

There are two ways in which organizations provide opportunities for accomplishments that are beyond the reach of individuals. These two reasons for organizing, defined in Figure 1–1, are effectiveness and efficiency.

Effectiveness	**Effectiveness** is the ability of an organization to accomplish an important goal, purpose, or mission. A 24-hour dry cleaning service is effective if it can dry clean its customers' clothes in 24 hours or less. A full-service stock brokerage house is effective if it can provide customers a full range of promised financial services. A university instructor is effective if students learn the subject matter of the course. People can achieve some goals and objectives only by combining their talents or coordinating their efforts. A full-service stock brokerage house, for instance, tries to provide its clients with a dizzying array of financial services. Included would be information and purchasing arrangements for stocks, bonds, options, futures, commodities (like wheat and corn), and retirement accounts.

FIGURE 1–1	▶ Two Reasons for Organizing

1. **Effectiveness** The ability of an organization to accomplish an important goal, purpose, or mission. Organizations combine the efforts and talents of many individuals and thereby bring into reach objectives that would be out of reach for individuals.
2. **Efficiency** The ability of an organization to maximize productivity per unit of resources (labor and capital). Organizations allow individuals to accomplish a few tasks more quickly and with fewer mistakes than if that individual had many more responsibilities.

To be effective—that is, to deliver *all* of these financial services to its customers—the stock brokerage house must have a source of expertise for each of its offered services. The amount of expertise and up-to-date knowledge needed to deliver all these services is beyond the capacity of a single individual. To provide the six mentioned services, a full-service brokerage house would need six experts working together, one for each of the six offered financial services. This example demonstrates that effectiveness often can be attained only by combining the talents of multiple individuals. No single individual can be a full-service financier, but an organization of individual experts can provide a full range of services.

Efficiency

Efficiency is a second reason why people come together in organizations. Efficiency is determined by the amount of effort required to deliver a promised good or service. Organizations have opportunities to increase efficiency through specialization. Because specialists are extremely familiar with their tasks, they can accomplish more work per hour than other workers whose efforts are less focused.

Organizations also may have access to more efficient production technologies than those available to individuals. In production circles, this is known as an *economy of scale*. When a lot of something is needed, organizations can use more efficient production technologies to produce it. A cobbler is effective in making shoes for his customers, but a large corporation can be more efficient. A corporation like Nike Shoes can purchase machinery to make shoes very quickly and at much lower cost than the individual cobbler.

The fact that organizations can achieve greater effectiveness and efficiency than individuals no doubt provided the foundation for the first and most basic form of organization—the clan. Primitive men and women may have tried to go it alone, perhaps distrusting the intentions of their neighbors. The survivors no doubt were those men and women who first realized that everyone eventually has to sleep. Thus, individuals could obtain round-the-clock protection from the ravages of the wild only by combining their talents and efforts into an organization.

Efficiency and effectiveness, though tied together as the twin justifications for organizing the talents and efforts of individuals, are not always achieved hand in hand. An organization can be effective (that is, provide a highly desired good or service) without doing so efficiently. On the other hand, an organization may succeed in producing a good or service very efficiently only to find that no customer wants it. Since both effectiveness and efficiency are critical to the survival of an organization, maintaining a healthy balance between them is another important challenge in managing behavior in organizations.

Management Functions

The importance of managing behavior in organizations to achieve effectiveness and efficiency has led researchers to identify primary managerial functions. Managers must accomplish these functions if their organizations are to outperform individuals. Henri Fayol is credited with first identifying these **managerial functions** in 1916.[2] As shown in Figure 1–2, Fayol's five functions include planning, organizing, coordinating, commanding and controlling.

---

[2] H. Fayol, *General and Industrial Management* (London: Pitman, 1961).

FIGURE 1–2	▶**Fayol's Management Functions**

Fayol's five management functions represent a prescription for managing behavior in organizations.

Planning	Thinking before taking action
Organizing	Arranging for material and personnel resources
Coordinating	Setting up the policies and procedures that govern worker behavior
Commanding	Motivating and directing the efforts of the work force in pursuit of the organization's plans
Controlling	Monitoring and correcting progress toward the organization's goals

Planning   The thinking that precedes action in an organization is **planning**. Planning takes place on at least two levels. The first level is concerned with the purpose, mission, or goals of the organization. What good or service will this organization produce and market? Who and where are the potential consumers of this good or service? What characteristics must the good or service have to satisfy the needs of its potential consumers? Management must answer all of these questions for an organization to be effective. The missions or purposes of an organization are often abstract, long-term objectives, such as becoming the biggest or best supplier in an industry. Goals are the concrete stepping-stones that the organization must achieve along the way to ensure that the mission is fulfilled.

The second level of planning is concerned with how the organization will produce or provide the good or service that is its mission. We might think of this as planning the strategies and tactics that will allow the organization to attain its goals and fulfill its mission efficiently. What resources (including people) are necessary to produce or provide the goods or services central to the organization's mission? How will these resources be obtained?

Organizing   Once the organization has an action plan in hand, organizing must take place. **Organizing** occurs when the organization arranges for the material and personnel resources needed to accomplish the plan. **Staffing,** for example, is the process of supplying a work force (people) to fill the organization's designed structures. Staffing consists of three components. First, a selection procedure must be designed and implemented to fill job descriptions identified in the organizing function. Second, those hired must be trained and socialized so that they can contribute to the organization's attainment of its goals and accomplishment of its mission. Third, an employee support system (including a wages-and-benefits package) that satisfies at least the minimum requirements and needs of the work force must be put in place. In concert, these three staffing activities provide the organization's human resources.

Coordinating   Creating a structure through which the members can produce the organization's central goods or services is **coordinating**. We can think of this structure as having several distinct components. First, there is the structuring of individual job responsibilities and duties. Who will do what and how will they do it? Next is the structuring of relationships among the individual jobs. What are the reporting relationships in the organization to be like? Who will be supervising whom? What kinds of departments will be necessary? How will these departments interact with each other? Finally, there is the physical structuring of the facility. Given the nature of individual jobs and the desired departmental structures and reporting relationships, what is the best way to arrange everyone physically? Should there be walls between desks to provide privacy, or should supervision be "line-of-sight"? If there is production machinery, where and how should it fit into the physical layout? All three of these organizing structures—individual, group, and physical—represent the first concrete stage of implementing the organization's action plan.

Commanding   Once the operating structures have been put in place and the work force has been hired to make the operating structures go, the manager must control the work force's execution of the work. **Commanding** includes directing and motivating the work force, often by generating direction and enthusiasm for work through leadership. Incentive systems or rewards and discipline or punishment procedures also can be used to both motivate and direct the behaviors of the work force.

Controlling   Monitoring the progress of the organization toward its stated goals and mission is **controlling.** Controlling requires measuring organizational performance, comparing performance against standards, and taking corrective action when performance turns out to be substandard. Corrective actions may include those taken to get the work force back on track (such as changes in leadership patterns or incentive systems). Corrective actions also may be directed toward revising the organization's action plan, thereby giving rise to consequent changes at the levels of organizing and staffing.

ORGANIZATIONAL BEHAVIOR: A DESCRIPTIVE VIEW ◆◆◆◆◆◆

Defining organizational life in terms of effectiveness, efficiency, and the five managerial functions used to pursue them—planning, organizing, coordinating, commanding, and controlling—paints a picture of the organization as a production system. This picture suggests that managers consider all the relevant inputs; formulate plans; design and put in place people and systems to execute the plans; give a few pep talks; and fine-tune the people, systems, and even the plan itself if outcomes are less than optimal. The image is one of deliberate and thoughtful pursuit of organizational effectiveness and efficiency.

This prescriptive view of organizational behavior is incomplete in several important ways. To begin with, organizations are not just production systems, they are also *social* systems. People do not join organizations just to be more efficient and more effective. People also join organizations because they want to *belong* to groups and because they enjoy sharing their efforts with others. As the Greek philosopher Aristotle once noted, "Man is by nature a social animal." Aristotle believed that any individual who does not feel the need to join with others in organizations "is either a beast or a god."[3] Since most of us are neither

---

[3] Aristotle, *Politics*, 328 B.C.

beasts nor gods, good management must take into account the fact that social aspects of organizations are important to an organization's members.

Fayol's functional view of behavior in organizations also is incomplete because it *underestimates* the disjointedness of organizational life. Life in organizations is hardly an orderly progression of activities, each following logically from the one preceding it. Finally, defining organizational life in terms of the five managerial functions is misleading because it *overestimates* the extent to which organizations pursue deliberate, planned activities focused on production efficiency and effectiveness.

There is more to organizational life than thoughtful, orderly planning and execution. A complete portrait of behavior in organizations includes three additional elements: conflict, uncertainty, and complexity.

Conflict

The functional approach to managing behavior in organizations assumes that all members share identical perceptions, beliefs, and goals. However, as noted by Stanford political scientist James March, we should not expect agreement among organizational members. We should expect **conflict:** differences among the perceptions, beliefs, and goals of organization members.[4]

The inevitability of conflict in organizations suggests that they are more than just production systems. Organizations also are political systems. A **political system** is a collection of individuals or groups that must work together and speak with one voice even though each has a private agenda to pursue.

The U.S. Senate is a more classic example of a political system. Each member of the Senate has a constituency (home state). The constituency has goals that it wants its senator to pursue. Each senator also has personal goals to pursue. And the United States (as an organization) has goals that it would like the Senate to pursue as well. Yet with all of these goals to balance, the Senate must speak with one voice by passing only one law for any issue. How does the Senate, given these multiple goals, ever come to a decision?

In a political system like the U.S. Senate, actions are a function of power. In its simplest form, **power** is the ability to influence the behaviors of others, usually through the control of resources. (Power and its use will be discussed in detail in Chapter 8.) In a political system, an individual with more power can impose his or her will on an individual with less power. That means that when goals conflict in a political system, which goals get pursued are a function of who has the power in the system.

Often, goal inconsistencies and incompatibilities remain unresolved within an organization. Rather than foster conflict by confronting them, managers make plans and decisions on an issue-by-issue basis. This strategy of considering issues *serially* and ignoring their long-term implications or interrelationships avoids conflict *in the short run*. However, it also renders meaningless any sense of legitimate overall goals for the organization.

Because organizations are collections of individuals with inconsistent or even conflicting goals, decisions are often made and actions taken according to who has power or who can best use power. Not surprisingly, decisions and actions often are terrible compromises. Individuals and groups bargain away

---

[4]J. G. March, "Business Firm as Political Coalition." *Journal of Politics* 24 (1962): 662–678.

what is important in exchange for being able to keep what they cannot live without.

The tragic explosion of the space shuttle Challenger provides a revealing example. In a major space launch, many different groups and individuals have many different goals and differing amounts of power. Some people saw the Challenger's space mission as an important public relations tool for NASA's public image and funding and for the career advancement of NASA personnel—but *only* if the launch proceeded on schedule! Others working on the project saw the possibility of danger, but also the possibility of losing their jobs if they pushed the matter too far and were wrong. The action eventually taken—the ill-fated launch of the Challenger—could not fulfill all the conflicting goals of the individuals and groups working on the project. Instead, the decision represented the underlying power realities of those working with NASA on the launch. Apparently those wanting the launch to proceed had more power (or made better use of what power they had) than those who did not want the launch to proceed. In retrospect, it appears that the decision was less a function of what was the right thing to do than a function of which group or individual had the power to decide which goals to pursue.[5]

The idea that organizations are political systems emphasizes the importance of interpersonal relationships and the behavior of individuals in groups (which will be discussed in Chapter 7). It also identifies two critical tasks in managing organizational behavior. First, because organizations consist of groups and individuals with inconsistent and conflicting goals, it is important that managers see conflict management as an important organizational task. (Conflict management will be discussed in Chapter 6.) Along these lines, one study of managers' behavior found that managers spend a substantial part of each day discussing apparently irrelevant topics with their superiors, subordinates, and coworkers.[6] The researchers labeled this activity "socializing and politicking," thereby suggesting that its purpose was building rapport, relationships, and allegiances to weather the storms of later conflicts. As noted in the "INTERNATIONAL FOCUS ON: Conflict," multinational work forces present managers with another dimension of conflict—cultural differences—which must be managed as well. Second, political decision-making processes hold the potential of undermining organizational efficiency and effectiveness. Leadership is important in keeping all organizational members focused on the organization's goals, in addition to any personal agendas. (Leadership will be the focus of Chapter 10.)

Uncertainty

One of the subtle assumptions of Fayol's managerial functions is that there is enough information available for orderly and deliberate planning to take place. But is this a good assumption? In reality, organizations are plagued by uncertainty that makes planning a very difficult enterprise.[7]

Uncertainty is not knowing for sure. Would a better motivated work force make a difference? Would new incentive or training programs help? What values will interest any particular work-force member? History or research may *suggest* answers to these questions, but in practice their answers can be known

---

[5] "Space Shuttle Probe Throws Shower of Sparks," *US News & World Report*, March 3, 1986, 6–7.

[6] J. P. Kotter, *The General Managers* (New York: Free Press, 1982).

[7] R. M. Cyert and J. G. March, *A Behavioral Theory of the Firm* (Englewood Cliffs, N.J.: Prentice-Hall, 1963).

INTERNATIONAL FOCUS ON

Conflict

When Worlds Collide An important by-product of the globalization of business in the late 20th century has been the birth of the multicultural work force. Japanese companies currently employ over 400,000 workers in the United States, and more than 200,000 Japanese immigrants have settled around the U.S. as employers, employees, and neighbors. Japan's expatriates are spread all over the United States. More than a third live on the West Coast, particularly in California, where 20 percent of all Japanese-owned factories are located. Roughly a quarter have gathered in New York City and its suburbs. The rest are scattered about in some unlikely places—the Japanese Chamber of Commerce of Georgia, for instance, has almost 300 members.

A disproportionate number of the Japanese expatriates who live around New York City have gathered in a couple of communities, where Japanese and American cultures often clash. That is the case in Scarsdale, New York, a wealthy and formerly homogeneous suburb that is somewhat stunned by the sudden influx from Japan. At Scarsdale High, Principal Judy Fox is trying hard to promote harmony by preparing a course in Japanese language and culture, putting Japanese-English dictionaries in every classroom, and hiring "bias-reduction consultants" who encourage students to talk out their differences. The efforts, though well-intended, have yet to bear fruit.

Japanese companies in the area are trying to address the problems as well. Hitachi, for one, now advises its expatriate employees to spread out instead of congregating in the U.S. equivalent of foreigners' "ghettos." The company also suggests that its expatriate employees take part in community activities, and some have taken the hint: Yasushi Sayama, a general manager of corporate administration at Hitachi, joined a local Lutheran church even though he's not a Christian.

For American Karen Satterly, a born-again Baptist who assembles circuitboards at Hitachi, the lesson is more personal. In her high school, she sensed that many of her fellow Americans felt inferior to their few Japanese classmates. "I think . . . that tends to make [Americans] a little mean," she says. "That's just something they have to overcome." Insights like that could provide important turning points for the grass roots of the American work force. Experiences like Karen's have become part of Japan's growing presence in America—an accumulation of small personal discoveries that could add up to more harmony and less conflict.

Source: Adapted from S. P. Sherman, "Japan's Influence on America," *Fortune,* June 17, 1991, 115–124.

only by trial and error. Managing this uncertainty is another key component of the challenge of managing organizational behavior. As shown in Figure 1–3, uncertainty comes from a variety of internal and external sources.

Internal Sources of Uncertainty   Much of the uncertainty faced by individuals both in and outside of organizations arises from perception—the collecting of information from the environment. (The perception process will be the focus of Chapter 3.) The behaviors of fellow workers can be a constant source of confusion. Was that friendly greeting by my supervisor a sign that I have been doing a good job? Or did my supervisor just have a good time at the company party last night? Is he being nice to me because he's about to give me an awful work assignment? Or is he grooming me to take over his position when he leaves? The inputs we receive from the environment are just inputs. They come to have meaning only by the interpretations we assign to them. We must act on the interpretations we make. If we have made the wrong interpretations, our actions will be wrong as well. Even an army as well-managed as Schwarzkopf's occasionally will fire on its own troops by accident.[8]

Uncertainty also exists in the understanding of means-ends relationships. A means-ends relationship is the probability that an outcome (the end) will occur if an action (the means) is taken. For example, if we replace all our typewriters with word processors, will the productivity of our work force go up or down? Will our employees be more or less satisfied with their jobs? Means-ends relationships are filled with uncertainty. Past experiences may tell us what to expect, but they can never tell us *for sure* what will happen. Taking action, then, always contains an element of rolling the dice and holding your breath.

Again, the case of the Challenger space shuttle is revealing. No one would have launched the Challenger knowing *for certain* that it would blow up. But then no one *ever* knows for certain that something is going to happen. A few engineers thought there might be a major problem, but was that likelihood enough to abort the launch? What probability of disaster could be assigned to their concerns? And what actions *should* have been taken based on these probability estimates? Is a 50 percent chance of an accident enough to warrant aborting the launch? How about 10 percent? And how would you know if the probability were closer to 50 percent or 10 percent?

Within an organization, goals also may be uncertain. Individuals may not know what they want out of their jobs, or what they want may change from day to day. (Individual uncertainty in motivation will be discussed in more detail in Chapter 4.) Similarly, different members of an organization may have quite different ideas of the organization's goals. Or the goals may have to be changed when changes occur in the organization's environment. Imagine how difficult planning must be if organizational goals are not stable or agreed upon!

External Sources of Uncertainty   A lot of uncertainty faced by managers is external to their organizations. It comes from the constantly changing and evolving environment in which the organization must function. While the role of the environment will be discussed in much greater detail in Chapter 14, there are several primary sources of environmental uncertainty that the modern manager must keep in mind.

[8]D. H. Hackworth, "Killed by Their Comrades," *Newsweek*, November 18, 1991, 45–46.

FIGURE 1–3	▶ Sources of Uncertainty

Internal

Individual:	Perceptions
	Goals/motivations
Organizational:	Means-ends relationships
	Organizational goals
	Responsibility/authority

External

Constant changes:	In the work force
	In values and expectations
	In technology
	In the legal environment

Changes in the Work Force   As if the management of organizational behavior were not already complex enough, the manager must deal with changes in the kinds of people who become employees. The modern work force, for example, is more educated than it has ever been. In 1980, 67 percent of U.S. adults age 25 and older had completed high school and 16.4 percent had completed four or more years of college. By 1990, more than 77 percent of U.S. adults age 25 and older had completed high school and more than 20 percent had completed four or more years of college.[9] Rising levels of education mean workers will demand more challenging and involving jobs.

Other significant characteristics of the modern work force also are changing. For instance, women have been entering the U.S. work force in recent years at a much faster pace than males. In 1960, only 33 percent of the work force was female. By 1980, the number was 50.5 percent and 58.3 percent by 1990.[10] Further, in 1960 only 19 percent of all mothers of children under six worked outside the home;[11] by 1988, 56 percent of mothers with children under six were employed outside the home, and 73 percent of mothers with children between the ages of six and seventeen were employed outside the home.[12]

The U.S. Census Bureau estimates that the Hispanic population in the United States grew from 14.6 million in 1980 to 21.9 million in 1990—50 percent in 10 years. Work-force participation of Hispanics consequently has grown from 4.5 percent of the total U.S. work force in 1976 to 7.4 percent in 1988, and it is expected to reach 10.1 percent by the year 2000. Participation in the U.S. work force by individuals of Asian descent also has increased, from 1.9 percent in 1976 to 3 percent in 1990. By the year 2000, it is expected that 4 percent of U.S. workers will be of Asian descent.[13]

Changes in Worker Values and Expectations   As the face of the U.S. work force and its educational level have changed, so too have workers' values and expectations. First, modern workers are more likely to want work to be meaningful

[9]J. Waldrop and T. Exter, "What the 1990 Census Will Show," *American Demographics*, January 1990, 20–30.

[10]J. Waldrop and T. Exter, "What the 1990 Census Will Show," *American Demographics*, January 1990, 20–30.

[11]C. Wallis, "The Child Care Dilemma," *Time*, June 22, 1987, 54–60.

[12]N. Darnton, "Mommy vs. Mommy," *Newsweek*, June 4, 1990, 64–67.

[13]J. F. Coates, J. Jarratt, and J. B. Mahaffie, "Future Work," *The Futurist*, May/June 1991, 10–19.

and involving, rather than just a way to get a paycheck. Management has had to respond with job enrichment programs that provide workers more opportunities to get involved in work. (These problems will be discussed in Chapter 12.)

Second, workers now seem more interested in fitting work into a larger sense of their lives than in devoting their lives to the organization. As noted in the "FOCUS ON: Changes in Work-Force Values," interest in the flexibility of *temporary* employment—even temporary *executives*—has reached an all-time high and promises to continue growing. Also, the mobility boom of the 1950s and 1960s is drawing to a close. Young executives no longer are ready and willing to uproot a family in the name of career advancement. Dual-career marriages and housing costs are encouraging more sedentary life-styles, even on the corporate fast track.[14]

Along with changing values, the modern work force also has changing expectations. Gone are the days when employees felt some sense of gratitude for the opportunity to work. In its place is a new feeling, the "entitlement" mindset. Employees in the modern work force see themselves as entitled to certain rights, such as privacy, fair treatment, and even interesting work.[15]

Changes in Technology In 1967, computers were bulky boxes of poorly understood electronic hardware. More than 25 years later, it is probably hard for managers and clerical staff in many sectors of American industry to remember what it was like to work without computers. The advent of the computer serves as a striking reminder that the possibility of technological change is a critical source of uncertainty for organizations. (The importance of technology to the management of organizational behavior will be addressed in more detail in Chapter 15.)

Advances in computer networking are even creating alternatives to the nine-to-five job at the office. Instead workers may be "dialing in" to work and doing their work over a telephone computer link.[16] Technological developments of this magnitude can have profound effects on the best-laid organizational plans. Thus, if managers hope to keep on top of their organization's efficiency and effectiveness goals, they must keep an eye on the most recent changes in available technologies.

Changes in the Law Many of the rights to which employees now feel entitled, such as the right to form unions for the purpose of collective bargaining, have been codified into law. The legal environment in which organizations must function represents another source of uncertainty. Laws that influence the day-to-day workings of organizations include those affecting hiring (the Equal Employment Opportunities Act), compensation (the Equal Pay Act), and maintenance (the Occupational Safety and Health Act). As our society has become increasingly litigious, greater emphasis has been placed on the development of

---

[14]"Farewell, Fast Track," *Business Week*, December 10, 1990, 192–203.

[15]A. Katzell, "Changing Attitudes toward Work," in *Work in America: The Decade Ahead*, eds. C. Kerr and J. Rosow (New York: Van Nostrand, 1979): 35–57.

[16]R. Perez-Peña, "Office for Weary Commuters a Long Way from the Office," *New York Times*, January 7, 1992, A-10.

Focus on

Changes in Work-Force Values

Rent-an-Exec With job jumping ever more common, companies can quickly find themselves without crucial top-level executives. Hurriedly filling a position with a replacement from inside the company often creates problems of its own, such as opening another hole further down the corporate hierarchy. But today, companies are trying a new tack: hiring senior managers, even chief executives, from the outside on a *temporary* basis.

Chief executive officers as office temps? Consider the advantages. Lining up a temporary replacement can be quick, because the person doing the hiring does not have to decide whether or not the individual would fit into the company on a long-term basis. It is also a way to rent before you buy; perhaps 25 percent of temporary executives take on their assignments permanently. Lastly, hiring a temp gives a company time to groom younger executives for eventual ascension to a top job.

The temporary executive route is working well for USGI, a Connecticut-based mortgage service company. USGI's vice-president of planning left last spring, and William Gow, USGI's chairman, didn't want to risk taking on a full-timer only to find that the new hire didn't work out. He felt it would depress company morale. He also felt the job might eliminate itself eventually. So Gow was in the market for a temporary executive. Gow went to New York-based Interim Management Corporation (Imcor), a temporary executive outfit he had heard about. In business a year and a half, Imcor says it has placed 35 executive temps.

Within two weeks, Imcor had selected four candidates from the 2,500 names in its files and dispatched them to Connecticut. Of the candidates introduced to Gow, one stood above the rest: Matthew Lind, 47, a man to whom an independent lifestyle is more important than steady advancement inside the corporate bureaucracy. An engineer

with a doctorate in applied mathematics, Lind was co-owner of a small investment banking firm and was working out of his home. He was itching for something else to do, as long as he did not have to commit to permanent employment.

Temporary executives have long been hired for specific projects—launching a product, say, or closing down a plant. But Lind represents something new—corporate managers who have reached a point in their careers where they don't need or necessarily want a steady job. Like most of the people in Imcor's talent pool, Lind has reached the point where money is no longer a compelling carrot. What Lind enjoys about his arrangement with USGI is being able to do so much of his work on his computer at home. He often gets up to work at 3 A.M. and by noon is able to spend some time with his four-month-old son or play his piano.

For his part, Gow sees Lind's "outsider" status as an advantage. Because interim employees like Lind are not seen as competitive threats to permanent employees, the temporary executives can rise above politics and concentrate more on the task at hand.

laws that protect employee rights. Since 1900, the legal environment in which organizations must function has evolved from an emphasis on the rights of management, to an emphasis on the rights of unions, to an emphasis on the rights of the individual employee. Further, ethical standards have changed and also have found their way into the laws that govern the behavior of organizations and their members (such as the laws against insider trading).[17]

All of these evolving elements in the organization's external environment combine with the internal sources of uncertainty described earlier to create an organizational environment in which nothing seems very certain. All this uncertainty often leads to managers behaving in ways that do not much resemble Fayol's portrait of deliberate and orderly planning and execution.[18]

Complexity

With all this conflict and uncertainty that managers must face, it should not be surprising that complexity is also a defining feature of life in organizations. **Complexity** refers to the overwhelming number of concerns that managers must keep track of and manage. Part of this complexity arises in the fact that in any organization there are really two organizations: the formal and the informal. As shown in Figure 1–4, the formal organization consists of the procedures and structures suggested by the functional approach to managing behavior in organizations. In effect, the formal organization represents the organization's perceptions, beliefs, and goals. Yet it is only the "tip of the iceberg."

The informal organization represents the rest of the organizational iceberg. The **informal organization** encompasses the interpersonal realities of an organization (such as employees' personal goals, perceptions, and beliefs), realities that typically are *not* part of the organization's action plan and yet are very much a part of the organization. These characteristics of the organization's members must be taken into account in managing their behavior to achieve organizational efficiency and effectiveness.

The complexity of organizational life has been captured and documented by several studies of what managers actually do on a minute-to-minute basis during the course of their workdays. Perhaps the best-known historical study describing the lives of managers in organizations was conducted by Henry Mintzberg.[19] Mintzberg carefully observed several weeks in the lives of five upper-level managers.

Mintzberg's findings about managerial work stand in stark contrast to the calm and orderly portrait of behavior in organizations suggested by Fayol's managerial functions. Mintzberg found that his managers' workdays were characterized by variety, brevity, and fragmentation. Mintzberg's five managers worked on many different things during a typical working day and worked on each only briefly. Many of the activities they worked on had little apparent connection to each other. Telephone calls were short and to the point, lasting on the average only 6 minutes. Desk work and unscheduled meetings were similarly brief, each lasting less than 15 minutes on the average.

---

[17] V. Cahan, "What Is Insider Trading? An Answer May Be on the Way," *Business Week*, June 29, 1987, 28.

[18] Cyert and March, *A Behavioral Theory of the Firm*.

[19] H. Mintzberg, *The Nature of Managerial Work* (New York: Harper & Row, 1973).

FIGURE 1–4	▶ The Organizational "Iceberg"

In any organization there are really two organizations: (1) the formal organization, consisting of the formal reporting relationships, rules, and procedures, and (2) the informal organization, consisting of what really goes on in the organization, including beliefs and social relationships.

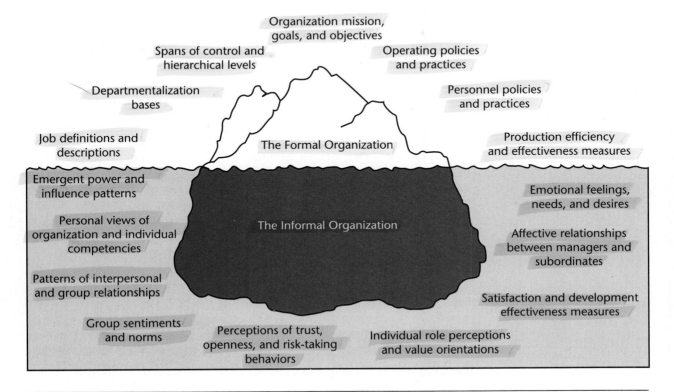

Source: R. J. Selfridge and S. L. Sokolik, "A Comprehensive View of Organizational Development," *MSU Business Topics* (1975): 47.

Mintzberg found that his upper-level managers spent 78 percent of their time engaged in verbal communication. Other studies have estimated that managers spend anywhere from 66 percent to 80 percent of their time in verbal communication activities.[20] For Mintzberg's managers, more than 90 percent of these verbal contacts were arranged on an ad hoc basis.

The portrait of managerial activity provided by Mintzberg's study suggests that organizational behavior can be quite chaotic. Half of the activities engaged in by Mintzberg's executive managers lasted less than five minutes and only 10 percent lasted more than an hour. Further, many of these activities were terminated by the managers themselves so that they could push on to more pressing job demands.

Other studies of the work lives of managers have found similar results. One study of 50 foremen in the United States found that they averaged 583 distinct

---

[20]T. Burns, "The Directions of Activity and Communication in a Departmental Executive Group," *Human Relations* 7 (1954): 73+.

activities per 8-hour shift—about one new activity every 48 seconds.[21] Another study of 160 British managers found that only about once every two days did the managers work uninterrupted for more than one half hour.[22] In a more recent U.S. study,[23] the American Telephone and Telegraph Company (AT&T) examined the behaviors of 60,000 middle managers and 170,000 first-line managers. The results of this study support Mintzberg's claim that managerial life is extremely complex and fragmented. And, as noted in the "FOCUS ON: Complexity," there is never enough time for everything.

The intense and fragmented complexity of managerial life is perhaps best captured in a quote by Columbia Business School professor Leonard Sayles:

> [The manager] is like a symphony orchestra conductor, endeavoring to maintain a melodious performance in which the contributions of the various instruments are coordinated and sequenced, patterned, and paced, while the orchestra members are having various personal difficulties, stagehands are moving music stands, alternating excessive heat and cold are creating audience and instrument problems, and the sponsor of the concert is insisting on irrational changes in the program.[24]

Sayle's quote again emphasizes the disjointed complexity of managerial behavior. Managers are like jugglers, trying to keep many balls in the air at once. The increasing internationalization of business adds another dimension, foreign cultures, to the complexity of managing. Managing the complexity of organizational behavior is an important component of the management challenge.

Related Fields

Much of the conflict, uncertainty, and complexity that characterize life in organizations arises precisely because organizations are collections of people. Understanding the behaviors of the people in organizations, therefore, is critical to good management. The study of people's behavior in organizations—organizational behavior—is one of a family of scientific areas of study known as the behavioral sciences. The behavioral sciences all share both a scientific orientation *and* a focus on human behavior as the object of scientific study. (A brief discussion of the scientific orientation or "scientific method" is provided in Appendix A.) This focus on human behavior differentiates the behavioral sciences from "hard" sciences (such as geology and astronomy) that study physical processes and objects (such as rocks and stars).

Several behavioral sciences figure prominently in the study of organizational behavior. Included are psychology, the study of individual behavior; sociology, the study of group behavior; political science, the study of social power and social conflict; and anthropology, the study of the evolution of man. Within the broad field of psychology, experimental psychology in particular is concerned with learning, perception, and other processes through which individuals interact with their environment. Social psychology focuses both on group influences on individual behaviors and on the individual thought processes that

---

[21] R. H. Guest, "Of Time and the Foreman," *Personnel* 32 (1956): 478–486.

[22] R. Stewart, *Managers and Their Jobs* (London: Macmillan, 1967).

[23] C. MacDonald, *Performance Based Supervisory Development* (Amherst, Mass.: Human Resources Development, 1983).

[24] L. R. Sayles, *Managerial Behavior* (New York: McGraw-Hill, 1964).

The Stitch in Time that Saves Nine

Thirty years ago, Anthony Newley and Leslie Bricusse wrote the song, *Stop the World—I Want to Get Off*, which decried the growing complexity and busy bustle of life. That was before fax machines, cellular phones, beepers, notebook computers, and international overnight mail; before competition turned ruthless, markets went global, resources grew scarce; and before the unexpected presence of high technology, deregulation, a unified Germany, corporate raiders, program trading, and the green revolution. However fast the world was spinning then, it must be spinning ten times as fast today.

What does it take to be a good manager in such a dizzyingly complex world? Management theorist Peter Drucker has noted that while successful managers vary widely in temperament, interest, even ability, they all seem to have one trait in common: the courage and foresight to concentrate on critical tasks rather than trying to do it all.

It's a lesson CEO Ron Canion learned when he founded Compaq Computer. "I knew what everyone else was doing every hour of the day," he says. "But you can't do that with 9,000 employees. In the past eight years, I've had to reassess repeatedly what I felt was the most important area for me to spend my time in. You have to prioritize your activities again and again—otherwise something is going to snap." Like many effective executives, Canion pushes himself to look past the small, insistent demands and spend time thinking about the largest questions before him—in his case, plotting the future of his firm and watching out for competitors.

For Westinghouse CEO John Marous, setting priorities is a formal process with a similar result. Not only does Marous set priorities; he even gets input from his executive vice-presidents—the result of a companywide "total quality fitness review" that takes a critical look at the CEO's office right down to the effec-

tiveness of the secretaries and chauffeurs. As a result, says Marous, "I've come up with some pretty firm guidelines. I spend most of my time developing strategic vision and planning. The very last thing I burden myself with is specific problem solving."

Most managers hope—often in vain—for a few spare minutes. "I demand a cushion of time between appointments," says Marous with a laugh, "and the cushion always disappears." To make it up, most managers try to get to work early to catch up on paperwork, and they stay late, somewhat removed from the sound and fury, to return calls. American Airlines CEO Robert Crandall says that if appointments keep him busy until 5 or 6 o'clock at night, he'll stay until 9 o'clock returning calls and finishing paperwork. Laurel Cutler, vice chairman of the advertising agency FCB/Leber Katz, says she always gets to work before 8 A.M. because "I hope that I'll have at least an hour before the phone rings." Cutler is also a firm believer in the ultimate timesaving technique: saying no. "The path of my life and career has been learning to say 'No.' Perhaps taking 'No' lessons is the real key to time management."

Setting priorities requires forgoing activities that probably seem important, and saying no also requires displeasing people. But until science figures out how to add an hour to the day, these are probably the best time-management techniques any manager has.

Source: Adapted from E. Calonius, "How Top Managers Manage Their Time," *Fortune*, June 4, 1990, 250–262.

control individual behavior in groups. Cultural anthropology studies ways in which symbols are used to create and maintain belief systems.

Since organizations are made up of individuals and groups, knowledge from psychology, sociology, political science, and anthropology should be useful in understanding their behavior. Organizational behavior differs from these related fields, however, in its focus not just on individual or group behavior but specifically on individual and group behavior *in organizations*. Again, this is the challenge of organizational behavior—not just understanding individual and group behavior, but understanding how individual and group behavior relates to the smooth running of organizations.

Management is also related to organizational behavior. Management has been defined as getting things done through people. The relationship between organizational behavior and management is one of knowledge base and application. Organizational behavior provides a knowledge base for understanding and predicting the behavior of individuals and groups in organizations. The field of management is comprised of a series of skills and techniques (such as designing work systems and compensation plans) for managing the behaviors of individuals and groups. Hopefully, the skills and techniques of management reflect the accumulated knowledge base provided by the field of organizational behavior. Thus, management is the application of organizational behavior knowledge to the challenge of managing behavior in organizations.

ABOUT THIS BOOK

This book divides the study of organizational behavior into five parts. Part 1 (Chapters 1 and 2) defines the challenge of managing behavior in organizations. Chapter 1 has introduced the topic of organizational behavior and presented a description of life in organizations that highlights the importance for managers of understanding human behavior. Chapter 2 provides an historical perspective on organizational behavior. Several classic theories and studies in management are presented and their roles in the development of the field of organizational behavior are discussed.

Part 2, Individual Behavior, and Part 3, Behavior in Groups, represent the foundation knowledge of organizational behavior. Part 2 (Chapters 3 through 6) explores the individual behavior processes of perception, attitudes and personality, learning and motivation, individual decision making, conflict, and stress. Part 3 (Chapters 7 through 10) focuses on the behaviors of individuals when they behave in groups. The topics of Part 3 include group dynamics, communication, power, group decision making, and leadership.

Part 4, Managing for Performance (Chapters 11 through 13), applies the foundation knowledge of organizational behavior to the challenge of managing in organizations. Chapter 11 (Organizational Entry) examines how individuals are brought into organizations and how organizations welcome and socialize new members. Chapter 12 (Job Design) explores how task assignments in an organization can be arranged to reflect our understanding of individual and group behavior. Finally, Chapter 13 (Maintaining Performance) addresses the issue of maintaining workers' motivation and performance on the job, primarily through performance appraisals and programs such as goal setting.

The scope of any individual's focus in an organization is his or her personal behavior and the behaviors of those in the immediate work group. But individual and work-group behaviors occur in the larger context of entire organizations. Part 5 (Chapters 14 through 18) explores the larger context of organizations and its implications for our understanding of behavior in organizations. Chapters 14 and 15 look at the environment and technology as primary *external* influences on behavior in organizations. Chapter 16 examines the influence of organizational structure and design (such as formalization and departmentalization) on organizational behavior. Chapter 17 focuses on the critical issue of change in organizations and how change can best be managed from a human standpoint. Finally, Chapter 18 looks beyond the present to see what lies ahead for organizations and organizational behavior.

An explicit concern in this book is to help readers develop a *theory-based* understanding of behavior in organizations. Why are theories important? Theories provide causal explanations for *why* things happen. Theories typically can be expressed in the form, "if X then Y." For instance, social comparison theory (which will be discussed in Chapter 8) can be expressed as, "if people are uncertain, then they will depend on others for advice." Theories do more than help managers decide what procedures to use; they help managers understand why those procedures will work. Many of us have experiences or intuitions that tell us *what* to do, how to manage other people. For instance, you might believe that "two heads are better than one"—the more people involved in making a decision, the better that decision will be. Or you might think that if you want someone to behave in a specific way, all you have to do is promise to *reward* the individual for performing in that specific way. Unfortunately, many of our intuitions—like these two—can be more wrong than right.

Theories help us generalize our intuitions to new situations where we may have no intuitions. Theories also help us understand when our intuitions are wrong. For instance, social comparison theory (Chapter 8) tells us when two heads may be worse than one, and expectancy theory (Chapter 4) tells us when promising to reward a behavior will not make that behavior more likely to happen.

An implicit concern in this book is the importance of understanding organizations and organizational behavior in everyday life. Organizational behavior is not just the study of *work* organizations. Organizational behavior refers to behavior in all organizations, including social clubs, families, and even study groups at school. To that end, the practical examples of organizational behavior contained in this book are drawn from a variety of different organizations, and even a variety of different countries. Each chapter also ends with some additional suggestions for readings, in case you want to know more about what you have read. A sound understanding of organizational behavior is useful for managing your life at work, but it is also useful for managing your life outside work.

SUMMARY: THE CHALLENGE OF ORGANIZATIONAL BEHAVIOR ◆◆◆◆◆◆

The conflict, uncertainty, and complexity of organizational behavior stands in stark contrast to a functional view of managerial life as deliberate and orderly planning and execution. Probably the truth falls somewhere between the two. A functional approach to organizational behavior may tell us what a manager should be doing to manage behavior in the best of all possible organizations. Unfortunately, no manager manages in the best of all possible organizations.

Instead this chapter has suggested that managers manage in organizations made highly complex by people and their behaviors, in which conflict is inevitable, and in which the only certain-ties a manager can depend on are that nothing is certain and everything is changing. Managing an organization's human resources to achieve effectiveness and efficiency in the face of complexity, conflict, and uncertainty and constant change is the challenge of organizational behavior. Preparing you to meet that challenge is the goal of this book.

Key Terms

Commanding Management function of directing and motivating the work force, often by generating direction and enthusiasm for work through leadership.

Complexity Overabundance of inputs that managers must keep track of, consider, and manage.

Conflict Differences among the perceptions, beliefs, and goals of organization members.

Coordinating Management function of creating a structure through which members can produce the organization's central goods or services.

Controlling Monitoring and correcting the progress of an organization toward its goals.

Effectiveness Ability of an organization to accomplish an important goal, purpose, or mission.

Efficiency Amount of effort required to deliver a promised good or service; can be increased through specialization and economies of scale.

Informal organization Interpersonal realities of an organization, such as employees' personal goals, perceptions, and beliefs, that are not part of the organization's formal goals and plans but that must be taken into account to achieve organizational efficiency and effectiveness.

Management A prescriptive view of what organizations are supposed to accomplish and how they are supposed to accomplish it, including planning, organizing, coordinating, commanding and controlling.

Managerial functions Activities that must be performed for organizations to outperform individuals, including planning, organizing, staffing, and controlling.

Organization Form of human association for the attainment of a common purpose by combining the talents and efforts of its members.

Organizational behavior The description and explanation of how people behave in organizations.

Organizing In Fayol's management functions, arranging for an organization's material and personnel resources.

Planning Management thought processes that precede action in an organization.

Political system Collection of individuals or groups that must work together and speak with one voice even though each has a private agenda to pursue.

Power Ability to influence the attitudes or behavior of others, usually through the control of resources.

Uncertainty Not knowing for sure; may include future actions or events, or relationships between actions and consequences.

Discussion Questions

1. What is an organization? Why do people become members of organizations? Think of some organizations to which you belong. Why did you join these organizations? Think of an organization of which you are *no longer* a member. Why did you leave it?

2. Differentiate between efficiency and effectiveness. Why are Fayol's managerial functions an incomplete description of how organizations pursue these goals?

3. How would you characterize the life of a manager? How does your description fit in with the three defining characteristics of organizations (conflict, uncertainty, and complexity) presented in this chapter?

4. Consider your class as an organization. What sources of uncertainty exist for you as a student? What sources exist for your instructor? What goals do you and your instructor share? What goals might you and your instructor have that are incompatible?

If You Want to Know More

A summary of Henry Mintzberg's study of executive behavior patterns is provided in his article, "The Manager's Job: Folklore and Fact," published in the *Harvard Business Review* 53 (1975). Studs Terkel also has put together a collection of interviews of workers at all levels and types of American work organizations. The book is entitled *Working* (New York: Pantheon Books, 1974).

Though Henri Fayol first proposed the functional approach to management in 1916, his book on the topic *(General and Industrial Management)* was not translated from French into English until 1949 (London: Pitman Press). A more contemporary discussion of traditional approaches to management is contained in Peter Drucker's book, *Management: Tasks, Responsibilities, and Practices* (New York: Harper & Row, 1974).

The two alternative perspectives on managing behavior in organizations described in this chapter are discussed at length in Graham Allison's book, *The Essence of Decision* (Boston: Little, Brown, 1971). Allison uses the alternative perspectives to explain the U.S. foreign policy decisions preceding both the Bay of Pigs fiasco and the Cuban Missile Crisis. These two alternative perspectives on life in organizations also are discussed along with several others in Gareth Morgan's book, *Images of Organization* (Beverly Hills, Calif.: Sage, 1986). The political perspective is discussed in detail in Roger Hilsman's book, *To Move a Nation* (Garden City, N.Y.: Doubleday, 1967). Hilsman uses the political perspective to analyze U.S. government decision making under the Kennedy administration. The effects of uncertainty and politics on effectiveness are discussed in an article by Richard Hall, "Goals and Effectiveness," in B. Staw's volume, *Psychological Foundations of Organizational Behavior* (Glenview, Ill.: Scott, Foresman, 1983).

Two readings that detail the effects that change and uncertainty will pose to the challenges of management in the 21st century are Stan Davis and Bill Davidson's *2020 Vision: Transform Your Business Today to Succeed in Tomorrow's Economy* (New York: Simon & Schuster, 1991); and Henry Coleman, Jr.'s "Managing in the 21st Century," *Organizational Dynamics*, Winter 1992, 5–15.

Jean Auel's *The Clan of the Cave Bear* (New York: Bantam Books, 1980) is an entertaining novel about life in a primitive clan. Her descriptions of how the clan deals with both crises and daily routines provide valuable insights into the workings and justifications of modern organizations.

On Your Own

◆◆◆

The Organizational Behavior IQ Test Please fill out the following questionnaire. Your instructor will provide you with information about the meaning of your responses.

On the following pages are 24 pairs of statements. For each pair, circle the letter preceding the statement that you think is most accurate. Circle *one* and *only one* letter in each pair.

After you have circled the letter, indicate how certain you are of your choice by writing 1, 2, 3, or 4 on the line in front of each item according to the following procedure.

Place a "1" if you are *very uncertain* that your choice is correct.
Place a "2" if you are *somewhat uncertain* that your choice is correct.
Place a "3" if you are *somewhat certain* that your choice is correct.
Place a "4" if you are *very certain* that your choice is correct.

Do not skip any pairs.

_____ 1. **a.** A supervisor is well advised to treat, as much as possible, all members of his/her group exactly the same way.
b. A supervisor is well advised to adjust his/her behavior according to the unique characteristics of the members of his/her group.

_____ 2. **a.** Generally speaking, individual motivation is greatest if the person has set goals for himself/herself which are *difficult* to achieve.
b. Generally speaking, individual motivation is greatest if the person has set goals for himself/herself which are *easy* to achieve.

_____ 3. **a.** A major reason why organizations are not so productive as they could be these days is that managers are too concerned with managing the work group rather than the individual.
b. A major reason why organizations are not so productive as they could be these days is that managers are too concerned with managing the individual rather than the work group.

_____ 4. **a.** Supervisors who sometime prior to becoming a supervisor have performed the job of the people they are currently supervising are apt to be *more* effective supervisors than those who have never performed that particular job.
b. Supervisors who sometime prior to becoming a supervisor have performed the job of the people they are currently supervising are apt to be *less* effective supervisors than those who have never performed that particular job.

_____ 5. **a.** On almost every matter relevant to the work, managers are well advised to be completely honest and open with their subordinates.
b. There are very few matters in the workplace where managers are well advised to be completely honest and open with their subordinates.

_____ 6. **a.** On almost every matter relevant to the work, managers are well advised to be completely honest and open with their superiors.
b. There are very few matters in the workplace where managers are well advised to be completely honest and open with their superiors.

_____ 7. **a.** One's *need for power* is a better predictor of managerial advancement than one's *motivation to do the work well.*
b. One's *motivation to do the work well* is a better predictor of managerial advancement than one's *need for power.*

_____ 8. **a.** When people fail at something, they try harder the next time.
b. When people fail at something they quit trying.

_____ 9. **a.** Performing well as a manager depends most on how much *education* you have.
b. Performing well as a manager depends most on how much *experience* you have.

_____ 10. **a.** The most effective leaders are those who give more emphasis to *getting the work done* than they do to *relating to people.*
b. The effective leaders are those who give more emphasis to *relating to people* than they do to *getting the work done.*

_____ **11. a.** It is very important for a leader to "stick to his/her guns." **b.** It is *not* very important for a leader to "stick to his/her guns."

_____ **12. a.** *Pay* is the most important factor in determining how hard people work. **b.** The *nature of the task people are doing* is the most important factor in determining how hard people work.

_____ **13. a.** *Pay* is the most important factor in determining how satisfied people are at work. **b.** The *nature of the task people are doing* is the most important factor in determining how satisfied people are at work.

_____ **14. a.** Generally speaking the top level executives of major corporations can be expected to make decisions which *maximize the best interests of the organization* as a whole. **b.** Generally speaking the top level executives of major corporations can be expected to make decisions which *make them look good (or at least not look bad)* even if the interests of the organization as a whole are not maximized.

_____ **15. a.** Generally speaking it is correct to say that a person's *attitudes cause his/her behavior.* **b.** Generally speaking it is correct to say that a person's *attitudes are primarily rationalizations for his/her behavior.*

_____ **16. a.** Satisfied workers produce *more* than workers who are not satisfied. **b.** Satisfied workers produce *no more* than workers who are not satisfied.

_____ **17. a.** Generally speaking the *structure* of an organization determines the *technology it uses.* **b.** Generally speaking the *technology* of an organization determines its structure.

_____ **18. a.** The statement, "A manager's authority needs to be commensurate with his/her responsibility" is practically speaking a *very meaningful statement.* **b.** The statement, "A manager's authority needs to be commensurate with his/her responsibility" is practically speaking a *basically meaningless statement.*

_____ **19. a.** A major reason for the relative decline in American productivity is that the division of labor and job specialization *have gone too far.* **b.** A major reason for the relative decline in American productivity is that the division of labor and job specialization *have not been carried far enough.*

_____ **20. a.** The notion that most semiskilled workers desire work which is interesting and meaningful is most likely *incorrect.* **b.** The notion that most semiskilled workers desire work which is interesting and meaningful is most likely *correct.*

_____ **21. a.** People welcome change for the better. **b.** Even if change is for the better, people will resist it.

_____ **22. a.** Leaders are born, not made. **b.** Leaders are made, not born.

_____ **23. a.** Groups make better decisions than individuals. **b.** Individuals make better decisions than groups.

_____ **24. a.** Generally speaking the largest corporations would be more efficient if they were *larger.* **b.** Generally speaking the largest corporations would be more efficient if they were *smaller.*

Source: "Coping with 'It's All Common Sense'," by Robert Weinberg and Walter Nord, *Exchange*, 1982. Volume VII, Number 2, 32–33. Used with permission.

CHAPTER 1

THE MANAGER'S MEMO

FROM: J. Cox, Executive Vice President

TO: M. Berger, Manager, Swimwear Division

RE: Second Quarter Performance

In reviewing each division's performance for the second quarter, I note that our new Swimwear Division is failing to meet its planned goals. Sales are well below targeted levels. I understand from the sales department that our swimsuits have failed to incorporate the most recent fashion innovations introduced by our major competitors. In addition, we have been receiving complaints that the legholes of our swimsuits are often sewn shut.

How can you explain these problems? As I recall, when you started up the division last year you had prepared an impressively detailed plan and had organized the division for maximum efficiency. Can it be that the division's fashion designers are poorly qualified or that the production work force is not cooperating with your goals?

None of this really fits the orderly management of organizations I was led to expect in business school. Am I being naive about the realities of organizational life?

Case Discussion Questions

Based upon what you have learned about organizational behavior, assume you are the manager of the Swimsuit Division and respond to this memo. What are some possible causes of the division's problems?

◆◆◆◆◆◆

FACING THE CHALLENGE: HISTORICAL PERSPECTIVES

THEY PRACTICED WHAT THEY PREACHED ◆◆◆◆◆◆

Frank and Lillian Gilbreth, two of America's earliest and best-known efficiency experts, pioneered the use of motion pictures in the early 1900s to identify efficient production techniques. Their photographic time-and-motion studies were used to distinguish the basic component motions of work tasks and sought to simplify work tasks by eliminating unnecessary motions. Included in their successes was the simplification of a bricklaying task from 18 to 5 basic motions, yielding an increase in output from 120 to 350 bricks per hour and a net *decrease* in worker fatigue.

For Frank and Lillian Gilbreth, improving efficiency was more than just a way to make a living—it was a way of life. In the book *Cheaper by the Dozen*, two of the Gilbreth children popularized their parents' attempts to apply scientific management to life at home. In one particularly revealing description of life at the Gilbreths', the children noted:

> Yes, at home or on the job, Dad was always the efficiency expert. . . . He even used two shaving brushes to lather his face, because he found that by so doing he could cut 17 seconds off his shaving time. For a while, he tried shaving with two razors, but he finally gave that up.
>
> "I can save forty-four seconds," he grumbled, "but I wasted two minutes this morning putting this bandage on my throat."

The Gilbreths' focus on improving efficiency by eliminating unnecessary motions lives on today in concepts like process management at Motorola, a Baldrige quality award winner. It used to take *seven weeks* for a Motorola field auditor to deliver a final report to top management. The auditor would visit a plant, return to headquarters to draft a report, have it typed, revise it, send it to the supervisor for comments, revise it again, send it to the audit manager for comments, revise it *again*, send it to the auditee for comments, and finally incorporate any further changes in a final version. Each twist and turn of the process afforded new opportunities for delay and error.

To speed things up, a task force was formed to make radical suggestions that eliminated nonessential tasks and expanded the use of information technology. Today, the auditor writes a report in the field on a laptop computer and then solicits and incorporates comments from the auditee and an audit manager while still at the plant. Back at headquarters, a secretary does a quick cleanup of the report on disk and prints it out. The whole process now takes just five days. Using this new procedure, Motorola's audit department has reduced its supervisory and support staff by a third in the last five years and now saves $1.8 million per year in audit fees.

Sources: Adapted from R. Henkoff, "Make Your Office More Productive," *Fortune*, February 25, 1991, 72–84; F. B. Gilbreth, Jr. and E. G. Carey, *Cheaper by the Dozen* (New York: Thomas Cromwell, 1948), 2–3; and F. B. Gilbreth and L. M. Gilbreth, *Applied Motion Study* (New York: Sturgis & Walton, 1917).

INTRODUCTION

To understand organizational behavior as a field of scientific inquiry, one must first look back on the history of management thought and theory. Organizational behavior traces its roots to classical management theories (such as Fayol's functional approach to management). It came into being as a field when management practitioners began to recognize the impossibility of successfully carrying out Fayol's management functions without a sound understanding of human behavior in organizations. This chapter explores the origins and history of the field of organizational behavior by examining the evolution of management thought and theory up to the present day.

TRADITIONAL VIEWS

In the beginning there was the Arsenal. The Arsenal was not the *very* beginning, of course, but it could have been the beginning of modern management theory and practice. Therefore, it is with the Arsenal that we begin our review of the history of management. The Arsenal, opened in 1436, was the shipyard of Venice, Italy. By 1400, Venice had become a thriving center of commerce. To protect its fleet of commercial ships, the city of Venice set up its own shipyard to build, repair, and outfit warships. By 1500, the Arsenal shipyard employed almost 2,000 workers and covered more than 60 acres of the Venice waterfront. This shipyard was the forerunner of the modern industrial organization.[1]

The Arsenal was the first modern assembly line. A series of Arsenal warehouses were arranged along a Venice canal, each corresponding to a different set of tasks in the building, repair, and outfitting of warships. The warships were towed up the canal, from warehouse to warehouse, until required work was completed. When a warship reached a particular warehouse, needed parts and equipment were passed out windows onto the ship.

---

[1] F. Lane, *Venetian Ships and Shipbuilders of the Renaissance* (Baltimore: Johns Hopkins Press, 1934).

Bureaucracy

The Arsenal was a bureaucratic organization. The defining characteristics of a bureaucratic organization are presented in Figure 2–1. In a bureaucratic organization (or **bureaucracy**), there are clearly defined lines of authority and responsibility for employees. Behavior is tightly controlled by rules, policies, and job assignments. In the Arsenal, the warehouses had been placed carefully in sequence so that no backtracking in the "assembly line" would be needed. Standardization of parts, specialization of labor, and accounting and inventory control all were used to keep a tight rein on the Arsenal's production process.

Bureaucratic organizations like the Arsenal function like machines. In a machine, every part has a specific, well-defined role that is performed in concert with all other parts of the machine. There are no extra parts, nor are there parts which function independently from the rest of the machine.

Max Weber, a German sociologist, was a great admirer of the bureaucratic model of organizations and wrote extensively on its characteristics during the latter nineteenth and early twentieth centuries. As shown in the following passage from *Legitimate Authority and Bureaucracy*, Weber believed that the bureaucratic organizations represented something of an *ideal* organizational form for proper management:

> Experience tends universally to show that the purely bureaucratic type of administrative organization . . . is, from a purely technical point of view, capable of attaining the highest degree of efficiency and is in this sense formally the most rational known means of carrying out imperative control over human beings. It is superior to any other form in precision, in stability, in the stringency of discipline, and in its reliability. It thus makes possible a particularly high degree of calculability of results for the heads of the organization and for those acting in relation to it. It is finally superior both in intensive efficiency and in the scope of its operations.[2]

To Weber's way of thinking, bureaucracy provided the ideal means of impersonal control, and thereby the surest path to organizational efficiency. Bureaucratic control enhances efficiency by ensuring that all worker effort is properly channeled toward the accomplishment of organizational goals.

Impersonal control in a bureaucracy means control that is achieved through rules, regulations, and job descriptions that clearly dictate proper conduct in the organization. This impersonal control stands in contrast to *personal* means of control, such as charisma or social persuasion. From the bureaucratic perspective, personal means of organizational control are far too dependent upon individuals for getting things done, and therefore are far too unreliable. In a bureaucracy, control is a function of the *system* (the rules and regulations) rather than of the people in the system. Control occurs because of authority vested in a position by the rules and regulations. This means that the system should be able to survive changes in personnel with no loss in efficiency. This is highly desirable from the viewpoint of reliability. It also means that the personalities and personal motivations of officeholders should be largely irrelevant to understanding behavior in a bureaucracy.

The prevailing view of workers in bureaucratic organizations is mechanical or mechanistic. Management views each worker as a collection of skills and abilities—a cog in the machine with performance potential. Management uses pay to fuel each cog's contributions to the functioning of the machine. In a bureau-

---

[2]M. Weber, *Essays in Sociology* (New York: Oxford University Press, 1946).

FIGURE 2–1	▶ Characteristics of a Bureaucracy

1. Each office has fixed official duties.
2. Conduct is governed by impersonal rules and regulations.
3. Effort is coordinated through a hierarchy of levels of authority.
4. Order and reliability are maintained through written communication and files.
5. Employment is a full-time occupation for members of the organization.
6. Appointment to office is made by superiors.
7. Promotion is based upon merit (that is, who does the best job).

Source: M. Weber, *Essays in Sociology* (New York: Oxford University Press, 1946).

cracy, management pays little if any attention to the fact that workers might be *thinking* about the work they are doing. Once again, this implies a limited view of employee motivation.

Despite the enormous efficiency advantages available through the use of bureaucratic organization, the model provided by the Arsenal shipyard was not widely adopted until the invention of the steam engine. When the steam engine was introduced in England, it became possible for the first time to design highly efficient, large-scale production technologies. In place of craftsmen working at home in cottage industries, large factories were built to house the new machines and the armies of workers necessary to run them. The Industrial Revolution had arrived.

Scientific Management

With the Industrial Revolution came the acceptance of large industrial factories and bureaucratic organizations as appropriate institutions for doing business. Managers were uncertain, however, about how to run these factories and organizations and take advantage of their tremendous efficiency potential. After all, workers were familiar primarily with "craftsman" models of production in which skilled individuals worked independently. Large industrial factories used greater job specialization, required increased standardization of work, and were structured around a differentiation between labor and levels of management. These new arrangements were unfamiliar and required a new approach to getting work done.

That new approach was a theory of management. The new challenge was planning, organizing, commanding, and controlling. Frederick Taylor translated this new way of thinking into prescriptions for changing the behaviors of individual workers on the shop floor. Taylor's approach to planning, organizing, coordinating, commanding, and controlling work on the shop floor became known as scientific management. **Scientific management** took its name from the careful and systematic observational techniques it used to design jobs and arrange work for the rank-and-file factory worker.

While employed as a manager at the Midvale Steel Works in Philadelphia, Taylor became disgusted with the gross inefficiency and waste he found on the factory shop floor. A piecework compensation plan was the heart of factory labor management at the time. Workers were paid a fixed amount for every correctly produced item. Unfortunately, Taylor observed, workers were ill-equipped, inadequately trained, and poorly supervised. Moreover, it was obvious that workers were restricting their output *intentionally* to keep management's productivity expectations low and piece rates high. Taylor suspected that with a more careful and systematic approach to labor management, worker productivity could be increased dramatically, perhaps more than tripled.

Taylor's attempts to correct the problems he found led to the four principles shown in Figure 2–2. First, Taylor popularized **time-and-motion studies.** Using a clipboard and stopwatch, Taylor observed different workers' ways of accomplishing the same task. He would time each worker's attempts and use the results to determine which methods were the most efficient. Taylor often would instruct a worker to try different methods for accomplishing a task while Taylor watched, timed, and recorded observations. For instance, in order to identify the most efficient method for shoveling coal, Taylor systematically manipulated such factors as the size of the shovel, the amount of coal in the shovel, the number of shovels between rest breaks, and the length of the rest breaks. Taylor's time-and-motion experiments identified the most efficient means for accomplishing a work task.[3]

Second, when the time-and-motion study of a work task had been completed, Taylor used this information to establish work standards. **Work standards** included specific instructions to workers for doing a work task, expected time to complete a task, and expected volume of output. Taylor used these standards to establish what he called "a fair day's work." "A fair day's work" was defined as the amount of production that could be expected from a worker who followed Taylor's directions and worked diligently throughout the entire workday. The standards Taylor provided made it clear to workers what was expected of them both in quality and method.

Third, Taylor emphasized the importance of the systematic **selection** and training of workers. Having identified (using time-and-motion studies) the most efficient method for completing a task, Taylor thought it critical to select workers capable of working according to the identified instructions. Then, careful training of those workers would ensure that they knew the correct method for accomplishing the work task.

Finally, Taylor firmly believed that what workers "want most from their employers beyond anything else is high wages."[4] As noted earlier, Taylor felt that workers intentionally restricted output to keep management productivity expectations low and piece rates high. To reverse this trend, Taylor offered workers a piece-rate differential. Whenever the daily output of a worker exceeded the calculated "fair day's work," the piece rate received by the worker would be higher. For example, a worker whose output exceeded the calculated "fair day's work" might receive 6¢ per piece produced instead of 5¢. Further, this higher piece rate would be paid for *all* the pieces the worker produced during the day in which the "fair day's work" was exceeded. Because Taylor believed that money was the only important motivator of workers on the job, he felt this incentive would be too attractive to pass up and workers would work hard to obtain it.

Using these four techniques—time-and-motion studies and experiments, work standards, systematic selection and training, and piece-rate differentials—

[3]F. W. Taylor, "The Principles of Scientific Management," *The Bulletin of the Taylor Society* (December 1916): 13–23.

[4]F. W. Taylor, *Shop Management* (New York: Harper and Brothers, 1911).

FIGURE 2-2	▶ **Features of Scientific Management**

1. *Time-and-motion studies.* Using a clipboard and stopwatch, Taylor calculated the speed of different approaches to a task. He also conducted experiments in which he varied approaches to a task to see which was most efficient.
2. *Work standards.* A "fair day's work" was the amount of production that could be expected of an industrious worker who followed Taylor's directions for completing a task efficiently.
3. *Selection and training.* Taylor emphasized that the selection of qualified workers and their careful training were essential to the achievement of highly efficient production.
4. *Wages.* Taylor believed that workers should share in the production gains attained by their highly efficient work. Taylor pioneered the use of wage differentials, which paid a worker extra for production beyond "a fair day's work."

Taylor's applications of scientific management at Bethlehem Steel produced stunning increases in efficiency. In some recorded cases, Taylor increased worker output from 12½ to 47 tons of pig iron loaded in a ten-hour day, even though he instructed workers to rest 57 percent of the time. Taylor is credited with saving Bethlehem Steel as much as $80,000 per year in pig-iron handling costs while simultaneously increasing workers' wages by more than 50 percent.[5]

Later research raised questions about the accuracy of Taylor's reported successes using scientific management at Bethlehem Steel.[6] Nevertheless, scientific management caught on big. In 1914, Ford Motor Company raised basic wages to $5 per day—an unheard-of sum that Ford attributed to the successes of its scientific management cost-cutting programs.[7]

Taylor's pioneering principles can be found today in the fields of operations management and human factors psychology. Operations management is a sister field of organizational behavior within the discipline of management. While organizational behavior is concerned with management of an organization's *human* resources, operations management focuses on the organization's *technical* resources (such as machinery, raw materials, and plant layout). Typical topics of study in operations management include purchase and storage of materials, work-flow and delivery scheduling, and quality-control issues. Human factors psychology is concerned with the importance of human characteristics and limitations in the design of training programs, work environments, and technologies.

Careful employee selection and training, standard setting, and financial incentives all remain powerful tools in today's management repertoire.[8] Scientific management did fall out of vogue, however. While the productivity gains it achieved were impressive, some were concerned that they represented a subtle

---

[5]W. J. Duncan, *Management* (New York: Random House, 1983).

[6]C. Wrege and A. Perroni, "Taylor's Pig-Tale: An Historical Analysis of Frederick W. Taylor's Pig-Iron Experiments," *Academy of Management Journal* 17 (1974): 6–27.

[7]Duncan, *Management*, 19.

[8]E. A. Locke, "The Ideas of Frederick W. Taylor: An Evaluation," *Academy of Management Review* 7 (1982): 14–24.

Frederick Taylor used the principles of scientific management (including time-and-motion studies, work standards, careful selection and training, and a piece-rate differential wage package) to dramatically increase the productivity of workers such as these employees of Bethlehem Steel.

form of worker exploitation. Further, the application of Taylor's techniques often resulted in layoffs, making scientific management at times unpopular in local communities.

Scientific management also lost popularity because Taylor built his theory of management around the assumption that money was the key way to motivate shop-floor workers. As noted earlier, Taylor's work also acknowledged the role of noneconomic factors in work settings. In particular, Taylor reported the existence of worker norms to restrict output intentionally. However, Taylor believed that these social concerns (and other noneconomic worker motives) were relatively unimportant and would be overwhelmed by financial incentives. The critical importance of noneconomic worker motivation was brought to light by a series of studies in the 1920s—the Hawthorne studies.

THE HAWTHORNE STUDIES

Elton Mayo, a professor at Harvard University, headed a research team investigating the high turnover in a Philadelphia textile mill. The year was 1923. After careful study, Mayo's team reorganized the work schedule to include more rest periods—a procedure not unfamiliar to the scientific management practitioners of Mayo's era. The major effects of adding the rest periods were to reduce turnover while substantially boosting worker morale.[9]

While the reduction in turnover was expected, the improvement in morale was a surprise. The unexpected morale increases highlighted for Mayo the importance of noneconomic motives for American workers. Mayo left the textile mills with a new sensitivity to the viewpoint of the worker. He did not have to wait long to apply his new insight. His Harvard research group had been asked to help unravel a perplexing mystery then unfolding at the Hawthorne plant of the Western Electric Company.

[9]E. Mayo, *The Social Problems of an Industrial Civilization* (Boston: Harvard University Press, 1945).

The Illumination Studies

Before Mayo and his colleagues arrived at the Hawthorne plant, an initial study there had explored the effects of workplace illumination (lighting) levels on worker productivity. Tungsten-filament electric lamps recently had been invented and quickly were displacing gas lamps as the favored lighting source in industrial plants. Electric companies, fearing substantial revenue losses from the highly efficient tungsten bulbs, wanted to encourage industrial electricity usage by suggesting that higher levels of illumination would increase worker productivity on the shop floor.

To test this "illumination" hypothesis, researchers selected two groups of about six female workers each from the shop floor. One group (the control group) was placed in a test room where the illumination level remained constant throughout the study. The other group (the experimental group) was placed in a test room where the amount of work-area illumination was varied systematically.

In the test room where illumination levels varied systematically, worker productivity increased when work-area illumination increased. This was expected. However, productivity also increased for this group when work-area illumination *decreased*, even to the level of moonlight intensity. Furthermore, the productivity increases achieved by the experimental group were matched by the *control* group, even though the control group's illumination levels remained constant throughout the study!

Elton Mayo and his Harvard colleagues were brought in to help solve this mystery. They noticed a subtle but important parallel with their findings in the Philadelphia textile mills. In both cases, simple economic views of worker motivation—consistent with the orientation of scientific management—were unable to explain the results. These failures of scientific management at Hawthorne led Mayo and his colleagues to a new understanding of the rank-and-file factory worker that encompassed more human attributes.

Mayo and his colleagues pursued his new vision of the factory worker through additional research at Hawthorne. By 1932, when research at Hawthorne ended, seven studies had taken place and more than 20,000 Western Electric employees had participated as subjects. Next to the illumination studies, the most provocative research results came from a study of workers wiring telephone connection terminals (or "banks").

The Bank Wiring Room Study

The bank wiring room study began with careful observation of the productivity of the bank wiring workers. According to the results of a time-and-motion analysis of bank wiring, industrial engineers had arrived at a standard of two and one-half completely wired telephone connection terminals per day per worker. In fact, the workers produced on the average only two completed terminals per day.

The workers in the bank wiring room offered several explanations for their "restriction of output." None of these explanations was particularly novel or noteworthy. What did command the researchers' attention was the manner in which output restriction was being achieved. Apparently the bank wiring group was a tight *social* group, in addition to a work group. There seemed to be an unstated conviction that *all* members of the group had family responsibilities and needed to remain employed. So the slower workers were protected by the

The Hawthorne studies are an important part of the history of organizational behavior. While their scientific validity remains in doubt even today, there is little doubt that the results of these studies forced management theorists to reexamine their assumptions about human motivation.

work group—no one outproduced the slowest workers enough to get them in trouble.

Protection of the slower workers was achieved by group members applying social pressure on the "rate busters." Group members might tease or ridicule a particularly fast worker who seemed to be on the verge of violating the group's informal production norm of only two completed terminals per day. If a fast worker's productivity really got out of hand, the group members might resort to "binging." Binging was a game in which one worker would punch the rate buster, setting off a chain reaction of returned punches. While the punching was all in good fun, "binging" did serve to distract fast workers from the task at hand and to convey the message that an important group expectation (productivity level) was being violated.

What did Elton Mayo and the management community learn from the Hawthorne studies? The results of the illumination studies demonstrated that purely economic views of worker motivation do not take into account the complexities that drive worker behavior. Scientific management could explain why productivity would go up when work area illumination was increased, but not why productivity would go up when illumination was *decreased* or *remained unchanged*. Perhaps of greater importance, the bank wiring group study demonstrated the power of the informal social structure of a work group. Though the bank wiring group workers were paid on an individual piece-rate plan, social pressures proved quite effective in restricting output of the work group's members.

As the years have passed, the scientific quality of the Hawthorne studies has come under attack. The celebrated Hawthorne effect, a concept learned in all introductory psychology classes and detailed in the "FOCUS ON: The Hawthorne Studies" is now believed to be a misinterpretation of the original findings. In retrospect, even Fritz Roethlisberger, one of the central research figures in the studies, admits that some of the Hawthorne study conclusions are questionable.[10] Nevertheless, the Hawthorne studies played a major role in shifting the emphasis of management theory away from simple mechanistic and economic views of worker motivation.

[10]F. J. Roethlisberger, *The Elusive Phenomena* (Cambridge, Mass.: Harvard University Press, 1977).

The Hawthorne Studies

Legacy of the Legend   "It looked as if the workers were reacting more to the positive concern of the experimenters about their working conditions than to the actual physical changes in illumination." With these words, Fritz Roethlisberger summarized a widely held belief about the importance of the Hawthorne studies at Western Electric. While this explanation of the findings of the Hawthorne studies has fallen into disrepute over the years, its message remains critical to the practice of behavioral science research. Subjects in experiments do not always act like workers on the job. This change in the behavior of subjects who know that an experiment is taking place is called *the Hawthorne effect.*

A. H. Pierce first noted this effect in 1908, when he wrote that subjects who know they are involved in experiments often take on a "cheerful willingness to assist the investigator in every possible way by reporting to him those very things which he is most eager to find." This willingness of subjects to help out or please the researcher was dramatically demonstrated in a series of studies conducted by Martin Orne. Orne asked subjects to perform serial additions of adjacent rows on sheets of paper filled with rows of random numbers. To complete just one would require 224 separate additions. After completing a page, the subject was "to tear up the sheet of paper which you have just completed into a minimum of thirty-two pieces and go on to the next sheet of paper."

Orne was looking for a particularly objectionable task to use in some other research he was pursuing. He expected that subjects would quit when they realized that the sheets were identical and that each finished sheet had to be destroyed—in short, when they realized that the task was meaningless. Instead subjects persevered at this task for *several hours,* showing no signs of hostility. Apparently subjects feel there is an implicit contract with the experimenter that they are duty-bound to honor.

Outside of the behavioral science laboratory, it seems inconceivable that an adult human being would put up with such nonsense. That it happens even in a behavioral science laboratory provides a testament to the power of the Hawthorne effects—and a caution about interpreting the results of experiments that are clearly defined as such to their subjects.

Sources: M. Orne, "On the Social Psychology of the Psychology Experiment: With Particular Reference to Demand Characteristics and Their Implications," *American Psychologist* 17 (1962): 776–783; F. J. Roethlisberger, *The Elusive Phenomenon* (Cambridge, Mass: Harvard University Press, 1977).

HUMAN RELATIONS

By demonstrating the power of social relationships in work settings, the Hawthorne studies created a need for new ways of thinking about management. Judging from the behavior of the workers in the bank wiring group at Hawthorne, social relationships could be even stronger motivators than management's economic incentives. Approaches to managing behavior in organizations now had to incorporate a more complex, and indeed more *human*, vision of the American worker. The new approach to management that emerged emphasized the importance of workers' personal and social needs. It came to be known as **human relations.**

A big problem for managers stood at the center of this new way of thinking. The application of high-efficiency management techniques often resulted in jobs that were efficient but not very interesting for the workers. Insufficiently stimulated by their work, workers turned to social fulfillment in the workplace.

Managers needed to direct worker attention and effort toward the job. This meant that the real problem was how to keep workers' search for noneconomic fulfillment from interfering with their accomplishment of the organization's objectives.

Human relations management offered some solutions to these problems. The human relations approach took two factors that had been ignored in previous theories about worker behavior in organizations and put them front and center. First, human relations embraced a broader concept of human needs and desires. Gone were purely economic approaches to understanding worker behavior. Human relations also accepted the informal organizational structures (such as social networks and group memberships) as critical components of organizational life. Human relations viewed bureaucratic models of organizational life, which ignored the humanity of workers, as inadequate. From the perspective of the human relations movement, the worker had social, personal, *and* economic motivations, and the organization was a complex network of work *and* social relationships. The business of managing for effective and efficient productivity had some new challenges.

The new emphasis on human relations in management was reflected in several developments: (1) Walker and Guest's research concerning organizational life for *The Man on the Assembly Line*, (2) Douglas McGregor's Theory Y, and (3) Rensis Likert's System 4 theory of management.

The Man on the Assembly Line

One highly visible research effort that came out of the new focus on human relations in the workplace was a series of studies conducted by Charles Walker and Robert Guest entitled *The Man on the Assembly Line*.[11] These studies became the forerunners of all current research on *job design* (a topic that will receive more attention in Chapter 12 of this book).

Walker and Guest's studies differed from virtually all previous management research. Following the lead of the Hawthorne studies, Walker and Guest focused their research on discovering what made workers interested and involved. Walker and Guest interviewed 180 workers at an American automobile assembly plant that was considered one of the most modern and technologically sophisticated in the world.

Walker and Guest studied many of the same job aspects as scientific management practitioners. However, they also looked at what they called the total job situation. The **total job situation** included the seven characteristics shown in Figure 2–3. The influence of the Hawthorne studies should be apparent in this list of research topics. A primary emphasis of human relations management was the inclusion of workers' *social relationships* (for instance, with other workers and with the union) in a theory of worker behavior in organizations.

The role of social relationships in organizational behavior was only one important emphasis of the research conducted by Walker and Guest. They also were interested in worker alienation. *Alienation* refers to a worker's feelings of boredom and underutilization of mental capacity. Walker and Guest were convinced that alienation occurred when workers were assigned highly specialized, highly routinized, and highly repetitive tasks—the very kinds of tasks designed

---

[11]C. R. Walker and R. H. Guest, *The Man on the Assembly Line* (Cambridge, Mass.: Harvard University Press, 1952).

Walker and Guest's studies of assembly-line workers in the 1950s led them to conclude that workers became alienated when they were assigned specialized, routinized, and repetitive tasks—the very kinds of tasks recommended by the principles of scientific management.

into assembly lines by scientific management practitioners to achieve efficiency. Walker and Guest also felt that workers' beliefs that management saw them only as production labor were at the root of alienation. Many workers apparently felt that the regimentation of their jobs made it possible for management to replace them at any time. It was, after all, the *system* rather than the workers that produced the cars. Walker and Guest found that jobs that scored high on alienating characteristics (for instance, assembly-line jobs) typically suffered *twice as much* turnover and absenteeism.

Walker and Guest interpreted their findings as a mandate for management to increase the mental role of workers in production. In fact, they came out clearly in favor of allowing workers some say in the arrangement and pacing of

FIGURE 2–3	▶ Features of the Total Job Situation

The human relations movement brought with it a broader sense of a job that went beyond work tasks. In their study of assembly-line jobs, for example, Walker and Guest defined the "total job situation" in terms of seven characteristics, which included social relationships on the job.

1. The worker's immediate job
2. The worker's relation to fellow workers
3. The worker's relation to supervisors
4. The worker's relation to the union
5. Pay and job security
6. Promotion and transfer
7. Working conditions in the plant

Source: C. R. Walker and R. H. Guest, *The Man on the Assembly Line* (Cambridge, Mass.: Harvard University Press, 1952).

their work. They suspected that "gains in quality and a drop in turnover or absenteeism may balance some decrease in output, if it occurs."[12]

The issue of worker participation in decision making on the shop floor provides a strong contrast between human relations and scientific management; Frederick Taylor had maintained that, "all possible brain work should be removed from the shop and centered in the planning or lay-out department. . . . The time during which the [worker] stops to think is part of the time that he is not productive."[13]

A second, parallel set of studies of manufacturing workers confirmed many of Walker and Guest's conclusions. In 1944 and 1945, Donald Roy worked as a radial drill operator for the Geer Company.[14] His observations and the descriptions of his work there have provided valuable insights for students of organizational behavior. Twenty years later, Michael Buroway returned to the same company to see if behavior at the Geer Company, as described by Roy, had changed much over the years.[15] While the manufacturing technology at Geer had changed dramatically (and the company had changed its name!), Roy's most important insights about worker behavior remained true.

Both Roy and Buroway found that while the pace of work for the typical rank-and-file laborer was fast, the work was not involving. The highly repetitive, routinized, and specialized jobs characteristic of high-efficiency manufacturing companies apparently are *not* difficult enough to challenge the intellectual capabilities of many manufacturing laborers. Absenteeism, turnover, and a general sense of alienation result. As one well-known job design expert has noted in describing this situation, most American workers are "underutilized and underchallenged at work."[16]

Both Roy and Buroway found that because work on the shop floor did not sufficiently tax the intellectual capacities of the workers, the workers would devise games and rituals or ceremonies to pass the time and make their jobs more bearable. Roy and Buroway agreed that these games and rituals generally were counterproductive in terms of the organization's effectiveness and efficiency goals. They concluded that there exists in every worker an untapped reservoir of intellectual energy. If the manager cannot usefully harness this energy, it will be turned to counterproductive purposes.

It is interesting to note that neither Roy nor Buroway concluded that American factory workers are lazy. On the contrary, they both believed that the reservoir of intellectual energy in the American worker is a potential source of heightened productivity waiting to be tapped. This conclusion is consistent with results of surveys of American workers. Surveys have shown both that American workers report not working as hard as they might, and that they would be willing to work harder if their jobs were more interesting and involving.[17]

---

[12]Ibid., 151.

[13]F. W. Taylor, *Scientific Management* (New York: Harper & Row, 1947). 98–99, 262.

[14]D. Roy, "Banana Time: Job Satisfaction and Informal Interaction," *Human Organization* 18 (1958): 1960.

[15]M. Buroway, *Manufacturing Consent* (Chicago: University of Chicago Press, 1979).

[16]R. J. Hackman, "The Design of Work in the 1980s," *Organizational Dynamics* (Summer 1978): 2–17.

[17]"Most Workers Really Want to Work Harder," *Nation's Business* (June 1980): 18.

Theory Y

Walker and Guest's research represents only a sample of work at the time of the human relations movement. The human relations movement represented a fundamental shift in the focus of managing organizational behavior. This shift found its strongest voice in the writings of two management theorists: Douglas McGregor and Rensis Likert.

McGregor was the executive director of industrial relations at the Massachusetts Institute of Technology during the 1940s and later became the president of Antioch College. McGregor felt that productivity problems in American manufacturing were largely due to management not providing workers the opportunity to fulfill any but their economic needs. He believed that managers did not provide opportunities to fulfill these other needs because they operated on the wrong *assumptions* about human nature. In the preface to *The Human Side of Enterprise*, McGregor noted that successful management of behavior in organizations is to a very large degree:

> . . . the result of management's conception of the nature of its task and all the policies and practices which are constructed to implement this conception. The way a business is managed determines to a very large extent what people are perceived to have "potential" and how they develop. . . . The blunt fact is that we are a long way from realizing the potential represented by the human resources we now recruit into industry.[18]

McGregor called management's traditional view of the worker Theory X. As shown in Figure 2–4, **Theory X** consists of a set of assumptions about what drives the behavior of the rank-and-file worker, such as his motive to avoid hard work. McGregor believed that these assumptions were not only incorrect but "unnecessarily limiting." He felt that by accepting such a limited view of workers' human potential, management constructed systems to control organizational behavior that made the realization of human potential impossible. A worker believed by management to be inherently lazy and averse to taking responsibility never will be given responsibility and never will flourish as an employee.

McGregor also believed that by accepting Theory X assumptions about the worker, management defined its role in the organization as the director and controller of labor through its exercise of authority. Having authority in an organization simply means having a position that confers the right to give orders to other workers and to punish workers who don't obey. The use of authority as a way of getting things done will be discussed in detail in Chapter 8.

McGregor felt that getting work done through the exercise of authority was exceptionally short-sighted. After all, authority will force action only when (1) workers have no choice but to go along, and (2) failure to obey can be detected and punished effectively (for instance, through dismissal). On the question of workers having no choice but to go along with orders (or get punished or fired), McGregor felt that Theory X assumptions were out of date. By 1940, legislation had begun to protect worker rights and the union movement in America was growing in strength. As a result, management was just beginning to realize

---

[18]D. McGregor, *The Human Side of Enterprise* (New York: McGraw-Hill, 1960), iv.

| FIGURE 2–4 | ▶ Assumptions of Theory X and Theory Y |

McGregor offered Theory X and Theory Y as two different approaches to the business of management. McGregor felt that a flexible but not permissive style like that represented by Theory Y was necessary to fully develop employees as organizational resources.

Theory X:
1. Management is responsible for organizing the elements of productive enterprise—money, materials, equipment, people—in the interest of economic ends.
2. With respect to people, management must direct their efforts, motivate them, control their actions, and modify their behavior to fit the needs of the organization.
3. Without this active intervention by management, people would be indifferent—even resistant—to organizational needs. They must therefore be persuaded, rewarded, punished, and controlled.
4. The average worker is by nature indolent—he works as little as possible. He lacks ambition, dislikes responsibility, prefers to be led. He is inherently self-centered, indifferent to organizational needs. He is by nature resistant to change. He is gullible, not very bright, the ready dupe of the charlatan and the demagogue.

Theory Y:
1. The expenditure of physical and mental effort in work is as natural as play or rest.
2. External control and the threat of punishment are not the only means for bringing about effort toward organizational objectives. Individuals will exercise self-direction and self-control in the service of objectives to which they are committed.
3. Commitment to objectives is a function of rewards associated with their achievement. The most significant of such rewards . . . can be the direct products of effort directed toward organizational objectives.
4. The average human being learns under proper conditions not only to accept but to seek responsibility.
5. The capacity to exercise a relatively high degree of imagination, ingenuity, and creativity in the solution of organizational problems is widely, not narrowly, distributed in the population.
6. Under the conditions of modern industrial life, the intellectual potential of the average human being is only partially utilized.

Source: D. McGregor, "The Human Side of Enterprise," *Management Review* 46 (1957): 22–28, 88–92.

that it depended on workers for productivity just as much as workers depended on management for jobs.

On the enforcement side, McGregor noted that continual observation of an organization's entire work force is out of the question. Compliance in the open might be followed by foot-dragging or even sabotage when the supervisor is out of sight. Further, it is possible for workers to go along with the *letter* of an order without fulfilling the *spirit* of what was intended. Worker compliance with orders is not really what management wants; management wants productivity. Cracking the whip is likely just to bring out the worst in the work force.

McGregor felt that this vicious cycle could be broken only with a more flexible management philosophy. To get the most out of workers, McGregor believed it was necessary for managers to assume that there was a lot to get out. McGregor provided an example of a more flexible set of assumptions in his Theory Y. As shown in Figure 2–4, **Theory Y** differed from Theory X primarily by presenting a much more *optimistic* view of human nature. A manager with a Theory Y view of his work force would be likely to give his workers opportunities to succeed and flourish, and thereby discover untapped potential. In contrast, a manager with a Theory X view of his workers never would trust his workers enough to give them a chance.

Under the Theory Y view of the worker, McGregor saw the role of management as integration. **Integration** means "the creation of conditions such that members of the organization can achieve their own goals *best* by directing their efforts toward the success of the enterprise."[19] Integration removes the necessity for punishment by management when workers ignore management's orders. If work is arranged so that the worker's goals are achieved when the organization's goals are achieved, failure to achieve the organization's goals will mean failure to achieve the worker's goals, which already should be punishment enough for the worker.

McGregor went to great lengths to point out that the distinction between Theory X and Theory Y was not like that between "hard" and "soft" approaches to administration. For McGregor, "hard" approaches to management were those in which managers maintained *control* over agendas and decision making; "soft" approaches to management were those in which control was delegated or even abdicated. McGregor was openly critical of "soft" management styles such as "industrial democracy" that turned decision making over to the workers. McGregor placed the blame for the 1957–1958 recession squarely on the shoulders of such *permissive* approaches to management. Theory Y does not represent an abdication of the right nor the obligation to manage. McGregor felt that management needed to retain control, but not through authority, threats, and punishment, as suggested by Theory X. Rather, Theory Y suggested that control was a matter of aligning manager and worker goals. If workers could get what they wanted by accomplishing what the organization needed, they would work hard and everyone would prosper.

Douglas McGregor intended his Theory Y to be speculative, and it was never scientifically tested or validated. Nevertheless, McGregor's work had a significant impact on management thinking in the United States, and several of his recommendations concerning job enlargement, delegation, the use of performance appraisal, and worker participation in organizational decision making today remain part of American management theory.

System 4

While McGregor's Theory Y was mostly speculation, Rensis Likert's **System 4** theory of management was heavily anchored in behavioral science research. Likert was a social psychologist and the director of the Institute for Social Research at the University of Michigan. Likert had uncovered important differences between the behaviors of superior and mediocre or inferior managers. He characterized the work units managed by superior managers as coordinated, motivated, and cooperative social systems with the following features:

1. a favorable climate, with lots of mutual confidence and trust among workers and supervisors
2. management attention to multiple motivations of workers
3. highly cohesive and participative work groups
4. the availability of performance feedback for worker self-guidance[20]

---

[19]Ibid., 49.

[20]R. Likert, *New Patterns of Management* (New York: McGraw-Hill, 1961).

Likert proposed that the two common threads linking all superior work units were an optimistic, supportive, and humanistic view of workers by management and the use of work groups. Likert thought it was particularly important for every worker to belong to a highly cohesive and participative work group with high performance goals and expectations. His System 4 ("group-participative") theory of management emphasized these characteristics. Likert's System 1 and System 2 referred to punitive and benevolent authoritarian management; System 3 was consultative management, in which management consulted with workers but retained its decision-making responsibility.

In a review of 20 years of research and several hundred studies concerning System 4 management, Likert found substantial support for his views, including higher productivity and production quality, higher levels of employee satisfaction and health, better labor relations, and lower absenteeism and turnover.[21] With Likert's System 4, management theory had come full circle from the Hawthorne studies. At Hawthorne, Elton Mayo had discovered that social relationships were an impediment to traditional management practice; in his System 4, Rensis Likert made those same social relationships the centerpiece of management theory.

BEYOND HUMAN RELATIONS   ◆◆◆◆◆◆

The human relations movement treated participation primarily as a way to satisfy workers. As noted by Reinhard Bendix in *Work and Authority in Industry*, the rallying cry of human relations was that "failure to treat workers as human beings [was] the cause of low morale, poor craftsmanship, unresponsiveness, and confusion."[22] Workers had become something more than mere bundles of skills and strength. Workers needed to be respected and to feel useful to the organization. By consulting with workers on decisions such as the distribution of tasks within work groups, work group leadership, and even production method design and scheduling, managers believed they were providing their workers a sense of being useful and important.

In its early stages, worker participation was meant to advise, not replace, management's decisions. In its most cynical form, human relations cast worker participation as the "lubricant which oils away resistance to formal authority."[23] This comment implies that managers may have believed it to be easier and better to make decisions *without* worker input. Nevertheless, workers were involved to boost morale and insure their later cooperation. As noted by one management theorist, this is not a complimentary view of the workers' capacity to contribute something useful through participation:

> The manager "buys" worker cooperation by letting his subordinates in on departmental information and allowing them to discuss and state their opinions on various departmental problems. He "pays a price" for allowing his subordinates the

---

[21]R. Likert, "Retrospective Comment," in *The Great Writings in Management and Organizational Behavior*, eds. L. Boone and D. Bowen (Tulsa, Okla.: Penwell Books, 1980), 249.

[22]R. Bendix, *Work and Authority in Industry* (New York: Wiley and Sons, 1956), 294.

[23]R. E. Miles, "Human Relations or Human Resources?" *Harvard Business Review* (July/August 1965): 148–163.

privilege of participation in certain decisions and exercising some self-direction. In return, he hopes to obtain their cooperation in carrying out these and other decisions for the accomplishment of departmental objectives.[24]

From the human relations perspective, then, worker participation had become a way to satisfy workers and thereby secure their cooperation and compliance. Outside the United States, however, worker participation in organizational decision making was taking on a different flavor altogether.

Worker Participation in Europe

In European management circles, worker participation in decision making became the centerpiece of the policy known as codetermination. **Codetermination** refers to allowing workers a say in major organizational policy decisions—not just minor or trivial operational decisions. It gives workers the chance to work with management to determine together the direction taken by a company.

Perhaps owing to the strength of the socialist labor movement in Europe (which campaigns for power for the rank-and-file worker), worker participation in European industry has for some time been considered a *right* of workers rather than a bone that management might throw them. In Germany for instance, worker participation in policy decisions was institutionalized and *legally guaranteed* through the Codetermination Law of 1951. According to this law (designed only for organizations of more than 2,000 employees), corporate employees and shareholders have an indirect influence over corporate governance. As shown in Figure 2–5, shareholder and employee groups separately elect representatives to a board of supervisors. The board of supervisors in turn elects a board of management. The board of management assumes responsibility for day-to-day operations of the corporation, subject to review by the board of supervisors. The board of supervisors also must be kept continually informed of the current and projected state of the corporation. Thus, the

Industrial democracy in Europe has taken the human resources philosophy far beyond participative management practices in the United States. In Europe, laws often require management to give employees a say in organizational decision making.

[24]Ibid.

| FIGURE 2-5 | ▶ A Model for Industrial Democracy in Germany |

Worker participation in organizational decision making has been taken much further in European management circles than in the United States. In the model for industrial democracy in Germany, workers have a say in electing the board of supervisors, which in turn elects a board of management to manage the company.

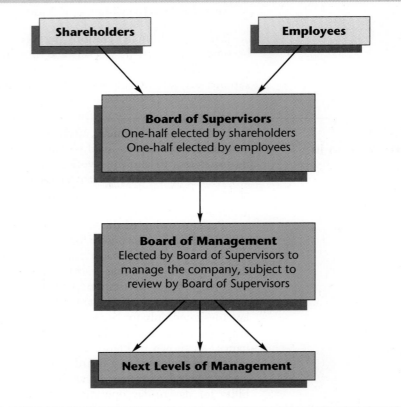

Source: K. E. Agathe, "Mitbestimmung: Report on a Social Experiment," *Business Horizons* 20 (1977): 5–14.

employees indirectly maintain a voice in corporate governance through their elected representation on the board of supervisors.[25]

The form that codetermination takes varies across Europe. European CEOs seem to agree that *de*centralized corporate decision making (featuring a lesser role for management and a greater role for workers) is both inevitable and desirable—desirable because it enhances an organization's flexibility and responsiveness.[26] In Ireland, corporate heavyweights Team Aer Lingus (an airline), Guinness (a brewery), and Amdahl Ireland (a computer manufacturer) all have begun using worker participation programs focused on employee involvement teams.[27] In Norway, rank-and-file workers (or their union representatives) have been given seats on boards of directors. But in these cases, work force productivity has not increased and work force alienation has not decreased.[28] As shown in the "FOCUS ON: Worker Participation in Europe," some Eastern European countries have begun to look elsewhere for answers.

[25]K. E. Agathe, "Mitbestimmung: Report on a Social Experiment," *Business Horizons* 20 (1977): 5–14.

[26]"Metamorphosis of the Manager," *Management Today*, August 1992, 72–75.

[27]C. Hannaway, "Why Irish Firms Are Smiling," *Personnel Management*, May 1992, 38–41.

[28]Work in America: Report of a Special Task Force to the Secretary of Health, Education, and Welfare" (Cambridge, Mass.: MIT Press, 1973).

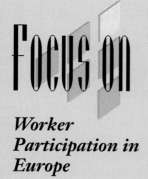

Focus on

Worker Participation in Europe

The East-Meets-West M.B.A. Before free-market economics can be practiced, it first must be taught. That's the idea behind the newly formed U.S. Business School in Prague, Czechoslovakia, where 66 students study for American-style M.B.A.'s under the tutelage of the "Chicago School" economists who provided the theoretical underpinnings of Reagan's economic revolution.

Visiting professors from the U.S. include Victor Tabbush from the University of California at Los Angeles and Roman Weil from the University of Chicago. The students include mathematicians, physicists, nuclear engineers, and professors, all of whom speak their instructors' native tongue, English.

Tuition is steep: about four months pay for the average worker. As in America, the full-time course of study entails financial hardship, because many students quit their jobs to enroll. And the potential benefits are in doubt. "My dean said it was absolutely useless to go to a school like this," said 40-year-old Marian Zajko, who quit a tenured post at the Bratislava School of Economics to attend the U.S. school. Yet Mr. Zajko sees the educational transition as vital to his and his nation's future.

Products of the school—around 70 new MBA's every nine months—will wear many hats:

—Krzysztof Biczyk, 29, will return to his job in Poland's Transportation Ministry with new ideas on the role of regulation.

—David Kyjovksky, 28, is already a successful entrepreneur by Western standards. He is attending school and wheeling and dealing at the same time.

—Iva Halouskova, 28, works at an advertising agency recently acquired by the U.S. advertising giant Young & Rubicam, Inc. She already has an advanced degree in psychology, and believes her M.B.A. will be "part of my entrance ticket to the civilized world."

The school officially granting the degrees is the Rochester Institute of Technology. In contrast to its American counterpart, the Prague location is cramped, underfunded and underequipped. But just as in America, students hear about Adam Smith's invisible hand, work endless accounting problems, and find themselves on the receiving end of business professor one-liners, such as Weil's "Accountants like to measure irrelevant things with precision."

Heads spinning, these hardy competitors are getting ready to run a race familiar to Americans. But winning while the rules change before their eyes will present unique challenges.

Source: J. F. Siler, "Adam Smith Goes to Czechoslovakia," *Business Week*, May 13, 1991, 78–79.

The Japanese Experience

If satisfying workers' needs had been the only impetus for management's turning to worker participation, participation's role in the history of organizational behavior would have been minor and short-lived. However, *organization* need satisfaction became the justification for allowing worker participation when organizations realized the instrumental value of worker participation. Worker participation could be more than a way for managers to keep workers satisfied and productive. Worker participation could be a tool used by management to *improve* the organization's decisions and plans. With this insight, human relations management gave way to a new view of managing organizational behavior—the human resources view.

Human resources differs from human relations management in its emphasis on participation as a means to productivity improvement through better, more informed organizational planning and decision making. Advocates of human resources see the workers' mental capabilities as *key resources* in the constant battle to improve organizational efficiency and effectiveness. Rank-and-file workers are closest to the work and possess much useful information—useful, that is, if only they are given a chance to share it!

The human resources orientation was strongly supported by the experiences of Japan. In 1950, W. Edwards Deming and a delegation of industrial engineers were sent to Japan to teach statistical quality control to the Japanese. Statistical quality control is a method for assessing whether a production system is performing correctly or needs to be adjusted. The delegation was charged with helping to modernize and westernize Japan's industrial base, which had been largely destroyed at the conclusion of World War II. Deming's lessons on statistical quality control were eagerly absorbed by the Japanese. If statistical quality control was part of the American success story, they reasoned, it should become the foundation for similar successes by Japanese industry.[29]

The Japanese took statistical quality control ideas further than even Deming might have imagined. Statistical quality control, as practiced in America at that time, was a procedure performed by specialists for the exclusive consumption of management. The Japanese reasoned that if it was useful for managers to have statistical quality control information, it made sense for *everyone* to be collecting, interpreting, and applying it. Soon worker groups, called "quality circles," began appearing in a few of Japan's industrial enterprises. In a quality circle, rank-and-file workers would get together to discuss their quality-control statistics and the implications for manufacturing practice. Worker participation had come to Japan.

It should be emphasized that training rank-and-file workers in statistical quality control techniques and providing an arena for using the information was but one feature of the new Japanese orientation toward workers. In reality, these practices are used by only 1 percent of Japanese companies, so it would be misleading to attribute Japan's recent enormous industrial success to them alone.[30] As noted in the "INTERNATIONAL FOCUS ON: The Japanese Experience," Japanese management may not always be as ideal as it seems. Nevertheless, the advent of these labor practices in Japan coincided with substantial gains in Japanese industrial productivity. By some estimates, productivity gains in Japan have been more than twice those in the United States in the past two decades.[31]

As Japan has gained strength as an industrial power, it has threatened U.S. dominance of international and even domestic markets. Not surprisingly, Japanese successes have focused the attention of U.S. companies on the management practices that helped Japan gain its position, and has encouraged many U.S. manufacturers to look for better ways to use the enthusiasm and expertise of the lower levels of the work force. Some U.S. companies even have successfully imported Japanese techniques to manage their own companies. Lockheed, for instance, tried quality circles. With only 30 circles in place, the company's estimated savings exceeded $3 million and defects were down by two-thirds.[32] Others have attempted to mold the Japanese human resources philosophy to fit the needs and character of U.S. workers.[33]

[29]A. Gabor, "The Man Who Changed the World of Quality," *International Management* (March 1988): 42–46.

[30]T. K. Oh, "Japanese Management: A Critical Review," *Academy of Management Review* 1 (1976): 14–25.

[31]E. E. Lawler III, *High-Involvement Management* (San Francisco: Jossey-Bass, 1986), 33.

[32]R. E. Cole, "Made in Japan—Quality Control Circles," *Across the Board* 16 (1979): 72–78.

[33]S. M. Young, "A Framework for Successful Adoption and Performance of Japanese Manufacturing Practices in the United States," *Academy of Management Review* 17 (1992): 677–700.

INTERNATIONAL FOCUS ON

The Japanese Experience

Japanese Management: Myth versus Method Years ago, the label "Made in Japan" left Americans snickering. Today, Japanese products command respect. Over the last decade, Japan's high-quality exports and our daunting deficit have underscored Japan's awe-inspiring economic growth. Searching for explanations, experts have attributed Japan's success to its highly praised business culture: lifetime employment, corporate paternalism, and machine-like efficiency. But recently, the media have begun depicting another Japan. Books like *The Enigma of Japanese Power* by Karel van Wolferen and *The Sun Also Sets* by Bill Emmott have forced us to reconsider our views of Japan as a social and economic utopia.

Certainly, some Japanese business practices are worthy of emulation. The practice of taking a long-term perspective may be Japanese management's most powerful lesson for America. For example, Sony's first offering in the highly-competitive personal computer market—Hit Bit—badly lagged behind market leaders and looked to be a sure money loser. But Sony's long-term thinking enabled it to take into account just how important Hit Bit's digital technology would be in developing products for the 1990s. Sony was able to commit resources to a long-term winner because it didn't have to worry about the short-term orientation of its stockholders, banks, and venture capitalists.

Similarly, teamwork is the key to effective and efficient product design in Japan, and it is a skill that U.S. firms desperately need to adopt. American companies typically design products by sequentially transferring a developing item between departments. Japanese companies, on the other hand, link all departments from the start via interdepartmental teams. Not only does this practice keep everyone involved; it facilitates communication and assures a design everyone can live with.

Not all Japanese practices bear up so well under scrutiny, however. The celebrated loyalty of Japanese workers may derive more from fear than commitment. Most Americans don't realize that if a Japanese worker leaves a large company, he or she will never be hired by another large company. Similarly, the Japanese policy of life-time employment may be misleading. The life-time employment guarantee covers only a fraction of Japan's work force—and only men. Even the benefits of Japan's highly-touted "just-in-time" inventory practice may be somewhat illusory. Large Japanese corporations do lower carrying costs by reducing their inventories. But they can afford this luxury because they surround themselves with completely dependent networks of vendors, and these vendors keep large inventories on hand so that the giant companies won't have to.

The management style of the Japanese is not the panacea we once thought it to be. But there's still plenty that Americans can learn from the Land of the Rising Yen. With a blend of disparate Eastern and Western styles, perhaps we can take advantage of the best of both worlds.

Source: Adapted from G. Katzenstein, "Japanese Management Style," *Working Woman,* February 1991, 49–50+.

In Search of Solutions

The themes of this latest wave of management theory—the human resources wave—have found highly vocal support in the writings of management evangelists Tom Peters and Bob Waterman.[34] Their 1982 best-seller, *In Search of Excellence,* sold over five million copies and was arguably the most-quoted management book of the 1980s. The book details a survey of 43 of the "best" U.S.

---

[34]T. J. Peters and R. H. Waterman, *In Search of Excellence* (New York: Harper and Row, 1982).

companies and concludes that employee involvement and participation programs are prominent features in these companies. The proof that Peters and Waterman offer for their views is largely anecdotal, however, and their findings have been questioned because of their survey's lack of systematic observation and analysis.[35]

Scientific attempts to ascertain the value of worker participation programs have proven less supportive. In one comprehensive analysis of 89 studies examining the value of participative management techniques, 78 percent of the studies included in the analysis found no positive effects of participation programs on productivity. Fully 60 percent of the studies did report positive effects on worker satisfaction, however.[36]

In a study of the U.S. metalworking industry, 70 percent of the plants surveyed had set up employee-involvement committees. While both management and labor praised the programs, plants using the programs proved to be 25 percent to 45 percent less efficient than plants not using the programs. Unions, on the other hand, tended to increase plant productivity.[37]

The most recent wave in the ebb-and-flow of human resources innovations is **total quality management (TQM).** Traditionally, quality has been "inspected in" during the final stages of a production process by quality-control specialists. When quality is "inspected in," poor quality items are identified and sent back to be reworked or scrapped. TQM instead calls for management practices that continuously "build in" quality at *every* state of a production process. TQM also shifts the responsibility for quality away from quality specialists and into the hands of the production work force.[38] At BMW, this shift in philosophy about quality has resulted in a shrinking of the "quality control" department from 1,200 to 65 employees in the last 15 years.[39] And TQM has claimed some significant successes: 20 surveyed U.S. companies using TQM reported an average drop in customer complaints of 11.6 percent, an average decline in defects of 10.3 percent, and an average increase in employee suggestions of 16.6 percent.[40]

TQM may represent management practice in the United States coming full circle. It has much of the flavor of Taylor's scientific management, but it is practiced by shop-floor workers rather than just their managers! TQM is scientific management adjusted to a human resources understanding of shop-floor workers. Critics, however, see TQM simply as the latest fad in American management's evolving understanding of employee participation.[41]

What conclusions should be drawn from these findings? Perhaps the safest comment on the human resources approach would be to echo the summaries

---

[35]M. A. Hitt and R. E. Ireland, "Peters and Waterman Revisited: The Unended Quest for Excellence," *Academy of Management Executive* 1 (1987): 91–98.

[36]E. A. Locke and D. M. Schweiger, "Participation in Decision Making: One More Look," in *Research in Organizational Behavior*, vol. 1, ed. B. Staw (Greenwich, Conn.: JAI Press, 1979).

[37]G. Koretz, "Worker Involvement: It Sounds Like a Good Idea, but . . .," *Business Week*, April 1, 1991, 18.

[38]J. E. Watson and T. W. Hopp, "The Private Sector's Experience with Total Quality Management," *The GAO Journal* (Winter 1991/1992): 34–38.

[39]J. Templeman, "Grill-to-Grill with Japan," *Business Week*, October 25, 1991, 39.

[40]Watson and Hopp, "The Private Sector's Experience."

[41]"The Cracks in Quality," *The Economist*, April 18, 1992, 67–68.

about human relations and scientific management: It provides no final solution. The uncertain value of any of these approaches has led to yet another approach to management—contingency theory. According to **contingency theory,** which management technique is appropriate depends on the particular situation. Each of the approaches we have reviewed—scientific management, human relations, and human resources—can be quite valuable, but under different circumstances. A contingency framework for understanding when participative management techniques would be appropriate will be presented in Chapter 9.

OPEN SYSTEMS THEORY

More than just management's understanding of the rank-and-file worker has evolved during the twentieth century. Also changing has been management's understanding of the organizations in which these rank-and-file workers labor. For much of the twentieth century, theories about organizational behavior have focused on the challenge of managing worker behavior *within* organizations to achieve efficiency and effectiveness. It has become apparent, however, that changes in the environment in which organizations function have a direct impact on behavior *within* organizations. An organization's environment (which will be the focus of Chapter 14) includes anything outside the organization's boundaries that might influence that organization, including competitors, suppliers, customers, laws and regulating agencies, and even social trends. Organizational theorists have now turned their attention to the challenge of managing the relationship between organizations and their environments. Our understanding of this relationship is encompassed in open systems theory.

Open systems theory, as described by Katz and Kahn in *The Social Psychology of Organizations,*[42] focuses on two assumptions. The first assumption is that organizations are social systems, meaning that changes in one part of the organization necessarily are reflected in changes in other parts. The system perspective differs from a traditional *mechanistic* view of organizations, which likens organizations to machines. In a machine, failure by one part *stops* the machine. Thus, all parts of the machine are equally essential to the machine's functioning. In contrast, in a system, failure in any part (or subsystem) of the system *perturbs* the system, forcing a reaction. However, only rarely does a subsystem failure stop a system. Instead, the system adjusts to accommodate the failure and continues to function, though it probably will never be the same again.

Imagine, for instance, that a firm's marketing director suddenly resigns to start a new company. Business at the firm does not grind to a halt. The firm adjusts to the loss and carries on. An acting director is appointed to keep things going, a search is initiated to find a permanent replacement, and precautions are taken to decrease the impact of such a loss should it recur. The loss perturbs the system; the system adjusts and continues functioning.

The system notion also implies a hierarchy of subsystems. Not all of a system's parts are equally essential, hence changes or failures at higher levels of the organization's subsystem hierarchy will have a greater impact on the system and will necessitate greater adjustments.

The second assumption is that organizations are systems open to influence from the environment. An organization's reason for being comes from the needs

---

[42]D. Katz and R. L. Kahn, *The Social Psychology of Organizations* (New York: Wiley and Sons, 1966).

of the environment, and its ability to meet those needs derives from the environment's supply of resources. McDonald's hamburgers would be nowhere if Americans didn't want hamburgers, or if McDonald's couldn't find the beef, the buns, or the brawn to make them.

The open systems perspective is important to understanding and management of organizational behavior because of the contingent character of social systems. The environment cannot be assumed to be a constant or dependable source of inputs. Thus, the turbulence of the environment, and the effects of this turbulence on organizational behavior, are critical areas of study.[43] The implications of open systems theory for organizational behavior and the contingent character of organizations it implies provide the focus for Part 4 of this book.

SUMMARY   ◆◆◆◆◆◆

Most written histories share several important characteristics. First, they are incomplete. They contain only a *selection* of the facts about *some* of the events and people of the past. This chapter's history of management thought and theory is no exception. It has presented only the most striking attempts to face the management challenge of organizational behavior up to and into the twentieth century. The remainder of this book will elaborate on these major themes, and in doing so will fill in the important gaps in the story.

Second, written histories make events appear to have been much more of a *sensible and orderly progression* than they actually were. Fads and fashions come and go in the field of organizational behavior. Ideas explode into prominence and then disappear. Some are rebirths and rediscoveries of old themes; some are too new and revolutionary. Most never command the field's attention, but many nevertheless have an influence. Histories are an attempt to make sense of these ebbs and flows of people, ideas, and events. In retrospect, overall directions are remembered.

In management thought and theory, there have been two major changes in the twentieth century. The first change has occurred in management's understanding of the rank-and-file worker. Replacing a predominantly economic view of worker motivation are human relations and human resources—two philosophies about human nature that are optimistic about workers' capacity to contribute meaningfully to organizational efficiency and effectiveness. Moreover, the definition of management's task has taken a subtle but significant turn. Managers must now manage workers as a *mental* resource as well as a physical resource.

The second change has occurred in management's understanding of the organization itself. Bureaucratic views of the organization focused attention on internal aspects of the management challenge. Open systems theory casts the organization as a ship adrift in a sea of external influence. Keeping it afloat means extending the management challenge—and our knowledge of organizational behavior—beyond the boundaries of the organization itself.

---

[43]Ibid., 3.

Key Terms

Bureaucracy   Form of organization in which there are clearly defined lines of authority and responsibility for members, and behavior is tightly controlled by rules, policies, and job assignments.

Codetermination   Policy of allowing workers a say in major organizational decisions, not just minor operational decisions.

Contingency theory   Approach to organizational behavior stating that choice of appropriate management technique is dependent on the particular situation.

Human relations   An approach to management that emphasizes workers' personal and social needs.

Human resources   View of workers' mental capabilities as key resources in organizational efficiency and effectiveness; emphasizes worker participation for more informed organizational planning and decision making.

Integration   Role of management defined by D. McGregor as the creation of conditions such that members of the organization can best achieve their own goals by directing their efforts toward the success of the enterprise.

Open systems theory   Management theory proposed by D. Katz and R. Kahn, which focuses on the assumptions that organizations are (1) social systems in which changes in one part are reflected by changes in other parts, and (2) open to influence from the environment.

Scientific management   Frederick Taylor's theory of careful and systematic observations and prescriptive techniques for designing jobs and incentive pay schemes for rank-and-file factory workers.

System 4   Management theory of Rensis Likert proposing that in superior work units management has an optimistic, supportive, and humanistic view of workers, and every worker belongs to a highly cohesive and participative work group with high performance goals and expectations.

Theory X   Management's traditional view of workers, including the assumptions that workers are naturally lazy, self-centered, and resistant to change and will avoid responsibility, and management must direct, motivate, and control them.

Theory Y   View of workers as naturally motivated to work as much as to rest or play; workers will exercise self-direction and self-control in the service of objectives to which they are committed.

Time-and-motion studies   Scientific management technique of timed observations and experiments to identify the most efficient means for accomplishing a task.

Total job situation   Seven characteristics of a job derived by C. R. Walker and R. H. Guest, including the worker's immediate job, relation to fellow workers, relation to supervisors, relation to the union, pay and job security, promotion and transfer prospects, and working conditions in the plant.

Total quality management   A philosophy about production that emphasizes "building" quality, and that makes quality the responsibility of all workers.

Work standards   Scientific management technique of providing specific instructions to workers for doing a task, including expected time for completion and expected volume of output.

Discussion Questions

1. What is a bureaucracy? Why did Max Weber believe that bureaucracies were the ideal organizational form?

2. What is scientific about "scientific management"? What assumptions does scientific management make about rank-and-file workers and how to manage them?

3. What were the contributions of the Hawthorne studies? In what ways did they alter current thinking about managing organizational behavior?

4. What did studies of rank-and-file workers in the 1950s reveal about worker motivation?

5. Distinguish between the human relations and human resources approaches to managing organizational behavior. What differing assumptions does each approach make about the relationship between worker satisfaction and performance?

6. Describe McGregor's Theory Y and Likert's System 4 approaches to management. What assumptions do their views make about worker motivation?

7. In what ways are the worker democracy movement in Europe and Japanese management examples of human resources approaches to management?

8. Describe the fundamental assumptions underlying open systems theory. How does the open systems theory approach to understanding organizations differ from Weber's notion of the bureaucratic organization?

If You Want to Know More

Excepts from the writings of the traditional theorists including Taylor (on scientific management) and Weber (on bureaucracy) are contained in the volume, *The Great Writings in Management and Organizational Behavior* (Tulsa, Okla.: Penn Well Books, 1980). Each reading includes retrospective comments by contemporary researchers in organizational behavior. Charles Wrege and Ronald Greenwood provide a recent review of Taylor's contributions to management theory and practice in *Frederick W. Taylor, Father of Scientific Management: Myth and Reality* (Homewood, Ill.: R. D. Irwin Press, 1991).

An excellent review of the Hawthorne studies, the origins of the human relations movement, and the beginning of the field of organizational behavior are provided in Fritz Roethlisberger's autobiography, *The Elusive Phenomena* (Cambridge, Mass.: Harvard University Press, 1977), which reads much more like a novel than a textbook. A latter-day critique of the scientific value of the Hawthorne studies appears in the *Psychology Today* article, "The Haw-

thorne Defect: Persistence of a Flawed Theory," by B. Rice (February 1982).

A condensed version of McGregor's views on Theory X and Theory Y is provided in his article, "The Human Side of Enterprise," which appeared in *Management Review* (November 1957). An attempt to test the assumptions of Theory Y and its implications for management is described by Byron Fiman in his article, "An Investigation of the Relationships among Supervisory Attitudes, Behaviors, and Outputs: An Examination of McGregor's Theory Y," which appeared in *Personnel Psychology* (26, Spring 1973). A field test of Theory Y is detailed in Erwin Malone's article, "The Non-Linear Systems Experiment in Participative Management," which appeared in the *Journal of Business* (48, January 1975).

Ray Miles, in his July/August 1965 *Harvard Business Review* article, "Human Relations or Human Resources?," summarizes the features that distinguish between these two schools of management thought. A more contemporary look at the profusion of management techniques emanating from human relations and human resources is provided in John Byrne's *Business Week* cover story, "Business Fads: What's In and What's Out?" (January 20, 1986, pp. 52–61). This article also is a good source for additional readings about human resources approaches to managing organizational behavior. A good introduction to the issues surrounding total quality management is provided in a special issue of *Organizational Dynamics* (Spring 1992). Some examples of the application of the total quality management philosophy in industry are described in a special issue of *Business Week* (October 25, 1991).

An excellent review of open systems theory is provided in Chapter 6 of John Miner's volume, *Theories of Organizational Structure and Process* (Hinsdale, Ill.: Dryden Press, 1982). An application of this theory in an organizational setting is detailed in Ned Rosen's article, "Open Systems Theory in an Organizational Subsystem: A Field Experiment" (*Organizational Behavior and Human Performance* 5 (1970): 245–265).

On Your Own

Management Practices Questionnaire   Complete the following questionnaire. Indicate your agreement or disagreement with each of the eight statements by circling the number on the scale below each statement. Determine the appropriate score by noting the points for the response you made to each statement. For example, if your response to Question 1 was strongly agree, you would give yourself five points; disagree is worth two points; and so on. Add the eight scores together.

1. The average human being prefers to be directed, wishes to avoid responsibility, and has relatively little ambition.

(5)	(4)	(3)	(2)	(1)
Strongly Agree	Agree	Undecided	Disagree	Strongly Disagree

2. Most people can acquire leadership skills regardless of their particular inborn traits and abilities.

(5)	(4)	(3)	(2)	(1)
Strongly Agree	Agree	Undecided	Disagree	Strongly Disagree

3. The use of rewards (for example, pay and promotion) and punishment (for example, failure to promote) is the best way to get subordinates to do their work.

(5)	(4)	(3)	(2)	(1)
Strongly Agree	Agree	Undecided	Disagree	Strongly Disagree

4. In a work situation, if the subordinate can influence you, you lose some influence over them.

(5)	(4)	(3)	(2)	(1)
Strongly Agree	Agree	Undecided	Disagree	Strongly Disagree

5. A good leader gives detailed and complete instructions to subordinates rather than giving them merely general directions and depending on their initiative to work out the details.

(5)	(4)	(3)	(2)	(1)
Strongly Agree	Agree	Undecided	Disagree	Strongly Disagree

6. Individual goal setting offers advantages that cannot be obtained by group goal setting, because groups do not set high goals.

(5)	(4)	(3)	(2)	(1)
Strongly Agree	Agree	Undecided	Disagree	Strongly Disagree

7. A superior should give subordinates only the information necessary for them to do their immediate tasks.

(5)	(4)	(3)	(2)	(1)
Strongly Agree	Agree	Undecided	Disagree	Strongly Disagree

8. The superior's influence over subordinates in an organization is primarily economic.

(5)	(4)	(3)	(2)	(1)
Strongly Agree	Agree	Undecided	Disagree	Strongly Disagree

☐ Total Score

Scoring Key: A score of greater than 32 points indicates a tendency to manage others according to the principles in Theory X. A score of less than 16 points indicates a tendency to manage others according to the principles in Theory Y. A score somewhere between 16 and 32 indicates flexibility in the management of others.

Source: Adapted from M. Haire, E. Ghiselli, and L. Porter, *Managerial Thinking: An International Study*, Appendix A. Copyright © 1966 by John Wiley & Sons, Inc. Reprinted with permission of John Wiley & Sons, Inc.

CLOSING CASE

CHAPTER 2

THE MANAGER'S MEMO

FROM: R. Wolferman, Manager, Water Sports Department

TO: F. Crane, Line Supervisor, Canoe Production

RE: Worker Performance and Turnover

Congratulations! You have met this year's goal of a 15 percent increase in canoe production using the same number of worker-hours as you did last year. It appears that your ideas for production efficiency have paid off in a big way—specifically, a $780,000 increase in the value of goods produced for the year.

Nevertheless, a review of our financial performance for the past year raises some concerns. I see that we spent $1.2 million for hiring and training last year, an $800,000 increase over the year before. According to the personnel department, this increase does not reflect a new training program, but rather the fact that turnover among canoe production workers tripled last year.

Could there be a link between the efficiency effort and the increased employee turnover? As I recall, your plans included making tasks more routine and specialized, as well as training workers to accomplish each task more quickly. While I know you put in many lonely hours developing these efficiencies, I wonder whether some workers have left as a result of them.

You have every right to be proud of the efforts that led to accomplishing the goal of higher output, and achievement of this goal will be reflected in your annual bonus. However, for the next year, I would like to develop a goal of reducing the cost of employee turnover while attempting to maintain at least some of the gain in worker output. To that end, please recommend some ways in which we can reduce next year's hiring and training costs. We'll discuss those ideas at our next meeting.

Case Discussion Questions

Assume you are the line supervisor, and write a response to the department manager's memo. Consider the management theories described in this chapter, and look for ways in which each can shed light on the circumstances of the memo. Can the supervisor maintain the increased efficiency while improving employee turnover? If so, how? If not, how can the supervisor strike a balance between these two concerns?

EXERCISE

PART 1:
Bridge Building

For this exercise, your instructor will divide the class into groups of about 8 to 10 students. One group will act as observers; the remaining groups will be "bridge builders."

The task of the bridge-building groups will be to build a bridge spanning two desks in your classroom. Your instructor will give each bridge-building group a package of "construction materials." This package will contain:

- 5 straws
- 1 newspaper
- 2 pencils
- 1 blue felt-tip pen

- 5 rubber bands
- 1 box of paper clips
- 1 red felt-tip pen
- 1 pad of "Post-it" notes

Additionally, your instructor will have a pair of scissors, a roll of tape, and a stapler that the bridge-building groups will have to share.

The bridge-building groups will have about 15 minutes to construct their bridges. At the end of the allotted construction time, all bridge builders will leave the classroom so that the observer group can evaluate the constructed bridges. Using the evaluation form provided, the observer group will evaluate the bridges on the basis of five criteria: length, width, height, strength, and beauty.

The observer group will also have responsibility for observing the **processes of group interaction** that occur as the bridge-building groups build their bridges. Your instructor will provide the observer group members with an "Observation Checklist" for that purpose.

▶ Evaluation Form: Bridge Building

Evaluate each bridge on the following criteria (circle a number):

1. **Length**
   (1)   (2)   (3)   (4)   (5)   (6)   (7)   (8)   (9)   (10)
   Very Poor   Outstanding
2. **Width**
   (1)   (2)   (3)   (4)   (5)   (6)   (7)   (8)   (9)   (10)
   Very Poor   Outstanding
3. **Height**
   (1)   (2)   (3)   (4)   (5)   (6)   (7)   (8)   (9)   (10)
   Very Poor   Outstanding
4. **Strength**
   (1)   (2)   (3)   (4)   (5)   (6)   (7)   (8)   (9)   (10)
   Very Poor   Outstanding
5. **Beauty**
   (1)   (2)   (3)   (4)   (5)   (6)   (7)   (8)   (9)   (10)
   Very Poor   Outstanding

CASE

PART 1:

The Ultimate Frisbee Team's Dilemma

Harry, Jere, George, and Bob L. were students at Centerville University who enjoyed playing Ultimate Frisbee, a game requiring two teams of seven. Since it was hard to round up 14 players every time they wished to play, they decided to start a regular frisbee team. Their hopes were to get some potentially good frisbee players together and teach them how to play Ultimate. They realized they would need to publicize the team. One of them, Jere, spoke to a reporter from the school newspaper, and a short article appeared about the team (see Exhibit 1). In the interview, Jere stated, "The team is open to all students, especially girls." Any of the four could have spoken to the reporter, but Jere took the initiative. Jere also announced a practice through the newspaper. Eleven people came to that initial practice: Jere, Fred, Roger (Fred's roommate), Jim H., Jean, Bob L., George, Pete C., Pete R., Paul, and Harry. Jere took their names, addresses, and telephone numbers and announced that practices would be held at 4 P.M. on Tuesdays and Thursdays (at a time that was convenient for Jere). It wasn't clear why Jere should be the one to decide this, but since Jere was taking names, he was the one asked by the newcomers.

At the second practice some new people showed up: Chas, Alex, Bert, Gene (all of whom lived together), Bob M., Linda, Sharon, and Jack. However, some people from the first practice didn't come because they had conflicting classes. Jere took these new people's names and toyed with the idea of taking attendance, but nothing came of it because, as he said to his roommate, "I didn't want to turn people off or make them feel they had to come." However, many

---

EXHIBIT 1 ▶ The *Centerville News*, March 1, 1984

"Ultimate Frisbee" Arrives with Spring
By Janice M. Dupre

Springtime is just around the corner, and for frisbee lovers it's time to warm up the old throwing arm.

This spring a group of frisbee enthusiasts are trying to get together a frisbee team at Centerville University (CU). Originator of the team is Jere Harris.

Many people are familiar with the frisbee as simply a plastic disc used for throwing around on a beach.

But there is an official game played with a frisbee. It's called Ultimate Frisbee, and it's like soccer in many ways.

"In Ultimate Frisbee there are seven players per team on the field. There is a kickoff, but you can't run with the frisbee in your hand," explains Harris. "It's an extremely fast game with two 24-minute halfs."

According to Harris, a Middle States Frisbee League is now being formed by a student from Amenon College. Colleges that already have teams and will hopefully be joining the league include Western Re-serve, Ohio Wesleyan, Wayne University, and Clarke. One of the best frisbee teams in the area is the New Hampton College team.

In past years individuals from CU have gotten together to play other schools, but there never has been an official team. "I've been playing frisbee all my life, but I never heard of Ultimate Frisbee until a friend of mine told me about the game last year. It's really a fast-moving game with lots of collisions because the frisbee is always in the air with everyone diving for it," said Harris, a junior hospital administration major.

Ultimate Frisbee is by no means a gentle game. At this moment Bob LaPointe, future cocaptain of the forming CU team has a dislocated shoulder from a frisbee game he recently played in.

The friend that introduced the game to Jere Harris last year was a graduate of Columbia High School in New Jersey. It was at Columbia where the first game was played.

"The Columbia-High team can beat any team in the nation," said Harris. "They won over 30 games at the national tournament held in Michigan last year. Columbia High School also publishes the Ultimate Frisbee rule book.

Each year a national frisbee tournament is held at Copperhopper, Michigan. Hundreds of Ultimate Frisbee teams from the United States and Canada come to take part in the tournament. The game of Frisbee is not confined to North America; it's very popular overseas and according to Harris is just being introduced to Red China.

So far the CU Frisbee team comprises about 10 members. Harris is hoping to get the team off the ground and start practicing soon. He is planning to announce practices as soon as he can arrange a time in the indoor track and as soon as the weather is nice.

"Frisbee is open to women," stresses Harris. "To play you don't have to be a super frisbee thrower; you just have to be able to throw and catch the frisbee and to run."

Along with all the food, energy, and political crises there is also a frisbee crisis. Frisbees are made with plastics, and since there is a plastic shortage the frisbees are an endangered species. Harris said that the major frisbee companies such as Whamo are urging people to buy their frisbees now because soon they will be hard to come by.

But until that time comes, frisbees will continue to fly in the sky on warm spring days at Centerville.

---

players made a mental note of who was there and who wasn't. Different people came and went like this at each practice thereafter.

Jere and several others knew how to play Ultimate and spent the first few practices teaching the others. Jere dominated the direction of these early practices, but after a short time the rest of the players were as good and some even better. Everyone had a lot of fun learning and playing. Jack and Chas were two players who stood out at practice. Jack (a grad student) was calm and collected, never became angry, and always played fairly. Chas had been the captain of his high-school football team and always organized the team he was on, deciding who should play and who should sit out.

Jere dealt with much of the administrative work such as announcing to the school radio and newspaper where and when practices would be held. No one asked Jere to do this, but attendance was sporadic and he hoped to get new people to fill the gaps at practice. However, response to the newspaper and radio announcements was minimal; consequently, Jere felt there should be an organizational meeting at night that he hoped would generate interest and attract more players. At the next practice Jere announced the meeting and explained that it was also to set up officers, dues, and so forth. Jack had 200 fliers printed up and he and Chas posted them around campus.

Jere came to the meeting late and found that strong opposition had developed against dues and against organization in general. Jere tried to explain that in order to receive funding from the university or to use university vehicles, the team must be organized with officers and a constitution, saying that the sports director for the university had told him this. A vote on dues barely passed whereupon several members left the meeting vowing they had quit. Jere followed them into the hall pleading with them to be sensible but could overhear two other members saying. "So what, we don't need them anyway." A debate ensued for a few minutes, and Jere called an end to the meeting, putting off a vote on a captain because he feared it would create further division among the team, since either Jere, Jack, or Chas might have made a good captain. Many new people who had shown up to the meeting explained they couldn't make practices as currently scheduled. Jere shrugged and said he'd try to set up alternative practices; however, this was never done.

A new group of players arrived after about 10 practices: Stan, Reggie, Mark, Bill T., and Howie. They always came and left together and often played on the same team. They were good players and talked about the coming games and their anticipated role in them. Reggie asked Jere at his first practice. "Do you think I'll start the first game?" Jere just shrugged.

By this time over 20 people had come out for the team, including 3 women (see Exhibit 2). The players fell into five friendship groups as shown in Exhibit 3. As practices continued, they became hard and competitive, and a lot of the fun which had been evident in the beginning seemed to disappear. One day Jere enraged Sharon by taking the frisbee away from her and throwing it himself. She started to walk off the field, but Jere called her back and the two had an argument right out in the middle of the field where everyone could see and hear it. She stayed at practice but was silent the rest of the day.

As the date for the first game drew near, all of the dues money was used to rent a 15-seat bus for the 50-mile trip to the other school. The day before the game about 12 people attended a meeting to discuss travel plans. Jack brought a letter written by Sharon. It was addressed to the team, but started:

EXHIBIT 2 ▶

Name	Attendance[a]	Initial Appearace	Ability[a]	Age	Class	Showed Up for Bus
Jack	regular	2nd practice	A	23	Grad.	XX
Fred	regular	1st practice	A	19	Fresh.	XX
Jere[b]	regular	1st practice	B	20	Jr.	XX
Jean	regular	1st practice	C	19	Soph.	XX
Harry[b]	regular	1st practice	A	21	Sr.	XX
Roger	sporadic	1st practice	B	21	Sr.	XX
Reggie	regular	10th practice	A	18	Fresh.	XX
Mark	regular	10th practice	A	18	Fresh.	XX
Howie	regular	10th practice	A	18	Fresh.	XX
Stan	regular	10th practice	A	19	Soph.	XX
Paul	sporadic	1st practice	B	19	Soph.	XX
Jim H.	regular	1st practice	A	19	Jr.	XX
Chas	regular	2nd practice	A	20	Soph.	XX
Gene	sporadic	2nd practice	B	20	Soph.	XX
Bert	sporadic	2nd practice	B	19	Soph.	XX
Sharon	regular	2nd practice	C	20	Jr.	XX
Linda	sporadic	2nd practice	C	18	Fresh.	XX
George[b]	regular	1st practice	A	19	Soph.	XX
Bob L.	sporadic	1st practice	B	19	Soph.	XX
Bob M.[b]	sporadic	2nd practice	B	20	Jr.	XX
Pete C.	sporadic	1st practice	B	19	Fresh.	XX
Bill T.	regular	10th practice	C	19	Soph.	XX
Alex	sporadic	2nd practice	C	19	Soph.	
Peter R.	sporadic	1st practice	C	18	Fresh.	XX

[a]Based on Jere's "mental notes."
[b]Founders of the team.

EXHIBIT 3	▶ **Subgroups (with spokesperson listed first)**

Group A: Jere, Harry, Bob L., George
Group B: Chas, Gene, Alex, Bert
Group C: Jack, Jean, Linda, Sharon, Jim H.
Group D: Stan, Reggie, Mark, Howie, Bill T.
Group E: Fred, Roger, Pete C., Paul

All the rest are independents, coming under no group.

Dear Jack:

The incident at this afternoon's practice was the last straw, but, I would like to impress, it was far from the only one. I'm writing this to you because you are the only one on the team who ever gave me any encouragement or made me feel like a real live person and not a bumbling incompetent.

I joined the frisbee team because I enjoy playing vigorous frisbee in the comradeship of others, and because I wanted to develop my own skill and confidence; but none of these is achievable under the present conditions.

How can I enjoy and concentrate on the game when not a minute goes by that I must force myself to ignore and rise above degrading and humiliating sexist treatment? It's often said that a female, be it a filly race horse or me on the frisbee team, must be three times as good as a male in order to be considered equal. Nothing truer has ever been said. Even Jere, who's practiced with me so much and encouraged my progress, turns overtly sexist in the presence of his teammates. Certainly the issues are not completely imagined in my mind—ask the other female players.

I am not against competitiveness as long as the competition element stimulates constant improvement. But when point-making takes priority over the freedom to make mistakes or try new things, then I think something is wrong. Maybe, if anyone cares you could let them in on this. . . .

With this Sharon announced her resignation from the team. The letter was received with much debate by the team, and some players refused to read the letter. Jack sided with the opinions stated in the letter and was joined in this opinion by many of the original members, including the two remaining women. Jere remained silent, unable to side with one view or the other.

Obviously some choice had to be made as to who would go on the bus. Group D insisted on "sending down the best 15," in which case all of them would go. Group C said, "Take those who have come to the most practices." Jere felt that this was the fairest solution, but it was hard to implement since no one was sure as to who had attended how many practices.

Jere, Jack, and Stan sat down and wrote up several lists of 15 (see Exhibit 4), but none was acceptable to all of the groups. Jere put off making any decision; several people got quite sore. Jere felt caught in the middle, and it was not something he could shrug off. He tried to act as the moderator of the dispute but kept saying, "Does anyone have any ideas?" Argument continued and people began to leave very upset when no decision was reached. Jere felt that he had been responsible for letting the scene get out of hand.

The day of the game came, and 19 people stood outside near the bus. Everyone wondered what to do. Some expressed the opinion that a captain should be elected to make the decision.

EXHIBIT 4	▶ Comparative Lists: Who Should Go to the Game

Jack's List	Group D's List
Jere	Reggie
Jack	Mark
Fred	Howie
Jean	Stan
Roger	Paul
Jim H.	Jere
Sharon	Jack
Linda	Fred
Bob L.	Roger
George	Jim H.
Harry	Chas
Paul	Gene
Pete R.	Bert
Chas	George
Gene	Harry

Questions for Discussion

1. Why has the Ultimate Frisbee Team had so much trouble getting organized?
2. Think about the traditional management functions of planning, organizing, staffing, and controlling. Has the Ultimate Frisbee team failed to do any or all of these?
3. How have uncertainty, conflict, and complexity contributed to the Ultimate Frisbee team's dilemma?

Source: A Cohen, S. Fink, H. Gadon, and R. Willits, eds., *Effective Behavior in Organizations*, 4th Edition (Homewood, Ill.: Irwin, 1988), 910–915. Reprinted with permission.

PART

TWO

INDIVIDUAL BEHAVIOR

3 ▶ **Foundations: Perception, Attitudes, and Personality**

4 ▶ **Learning and Motivation**

5 ▶ **Individual Decision Making**

6 ▶ **Conflict and Stress in Organizations**

◆◆◆◆◆◆

FOUNDATIONS: PERCEPTION, ATTITUDES, AND PERSONALITY

Do Women Manage Differently?   ◆◆◆◆◆◆

Here's a twist: Suddenly *men* have to worry about gender equality. A cadre of consultants, academics, and executives say Mr. Macho Hardcharging Manager could soon be out of a job. In his place they see a more nurturing, empathic sort, a born consensus builder. She—emphatically *she*—shuns the trappings of power and prefers "centrarchies" to hierarchies. Sally Helgesen's *The Female Advantage*, the bible for this new brand of feminism, claims that with their superior management instincts, women "may be the new Japanese."

The assertion that women are ideally suited to the flattened organizations of the 1990s, where teamwork and a free flow of information are paramount, is certainly a welcome message to some, considering the paltry progress women have made in the executive offices of business. As the 1990s began, less than .05 percent of the highest officers and directors in America's largest public companies were women.

But beware the siren call. In a thorough review of dozens of research studies, Gary Powell, management professor at the University of Connecticut, concluded that the similarities among men and women managers far outweigh the differences. "Those who choose managerial careers, like firefighters, have a lot in common. The best embody the stereotypes of both genders."

Not even all feminists are buying the new line. Many feel that today's Ms. Corporate Success Story is no less a caricature than past characterizations of female managers. Notes Cynthia Fuchs Epstein, sociologist and author of *Deceptive Distinctions*, "The notion at the base of this debate is that women have a single personality. That doesn't capture the rich variation in people."

Consider the reverse stereotypes in Herb and Marion Sandler, the husband and wife team who run Golden West Financial, a vibrantly healthy California savings-and-loan. Says she: "I'm less likely to compromise than my husband is when people don't perform to our standards." Says he: "I'm what you'd call soft." Both call the notion of male and female management styles nonsense.

"Do Women Manage Differently?" J. Fierman, *Fortune*, December 17, 1990, 115–118.

INTRODUCTION ◆◆◆◆◆◆

Organizations are made up of individuals who are trying to combine their efforts for mutual benefit. The better a manager understands how and why individuals act the way they do, the better that manager can help individuals work together efficiently and effectively.

The most fundamental principle of individual behavior is captured in psychologist Kurt Lewin's[1] equation:

$$B = f(P,S)$$

This equation proposes that all individual behavior (B) can be explained as a function (f) of (is caused by) something *inside* the person (P) and something *outside* the person in the situation (S) or context. For example, Lewin's equation suggests that differences in the ways that men and women manage (discussed in the opening vignette to this chapter) could be a function of something inside men and women (differences in their values and preferences). Or differences in the ways that men and women manage could be a function of something in the situation—differences in the ways that men and women are treated as managers. The management styles of women and men are the behaviors (B), the values and preferences of men and women are the something inside the person (P), and the ways women and men are treated as managers are the something outside the person (S).

The challenge of being a good manager is to encourage effective and efficient behaviors by other members of the organization. In the terms of Lewin's equation, a manager must know two things: what people bring to the organization (P), and what situations (S) must be created in the organization in order to encourage appropriate behaviors (B).

This chapter provides the foundation for answering that management challenge. The chapter begins by addressing the question, "How do individuals come to know the situations (S) in which they find themselves?" **Perception** is the process by which individuals come to know the situations in which they find themselves. Second, the chapter turns to the question, "What do individuals bring (P) to the organization?" This chapter explores two important aspects of what individuals bring to organizations: attitudes and personality. **Attitudes**—the way that individuals feel about things—are important to organizational behavior because they reflect an individual's tendencies to act. **Personality** is also about an individual's tendencies to act, but at a more general and enduring level than attitudes. This chapter concludes by exploring how an individual perceives the attitudes and personalities that *other* individuals bring to the organization. Subsequent chapters examine other important aspects of what an individual brings to organizations: learning and motivation (Chapter 4), decision-making tendencies (Chapter 5), and conflicts and stress (Chapter 6).

THE PROCESS OF PERCEPTION ◆◆◆◆◆◆

Perception is an individual's window to the world. When you look at this book, you *perceive* the words written in it. When you start a fire in the fireplace, you

---

[1] K. Lewin, "Behavior and Development as a Function of the Total Situation," in *Manual of Child Psychology*, ed. L. Carmichael (New York: Wiley, 1970), 791–844.

perceive the warmth the fire gives off. When you interact with someone, you *perceive* the kind of person that individual is, and you *perceive* the causes of his or her actions. Perception is the process by which we come to know the world so that we may act upon it.

The world comes to us through the firing of our nerve endings—a process called **sensation.** When you put your hand on a hot stove or someone calls your name, your nervous system comes alive and your nerve endings send inputs back to your brain. But there is no meaning attached to the firing of nerve endings. As William James noted in 1909, at the level of sensation the world must appear as something of a "buzzin', blooming confusion."[2] Perception is the process of making sense of the firing of our nerve endings by attaching meaning to sensations. As noted in Chapter 1, uncertainty is a defining feature of organizational behavior. More is always going on in an organization than any one person can digest, and much of what happens is ambiguous. If managing the uncertainty and confusion of the world around us is a central challenge of organizational behavior, perception is the first step in facing that challenge.

Psychologist Jerome Bruner is largely responsible for our current views of the perception process. In the 1940s and 1950s, Bruner and his colleagues wrote several articles concerning the "new look" in perception.[3] This "new look" ended the view of perception as a passive process in which the observer simply receives inputs from the environment. Instead it emphasized that perception is an *active* process—the perceiver plays an important role in determining what view of the world is provided by sensory inputs. This active view of perception also led researchers to look for new ways of understanding differences in perception among individuals.

The best way to understand perception is to remember that the act of perceiving is like painting a picture of the world with canvas and paints. Painting is a stylized activity, one in which the personal and unique style of the painter plays an active and important role. The painter selects which aspects of the event to include in the painting. Usually not all aspects are included—only those that the painter sees as central to constructing a representation of the event. The painter's representation of an event is not a true recording of that event. It is an interpretation of the event through the eyes of the painter. This is the essence of the perception process: perception is the selective construction of an interpretation of the world. The roles of each of these three component perception processes—attention, construction, and interpretation of sensory inputs—are captured in the model of perception shown in Figure 3–1.

Attention

It is easy to forget that our sensory systems are constantly bombarded with potential inputs. Walking down the street, we are exposed to signs, people, buildings, and cars. The work setting offers any number of potential inputs, including bosses, subordinates, pieces of furniture, reports, newspapers, and production machines. **Attention**—where we choose to direct our sensory input system—is a scarce resource that we direct and ration.

Psychological research repeatedly has demonstrated the limitations of our sensory input system. Imagine yourself walking along the street. A car drives

---

[2] W. James, *The Principles of Psychology* (New York: Henry Holt and Company, 1925).

[3] J. S. Bruner, "On Perceptual Readiness," *Psychological Review* 64 (1957): 123–152.

FIGURE 3-1 ▶ **Processes of Perception**

Perception is an active process in which the perceiver plays an important role. The perceiver selectively attends to sensory inputs, constructs a representation of the inputs, and interprets the meaning of the construction. These three processes each can be influenced by both the perceiver and the source of the sensory inputs—either the object of perception or the context in which perception occurs. Perceptions then become the inputs to subsequent actions of the perceiver.

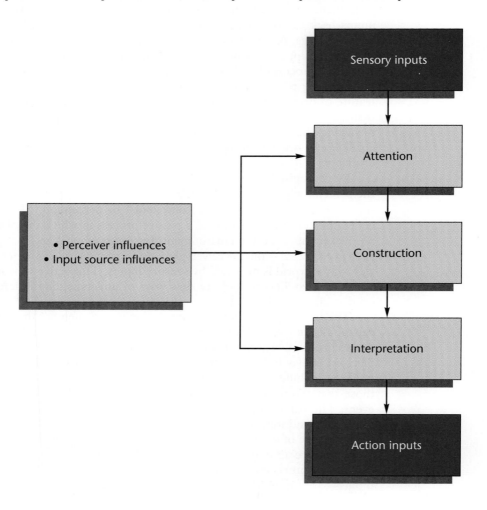

by. You are in a position to notice the license plate, features of the car, and characteristics of the driver. But do you perceive these things? While we are exposed to an infinite number of sensory inputs, only a limited number can be processed by our perceptual system. We can attend to only a limited selection— a sample—of all the available inputs, and hope we get a sample that is representative of the inputs we could *not* consider. Some of the directing and rationing of our attention comes from within; for instance, from our expectations and agendas. Some of the directing of our attention comes from characteristics of the sources of sensory inputs themselves.

The most important selection procedure for choosing among the infinite number of available sensory inputs is called accommodation. Accommodation occurs when a perceiver ignores a sensory input because the input is *not changing*. A sensory input that is not changing is not providing new information, so it can be ignored. For example, we all accommodate the habits and eccentricities of our coworkers, including the clothing they typically wear. Only when something out of the ordinary occurs—a particularly nasty coworker acts pleasant, or the boss comes to the office in shorts—are we likely to take notice.

With so many sensory inputs to choose from, the inputs that don't provide new information usually are the first to be ignored. Accommodation, however, is only one of several processes that determine which sensory inputs are processed.

Perceiver Influences   What a perceiver attends to can be influenced tremendously by theories that the perceiver harbors about the way the world works. For instance, the "FOCUS ON: Perceiver Influences on Attention" suggests that some perceivers consider clothing to be an important cue about what kind of person a job candidate might be. An individual who believes that clothing says something important naturally will be more likely to notice (*attend* to) the clothing other people wear.

The needs and motivations of a perceiver can have a similar influence on the rationing of attention. A hungry individual entering a dining room probably will notice what kinds of foods are available. A single and lonely young male more likely would notice the number and location of attractive females in the room. Needs and motivations also can lead a perceiver to look more carefully at objects or events, carefully enough to pick up fine nuances or distinctions that otherwise would be missed. An aspiring junior executive, for example, likely will pay extra attention to the boss's actions (and perhaps thereby gain some important insights into the boss's behavior) in the hopes of gleaning some hints about how to get promoted.

Are these perceiver influences on attention problematic? Certainly they can be. An interviewer whose expectations focus attention on unimportant characteristics of job candidates may miss critical information that could predict the job success or failure of the candidate. However, such influences also are unavoidable and even necessary. Because we all are exposed to an unlimited number of sensory inputs, we must have a way to decide which inputs to attend to and which to ignore. An interviewer who attends to a job applicant's clothing may be wrong about whether clothing tells you something important about an individual. However, it is impossible to conduct a selection interview without *some* theory to direct the information collection process. The perception process has to start with a rule for selecting which of the infinite number of available sensory inputs will be attended to. This means that good perceptions of the world begin with good theories of the world. Only with good theories are we likely to attend to the most valuable available sensory inputs.

Input Source Influences   Sometimes a perceiver's attempts to direct attention with theories about what to look for are upstaged by characteristics of the source objects or events, or **input source influences.** An object or event that is particularly eye-catching is said to be salient: It commands a perceiver's atten-

Focus on

Perceiver Influences on Attention

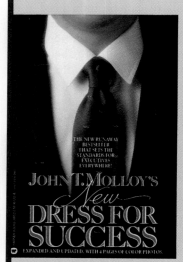

THE NEW RUNAWAY BESTSELLER THAT SETS THE STANDARDS FOR EXECUTIVES EVERYWHERE!

JOHN T. MOLLOY'S
New
DRESS FOR SUCCESS

EXPANDED AND UPDATED, WITH 4 PAGES OF COLOR PHOTOS.

Wardrobe Passages   In 1975, John Molloy published his landmark book, *Dress for Success.* Molloy's central message was that "the clothes make the man" (or woman); the initial image communicated by a businessperson is through his or her clothing. In 1977, Molloy followed up with *The Woman's Dress for Success Book,* which focused on the importance of clothing to would-be executive women. The message was that if a woman wanted to succeed in a man's world (that is, the business world), she would have to dress like a man. As a result, women's business fashions turned toward blue and gray suits.

There is evidence that the tide turned in the 1980s. In a 1985 article for *Working Women,* Heather Twidale noted that as women have achieved the rarefied atmosphere of the executive suite the basic blue and gray suits have given way to self-assured elegance in fashion. The corporate uniform—white shirt and blue suit—may be necessary at first to gain credibility and legitimacy. Beyond initial successes, however, cultivating some individual style can be crucial. Blue suits may send the appropriate message when a new executive is starting out, but leaders have a style all their own.

Professional sports teams have similarly considered the role of clothing. Here the question is whether replacing brightly colored uniforms with basic black can turn up players' intensity and reshape a pro team from wimps to winners. Compelling evidence suggests that clothing color does make a difference. Two hockey teams that switched to black uniforms went from the 14th and 9th to the 7th and 3rd most penalized teams in the league in just one year. Two possible explanations for this are that playing in black makes players more aggressive, or that their actions in black are *perceived* as more aggressive. Interestingly, research has backed up both views.

How much credit do the players give the colors of their uniforms? Most seem to believe that black uniforms only make them *seem* more aggressive, yet none are willing to discount color as a force. Black, almost everyone seems to agree, makes a team look formidable to the opposition. And that might be the real psychological power of the black uniform—it intimidates.

But do clothes really make the man? Says ex-Oakland Raider Ben Davidson, "If black jerseys could do all that, they would wear them in the executive suites."

Sources: Adapted from J. T. Molloy, *Dress for Success* (New York: P. H. Wyden, 1975); J. T. Molloy, *The Woman's Dress for Success Book* (Chicago: Follet Publications, 1977); H. Twidale, "The Triumph of Executive Chic," *Working Woman,* November 1985, 138–140; and S. Boxer, "Dark Forces," *Sports Illustrated,* April 17, 1989, 52–56.

tion. Several characteristics of objects or events will make them more likely to command attention.

Distinctiveness and novelty contribute to the salience of an object or event. Distinctiveness and novelty are the flip side of accommodation. The expected often is ignored or overlooked; new and novel sensory inputs demand attention. The first black executive in a company, the first female worker on a construction site, and the first male nurse in a hospital each command more than their fair share of attention. They are different from those around them—or at least novel in their positions—so they stand out more in the eyes of their beholders.

Vividness also contributes to the salience of an object or event. Vividness has to do with the visual intensity of an object of the perception process. An object or image may be particularly vivid, meaning that the colors are bright and memorable and our eyes are drawn to the image. In a written report, word-

No doubt your eye was drawn to this picture when you first turned the page. The picture's vivid colors and distinctive patterns make it particularly salient, or eye-catching. Without the correct perceptual set, however, it would take you a few seconds to arrive at a correct perception of the picture. It's the S&P 500 Index trading pit on the floor of the Chicago Mercantile Exchange.

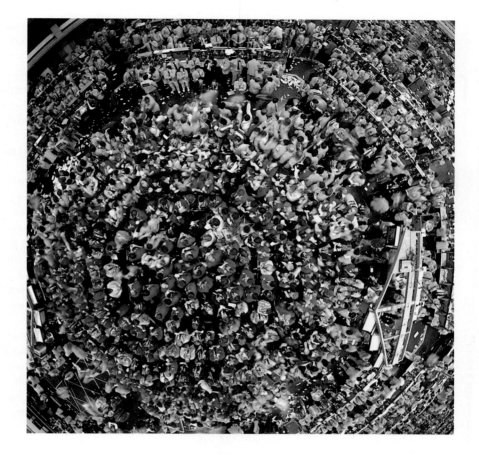

ing also may be vivid in that it calls forth vivid images. Vividness commands the attention and information processing of a perceiver.

Personal perspective also can profoundly influence which sensory inputs are considered. An individual's own contributions to something (such as a task force report) are much more salient than the contributions of others. That's because you never miss what you yourself contribute, but you may miss what others contribute. It is not surprising, then, that group members asked to evaluate the percentage of their contribution to a joint project routinely provide answers that sum to more than 100 percent. We all think we do more than our fair share because our share is more salient to us than others' contributions.

Differences in personal perspective can go a long way toward explaining how conflicts occur in organizations; for example, consider the consequences of the differences between supervisor and subordinate perceptions shown in Figure 3–2.

Source characteristics have their greatest influence on attention under conditions of information overload. **Information overload** occurs when there are too many attention-grabbing sensory inputs. In familiar surroundings, where many features of the environment are well known and need little attention, plenty of attention is available for new or unusual objects or events. In novel situations, where a perceiver has few theories about where to direct attention and receives many unusual inputs, characteristics of objects and events that command attention (for instance, motion or vividness) will play a major role in what information gets attended to and processed.

Construction

Once sensory inputs have been selected for further processing, the perceiver uses them to construct a representation of the event or object being attended to. The **construction** process organizes and edits the sensory inputs in a way that makes them potentially meaningful. The construction process also is subject to both input source and perceiver influences.

Perceiver Influences The perceptual construction process can be influenced tremendously by perceptual set. **Perceptual set** refers to the expectations that a perceiver brings to the perception task. What a perceiver expects or wants to see plays a major role in the perception he or she constructs.

A visual demonstration of perceptual set is provided in Figure 3–3. If you were led to expect to see an old woman in the large picture, you would see an old woman. If you were told to expect to see a young woman, you would see a young woman. In fact, this picture can be seen as *either* an old woman or a young woman. The expectation determines which construction a perceiver makes from the same sensory inputs.

Experiences can be the source of perceptual sets. If an individual were shown the drawing in the middle before seeing the large "old woman/young woman" picture, a young woman would be likely to emerge from it. But if an individual were shown the drawing on the left before seeing the large "old woman/young woman" picture, an old woman likely would emerge from it. In this case there is no "right" answer. The picture can be seen as either an old woman or a young woman. What is important is that the perceiver's prior experience (seeing the unambiguous old woman or young woman picture) creates a

FIGURE 3–2	▶ Differences in Perception between Supervisors and Subordinates

Supervisors and subordinates have different needs, different expectations, and different personal perspectives, so it's no surprise that their perceptions differ in important ways. Reconciling these differences in perception—for instance, by openly discussing them—can help supervisors avoid conflicts with their subordinates.

Types of Recognition	Frequency with Which *Supervisors* Say They Give Various Types of Recognition for Good Performance	Frequency with Which *Subordinates* Say Supervisors Give Various Types of Recognition for Good Performance
Gives privileges	52%	14%
Gives more responsibility	48	10
Gives a pat on the back	82	13
Gives sincere and thorough praise	80	14
Trains for better jobs	64	9
Gives more interesting work	51	5

Source: Adapted from R. Likert, *New Patterns in Management* (New York: McGraw-Hill, 1961), 91.

| FIGURE 3-3 | ▶The Young Woman and the Old Woman |

Expectations can lead us to perceive what we expect. In these pictures, most people who first see the young woman in the middle see another young woman in the large, ambiguous picture. In work organizations, training and socialization create important expectations that help workers perceive apparently novel and insoluble problems as familiar situations they are well prepared to handle. Expectations can be dangerous if they lead us to perceive what really isn't there.

Source: R. Leeper, "A Study of a Neglected Portion of the Field of Learning—The Development of Sensory Organization," *Journal of Genetic Psychology* 46 (1935): 41–75.

perceptual set; the perceptual set in turn determines which subsequent perceptions are likely to be constructed.

Nobel Prize winner Herbert Simon describes a graphic example of the effects of perceptual set in the book *Administrative Behavior*.[4] Executives from different departments of major companies read a case study. The case study described the problems faced by the chief executive officer (CEO) of a major corporation. After they had read the case, the executives were asked to analyze the cause of the CEO's problems. Not surprisingly, each executive perceived the cause of the CEO's problems to be within his or her own specialty. For example, the marketing executives saw a marketing problem, the finance executives saw a finance problem, and so on. Each executive brought to the perception task a perceptual set—his or her own business specialty—which in turn determined the perception of the CEO's problems that each executive constructed. Another example of the influence of perceptual set on perceptual constructions, in the domain of college sports, is shown in the "Focus on: Perceiver Influences on Construction."

Prejudice represents a particularly dangerous form of perceptual set influences on construction. Prejudice refers to the tendency of an individual to prejudge the actions of another individual according to a set of beliefs. For instance, if a male executive believes that women make poor managers, he will be likely to perceive all attempts to manage by women as inappropriate. As we

---

[4]H. Simon, *Administrative Behavior* (New York: MacMillan, 1945).

Focus on

Perceiver Influences on Construction

They Saw a Game The role of perceiver motivations in constructing perceptions is regularly on display when a perceiver's self-image is on the line. For example, if a perceiver *identifies* with a sports team—takes pride in the team's wins and wallows in misery when the team loses—the perceiver has a *vested interest* in the team's actions being right and good. This vested interest dramatically affects constructed perceptions about the team's actions, as demonstrated in the following study of fan reactions to a football game:

> Anyone who has observed the spectators at athletic events can't help noticing that two apparently reasonable people can experience a play in football or basketball in very different ways as a function of having been "tuned" by different expectations and purposes. This fact of experience was illustrated by a case study of a football game. It so happened that Dartmouth and Princeton played each other in football one November afternoon. The game turned out to be very rough, and tempers flared both during and after the game. Immediately following the game, partisans for both schools made accusations that the other school had played rough and dirty football. The school papers, the school alumni magazines, and a number of the metropolitan newspapers highly publicized the whole affair. There was clearly a very real disagreement as to what had actually happened during the game. What is of special interest . . . were the results of showing a movie of the game to a group of Dartmouth students and a group of Princeton students. Keeping in mind that an identical movie was shown to both groups of students, it is interesting to [note] the number of infractions perceived in the same film by two groups of people with different loyalties and different expectations. Students . . . tended to see the team from the other university as having committed the most infractions.

Source: D. J. Schneider, A. H. Hastorf, and P. C. Ellsworth, *Person Perception* (Reading, Mass.: Addison-Wesley, 1979).

shall see later, perceptual sets influence not only perceptual constructions, but also the meanings people attach to these constructions.

Input Source Influences Characteristics of the source of sensory inputs—the object or event being perceived—also can influence the perceptual construction process. Three examples of input source influences on perceptual construction are contrast, anchoring-and-adjustment, and "halo" effects. All three arise when one sensory input influences the construction of perceptions of other sensory inputs.

Contrast effects occur when an individual sees something as larger or smaller than it really is because of a comparison to a very small or very large reference point. Think about how you would feel about a $3,000 increase in your annual salary. If your last salary increase was only $1,000, this raise would seem generous *in contrast*. If you learned that a coworker had received a $10,000 increase, your $3,000 would seem pretty paltry. Of course, $3,000 is $3,000. It's the contrast with either $1,000 or $10,000 that makes it seem big or small.

Anchoring-and-adjustment effects are the flip side of contrast effects. Contrast effects occur when our perceptual system constructs two sensory inputs to be more dissimilar than they really are; anchoring-and-adjustment effects occur when our perceptual system constructs two sensory inputs to be more *similar* than they should be. Imagine you are trying to assign a value to something—for instance, how much a particular employee should be paid. A friend suggests that you pay the new employee $50,000, which you reject as too high. This "suggestion," even though you rejected it, nevertheless has an effect. Knowing the suggestion to be too high, you would *adjust* away from it (lower) in formulating your perception of what would be fair. However, research repeatedly has demonstrated that adjustments of this sort are almost always *insufficient*. In this case, insufficient adjustment down from the $50,000 suggestion would result in a higher salary actually assigned to the new employee. The $50,000 suggestion anchors your perception of what would be a fair wage for the new employee, even though the suggestion itself is obviously inappropriate. If the suggestion had been $5,000, you would have rejected it as well and adjusted upward. Again, however, the adjustment would be insufficient, producing a bias now to perceive a *lower* salary as fair.

Interestingly, the ability of an "anchor" (such as a suggested salary) to influence perceptual construction does not seem to depend on its being a sensible clue to the correct answer. In one study of anchoring-and-adjustment effects, students were asked to estimate the proportion of African countries in the United Nations. Before making their estimates, however, each student was given a number to consider from one spin of a "wheel of fortune." Obviously this random number obtained from a spin of the wheel could not be a useful clue in deciding the correct proportion of African countries in the United Nations. Nevertheless, the numbers obtained from the spin of the wheel clearly influenced the students' estimates.[5]

Halo effects occur when the perception of an object or event on one dimension influences the construction of perceptions of that object or event on other dimensions. A physically attractive individual, for instance, may be perceived as more competent than another worker who is less physically attractive. Why? Physical attractiveness is positive, so it creates a positive "halo." Other traits of the attractive individual (such as ability or accomplishments) are perceived as more positive because of the positive "halo." Perception of the individual on one dimension (physical attractiveness) influences the perception of the individual on other dimensions (such as ability or accomplishment). Unfortunately, "halo" effects also probably are responsible for people thinking that their friends can do no wrong. Friendship creates a positive "halo" that can seriously compromise an individual's evaluations of a friend's actions.

Contrast, anchoring-and-adjustment, and "halo" effects all are examples of the influence of one sensory input on the constructed perception of another. These effects arise, of course, as a reaction to uncertainty. Your perception of your own age is not likely to be influenced by anchoring and adjustment. Nor is your perception of your own physical attractiveness likely to influence your perception of your own age. But your own age is something you *know*. Most things you cannot know; you can only construct perceptions of them. The perceptual construction process is an uncertain one, because you never know if you are seeing things the way they really are. It is this uncertainty that makes perceptual construction vulnerable to influence.

---

[5]A. Tversky and D. Kahneman, "Judgment under Uncertainty: Heuristics and Biases," *Science* 185 (1974): 1124–1131.

| Interpretation |

The selection and construction processes provide the perceiver with only a representation of what object or event has occurred in the world. A final stage in the perception process is **interpretation** of the representation to assign meaning to what the perceiver has perceived.

One process people use to assign meaning to actions and their outcomes is attribution. **Attribution** is the process of perceiving the *causes* of actions and outcomes. When a foreman yells at a worker, what *caused* the yelling behavior? Was it something the worker did? Something the worker didn't do? Something the foreman ate? Perhaps the foreman just likes to yell at everyone. These are important distinctions because they help us determine the meaning of the yelling. Should the worker take yelling as important criticism, write it off as a bad day for the foreman, or believe that yelling is something everyone on this job needs to learn to live with? Determining whether the foreman is yelling (as opposed to talking normally) is a matter of attention and construction. Yelling in and of itself is not an important sensory input. The *meaning* of the yelling is what counts.

Attributions are particularly useful because they provide models of how the people around us function, what their motives are, and what determines their behavior. These models in turn reduce our uncertainty in social interaction. If we understand how others are likely to behave and why, we can use this knowledge to achieve our goals. Attributions help us understand cause-and-effect relationships, such as what caused the foreman to yell and therefore when he is likely to yell again. Attributions allow us to predict the future behavior of others based upon our understanding of the causes of their past and present behavior. Attributions then are critical to formulating action plans for the future.

Processes of Attribution   The central principle of attribution is **covariation.** Psychologist Harold Kelley, the founding father of the theory of attribution, explained covariation by noting that "an effect is attributed to that condition which is present when the effect is present and absent when the effect is absent."[6] In other words, if a condition is present when an effect occurs but absent when the effect fails to occur, the condition is said to *covary* with the effect. Conditions that covary with an effect will be perceived to *cause* the effect. To take a concrete example, if a worker's performance is good (the effect) when the worker is supervised (the condition) but poor when the worker isn't supervised, then supervision will be perceived as the cause of good performance. People judge covariation three ways: via distinctiveness, consensus, and consistency.

Imagine that your boss has just complimented you (the effect) on a report that you recently submitted. You are wondering what to make of this compliment. What *meaning* should you attach to your boss's remark, and what implications does that meaning hold for your future behavior? Was the quality of your report the *cause* of your boss's compliment? To sort out this uncertainty, first you would want to note whether the compliment was *distinctive:* Does your boss compliment people all the time or is this a rare event? If an effect occurs all the time (for instance, if everyone compliments everyone else in this company all the time just as a matter of politeness), then it is pointless to look for

[6]H. H. Kelley, "Attribution Theory in Social Psychology," in *Nebraska Symposium on Motivation* 15, ed. D. Levine (Lincoln, Neb.: University of Nebraska Press, 1967).

causes of the effect. Attribution is a worthwhile activity only if an effect occurs some but not all of the time. Then situations in which the effect occurs are distinctive (they differ from other situations), and it is useful to ask what *causes* the effect to occur sometimes but not others.

Consensus has to do with whether the condition produces the effect for other people. Assume for the moment that your boss's compliment was distinctive and therefore merits further search for a cause. If other people read the report and also compliment it, that would be evidence of covariation of the report and the compliment *across people*—a consensus that the quality of the report (the condition) causes the compliment (the effect).

Finally, you might look at the *consistency* of your boss's compliments across time and across situations. Does your boss compliment all your reports, or did she single out this report in particular? Has she similarly complimented other reports on this same topic? Has she similarly complimented other reports written in this same style? These questions all attempt to isolate the cause of the boss's compliment by finding consistencies between appearance of the effect and plausible causes.

Attributions are important because different attributions for actions or events merit different responses. Figure 3–4 provides a framework for the different types of attributions you might arrive at for a subordinate's performance. This framework has two dimensions: location of the cause and stability of the cause. Location can be internal (the individual) or external (outside the individual); stability can be permanent or temporary. As shown in Figure 3–4, these

---

FIGURE 3–4   ▶ **Attributions**

The attributions we make for the causes of events (actions and their outcomes) are critical to our responses to those events. This table provides a framework for our attributions and the responses those attributions will occasion. For example, we are likely to punish an employee who failed if we think he or she didn't make an effort. On the other hand, we may be likely to help an employee who failed if we think he or she doesn't have the ability.

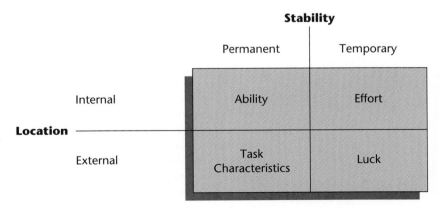

	Stability	
	Permanent	Temporary
Location — Internal	Ability	Effort
External	Task Characteristics	Luck

Source: B. Weiner, *Achievement Motivation and Attribution Theory* (Morristown, N.J.: General Learning Press, 1975).

two dimensions yield four different causes for behaviors: luck, effort, task characteristics, and ability/personality. Each cause carries with it a different recommendation for action.

Consider a worker whose performance is disappointing. Before a supervisor can decide what to do to correct the poor performance, the supervisor must determine its cause. If the supervisor observed that other workers handled this task well, the supervisor would make an internal attribution—decide that the worker's failure was due to either lack of effort or lack of ability. If the worker did fine at other tasks, lack of effort could be ruled out as an explanation. Having determined lack of ability to be the cause of the poor performance, the supervisor could reassign the worker to a task more suitable to the worker's abilities.

If on the other hand the supervisor noted that the worker had done fine on this job in the past but *only recently* had performed poorly, the supervisor would have to conclude that the cause of the performance failure was unstable. The supervisor then might see if other workers recently had experienced similar difficulties, or if only *this* worker was having trouble. If only this worker was having trouble, that would suggest that perhaps something was temporarily causing the worker not to give as much effort as before. A new assignment would not be necessary: a personal pep talk would be more appropriate.

Finally, what if further investigation by the supervisor revealed consensus—that lots of workers were having similar performance problems? That would suggest an external cause of poor performance. Perhaps the design of the task might be at fault, or training for the entire work force might be inadequate.

That attribution is a *perception* process should be obvious from this example. The sensory input is the same in all cases: the employee's performance is disappointing. What varies is the interpretation of this performance. Is the cause of the performance failure internal or external to the individual, and is the cause permanent or only temporary? Each attribution carries with it a different prescription for resolving the performance problem.

The framework of possible attributions also suggests how we come to understand the personality of another individual. Personality is used to describe the tendency of an individual to behave consistently across situations and across time. We attribute an individual's behaviors to stable internal causes when that individual behaves similarly across situations and across time, and unlike other people. In effect, personality is the cause assigned to consistent behavior that cannot be explained otherwise. (The process of perceiving others will be discussed in greater detail later in this chapter.)

Perceiver Influences   Attribution is not the discovery of true causes of behavior, merely an individual's interpretation of the likely causes of behaviors and outcomes. Attribution represents the attempts of an individual to make causal sense of the world. Unfortunately, like the perceptual processes of attention and construction, attribution is subject to influences.

One important source of attributional influence is personal perspective. When we observe the behaviors of another individual, the most salient plausible cause of that individual's behaviors is that individual. That other individual is always front and center stage in the production of his or her own behaviors. When we ourselves act, our own persona is *not* a salient component of the visual landscape. In fact, most of us rarely see ourselves behaving at all. Instead, we see only the environment to which we are responding.

Furthermore, we see our own behaviors in a variety of different settings—at home, at work, at play. Many of the other individuals with whom we interact we see only in a considerably more limited number of circumstances. Some, for instance, we may see only at work. As a result, the diversity of circumstances in which we observe their behaviors will be quite limited. We may mistakenly see their behavior as very consistent across circumstances when in fact their behavior is consistent only over an extremely limited set of circumstances.

These consequences of personal perspective—greater visual salience of others as plausible causes of their behaviors and limited diversity of circumstances in which to view others' behaviors—give rise to an important perceptual bias known as the fundamental attribution error.[7] The **fundamental attribution error** is the tendency of a perceiver to see others' behaviors as caused primarily by stable, internal characteristics (such as personality) while seeing his or her own behavior primarily as a response to environmental circumstances. The fundamental attribution error suggests that explanations for actions typically will take the form, "*I* did it because the circumstances demanded it; *he* did it because that's the kind of person he is."

The fundamental attribution error is important because of the role (described earlier) that a supervisor's attributions play in evaluating employee behaviors. Supervisors are likely to conclude that a subordinate's behaviors reveal something about the subordinate, and therefore are worthy of blame or praise. The subordinate is instead likely to believe that those same behaviors are simply sensible reactions to environmental cues—what anyone would have done under the same circumstances.

Input Source Influences   Sometimes we forget that *other people* represent a significant feature of the perceptual field in which actions and consequences occur. Because others often are present when we are trying to interpret ambiguous sensory inputs, actions of others also can influence our perceptions. If a classmate says that a test the two of you just took was difficult, you may also be disposed to see the test as having been difficult—especially if you weren't sure what to think. In effect, the comments and opinions of others can anchor our perceptions and judgments.

This process of having one's perceptions influenced by the comments and perceptions of others is called **social comparison.** Social comparison will be discussed in greater detail in Chapter 8.

ATTITUDES

If perception is an individual's window to the world, then attitudes are the world's window into that individual. **Attitudes** are "predispositions to respond in consistently favorable ways to certain people, groups, ideas, or situations."[8] This definition of attitudes implies the three components of attitudes shown in Figure 3–5. First, attitudes are about specific things and therefore include *beliefs*

[7] E. E. Jones and R. E. Nisbett, "The Actor and the Observer: Divergent Perceptions of the Causes of Behavior" in *Attribution: Perceiving the Causes of Behavior,* eds. E. E. Jones et al. (Morristown, N.J.: General Learning Press, 1972).

[8] R. L. Crooks, and J. Stein, *Psychology: Science, Behavior, and Life* (Fort Worth, Tex.: Holt, Rinehart, and Winston, 1988).

FIGURE 3–5 ▶ **Attitudes**

Attitudes represent an evaluation of our perceptions against our internal belief systems and values. Attitudes include beliefs, affect, and tendencies to act.

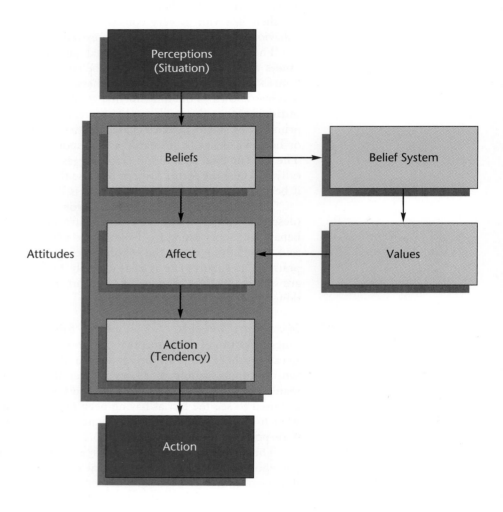

---

about those things. If I have an attitude about working in groups, that implies that I know something about working in groups—that I have some beliefs about working in groups. Second, attitudes include some *affect*—a favorable or unfavorable evaluation of those beliefs. If I have an attitude about working in groups, then I must have some negative or positive feeling about working in groups. Finally, attitudes include a *tendency to act*. If I have an attitude about working in groups, then my attitude should tell you whether I would choose to work in groups or alone.

Where do attitudes come from? Figure 3–5 suggests that attitudes are simply a reflection of our perceptions. We perceive something in our organization—a situation, for example. That perception leads us to have beliefs and affects about the situation, and those beliefs and affects in turn predispose us to act in a particular way toward that situation.

Unfortunately, attitudes are not nearly so simple. Attitudes are not just a reflection of our perceptions—they are an *evaluation* of our perceptions. Consider the attitude you have toward committees. Perhaps you avoid committees (a tendency to act) because you have negative feelings about them (an affect) and you think that committees are a waste of time (a belief). Notice that this suggests that your action (avoidance) is a function of your affect (negative), which is in turn a function of your belief (that committees are a waste of time).

But does this really explain your attitude toward committees? Why do you have negative feelings about wasting your time? Probably because you *believe* that if you waste your time, you will not be able to accomplish other things, and you *value* those other things. This suggests that attitudes arise when our perceptions are evaluated against our belief systems and our values. Our **belief system** is our stored set of theories and expectations about how and why the world works; our **values** represent our core understanding of what is important to us. What makes us feel negatively about committees are not just our beliefs about committees (they waste time) but also our *beliefs about those beliefs* (wasting time means you can't accomplish other things) and the *value* we attach to those beliefs (it is important to accomplish other things). Thus, our attitudes are not just a reflection of our perceptions—attitudes also reflect our belief system and our values. Attitudes are the world's window to our beliefs and values. Since values are relatively stable and enduring personal characteristics, it should not be surprising that some of our attitudes—for instance, satisfaction with our jobs—also turn out to be quite stable over many years.[9]

Self-Perception

Unfortunately, even this may be too simple an explanation of where attitudes come from. Figure 3–5 suggests that we always perceive, form attitudes, and then act accordingly—that actions are a *result* of attitudes. Sometimes, however, uncertainty, complexity, and conflict may reverse this causal chain. Sometimes we act and only later try to understand why we did so—what our attitude must have been. In this case, our *own action* is the perception that we evaluate to form an attitude. When we examine our own actions to decide what our attitudes must be, we are engaging in **self-perception**. We are trying to "make sense of" our own behaviors, a process known as rationalization. Rationalization occurs in a couple of different ways. A **self-serving bias** is the tendency of individuals to attribute the causes of actions or their outcomes in a way that reflects well on them or absolves them from responsibility for poor outcomes. Self-serving attributions take one or two forms: (1) they explain an action as a sensible response to situational demands or constraints (thereby excusing the outcome), or (2) they explain the outcome as the result of causes external to the individual (such as the interfering behaviors of others). These two forms of self-serving bias differ in that the first form admits that the action taken was wrong, but excuses it as a sensible reaction to the situation; the second form

[9]B. M. Staw, N. E. Bell, and J. A. Clausen, "The Dispositional Approach to Job Attitudes: A Life-Time Longitudinal Test," *Administrative Science Quarterly* 31 (1986): 56–77.

suggests that the action taken might even have been *correct* and that it didn't produce a good outcome for reasons beyond the individual's control.

In one demonstration of self-serving attribution bias, several groups of students played a game in which they were responsible for governing a fictitious nation torn by revolution. Many decisions were required during the game, and the researcher arranged for each group of students to meet with some significant successes and some significant disasters. The researchers found that students tended to place blame for the failures on situational circumstances, but claimed responsibility for the successes.[10] Similar self-serving attributional biases have been demonstrated by teachers who credit their high-quality instruction for their students' successes but blame the students' lack of effort for their failures.[11] Research also has shown that in their annual reports to stockholders, unstable corporations often attribute their past successes and failures in ways that emphasize management's ability to control corporate performance and therefore improve it in the future.[12]

Self-perception also comes into play when an individual acts quickly and only later reflects back on why the action was taken. If we engage in actions that are to ourselves mysterious (for instance, because we do not wish to admit to our subconscious motives), we arrive at an understanding of our own attitudes that explains our actions. Imagine that you do something with a friend that you know you should not do—trading on the stock market based on inside information, for example. After the fact, you might convince yourself that it was important to go along with the friend, rather than admitting that you really did want to take advantage of the inside information. You have rationalized your behavior (made it appear sensible) by deciding what your attitude must have been. If there are environmental forces (such as incentives or requests by powerful others) that could have "caused" our behaviors, we will be unlikely to attribute the actions to our own attitudes.

Personal perspective is an important source of differences in our self-perceptions and the perceptions other individuals have of our behaviors. Self-perception biases can be alleviated by encouraging an individual to see his or her actions as others would.

Objective Self-Awareness Making an individual more aware of his or her own role in causing actions or their consequences means making that individual more aware that the actions or their consequences are the product of personal motivations and preferences rather than simple reactions to environmental demands. An actor's awareness of his or her own role in causing behaviors and their consequences is called **objective self-awareness.**[13] Studies have shown that without objective self-awareness individuals will make more *situational* attributions for their actions and consequences (as discussed in the fundamental

[10] S. Streufert and S. C. Streufert, "Effect of Conceptual Structure, Failure, and Success on Attribution of Causality and Interpersonal Attitude," *Journal of Personality and Social Psychology* 11 (1969): 138–147.

[11] T. J. Johnson, R. Feigenbaum, and M. Weiby, "Some Determinants and Consequences of the Teacher's Perception of Causality," *Journal of Educational Psychology* 55 (1964): 237–246.

[12] G. R. Salancik and J. R. Meindl, "Corporate Attributions as Strategic Illusions of Management Control," *Administrative Sciences Quarterly* 29 (1984): 238–254.

[13] R. A. Wicklund, "Objective Self-Awareness," in *Advances in Experimental Social Psychology* 8, ed. L. Berkowitz (New York: Academic Press, 1975).

attribution error). What happens, however, when individuals instead are given feedback that highlights their own roles in the actions? What happens, for example, when individuals view videotapes of their behavior? Individuals then attribute more of their behaviors and consequences to themselves—to their own attitudes—just as an impartial observer would. Objective self-awareness helps an individual see himself or herself at the center of the action and thereby eliminates a major source of differences between processes of perception applied to the self and to others.

The Satisfaction-Performance Controversy	One of the central concerns about attitudes in organizations is the relationship between worker performance and an important workplace attitude: job satisfaction.[14] Does a worker's satisfaction with the job lead to superior work performance? Does superior work performance make a worker more satisfied? Or is there perhaps something else that makes workers both satisfied and productive? At issue, of course, is the task of the manager. The view that "satisfaction causes performance" suggests that the manager's role is to make organizational life satisfying for workers in the hopes of eliciting superior worker performance. The logic of this belief is compelling:

> . . . the degree of job satisfaction felt by an employee determines his performance, that is, satisfaction causes performance. This proposition has theoretical roots, but it also reflects the popular belief that "a happy worker is a productive worker" and the notion that "all good things go together." It is far more pleasant to increase an employee's happiness than to deal directly with his performance whenever a performance problem exists. Therefore, acceptance of the satisfaction-causes-performance proposition as a solution makes good sense, particularly for the manager because it represents the path of least resistance. Furthermore, high job satisfaction and high performance are both good, and, therefore, they ought to be related to one another.[15]

One explanation for the belief that worker satisfaction *causes* superior performance is exchange theory.[16] According to exchange theory, life is a series of transactions. The values of the things being traded (for example, flattery in exchange for the favors of an attractive companion) may not be easily compared, but everyone tries to keep score. If someone gives you something of value, you are obligated by the unwritten rules of social interaction to give something of comparable value in return. If an organization treats a worker well and the worker is satisfied, the worker is likewise obligated to return comparable value in the form of hard work and productivity.

Exchange theory is not alone in suggesting a link between worker satisfaction and performance. An early review of 23 studies of the relationship between worker satisfaction and performance revealed *only one study* in which satisfaction

---

[14] See, for example, C. D. Fisher, "On the Dubious Wisdom of Expecting Job Satisfaction to Correlate with Performance," *Academy of Management Review* 5, (1980): 607–612; and M. T. Iaffaldano and P. M. Muchinsky, "Job Satisfaction and Job Performance: A Meta-Analysis," *Psychological Bulletin* 97 (1985): 251–273.

[15] C. H. Greene, "The Satisfaction/Performance Controversy," *Business Horizons* 15 (1972): 31–41.

[16] A. W. Gouldner, "A Norm of Reciprocity: A Preliminary Statement," *American Sociological Review* 25 (1960): 161–178.

and performance were not positively related to each other.[17] On the other hand, the relationships found between satisfaction and performance, while consistently positive, rarely have been strong. This, too, is not surprising. There are *lots* of unproductive or even *counterproductive* ways for workers to find satisfaction in work. Donald Roy and Michael Buroway's chronicles of life on the assembly line (described in Chapter 2) detailed the unproductive games that shop-floor workers often play. These games are a way of making uninteresting work interesting—a way of gaining satisfaction *on* the job when satisfaction *with* the job is not available. This sentiment is echoed in one writer's comments concerning his own experiences in the blue-collar labor force:

> At first I was surprised at how skillful people were in using up the time of day and yet producing so little. I have now become intrigued with the notion that most of us want a job with security, as in the military; we want good pay and maximum benefits, tenure and seniority, but there seems to be a powerful inclination to do as little work as possible. If we have job security and basic needs are being met, do we lose our motivation to work? My experience has given rise to serious doubts regarding humans' intrinsic desire to work at all.[18]

Research does support the importance of job satisfaction to the management of organizations. Job satisfaction has been shown to be related to worker turnover and absenteeism.[19] Both of these are critical considerations for managers because of the costs they entail. An absent worker cannot be a productive one, and a worker who leaves the organization—whether voluntarily or not—must be replaced, resulting in lost productivity and selection and training costs for the replacement. Thus, even though greater job satisfaction may not *cause* better performance, job satisfaction certainly has an *indirect* effect on organizational performance. As noted in the "FOCUS ON: Attitudes," some companies understand the benefits of having satisfied employees and are working hard to realize those benefits.

One view of the relationship between job satisfaction and performance is that superior performance leads to desired rewards and the receipt of those rewards results in worker satisfaction.[20] This view of the relationship between satisfaction and performance means that the task of the manager is to encourage superior worker performance and reward it when it occurs. Superior worker performance then leads to rewards and thereby to job satisfaction, low turnover, and low absenteeism—not to mention organizational efficiency and effectiveness. This view suggests an important alteration of McGregor's Theory Y. It is not hard work that is natural to workers; what is natural to workers is the dogged pursuit of satisfaction. In that dogged pursuit the worker may become all the things that McGregor hoped for—creative, industrious, and accepting if not desirous of responsibility. It is the task of the manager to arrange work so that the surest path to a worker's satisfaction runs through actions that are productive for the organization.

[17] V. H. Vroom, *Work and Motivation* (New York: Wiley and Sons, 1964).

[18] R. Schrank, *Ten Thousand Working Days* (Cambridge, Mass.: MIT Press, 1978).

[19] See, for instance, J. L. Cotton and J. M. Tuttle, "Employee Turnover: A Meta-Analysis and Review with Implications for Research," *Academy of Management Review* (January 1986): 55–70.

[20] E. E. Lawler III and L. W. Porter, "The Effect of Performance on Job Satisfaction," *Industrial Relations* 7 (1967): 20–28.

Focus on Attitudes

All Work and No Play . . . Isn't Even Good for Work? Does job satisfaction need to directly improve employee productivity for it to be a priority for managers? Outdoor products manufacturer Patagonia and electronics giant Texas Instruments don't think so. They have discovered that workers in their 20s often use quality of worklife and job satisfaction, rather than financial reward or opportunity for career advancement, as the determining factors in selecting and remaining with an employer. Firms like Patagonia and TI have learned that if you want to keep your best employees productive, first you have to keep them. And that means keeping employees satisfied with what their jobs have to offer—for instance, by offering employees educational assistance programs or a nontraditional office environment.

Other companies have even found *direct* productivity benefits from nontraditional office environments that emphasize employee satisfaction. Joy Committees at the office? Hula-hoop contests? These seemingly incongruous

additions to the business scene represent a new approach to increasing productivity. Playfulness, researchers are finding, can help people take a better, more creative approach to the way they work. The serious benefits of fun are so well established that a number of firms have made it part of their corporate culture.

Ben & Jerry's Homemade, for example, set up an official Joy Committee. Tacky Dress-Up Day, complete with plaids, paisley, and polyester, blinded the staff one day last year. Earlier, during the busiest time of the summer, the ice cream company hired masseuses to ease the tension. "People could go out, have a massage and relax for half an hour," says Peter Lind, head of research and development and grand poobah of the committee. Lind feels joy improves productivity in part by making employees feel comfortable with one another: "There's not a hierarchy here. People can share ideas." Another perk, naturally enough, is free ice cream.

At Odetics, a high-technology robotics firm in California, fun is part of an overall commitment to keeping employees happy and healthy. The company has a Fun Committee, and a repertory theater, a weight room, a pool, and tennis and volleyball courts. Employees' use of the facilities is believed to increase employee communication and enhance good employee relations.

Research supports the idea that joy and play can be especially beneficial to creativity. Psychologist Alice Isen and her colleagues at the University of Maryland, for example, found that people who "felt good" after seeing a humorous film solved problems more creatively. Similarly, Mary Ann Glyn, a professor of organizational behavior at Yale University, discovered that people who see problems as games come up with more creative solutions than those who consider the same problems work.

Sources: Condensed from "All Work and No Play . . . Isn't Even Good for Work," *Psychology Today,* March 1989, 34–36; and C. M. Solomon, "Managing the Baby Busters," *Personnel Journal* 71 (3) (1992): 52–59.

PERSONALITY ◆◆◆◆◆◆

If attitudes are a reflection of an individual's values and belief system, then **personality** *is* an individual's values and belief system. Personality has been defined as the characteristics of an individual that cause consistent patterns in that individual's behaviors over time.[21] Personality represents a predisposition to have particular beliefs, attitudes, and behaviors. While attitudes often change, and values may evolve over time, personality is usually thought of as more enduring and stable.

Personality is typically discussed in terms of **traits.** A trait is a characteristic, usually expressed as a dimension on which every person can be measured. Height, for instance, is a trait because everyone has a height that can be measured in terms of feet and inches; height is a *physical* trait rather than a personality trait, however. Personality traits refer to relatively enduring characteristics inside an individual (such as the ability to manage time featured in the "FOCUS ON: Personality") that we think are likely to predispose that individual to particular beliefs, attitudes, and behaviors.

Primary Personality Traits

Psychologist Raymond Cattell was a pioneer in the search for a universal set of primary personality traits.[22] He used direct observations of large numbers of people in everyday life and a variety of questionnaires to identify sixteen primary personality traits. He expressed these sixteen traits in terms of pairs of polar opposite words, such as relaxed versus tense. Along with his colleagues, Cattell used his sixteen primary traits to create a questionnaire to measure personality. The questionnaire allowed Cattell to create a personality profile for any individual. The profile indicates where an individual's personality was located on each of the sixteen primary traits. The average personality profiles for three different occupations—writers, airline pilots, and business executives—are provided in Figure 3–6. Not surprisingly, Cattell's personality profiles for these three occupations are all quite different. In a study of 180 married couples, Cattell also found that married couples were most satisfied when they were most alike in their personality profiles.[23]

The most recent development in the search for a universal set of primary personality traits has been the apparent confirmation of a "Big Five"—a set of five primary dimensions of personality. These five primary personality traits include extraversion/intraversion, emotional stability, agreeableness, conscientiousness, and openness to experience.[24] The first dimension, extraversion/introversion, is best understood in terms of the two personality types that define its endpoints. Extraverts are gregarious, assertive, talkative, and socially active, while introverts are shy and inwardly directed. Characteristics commonly associated with the second dimension, emotional stability, include anxiousness, inse-

---

[21] L. A. Pervin, *Personality* (New York: Wiley, 1984); and W. Mischel, *Introduction to Personality* (New York: Holt, Rinehart, and Winston, 1986).

[22] R. Cattell, D. Saunders, and G. Stice, *The 16 Personality Factor Questionnaire* (New York: Academic Press, 1950); and R. Cattell, *The Scientific Analysis of Personality* (Baltimore: Penguin Books, 1965).

[23] R. Cattell, "Personality Pinned Down," *Psychology Today*, July 1973, 40–46.

[24] J. M. Digman, "Personality Structure: Emergence of the Five-Factor Model," *Annual Review of Psychology* 41 (1990): 417–440.

FIGURE 3–6 ▶ **Personality Profiles**

These personality profiles are based on Cattell's *16 Personality Factor Questionnaire* for three occupational groups: writers, airline pilots, and business executives.

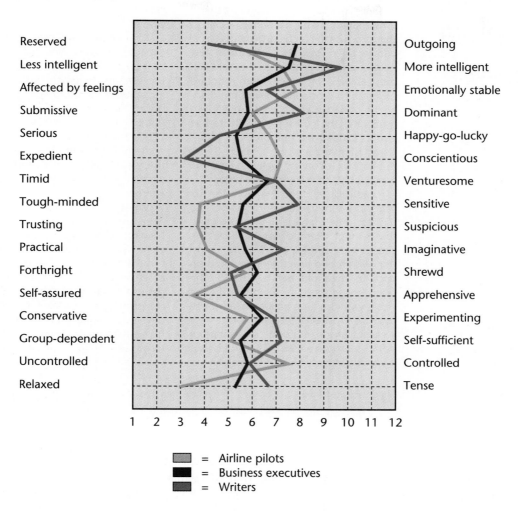

= Airline pilots
= Business executives
= Writers

curity, and susceptibility to embarrassment and depression. Individuals scoring high on the third dimension, agreeableness, are generally courteous, cooperative, and flexible. Conscientiousness, the fourth dimension, reflects the thoroughness and dependability of an individual. Finally, individuals high on the fifth dimension, openness to experience, are thought to be imaginative, curious, and intelligent. Of these five primary personality dimensions, only conscientiousness has shown to be consistently related to job performance across a variety of occupational groups.[25]

[25] M. R. Barrick and M. K. Mount, "The Big Five Personality Dimensions and Job Performance: A Meta-Analysis," *Personnel Psychology* 44 (1991): 1–26.

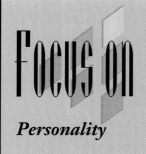

Personality

Time Management: Trait or Technique? Given the dizzying complexity of the world they face, it should hardly be surprising that record numbers of managers are signing up for time-management seminars—classes that promise to teach participants to organize their lives and squeeze a few extra hours out of the day. Students almost always come away with a bound organizer designed to make time management easier, and more than a dozen firms offer the courses—which start at about $500—and hundreds of thousands of managers have taken them. But can such courses really change the way executives manage their time?

Diana Hunt, who worked for six years as a seminar leader for one of the biggest time-management companies, thinks not. "People would leave the classes very motivated. But we found that within two years people would go back to their old habits." As for the bound organizers, they end up in the closet with the running shoes, language tapes, and other good intentions.

Jack Gordon, editor of *Training Magazine,* is also skeptical. "The truth is that if you are already kind of logical, linear, and organized, a time-management course will make you more logical, linear, and organized," he says. "If you're not—if you don't want to organize your life into A, B, and C priorities—then you won't."

Further criticism comes from an unexpected source: Alec Mackenzie, author of the book *Time Trap* that started the time-management boom in 1972. "In spite of the hundreds of millions of dollars spent on it, time-management training isn't working," says Mackenzie. "They say that 50% of all women become interested in diets, and 2% keep the weight off. That's pretty close to what I've found with time management."

What's the final word on time-management training? Graduates say the training works, and the courses do offer some wisdom and hints. But consider this: When Mackenzie spoke with us, he asked if we had tried his Time Tactics organizer. "You really should," he urged. He promised to mail it the following day. But despite Mackenzie's theories, his best-selling book, and his system, he forgot to send it.

Source: Adapted from E. Calonius, "The Trouble with Time-Management Courses," *Fortune,* June 4, 1990, 262.

Organizational Personality Traits

The most direct application of primary personality traits in organizational behavior has been attempts to match personality profiles with types of jobs and organizations.[26] For example, Holland's Vocational Preference Inventory questionnaire consists of 160 occupational titles. Individuals completing the questionnaire indicate which of the occupations they like and dislike, and these responses are used to assess an individual's personality.[27] Using Holland's questionnaire, an individual's personality profile is expressed as a location in the hexagon shown in Figure 3–7. The hexagon arises from six primary personality types: realistic, investigative, social, conventional, enterprising, and artistic. Each of these six personality types matches a particular occupational environ-

[26]J. A. Chatman, "Matching People and Organizations: Selection and Socialization in Public Accounting Firms," *Administrative Science Quarterly* 36 (1991): 459–484.

[27]J. L. Holland, *Making Vocational Choices: A Theory of Vocational Personalities and Work Environments* (Englewood Cliffs, N.J.: Prentice-Hall, 1985).

FIGURE 3-7	▶ Relationships Among Occupational Personality Types

Holland's Vocational Preference Inventory expresses an individual's personality as a location in this hexagon of six primary personality types.

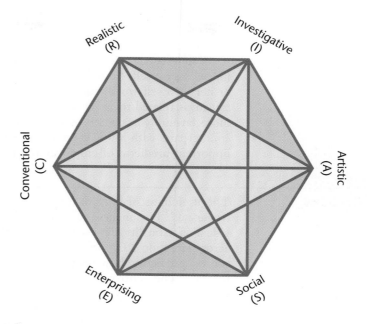

Source: J. L. Holland, *Making Vocational Choices: A Theory of Vocational Personalities and Work Environments*, 2nd ed. (Englewood Cliffs, NJ: Prentice Hall, 1985). Used by permission. This model originally appeared in J. L. Holland et al., "An Empirical Occupational Classification Derived from a Theory of Personality and Intended for Practice and Research," ACT Research Report No. 29 (Iowa City: The American College Testing Program, 1969).

ment. For example, social personality types should perform best in work environments that emphasize interpersonal rather than intellectual or physical activities. Research has shown some support for using Holland's questionnaire to match people to jobs.[28]

Many organizational researchers have been less interested in deriving primary personality traits than in identifying specific personality characteristics that predict organizational outcomes. Two personality characteristics that have been of particular interest to organizational researchers are locus of control and self-esteem.

Locus of control is the degree to which people think they can control the consequential events in their lives.[29] An individual who has a strong internal locus of control believes that the important events in life can be (for the most part) controlled by his or her own actions. An individual who has a strong external locus of control believes that the important events in life are (for the most

---

[28]A. R. Spokane, "A Review of Research on Person-Environment Congruence in Holland's Theory of Careers," *Journal of Vocational Behavior* (June 1985): 306–343.

[29]J. B. Rotter, "Generalized Expectancies for Internal Versus External Control of Reinforcement," *Psychological Monographs* 1 (609) (1966).

part) beyond his or her control—for instance, controlled by fate, chance, or other people. Studies have found that internal locus of control individuals are more satisfied with their jobs, more interested in opportunities to participate in organizational decision making, and more likely to be managers.[30] Managers high on internal locus of control also have been shown to adjust more easily to international transfers.[31]

Self-esteem refers to the amount of self-respect an individual holds for himself or herself. An individual with high self-esteem has a strong belief in his or her own self-worth and tends to be less easily influenced by others.[32] Self-esteem is related to occupational choice. Individuals with high self-esteem are more favorably evaluated by recruiters and receive more job offers than their counterparts with low self-esteem.[33] Self-esteem also has been shown to be an important predictor of employee burnout.[34]

Qualifications

The usefulness of personality as a concept in organizational behavior is controversial.[35] Personality is a useful concept to the extent that measuring an individual's personality allows us to predict that individual's behaviors over time and across situations. Unfortunately, researchers generally have had only modest success predicting how people will behave using personality assessment instruments.[36] The controversy over the use of personality traits as a way of understanding behavior in organizations has led to two interesting developments.

The first of these developments is the notion of strong versus weak situations.[37] A **strong** situation is one in which the demands of the situation are likely to cause everyone to behave the same way. A **weak** situation, on the other hand, is one in which the appropriate behavior is not at all obvious and in which people are pretty much free to decide for themselves what to do. Personality traits are likely to be much more predictive of behavior in weak situations. A lecture is an example of a strong situation; most students, *regardless of personality type*, are likely to sit quietly and listen to a lecture because that's what the situation demands. Social gatherings, on the other hand, are weak situations—a wide variety of behaviors could be appropriate at a social gathering. Thus, an

[30] T. R. Mitchell, C. M. Smyser, and S. E. Weed, "Locus of Control: Supervision and Work Satisfaction," *Academy of Management Journal* (September 1975): 623–631; and R. W. Renn and R. J. Vandenberg, "Differences in Employee Attitudes and Behaviors Based on Rotter's (1966) Internal-External Locus of Control: Are They Valid?" *Human Relations* 44 (11): 1161–1178.

[31] J. S. Black, "Locus of Control, Social Support, Stress, and Adjustment in International Transfer," *Asia Pacific Journal of Management* (April 1990): 1–30.

[32] G. B. Northcraft and S. J. Ashford, "The Preservation of Self in Everyday Life: The Effects of Performance Expectations and Feedback Context on Feedback Inquiry," *Organizational Behavior and Human Decision Processes* 47 (1990): 42–64.

[33] R. A. Ellis and M. S. Taylor, "Role of Self-Esteem with the Job Search Process," *Journal of Applied Psychology* 68 (1983): 632–640.

[34] J. G. Rosse, R. W. Boss, A. E. Johnson, and D. F. Crown, "Conceptualizing the Role of Self-Esteem in the Burnout Process," *Group and Organization Studies* 16 (4) (1991): 428–451.

[35] See, for example, A. Davis-Blake and J. Pfeffer, "Just a Mirage: The Search for Dispositional Effects in Organizational Research," *Academy of Management Review*, 14 (3) (1989): 385–400.

[36] W. Mischel, *Introduction to Personality* (New York: Holt, Rinehart, and Winston, 1986).

[37] A. Davis-Blake and J. Pfeffer, "Just a Mirage: The Search for Dispositional Effects in Organizational Research," *Academy of Management Review*, 14 (3) (1989): 385–400.

individual's behaviors at a social gathering are much more likely to reflect that individual's personality than that same individual's behavior at a lecture. Knowing whether a situation is strong or weak can help us understand whether personality will be useful for predicting individual behavior in that situation.

The second development in understanding the usefulness of personality is the idea of using personality as a **moderating variable** in explaining individual behavior.[38] A moderating variable does not by itself influence behavior; rather, a moderating variable influences the effect of *another* variable on behavior. An example of a moderating variable is the personality trait *growth need strength* (GNS).[39] GNS refers to an individual's interest in growing and developing on the job. GNS has been used to predict how individuals will behave on the job. However, GNS itself does not predict how people will behave on the job; instead, GNS predicts how particular job features will influence an individual's behavior on the job. For instance, feedback is more likely to improve the performance of an individual high in GNS than an individual low in GNS. GNS moderates the influence of feedback on an individual's performance. (GNS will be discussed in more detail in Chapter 12.) Locus of control and self-esteem also have demonstrated moderating effects on important organizational outcomes.[40] Together, the distinction between strong and weak situations, and the possible moderating role of personality traits, has rekindled interest in the usefulness of personality in organizational behavior.

PERSON PERCEPTION ◆◆◆◆◆◆

Because what people bring to the organization (for instance, attitudes and personality) is an important cause of their behaviors, getting to know the attitudes and personalities of other people is a primary perceptual task for all members of organizations. Where do our impressions of other organizational members come from? The answer is that we build our perceptions of others from both (1) evidence we gather about the person and (2) beliefs we have about the evidence we gather. Often this building process involves stereotypes.

| **Stereotypes** | A **stereotype** is a complex set of expectations and beliefs associated with specific personal characteristics, such as gender, race, or occupation. The opening vignette for this chapter suggests that people have a variety of stereotypes of women as managers. As noted in the "INTERNATIONAL FOCUS ON: Person Perception," men in Thailand have very strong stereotypes concerning the ability of women to hold certain jobs. Perhaps more close to home, there is also a stereotype associated with having a master's degree in business administration |

[38] H. M. Weiss and S. Adler, "Personality and Organizational Behavior," *Research in Organizational Behavior,* vol. 6, ed. B. Staw and L. Cummings (Greenwich, CT: JAI Press, 1984), 1–50.

[39] J. R. Hackman and G. R. Oldham, "The Job Diagnostic Survey: An Instrument for the Diagnosis of Jobs and the Evaluation of Job Redesign Projects," Tech Report #4, Department of Administrative Sciences, Yale University, 1974.

[40] See, for example, T. J. Newton and A. Keenan, "The Moderating Effect of the Type A Behavior Pattern and Locus of Control upon the Relationship between Change in Job Demands and Change in Psychological Strain," *Human Relations* 43 (12), (1990): 1229–1255.

INTERNATIONAL FOCUS ON

Person Perception

A Woman's Place in Thailand

There are those who would have us believe that a Thai deputy district officer (DDO) is something like a sheriff in the Old West: It takes a tough *man* who is quick on the draw to fill the shoes of a DDO and, therefore, no *woman* can do the job.

The fact that some women in the United States now hold jobs as sheriffs has done nothing to shake the conviction of these people. As far as they are concerned, DDO is and always will be a man's job.

In reality, women are barred from applying for this job and only lately has this become a subject of sometimes heated debate. Some officials within the Interior Ministry Local Administration Department (LAD) of Thailand, which is the body that appoints DDOs, are convinced that only men can qualify for this job.

"The job does not end in the office," notes a male LAD official. "It is around-the-clock work. It's a man's job. What happens when the DDO is required to witness an autopsy as he would be if unnatural causes are suspected in a death? Would a woman dare to do this?" He adds that a woman's commitments as a mother and housewife would also interfere with her work as a DDO. "She would not be able to devote enough time to her job and this would put a heavier burden on the shoulders of her colleagues."

At the village level, where the DDO would have to function, there is also strong sentiment that a woman should not occupy such a position. "Women are the weaker sex," says Suwan Jansud, a village headman. "Women do not have the confidence it takes to solve problems. They change their minds all the time." Even some male university students are against the idea of a woman DDO. "I accept that women nowadays are more capable and speedy workers. But they still cannot defend themselves if they are physically attacked by gangsters. Men should do these difficult jobs—they should be responsible for protecting women," says Chetthawat Taweemaitree, a student at Thammasat University.

Khunying Dr Saisuree Chutikul, a minister to the Prime Minister's Office in Thailand, maintains that the real reason that women are barred from certain jobs is simply the prejudice that exists in Thai society. It is, she says, the traditional concept that women are the "elephant's hind legs" and that the men are the "fore legs" and should lead the way. She says that men should start looking at women as "partners" and not lead women but work together with them. She concludes, "If the LAD wants to make sure that their candidates for DDO are physically able to handle the job, it can make its physical fitness test tougher."

Source: Adapted from "A Woman's Place . . .," M. Traisawasdichai and S. Phettae, *The Nation*, Bangkok, August 9, 1991, C1–C2.

(MBA).[41] All of these stereotypes suggest that if you know just one character-istic of an individual, then that characteristic brings forth an entire set of beliefs and expectations about that individual. Knowing that an individual has an MBA, for instance, may suggest to you that the individual is arrogant, impatient, self-centered, and highly focused on money.

Where do stereotypes come from? Some may come from experience, such as from having met a few MBAs who were self-centered or a few hard-charging female managers. Stereotypes also come from other people. You may be told that MBAs are arrogant and impatient by your friends. The accuracy of ste-reotypes is always problematic. Obviously, not *all* MBAs are arrogant, impa-tient, self-centered, and money-focused. Further, having a stereotype will lead us to see things in individuals (through the stereotype's influence on attention, construction, and interpretation) that are not really there. So why do we have stereotypes at all? There are two reasons: uncertainty and projection.

Uncertainty   When you meet a new member of the organization for the first time, you have no idea how that person will act. Will the new worker be trust-worthy? Will the new worker be responsible? Will the new worker be fun to work with? You cannot *know* these things until you have worked with the new person for a while and gotten to know him or her better.

But what do you do in the meantime? Getting to know someone means working together and sharing experiences. To do this, you must make some assumptions about how the person is likely to act. What does this person—say, a young man—consider to be "forward" behavior? Would you be perceived as "obnoxiously aggressive" if you asked him out to lunch his first day on the job? If you act too friendly will he think you want to borrow money from him? To interact with the individual at all, you have to make some inferences about him based on whatever small amount of information you have about him. The ques-tion is not *whether* you should assume anything about the new person, but *how much* you should assume.

Stereotypes assume a lot. But having a stereotype doesn't necessarily mean *acting* on the beliefs it dictates. For many of us stereotypes serve as hypotheses or speculations we can test about what kind of person the new person *might* be. If the new worker has an MBA, we might watch at lunch and see if he is impa-tient with the waiter or obsessed about the bill. In effect, stereotypes provide a way to learn about another person by providing a series of hypotheses to test.

Self-Fulfilling Prophecies   The problem with having hypotheses about a person is that we cannot test them objectively. Hypotheses about how a person is likely to act, even innocent and tentative ones, give rise to self-fulfilling prophecies.[42] A **self-fulfilling prophecy** occurs when an expectation about how someone is likely to act *causes* that person to confirm the hypothesis or fulfill the expectation. Self-fulfilling prophecies were popularized by a stage play called *Pygmalion*. In the play, a bet was made (and won) by an English lord that a common servant girl would blossom into a beautiful and sophisticated princess *if only she were treated as one.*

---

[41] M. R. Louis, "MBAs in the Press: Stereotypes and Unscientific Samples," *Wharton Magazine*, Volume 6 (1981): 12–18.

[42] R. Rosenthal and L. Jacobson, *Pygmalion in the Classroom* (New York: Holt, Rinehart and Winston, 1968).

There are two kinds of self-fulfilling prophecies: passive and active. In a passive self-fulfilling prophecy, the perceiver's expectations do not actually change the "target" individual's behaviors, but only the perceiver's perceptions of that behavior. If a perceiver expects MBAs to be arrogant and meets an MBA, the perceiver's attention will be biased to search for evidence of arrogance, and the perceiver will be more likely to construct and interpret ambiguous actions as arrogance. The expectation of arrogance will likely be fulfilled because the expectation will *drive* the attention, construction, and interpretation processes. And not coincidentally, confirmation of the "arrogant MBAs" expectation should strengthen this passive self-fulfilling prophecy and make it *even more likely* to be confirmed in the future.

In a passive self-fulfilling prophecy, the perceiver and the perceiver's expectations are somehow insulated from the real world. The expectations do not influence another's actions, but only the perceiver's perceptions of those actions. Active self-fulfilling prophecies, on the other hand, are more dynamic. In an active self-fulfilling prophecy, the expectations of the perceiver actually *change* the behaviors of the "target" individual so that they fulfill the perceiver's expectations.

Consider what happens when a supervisor has a high opinion of a new worker. The supervisor acts friendly toward the new worker, gives the new worker opportunities to assume responsibility, and checks on the new worker to see if things are going well or if the new worker needs some assistance. If the new worker fouls something up, the supervisor will see the failure as a learning experience and urge the new worker to shrug it off. In fact, failures by the new worker are likely to be seen as not the new worker's fault—or not even failures!—by the supervisor. In short, positive expectations lead the supervisor to provide the new worker with a supportive climate that includes every possible opportunity to succeed. No doubt such a supportive climate would not be lost on the new worker, and that is how expectations become *actively* self-fulfilling. If treatment of the new worker makes a difference (for instance, confidence leads to better performance), then the supportive climate provided by the supervisor with high expectations will yield a performance that fulfills the supervisor's high expectations.

Compare this scenario to what happens if the supervisor has *low* expectations for the new worker. If the supervisor doesn't trust the new worker to do a good job, the supervisor probably will watch the new worker constantly. All this attention may make the new worker nervous, and thereby more likely to fail on the job. The new worker's behavior will fulfill the supervisor's low expectations. Douglas McGregor summed up the problem of self-fulfilling prophecies succinctly in his comment that in our attitudes toward our subordinates "we may be caught in a web of our own weaving."[43]

Self-fulfilling prophecies highlight the importance of *first impressions* in person perception. The first information received about an individual may evoke expectations (for instance, a stereotype) that lead (through self-fulfilling prophecies) to their own confirmation. It should not be surprising, then, that corporations are willing to spend millions of dollars annually on image advertising. Image advertising (such as the advertisement shown in Figure 3–8) tries to con-

---

[43] D. McGregor, *The Human Side of Enterprise* (New York: McGraw-Hill, 1960), 42.

▶ **Favorable Perceptions**

Organizations use image advertising to create a favorable perceptual set that will influence attention, construction, and interpretation of perceivers' sensory inputs about them. In this ad, the Navy encourages young people to think about careers in the Navy through the perceptual set "adventure."

vey a positive image of an organization—for example, that the company is friendly and helpful or likes children. This image acts as an expectation that leads customers into positive self-fulfilling prophecies (or so the organization hopes) when they interact with the organization or read about it in the news.

The potency of first impressions also explains why so much attention in corporate circles is accorded to clothing. John Molloy's dictum that "the clothes make the man" forced people to realize that clothing is an important component of any first impression. One of the first things most people learn about a new member of an organization is the way the person dresses. When a new person first enters the hallowed halls of the organization, how the person is dressed is immediately salient—perhaps as salient as the person's sex or race, and certainly more salient than educational background or work experience. Blue three-piece suits convey a certain image—of power, knowledge, seriousness—that can significantly influence later perceptions of and actions toward a new organizational member. While the dictates of fashion may change as executives move up the corporate ladder (see "Wardrobe Passages" at the beginning of this chapter for an example), the role of clothing in those important first impressions remains a constant. Clothing is one way to manage the uncertainty of first impression formation.

Projection   In addition to helping sort out how to deal with a new person, stereotypes also serve symbolic purposes. Stereotypes can symbolize how one group of people *feels* about another group of people; that is, what the first group would *like* to think is true about the second group, rather than what *is* true. For example, unfavorable stereotypes about new MBAs in an organization may symbolize the feelings of the organization's "old guard" toward the organization's new generation of managers. If the older workers are jealous of the successes of the new MBAs, envious of their higher salaries, upset that the new MBAs didn't have to "work their way up from the shop floor," these feelings may surface in negative stereotypes. The older workers are projecting their negative feelings into their image of the new MBAs in the organization. In this example, the older workers' negative stereotypes do not represent actual characteristics of the new MBAs (though, through self-fulling prophecies, they certainly could!). The negative stereotypes instead represent the older workers' feelings about the new MBAs in the organization.

It is important to realize that symbolic stereotypes do not always translate into prejudicial public behavior. In 1937, when sentiment against Asian-Americans was running high in the United States, one adventurous researcher decided to test the relationship between stereotypes and action. The researcher had a Chinese couple visit 250 restaurants and hotels in the western United States. The researcher also contacted each establishment to ask if it would provide service to Asian-Americans. While 90 percent of the responding proprietors reported that they would refuse to serve Asian-Americans, only once was the couple actually refused service in person. Apparently stereotype beliefs and behaviors don't always match.[44]

If stereotypes serve symbolic functions, mismatches between behaviors and (apparent) beliefs should not be surprising. The negative stereotype may represent people's attempt to let off steam in a way that they would never direct at any individual. Another possibility is that negative stereotypes often present such horrible images that actual individuals provide a stark contrast. The new person then can be treated as an *exception* to the stereotype—an MBA who is "one of the guys," for example. This allows the stereotype to remain intact and continue to fulfill its symbolic function while the new worker gets treated according to beliefs about his or her *other* characteristics.

Unfortunately, the failure of women and blacks to attain positions of corporate leadership in the 1960s and 1970s suggests that unfavorable stereotypes can have damaging consequences as well. Further, unfavorable stereotypes always claim more victims than just those individuals discriminated against. The organizations that allow stereotypes to be the basis of their personnel decisions are also casualties, as they forgo the valuable contributions of the individuals they erroneously reject.

[44]R. T. LaPiere, "Attitudes and Action," *Social Forces* 13 (1934): 230–237.

SUMMARY ◆◆◆◆◆◆

Perception is the prelude to action in organizations. Before we can act—before we even can decide what action to take—we must perceive what is going on around us.

Perception is an active process. Perceptions are the product of selection, construction, and interpretation activities by the perceiver. First, the perceiver must sample inputs from the infinitely complex "buzzin', blooming confusion" that is reality. After a manageable set of inputs has been selected, a representation of what is going on must be constructed. Finally, this representation must be interpreted to give it meaning. The meaningful representations of reality that become the output of the perceptual process become the inputs to our decisions and actions.

Because perception is an active process, it is susceptible to influence. Perceiver theories, beliefs, and expectations necessarily influence (and sometimes bias) all three components of the perception process. In fact, without some preconceptions on the part of perceivers, perceptions could not occur at all. Characteristics of the objects of perception, as well as the context in which perception occurs, also influence the perceptual outcome.

Attitudes are the world's window to an individual. Attitudes are an evaluation of our perceptions, including beliefs, affects, and a tendency to act. Sometimes our attitudes come from observing and trying to understand our own behaviors.

Personality consists of the characteristics that lead an individual to behave in consistent ways over time. Personality is typically discussed in terms of traits, like locus of control. Personality and attitudes both figure prominently in our attempts to perceive and understand other individuals in organizations.

Key Terms

Anchoring-and-adjustment effect Tendency of individual perceptions or judgments to be similar to a reference point even when the reference point is arbitrary or irrelevant.

Attention Individuals' choice of where to direct and how to ration their limited sensory input system.

Attitudes Beliefs and feelings that lead an individual to respond consistently to people, ideas, and situations.

Attribution Process of perceiving the causes of actions and outcomes; provides models of how other people function, what their motives are, and what determines their behaviors.

Belief system Stored set of theories and expectations about how and why the world works.

Construction Process of perceiver organizing and editing sensory inputs in a way that makes them potentially meaningful; subject to both input source and perceiver influences.

Contrast effect Tendency of individual perceptions or judgments to be seen as very different from an extreme reference point.

Covariation Central principle of attribution theory, stating that behaviors are attributed to causes that are present when the behaviors are present and absent when the behaviors are absent; covariation is judged by distinctiveness, consensus, and consistency.

Fundamental attribution error
Tendency of individuals to perceive others' behaviors as caused primarily by stable, internal characteristics (such as personality) and to perceive their own behavior as primarily a response to environmental characteristics.

Halo effect Tendency for an individual's perception of an input on one dimension to influence his or her perceptions of that input on other dimensions.

Information overload State of perceivers when their sensory input systems are overwhelmed with new, unusual, attention-grabbing inputs.

Input source influences Characteristics of a source object or event that affect perceivers' attempts to direct their attention, including motion, distinctiveness, novelty, vividness, contrast effect, anchoring-and-adjustment effect, and halo effect.

Interpretation In perception, the process of assigning meaning to a constructed representation of an object or event.

Locus of control A trait which represents the extent to which people think they can control the consequential events in their lives.

Moderating variables A variable which influences the effects of another variable on behavior.

Objective self-awareness Individuals' perceptions of their own roles in causing behaviors and their consequences.

Perception Process by which individuals receive and interpret sensations from the environment so they may act upon it.

Perceptual set Expectations that a perceiver brings to the perception task, based on suggestions, beliefs, or previous experiences.

Personality The characteristics that lead an individual to behave in consistent ways over time.

Self-esteem A trait which represents the amount of self-respect an individual has.

Self-fulfilling prophecy Expectation about how someone is likely to act that actually causes the person to meet the expectation.

Self-perception Examination of own actions to decide attitudes.

Self-serving bias Tendency of perceivers to attribute the causes of actions or their outcomes in a way that reflects well on the perceivers or absolves the perceivers from responsibility for poor outcomes.

Sensation Process of nerve endings sending inputs to the brain with no meaning attached.

Stereotype Complex set of expectations and beliefs associated with specific personal characteristics, such as sex, race, or occupation.

Strong situation A situation in which contextual demands are likely to cause everyone to behave the same.

Values An individual's core understanding of what is important to himself or herself.

Trait A characteristic, usually expressed as a dimension on which every person can be measured.

Weak situation A situation in which the appropriate behavior is not at all obvious and in which people therefore are pretty much free to decide for themselves what to do.

Discussion Questions

1. In what ways is perception an *active* rather than passive process?

2. Why are good theories about reality a necessary prerequisite to accurate perceptions of reality?

3. Which of the following statements is more defensible, given the view of perception developed in this chapter: "A little knowledge is a dangerous thing," or "A little knowledge is a necessary thing"?

4. Drawing only on your understanding of the perceptual process, provide three explanations for the phrase, "There's no accounting for taste."

5. In what way might the attributions we make about the consequences of our behaviors be more important than the consequences themselves?

6. How are our perceptions of our own actions different from our perceptions of the actions of others?

7. Why is it important for managers to have confidence in and expect a lot from their subordinates?

8. How do attitudes and personality provide similar explanations for why individuals behave consistently over time? How do they differ? Why are people more likely to use attitudes and personality to explain *others'* behaviors than to explain their *own* behaviors?

If You Want to Know More

A classic article on influences on attention and input selection is provided by Bruner and Goodman, "Value and Need as Organizing Factors in Perception" (*Journal of Abnormal and Social Psychology* 42, 1947: 33–34).

Allport's article, "Prejudice, a Problem in Psychological and Social Causation" (*Journal of Social Issues* 4, 1950), provides a good foundation for understanding the role of stereotypes in person perception. Lord and Kernan provide a similar foundation for understanding the role of scripts in action perception in their article, "Scripts as Determinants of Purposeful Behavior in Organizations" (*Academy of Management Review* 12, 1987: 265–277).

The role of attributions in organizational perception is discussed in an article by Bartunek entitled, "Why Did You Do That? Attribution Theory in Organizations" (*Business Horizons* 24, 1981: 66–71). Pettigrew provides some interesting insights into what happens when attributional processes are driven by stereotypes in, "The Ultimate Attribution Error: Extending Allport's Cognitive Analysis of Prejudice" (*Personality and Social Psychology Bulletin* 5, 1979: 461–476).

A particularly good example of self-fulfilling prophecies at work in organizations is provided by Word, Zanna, and Cooper in their article, "The Nonverbal Mediation of Self-fulfilling Prophecies in Interracial Interaction" (*Journal of Experimental Social Psychology* 10, 1974: 109–120). The role of attributional processes in fueling self-fulfilling prophecies is described in detail by Storms and McCaul in, "Attribution Processes and Emotional Exacerbation of Dysfunctional Behavior" (in Harvey, Ickes, and Kidd, eds., *New Directions in Attribution Research*, Hillsdale, N.J.: L. Erlbaum Associates, 1976).

Goffman's classic, *The Presentation of Self in Everyday Life* (Edinburgh University Press, 1956), offers some interesting insights into the application of perception to the process of impression management. A good book about the face as a source of nonverbal communication is Ekman and Friesen's *Unmasking the Face* (Englewood Cliffs, N.J.: Prentice-Hall, 1975). A good general introduction to communication in business is Mary Munter's *Business Communication: Strategy and Skill* (Englewood Cliffs, N.J.: Prentice-Hall, 1987).

The tenets of self-perception processes are laid out by Bem in "Self-Perception Theory" (in Berkowitz, *Advances in Experimental Social Psychology* 6, 1972). A summary of some of the relevant research studies on this topic appears in Wicklund and Frey's "When the Self Makes a Difference" (in Wegner and Vallacher, *The Self in Social Psychology*, Oxford University Press, 1980).

There is some controversy about the degree to which job satisfaction is induced by characteristics of the work environment, or whether instead job satisfaction is a more stable and enduring personality characteristic. A review of the arguments is provided in "Job Satisfaction: Dispositional and Situational Influences" by R. D. Arvey, G. W. Carter, and D. K. Buerkley (in C. L. Cooper and I. T. Robertson, eds., *International Review of Industrial and Organizational Psychology* 6, [1991] 359–383).

A recent review of the issues surrounding the importance of personality variables in organizational behavior is provided by Jennifer George in her article, "The Role of Personality in Organizational Life: Issues and Evidence" (*Journal of Management* 18 [2], 1992: 185–213). The extent to which our self-esteem is tied to our feelings of self-worth *at work* is explored in an article by Jon Pierce, Donald Gardner, Larry Cummings, and Randy Dunham entitled, "Organization-Based Self-Esteem: Construct Definition, Measurement, and Validation" (*Academy of Management Journal* 32 (3), 1989: 622–648).

On Your Own

Locus of Control   For each of the ten statements below, indicate your agreement or disagreement using the following scale:

1 = strongly agree
2 = agree
3 = slightly agree
4 = neither agree nor disagree
5 = slightly disagree
6 = disagree
7 = strongly disagree

_____   **1.** People's misfortunes result from their mistakes.

_____   **2.** Getting a good job depends mainly on being in the right place at the right time.

_____   **3.** In the long run, people get the respect they deserve.

_____   **4.** Many times I feel that I have little influence over the things that happen to me.

_____   **5.** Most misfortunes are the result of lack of ability, ignorance, laziness, or all three.

_____   **6.** Most people don't realize the extent to which their lives are controlled by accidental happenings.

_____   **7.** Capable people who fail to become leaders have not taken advantage of their opportunities.

_____   **8.** Who gets to be the boss often depends on who was lucky enough to be in the right place at the right time.

_____   **9.** Becoming a success is a matter of hard work. Luck has little or nothing to do with it.

_____   **10.** The world is run by the few people in power and there is not much any individual can do about it.

To determine your locus of control: Subtract each of your responses to the even-numbered questions from 8. (For instance, if you answered "5" for question 10, your final score for question 10 would be $8 - 5 = 3$.) Add the total of your corrected scores for the even-numbered questions to the total of your actual responses to the odd-numbered questions. The lower your score, the more internal your locus of control; the higher your score, the more external your locus of control.

Adapted from: J. B. Rotter, "Generalized Expectancies for Internal versus External Control of Reinforcement," *Psychological Monographs: General and Applied* (80) 1, 1–28.

CHAPTER 3

THE MANAGER'S MEMO

FROM: P. Clydesdale, President

TO: A. Jablonski, Comptroller

RE: Reports from the Finance Department

I am getting tired of being bombarded with incomprehensible reports from the Finance Department. Your hotshot MBAs may think they are impressing me with their fancy words and long columns of numbers, but they are just telling me they are too big for their britches.

Just last week, I received five more reports from different members of your staff. One report was 23 pages long. When do these people think I have time to read this stuff?

Long as the reports are, they are woefully short on policy ideas. So what if gross margin return on investment is up 3 percent over the last quarter? What does that tell us about our business of selling fire-fighting equipment? Believe me, having started this business from scratch, I could tell your pinstriped people a lot about fire-fighting equipment!

Please establish some guidelines to stem this tidal wave of paper, and then let me know what you've done.

Case Discussion Questions

Assume you are the comptroller, and respond to the president's memo. In setting guidelines that will meet the president's needs, consider what you have learned about perception. In writing your response, try to follow any relevant guidelines you have set for your staff members to follow in *their* writing.

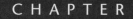

LEARNING AND MOTIVATION

FEELING STUCK? CREATE A NEW BUSINESS! ◆◆◆◆◆◆

In the 1960s, a sharp manager trainee could be in charge of a Hyatt hotel within three years or so. Now, with most of its growth behind Hyatt Hotels Corporation, the flagship of the Pritzker family empire, would-be general managers can wait up to eight years or longer for their own property. That creates a motivation problem for sharp trainees. One way the $2.2 billion hotelier retains its strong young talent is by setting up freestanding companies, outside the core hotel business, for the entrepreneurial thinkers in its ranks. John Allegretti was ready to quit Hyatt after two years when vice president Don DePorter asked him to head a waste reduction project. That turned into a new company called International ReCycleCo. Allegretti now has 24 clients in 8 states in addition to several large Hyatts.

As a director of sales development for Hyatt Hotels, James E. Jones noticed that party planners had a lucrative business providing outside catering and entertainment. With his contacts in professional sports, Jones was ready to start his own business. Instead, Hyatt provided him with $780,000 to start the events planning outfit Regency Productions by Hyatt. Soon after, Jones won a contract to manage corporate hospitality tents for the NFL Super Bowl, and a catering contract with the U.S. Open golf tournament.

In addition to startup capital, Allegretti and Jones get plenty of freedom to sink or swim, but no equity stake in the businesses. The program is popular, attracting a surfeit of business ideas from employees. But senior executives often have to manage the more promising ideas through the process of writing a business plan, including a plan for operating contingencies if revenue projections aren't met. It's time-consuming, but it's one way to leverage employees' expertise in the hotel business into some other kind of venture. As Hyatt president Thomas J. Pritzker says, "It's always better to have a racehorse you have to rein in than a donkey that you have to whip."

Source: J. E. Ellis, "Feeling Stuck at Hyatt? Create a New Business," *Business Week*, December 10, 1990, 195.

INTRODUCTION

For a manager in an organization, the challenge of managing employee behavior is more than just providing work for employees to do. The manager also must motivate the employees to do the work. Learning and motivation are the processes of directing and energizing behavior at work.

Motivation presents a particularly complex challenge for the modern manager. To begin with, no two employees—not even two employees working the same job—are alike. At any point in time, different employees will have different needs and different desires. What turns one employee on to work may not turn on another employee at all. Further, as highlighted in the "FOCUS ON: Changing Motivations of the American Work Force," today's employees are different from their predecessors. What works for an employee today—what motivates that employee to do his or her work and do it well—may not "turn on" that same employee next year, next week, or even next hour! Motivating employees is a process fraught with uncertainty.

However, motivating employees also is a process filled with promise. Surveys of worker attitudes reveal that most American workers could work harder if they really wanted to do so.[1] They just don't want to. Instead, workers often play the kinds of counterproductive games described by Donald Roy and Michael Buroway in their studies of American industry, discussed briefly in Chapter 2.

What happens if employees do work hard? When managers properly motivate their workers, worker performance and satisfaction can both improve dramatically. Everyone benefits. At Parsons Pine Products, a simple motivational intervention (an extra day's pay each month for perfect on-time attendance) reduced absenteeism by 30 percent.[2] Management at Union National Bank also has discovered the power of properly motivating its work force. In 1985, Union's wide variety of individualized motivational programs paid workers $1 million in incentives, while increasing productivity between 200 and 300 percent.[3] At Hyatt, top management (like Hyatt Vice-President Don DePorter, described in this chapter's opening vignette) have found that attention to employee motivation can pay a *triple* dividend: good performance, retention of the company's best employees, and even the creation of successful new lines of business.

This chapter explores two pieces of the employee motivation puzzle. First, motivating employees means that employees must feel they will gain something personally through their actions. It is not enough that accomplishment of a task is important for the welfare of the organization. To energize an employee, managers must make the accomplishment of work tasks contribute to the welfare of the employee as well. This is the realm of content theories of motivation. **Content theories of motivation** outline what workers want and need and therefore what tools managers can use to energize their subordinates' behaviors.

---

[1] B. Davis and D. Milbank, "If the U.S. Work Ethic is Fading, 'Laziness' May Not Be the Reason," *Wall Street Journal*, February 7, 1992, 1, 5.

[2] "Bonuses for Just Showing Up," *Time*, August 7, 1978, 67.

[3] W. Dierks and K. A. McNally, "Incentives You Can Bank On," *Personnel Administrator* (March 1987): 60–65.

Focus on

Changing Motivations of the American Work Force

What 25-Year-Olds Want in the 1990s Angela Azzaretti, 25, graduated from the University of Illinois and took a job at Caterpillar's headquarters in Peoria during the summer of 1987. Caterpillar trained her for a year, then assigned her to the engine plant in Mossville, Illinois. She did well in Mossville, and soon she was offered a promotion to the staff of Caterpillar's headquarters. Angela turned it down. Then she was offered another promotion—a move to a new plant. She turned that down, too. "Job satisfaction is the most important thing to me," says Angela.

After studying economics at the University of Iowa, Rick Watkins took an investment banking job at Merrill Lynch in 1988. "It was a nonsensical, 100-hour-week, cram-it-down-your-throat, no-social-life world," he says. Rick quit after a year, despite assurances from higher-ups that he had the skills to follow in their footsteps, with all the rewards and privileges that implied. Now he puts in 40-hour weeks on the floor for Susquehanna Investment Group, a small speciality firm. Says Rick, "I want to be happy and fulfilled—socially and culturally—and to progress in the work world to the point where I'm happy with myself."

What, you ask, has gotten into the newest cohort of businessmen and businesswomen? Nothing less than a new attitude toward life and work—an individualism that is characteristic of the baby busters. The leading edge of this smaller, overshadowed generation was born in 1965. Now, as the oldest of them reach their late 20s, they are arriving in corporate America and struggling to recast the rules according to their own demands. They are the Employees Who Can Say No, a novel breed that apparently won't be easily manipulated into workaholism by the traditional lures.

Let's call them yiffies—young, individualistic, freedom-minded, and few. Yiffies insist on getting satisfaction from their jobs but refuse to make personal sacrifices for the sake of the corporation. Their attitude seems to be that other interests—leisure, family, and lifestyle—are as important as work.

Some managers might want to laugh the first time one of the company's youngest employees insists on working "just" a 40-hour week so she can go scuba diving or so he can learn a new language. But, says Glenn Blake, director of employment and management development at General Mills, "There's a stronger sense of balance in their lives. Quality of life is more important to them than it was ten years ago."

In 1980, 25-year olds vaunted their ambitions. Arrogant and impatient, they believed that business offered "the fastest means of gratifying their frankly materialistic requirements." Corporate America's latest legion of recruits sounds very different.

Source: A. Deutschman, "What 25-Year Olds Want, *Fortune,* August 27, 1990, 42–50, 73.

Second, motivating employees means that their actions must be properly *directed.* This implies that the employees have learned what needs to be done, and how and when to do it. Directing behavior is the realm of process theories of motivation. **Process theories of motivation** describe how managers can use knowledge of subordinates' needs and desires to direct subordinate behavior appropriately. Taken together, content and process theories of motivation provide managers a foundation for managing the motivations of a work force. The specific application of these theories to management tasks such as socializing new employees, designing jobs, and providing incentives for exceptional performances will be the focus of Part 4 of this book.

ENERGIZING BEHAVIOR:
CONTENT THEORIES

Motives, needs, wishes, and desires are all terms used (for the most part interchangeably) to describe the reasons behind worker behaviors. In some cases these terms refer to physiological necessities (such as the need for food and water); in other cases they refer to outcomes that individuals would like to have but certainly could live without (such as power and achievement).

Content theories of human motivation summarize the kinds of motives that energize worker behaviors. Since different people seem to have different needs, wishes, and desires that are constantly changing, managers need to have a framework for understanding what motives people are likely to act upon and how those motives are likely to evolve over time. These issues are within the realm of content theories of motivation. There are a number of content theories. We will examine several in this chapter; Maslow's need hierarchy, Alderfer's ERG, Herzberg's two-factor theory, and McClelland's learned needs. We will examine the basic tenets of each theory, and their unique contributions to our understanding of human motivation.

Maslow's Need Hierarchy

Abraham Maslow was a psychologist at Brandeis University, and he was not interested in organizational behavior. Instead, his theory of motivation was simply the most prominent of many reactions to economic and mechanistic views that had dominated the field of psychology prior to the 1940s. Maslow's theory of human motivation was based on several assumptions. First, Maslow believed that there was a *hierarchy* consisting of at least five distinct categories of human wants and needs:[4]

1. *Basic physiological needs.* These include hunger, thirst, and sex drives.
2. *Safety needs.* Concern about protection from physical sources of harm, including shelter from the weather.
3. *Belonging/affiliation needs.* The need for interpersonal relationships with others that include personal liking, affection, care, and support.
4. *Esteem needs.* The need for respect, positive regard, status, and recognition from others.
5. *Self-actualization needs.* The need to fulfill one's potential—to be all that one can be.

Second, as shown in Figure 4–1, Maslow believed that there was a specific order in which individuals would pursue the fulfillment of these needs. For instance, since the basic physiological needs are the most primary needs, attention will be focused first on their fulfillment. Only after these basic physiological needs have been met will an individual's attention turn to the fulfillment of needs higher up on the need hierarchy. From Maslow's perspective, then, self-actualization is a need that individuals will pursue only after *all* their other needs have been met. Unfulfilled lower-order needs take precedence over unfulfilled higher-order needs, and fulfillment of lower-order needs leads to a progression

---

[4]A. H. Maslow, "A Theory of Human Motivation," *Psychological Review* (July 1943): 370–396.

FIGURE 4–1	▶ Maslow's Hierarchy of Needs

Maslow's need hierarchy helps explain differences in needs among employees and across time. According to Maslow's theory, employees turn their attention to higher-order needs only when lower-order needs have been fulfilled.

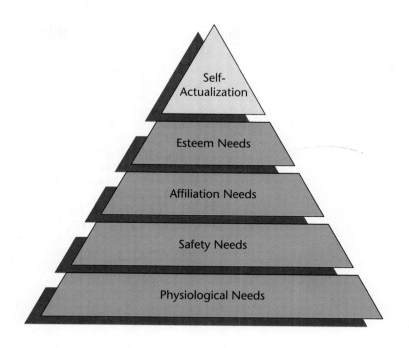

of attention up the hierarchy to higher-order needs. An example of how companies are working to satisfy the basic needs of a working-parent work force is provided in the "FOCUS ON: The Hierarchy of Needs."

Maslow's need hierarchy was the prototype of *hierarchical* theories of human motivation. It represented a significant departure from economic theories of worker motivation. As a result, the theory had an important impact in three ways. First, Maslow's need hierarchy presented an entire array of *noneconomic* worker needs. If an employee doesn't respond to economic incentives, managers have alternate sources of employee motivation to consider. Second, Maslow's hierarchy provided an important explanation for the changing motivations of workers over time. When a new employee first starts on the job, needs lower on the hierarchy—physiological or safety needs—are likely to command the most attention. Later, as these needs are fulfilled, the employee's attention will turn to the fulfillment of higher-order needs, such as gaining the acceptance and respect of coworkers. Finally, Maslow's need hierarchy explained the motivational differences among employees. Though the need hierarchy is the same for all individuals, at any point in time individuals are likely to be at different levels of the hierarchy, depending upon which of their needs have been fulfilled and which have not.

Research has not been kind to Maslow's need hierarchy theory. A general review of need hierarchy studies revealed no consistent support for Maslow's

Focus on

The Hierarchy of Needs

Satisfying the Basic Needs of Parents   Some parents get to take their school-age children to work every day, and it makes them very happy. No, it's not child labor. Companies have begun to provide more than day care for employees' children. They're going the next step and bringing public school classes onto company property. At the Miami, Florida offices of American Bankers Insurance Group the company-owned school, called the ABIG Learning Center, is staffed with teachers from Miami's school district, and uses the same curriculum as the rest of the school district. The difference is the students ride to work with their parents and when they arrive at the office, the kids go to school. Nine other programs in Florida and Minnesota are modeled after the ABIG Learning Center, and the concept has caught the attention of other school boards in California, New York and New Jersey.

The insurance company, responding to community officials, put up $350,000 to construct the school building. They also pay operating expenses of about $60,000 annually. After third grade, students are switched to a regular school. Insurance liability is split between the school district and the company.

At ABIG, parents pay for after-school care. But at the Clearwater, Florida school inside Honeywell, the company pays. At the Twin Towers Hotel and Convention Center in Orlando, Florida, the company pays for the school children's lunch, whereas at ABIG, parents pick up the tab.

The results of these programs have been impressive, ranging from less worker tardiness to more productivity. Parents know their children are close by, close enough to even meet them for lunch. They find this an enhancement of the workplace, so there are recruiting benefits for the company as well.

School districts can save big money with this kind of cost sharing. And in Florida, companies which build such schools can get property taxes forgiven on the school portion of their property. That makes it a good deal for everyone, except when it comes time to graduate. Trading the low student-teacher ratio for a higher one at a regular school could cause adjustment problems among students, some parents think. But such adjustments are to be expected from a working alternative to the mainstream.

Source: I. Recio, "Beyond Day Care: The Company School, *Business Week,* May 20, 1991, 142.

five need categories or for Maslow's hierarchical satisfaction rule.[5] These studies suggest that workers can distinguish only between broad categories of lower-order and higher-order needs. Within these broad categories, there seems to be little relationship between fulfillment of one need and attention to another.

Alderfer's ERG

A modification of Maslow's need hierarchy was proposed by Clay Alderfer. Alderfer's views on motivation arose from the results of questionnaires he gave to over 100 employees at several levels of responsibility in a bank.[6] Alderfer's work led him to propose that there are *three* (rather than Maslow's five) primary categories of human needs:

1. *Existence.* The basic physiological needs (hunger and thirst) and protection from physical danger.
2. *Relatedness.* Social and affiliation needs, and the need for respect and positive regard from others.
3. *Growth.* The need to develop and realize one's potential.

By establishing these broader categories of human needs, Alderfer created a less rigid version of Maslow's hierarchy of needs. For example, since Maslow's social and esteem needs are grouped together in Alderfer's model under the umbrella of "relatedness" needs, neither takes fulfillment precedence over the other.

In contrast to Maslow's theory, Alderfer proposed that when fulfillment of a higher-order need is blocked—if something prevents the higher-order need from being fulfilled—an individual's attention will *regress* back toward further fulfillment of needs *lower* in the hierarchy. For instance, if relatedness needs are relatively fulfilled but growth-need fulfillment is blocked, an individual's attention will return to fulfillment of relatedness needs. Finally, Alderfer's model also assumes that some needs become *more* rather than less important as they become fulfilled.

Research on Alderfer's modifications to Maslow's theory has been supportive. Both laboratory and field studies have generated support for Alderfer's three categories and their hierarchical fulfillment relationship.[7] Other studies have supported Alderfer's contention that needs can become *more* important as they are fulfilled.[8]

Herzberg's Two-Factor Theory

Another major content theory of motivation is the **two-factor theory.** The two-factor theory traces its origins to Frederick Herzberg's study of 200 white-collar engineers and accountants.[9] Unlike other content theories of motivation,

---

[5] M. A. Wahba and L. G. Bridwell, "Maslow Reconsidered: A Review of the Research on the Need Hierarchy Theory," *Organizational Behavior and Human Performance* 15 (1976): 212–240.

[6] C. P. Alderfer, "An Empirical Test of a New Theory of Human Needs," *Organizational Behavior and Human Performance* 4 (1969): 141–175.

[7] J. P. Wanous and A. Zwany, "A Cross-Sectional Test of Need Hierarchy Theory," *Organizational Behavior and Human Performance* 18 (1977): 78–97.

[8] C. P. Alderfer, R. E. Kaplan, and K. K. Smith, "The Effect of Variations in Relatedness Need Satisfaction on Relatedness Desires," *Administrative Sciences Quarterly* 19 (1974): 507–532.

[9] F. Herzberg, *Work and the Nature of Man* (Cleveland: World, 1966).

the two-factor theory is framed in terms of factors that affect work satisfaction (rather than needs). Two categories of factors are proposed in the two-factor theory.

1. *Hygiene factors.* A broad category of working conditions, including safety and amount of pay, quality of supervision, and the social environment of work.
2. *Motivators.* Factors associated with the performance of work, such as recognition for a job well done, achievement, autonomy, and responsibility.

The two-factor theory of needs specifically applies to understanding job satisfaction in work settings. As shown in Figure 4–2, the two-factor theory proposes that the determinants of job satisfaction and job dissatisfaction are not the same. According to the theory, dissatisfaction results when the work setting does not fulfill the worker's basic needs—the **hygiene factors** in the terms of the theory. A worker who is worried about safety on the job, or basic pay, cannot devote attention to the task at hand and therefore cannot do a good job. However, fulfillment of these hygiene needs *does not* satisfy workers. Rather, fulfillment of these basic needs simply *prevents* dissatisfaction. Satisfaction depends on a second set of factors, **motivators,** which include the opportunity for achievement, responsibility, and recognition through work.

Like Maslow's need hierarchy and Alderfer's ERG model, the two-factor theory subscribes to a form of the "satisfaction-progression" hypothesis. In the two-factor theory, hygiene factors are *preconditions* for job satisfaction. Management cannot satisfy workers by fulfilling worker hygiene needs, but unfulfilled hygiene needs can prevent workers from being satisfied. Motivators, on the other hand, satisfy workers, but only when management has also fulfilled their hygiene needs.

Herzberg's two-factor theory has come under fire for a variety of reasons.[10] The studies on which it is based have been challenged on methodological grounds. For instance, people may want to perceive and blame features of the work setting as the causes of their job dissatisfaction, even if this is not true. Further, Herzberg's separation of factors affecting dissatisfaction and satisfaction has not stood up to empirical scrutiny. Studies have shown that achievement and recognition—two motivators related to satisfaction according to the theory—also influence job dissatisfaction. Finally, the importance of the two-factor theory revolves around the idea that job satisfaction and dissatisfaction are critically related to work motivation and performance. As discussed in Chapter 2, this is at best a tenuous assumption.

McClelland's Learned Needs

David McClelland's work on **learned needs** provides a final content theory of motivation. McClelland's work focused on three categories of needs:

1. *Need for affiliation.* Concern for establishing and maintaining social relationships.
2. *Need for power.* Concern for reputation, responsibility, influence, and impact.
3. *Need for achievement.* Concern for establishing and maintaining high levels of performance quality.

---

[10]R. J. House and L. A. Wigdor, "Herzberg's Dual-Factor Theory of Job Satisfaction and Motivation: A Review of the Evidence and a Criticism," *Personal Psychology* 20 (1967): 369–390.

| FIGURE 4–2 | ▶A Summary of Factors Affecting Job Satisfaction and Dissatisfaction |

Herzberg's research suggests that job dissatisfaction and job satisfaction are caused by different aspects of the work setting. Job dissatisfaction is high when hygiene factors (like work conditions and supervision) are inadequate. Job satisfaction is high when motivators (like achievement and recognition) are present.

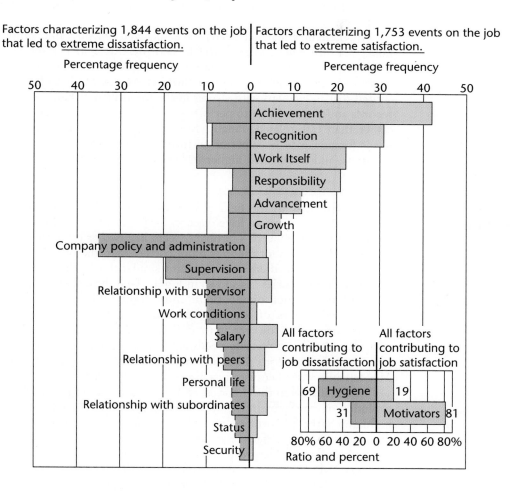

Source: Frederick Herzberg, "One More Time: How Do You Motivate Employees?" *Harvard Business Review*, January/February 1968. Copyright © 1968 by the President and Follows of Harvard College.

McClelland's approach to motivation differs from that of the other content theories discussed. McClelland emphasizes that affiliation, power, and achievement are *learned* needs rather than instinctive desires. In a dramatic demonstration that needs can be learned, McClelland attempted to improve the economic climate of Kakinada, India, by training 50 of its businessmen to have greater needs for achievement. The training group was encouraged to imagine positive outcomes of aggressive investment strategies, to imagine how these strategies would fulfill their personal needs, and to set goals. Follow-up studies several years later revealed that the "trained" businessmen had invested more money in local business ventures, started more new businesses, participated in more community development activities, and created more new jobs in the community than their untrained counterparts.[11]

Because the needs for affiliation, power, and achievement are learned, McClelland contends that they fit into no static hierarchical ordering. Instead, different individuals feel different needs in differing degrees. Thus, there are no "satisfaction-progression" or "frustration-regression" relationships among the needs.

McClelland's learned needs have received considerable support. In his book, *The Achieving Society*,[12] McClelland presents evidence for a relationship between the current state of economic development of countries and measured levels of need for achievement in those countries. Studies also have demonstrated that individuals with strong needs for affiliation have better attendance records and respond best to performance feedback that is personally supportive rather than task-related. Finally, research has shown individuals with strong needs for power to be superior performers, more likely to occupy supervisory positions, and to be rated higher in leadership by coworkers.[13]

Implications of Content Theories

To a student new to the field of organizational behavior, the several content theories of motivation we have discussed—the need hierarchies, the two-factor theory, and learned needs—probably seem like two or three theories too many. Is one of these content theories more correct than the others?

To begin with, there are important similarities in the *types* of needs proposed by these theories. As shown in Figure 4–3, these theories propose similar types of needs, but divide them into slightly different categories. Only McClelland's theory of learned needs does not hypothesize any hierarchical ordering of needs. However, in modern industrial America, fulfillment of physiological, safety, and security needs is virtually guaranteed by government legislation. It is therefore plausible that these needs simply did not surface in McClelland's work because they are generally fulfilled.

In all fairness to the theories, each has served an important function in the evolution of management theories of work motivation. Need-hierarchy theories highlighted the importance of noneconomic needs—such as Maslow's self-esteem needs or Alderfer's relatedness needs—in motivating workers. Although it hasn't enjoyed widespread support, Herzberg's two-factor theory raised in managers' minds an important distinction between extrinsic (work context) and intrinsic (inherent in the work) sources of motivation. Finally, McClelland's theory drove home the idea that some needs are learned. As noted in the "INTERNATIONAL FOCUS ON: Energizing Behavior," McClelland's view that some needs are learned also explains a few important differences among cultures and allows room for hope if a culture's motivational focus seems problematic.

Taken together, all three content theories emphasize the variety of possible worker needs. This has two important implications for the challenge of man-

---

[11] D. C. McClelland and D. G. Winter, *Motivating Economic Achievement* (New York: Free Press, 1971).

[12] D. C. McClelland, *The Achieving Society* (Princeton, N.J.: Van Nostrand, 1961).

[13] R. M. Steers and N. D. Braunstein, "A Behaviorally Based Measure of Manifest Needs in Work Settings," *Journal of Vocational Behavior* 9 (1976): 251–266; E. French, "Some Characteristics of Achievement Motivation," *Journal of Experimental Psychology* 50 (1955): 232–236.

FIGURE 4–3	▶ A Comparison of Four Content Theories of Motivation

There are a variety of content theories of motivation, but the sources of motivation proposed by each bear many similarities. All theories propose self-development needs and social affiliation needs. Only McClelland's "learned" needs do not posit any basic physiological needs, perhaps because they do not need to be learned.

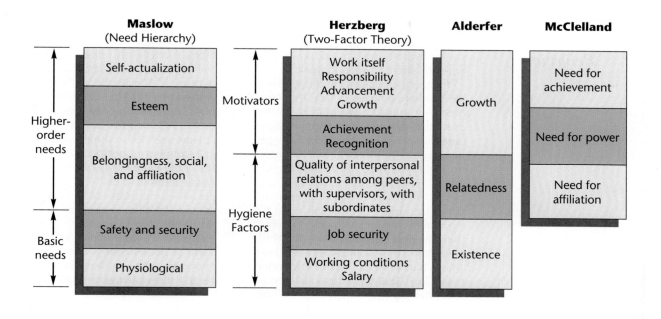

Source: James L. Gibson, John M. Ivancevich, and James H. Donnelly, Jr., *Organizations: Behavior, Structure, Processes*, 6th ed. (Plano, Tex.: BPI, 1988), 127.

aging behavior in organizations. First, these theories remind managers that there is no such thing as an ideal job design. While our later discussions of job design will focus on how to make jobs more motivating, it should always be remembered that more of any of these job features is only better for a worker who wants or needs more. This conclusion has led some management theorists to suggest that an important part of selecting a new employee is finding one whose needs fit what the job has to offer.[14]

A second implication of content theories for management practice is the need to tailor compensation schemes to different individual needs. "Cafeteria" benefit plans, which allow workers to individually tailor their mix of fringe benefits, and incentive schemes that allow workers to choose their own rewards both acknowledge this important contribution of content theories of motivation.[15] These issues will be discussed in greater detail in Chapter 13.

[14] E. E. Lawler III, "For a More Effective Organization—Match the Job to the Man," *Organizational Dynamics* 3 (Summer 1974).

[15] A. Brown, "Today's Employees Choose Their Own Recognition Awards," *Personnel Administrator* 31 (1986): 51–58.

INTERNATIONAL FOCUS ON

Energizing Behavior

A Cure for Workaholics? Employees of Isetan Company, a Japanese retailer that caters to the mink-and-Mercedes crowd, average fewer than 37 hours a week behind the counter. They work five days a week and must use all of their paid vacation. To make sure they do, each department posts a schedule of all staff holidays six months in advance. Isetan is a pacesetter in Japan's newborn drive to adopt a Western-style, five-day working week.

In Japan, complaints about working too hard are no joke. In fact, the Japanese have coined a word for death by overwork: *karoshi*. The average Japanese worker typically has spent 52 hours per week on the job, or about 400 more hours per year than his American counterpart. There are no official statistics, but in 1989 more than 1,300 Japanese families requested information about filing claims for family members who, they say, died from overwork. And they are winning their claims. Last year a Japanese court ordered the Labor Ministry to pay $210,000 to the family of a post-office manager who died of a cerebral hemorrhage after putting in several months of overtime.

Increasing leisure time was a common plank in the platforms of all three men who tried to succeed Yasuhiro Nakasone as prime minister when his term expired in October 1988.

Change will not happen overnight. In 1988, the Japanese workweek was cut to 46 hours, with a further reduction to 44 hours to come in the early 1990s. A 40-hour week probably won't become the norm at major corporations before the mid-1990s. Small companies will take much longer to fall into line. Still, says University of Tokyo law professor Kazuo Sugeno, "It's a turning point for Japanese society."

The growing and widespread support for a shorter week reflects a pervasive feeling in the country that Japan has come of age. "After World War II, people worked very hard to reconstruct the country," notes Koichi Sato, director of research for Domei, the Japanese labor confederation. "But as the economy of Japan becomes stronger, people start to wonder if the living standard is really as enjoyable as it should be."

The awesome task of rebuilding Japan made long hours an integral part of post-World War II Japanese culture. "The ethic for my generation was 'work hard and be dedicated to a company'," says Sugeno, who was born in 1943. That's still the watchword of most of Japan's salaried employees. Although they are entitled to 15 paid holidays a year, they actually take only half that number, and few take more than four days off at a time. Peer pressure and fear of burdening coworkers are the main reasons.

Younger Japanese are leading the assault on workaholism. While their parents save compulsively and toil long hours without complaining, young people are free spenders out to have a good time. They crowd into expensive health clubs and discos after work, and they flee their offices at 6 p.m. on Fridays in winter to catch a train to ski slopes in the mountains. Many spend their holidays touring Europe or windsurfing in Hawaii.

"Young people today are a completely different species," says Sugeno. "My 18-year-old son can enjoy music, plays, art, novels, and so on. He knows how to use his vacation time. I don't."

Sources: "Japan Seeks a Cure for Workaholics," *International Management,* January 1988, 32–33, and S. B. Laporte, "Japanese Executives: Worked to Death?" *Working Woman,* September 1990, 66.

DIRECTING BEHAVIOR: PROCESS THEORIES

Once a manager has identified the needs that will energize subordinates on the job, the next challenge is to use that knowledge to *direct* worker actions appropriately. An employee with needs will act to fulfill them. It is up to the manager to make sure that worker need fulfillment is in concert with fulfillment of the organization's needs. Process theories describe how managers can use knowledge about their subordinates' needs to direct subordinates. Process theories also provide the foundation for many of the specific management techniques (such as goal setting and job design) that will be the focus of Part 4.

The challenge of directing worker behavior really boils down to two forms of learning. Many on-the-job tasks require behaviors that are already within a worker's repertoire or require only minimal instruction. For example, having a subordinate make marks on a check sheet for each unit produced is a simple behavior that requires minimal instruction. The learning that must take place in these cases occurs when the employee learns which simple behaviors will accomplish the organization's goals and therefore will be rewarded. This type of learning is called **conditioning.**

A second kind of learning occurs when on-the-job tasks require complex behaviors that are not in the worker's behavioral repertoire. Interviewing, for example, requires a variety of verbal and nonverbal skills that a new interviewer has not yet acquired. The **complex learning** that must take place in these cases is the acquisition of a new behavior.

Conditioning

As noted above, conditioning is concerned with eliciting appropriate work behaviors. In simpler terms, conditioning amounts to building good habits in workers. A habit is an automatic or routine behavior, such as brushing your teeth before you go to bed or cleaning a machine at the beginning of a work shift. In many cases, appropriate work behaviors are inconvenient and do not produce short-term personal benefits. However, they will produce long-term benefits for the organization. Therefore, the manager needs to strengthen the appropriate behaviors in the worker. The manager needs to create good worker habits.

The "Law of Effect"   How are good work habits created? The primary principle for building good work habits is Thorndike's "law of effect." The law of effect states that:

> Of several responses to the same situation, those that are accompanied or closely followed by satisfaction . . . will be more likely to recur; those which are accompanied or closely followed by discomfort . . . will be less likely to occur.[16]

The two central concepts of the law of effect are **contingency** and **consequences.** If good consequences are contingent upon (follow) a behavior, the probability of that behavior occurring again will be strengthened: it will become a habit or routine. If bad consequences are contingent upon (follow) a behavior, the probability of that behavior occurring again will be weakened: the behavior

---

[16]E. L. Thorndike, *Animal Intelligence* (New York: Macmillan, 1911), 244.

will be avoided and will not become habitual. Simply stated, the law of effect says that worker behaviors are a function of the consequences they produce.

In practice, there are two different contingencies. First, there is a contingency between performance and consequences. What level of performance is required to merit desired consequences? Second, there is a contingency between behavior and performance. Which behavior will produce the level of performance required?

An important qualification of the law of effect is satiation. The law of effect assumes that if the consequences of a behavior are desirable, the worker will perform the behavior again in order to obtain more of the consequences. However, if the consequences fulfill the need completely, the worker is said to be *satiated*. The need disappears and will not motivate further behavior to fulfill it.

The law of effect became the basis for J. B. Watson's theory of "behaviorism" in the 1920s.[17] **Behaviorism** is a radical view of human motivation that contends that *all* behavior can be understood by examining only contingencies and consequences. According to behaviorism, thoughts and beliefs are irrelevant to understanding behavior. Behaviorism was popularized by B. F. Skinner in the 1960s through his book, *Walden II*, which described a fictional experimental community run according to the principles of behaviorism.[18] *Walden II* offered readers new insights into the importance of the law of effect in understanding and controlling everyday behavior.

Walden II also touched off a storm of controversy. Behaviorism, some said, presented a degrading view of the human condition. The argument was that if human behavior was controlled exclusively by contingencies and consequences, there was no such thing as free choice: all behavior was controlled. Without free choice, there in turn could be no dignity or humanity, since they existed only when an individual *freely chose* to be moral in the face of immoral temptation. In another of Skinner's popular books of the 1960s, *Beyond Freedom and Dignity*, Skinner responded to this critique of behaviorism.[19] He argued persuasively that there was no question that human behavior was controlled by contingencies and consequences, only whether behavior was controlled well or poorly.

Reinforcement Theory   How can the law of effect be put into practice to direct worker behavior? The answer is simple: a manager should reinforce appropriate worker behaviors and not reinforce (or even punish) inappropriate behaviors. **Reinforcement** occurs when a manager gives a worker something the worker wants or needs (or takes away something the worker dislikes) when the worker behaves appropriately. This makes the appropriate behavior more likely to occur in the future. Providing approval or recognition to a worker with a high need for achievement will increase the probability that the worker will repeat the desired behavior. Similarly, if a worker has a high need for safety, removing a potential hazard in the workplace following appropriate work behavior reinforces that behavior. The "FOCUS ON: Reinforcement Theory"

---

[17] J. B. Watson, *Psychology, From the Standpoint of a Behaviorist* (Philadelphia: Lippincott, 1919).

[18] B. F. Skinner, *Walden II* (New York: Macmillan, 1948).

[19] B. F. Skinner, *Beyond Freedom and Dignity* (New York: Knopf, 1971).

Recognition awards (such as plaques or certificates) increase the probability of appropriate work behaviors only if the awards are desired by employees and are awarded to correctly behaving employees. If employees desire recognition and accomplishment, any acknowledgment of their contribution may be greatly prized.

describes the difficulty of using reinforcement theory correctly—and the costs of using it incorrectly.

Punishment occurs when a manager gives a worker something the worker dislikes (for example, a suspension or a punch in the nose) in response to *inappropriate* work behaviors. A worker with a high need for affiliation could be punished by isolation—removal from social contacts. The use of punishment will be discussed in more detail later in this chapter.

In applying Thorndike's law of effect to managing behavior in organizations, it is critical to distinguish among several different kinds of consequences of individual work behaviors:

1. Consequences of individual work behaviors for the organization (for example, efficiency, effectiveness, productivity)
2. Consequences of individual work behaviors provided by the organization for the individual (such as wages or promotions)
3. Consequences of individual work behaviors provided informally by coworkers (such as praise or criticism)
4. Consequences of individual work behaviors that occur as part of the behaviors (such as fatigue and social interaction).

What makes an appropriate behavior appropriate is that it produces good consequences. If you brush your teeth, you are less likely to get cavities (a good consequence). If you thank a coworker (a good consequence) for doing something nice, the coworker is more likely to do something nice again. Some behaviors are even intrinsically rewarding—they are their own reward. (These **intrinsic rewards** are what Herzberg's two-factor content theory called "motivators.") For example, the worker pictured in Figure 4–4 enjoys making noise and can't help but do so when using his jackhammer.

Whether that worker is tearing up the *correct* road with his jackhammer is, of course, a different matter altogether. What makes an appropriate *work* behav-

Focus on

Reinforcement Theory

Rewarding A and Hoping for B

Thorndike's "law of effect" seems a very obvious principle of behavior. Yet it also may be the most widely ignored.

Virtually everyone knows at least one parent who is despondent over a teenager's unwillingness to accept the mantle of adult responsibilities. Or one friend whose love affair has gone sour. What is a typical response to these tragic circumstances? Far too often, the strategy is to give, give, give. The disappointed parent feeds, clothes, shelters, and generally supports the recalcitrant teenager, hoping to get him or her back on the right track; the disappointed lover showers the standoffish partner with gifts and affection, trying to convince the partner of the error of breaking up. While at first blush these actions seem natural and appropriate, the consequences they give rise to are, predictably, disastrous. The teenager *learns* to be a bit more lazy every day; the lover's partner *learns* to pout.

The problem, of course, lies in ignoring the relevant contingencies. Reward children for being a disappointment and they will learn to be a disappointment. Reward a lover for being distant

and the lover will learn to be distant. This is the law of effect in its simplest form.

In his article, "The Folly of Rewarding A, While Hoping for B," Steven Kerr has documented examples of this backwards treatment of contingencies in organizations. Two examples he mentions are budget allocations and worker cooperation. When allocating financial resources, most corporations hope for sensible and frugal spending. Yet new annual allocations often are made on the basis of the amount spent during the previous year. Divisions therefore are rewarded with budget increases for doing exactly what no one in the company wants them to do—overspend. Similarly, managers often bemoan the failures of their work force to work together like a team. Yet the basis of most corporate compensation systems is *individual* effort. If individual effort is what the organization rewards, is it really any surprise that individual effort—rather than work-group cooperation—is what the organization gets?

Thorndike's law of effect is easy to understand. For some reason, it is not always easy to follow.

Source: S. Kerr, "On the Folly of Rewarding A, While Hoping for B," *Academy of Management Journal* 18 (1975), 769—783.

ior appropriate is that it produces good consequences *for the organization.* Unfortunately, the individual work behaviors that produce consequences needed and desired by the organization often are not the same as the behaviors that produce consequences needed and desired by employees. If they were, employees would be called players instead of workers. Many intrinsic consequences of work behaviors (such as fatigue) are not desired by the worker. This has important implications for managers.

Managers need to ensure that appropriate work behaviors will be followed by consequences desirable to the workers, so that these behaviors will be more likely to be repeated. This means finding out what workers want or need and making fulfillment of those wants or needs contingent on appropriate on-the-job behaviors. If John likes lottery tickets, his manager could give John a lottery ticket when he shows up on time for work.

While this strategy may look good on paper, overall it is terribly impractical. No manager can reinforce the appropriate behaviors of *all* his or her employees *every time* they occur. There just isn't that much time in the day. That is why conditioning is important. The manager must use reinforcement

FIGURE 4–4 ▶

The rewards for work behaviors can be either extrinsic or intrinsic to the actual performance of the task. Wages and compliments are two forms of extrinsic rewards: rewards the organization gives employees in exchange for appropriate work behaviors. The employee in this picture also has found some intrinsic rewards: rewards he receives as part of performing his job, such as exercise and "the opportunity to make lots of noise."

"I FIND THIS WORK TRULY FULFILLING IN MANY WAYS — THERE'S THE EXERCISE, THE SENSE OF ACCOMPLISHMENT, AND, MOST IMPORTANT, THE OPPORTUNITY TO MAKE LOTS OF NOISE."

Source: © 1975 by Sidney Harris–*The Wall Street Journal.*

and the law of effect to condition good work habits into the workers. As noted earlier, a habit is a routine behavior. You don't ask whether there will be good consequences every time you brush your teeth; brushing your teeth is a habit. That means you do it whether it is immediately followed by good consequences or not.

Habits are developed through partial reinforcement. **Partial reinforcement** means that an appropriate behavior is followed by a reinforcer only *part* of the time. This is in contrast to continuous reinforcement, in which *every* occurrence of appropriate behavior is reinforced. If managers had the time and resources to observe and reinforce *every* appropriate worker behavior, habits would be unnecessary. Habits—the tendency of workers to behave appropriately without hope of immediate reward—take the place of continuous reinforcement. Habits keep workers behaving appropriately even when the boss isn't around to observe and immediately reinforce appropriate behavior.

Partial reinforcement can be provided on a variety of reinforcement schedules. Reinforcement can be provided on a fixed or variable ratio of appropriate behaviors (for instance, after every fifth appropriate behavior) or following the first appropriate behavior after a fixed or variable interval of time (for instance, the first appropriate behavior after five minutes). These different types of reinforcement schedules have different effects on worker behaviors, as summarized in Figure 4–5.

| FIGURE 4-5 | ▶ Reinforcement Schedules and Their Effects on Behavior |

Different schedules of reinforcement have dramatically different effects on behavior. Continuous reinforcement means rewarding a subordinate after every correct behavior and is the fastest way to teach someone a new behavior. Variable reinforcement schedules (variable ratio or variable interval) reward correct behaviors only occasionally and promote their persistence even when rewards are not available.

Schedule	Description	When Applied to Individual	When Removed by Manager	Organizational Example
Continuous	Reinforcer follows every response	Fastest method for establishing new behavior	Fastest method to cause extinction of new behavior	Praise after every response, immediate recognition of every response
Fixed Interval	Response after specific time period is reinforced	Some inconsistency in response frequencies	Faster extinction of motivated behavior than variable schedules	Weekly, bimonthly, monthly paycheck
Variable interval	Response after varying period of time (an average) is reinforced	Produces high rate of steady responses	Slower extinction of motivated behavior than fixed schedules	Transfers, promotions, recognition
Fixed ratio	A fixed number of responses must occur before reinforcement	Some inconsistency in response frequencies	Faster extinction of motivated behavior than variable schedules	Piece rate, commission on units sold
Variable ratio	A varying number (average) of responses must occur before reinforcement	Can produce high rate of response that is steady and resists extinction	Slower extinction of motivated behavior than fixed schedules	Bonus, award, time off

Source: O. Behling, C. Schnesheim, and J. Tolliver, "Present Theories and New Directions in Theories of Work Effort," *Journal of Supplement Abstract Service of the American Psychological Association*, 1974, 57.

No form of partial reinforcement is as effective as continuous reinforcement for getting a behavior to occur initially. Every reinforcement of an appropriate work behavior increases the likelihood that the behavior will occur again. Similarly, every occurrence of the appropriate behavior that is *not* reinforced decreases the likelihood that the appropriate behavior will occur again. Continuous reinforcement is useful for initially building up the probability of occurrence of the appropriate behavior. Then, gradually, reinforcement can be given less and less often, just often enough to keep the habit in place.

Consider how you might handle a worker in your organization who is habitually late. You might start out with continuous reinforcement. You could find out what the worker needs or desires and provide it every time the worker is on time. If the worker wants recognition, you might stop by the worker's work station and provide praise each day the worker shows up on time. After a while, the worker's habit of showing up on time should be strong. You could gradually decrease the frequency of reinforcement, reinforcing only once every few times the worker showed up on time. Eventually you might be able to maintain his or her punctual behavior by praising punctuality only during scheduled performance reviews, once every several months. This is partial reinforcement and the law of effect at work.

Punishment   On the other hand, you might start out by punishing your tardy worker every time the worker showed up late for work (for example, docking the worker's pay). What would be the likely consequences of this conditioning strategy? Punishment has several undesirable effects. The point of punishment is to stop inappropriate behavior. But that is *not* the goal of the organization. The goal of the organization is to increase the probability of appropriate behavior. Two possible outcomes of punishing tardiness are that the worker will simply not show up at all or will show up on time but drunk. In both instances, punishment has stopped the original behavior (showing up sober but late) but the behavior that has occurred instead is equally (if not more) inappropriate.

These unfortunate and equally inappropriate new behaviors are not so unlikely, either. One side effect of punishment is to generate resentment that surfaces as "acting out." If a worker feels humiliated for being punished, the worker may act out resentment through different but equally inappropriate behaviors (such as showing up on time but drunk or not showing up at all). Worse yet, the worker may decide to get even with the punisher through subtle forms of interpersonal or organizational sabotage.

Punishment also tends to build an interpersonal wall between the punisher and the worker. The punished worker will be less likely to discuss work with the punisher. Other problems that might have been prevented may blossom into full-fledged crises.

One problem with punishment is that it creates the wrong choice for the worker. As we noted in the beginning of this chapter, behaviors occur for a reason. If a worker is always late for work, the worker must be getting some benefit out of being late (for example, a little more sleep). Punishing this inappropriate behavior means lateness now is *both* punished and reinforced, giving it an expected value of zero—and a *lower value than it had before*. The worker has lost value, leading to resentment and acting out.

Now consider the outcomes of counterconditioning: reinforcing the appropriate behavior (rather than punishing the inappropriate behavior) in the hopes of substituting appropriate behaviors for inappropriate ones. Reinforcing appropriate behavior (punctuality) creates a different choice for the worker. From the worker's perspective, counterconditioning substitutes the reinforcement of appropriate behavior for the foregone reinforcement of inappropriate behavior. The net expected values of appropriate and inappropriate behavior now are equally positive for the worker, so the worker might as well come to work on time. From the perspective of the organization, counterconditioning substitutes appropriate for inappropriate worker behavior. The probability of appropriate worker behavior is increased *without* risking the undesirable consequences of punishment.

This is not to suggest that punishment does not have its uses. It does suggest, however, that punishment alone is not a complete strategy for managing subordinate behavior. Punishment is most appropriate when a manager can use it to immediately stop counterproductive behaviors—for example, by suspending an employee who shows up for work drunk. Unfortunately, managers cannot immediately punish inappropriate behaviors they don't witness, and punishment becomes ineffective when it is delayed.

Further, as noted earlier, the use of punishment still begs the question of what motivated the inappropriate behavior in the first place. If a worker is sabotaging the assembly line because sabotage is more interesting than the job, punishment of the sabotage isn't going to make the job more interesting. At the least, punishment should be used together with counterconditioning, thereby giving the subordinate a greater incentive to perform appropriate work behaviors than already exists for inappropriate ones.

Finally, it should always be remembered that punishment in organizations typically is a *social* phenomenon, an event that influences the thoughts and behaviors of *unpunished* as well as punished individuals. Of particular interest to bystanders of a punishment episode will be such issues as: Did the punished individual get a fair chance to explain or defend his or her actions? And did the punishment fit the crime? Attempting to "punish in private" cannot eliminate these concerns. An organization's informal communication grapevine no doubt will carry the news. Ignoring the social aspects of punishment may only mean that a manager has foregone the opportunity to build favorable and productive perceptions of the episode in the minds of the work force.[20]

OB–Mod   The systematic application of simple conditioning and reinforcement theory principles to the management of organizational behavior is known as **organizational behavior modification (OB–Mod).** OB–Mod encompasses the important aspects of conditioning and reinforcement theory in a simple framework that a manager can apply to any behavioral problem. Five steps are used to establish an OB–Mod behavioral-change program:[21]

1. *Define the target behavior.* This must be a clear and unequivocal statement of the desired behavior. For example, "at work on time" would be defined explicitly: "checked in, work smock on, at your workbench, and ready to begin work when the plant time clock reads 8:00 A.M." This means that a manager must be able to state desired performance in terms of precise events. After all, if the manager can't decide what the desired behavior is supposed to be, how should a subordinate know?

2. *Measure the frequency of behavior.* The success of a change effort needs to be measured against a baseline of normal performance. This is important so that both management and the worker will be able to tell whether progress is being made, and they will know when to reinforce the behavior.

3. *Set reasonable performance goals.* If the subordinate's behavior is to be changed, a goal will give the employee something to think about and shoot for. (The importance of goals in motivating work behavior will be discussed in detail in Chapter 13.)

4. *Monitor behavior.* Keep track of the frequency of occurrence of the appropriate behavior. Requiring the subordinate to collect this information will help maintain the subordinate's involvement in the behavior change effort.

5. *Administer rewards.* Since OB–Mod is based on conditioning and reinforcement theory, the final and most important step is to reward appropriate behaviors. The manager must reward acceptable progress toward

---

[20]L. K. Trevino, "The Social Effects of Punishment in Organizations: A Justice Perspective," *Academy of Management Review,* 17(4) (1992): 647–676.

[21]F. Luthans and R. Kreitner, *Organizational Behavior Modification and Beyond* (Glenview, Ill.: Scott, Foresman, 1985).

or achievement of the performance goals. This increases the likelihood that these desired behaviors will become habits.

Has OB–Mod proven successful? Two researchers identified ten organizations that have used OB–Mod approaches to deal with behavioral problems; in nine of the ten organizations, OB–Mod was successful. Interestingly, in many of the organizations where OB–Mod had been successfully implemented, social rewards (such as praise) were commonly used instead of money to reinforce appropriate behaviors.[22]

Complex Learning

Complex behaviors are behaviors unlikely to occur naturally or without substantial training and practice. Complex behaviors present a problem for managers because they cannot be simply conditioned. As an example of a complex behavior, consider the golf swing. How would you condition someone to swing a golf club correctly? You could punish poor swings and reinforce good swings, hoping to increase the probability of good-swing recurrence. Unfortunately, a good golf swing is sufficiently complex that you might wait *forever* for a good swing—especially if you were training someone who was just learning to play golf. So what might you do instead? Two options are considered here: **successive approximation** and **vicarious learning**.

Successive Approximation   Conditioning and the law of effect also can be used to help workers acquire complex behaviors required on the job. Since the appropriate behavior is unlikely to occur at first, it is conditioned by reinforcing successively better approximations of the final desired behavior.

One variant of successively reinforcing better approximations of the final desired behavior is *shaping*. In shaping, the entire desired behavior is reinforced or not reinforced, but the requirements for reinforcement become more stringent over time. Shaping a golf swing, for instance, would entail at first reinforcing almost any swing, then only reasonable approximations of the final correct swing, then only good approximations of the final swing, and finally only the correct swing. As the reinforcement criteria become more stringent, the behavior of the learner is being "fine-tuned" to more closely approximate the final desired behavior.

Another form of successive-approximation conditioning is *chaining*. In chaining, the desired complex behavior is broken down into component behaviors; successively more complete demonstrations of the desired behavior chain then are reinforced until the final desired behavior is acquired. A golf swing, for instance, could be broken down into five parts: the address, the take-away, the backswing, the downswing, and the follow-through. To chain a correct golf swing, you would start by reinforcing only a good address; then a good address and take-away; then a good address, take-away, and back swing; and so on, until you were reinforcing only good examples of the *entire* chain.

In practice, chaining and shaping often are used together. Extremely complex work behaviors can be broken down into components and (using chaining)

[22] W. C. Hamner and E. P. Hamner, "Behavior Modification on the Bottom Line," *Organizational Dynamics* 4 (1976): 3–21.

Complex work behaviors often are acquired by observation of other workers. Placing new workers next to good role models may increase the speed with which they learn appropriate work behaviors. Vicarious or social learning may help these air-traffic controllers pick up an initial approximation of their complicated task, which is later reinforced with conditioning.

acquired one component at a time. Within the process of learning each component, shaping may be used to encourage acquisition.

Vicarious Learning Largely ignored to this point in our discussion of work motivation is the role of workers' cognitions (thoughts) in acquiring and performing appropriate work behaviors. The image of learning offered by conditioning, reinforcement theory, and behaviorism is learning by doing or learning by trial and error. The worker tries behaviors; appropriate work behaviors are acquired when workers are reinforced for trying them. A major criticism of behaviorist approaches to learning is that they ignore the fact that workers learn many behaviors without ever doing them, just by observing others engaged in these behaviors. This criticism has been voiced by psychologist Albert Bandura, a noted expert in behavior modification:

> . . . It is doubtful if many classes of responses would ever be acquired if [learning] proceeded solely by the method of successive approximations through differential reinforcement of emitted responses. The technique of reinforced shaping requires a subject to perform some approximation of the terminal response before he can learn it. In instances where a behavioral pattern contains a highly unusual combination of elements . . . the probability of occurrence of the desired response, or even one that has some remote resemblance to it, will be zero. . . . In cases involving intricate patterns of behavior, modeling is an indispensable aspect of learning.[23]

Learning by observing others is called **vicarious learning.** Vicarious learning can refer either to acquiring complex behaviors (such as a golf swing) or to learning which behaviors (simple or complex) will be reinforced, which will not, and even which behaviors will be punished. Vicarious learning also is called *social learning* because it always involves observing behaviors modeled by others.

---

[23] A. Bandura, *Principles of Behavior Modification* (New York: Holt, Rinehart, & Winston, 1969), 143–144.

Behavior acquisition through vicarious learning must be different from behavior acquisition through conditioning. Acquisition of appropriate behaviors through conditioning can occur through what is essentially "muscle memory." Imagine that you engage in an appropriate behavior and the behavior is reinforced. The reinforcement strengthens the probability that you will repeat the same component motions of the reinforced behavior the next time you get a chance. With vicarious learning, someone else has engaged in the reinforced behavior, so the appropriate motions cannot be stored in your muscles.

Vicarious learning involves symbolic storage of the appropriate behavior. Symbolic storage of an action is storage of a representation of the behavior, rather than storage of the behavior's component motions themselves.[24] If you observe someone else engaging in the appropriate behavior, the observation creates an image in your mind that you retain. If you think or talk about this image or the behavior itself, the words you think or speak also are retained as verbal representations of the behavior. These verbal representations and images of behaviors then serve as templates (road maps or instructions) to later help you correctly engage in the appropriate behavior yourself.

These two different forms of behavior storage—"muscle memory" and symbolic storage—explain why occasionally an individual can do something quite complex without being able to describe how. For instance, can you describe how to maintain your balance? Probably not. Yet, maintaining your balance is quite easy. Maintaining balance is a habit that we learn from doing—from trial and error—and we have "muscle memory" for engaging in the appropriate motions. We do not have good symbolic representations of this behavior, however, so we can do it much better than we can explain it.

Vicarious learning and conditioning are complementary forms of learning. As Bandura noted, it is inconceivable that certain complex behaviors could be learned by trial and error conditioning. Vicarious learning explains how initial approximations of complex behaviors occur. Reinforcement then can make correct initial approximations more likely to recur.

Vicarious learning is also limited, however. Watching another individual engage in a complex behavior provides a symbolic representation of a gross approximation of the appropriate behavior. However, symbolic representations are exactly that—gross. The subtle nuances of an appropriate behavior often cannot be observed easily. Observation may provide a good first approximation; reinforcement of successively better approximations is required to fine-tune the appropriate component motions.

Interestingly, the sequence of these two types of learning—vicarious learning first, conditioning later—can be reversed to further fine-tune complex behaviors. Some work behaviors are so foreign to new workers that even after a cycle of symbolic acquisition followed by conditioned fine-tuning, the behaviors remain only grossly acquired. In these circumstances, further vicarious observation of others *or even of oneself* (for instance, by videotape) can be helpful in fine-tuning the symbolic representation of the appropriate behavior. Observation of one's own behavior at this point also may reveal differences between the actual and intended implementation of the behavior. In such cases, vicarious learning and conditioning become complementary components of complex behavior acquisition.

---

[24]R. Wood and A. Bandura, "Social Cognitive Theory of Organizational Management," *Academy of Management Review* 14(3) (1989): 361–384.

COGNITIVE QUALIFICATIONS

Are contingencies and consequences all there is to understanding work motivation? If a manager knows what workers need and makes the fulfillment of those needs contingent on appropriate behaviors, *will* appropriate behaviors occur? As noted in some further comments by Bandura, this is far too simple a view of human behavior:

> A valid criticism of extreme behaviorism is that . . . it has neglected determinants of behavior arising from cognitive functioning. . . . A theory that denies that thoughts can regulate actions does not lend itself readily to the explanation of human behavior. Although cognitive activities are disavowed in the [behaviorist] framework, their role in causal sequences cannot be eliminated.[25]

Vicarious learning presents undeniable proof that **cognitions** (beliefs and thoughts) are critical to understanding worker motivation and performance. Having thus opened the Pandora's box of cognition, we must examine its further role in determining behavior. In particular, if appropriate work behaviors have been acquired by the worker and outcomes desired by the worker have been made contingent upon their execution, can worker thoughts and beliefs *prevent* the appropriate behavior from occurring? The answer is yes. Two such worker cognitions will be considered in the remainder of this chapter: expectancy and equity.

Expectancy

The basic principles of **expectancy theory** are presented in an early statement of the theory:

> If a worker seeks high productivity as a path leading to the attainment of one or more of his personal goals, he will tend to be a high producer. Conversely, if he sees low productivity as a path to the achievement of his goals he will tend to be a low producer.[26]

The contrast between this expectancy view of worker motivation and the law of effect discussed earlier is both subtle and striking. The law of effect states that if managers make desired consequences contingent upon appropriate work behavior, appropriate behaviors will occur. Expectancy theory instead proposes that if workers *believe* that a consequence they *believe* they need is contingent upon work behaviors they *believe* they can do, they will engage in those work behaviors. The key difference between these two perspectives is the central role of beliefs in expectancy theory. According to expectancy theory, it is not enough that desired consequences are contingent upon appropriate behavior; the worker must *believe* that the consequences are desirable, *believe* that the behavior will produce them, and *believe* that the behavior can be done.

The differences between behaviorist and expectancy theories of work motivation are outlined in Figure 4–6. The orange boxes in the figure present a simple behaviorist model of worker motivation. If contingent consequences are desired, they will reinforce the worker's behavior, making the behavior (short of satiation) more likely to occur again. Each experience of the contingency also

---

[25] A. Bandura, *Social Learning Theory* (Englewood Cliffs, N.J.: Prentice-Hall, 1977), 10.

[26] B. S. Georgopoulos, G. M. Mahoney, and N. W. Jones, "A Path-Goal Approach to Productivity," *Journal of Applied Psychology* 41 (1957): 346.

FIGURE 4-6	▶ Expectancy Theory

Expectancy theory captures the importance of cognitions (beliefs and thoughts) to motivation. A worker may be capable of superior performance and superior performance may be rewarded. But if the worker does not *believe* that he or she can do the work, or that the work will be rewarded, he or she will not be motivated.

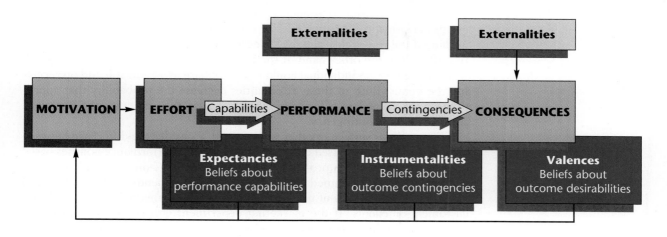

adds to the worker's learning ("muscle" or symbolic memory) about the contingency.

The teal boxes in the figure present an expectancy model of worker motivation. The expectancy model adds three "belief" components to the behaviorist model: valence, instrumentality, and expectancy. **Valence** refers to the value of a behavior's consequences, as perceived by the worker. What workers really need is only as important to determining behavior as what workers *think* they need. What people actually need—help, for instance—is often quite different from what they think they need. For better or worse, what people think they need is what they are willing to work for.

Expectancy refers to the worker's belief that his or her own efforts are capable of producing the required levels of performance. **Instrumentality** refers to the worker's belief that attaining the required levels of performance will produce desired personal outcomes (such as monetary rewards or praise). If the worker believes that performance is not really contingent on effort, or that the desired rewards are not really contingent on performance, the worker will not be motivated to engage in the behavior, even if it really would produce the desired consequences. The worker's *beliefs* about contingencies are more important than the contingencies themselves.

What influences beliefs in motivating worker behaviors? Externalities have a big impact on expectancy and instrumentality beliefs. As noted in Figure 4–5, **externalities** are the causes of a worker's behaviors or the consequences of those behaviors that are beyond the worker's control, such as the behaviors of another worker or the reliability of a machine. Imagine that you work as a salesperson and a performance bonus is available, contingent upon the sales volume of the entire sales force reaching a predetermined level. You cannot achieve the bonus through your own behaviors alone. Instead, you are dependent upon other members of the sales force working hard and making their own contributions to the group's sales volume. What would expectancy theory predict about sales force motivation with this kind of bonus?

Externalities decrease worker motivation because they introduce uncertainty into the perceived causal relationship between individual behavior and attainment of desired consequences. If the bonus will be awarded based upon group performance, it is possible for one individual to work very hard and get nothing if the rest of the sales force doesn't come through with an equally effective effort. On the other hand, if the rest of the sales force does come through with a big effort, an individual could not work hard at all and still end up receiving the bonus. Both of these externalities decrease the probability that appropriate work behaviors will occur simply because they decrease the perceived strength of the contingency.

Externalities surface in other ways as well. Consider the difference between performance bonuses based upon profit sharing and performance bonuses based upon cost savings. With profit sharing, the receipt of a bonus not only depends on the behaviors of immediate coworkers; it also depends on the (uncertain) behaviors of other parts of the organization, other competitors in the field, and customers or clients. If the marketing department chooses a poor marketing strategy, for example, profits may disappear (and any profit-sharing bonus with them!) even while the production workers are producing at record efficiency. A cost-savings bonus, on the other hand, is a matter of production efficiency alone and reduces a production worker's perceived dependency on a host of other organizational actors.

The inhibiting effects of externalities on worker motivation can be decreased in two ways. First, if management can identify individual contributions to work outcomes, workers will be able to tell who in the work group is pulling their weight and who is not. The work group then can bring pressure to bear on poor contributors. Workers also then can calculate better the likely impact of their own effort on the group's performance.

Second, if individual contributions to the group effort can be measured, managers can separately reinforce them. If workers really are dependent on each other, however, it will not make sense to do away with group incentives. Reinforcing only individual performance predictably trains workers to be concerned only with individual accomplishments, even at the expense of group accomplishments. Maintaining both individual and group-based reward systems encourages both individual effort and group collaboration.

Attributions also play a major role in instrumentality beliefs. Instrumentality beliefs are perceptions of the relationship between individual behaviors and desired consequences. And there is enough uncertainty in the behavior-performance-consequences chain that hopelessly incorrect attributions are always possible. For example, **superstitious behavior** occurs when a worker believes a behavior will be rewarded even though that behavior is in fact irrelevant. A worker may engage in a behavior (such as saying, "Have a nice day!" to the boss first thing in the morning) while *also* engaging in the appropriate behavior. Since both behaviors are paired with the reinforcement, the probability of both increases, even though one is completely irrelevant. Attributions can lead to two other forms of instrumentality beliefs—self-efficacy and learned helplessness—that are critical to a worker's willingness to activate appropriate work behaviors.

Self-Efficacy   Self-efficacy is a worker's belief that he or she can produce required levels of performance by engaging in appropriate work behaviors.[27] **Self-efficacy** beliefs arise in workers' observations of their work behaviors and the attributions they make about their role in controlling levels of performance. Workers with high self-efficacy believe that (1) they have the ability needed, (2) they are capable of the effort necessary to produce a required level of performance, and (3) no outside causes will prevent their behavior from attaining the required performance level. If workers have low self-efficacy, they believe that no matter how hard they try, something (insufficient ability, inadequate effort, or outside interference) ultimately will prevent them from reaching their performance goal.

As perceptions, self-efficacy beliefs can be incorrect. Even if a worker achieves the required performance, he or she may attribute the accomplishment to causes other than personal efforts or abilities—beginner's luck or ease of the task, for example. On the other hand, even if the worker fails to reach the required level of performance, he or she may find causes for the failure (such as interference from other workers, lack of time, or even lack of personal effort) that excuse the failure and allow the worker to continue to believe that the required performance level is well within reach.

In either case, the worker will have arrived at a self-efficacy belief that is in stark contrast to the latest consequences received. Such attributions can be tremendously useful. High self-efficacy will encourage a worker to persevere in the face of failure and to continue with a successful strategy that accidentally has produced poor performance. Similarly, accurate low self-efficacy beliefs should force a worker to reevaluate his or her approach to a problem, find ways to exert greater effort, or perhaps just convince the worker that assistance (perhaps in the form of additional training) is necessary.

Inaccurate self-efficacy beliefs can be a nightmare for a manager. There is almost nothing worse than subordinates or coworkers who believe that their behaviors are appropriate to obtain the required level of performance—who believe that they have the correct strategy for the task at hand and are exerting the necessary effort—and are *wrong*. In such circumstances, workers will not entertain proposals to alter their task strategy, exert more effort, or seek assistance. The performance failures that have occurred will occur again and again because the workers have neutralized the law of effect with their cognitive rationalizations. For a manager, there could be only one worse motivational headache: workers whose attributions cause them to give up when in fact required performance levels are well within reach.

Learned Helplessness   When workers believe that they are incapable of producing the required performance, or that the required performance (even if produced) would not lead to desired consequences, motivation to engage in appropriate work behaviors will be low. When work motivation is low enough

[27] M. E. Gist and T. R. Mitchell, "Self-Efficacy: A Theoretical Analysis of Its Determinants and Malleability," *Academy of Management Review* 17(2) (1992): 183–211.

that workers give up—don't even bother to try—**learned helplessness** has occurred.[28]

Learned helplessness is more tragic than inappropriately high self-efficacy. Repeated failures eventually should lead even the most confident incompetent to see the error of his or her ways. And the confident incompetent at least is trying, so a manager always retains the hope (however dim) that accidentally appropriate behaviors will change everything (performance and expectancies) for the better. Workers who are suffering from learned helplessness never try, however, or try only hard enough to confirm their suspicions, and so never find out that they are capable or with some assistance could be. Learned helplessness thus takes on all the characteristics of a classic self-fulfilling prophecy, and the kind of self-fulfilling prophecy that every manager should be desperate to avoid.

How can overly optimistic self-efficacy beliefs and overly pessimistic learned helplessness beliefs be avoided? Not surprisingly, there are two answers: one behavioral and one cognitive. The behavioral answer is that self-efficacy and learned helplessness beliefs are based on individuals' perceptions of their own behaviors. A manager can help a subordinate alter inaccurate perceptions by altering what the individual sees. If a subordinate's expectancies are inflated, the subordinate will not be as careful or try as hard as possible. Encouraging the subordinate to carefully keep track of performance can lead to a more realistic perception of his or her accomplishments. On the other hand, if an individual feels unable to do anything well and seems to have given up, a few easy tasks (with perhaps a little extra supervision) may be just the way to get the worker's expectancies back on the road to recovery.

The cognitive answer to inappropriate expectancies is communication. Managers should encourage their subordinates to talk about their perceptions of the contingencies at work. At the very least the manager should make sure that subordinates understand the contingencies as management sees them and as the organization has laid them out. What behaviors are likely to produce the required performance? What levels of performance are going to be rewarded and how? Misperceptions of work contingencies often are a function of uncertainty. A little communication can go a long way in curing these misperceptions.

Problems arising from self-efficacy and learned helplessness also highlight the importance of performance appraisal as a managerial tool. While performance appraisal often is viewed primarily as a means of assigning compensation, it also can play a major role in diagnosing the causes of and correcting performance deficiencies. Performance appraisal provides the manager a tremendous opportunity to help a worker who is spiraling into learned helplessness to rethink the way to successful new task strategies. These motivational aspects of performance appraisal will be discussed in detail in Chapter 13.

Equity

Expectancy deals with how workers answer the questions: "Can I obtain the outcomes I want at work? What do I really think the contingencies are? And do I want what I can get?" **Equity** deals instead with the questions: "If I can get the outcomes I want, will they be worth the price I pay? Do I really want them?" Just because a reward is desired does not mean it is desired at the *cost* of the behavior demanded.

---

[28] M. E. P. Seligman, *Helplessness* (San Francisco: W. H. Freeman, 1975).

Animal psychologist Edward Tolman's experiments with monkeys in the 1930s provided a first glimpse at the importance of equity to the motivation of behavior.[29] Tolman was interested in the ability of monkeys to recognize symbols. He would put different symbols on each of several cups. Then, over many trials, he would consistently put bananas under the cup with a particular symbol and observe whether the monkey could use the symbol to find the banana.

As the story goes, one day Tolman tried to substitute "monkey chow" for the banana under the cup. Monkeys like "monkey chow," but monkeys *love* bananas. So what happened when Tolman's clever monkey picked the correct symbol and turned over the cup, only to find "monkey chow" instead of a banana? Just like any self-respecting human being under the same circumstances, the monkey got hysterical, threw a temper tantrum, and refused to play Tolman's game any more.

Why was this outcome so upsetting for the monkey? Why would it be upsetting if it happened to you? The consequences were desirable, and the contingencies were not violated. The problem was that the outcome wasn't fair. The monkey had been led to believe he *deserved* a banana for the difficult task of identifying the correct symbol. When you deserve a banana, getting paid off in "monkey chow" just isn't fair.

Equity has to do with fairness judgments and how those judgments influence a worker's willingness to work. Equity theory views behavior as a process in which workers exchange appropriate work behaviors for desired consequences. This means workers are aware of more than just which behaviors are appropriate and which desired consequences they will merit. It means that workers also are aware of the *relationship* between appropriate behaviors and desired consequences, of just how much need fulfillment they receive in exchange for how much appropriate behavior.

J. Stacey Adams first developed and tested the ideas underlying equity theory while working as a researcher with the General Electric Company in Crotonville, New York. His research led Adams to conclude that equity is an important component of work motivation. Workers strive to maintain equity in their exchange relationships at work; when they perceive inequity, workers will strive to reestablish equitable exchange arrangements.[30]

Judging Equity   Equity is a function of the perceived *ratio* between the inputs a worker puts into the job and the outcomes (consequences) he or she receives in exchange. For instance, if you worked four hours (your input) and received $60 in exchange (your outcomes), your equity ratio (outcomes/inputs) would be 60/4, or 15. In practice, of course, equity ratio calculations are much more abstract and complex. A list of possible work inputs and outcomes is provided in Figure 4–7. It should be understood that this is not meant to be a complete list, nor does any worker necessarily think of all these outcomes and inputs when deciding if the offered contingencies are equitable. This list does, however, provide some idea of the outcomes and inputs that typically are considered by workers in equity calculations.

---

[29]E. C. Tolman, *Purposive Behavior in Animals and Men* (New York: Century, 1932).

[30]J. S. Adams, "Toward an Understanding of Inequity," *Journal of Abnormal and Social Psychology* 67 (1963): 422–436.

FIGURE 4–7	▶ Possible Inputs and Outcomes Considered in Equity Calculations

An individual decides whether the consequences contingent upon work behaviors are equitable by comparing work outcomes (the rewards received from the work) to work inputs (what the worker brings to or puts into the job). Work outcomes include both those extrinsic rewards provided by the organization, such as wages, and rewards intrinsic to the job, such as the possibility of personal growth and development.

Inputs	Outcomes
Quality of work performed	Job security
Reliability	Pay
Acceptance of responsibility	Competent supervisor
Job knowledge	Possibility of growth
Cooperation with others	Fair supervisor
Self-improvement	Recognition
Attitude	Adequate working conditions
Quantity of work performed	Interpersonal relations with
Initiative	Supervisor
Adaptability-versatility	Peers
Judgment	Adequate planning/management
Intelligence	Adequate personnel policies
Experience	Amount of work
Personal appearance	Responsibility
Oral communication skills	Advancement
Education	Routine work
Written communication skills	Status
Personal involvement with work	Difficult work
	Personal life

Source: D. W. Belcher and T. J. Atchinson, "Equity Theory and Compensation Policy," *Personnel Administration* 33 (3) (1970): 28; Belcher and Atchinson, "Equity, Rewards, and Compensation Administration," *Personnel Administration* 34 (2) (1971): 34.

One key concern in worker equity calculations is how a worker decides whether a particular outcome/input exchange ratio is or is not fair. A worker decides whether an outcome/input exchange ratio is fair by comparing it to other exchange ratios. Several comparisons are likely: to personal or absolute standards, to the ratios of other workers in the organization, and to the ratios of other workers outside the organization. Personal standards might include an individual's actual living costs; a full-time job that cannot cover living expenses will be perceived as inequitably compensated. Absolute standards would include the federally established minimum wage. When equity comparisons are made either within an organization or to those of workers in other organizations, an individual might compare outcome/input ratios with those of other workers who have the same or similar jobs, have equal seniority, or have jobs with similar selection requirements.

Most likely, equity comparisons are made on the basis of salience and availability. If another worker's outcome/input ratio for some reason becomes salient (for example, because salary is mentioned in conversation), an equity comparison is likely to be made. If workers feel that their outcome/input ratio is out of line, comparisons are likely to be made using the most available comparison

ratios—those of the workers' acquaintances both within and without the organization.

Regardless of the basis for comparison, it is important to remember that
equity judgments are based on *perceptions* of outcomes/inputs and therefore are
susceptible to error. As noted in Chapter 3, workers generally *overestimate* their
own contributions at work relative to other workers; workers see more of what
they themselves accomplish and less of what others do. This should encourage
judgments of inequitable treatment.

Many organizations have attempted to prevent judgments of inequitable
compensation from occurring by keeping compensation levels secret. Maintaining pay secrecy will render equity judgments difficult, since the outcomes
received by coworkers can only be estimated. Unfortunately, keeping pay levels
secret only makes matters worse. When pay is secret, workers tend to *overestimate* compensation levels received by other workers, fostering perceptions
of inequity.[31] If an organization is compensating its employees equitably, its best
defense against inequity perceptions should be communication. A performance-
review system that leads workers to an accurate perception of their work contributions and publicized rules about the relationship between work contributions and compensation should reduce the probability of inaccurate equity
perceptions.

There is growing evidence of a significant difference in the ways that
women and men arrive at equity judgments at work. While at career entry
women may have better credentials for first jobs than their male counterparts
(for example, higher GPAs or better verbal skills), men generally perceive themselves as bringing more or better job inputs. Males also have higher performance expectations than females, even in female-dominated occupations. Further, while women don't value pay or promotion less than men, they do place
more value on *nonfinancial* job outcomes (like interpersonal factors). Not surprisingly, then, since women perceive themselves to be making less inputs and
are willing to count more outputs as compensations of a job, women (compared
to men) see less pay as equitable.[32]

Restoring Equity   How do workers react to perceived inequities in the workplace? They will strive to restore equity, to get their personal outcome/input
ratio more in line with the ratios of relevant others. Exactly how equity is
restored depends on whether the inequity comes from overreward or
underreward.

Overreward means that a worker believes he or she is receiving *more* compensation than that deserved for services rendered (inputs). Perhaps surprisingly, overreward is distressing to workers because it leads to "insecure non-
reliance upon the continuance of earnings, provokes fear of rivalry in others
who are not favored, and stimulates an anxious and selfish desire further to
improve the favored position."[33] Several research studies have demonstrated
that workers often react to overreward by increasing their work inputs. For

[31] E. E. Lawler, *Pay and Organizational Effectiveness: A Psychological View* (New York: McGraw-Hill, 1971).

[32] L. A. Jackson, P. D. Gardner, and L. A. Sullivan, "Explaining Gender Differences in Self-Pay Expectations:
Social Comparison Standards and Perceptions of Fair Pay," *Journal of Applied Psychology* 77(5) (1992): 651–663.

[33] E. Jaques, *Equitable Payment* (New York: Wiley, 1961), 142–143.

Focus on

Equity

The Trust Gap   Just when top management wants everyone to begin swaying to a faster, more productive beat, employees are loath to dance. Observes David Sirota, chairman of the corporate polling firm Sirota Alper & Pfau, "CEOs say, We're a team, we're all in this together, rah, rah, rah. But employees look at the difference between their pay and the CEO's. They see top management perks—oak dining rooms and heated garages versus cafeterias for the hourly guys and gals and parking spaces half a mile from the plant. And they wonder: Is this togetherness?" As the disparity in pay widens, the wonder grows.

The rate of increase in top management's compensation parted company from workers' in the late 1970s. Top executives who make 100 times the average shop-floor worker are no longer rare. European and Japanese CEOs, who seldom earn more than 15 times the employee average, are amazed by the disparity.

J. P. Morgan and Co. discovered that its poorly performing clients had one characteristic in common: "Each company's top executive was paid more than 130 percent of the people in the next echelon, and these, in turn, more than 130 percent of the compensation below them." Morgan concluded that disproportionately high executive salaries disrupted teamwork.

Companies with big pay gaps pay another price they typically don't care to discuss. Michael Crino, professor of management at Clemson University, explains: "If people feel somehow that their side of the scale isn't balanced with yours, they may go to extremes to balance it. If management is arrogant, if it keeps all the perks to itself when the company does well, then pushes all the disasters downhill when times are bad, then there are certain collateral behaviors you can expect to see." He means sabotage.

Some companies have woken up to the hidden costs of the trust gap. When Nucor, a North Carolina steel company, went through tough times, President Ken Iverson took a 60 percent cut in pay. Notes Jude Rich, president of a compensation consulting firm, "It makes a real difference if employees see that their CEO is willing to take it in the shorts along with them."

Herb Kelleher, CEO of Southwest Airlines, agrees. "If there's going to be a downside, you should share it. When we were experiencing hard times two years ago, I went to the board and told them I wanted to cut my salary. I cut all the officers' bonuses 10 percent, mine 20 percent." Analysts rate Southwest's employees the most productive of any airline. Why are they? Says Kelleher (pictured here), "Because they know we aren't trying to milk them in order to swell the bottom line."

Source: Adapted from A. Farnham, "The Trust Gap," *Fortune*, December 4, 1989, 56–78.

example, if workers believe they are being paid too much per completed unit on a piecework compensation schedule, they will increase the *quality* of the units produced. By raising the quality of the completed units, the workers are increasing personal work contributions and thereby justifying the overpayment.

Because equity judgments are perceptions of the ratio of work contributions and of the value of consequences received, overreward also may be justified simply by adjusting perceptions. If workers think they are overpaid, the easiest path to reconciling this inequity is to become convinced that either (1) their work contributions were more substantial than earlier believed, or (2) the consequences received were not (upon reflection) nearly as valuable as initially suspected. In sum, workers often sort out overreward inequities by convincing themselves that their work merited the extra compensation after all.

Inequity judgments arising from *underreward* pose a more serious threat. Workers' feelings of inequity stemming from perceived underreward have been linked with absenteeism, turnover, and even (as noted in the "FOCUS ON: Equity") sabotage. Any of these could prove disastrously expensive for the organization. How a worker resolves underreward inequity depends upon the financial incentives available for the work force. If workers are paid on an hourly basis, underreward leads to decreased quantity of production. This decreases the worker's perceived contributions and thereby lowers the outcome/input ratio.

If workers are paid on a piece-rate basis, underreward inequity is resolved a little differently. From the perspective of the workers, lowering their production output would be personally counterproductive. On a piece-rate compensation schedule, lowered production means lower wages at the end of the pay period. For reasons of self-interest, then, lowering production quantity is an unlikely equity-resolving path for workers paid by units completed. Instead, under piece-rate compensation schedules, production *quantity* is maintained while unit *quality* quietly erodes. As unit quality slips, perceived inputs decrease and equity ratios fall to acceptable levels.

SUMMARY ◆◆◆◆◆◆

Motivation is the process of energizing and directing worker behavior. Content theories of motivation provide an understanding of what types of needs and desires are likely to energize behavior in organizations. Behaviorism and reinforcement theory provide a model for directing worker energies toward the fulfillment of organizational needs through appropriate work behaviors. Workers will pursue organizational objectives when personal need fulfillment is contingent upon appropriate work behaviors.

Unfortunately, contingencies and consequences present far too simplistic a view of the challenge of motivating worker performance in organizations. Expectancy concerns qualify behaviorist theories of energizing and directing behavior. Contingencies between desired consequences and appropriate behaviors will energize appropriate work behaviors only if the worker believes they will lead to personal need fulfillment. Equity concerns provide a qualification to energizing behavior. A desired consequence will be pursued by a worker only if the price (worker inputs) is equitable. Expectancy and equity concerns both are perceptions of motivational arrangements at work. These perceptions play an important role in a worker's decision to engage in appropriate work behaviors.

Theories of motivation provide managers a foundation for motivating a work force. The specific application of these theories to management tasks (such as socializing new employees) will be the focus of Part 4 of this book.

Key Terms

Behaviorism View of human motivation that all behavior can be understood by examining only contingencies and consequences.

Cognitions Beliefs and thoughts: the information processing that goes on inside an individual's head.

Complex learning Form of learning requiring acquisition of new behaviors not yet available in a worker's behavioral repertoire.

Conditioning The use of reinforcement and punishment to create habits.

Consequences A central concept of the law of effect: the good or bad results following from a behavior.

Content theories of motivation Theories that focus on the factors within people that motivate them to perform; for example, the theories of Maslow, Herzberg, and McClelland.

Contingency A central concept of the law of effect: the relationships between actions and their outcomes.

Equity Workers' judgments of fairness based on the ratio of work outcomes to work inputs.

Expectancies Workers' cognitions concerning the likely consequence of their actions.

Expectancy theory Theory stating that worker behaviors are a function of workers' *beliefs* about consequences and contingencies.

Externalities Causes of a worker's behaviors or the consequences of those behaviors that are beyond the worker's control.

Hygiene factors In two-factor theory, workers' basic needs of pay, safety on the job, quality of supervision, and social environment, fulfillment of which prevents dissatisfaction.

Instrumentality Workers' belief that attaining the required levels of performance will produce desired personal outcomes.

Intrinsic rewards Rewards that occur naturally as the product of engaging in a behavior.

Learned helplessness Workers' beliefs that they are incapable of producing a required performance or that the required performance, even if produced, would not lead to desired consequences; causes the worker to stop trying.

Learned needs Content theory of motivation proposing that three categories of needs—affiliation, power, and achievement—are learned, not innate, desires.

Motivators In two-factor theory, factors that provide worker satisfaction, such as the opportunity for achievement, responsibility, and recognition through work.

Organizational behavior modification (OB–Mod) Systematic application of simple conditioning and reinforcement theory principles to the management of organizational behavior.

Partial reinforcement Rewarding an appropriate behavior in a noncontinuous or variable manner, serving to develop desirable work habits that are more resistant to extinction than those acquired under continuous reinforcement.

Process theories of motivation Theories that focus on the process by which rewards direct behavior; for example, expectancy, equity, and reinforcement theories.

Punishment Administering an unpleasant consequence (for example, docking a worker's pay) in response to inappropriate work behaviors.

Reinforcement Reward for a behavior that increases the probability that the behavior will be repeated.

Self-efficacy Workers' beliefs that they can produce required levels of performance by engaging in appropriate work behaviors.

Successive approximation Reinforcing increasingly better attempts at a final desired behavior; may include shaping or chaining.

Superstitious behavior Belief that a behavior will be rewarded even though the behavior is in fact irrelevant.

Two-factor theory Content theory of motivation framed in terms of factors that affect work dissatisfaction and satisfaction: hygiene factors and motivators.

Valence The perceived value of a behavior's consequences.

Vicarious learning Acquiring desirable behaviors by observing the behaviors of other people; also called *social learning*.

Discussion Questions

1. Think about the phrase, "Spare the rod and spoil the child." Given your understanding of the principles of motivation, does this sound like a sensible approach to raising children? Does it sound like a sensible approach to directing workers?

2. Is compassion incompatible with the principles of motivation?

3. In what way might behaviorism be thought to be dehumanizing? Does adding the expectancy and equity qualifications to behaviorism produce a theory of worker motivation that is *less* dehumanizing?

4. One criticism of behaviorism in particular (and of the application of reinforcement theory to motivating workers in general) is that behaviorism is "manipulative." Are the tenets of behaviorism incompatible with free will and freedom of choice?

5. Compare and contrast the assumptions underlying the content theories of motivation discussed in this chapter. Why hasn't one of these theories simply "won out" as the best theory?

6. Why is conditioning (or behaviorism) an inadequate explanation of the acquisition of complex behaviors?

7. Why is it difficult to predict whether a worker's performance of appropriate work behaviors will be undermined by equity or expectancy concerns? How can a

manager prevent equity and expectancy concerns from undermining appropriate work behavior?

8. Why is it important to avoid the use of punishment as a means of directing work behaviors?

If You Want to Know More

Many reviews of each of the content theories of motivation are available. Wahba and Bridwell provide a critical analysis of Maslow's need hierarchy perspective in their article, "Maslow Reconsidered: A Review of Research on the Need Hierarchy Theory" (*Organizational Behavior and Human Performance* 15 [1976]: 212–240). Herzberg's theory is reviewed and critiqued in House and Wigdor's piece, "Herzberg's Dual-Factor Theory of Job Satisfaction and Motivation: A Review of the Evidence and a Criticism" (*Personal Psychology* 20 [4] [1967]: 369–380). A more general review and critique of content theories of motivation and their role in understanding work motivation is provided by Salancik and Pfeffer in, "An Examination of Need-Satisfaction Models of Job Attitudes" (*Administrative Science Quarterly* 22 [3] [1977]: 427–456).

The general principles of directing behavior discussed in this chapter are summarized in two books by Albert Bandura. *Principles of Behavior Modification* (New York: Holt, Rinehart and Winston, 1969) provides excellent discussions of the basic behaviorist principles of reinforcement theory. *Social Learning Theory* (Englewood Cliffs, N.J.: Prentice-Hall, 1977) provides a concise summary of research and theory on vicarious forms of learning and motivation. An application of reinforcement theory principles in an organization setting is detailed in an article by Fred Luthans and Jason Schweizer, "OB Mod in a Small Fac-

tory: How Behavior Modification Techniques Can Improve Total Organizational Effectiveness," in *Management Review* (September 1979): 43–50. The importance of supportive management practices to learning by employees *and their managers* is discussed in "Management Practices in Learning Organizations," by Mick McGill, John Slocum, and David Lei (*Organizational Dynamics* [Summer 1992]: 5–17).

The tenets of expectancy theory are developed by Vic Vroom in his book, *Work and Motivation* (New York: Wiley, 1964), and updated in Chapter 7 of Craig Pinder's book, *Work Motivation* (Glenview, Ill.: Scott-Foresman, 1984). An interesting application of the theory to life in organizations is provided by P. J. Andrisani in his article, "Internal and External Attitudes, Personal Initiative, and the Labor Market Experiences of Black and White Men" (*Journal of Human Resources* 12 [1977]: 308–388). The article discusses the relationship between self-efficacy and earning potential in males.

An update on the latest developments and issues in equity theory is provided in the book, *Organizational Justice: The Search for Fairness in the Workplace*, by Blair Sheppard, Roy Lewicki, and John Minton (New York: Lexington Books, 1992); and in Boris Kabanoff's article, "Equity, Equality, Power, and Conflict" (*Academy of Management Review*, 1991, 16 [2]: 416–441).

On Your Own

Assessing Your Work Motivation This exercise will give you two different ways to assess your own work needs and motivations. First, fill out the following questionnaire. Scoring instructions will be provided by your instructor. Next, take a look at the woman in the photograph. Is she relaxing, worrying, daydreaming? Just what is going through her mind? Write a one-paragraph description of what you think is going on in this picture.

This picture is an example of a projective test, in which the respondent *projects* his or her inner feelings into the description of the picture. There is no right answer to the question, "What is going through the young woman's mind?" The picture is intended to be ambiguous, so that the respondent's answer will reflect what is at the forefront of his or her mind. Projective tests have been used extensively to assess affiliation, power, and achievement motives.

Motivation Questionnaire You are to indicate how important each characteristic is to you. Answer according to your feelings about the most recent job you had or about the job you currently hold. Circle the number on the scale that represents your feeling—1 (very unimportant) to 7 (very important).

1. The feeling of self-esteem a person gets from being in that job 1 2 3 4 5 6 7
2. The opportunity for personal growth and development in that job 1 2 3 4 5 6 7
3. The prestige of the job inside the company (that is, regard received from others in the company) 1 2 3 4 5 6 7
4. The opportunity for independent thought and action in that job 1 2 3 4 5 6 7
5. The feeling of security in that job 1 2 3 4 5 6 7
6. The feeling of self-fulfillment a person gets from being in that position (that is, the feeling of being able to use one's own unique capabilities, realizing one's potential) 1 2 3 4 5 6 7
7. The prestige of the job outside the company (that is, the regard received from others not in the company) 1 2 3 4 5 6 7
8. The feeling of worthwhile accomplishment in that job 1 2 3 4 5 6 7
9. The opportunity in that job to give help to other people 1 2 3 4 5 6 7
10. The opportunity in that job for participation in the setting of goals 1 2 3 4 5 6 7
11. The opportunity in that job for participation in the determination of methods and procedures 1 2 3 4 5 6 7
12. The authority connected with the job 1 2 3 4 5 6 7
13. The opportunity to develop close friendships in the job 1 2 3 4 5 6 7

Now that you have completed the questionnaire, score it as follows:

Rating for question 5 = _____. Divide by 1 = _____ security.
Rating for questions 9 and 13 = _____. Divide by 2 = _____ social.
Rating for questions 1, 3, and 7 = _____. Divide by 3 = _____ esteem.
Rating for questions 4, 10, 11, and 12 = _____. Divide by 4 = _____ autonomy.
Rating for questions 2, 6, and 8 = _____. Divide by 3 = _____ self-actualization.

The instructor has national norm scores for presidents, vice-presidents, and upper middle-level, lower middle-level, and lower-level managers with which you can compare your *mean* importance scores. How do your scores compare with the scores of managers working in organizations?

Source: Lyman W. Porter, *Organizational Patterns of Managerial Job Attitudes* (New York: American Foundation for Management Research, 1964), 17, 19.

CLOSING CASE

CHAPTER 4

THE MANAGER'S MEMO

FROM: R. Prince, Manager, Word-Processing Center

TO: E. Switzer-Greer, Manager, Personnel Department

RE: Department Policies

Unfortunately, some members of my staff are less than conscientious when it comes to arriving on time in the morning and after their lunch break. In addition, some of the word-processing staff are not very motivated to do their best.

I think that the most effective way to reduce this problem would be a clear, simple, understandable policy to motivate the employees. I have developed the following guidelines for punctuality and output:

- All employees are to be punctual. At 8:30, which is starting time, I will patrol the word-processing department and make a note of anyone who is late. Anyone who is late three times will be laid off.
- All employees are to let me know when they go to lunch. They must be back at their desks within one hour. Anyone who is late three times will be laid off.
- Based on five years' experience with this department, a reasonable quantity of work is 15 pages a day of original typing or 30 pages of revisions. Employee's annual raises will be based on whether they exceed, meet, or fall below this level of output.
- Raises will be computed as follows: An employee who exceeds the standard level will receive a 6 percent raise. An employee who meets the standard will receive a 3 percent raise. An employee who falls below the standard level will receive no raise for the year.

I believe this four-point policy is easy to remember and understand. Please let me know whether you think the policy will be effective in motivating employees to be on time and to work diligently while they are here. Also, I'm interested in seeing any suggestions you have for improving this policy.

Case Discussion Questions

Assume you are the manager of the personnel department, and write a response to this memo. To support your position, refer to the motivation theories and research described in the chapter. In phrasing your response, keep in mind that you can benefit by reinforcing certain behaviors of the word-processing manager (such as seeking good policies and consulting you).

INDIVIDUAL DECISION MAKING

SHUTTLE PROBE THROWS SHOWER OF SPARKS ◆◆◆◆◆◆

The investigation into the explosion of the space shuttle Challenger became deeper, wider, and more embarrassing almost overnight as threats of subpoenas and talk of cover-ups ricocheted through Washington. The search for the cause of the January 28 disaster yielded shocking disclosures that abruptly shifted the focus from technical failure to human error. Testimony and documents appeared to point to critical gaps in the chain of command at the National Aeronautics and Space Administration (NASA).

Pronouncing himself both "surprised and appalled" at a decision-making process that may have been flawed, presidential commission chairman William Rogers issued directives that heightened the suspicion: All NASA personnel involved in the decision to launch Challenger were removed from the space agency's own internal probe. . . .

Among commission members, there remained little question that a technical failure caused the fatal explosion. . . . Still, there were increased fears that NASA officials may have overridden strong objections from engineers—who were concerned by potentially lethal faults in the O-ring seals of the booster rockets—and ordered an over-hasty launch of Challenger. Some even hinted that NASA may have tried to mask any chain-of-command error in the decision to press ahead with the launch.

The most damning testimony yet came from engineers at Morton Thiokol, manufacturers of the solid rockets that power the shuttle during its first two minutes and eight seconds of flight. In interviews, Thiokol engineers told of trying to talk their superiors out of giving an "all clear" for the launch amid an unusual Florida cold snap, yet watching as NASA "bullied" company officials into giving a "go" for the launch.

"I fought like hell to stop that launch," one engineer told National Public Radio. "I'm so torn up inside I can hardly talk about it." Another said he was so worried about the O-rings that on the eve of the launch, "I kept having fantasies that at the moment of ignition, the shuttle would blow up instantly."

In talks with Lawrence Mulloy, chief of the solid-rocket-booster program at the Marshall Space Flight Center in Alabama, Thiokol engineers angrily insisted that NASA wait until temperatures climbed into the 50s before launching. They told NPR that Mulloy responded, "My God, Thiokol, when do you want me to launch? Next April?" After hours of discussion, top Morton Thiokol officials overruled their engineers and signed a launch approval.

NASA has not revealed details of the launch discussions, except to confirm that the three highest-ranking NASA officials were not informed about the debate over the low temperatures.

NASA itself began what some observers called a classic response of a bureaucracy under fire: It reorganized. A respected 20-year agency veteran, general manager Phil Culbertson, was fired by NASA chief William Graham. . . .

NASA's Houston center, meanwhile, brought in a psychologist to help employees deal with their worries about an agency suddenly adrift. Declared former astronaut Joe Allen, now with Space Industries, Inc., in Houston, "Any government agency in difficult times needs real strong leadership. These are very difficult times. The fact of the matter is, it isn't clear who is running the agency."

Source: *US News & World Report*, March 3, 1986, 6–7.

INTRODUCTION ◆◆◆◆◆◆

Even though the Challenger accident happened in 1986, many of us can remember the event in great detail. Was the decision to launch the Challenger that cold morning a good decision or a bad one? One might suggest that because of the outcome and the death of the six astronauts and Christa McAuliffe, the decision was clearly the wrong one. Judging a decision based on what eventually resulted from it may be one way to evaluate the quality of decisions. However, relying only on the outcomes requires us to hold ourselves or our subordinates responsible for factors that we simply cannot control. It may be that the choice of a particular option is the correct one—at the time the choice is made—but because of unforeseeable events, the outcome of that decision is bad. Employees in all organizations, whether they work for Morton Thiokol, NASA, or other companies, are making decisions that have a significant impact on the very viability of their employers. In this chapter, we will examine the processes of individual choice and decision making and the psychological and cognitive factors that go into the selection of one choice over another.

The complete cycle of organizational decision making is illustrated in Figure 5–1. Individual decision making is one component of the larger context of organizational decision making. The four components of organizational decision making can be described as follows:

1. Decision making begins when individuals perceive a discrepancy between how their organization could or should be and how it actually is. This perceived difference between what is and what could or should be precipitates decision making and action.

| FIGURE 5-1 | ▶ Organizational Decision Making |

Organizational decision making is cyclical. Individuals (1) think and (2) choose. Individual choices add up to (3) organizational choices, which invite (4) environmental responses. These responses in turn influence individual thought.

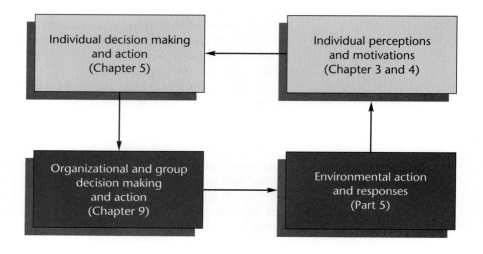

2. Individuals respond to these perceived discrepancies by making decisions and taking actions. This chapter focuses on the nature and importance of these individual decisions in the larger organizational context.
3. The process through which individuals' choices and actions come together to produce group or organizational choices and actions—group decision making, for instance—is the focus of Part 3. It should be noted that at the group or organizational level, good decisions do not always produce good actions. When lots of people are involved, even good decisions can be implemented incorrectly.
4. Finally, the larger environment in which the organization functions responds to behavioral changes. The importance of the environment and its responses to and influences on organizations is the focus of Part 5. These responses by the environment provide inputs that lead individuals to new perceptions, choices, and actions.

MAKING DECISIONS

The focus of this chapter is the individual decision-making component of organizational decision making. Decisions are responses to problems—differences between what is and what could or should be. Problems may vary in importance from figuring out which job you should accept after graduation to deciding which brand of toothpaste you should buy.

Five Steps of Decision Making	**Recognition and Definition of the Problem** Perceiving a discrepancy between what is and what could or should be is problem recognition, and provides the foundation for all individual decision making. Problem recognition requires the decision maker to (1) understand goals and objectives (either of the organization or of the individual), (2) monitor accomplishment of those goals (performance discrepancies), and (3) evaluate the importance of the discrepancy. Problem recognition is a critical aspect of individual decision making. If a manager identifies the wrong problem or erroneously evaluates its importance, then the final decision will not address the real concerns of the organization.

Defining the problem correctly is critical to successful decision making. Because problem recognition is a *perceptual* process, managers may not come up with accurate assessments of the problems at hand, which gets decision making off on the wrong foot. Managers often make poor decisions because (1) they allow available solutions to define the problem, (2) they focus on aspects of problems they know they can solve and ignore the larger, more difficult issues confronting them, or (3) they diagnose problems in terms of the most obvious symptoms.[1] In other words, decision makers often get sidetracked by tangential aspects of the real problem and by their beliefs about what problems they know they can solve.

Information Search   If a perceived discrepancy is important, then the decision maker will implement a second stage of the decision-making process: determining why the problem occurred. The decision maker must gather information about the problem or discrepancy and possible ways to solve it. At this point, the decision maker should have a clear understanding of the problem and have collected sufficient information to begin the third phase of the decision-making process.

Alternative Generation   The third phase of individual decision making is developing or identifying potential courses of action. This phase requires that the information previously gathered be transformed into a set of alternatives. Identifying alternatives is a difficult task; it requires a considerable amount of creativity and mental flexibility. Often managers spend too little time on this phase because they are willing to choose among alternatives before they have generated a diverse range of options. Theoretically, managers should continue to generate alternatives until the potential for improving on them is too small to justify the added expense. More often than not, managers are willing to stop generating alternatives at the first sign of a potentially acceptable solution.

Evaluation and Choice   When a sufficient number of alternatives have been identified, the decision maker must evaluate them and make a choice. This evaluation can be accomplished in one of two ways. Either the decision maker can compare each alternative to every other alternative, or the decision maker can compare each alternative to the desired goal. While both methods have their strong points, the more clearly defined the problem and its antecedents (or causes) and the more specific the alternatives, the better the eventual choice.

---

[1]G. Huber, *Managerial Decision Making* (Glenview, Ill.: Scott, Foresman, 1980).

Implementation and Assessment   Once a choice has been made, the decision maker must implement the decision. While the choice process is important, decisions are worthless unless implemented. Individual decision makers are remiss if they do nothing to implement a decision after having devoted time, energy, and organizational resources to identify an appropriate course of action. However, decision makers also may be remiss if they make no attempt to assess the appropriateness of the chosen course of action. After implementing the choice, the decision maker can monitor the outcomes to determine what changes have occurred. Did the discrepancy between desired and actual states disappear? If not, perhaps the real problem was not solved. The problem information may have been incomplete, or the wrong alternative was selected. Do changes need to be made in how alternatives are evaluated? Perhaps the decision was not correctly implemented. Regardless of the cause, if the decision does not resolve the discrepancy, then the process may begin again. Figure 5–2 illustrates this complete cycle of individual decision making.

Rationality and Bounded Rationality	The five-phase cycle of individual decision making is often referred to as the "rational model." **Rationality** suggests that a decision has been based on the careful and calculated understanding of action alternatives and their consequences. In Western society, the term *rationality* also suggests high-quality decision making uninfluenced by irrelevant or fleeting considerations.

FIGURE 5–2   ▶ Individual Decision-Making Process

Individual decision making, like organizational decision making, can be represented as a feedback cycle. The individual defines the problem and collects information to generate alternatives. When a choice is made and implemented, the outcome provides feedback about whether the problem was defined correctly, and whether it was solved or needs further attention.

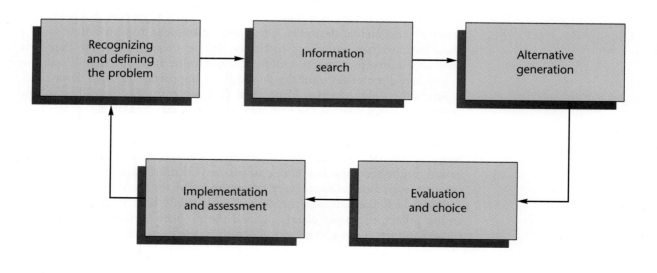

While this five-phase rational decision-making process represents an ideal to which decision makers aspire, it is also a difficult (if not impossible) ideal to achieve. To be a rational decision maker, a manager would have to compile a complete listing of all alternatives and their consequences. The manager would have to know how the world (or at least the organization and its environment) would be affected by each alternative. Even for apparently simple decisions of the organization, this places substantial demands on the information collection, storage, and integration powers of individual decision makers—such great demands that the information-processing requirements of rationality typically exceed the capabilities of the human mind. Thus, while rationality is an attractive ideal, actual decision making typically falls short of rationality in a number of ways:[2]

1. The rational ideal requires complete knowledge and anticipation of the consequences that will follow each choice. In practice, knowledge is always incomplete.
2. Since the consequences of actions occur in the future, they can only be imagined. In attaching preference or value to a particular outcome, then, decision makers must rely on imagination rather than experience. The attractiveness of a consequence can be anticipated only imperfectly through imagination. Only by actually experiencing the consequence can we know our preference for that consequence.
3. Rationality requires a choice among all possible alternatives. But the number of alternative actions in any situation is unlimited. In practice, decision makers have the time to consider only a few of the infinite possibilities.
4. Human decision makers can retain only a relatively small amount of information in memory.
5. Limited human information-processing capabilities constrain the ability of decision makers to perform the necessary calculations (even given all the necessary information) to determine the best alternative.
6. Rationality assumes that decision makers have a stable, specifiable, and consistent hierarchy of needs and motivations. As noted in Chapter 4, however, human needs and goals change over time, and individuals and organizations often simultaneously pursue apparently incompatible objectives.

Given these limitations on any decision maker's abilities, it should not be surprising that actual decision making often falls short of the rational ideal. However, because rationality is such an attractive goal, individuals are hesitant to give up their perceptions of themselves as rational decision makers. Much of the research on managers as decision makers has been based on managers' self-reports of how they claim to make decisions. Managers typically describe the process by which they make decisions as closely following the five-phase rational cycle of individual decision making.

When actual managerial decision behavior has been systematically observed, however, quite a different picture has emerged. In contrast with the perception that managers sit in their offices, carefully consider information and alternatives, and make calculated choices, observation indicates that managers'

---

[2]J. G. March and H. A. Simon, *Organizations* (New York: John Wiley & Sons, 1958).

decision-making processes are hardly ideal. One study found that in making decisions, managers tend to avoid hard (systematic or analytical) data and to rely on softer forms of information, such as gossip or speculation.[3] Since managers make hundreds of decisions daily, it seems likely that even approximating the systematic and time-consuming demands of rational decision making is beyond reach. A different decision-making model is required to capture the actual decision behavior of managers.

The rational model of decision making defines how a decision should be made, rather than describing how managers actually make decisions. In his Nobel Prize-winning work, economist Herbert Simon suggested that individual decision making is bounded in its ability to approach rationality by the limits of the human information-processing apparatus. Given these limitations, Simon argued that prescriptions for how decisions should be made (such as the five-step rational ideal pictured in Figure 5–2) are not nearly so useful for understanding and predicting actual individual decision behavior as are descriptions of how decisions are made.[4] Simon's notion of **bounded rationality** is a descriptive model of individual decision making. Bounded rationality diverges from the rational ideal in four important ways. Bounded rationality characterizes actual individual decision-making behavior as based on a limited perspective, the sequential evaluation of alternatives, satisficing, and the use of judgmental heuristics.

Limited Perspective   First, bounded rationality assumes that the information-processing demands of actual decision makers are managed by limiting the scope of decisions. Not all alternatives are considered, and not all goals are accommodated. Instead, the focus of the choice is limited to a manageable subset of goals, alternatives, and consequences. For example, bounded rationality assumes that a decision maker may simultaneously pursue multiple and conflicting goals. To reconcile the different goals, decision making is compartmentalized. Decisions at one point in time may attempt to achieve one goal; a second decision at some other point in time may help to achieve another, mutually exclusive, goal.

Consider, for example, a department head who issues a travel policy at the beginning of the fiscal year. The policy states that reimbursement for all company-sponsored travel will be limited to $500. The policy is designed to promote departmental budgetary goals. However, two weeks after the policy is put in place, an employee known for his "squeaky wheel" behavior requests reimbursement of $650 for a trip. After three meetings with the employee, the department head finally approves the $650 request. The decision satisfies the decision maker's need to limit further interactions with the troublesome employee—an important goal—but at the cost of violating the first goal of careful fiscal management. Limited-scope decision making reduces information search and processing demands and makes decision making manageable. But it has its costs.

[3] H. Mintzberg, "The Manager's Job: Folklore and Fact," *Harvard Business Review* (July-August 1975): 49–61; and "How Top Managers Manage Their Time," *Fortune*, June 4, 1990, 250–262.

[4] H. A. Simon, *Administrative Behavior* (New York: MacMillan, 1957).

Sequential Alternative Evaluation   The second way in which bounded rationality deviates from the normative model of decision making is in evaluation of alternatives. Rather than simultaneously considering all possible alternatives and their consequences and choosing the best possible alternative, decision makers evaluate alternatives sequentially. For example, two alternatives are considered and the better one is chosen. That alternative may then be compared to another alternative. This "pair-wise" comparison requires considerably less mental activity than comparing a number of alternatives simultaneously. In fact, a study of personnel-selection decision making found that individuals who evaluated candidates in a sequential manner took significantly less time than those who evaluated the same number of candidates simultaneously.[5]

Satisficing   Theoretically, a decision maker could continue making pair-wise comparisons of all possible alternatives until the optimal solution emerged. However, given the number of decisions that need to be made and the amount of time that would be consumed in such extended comparisons, another goal— taking timely action—must take precedence. Since the costs of finding an optimal course of action are too dear, decision makers must be willing to forego the best solution in favor of one that is acceptable or reasonable. That is, decision makers **satisfice** (a term derived from the words satisfy and suffice). They do not examine all possible alternatives. They look at a small number of familiar or likely solutions and choose one that produces an outcome that is "good enough."

Judgmental Heuristics and Biases   The fourth way in which bounded rationality differs from the rational ideal is its use of judgmental heuristics. **Judgmental heuristics** are rules of thumb, or shortcuts, that reduce the information-processing demands for decision makers. Judgmental heuristics summarize past experiences and provide an easy method to evaluate the present. Judgmental heuristics facilitate individual decision making by substituting rules or "standard operating procedures" for complex information collection and calculation. For the most part, heuristics save considerable mental activity. However, in certain situations, using these cognitive heuristics can result in systematically biased outcomes. To distinguish this misapplication of cognitive heuristics from their appropriate use, we will use the term *cognitive bias* to refer to the inappropriate use of cognitive heuristics that results in systematically biased decisions. Two examples of judgmental heuristics (or biases) are availability and representativeness, which will be discussed in the following sections.

Availability   Decision makers often assess the frequency or likelihood of an event's occurrence by how easily they can remember it.[6] This "rule" is based on the notion that frequently occurring events are familiar to us and, thus, are easy to recall. This heuristic is useful because familiar events often are more

---

[5]V. L. Huber, M. A. Neale, and G. B. Northcraft, "Decision Bias and Personnel Selection Strategies," *Organizational Behavior and Human Decision Processes* 40 (1987): 136–147.

[6]A. Tversky and D. Kahneman, "Judgment under Uncertainty: Heuristics and Biases," *Science* 185 (1974): 453–463.

easily recalled than less frequent events. However, biased outcomes result from dependence on this rule when the ease of memory recall is influenced by factors unrelated to the frequency of an event's occurrence. If an event evokes emotions, is vivid, easily imagined, or specific and concrete, it will be more "available" from memory than will equally occurring events that are unemotional, bland, vague, or difficult to imagine.

Problems 1, 3, and 4 in Figure 5–3 all provide examples of the use of the **availability bias.** For all three of these problems, most people chose option A. B is really the correct choice, however. The corporations represented by answer B in Problem 1 have over twice the sales volume of the companies listed in answer A. Because the first group contains consumer firms, they are more likely to be familiar to us as consumers. The second (B) group contains industrial firms or holding companies that are less familiar to us. If the availability bias did not influence us, our exposure to these two groups of companies would not alter our judgments.

For Problem 3, driving a car on a 400-mile trip is actually much riskier than flying 400 miles on a commercial airliner. However, media attention to

---

FIGURE 5–3 ▶ Decision-Making Quiz

1. The following 9 corporations were ranked by *Fortune* magazine to be among the 500 largest United States–based firms, according to sales volume for 1987:

   Group A: Gillette, Coca-Cola, Lever Brothers, Apple Computers, and Hershey Foods
   Group B: Weyerhaeuser, Northrup, CPC International, and Champion International

   Which group (A or B) had the largest total sales for the organizations listed?
2. The best student in the graduate organizational-behavior class writes poetry and is rather shy and small in stature. What was the student's undergraduate major: (a) Chinese studies or (b) psychology?
3. Which is riskier: (a) flying in a commercial airliner on a 400-mile trip or (b) driving a car on a 400-mile trip?
4. Are there more words in the English language that (a) begin with the letter "r" or (b) have "r" as the third letter?
5. On one day in a large metropolitan hospital, eight births were recorded by gender in the order of their arrival. Which of the following orders of births (B = boy, G = girl) was most likely to be reported?
   a. B B B B B B B B
   b. B B B B G G G G
   c. B G B B G G G B
6. A large car manufacturer has recently been hit with a number of economic difficulties, and it appears as if three plants need to be closed and 6,000 employees laid off. The vice-president of production has been exploring ways to avoid this crisis. She has developed two plans:
   a. Plan A will save one of the three plants and 2,000 jobs.
   b. Plan B has a one-third probability of saving all three plants and all 6,000 jobs, but it has a two-thirds probability of saving no plants and no jobs.
   Which plan would you select?

Source: M. H. Bazerman, *Judgment in Managerial Decision Making*, 2nd ed. (New York: Wiley, 1990).

airplane crashes has made them quite vivid in our memories. Little attention is given to automobile accidents, probably because they are so common.

The common response to Problem 4 is that more words in the English language begin with "r" than have "r" as the third letter. In fact, we can draw up a rather extensive list of words that begin with the letter "r." However, considerably more words have "r" as their third letter. In deciding how to answer this question, you probably tried to come up with a list of words that begin with the letter "r" and another list of words that have "r" as the third letter. Because of the way in which we store information in memory, it is much easier to generate examples of words beginning with "r." If we think of our memory as analogous to a card catalogue in the library, it is very easy to come up with all sorts of "r" words (just as it would be easy to generate from the card catalogue listing authors whose last name was "Woolf"). The card catalogue would be of little use to us in trying to identify words with "r" as the third letter, just as it would not help in trying to find authors whose first name was Virginia. Neither the catalogue nor our memories is designed to store and retrieve information in that way.

Representativeness   In Problem 2 in Figure 5–3, the most common response is that the undergraduate major of the student was Chinese studies. However, the correct response is that the individual majored in psychology. In selecting the first option, important base-rate information has been ignored. A base-rate probability is an overall probability that something will occur, all other things being equal. In this case, the base-rate probability that any MBA student is a psychology major is higher than the probability that the student is a Chinese studies major simply because overall there are a lot more psychology than Chinese studies majors. Thus, the rational choice is psychology because it so dominates Chinese studies. However, individuals who write poetry and are short in stature, studious, and shy more closely resemble our stereotypes of a Chinese person or the type of person who would be likely to major in Chinese studies. That individual, then, is representative of our stereotype. Thus, we decide that Chinese studies must be the major of the best student, regardless of the fact that there are many more psychology majors than Chinese studies majors.

Problem 5 provides another example of the **representativeness** bias. The most common response to this problem is that option c is the most likely birth order to be observed. The common reason given for this choice is that the third option looks random. The first and second options are too ordered and, thus, seem highly unlikely to occur. The correct response is that all three of the options are equally likely to occur. The problem here is that we believe that a sequence of independent events (such as eight births) generated from a random process should resemble the essential characteristics of a random process, even when the sequence is too short for that process to express itself statistically. This is referred to as the "law of small numbers." Decision makers expect a few examples of a random event to behave in the same way as large numbers of the event.

In large samples of births, the births of girls and boys occur about equally. However, there is no reason why one should not expect a run of eight boy births or four boy births followed by four girl births in a small sample. The premise that randomness has some specific order (or specific lack of order) requires the assumption that there is some relationship or dependence between one occurrence and the next. Yet the gender of Mother A's baby has no effect on the gender of Mother B's.

This belief that events have some sort of memory is rampant in the bias known as the *gambler's fallacy*. Assuming a fair (untampered with) roulette wheel, if the ball landed on a red number ten times in a row, how would you bet (red or black) on the next spin of the wheel? Many decision makers would bet on a black number, feeling that a black number was somehow due. Since there are an equal number of black and red numbers, the objective probability of the ball's landing on a red or black number must be exactly the same. The ball does not remember where it has landed in the past. While you may remember where the ball landed on the last spin of the wheel, from the ball's perspective each event is completely independent from the next. When examined in detail, the gambler's fallacy is obviously wrong, but it does have considerable intuitive appeal.

Decision Making Under Uncertainty

In addition to the information-processing demands it places on decision makers, rationality also assumes a complete understanding of means-ends relationships—what consequences occur as a result of actions. The bounded rationality perspective suggests that decision makers cannot possibly consider, evaluate, and integrate all means-ends information into decisions. Uncertainty raises an additional problem for decision makers: knowledge about means-ends relationships is often only fuzzy at best.

In Chapter 1, uncertainty was defined as "not knowing for sure." The terms **uncertainty** and **risk** both suggest that the consequences of an action can be known only in terms of a perceived likelihood of occurrence. A particular action may produce a desired consequence, but at the risk of other consequences. The consequences of the action are uncertain. Most decisions must incorporate this notion of risk or uncertainty. The number of certain means-ends relationships is very small.

Although individuals may wish their lives were filled with certainty, most of us are constantly faced with decisions among risky alternatives. Without complete knowledge, then, even the best plans and decisions are implemented at the risk of poor outcomes. Though we may try to ignore the risk inherent in our daily decisions, we often express our uncertainty about outcomes, saying "Chances are," "It seems likely that," "I think," and "I bet." A more formal way to express our uncertainty is through probabilities.

Probability (a statistical term) is a measure of the likelihood that a particular event will occur. Our confidence in a particular probability can be very high. For example, with a fair coin, most people would agree that there is a 50 percent probability of a tossed coin coming up heads. However, few people would agree on the probability that the Dow-Jones Industrial Average will be above 5100 on March 30, 1996. The difference between these two situations is that for the Dow-Jones average, we are forecasting the future without being able to understand or specify everything that could happen to affect it. When dealing with cards, coins, gambling, and games, it is much easier to produce accurate probabilities of an event's occurrence because we can identify all possible outcomes and all the processes that should affect them. The probability of a particular event's occurrence may be low, but it is knowable. For example, the probabilities of being dealt certain hands in a poker game are illustrated in Figure 5–4.

For some decisions, the amount of risk and uncertainty are well defined. The probability of being dealt a particular hand of cards, for instance, can be determined ahead of time. The probability that a new product line will be successful cannot be determined exactly.

Reactions to Risk   Decision makers' reactions to risk and uncertainty often do not reflect careful consideration of the consequences of alternatives. The rational ideal for decision making under uncertainty is to select the alternative with the highest expected value. The **expected value** of an action is the value assigned to each possible consequence of the action, multiplied by the probabilities that each of these possible consequences will occur.

As an example of expected value, imagine that you are deciding whether to insure your personal computer against theft. The insurance company's brochure indicates that the company will reimburse you for the full replacement cost of your computer less a $50 deductible charge if it is stolen. The cost of this insurance is $50 per year. If someone steals your computer and you have insurance, you lose $100. (The insurance company will replace your computer, but you

FIGURE 5–4	▶ **Chances of Being Dealt Different Poker Hands**

In poker, the probability of being dealt a pair (two of the same card—for instance, two kings) is one in 2.5, or 40 percent. If you were offered $1 if you could deal yourself one pair, your expected value would be ($1 × .4) + ($0 × .6) = $.40.

Straight flush	1 in	64,974
Four of a kind	1 in	4,165
Full house	1 in	694
Flush	1 in	509
Straight	1 in	256
Three of a kind	1 in	48
Two pair	1 in	21
One pair	1 in	2.5
No pair	1 in	2

Source: Excerpt from *Oswald Jacoby on Poker* by Oswald Jacoby, copyright 1940, 1947, 1981 by Doubleday, a division of Bantam, Doubleday, Dell Publishing Company, Inc. Used by permission of the publisher.

will still be out the $50 deductible and the $50 cost of the insurance.) If someone steals your computer and you have no insurance, you will lose $3,500 (the cost of replacing the computer). If you buy the insurance and no one steals your computer, you will lose $50 (the insurance premium). If no one steals your computer and you are not insured, you lose nothing. Should you purchase the insurance for your new $3,500 computer? The payoff matrix for this decision is presented in Figure 5–5.

At this point, you still do not have sufficient information to answer the question. What is missing is information concerning the probability that your computer will be stolen. After doing a little research, you discover that there is a 1-in-100 chance that your computer will be stolen. Armed with this information, you can calculate the expected value of buying and not buying insurance:

$$\text{Expected Value } (EV)_{\text{(buy)}}$$
$$= P_{\text{(stolen)}} \times \text{Net loss}_{\text{(stolen)}} + P_{\text{(not stolen)}} \times \text{Loss}_{\text{(not stolen)}}$$
$$= (.01)(-\$100) + (.99)(-\$50)$$
$$= -\$50.50$$
$$EV_{\text{(do not buy)}}$$
$$= P_{\text{(stolen)}} \times \text{Loss}_{\text{(stolen)}} + P_{\text{(not stolen)}} \times \text{Loss}_{\text{(not stolen)}}$$
$$= (.01)(-\$3,500) + (.99)(\$0)$$
$$= -\$35.$$

Based upon these calculations and the rule of choosing the option with the greatest expected value, you should not buy the insurance. In the long run (which may include losing an occasional computer to thieves), you will come out ahead by not buying the insurance.

Do decision makers rely on expected-value calculations when they make decisions? For the decision presented in Figure 5–6, the "rational" decision is to select the alternative with the highest expected value. For option A, the expected value (or EV) of taking the $10 million is the outcome ($10 million) multiplied by the probability of that outcome (100%), or $10 million. For option B, the expected value is the sum of the two possible outcomes ($22 million and $0 million) each multiplied by the probability of their occurrence (50% and 50%), or:

$$EV = (\$22 \text{ million} \times 50\%) + (\$0 \text{ million} \times 50\%) = \$11 \text{ million.}$$

FIGURE 5–5   ▶ **Payoff Matrix for Computer Insurance Purchase**

Insurance is a way of minimizing risk when outcomes are uncertain and stakes are high. As shown in this figure, a person who buys insurance spends a little to avoid losing a lot.

Choices	Stolen	Not Stolen
Buy insurance	−$100	−$50
Do not buy insurance	−$3,500	0

FIGURE 5–6	▶ Framing the Decision

Some choices bring out our aversion to risk; others, our attraction to it. When we have sure gains to protect (as in scenario 1), we are likely to avoid risks. When we are facing possible losses (as in scenario 2), we are likely to take chances to avoid these losses or break even.

1. You can (A) have $10 million for sure ($EV$ = $10 million) or (B) flip a fair coin and receive $22 million if heads appears and nothing if tails appears (EV = $11 million). The simple decision rule would select the "B" option. What would you do?

2. You are being sued for $5,000 and estimate a 50 percent chance of losing the case (EV = −$2,500). The other side, however, is willing to accept an out-of-court settlement of $2,400 ($EV$ = $2,400). Ignoring attorney fees, court costs, aggravation, and such, would you (A) fight the case or (B) settle out of court? The simple decision rule would lead you to settle out of court.

Source: M. H. Bazerman, *Judgment in Managerial Decision Making* (New York: Wiley, 1989).

Surprisingly, the most common response to this choice is the A option, even though A results in a smaller expected value. One explanation for this is that the typical decision maker is not **risk neutral.** Choosing the option with the highest expected value is a risk-neutral decision—it assumes that the decision maker is indifferent between risky and certain outcomes if they have the same expected value. However, in many situations, **risk averse** decision makers ignore the expected-value solution and choose the option in which there is less risk. The decision maker is willing to pay a premium (the $1 million difference in the first situation) to avoid the risk of the $22 million gamble. Paying such a premium to avoid risk is a common practice. The enormous size of the insurance industry is evidence of our willingness to pay money to avoid risks.[7]

Risk-seeking behavior is just the opposite. That is, a decision maker is risk seeking when he or she pays a premium to experience risk. Participating in gambling activities in Las Vegas is an example of risk-seeking behavior. Since objectively the odds of winning money are in favor of the "house," the risk-neutral (or expected-value) decision would be not to play. Given the odds and the risk inherent in the situation, the risk-averse decision would also be not to play. However, a visit to any of the casinos there reveals a large number of individuals who have made the risk-seeking choice to play. In making decisions, the risk or uncertainty that accompanies decision options influences the final selection. In fact, we all know people we would categorize as risk seeking or risk averse. However, it is much more difficult to know whether we ourselves are risk seeking or risk averse. That is, we can think of situations in which we take risks and situations in which we avoid risks. We may operate hang gliders and fly airplanes as hobbies yet religiously wear automobile seat belts and pay our life, health, liability, dental, pet, and credit-card insurance premiums.

What is an appropriate level of risk taking within an organization? Different constituency groups in an organization may lobby for different risk attitudes on the part of the manager. Stockholders or owners of the company may have their own view of appropriate levels of risk. Lower-level managers generally are more risk averse than upper-level managers. Further, managers indicate that

---

[7]C. Holloway, *Decision Making under Uncertainty: Models and Choices* (Englewood Cliffs, N.J.: Prentice-Hall, 1979).

their risk strategies mirror their best interests rather than the best interests of the company.[8] The credit department of an organization may be more risk seeking than the manufacturing department.

How, then, can an organization influence the risk strategies of its managers in the direction of the company's best interests? It may be that managers take risks inconsistent with the company's risk attitude because they are unaware of the organization's risk policy. In such cases, communicating the level of acceptable risk to the employees may generate a more consistent risk policy within the organization.

Second, managers may accept levels of risk that are in their own best interest (and not the company's) because of the incentive structure of the organization. If incentives are based on the individual's success and not the company's success, then it is little wonder that individuals make decisions consistent with their own best interests. The task here is to make the best interests of the organization and the best interests of the individual consistent. Chapter 13 will consider in detail the importance and impact of incentive systems on organizational performance.

Framing   One judgmental heuristic that decision makers use to deal with risk is **framing**. In Problem 6 in Figure 5–3, the typical response is to select Plan A. However, let's reconsider the problem, replacing the two original choices with the following choices:

c.   Plan C will result in the loss of two of the three plants and 4,000 jobs.
d.   Plan D has a two-thirds probability of resulting in the loss of all three plants and all 6,000 jobs but has a one-third probability of losing no plants and no jobs.

Which plan would you select? If you closely compare plans A and B to plans C and D, you will discover that they are *exactly* the same. Plans A and C both result in the loss of two plants (and 4,000 jobs) and the saving of one plant (and 2,000 jobs). Plans B and D both represent a gamble—a 1-in-3 chance that all the plants and jobs will be saved and a 2-in-3 chance that all the plants and jobs will be lost. Yet, when individuals see only Plans C and D, they typically choose Plan D. Although both sets of plans represent the same two options, changing the descriptions from potential gains (jobs and plants saved) to potential losses (jobs and plants lost) is sufficient to alter the average plan selection from the risk-averse choice of Plan A to the risky choice of Plan D. Why?

There is a fundamental difference in decision makers' responses to gains and losses. When we are confronted with the choice of losing $10 for certain or taking a gamble with an equal expected value, we are likely to take the gamble rather than incur the pain of losing for certain. Gains, however, are a different story. When we must choose between that $10 for certain or a gamble with an equivalent expected value, we will typically choose the certain $10. Consistent with the old adage that "a bird in the hand is worth two in the bush," we prefer choices that are certain (risk averse) when we can gain. Having that bird safely under control is worth more to us than the potential of twice as many birds. Further, it seems the pain associated with losing, say, $10 is greater

---

[8]K. MacCrimmon and D. Wehrung, *Taking Risks: The Management of Uncertainty* (New York: The Free Press, 1986).

than the pleasure associated with gaining that $10. Thus, as the potential losses get larger, we are likely to become more and more risky in our behavior. Conversely, as the potentials gains get larger, we are likely to forego more and more of them for the comfort of certainty.

Escalation   The impact of framing can be quite costly to organizations, as demonstrated in the following example.[9]

You are a bank loan officer. A seemingly good credit risk comes to you and asks for a $50,000 business start-up loan. After careful review of the application, you personally make the decision to grant the loan. Six months later, the same applicant shows up in your office and says, "I have bad news and I have good news. The bad news is that the company is having problems. In fact, without additional help, we are going under and you will lose the $50,000. The good news is that I am quite confident that if you lend us an additional $50,000, we can turn the whole thing around." Do you lend him an additional $50,000?

In this situation, the odds are that you will seriously consider the additional $50,000 loan. Why? One way to look at this situation is from the perspective of a negative frame. In this case, the loan officer is likely to view the situation as a choice between two options: (1) not loaning the additional money and losing the $50,000 for certain, or (2) loaning a second $50,000 to the business in hopes that it will survive to repay the loan and the interest. Viewing this scenario as a choice between (1) a loss for certain and (2) a gamble in which you may not lose is likely to induce you to make the second loan. Committing additional resources to failing causes based on the (slim) hope that there will be a dramatic change is called **escalation.**[10] Thus, escalation is continuing a commitment to a previous decision, when a "rational" decision maker would withdraw.

Examples of this sort of behavior are commonplace. Do you put more money into the repair of your old car? How long do you wait once you have been put on "hold"? How long do you wait for an elevator? How long do you persist in getting a degree once you realize there is no hope of getting a job after graduation? How many more resources (buying a house, having a baby) do you commit to a failing marriage? How many more soldiers was President Johnson willing to commit to what was obviously the losing proposition of the Vietnam War?

For escalation to exist, there must have been a previous commitment of resources. Because these resources were committed in the past, they are unrecoverable and should be ignored. That is, they are "sunk," or historical, costs. Objectively, a decision maker should be concerned only with the future costs and benefits associated with a particular course of action. Thus, it does not matter if you have invested 10 years in your current relationship; the primary consideration should be the future costs versus the future benefits of remaining in the relationship. This future-oriented perspective is likely to lead to a more optimal outcome.

In accounting, one of the major prescriptions is to ignore sunk costs. While we are involved in accounting tasks, it is quite easy to implement this rule.

[9]M. H. Bazerman, *Judgment in Managerial Decision Making* (New York: John Wiley & Sons, 1989).

[10]B. M. Staw, "Knee-Deep in the Big Muddy: A Study of Escalating Commitment to a Chosen Course of Action," *Organizational Behavior and Human Performance* 16 (1976): 27–44.

Decision escalation involves committing additional resources to a failing cause in hopes that the situation will improve. A loan officer might be tempted to provide additional funds to a failing business in hopes of recouping previous losses, where a "rational" decision maker would not.

However, when we are confronted with similar unrecoverable costs in our daily lives, we tend to include them in our mental calculations. In avoiding a certain loss, a decision maker may discount the negative information received in an attempt to justify the initial decision. In committing additional resources, the decision maker may believe that the downturn is temporary—that contributing more resources increases the chance that the initial decision will be proved correct. But such rationalizations may be very risky to the health of an organization.

An example of escalation is provided in the "FOCUS ON: Escalation." Victims of escalation do not include opportunity costs in their mental arithmetic. Opportunity costs are the costs of inefficient use of resources. Unlike out-of-pocket costs, which are very vivid and salient in nature, opportunity costs are passive and abstract. These costs are incurred by the passage of time. Ignoring them makes the option of continuing a failing project appear more positive and the option of abandoning the project appear more negative.[11]

While escalation is a very insidious process, the following recommendations can reduce its influence:[12]

1. Set limits on your involvement and commitment in advance, and stick to those limits.
2. Avoid looking to other people to see what you should do, since they are likely to be escalating their commitment inappropriately.
3. Actively reevaluate why you are continuing your commitment (escalation is often a function of impression management—we want other people to think that we know what we are doing).
4. Remind yourself of the costs involved; the opportunity costs or the costs of continuing are often ignored.

---

[11] G. B. Northcraft and M. A. Neale, "Opportunity Costs and the Framing of Resource Allocation Decisions," *Organizational Behavior and Human Decision Processes* (1986): 28–38.

[12] J. Brockner and J. Rubin, *Entrapment in Escalating Conflicts* (New York: Springer-Verlag, 1985).

Escalation

Robert Campeau In 1987, *Fortune* magazine named Robert Campeau one of its "Fifty Most Interesting Business People" after he had successfully taken over Allied Corporation—a company that was thirty times larger than his own Campeau Corporation, a Canadian real estate firm. Flushed with this success, Campeau began a hostile takeover attempt of Federated Department Stores on January 25, 1988, with a bid of $47 per share for the company that owned the most profitable retail store in the United States—Bloomingdale's.

But Campeau was not alone in his quest for Federated. Macy's under the leadership of CEO Edward Finkelstein, decided that it, too, wanted to own Federated. The much publicized bidding war became personal. In less than two months, the *Wall Street Journal* reported that David Weinstock, a public relations consultant working for Campeau, said "we're not dealing in price anymore, but egos. What's been offered is top dollar, and beyond what anyone expected. I knew that as the deal went on that he was either going to win or die. He was not going to be reasonable."

On March 31, it became clear that Federated's board clearly preferred selling to the head of Macy's, an individual who was more experienced and respected in the retail sales industry. The board was legally required to get the highest price for the stockholders and was about to declare Campeau the winner when Macy's final bid came in. Campeau then topped this final offer by

approximately $500 million. Reports following the late-night March 31 meeting indicated that Macy's had agreed to drop out of the bidding for Federated in exchange for the option of buying two of Federated's stores, I. Magnin's and Bullocks, for $1.1 billion as well as recovering about $60 million in fees and expenses.

Campeau may have won this auction, but the price of winning was that Campeau Corporation declared bankruptcy and sought protection under Chapter 11 of the U.S. Bankruptcy Code in January 1990. The price of a share of common stock in Campeau went from an all-time high of $26 in August 1987 to around $1 in late 1989. Robert Campeau's personal desire to win the bidding for Federated seems to have led to the downfall of his organization and damaged the financial position of two of the more productive retailers in the United States.

Sources: M. H. Bazerman and M. A. Neale, *Negotiating Rationally* (New York: The Free Press, 1992); "Suitors for Federated Department Stores Show Few Signs of Weakening Resolve in Bidding War," *Wall Street Journal,* March 25, 1988, 4; "Is Anyone Minding Federated's Store as Battle Rages to Take Over Retailer?" *Wall Street Journal,* March 25, 1988, 4; and Carol Loomis, "The Biggest Looniest Deal Ever," *Fortune,* June 18, 1990, 48–72.

Types of Decisions

If rationality is only an unattainable dream of decision makers, what determines how carefully a decision maker attempts to follow the rational model versus when (for instance) heuristics are used? What determines just how "bounded" a decision maker's efforts are likely to be?

Individual decisions cover a wide range of issues of varying importance to the organization. At one extreme, decisions can be made quickly—almost without the appearance of conscious thought. At the other extreme, decisions can involve many groups and considerable organizational resources. What influences the amount of cognitive and organizational resources allocated to making a decision? The time and effort put into the decision-making process are directly related to the importance of that decision for the individual and the organization.

The amount of time and resources spent on any decision-making process is a function of three factors: problem significance, solution irreversibility, and decision-maker accountability.[13] The more important the decision to the individual or the organization, the more irreversible the solution once implemented, and the greater the responsibility of the decision maker for the actual decision, the more organized, analytic, and purposeful the decision maker is in making a choice. Decisions that are trivial or easily reversible result in less organized decision-making strategies.

The familiarity of a decision also will influence the resources devoted to it. The routine problems that face organization decision makers allow the use of standard operating procedures, rules, and policies as substitutes for comprehensive decision making. If the same problem recurs regularly (for example, how much travel money to allow for any business trip), a policy can be established that makes the decision itself. Rather than confronting the problem anew each time it surfaces, the "automatic" decision greatly reduces information-processing demands for the decision maker. Without standard operating procedures, rules, and policies to direct the daily activity of organizational actors, it is unlikely that managers could ever cope with the minute-to-minute demands for decisions necessary to produce the goods or services demanded by the organization's customers.

Often, the selection of an appropriate outcome depends, in large part, on the attractiveness of the outcome. A major component of attractiveness is the parties' perception of the outcome's fairness. The general notion of fairness encompasses many different types of inputs into the decision-making process. In the next section, we will consider the broad concept of fairness as it relates to perceptions of justice within organizations, as well as the importance of ethics in managerial decision making.

FAIRNESS: ETHICS AND JUSTICE IN THE WORKPLACE ◆◆◆◆◆◆

The fairness of a decision cannot be judged objectively. However, while it is often quite easy for us to know whether we have been treated fairly, it is much more difficult for us to determine what others perceive as fair. When our expectations of fair treatment are not met, we often experience a strong emotional response. Consider this manager's experience:

---

[13] D. W. McAllister, T. R. Mitchell, and L. R. Beach, "The Contingency Model for the Selection of Decision Strategies: An Empirical Test of the Effects of Significance, Accountability, and Reversibility," *Organizational Behavior and Human Performance* 24 (1979): 228–244.

So often I am filled with so much rage and anger because of how I am treated . . . the broken promises and lies by my bosses, the undeserved recognition that others receive, or when I feel as manipulated as an accounting entry into our current fiscal year budget. . . . You know sometimes you want to grab them and shake them so hard that it hurts them as much as you feel hurt. . . . All I want here is a fair deal. . . . Yeah, I know there is no justice, but that makes it all the worse. With every day, it seems that revenge is becoming my only *real* option to gain some sense of justice.

—An assistant brand manager employed at a
Fortune 500 consumer products firm[14]

The employee quoted above is expressing outrage at the injustice he experiences at the hands of his employer. Examples of unfair practices and similar employee responses are common in organizations. Employee responses to perceived and real injustices can range from the trivial (gripe sessions when employees get together) to the critical (destruction of valuable company records by disgruntled employees) to the dangerous (employees who seek revenge on their employer through physical violence).

Interactive Justice

A number of researchers have identified important components of justice in the workplace. Employees may be concerned with **distributive justice** (the fairness of outcomes they receive)[15] or **procedural justice** (the process by which outcomes are allocated)[16] or **interactive** (or interpersonal) **justice** (the quality of the interpersonal treatment they receive).[17] While managers may have little to say about organizational rewards (distributive justice) or how they are allocated (procedural justice), they may have considerable discretion concerning how their employees are treated (interactive justice). For example, managers may be told that only a certain percentage of their employees may be given an outstanding rating and the concomitant salary increase. Thus, managers may be unable to reward employees equitably for their productivity. Or organizational policies may restrict managers' ability to gather input from the ratee when completing performance evaluations. Even when organizational impediments to fair treatment exist, whether or not employees *feel* justly treated will depend in large measure on the interpersonal treatment they receive from their managers *and* the managers' proper use of discretionary authority.[18]

Interpersonal Treatment In evaluating the quality of interpersonal treatment, individuals focus on whether they were treated politely and respectfully

---

[14] R. J. Bies, "The Predicament of Injustice: The Management of Moral Outrage," in *Research in Organizational Behavior*, vol. 9, ed. B. M. Staw and L. L. Cummings (Greenwich, Conn.: JAI Press, 1987), 290.

[15] See, for example, G. C. Homans, *Social Behavior: Its Elementary Forms* (New York: Harcourt Brace Jovanovich, 1961); and M. Deutsch, *Distributive Justice* (New Haven, Conn.: Yale University Press, 1985).

[16] See, for example, J. Thibaut and L. Walker, *Procedural Justice* (Hillsdale, N.J.: Erlbaum, 1975); and E. A. Lind and T. R. Tyler, *The Social Psychology of Procedural Justice* (New York: Plenum, 1988).

[17] See, for example, T. R. Tyler and R. J. Bies, "Beyond Formal Procedures: The Interpersonal Context of Procedural Justice," in *Advances in Applied Social Psychology: Business Settings* (New York: Erlbaum, 1988); and R. J. Bies and J. S. Moag, "Interactional Justice: Communication Criteria of Fairness," in *Research on Negotiations in Organizations*, vol. 1, ed. M. H. Bazerman, R. J. Lewicki, and B. Sheppard (Greenwich, Conn.: JAI Press, 1986), 43–55.

[18] Tyler and Bies, "Beyond Formal Procedures."

and whether the manager followed general principles of ethical conduct. In one study, students were asked whether they had been fairly or unfairly treated in job interviews. Students believed they were fairly treated to the extent that the interviewer was candid and honest, provided timely feedback about whether they would be made a job offer, treated them with respect, focused on appropriate topics and avoided such inappropriate issues as gender, race, and marital status, and adequately justified the decision whether to hire them.[19]

Use of Discretionary Power A manager's use of discretionary power will also influence an employee's perception of justice. For example, when a manager allows employees more participation in making decisions that affect them, they will perceive the decisions as being more fair. Alternatively, employees will be outraged if they discover that their involvement is not seriously considered—that the participation is a sham. Employees will react more negatively to this false participation than they would if their views had never been solicited.[20]

The attribution of a manager's intent can also significantly influence an employee's perception of fairness. Even fair procedures will be discounted if managers use them for their own gain. For example, suppose a manager benefits personally from some procedure. If workers are given an opportunity to voice their objections about this procedure and their objections are ignored, they will view the procedure as even more unfair than they would if they never had the opportunity to complain.

Because the *perceived* fairness of an outcome or procedure may differ from its *objective* fairness, the attribution of intent is critical to the perception of organizational justice. Managers should be concerned not only with being fair but also with "looking fair." Managing impressions of organizational justice is critical to being perceived as just.[21]

Managers may be perceived as more just or fair if they use tactics to reinforce the employees' perception of fairness. For example, managers can respond to threats to their fairness persona by using defensive tactics such as excuses ("Economic conditions necessitate my decision"), justifications ("I am punishing you for your own good!"), and apologies ("I am sorry I have to give you such a low rating"). These tactics distance managers from responsibility for their actions. In addition, managers may use more proactive tactics to portray themselves as fair and just. These include entitling and enhancement. **Entitling tactics,** the opposite of excuses, are attempts to gain responsibility for positive events and their consequences.[22] The "FOCUS ON: Looking Fair" illustrates a number of ways in which managers can increase their perceived responsibility for fair outcomes and, thus, their perception of being fair.

---

[19]R. J. Bies, "Identifying Principles of Interactional Justice: The Case of Corporate Recruiting," in the symposium Moving Beyond Equity Theory: New Directions for Research on Justice in Organizations, Academy of Management, Chicago, Ill.

[20]R. Cohen, "Power and Justice in Intergroup Relations," in *Justice in Social Relations*, ed. H. Bierhoff, R. Cohen, and J. Greenberg (New York: Plenum, 1986).

[21]J. Greenberg, "Looking Fair Versus Being Fair: Managing Impressions of Organizational Justice," in *Research in Organizational Behavior*, vol. 12, ed. B. M. Staw and L. L. Cummings (Greenwich, Conn.: JAI Press, 1990).

[22]E. D'Arcy, *Human Acts: An Essay on Their Moral Evaluation* (New York: Oxford University Press, 1963).

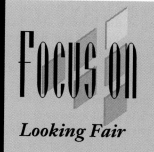

Looking Fair

Cultivating an Image of Justice
Jerald Greenberg asked 815 managers to describe the one thing they thought they could do to make their subordinates think management treated them fairly. The managers reported that they engaged in both *behavioral acts* (things done to look fair) and *social accounts* (things said to look fair) to create the perception that they were just.

Eighty-one percent of the managers reported that they could enhance their image of fairness by "publicly announcing all pay raises and promotions"—a behavioral act focused on outcomes. Fifty-one percent indicated that "allowing workers to participate in decision making"—a behavioral act that focuses on process—would enhance the workers' perception of managerial fairness.

Forty-three percent of the managers said they could enhance their reputations for fairness by "explaining why certain work assignments were made" (a social account focusing on outcome). Giving social accounts about such processes as "how pay raises are determined" would increase their level of perceived fairness for 76 percent.

Greenberg suggests that one of the more interesting aspects of this survey was managers' awareness of entitlement tactics—tactics designed to increase their perceived responsibility for positive outcomes.

Source: J. Greenberg, "Cultivating an Image of Justice," *Academy of Management Executive* 2 (1988).

Enhancements, the opposite of justifications, are attempts to augment the positive consequences of one's behavior.[23] That is, managers may frame their behavior in such a way as to make it appear more fair or positive than it objectively is. By presenting selective information about an ambiguous event, managers may socially construct the interpretation of that event as evidence of their fairness.[24] Individuals may manage their reputations for fairness by leaking information about their fair actions to opinion leaders or using informal communication channels to disperse specific interpretations or events.[25]

Both public and private benefits accrue to managers who appear fair. A reputation for fairness may enhance their self-esteem and self-concept. It also may aid in the development of their power base. The perception that managers are fair will encourage compliance on the part of subordinates. They may experience fewer challenges to their authority, and their credibility and trustworthiness will be enhanced.

Certain liabilities are associated with a reputation for fairness as well. If fairness is an integral part of a manager's identity, then hints of unfairness will be more damaging to that manager than to others for whom fairness is not an issue.[26]

But how should a manager behave to "appear fair"? One obvious way is to allocate valued resources among employees fairly. But, by what criteria should

---

[23] B. R. Schlenker, *Impression Management: The Self-Concept, Social Identity, and Interpersonal Relations* (Belmont, Calif.: Brooks/Cole, 1980).

[24] Bies, "The Predicament of Injustice," 289–319.

[25] Greenberg, "Looking Fair Versus Being Fair."

[26] Schlenker, *Impression Management.*

these resources be allocated?[27] One way to allocate surplus is by adhering to a norm of equality—each party gets the same amount of the benefit. Another option is to distribute resources based on the respective input of the relevant parties such that their ratios of contributions to rewards are equal. Or, it may be that the relative need of the parties determines the allocation of valued outcomes.[28]

Because the fairness of an outcome is important, the perceptions of fairness can play a major role in the relative attraction of a particular outcome or choice. A recent set of studies demonstrated that perceived fairness dominated purely economic considerations. Consider how you would judge the action of the hardware store owner in the following scenario:[29]

> A hardware store has been selling snow shovels for $15. The morning after a large snowstorm, the store raises the price to $20.

Would you rate this action as fair or unfair? It turns out that despite the economic rationality of raising the prices on the snow shovels, 82 percent of the respondents considered raising the price of the snow shovels as unfair.

In addition, cognitive biases also influence peoples' perceptions of fairness. For example, the same set of actions judged unfair in one context may be reframed and judged as more fair in a second context. Consider these two problems:

> Question A: A company is making a small profit. It is located in a community experiencing a recession with substantial unemployment but no inflation. Many workers are anxious to work at the company. The company decides to decrease wages and salaries 7 percent this year.

Sixty-two percent of the respondents thought that the company's behavior was unfair.

> Question B: A company is making a small profit. It is located in a community experiencing a recession with substantial unemployment and inflation of 12 percent. Many workers are anxious to work at the company. The company decides to increase wages and salaries 5 percent this year.

Here only 22 percent of the participants judged the company's action as unfair. Although the *real* impact on income was very similar, a wage cut was coded as unfair while a nominal gain (that did not cover inflation) was more acceptable. Thus, the frame or context of the decision influenced the perception of fairness.

Figuring out what is fair and what is unfair often requires the decision maker to consider, explicitly, the social situation. As such, a common way we determine fairness is by comparing what we got to what others have received. A vivid example of impact of another's outcome on our own perceptions of fair-

---

[27] Robert H. Franke (1988). *Passions within Reason* (New York: Norton and Company, 1988).

[28] J. S. Adams, "Inequity in Social Exchange," In *Advances in Experimental Social Psychology*, Vol. 2, ed. L. Berkowitz (New York: Academic Press, 1965); M. Deutsch, "Equity, Equality and Need: What Determines Which Value Will Be Used As the Basis of Distributive Justice?" *Journal of Social Issues* 31 (1975): 137–149; and M. Deutsch, *Distributive Justice* (New Haven: Yale University Press, 1984).

[29] D. Kahneman, J. Knetsch, and R. Thaler, "Fairness As a Constraint on Profit Seeking: Entitlement in the Marketplace," *American Economic Review* 76 (1987): 728–741.

ness and our subsequent choices was provided in a series of demonstrations of "ultimatum bargaining."[30] In this type of bargaining, two players (who do not know each other) are randomly assigned to be either Player 1 or Player 2. Player 1 is given a sum of money, say $10, that must be divided between the players. Player 1 must propose an allocation and Player 2 must either accept or reject this allocation. If Player 2 accepts the allocation, then the $10 is divided according to the agreed-on allocation. If Player 2 rejects the proposed allocation, then neither player gets any money at all. In this situation, if you were Player 1, how would you propose to divide the money? If you were Player 2, what is the minimum amount of money you would accept as a proposal from Player 1?

If concerns with fairness had no impact, then we might expect Player 1 to allocate the smallest possible amount, say 1 cent, to Player 2. Player 2 should accept this allocation because he or she is economically better off by gaining a penny than by refusing the allocation and, thus, gaining nothing. What typically happens to individuals in this situation is that Player 1 almost never proposes a $9.99/$.01 division of the money. In fact, a fifty-fifty split of the money was the most common allocation and very few Player 1's were willing even to propose a $9/$1 split. When Player 1 attempted to claim an excessive portion of the ten dollars, Player 2 typically refused to accept the proposed allocation, thus settling for nothing.

Even in a variation of this game called the Dictator Game, where Player 1 could unilaterally decide how to allocate the $10, there were very few instances where Player 2 received very little or nothing at all.[31] Only 36 percent of Player 1's took one hundred percent of the money. Thus, when acceptance by Player 2 was required, proposals become more equal; although sixty-four percent of Player 1's in the Dictator Game still chose to give the other party some portion of the resources. Thus, both a concern with being fair and the realization that being perceived as unfair can have future costs led participants in these games to alter their choices.

There is much evidence that the perception of fairness plays an important role in peoples' actions and decisions. One such example of the importance of determining what is fair is illustrated in the "INTERNATIONAL FOCUS ON: Fairness," which describes the character of the Russian people.

The importance of equality as a norm of fairness should not be underestimated, even in situations where we, as the Russians, may wish to maintain equality if only to make sure that things are equally bad for everybody. The desire to share equally in the good and bad is typically proposed by those who would be disadvantaged should some other allocation rule be invoked (such as equity—each based upon his or her contribution—or relative need).

Such an emphasis on self-interest—the ability to use "fairness" as a justification for making a particular choice—may seem to be inconsistent with good, ethical decision making. To this point, we have examined how an individual decision maker can generate consequences that are good for that individual. But, what happens when the self-interest of one party interferes with

[30]W. Guth, R. Schmittberger, and B. Schwarze, "An Experimental Analysis of Ultimatum Bargaining," *Journal of Economic Behavior and Organization* 3 (1982): 367–388.

[31]J. Ochs and A. Roth, "An Experimental Study of Sequential Bargaining," *American Economic Review* 79 (1989): 335–385.

INTERNATIONAL FOCUS ON
Fairness

The Russian People Russians are long-suffering people who can bear misery, so long as they see others are sharing it. But let someone become better off—even if it is through his own honest labor—and the collective jealousy can be fierce.

I came to see the great mass of Soviet people as protagonists in what I call the culture of envy—corrosive animosity that took root under the czars in the deep-seated collectivism in Russian lives and then was accentuated by Leninist ideology.

What is ominous for Gorbachev's reforms is that this free-floating anger of the rank and file often settles on anyone who rises above the crowd. This hostility is a serious danger to the new entrepreneurs Gorbachev is trying to nurture. It is a deterrent to modest initiative among ordinary people in factories or on farms. It freezes that vast majority into immobility of conforming to group attitudes.

I heard of a farmer outside Moscow whose horse and few cows were set free and whose barn was set afire by neighboring farm workers jealous of his modest prosperity. In the West, if an American sees someone on TV with a shiny new car, he will think, "Oh, maybe I can get that someday for myself." But if a Russian sees that, he will think, "This bastard with his car. I would like to kill him for living better than I do." Anatoly A. Sobchak, mayor of Leningrad said, "Changing that psychology is the hardest part of our economic reform. That psychology of intolerance toward others who make more money, no matter why, no matter whether they work harder, longer, or better—that psychology is blocking economic reform." They are so jealous of other people that they want others to be worse off, if need be, to keep things equal.

Source: Henrick Smith, "The Russian Character," *The New York Times Magazine,* October 28, 1990.

the interests or rights of another party or of the society as a whole? This is the issue of ethics.

Ethical Decision Making

The concept of self-interest as the basis for action has been justified by many scholars. One of the earliest was Adam Smith. As evidenced in the "FOCUS ON: Self-Interest," Smith believed that the general welfare of the society is promoted as a side-effect of people's self-interest. People will work harder for their own self-interests than if they are made to contribute directly to society.[32]

The justification of decisions in light of self-interest is compelling. First, it is unlikely that our capitalist system would function if individuals were truly altruistic and pursued the interests of others to the detriment of their own. Second, people are likely to be more highly motivated if they are encouraged to pursue their own self-interests. However, a distinction needs to be made between short-term, or immediate, self-interest and long-term, or enlightened, self-interest. When Adam Smith describes self-interest, he is referring to the long-term view of self-interest.[33] The conflict between these two perspectives is often referred to as a social dilemma. That is, when will the best long-term interests of the individual (and, simultaneously, the society) be served when they conflict with the immediate interests of the individual?

[32] R. Buccholz, *Isn't It All a Matter of Self-Interest?* Business Ethics series, Vol. V (Chicago, Ill.: Loyola Marymount, 1986).

[33] A. Smith, *The Wealth of Nations* (New York: Modern Library, 1937).

Focus on
Self-Interest

Adam Smith As the following comments show, Adam Smith believed that people promoted the general welfare only as a side-effect of promoting their own self-interest.

As every individual, therefore endeavors as much as he can both to employ his capital in the support of domestic industry, and so to direct that industry that its produce may be of the greatest value; every individual necessarily labors to render the annual revenue of society as great as he can. He generally, indeed, neither intends to promote the public interest, nor knows how much he is promoting it. By preferring the support of domestic to that of foreign industry, he intends only his own security; and by directing that industry in such a manner as its produce may be of the greatest value, he intends only his own gain, and he is in this, as in many other cases, led by an invisible hand to promote an end which was no part of his intention. Nor is it always the worse for the society that it was no part of it. By pursuing his own interest, he frequently promotes that of the society more effectually than when he really intends to promote it.

Source: A. Smith, *The Wealth of Nations* (New York: Modern Library, 1937), 43.

A common example of a social dilemma is provided in Figure 5–7, "The Tragedy of the Commons." Obviously it is in the best interest of the individual to graze as many dairy cattle as possible. However, with this strategy, the land quickly becomes unusable for the entire village.

The tragedy of the commons is not an unusual problem. Consider the typical experience in study groups or group projects. It is probably in the short-term self-interest of any individual not to contribute his or her fair share in group efforts, especially if the individual effort of each participant cannot be identified. In fact, people who exhibit this unwillingness to contribute to the larger good are termed **free riders.** Free riders are a common problem in work groups.

However, while a free-rider solution is initially attractive, let's consider some of the outcomes that may result from such a choice. First, if all the group members chose that option, then thousands of students in hundreds of colleges would receive poor grades and miss out on a useful learning experience. Alternatively, the individual who chooses this option may enjoy the benefits of receiving a grade without incurring the cost of contributing, but what happens

FIGURE 5–7	▶ The Tragedy of the Commons

A common grazing area is used freely by a town's dairy farmers. Increasing the number of cattle grazed in the area is obviously in the best interest of any particular farmer. However, if all the farmers keep increasing their herds, they will eventually overgraze the commons. Ultimately, they will kill the grass and diminish the collective interest; that is, they will reduce the value of the commons to the group as a whole as well as to themselves as individuals. What should (will) the individual farmer do?

Source: G. R. Hardin, "The Tragedy of the Commons," *Science* 162 (1968): 1243–1248.

if this person's behavior becomes public knowledge? The free rider may end up without a group to share the burden of future group projects.

Given these facts, why is it that some individuals will opt for short-term gain to the exclusion of long-term benefits? Why are short-term benefits chosen even in the face of considerable long-term costs? Three factors promote our selection of short-term gains or benefits. First, referring to our earlier discussion of the availability heuristic, immediate benefits are more likely to be vivid and salient to the individual. Time-delayed costs or benefits are likely to be less available to the decision maker. Thus, when deciding the likely outcome of a choice, decision makers may discount the probability of incurring those long-term costs or benefits. Therefore, decision makers will evaluate the short-term benefits as more attractive than the long-term rewards or costs.[34]

Second, choices that maximize short-term gain may be selected because of ignorance or limited cognitive capabilities. That is, from the bounded-rationality perspective, the information search may not have been sufficient for the decision maker to choose the "enlightened" alternative. For example, a fish swimming into a baited net does not know he cannot get out. The decision maker may not possess the cognitive capabilities to make the what-if analyses needed to maximize the long-term value of a complex decision.

Finally, short-term benefits may be very rewarding early on. However, these reinforcers may become less and less rewarding over time until they are eventually punishing. Examples of these sliding reinforcers might include drug and alcohol use/abuse, extramarital affairs, and excessive consumption of natural resources.[35]

Managing Organizational Ethics

A recent study by the Ethics Resource Center in Washington, D.C., found that 85 percent of 711 companies surveyed had policy statements or codes of conduct that were designed to clarify the limits of ethical and unethical behavior.[36] However, fewer than 10 percent of these companies had any mechanism in place to monitor their employees' adherence to these codes. Another recent survey conducted by a popular magazine found that 56 percent of those who answered the survey thought that the ethics of American business had deteriorated significantly in the last 10 years. This rather popular notion has been fueled by the publicity of many rather unsavory incidents. For instance, in 1990, John Borowski was sentenced to two years in prison and fined $400,000 for ordering employees of Borjohn Optical Technology, Inc., in Burlington, Massachusetts, to dump toxic wastes down the sewer. In September 1990, General Electric was ordered to pay a $10 million criminal fine and $20 million in civil charges for overbilling the government for computers. The National Bank of Greece was ordered to pay an $8 million fine for money laundering in a six-year scheme to hide cash deposits from the Treasury Department. There is even an investigation into the charge that operatives for Avon Products, Inc., were grilling the associates of top officers of rival Mary Kay Corp. These operatives

---

[34]M. A. Neale, "The Effect of Negotiation and Arbitration Cost Salience on Bargainer Behavior: The Role of Arbitrator and Constituency in Negotiator Judgment," *Organizational Behavior and Human Performance* 36 (1984): 97–111; J. Platt, "Social Traps," *American Psychologist* (August 1973): 641–651.

[35]J. Platt, "Social Traps."

[36]M. Galen, "Keeping the Long Arm of the Law at Arm's Length," *Business Week*, April 22, 1991, 104.

Focus on

*Competitive
Secrets and
Disgruntled
Employees*

The High Cost of Unethical Behavior 3M employee Phillip A. Stegora helped develop a new type of casting tape that would likely dominate the $200 million market for tape used by physicians to set broken bones. While Johnson & Johnson had been an early leader in this market with its plaster-of-Paris bandage roll, 3M became a major player when it introduced its new fiberglass cast. However, the resin needed to mold the fiberglass into a hard bandage became sticky and difficult to work when it was wet. In 1985, a slicker resin was developed and Stegora, hoping to benefit financially from his knowledge of this new product, sent samples to four of 3M's competitors. None of the competitors reported this incident, but when 3M eventually got wind of it, the FBI quickly traced the theft to Stegora and he served 22 months in prison.

While this may have been the end of the incident, it turned out that Johnson & Johnson had done some chemical analyses on the samples sent by Stegora. These reports were sent to several officials in the company's orthopedics group who failed to instruct their chemists not to use the results of the analyses in subsequent research. This resulted in Johnson & Johnson incorporating the information from the analyses of 3M's technology into its new casting tape, significantly reducing 3M's ability to dominate the casting bandage market.

Source: Kevin Kelly with Joseph Weber, "When a Rival's Trade Secret Crosses Your Desk . . . ," *Business Week*, May 20, 1991.

are also suspected of following Mary Kay's executives overseas, spreading harmful rumors, and raiding Mary Kay's trash in search of information.[37]

Recently, Johnson & Johnson may have experienced some of the long-term costs of short-term benefits. The "FOCUS ON: Competitive Secrets and Disgruntled Employees" describes why the United States District Court in Minneapolis has ordered Johnson & Johnson to pay 3M $116.3 million for infringing on patents and the misappropriation of trade secrets.

> . . . institutionalizing ethics may sound ponderous, but its meaning is straightforward. It means getting ethics formally and explicitly into daily business life. It means getting ethics into company policy formation at the board and top management levels and through a formal code, getting ethics into all daily decision making and work practices down the line, at all levels of employment. It means grafting a new branch on the corporate decision tree—a branch that reads "right/wrong."[38]

When asked to list factors that might lead to unethical decisions, respondents in a *Harvard Business Review* poll identified the behavior of their superiors as most influential. Other highly ranked factors included lack of a formal policy, the behavior of one's peers, society's moral climate, one's personal financial need, and even (as shown in Figure 5–8) the general ethical climate of the industry.[39]

---

[37]Tim Smart, with Michele Galen, Gail DeGeorge, and Paul Angiolillo, "The Crackdown on Crime in the Suites," *Business Week*, April 22, 1991, 102–104; and Wendy Zellner and Bruce Hager, "Dumpster Raids? That's Not Very Ladylike, Avon," *Business Week*, April 1, 1991, 22.

[38]T. V. Purcell and J. Wever, *Institutionalizing Corporate Ethics: A Case History*, Special Study No. 71 (New York: The Presidents Association of American Management Associations, 1979).

[39]J. Cullen, B. Victor, and C. Stephens, "An Ethical Weather Report: Assessing the Organization's Ethical Climate," *Organizational Dynamics* (Autumn 1989): 50–62.

FIGURE 5–8 ▶

For some decision makers, ethics provides absolute standards against which behaviors are judged. As noted in this cartoon, for others, ethics is just another input to the decision-making process.

Since managers are interacting with increasing numbers of cultures with different beliefs about what is ethical or standard practice, it is increasingly important for organizations to specify their ethical standards and expectations of conduct. Given the increasingly frequent occurrences of blatantly unethical and often illegal behavior within large and highly respected organizations, it is critical for managers and firms to promote the ethical conduct of business—that is, the institutionalization of ethics.

Institutionalizing Ethics

Within organizations, ethical principles can be institutionalized in a variety of ways. The goal of such activities is to ensure that ethical concerns are considered in the same routine manner in which legal, financial, and marketing concerns are addressed.

In some corporations, permanent board-level committees are created to monitor the ethical behavior of the organization. These committees, often called "social responsibility" or "public policy" committees, serve two functions within an organization. First, they lend legitimacy to the consideration of an ethics agenda at the highest level of organizational decision making. Second, they symbolically communicate to the employees and external stakeholders of the organization its commitment to ethical principles in conducting business.

Codes of ethics identify acceptable and unacceptable behavior in organizations, much as laws do for a society at large. Junk bond king Michael Milken, shown here leaving court, was indicted on 98 criminal counts and sentenced to ten years in prison for his part in the insider trading scandal at Drexel Burnham. Using confidential information for personal gain is not only unethical by the standards of most businesses, but illegal.

A second mechanism for institutionalizing ethics within an organization is the use of a **code of ethics.** Within an organization, this code describes the general value system of the organization, defines the organization's purpose, and provides guidelines for decision making consistent with these principles. Examples of behaviors routinely prohibited by typical ethics codes are described in Figure 5–9.

FIGURE 5–9	▶ **Percentage of Firms with Codes of Ethics Prohibiting Specific Employee Behaviors**

A corporate code of ethics captures the value system of an organization. It also may increase the probability of ethical behavior by providing guidelines for individual decision making.

Prohibited Behavior	Percentage of Firms
Extortion, gifts, and kickbacks	67%
Conflict of interests	65
Illegal political payments	59
Violation of laws in general	57
Use of insider information	43
Bribery	37
Falsification of corporate accounts	28
Violation of antitrust laws	25
Moonlighting	25
Legal payments abroad	23
Revealing company secrets	22
Ignorance of work-related laws	22
Fraud, deception	11
Justifying illegal behavior that serves the company	10

Source: R. Chatov, "What Corporate Ethics Statements Say," *California Management Review* 21 (1980): 22.

Focus on

Ethical Behavior

Following the Leader When E. F. Hutton speaks, its slogan claims, people listen. But in 1985, E. F. Hutton found itself deep in trouble because no one in Hutton was speaking or listening. What was not spoken about—or at least not questioned—was check kiting by Hutton's money managers. And what no one listened to was the voice of conscience whispering misgivings about an unethical and illegal practice.

The scheme was simple. A branch of E. F. Hutton would have, say, $70,000 on deposit in a small bank in Ohio. The Hutton branch would request a cash transfer from the account for $1 million. The bank, not wanting to lose Hutton's valuable business, would advance the money, and a day later Hutton would replace it. Hutton got the free use of $1 million of the bank's money for 24 hours.

While substantial account overdrafts occur from time to time in business banking, Hutton made a practice of them. On any given day, the firm overdrew its bank accounts to the tune of millions of dollars. The interest on that money became a major source of revenue for Hutton. When the U.S. Justice Department finally investigated, E. F. Hutton was cited on 2,000 counts of mail and wire fraud, received a $2 million fine, and had to set up a multimil-lion-dollar fund to reimburse banks for lost interest payments.

Few employees at E. F. Hutton seem to have questioned the practice before the federal investigation; once established among Hutton executive echelons, it was taken for granted. In fact, an internal memo from the corporate department in charge of cash management advised, rather blandly, "If an office is overdrafting their ledger balance consistently, it is probably best not to request an account analysis." In other words, the memo said they would rather not know about it—and rather the bank not notice, either.

Source: Daniel Goleman, "Following the Leader: Sometimes It's Folly to Go Along with the Boss," *Science '85* (October): 18–19.

A third method which has gained in popularity in recent years is the implementation of ethics training programs. Of 279 large companies responding to a 1985 survey conducted by the Center for Business Ethics at Bentley College in Waltham, Massachusetts, 20 percent said they were using seminars or workshops to reinforce good ethics.[40] Interestingly enough, the most visible companies in the ethics business are often those struggling to repair their damaged reputations. A check-kiting scheme implemented by E. F. Hutton and illustrated in the "FOCUS ON: Ethical Behavior" is an example of one of these companies. General Dynamics developed an ethics program so that it could remain eligible for its Navy contracts after allegations about improper contracting procedures surfaced. Corporations that have not been guilty of wrongdoing have

---

[40] P. Richter, "Big Business Puts Ethics in Spotlight," *Los Angeles Times*, June 19, 1986.

recently initiated formal ethics programs in an effort to avoid public-relations problems, raise employee morale and productivity, and make their organizations more honest.

When we broaden our perspective on institutionalizing ethics from the organization to the larger society, an interesting cycle is evident. Ethical issues for the organization or the individual are those for which society has not established clear-cut mandates. For example, the domain of ethics is completely separate from the legal domain. Business ethics, then, represent concepts of appropriate and inappropriate behavior that reflect how society views business practices that are not covered by legal principles.

Further, what composes the domain of ethical issues seems to change in decade-long cycles. Typically, what is part of an ethical agenda at one time becomes the focus of law in subsequent years. For example, protection of the environment was an ethical and moral issue beginning in the 1950s. The first major environmental legislation was passed in the 1960s. Concern about unethical behavior on the part of U.S. firms operating in foreign countries was an ethical issue in the 1960s, and the Foreign Corrupt Practices Act was passed by Congress in the 1970s. Issues of workplace safety and employment discrimination were ethical problems in the 1960s that resulted in major legislation in the 1970s. Concerns with sexual harassment in the workplace in the 1970s led to the implementation of laws in the 1980s.

Apparently, once ethical concerns gain sufficient attention, they become codified into law. However, this is not to suggest that one should ignore such dilemmas until they become law. Rather, this evolution is the process of individuals, organizations, and society at large forming a consensus about the appropriate form of conduct. Because the laws reflect many of society's attitudes, current ethical concerns will become the grist for future lawmakers. Each individual, then, has a responsibility to examine his or her behavior within the workplace and the community and incorporate ethical concerns into the decision-making process.

CREATIVITY

A final aspect of individual decision making is the individualistic, novel, idea-generating process known as **creativity.** In the past, most people believed that creativity was something you were born with. Recent research, however, suggests otherwise. Creativity now is viewed as a process of mental gymnastics. The creative process draws on all parts of the brain, from knowledge, logic, imagination, and intuition to the ability to see relationships between ideas and things.[41]

The notion that creativity can be learned has not been ignored by corporate America. A study of 25 major companies found that a majority had undertaken some sort of formal training in creativity within the last two years.[42] While a

[41] E. T. Smith, S. Yanchiniski, M. Sabin, and P. E. Simmons, "Are You Creative?" *Business Week*, September 30, 1985, 80–84.

[42] Reported in W. Kiechel, "Getting Creative," *Fortune*, July 25, 1983, 109–114.

number of different methods are used to teach creativity, four prescriptions are common to most creativity training programs:

1. Make sure you thoroughly understand the problem you are trying to solve. Sometimes problems elude solutions because they are poorly defined.
2. Relax. Stress reduces creative ability.
3. Try to think in terms of analogies or metaphors. For example, how is this problem similar to problems you have solved previously? If that doesn't help, try thinking about the problem as a paradox and find an analogy that solves it. In general, the idea here is to break out of rigid thinking patterns that may block new ideas. Some examples of creative ideas born of analogies and paradoxical thinking are described in the "Focus on: Creativity."
4. Pay attention to daydreams. Try to put together an image or piece of information that is outside the problem. Reconciling the two can force the mind to make new connections. Try, for example, consulting the dictionary. This worked for a greeting-card company. Combining the word *shrink* and the business (greeting cards) led to the development of business card-sized greetings that could be slipped into lunch boxes and shirt pockets.

Creativity can be cultivated. To do so, a decision maker must look at things in new and different ways. Creativity is a form of decision making that requires heuristics rather than logical, comprehensive calculation.

Focus on

Creativity

From Cats to Spoiled Beer One way to think creatively is to use analogies and paradoxes. Some successful users of these techniques include Eli Whitney, Sister Tabatha Babbett, and Adolph Coors Co. Eli Whitney conjured up the idea of the cotton gin by watching a cat try to catch a chicken through a fence—just the thing to comb seeds out of cotton bolls. Sister Babbett, while watching two men saw wood with a straight saw as she worked at her spinning wheel, figured that the job would be much easier if teeth were cut into the edge of a wheel—hence the development of the circular saw.

Or consider the small company that went to an expert in problem solving, William J. J. Gordon, to come up with a way to reduce the excessive space required for the storage and presentation of potato chips. Looking for an analogy in nature, the group saw a similarity between dried leaves and potato chips. Dried leaves (or chips), when packed too tightly together, will crumble. But, wet leaves can be packed together without crumbling. This analogy was the catalyst for slicing up potatoes before they dried into a uniform shape that could be easily stacked. The idea was developed and sold to Procter & Gamble as Pringles—potato chips in a can!

Paradox was the method by which the Adolph Coors Co. solved the problem of paying to dispose of gallons of spoiled beer. Inspired by the scene in *Tom Sawyer* in which Tom talks his friends into helping him whitewash the fence, Coors now sells its spoiled beer to the Japanese to be used as feed for their beef cattle.

Sources: "Are You Creative?" *Business Week*, September 30, 1985, 84; and Magaly Olivero, "Get Crazy: How to Have a Breakthrough Idea," *Working Woman*, September, 145–147.

SUMMARY

◆◆◆◆◆◆

Because human beings make thousands of decisions every day, the process of decision making appears to be deceptively simple. Upon closer examination, however, it is clear that making a good decision is often difficult and time-consuming. While individuals would like to perceive their decision process as rational, we are unable to meet the cognitive and information demands necessary to reach the optimal solution.

Although the demands of rationality exceed the capabilities of human decision makers, we still strive to make rational decisions. Decision makers adapt to their limitations by four means: conducting local rather than comprehensive alternative searches, evaluating alternatives sequentially rather than simultaneously, satisficing rather than optimizing, and using judgmental heuristics to reduce information-processing demands.

Attempts to improve our decision-making skills are made more difficult by the uncertain nature of our environment. Not knowing for certain what outcome will result from a particular decision alternative, we are forced to include elements of risk in our mental calculations. Expected value models and decision trees are useful mechanisms when probabilities are clear and outcomes can be assigned different values or utilities. However, many decision processes are not so clear. Even when a dominant solution can be identified by expected-value calculations or the decision tree, that option is not always selected. To understand how decisions are made, other factors, such as the risk preferences of decision makers—in addition to probabilities and preferences—need to be considered.

Given the inevitability of flawed decision making, how can we make better decisions? We must consider the ethical implications of decisions at the individual, organizational, and societal level. Attempts to ensure that ethical considerations be a routine part of organizational decision making have led to different organizational interventions. Some organizations have instituted board-level committees to tackle ethical issues, adopted official codes of ethics, and implemented ethics training for employees. In addition to these organizational efforts, society, through legislation, provides a final mechanism for reinforcing ethical decision making, removing the decision from the voluntary domain of ethics to the regulated area of law.

Key Terms

Availability bias Assessing the frequency or likelihood of an event's occurrence by how easily it is remembered, even though memory recall is influenced by factors unrelated to the frequency of an event.

Bounded rationality A model of individual decision making that diverges from the rational ideal in being based on a limited perspective, the sequential evaluation of alternatives, satisficing, and the use of judgmental heuristics.

Code of ethics Mechanism for institutionalizing ethics within an organization that describes the general value system of the organization, its purpose, and guidelines for decision making consistent with these principles.

Creativity Individualistic, novel, idea-generating process.

Distributive justice   Fair treatment of employees in awarding organizational rewards or in administering organizational punishment.

Enhancement   Attempt to augment the positive consequences of one's behavior to increase the perception of fairness among employees; the opposite of justification.

Entitling tactic   Attempt to gain responsibility for positive events and their consequences in order to increase the perception of fairness among employees; the opposite of excuse.

Escalation   Committing additional resources to failing causes based on the slim hope that there will be a dramatic change.

Expected value   Value of an option, determined by summing the values assigned to each possible consequence of an action, multiplied by the probabilities that each of these possible consequences will occur.

Framing   Judgmental heuristic that decision makers use to deal with risk in which they become increasingly likely to take risks when confronting potential losses and increasingly likely to avoid risks when confronting possible gains.

Free rider   Person who accepts the benefits of being a member of a group but is unwilling to contribute to the good of the group.

Interactive justice   Equitable treatment of employees in interpersonal treatment by managers.

Judgmental heuristics   Rules of thumb, or shortcuts, that reduce the information-processing demands on decision makers.

Procedural justice   Equitable treatment of employees in the processes by which organizational rewards are allocated and punishments are administered.

Rationality   Basing a decision on careful and calculated action alternatives and their consequences.

Representativeness   Decision heuristic based on the belief that an outcome should resemble its cause.

Risk   Amount of uncertainty associated with a particular decision alternative or choice.

Risk averse   Willingness of a decision maker to pay a premium to avoid risk, ignoring the expected-value solution.

Risk neutral   Indifference of a decision maker between risky and certain outcomes if they have the same expected value.

Risk seeking   Willingness of a decision maker to pay a premium to experience risk.

Satisficing   Foregoing the optimal solution in favor of one that is acceptable or reasonable in order to save the time and effort needed for extended comparisons.

Uncertainty   Consequences of an action can be known only in terms of a perceived likelihood of occurrence.

Discussion Questions

1. Think about your general strategies for making a decision. How do they change when you make a decision about your choice of breakfast foods, compared to what computer you will purchase? What are some of the critical differences in these very different decisions?

2. Even if we did have the cognitive mechanisms necessary to make optimal choices, why might we choose not to engage in a rational decision strategy?

3. What are the three ways in which an individual can achieve a "great" outcome? What differentiates the expert from the novice, if both can achieve "great" outcomes?

4. What is your general attitude toward risk? List some situations in which you are willing to take risks. List some situations in which you are not willing to take risks. In what general ways do these two groups of situations differ?

5. Ethical dilemmas can occur at all levels of organizations. Why is it difficult for individuals who are low in the organizational hierarchy to confront such issues? Why is it difficult for individuals who are highly placed in the organization to address these ethical concerns?

6. Why is it important that managers consider how employees will judge the fairness of their decisions? How can judgments of fairness and unfairness influence employees willingness to perform?

7. Consider the following poem:

   I am not free
   Nor want to be.
   I produce my claim to humanity
   Through my willingness to accept
   The unjustified demands
   Of duty.*

   What approach to decision making is implied by this poem? What are the implications for a manager? Would you want this person working for you?

8. Why might it be important for people to believe that they take action on the basis of rational decisions?

*J. G. March, *Academic Notes* (London: Poets' and Painters' Press, 1974).

If You Want to Know More

The study of individual decision making is currently enjoying great popularity in both the popular and academic press. Recent articles such as "Decisions, Decisions" by Kevin McKean, which appeared in the June 1985 issue of *Discover* magazine, focus on identifying the cognitive biases to which human decision makers are subject. Understanding risk was the basis for an article entitled "The Compleat Worrier: Staying Alive in the 20th Century" by William Allman, published in the October issue of *Science '85*. An interesting but older article on escalation entitled "Psychological Traps," by Jeffrey Rubin, appeared in the March 1981 issue of *Psychology Today*.

These articles provide excellent overviews of cognitive biases, risk, and escalation. However, for a more in-depth examination, one of the earlier (1957) books by Simon entitled *Administrative Behavior* certainly merits attention. More recent books on the topic of individual decision making include Bazerman's *Judgment in Managerial*

Decision Making (Wiley, 1989); Kahneman's, Slovic's, and Tversky's reader *Judgment under Uncertainty: Heuristics and Biases* (Cambridge University Press, 1982); and Hogarth's *Judgment and Choice* (Wiley, 1981).

For a more detailed exploration of ethics and ethical decision making within organizations, you may wish to read Blanchard's and Peale's *The Power of Ethical Management: You Don't Have to Cheat to Win* (Morrow, 1987); Mark Pastin's latest book, *The Hard Problems of Management: Gaining the Ethics Edge* (Jossey, Bass, 1986); or *The Way We Do Things around Here: Managers Talk Ethics* (Wiley, 1986) by Barbara Ley Toffler.

On Your Own

In a *Harvard Business Review* article, Laura Nash suggests that there are twelve questions that "draw upon the traditional philosophical frameworks [of ethics], but avoid the level of abstractions normally associated with formal moral reasoning." These are practical questions which, if answered honestly, may give you a general indication of the ethical nature of your decision.

1. Have you defined the problem accurately?
2. How would you define the problem if you stood on the other side of the fence?
3. How did this situation occur in the first place?
4. To whom or to what do you give your loyalty as a person and a member of the corporation?
5. What is your intention in making this decision?
6. How does this intention compare with the probable results?
7. Whom could your decision or action injure?
8. Can you discuss the problem with the affected parties before you make your decision?
9. Are you confident that your position will be as valid over a long period of time as it seems now?
10. Could you disclose without qualm your decision or action to your boss, your CEO, the board of directors, your family, or society as a whole?
11. What is the symbolic potential of your action if understood? If misunderstood?
12. Under what conditions would you allow exceptions to your stand?

The twelve questions are a way to articulate an idea of the responsibilities involved and to lay them open for examination. Whether or not a final policy emerges from this process, the process is useful for the following reasons:

▶ The process encourages talk in a group on a subject that traditionally has been reserved for one's conscience.
▶ It is a way of determining the values and goals of a company.
▶ It provides a mechanism for sharing information within an organization.
▶ It may uncover dramatic differences between values and the practicality of their implementation.
▶ It helps improve the nature and range of alternatives.
▶ It is cathartic.

Source: L. Nash, "Ethics without the Sermon," *Harvard Business Review* (November/December 1981): 78–90.

CLOSING CASE

CHAPTER 5

THE MANAGER'S MEMO

FROM: P. Dawson, Purchasing Manager

TO: F. Baumgartner, Vice President, Small-Car Division

RE: Alternative Supplier of Seat Belts

The representative of a potential supplier has informed me that his company can supply us with seat belts made of a new material. The primary advantage of using this supplier is that the new material is less expensive. At our present rate of production, switching to this manufacturer could save our company $3 million a year.

According to the sales rep, the new seat belts are like the standard ones in every way except that they are slightly less strong. In crash tests, the seat belts tear apart in one in 10,000 tests. This seems like a minor risk, although the standard seat belts never tear apart in crash tests. (As an aside, I checked with the legal department and learned that the average settlement for a death of a driver of one of our cars when we were held liable is $1 million.)

Considering the competitive pressure we are under, this alternative supplier may be a wise choice. I am, of course, aware that the company is considering closing the Mill City plant in order to cut costs. Perhaps the savings from this alternative supplier would enable us to keep the plant open, saving 500 to 1,000 jobs.

Please let me know whether you want to try the new seat belts in your division's cars.

Case Discussion Questions

Based on what you have learned about individual decision making, assume that you are the vice president of the Small-Car Division, and write a memo describing your decision. Consider whether your decision is a rational one and, if not, why it is not.

CONFLICT AND STRESS IN ORGANIZATIONS

DO YOU PUSH YOUR PEOPLE TOO HARD? ◆◆◆◆◆◆

Medical directors at over two hundred corporations reported that, on average, one-quarter of their employees suffered from stress-related disorders. According to the Research Triangle Institute, emotionally exhausted or depressed employees cost the United States over $183 billion annually in lost productivity, job errors, and doctor bills. The environment in which many organizations find themselves may enhance the stress experienced by employees as well as the burnout that often results from demanding more and more productivity from fewer individuals.

Consider the experience of a former store manager of Food Lion, one of the fastest growing supermarket chains in the United States. As one former Food Lion manager put it, "I put in more and more and more time—a hundred hours a week—but no matter how many hours I worked or what I did, I could never satisfy the supervisors." The Food Lion manager quit, and former coworkers of hers are supporting the attempts to unionize the 730 chain store. At Nordstrom, department sales clerks who are expected to go to extraordinary lengths to serve their customers (including delivering merchandise on their own time) are suing the company for back pay. Striking machinists drove Eastern Air Lines into bankruptcy when asked to make concessions once too often.

Digital Equipment Corporation, midway through its restructuring, invited employees to look for inefficiencies in their work. Employees themselves were able to identify tasks that could be eliminated. "Fear of their own layoffs slows them down a bit, but not much," says John F. Smith, DEC's senior vice-president for operations. Smith recommends specific rules to minimize the stress involved in downsizing:

1. Don't screw around and don't stretch it out. Employees need to know when the bad days will end and whether a second round of layoffs is coming.
2. If people see deadwood walking around—or out the door with a big package—watch out! If you play favorites, you'll lose employees' trust when you need it the most.
3. Make sure workers know what the new organization will look like, what part they will play in it, and why it will be healthy. That way, they can track gain, not pain.

Thomas Stewart, "Do You Push Your People Too Hard? *Fortune*, October 22, 1990, 121–128.

THE NATURE OF CONFLICT IN ORGANIZATIONS ◆◆◆◆◆◆

Conflict over resources and uncertainty about the future are the prime causes of stress among employees in organizations. In this chapter, we will consider different types of conflict and their impact on the organization and its members. We will also explore the causes and consequences of stress and ways of managing stress in the corporate environment.

Conflict—which results when an individual has separate but incompatible interests—becomes a critical determinant of organizational behavior in the face of perceived or real **resource scarcity.** That is, conflicts become important when there are not enough resources (food, love, attention, cars, clothes, autonomy, recognition, opportunities, and so on) for everyone to accomplish their goals. Consequently, individuals must compete with others for a share of those scarce resources. Competition can occur between family members and friends, among social groups, and within organizations. It should be noted that conflict does not always lead to competition, unless resources are scarce. If two marketing executives have conflicting ideas about how to sell a new product and the marketing budget can accommodate both ideas, the conflict generates no competition. For two individuals (or groups) to compete, they must perceive their goals to be mutually exclusive (that is, if one party gets what he or she wants, the other cannot). In the "FOCUS ON: Conflict," managers at First National Bank of Chicago experienced considerable conflict within their inner circle under the leadership of Robert Abboud. Employees avoided or played down the problems the bank was facing. No one seemed willing to confront the enormous level of destructive conflict within the organization, and as such, the performance of the bank was seriously compromised.

While managers such as Abboud may be guilty of creating conflict, they are more often associated with managing conflict. Of the ten managerial roles identified by Mintzberg, three specifically relate to conflict management duties.[1] Managers deal directly with organizational conflict in the roles of disturbance handler, negotiator, and resource allocator. In fact, if you ask managers how they spend each day, they will report that on average over 20 percent of each working day is spent in some form of conflict-management activity.[2]

The importance of conflict to organizational behavior was first highlighted in the 1920s by early management theorist Mary Parker Follett. In contrast to the mechanistic perspectives of her more famous contemporaries (such as Frederick Taylor), who focused on ways to structure organizations to avoid conflict, Follett believed that conflict was inherent and necessary for effective organizational performance. Much of her theorizing now serves as the basis for current perspectives on managing conflict in the workplace. An overview of her views and work is presented in the "FOCUS ON: The Nature of Conflict."

It is important to remember that while all organizational members are destined to be involved in a variety of conflicts and competitions, individual interests are not all incompatible nor is conflict uniformly bad or unwanted. As noted in Chapter 1, conflict occurs when individuals have differing perceptions,

---

[1] H. Mintzberg, *The Nature of Managerial Work* (New York: Harper and Row, 1973).

[2] K. Thomas and W. Schmidt, "A Survey of Managerial Interests with Respect to Conflict," *Academy of Management Journal* 19 (1976): 315–318.

beliefs, and goals. Such differences are both inevitable and healthy. Multiple and conflicting perspectives on a problem, when effectively managed, can reveal creative solutions and insights. Conflict, as with many other human conditions, is destructive in the extreme. When conflict is poorly managed and leads to hostility and infighting—as at the First National Bank of Chicago—it becomes destructive. However, too little apparent conflict often signals serious organizational or group problems as well.

Consider, for example, two married couples: one constantly fights and bickers, and another never fights. Both couples are likely to be having problems. The apparent absence of inevitable conflict often means that important differences between individuals are being suppressed or covered up. This does not mean that fighting is a good thing. It does mean that differences in perceptions, beliefs, and goals are inevitable and can be useful—but only if these conflicts are expressed so that they can be managed properly.

Examples of too much conflict are common in our society. Examples of too little conflict are much more difficult to identify. In his book *Groupthink*, Irving Janis suggests that disastrous foreign policy decisions often result when too little conflict is expressed within important decision-making bodies.[3] In a special task force, for instance, too little expressed conflict usually means that either inevitable conflicts are being suppressed or there are not enough diverse perspectives to generate insightful, high-quality decisions. Thus, moderate levels of conflict within organizations and between individuals are desirable if managed appropriately. Figure 6–1 illustrates the relationship between levels of conflict and organizational outcomes.

[3] I. Janis, *Groupthink: Psychological Studies of Policy Decisions and Fiascoes* (Boston: Houghton-Mifflin, 1982).

| FIGURE 6–1 | ▶ Conflict Intensity and Organizational Outcomes |

Conflict occurs because people differ in their perceptions, beliefs, and goals. Some conflict in organizations is not just inevitable, but useful and healthy, if appropriately managed.

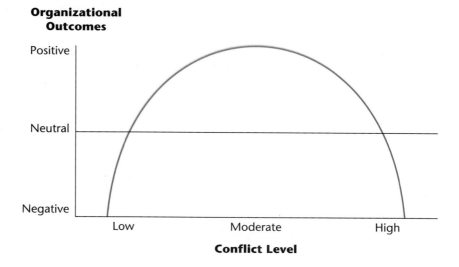

Source: L. D. Brown, *Managing Conflict at Organizational Interfaces* (Reading, Mass.: Addison-Wesley, 1983).

Focus on

Conflict

Infighting at the First National Bank of Chicago   In early May 1980, Robert Abboud was fired as chairman of the First National Bank of Chicago by its board of directors. The response on Wall Street and among the bank's employees was surprisingly positive. Employees were quoted as saying "people were singing 'Ding-dong, the witch is gone'," and bank executives and spouses were reportedly celebrating Abboud's dismissal with "steaks and champagne."

Such glee at the chairman's departure was predictable, for he had been abrasive, autocratic, and unpopular since being named to that position in 1975. When he was selected, two of the other three candidates for the position and more than two hundred bank officers resigned.

In his defense, the conflict did not begin with Mr. Abboud's tenure; rather, his selection as chairman may have exacerbated an already existing condition. One middle-level bank officer indicated that the tendency since 1972 was to take sides and take "swipes" at the other team. Individuals were defined based upon their affiliation with a particular "side." A rumor, since proved false, indicated that the First National Bank of Chicago's poor performance (a 47 percent drop in operating net income in the fourth quarter of 1979) was directly attributable to Edwin H. Yeo III, the top financial executive. The bank officer recalls, "I don't remember where I heard it, and I had no idea if any of it was true, but I passed it on anyway. Yeo was the enemy." (This particular employee was reported to be a supporter of Abboud.)

A few days before Yeo resigned, an unsigned memo was circulated which detailed complaints about Yeo's management style. No one knew who wrote the memo or how it got circulated; it was assumed to be written by a senior-level executive. Its wide circulation and implied legitimacy resulted in the perception that the accusations were, indeed, true.

Some observers suggested that the conflict at the First National Bank of Chicago was the result of Abboud's choice

Sources: Lawrence Roet, "Bank Politics: First Chicago with or without Abboud Is a Place of Tension," *The Wall Street Journal,* May 13, 1980; Todd Vogel, "Abboud Gets His Bank," *Business Week,* May 2, 1988, 38; and "Will Abboud Get The Boot?" In "Business This Week," ed. Harris Collingswood, *Business Week,* March 18, 1991, 40.

Too much conflict can be detrimental to organizations when it arouses anxiety in individuals, lowers job satisfaction levels, decreases productivity, increases turnover, and reduces the amount of information sharing and creative risk taking among employees. It may create a climate of mistrust or defeat. Too little apparent conflict hampers organizational functioning when it results from the suppression of critical (and useful) differences among organizational actors or the withdrawl of active involvement or commitment by organizational participants.

Conflict is useful to organizations in a variety of ways. Effectively managed, conflict promotes creative problem solving and the search for new ways of doing business. It increases employee interest and clarifies individual decisions and perceptions. In addition to its motivating and involving aspects, conflict can point up problem areas and signal the need for change within an organization. It allows a variety of perspectives to be brought to bear in finding new solutions to problems and identifying new directions for the organization. Thus, the suc-

of talented but ambitious outsiders for inner-circle positions. Others believed that Abboud's style was perceived as abrasive only by those who "didn't like to go in and face him because they felt they might be asked a question they couldn't answer."

Regardless of the basis of the conflict, the friction within the bank was regarded by many observers as so severe that it had seriously affected operations. While Abboud is given credit for strengthening the balance sheet and stabilizing the loan portfolio after the 1973–1975 recession, many employees contend that he intensified the conflict by playing executives off one another and criticizing subordinates in public. Because of this environment, the bank's top managers may have been so immersed in political infighting that they ignored the larger organizational issues. It was reported that, because of the organizational climate, bank executives refused to confront some of the bank's major problems. Instead, managers preferred to blame "bad data" or assume that the bank would "grow out of the problem." As a result, the bank's holding company had a reduction in net operating income of 12 percent in 1979 and 44 percent in the first quarter of 1980.

Although fired by the directors of the First National Bank of Chicago in 1980, Robert Abboud was selected to head the struggling First City Bankcorp of Texas in the second biggest bank bailout in U.S. history. His management style of personally approving almost every commercial loan considered by the bank, which irked many of his department heads, was hoped to be just what First City needed. However, on March 5, 1991, First City suspended dividend payments on all of its stocks in an attempt to improve its financial position in the wake of bad loans made under the leadership of Robert Abboud. By 1990, *Business Week* reported that bad loans accounted for nearly 6 percent of total loans, costing the bank about $158 million. Abboud was forced to begin downsizing and is looking for other ways to reduce debt and increase capital. With some analysts suggesting that First City's board of directors may be considering a new chairman, it does not seem that likely that Abboud's performance at First City will provide vindication for his 1980 ouster at First Chicago.

cessful manager is not the one who eliminates conflict in the organization. Rather, the successful manager is the one who manages moderate levels of conflict to achieve individual and organizational goals.

Conflict Between Individuals

Interpersonal conflict arises because of incompatible goals, ideas, feelings, or behaviors among two or more people. The most common form of interpersonal conflict is mixed-motive conflict. Mixed-motive conflict occurs when the participants have multiple interests at stake, some of which are best served by competitive behavior and others, by cooperative behavior. A common example of a mixed-motive situation is the prisoner's dilemma.[4] A description of the prisoner's dilemma is presented in the "FOCUS ON: Interpersonal Conflict."

[4]A. Rapaport and A. Chammah, *Prisoner's Dilemma: A Study in Conflict and Cooperation* (Ann Arbor, Mich.: University of Michigan Press, 1965).

Focus on

The Nature of Conflict

Mary Parker Follett The view that conflict can have a positive influence on organizational performance is usually considered a rather modern invention. Early management theorists tended to endorse the perception that conflict resulted in poor organizational performance. In fact, scientific management focused on reducing the amount of interaction and interdependence (and, thus, opportunities for conflict) among workers.

One management theorist provided a stark contrast to the prevailing view of conflict in the 1920s. Mary Parker Follett (1868–1933) believed that conflict provided management with an opportunity for creativity. She was one of the first management theorists to break away from the tenets of scientific management and to focus instead on developing philosophical and psychological foundations of management.

Follett defined conflict simply as difference. She noted, "As conflict—difference—is here in the world, as we cannot avoid it, we should, I think, use it. Instead of condemning it, we should set it to work for us." From Follett's perspective, conflict was neither good nor bad. She compared conflict to the necessary friction between the wheel of a locomotive and its track, suggesting that conflict was a critical component of organizational life.

The influence of her thinking is found in the work of many modern conflict-management theorists. She first introduced the concept of "integration" as her preferred method for dealing with conflict. Integration, she wrote, produced outcomes in which the desires of both parties are recognized and neither side has had to sacrifice. Such a strategy was compared to the other two forms of conflict management: domination and compromise. While her theorizing is consistent with more modern views of conflict, it is interesting to speculate why her work received so little attention for so long.

Source: M. P. Follett, "Constructive Conflict," in *Dynamic Administration: The Collected Papers of Mary Parker Follett,* ed. E. M. Fox and L. Urwick (New York: Hippocrene, 1982), 1–20.

In the prisoner's dilemma, two prisoners are faced with a choice to cooperate with their accomplice or to compete. Each prisoner must decide whether to (1) cooperate by remaining silent, thereby risking minor punishment if the accomplice also remains silent or major punishment if the accomplice confesses, or (2) compete (confess and earn either a minimal sentence if the accomplice "holds out" or a larger sentence if both confess). This situation illustrates two basic points about interpersonal conflict. First, the parties to a dispute are often interdependent—that is, the choices one makes influence the outcomes and choices of the other. Second, separate individual and joint outcomes may be mutually exclusive. The dominant (best) individual outcome results when the individual confesses. The dominant joint outcome occurs when both parties remain silent. Thus, whether to maximize the individual or the joint outcome is the nature of the prisoner's dilemma.

Conflict Between Groups

It would be simple if we could take what we know about interpersonal conflict and apply it directly to groups. While much of what we know about dyadic (two-person) conflict can be applied to groups, group conflict involves more than just summing the conflicts and motives of the individual actors. Although we will go into considerably more detail about groups in Chapters 7 and 9, it

Focus on

Interpersonal Conflict

The Prisoner's Dilemma Two suspects are taken into custody and separated. The district attorney (D.A.) is certain they are guilty of a specific crime but does not have sufficient evidence to convict them. She points out the alternatives to both prisoners—to confess to the crime that the police are sure they committed or not to confess. If both do not confess, then the D.A. will prosecute them on a minor charge for which they will both receive minor punishments. If they both confess, they will be prosecuted, but she will recommend less than the most severe sentence. If one turns "state's evidence" and confesses and the other does not, the confessor will receive a small sentence but the other will receive the maximum sentence. (The possible outcomes in years in prison are shown below. Each prisoner must make his decision *without* knowing what the other is doing.)

		A	
		Keep Quiet	**Confess**
B	**Keep Quiet**	−1, −1	−15, −3
	Confess	−3, −15	−10, −10

is important to consider the added dimensions that groups bring to the management of conflict.

Group conflict can occur within the group (intragroup) or between groups (intergroup). In day-to-day activities, it is often difficult to separate the effects of each of these forms of conflict, since one group rarely exists in isolation. Intragroup conflict occurs primarily because groups exert considerable influence on individual members. This influence usually takes the form of shaping the individual's behavior into a form acceptable to the group. Individual members may resist, resulting in conflicting goals (What is the nature or focus of our group?), ideas (What does this group stand for? What does it mean for me to be a part of the group?), emotions (How do I feel about being a part of this group?), and behaviors (How are we to accomplish our goals?). The more intragroup conflict, the less coordination, communication, and productivity.[5]

Intergroup conflict can also alter what is occurring within a particular group. In a study of interactions within and between groups, Sherif found that when two groups found themselves in conflict, behaviors within the groups changed in the following predictable ways:[6]

▶ Group cohesiveness increased.
▶ Task orientation increased.
▶ Loyalty to the group increased.
▶ Acceptance of autocratic leadership increased.

---

[5]M. Deutsch, "An Experimental Study of the Effects of Cooperation and Competition upon Group Process," *Human Relations* 2 (1949): 199–232.

[6]M. Sherif, *Intergroup Conflict and Cooperation* (Norman, Okla.: University Book Exchange, 1977).

In short, conflict with another group tends to coalesce or unify a group and make it better able to cope with external threats. Additionally, Sherif noted that conflict between groups often produces a "we/they" mentality that reveals itself in:

▶ Distorted perceptions and goals
▶ Negative stereotypes about the other group
▶ Reduced communication

Sherif and his colleagues collected much of their data on group conflict at a summer camp that they conducted. Known as the Robber's Cave experiments, Sherif's summer camp studies provide the basis for much of what we know about competition between groups, whether among adolescents or adults. These experiments are described in more detail in the "FOCUS ON: Group-Level Conflict."

Conflict Within Organizations

Organizational conflict embodies aspects of both group and individual conflict. The organization provides an arena for conflict to occur, as well as defines relationships and interdependencies among the disputants. However, conflict can

Group-Level Conflict

The Robber's Cave Experiments
Set up specifically for these experiments the Robber's Cave boys' camp recruited participants from different schools (to eliminate previous acquaintances) and screened for both physical and psychological health. During the first days of camp, the boys were allowed to develop friends spontaneously through a variety of campwide activities. The boys were then housed in two cabins. The population of each cabin was designed so that approximately two-thirds of an individual's best friends were in the other cabin. Within a few days, the pattern of interaction shifted dramatically. The boys tended to interact almost exclusively with their cabinmates and shared norms about group activities began to develop.

The researchers then arranged a series of competitive activities (such as football, baseball, and tug-of-war) in which the two cabins were pitted against each other. To increase the conflict, prizes were awarded to the winning team. During this time, the re-searchers noted that campers were developing hostility towards and stereotyped the behavior of members of the other cabin; they even planned ambushes and raids. New leaders emerged who were effective in combat, and intragroup solidarity increased dramatically.

The researchers devised situations specifically to promote conflict between the groups. At a campwide party, one group (the Red Devils) was allowed to arrive considerably earlier than the other group (the Bulldogs). The refreshments for the party consisted of two very different kinds of food. Half of the food was very fresh and appealing; the other half was old, ugly, and unappetizing. Because of the general level of competition that existed between the groups, the Red Devils consumed most of the attractive food, leaving the damaged food for their adversaries. When the Bulldogs arrived, they were so annoyed that the incipient conflict escalated from name-calling to a full-scale food fight.

Source: M. Sherif, *Intergroup Conflict and Cooperation* (Norman, Okla.: University Book Exchange, 1977).

Vertical conflict may involve groups at different levels or may occur between a group and an individual. Striking Eastern Airlines employees, shown here, were unhappy with Frank Lorenzo's cost-cutting measures. Unmanaged conflict between workers and management ultimately forced the airline into bankruptcy.

occur in a number of patterns—between two individuals, between an individual and a group, between two groups, or between two or more groups. Further, this conflict can occur in the same level of the organization's hierarchy (between two equal-status disputants), or it can occur across different levels of the organization (between supervisor and subordinate, for example).

Vertical conflict refers to conflict between people at different levels in an organization. The primary basis for this conflict is the differences in power across levels in the organization. For example, senior managers are likely to have very different personal and organizational expectations than assembly-line workers in the same organization. These expectations can color their experiences, beliefs, and interests, making the groups appear to be incompatible.

Horizontal conflict refers to conflict occurring at similar organizational levels. The more organizational units come into contact with each other, the more dependent they are on each other, and the smaller the amount of available resources, the greater the probability for horizontal conflict.[7] Three different types of group interdependence have been identified: pooled, sequential, and reciprocal interdependence.

Pooled interdependence exists when each department or unit contributes to the larger good but is not dependent upon the other. **Sequential interdependence** exists when the outputs of one unit become the inputs of another unit. The second unit is, then, quite dependent upon the first unit. **Reciprocal interdependence** exists when the outputs of one department become the inputs of a second; and the outputs of that second unit become the inputs for the first. Thus, both units are mutually dependent. As you might expect, reciprocal interdependence is likely to produce more conflict than sequential interdependence, and sequential interdependence is likely to produce more conflict than pooled interdependence.

---

[7] K. Thomas, "Conflict and Conflict Management," in *Handbook of Industrial and Organizational Psychology*, ed. M. Dunnette (Chicago: Rand McNally, 1976): 889–936.

Line-staff conflict is also a common organizational occurrence. Line employees are those directly involved in some aspect of producing the organization's product. Staff employees provide technical and advisory assistance to the line. As such, both groups have very different perspectives, goals, and statuses.

Traditionally, staff members tend to be more educated, better trained, and younger than line managers. Staff members tend to be professional, and as such have primary loyalty to their profession rather than to the organization. Staff members tend to be in lower organizational positions than the line managers they advise. Further, because the staff member is technically trained, he or she is familiar with a critical body of knowledge necessary for the effective functioning of the line manager. Thus, there may be an inherent conflict between the manager's authority to produce the product and the staff member's skill or knowledge necessary to produce the product.

It is easy to see the basis for this conflict. As organizational technologies become more complex, the demand for technically sophisticated staff members also will increase. Thus, the potential for conflict between line and staff members can only become more intense in the future.

Role conflict is a special form of organizational conflict. A role is a set of activities associated with a particular position. These activities are determined by the expectations of other organizational members (usually supervisors and coworkers), who make up the role set. When two or more role-specific activities are incompatible, then role conflict occurs.[8] In such cases, any attempt to comply with one set of expectations makes it impossible or difficult to comply with the other set of expectations. Unlike other forms of conflict, this form of conflict is organizationally based. That is, role conflict exists because expectations for job performance (as defined by the role set) do not coincide with the perception of appropriate job-related activities of either the role occupant or other members of the role set.

MANAGING CONFLICT ♦♦♦♦♦♦

By now it should be obvious that conflict is a common experience, regardless of whether we are by ourselves, with friends and relatives, or in work groups. What is important from both a personal and managerial perspective is how to manage it effectively. At the individual level, we need to know how to handle internal conflict as well as that between individuals with incompatible interests. In addition, we also need to know how to handle conflict within the groups and organizations to which we belong.

Negotiation: Interpersonal Conflict Strategies

A number of interpersonal conflict strategies can be brought to bear on disputes between individuals. Figure 6–2 illustrates five common strategies for resolving or managing conflict. The five strategies are competing, avoiding, accommodating, collaborating, and compromising. Notice that these five strategies are based upon differing levels of concern with maximizing your needs and maxi-

[8]D. Katz and R. L. Kahn, *The Social Psychology of Organizations* (New York: Wiley and Sons, 1978).

FIGURE 6–2 ▶ **A Two-Dimensional Model of Conflict Behavior**

The approach to interpersonal conflict can be characterized by individuals' concern with their own needs or concern for others' needs. Variations along these dimensions can give rise to five distinct conflict-resolution styles.

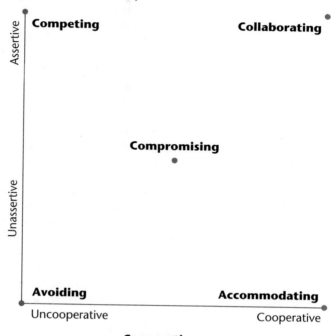

Source: K. Thomas, "Conflict and Conflict Management," in *Handbook of Industrial and Organizational Psychology,* ed. M. D. Dunnette (Santa Monica, Calif.: Goodyear Publishing Company, 1976), 900.

mizing the needs of the other party. Which conflict-management strategy you select depends upon where within the figure's two-dimensional space your interests lie.

If you are primarily concerned with getting what you want out of the exchange, then two strategies are likely to be most useful: competing and collaborating. If you are unconcerned with the other party's needs, **competing** may be the appropriate strategy. Other situations when you might need a competing strategy include when you are involved in an emergency or critical situation, when the other party is untrustworthy, or when you are sure of the correct solution.

If it is just as important that the other party's concerns be considered as that yours be considered, then **collaborating** may be a better strategic choice. Collaborating is a particularly useful alternative when the issue is too important to compromise, when you are trying to engender commitment among the parties to the dispute, or when you are trying to gain insight.

If you have little concern for your position or the position and desires of the other party, then it may be best to implement an **avoiding** strategy. If the issue at conflict is trivial or you are seriously outmatched by your opponent, you may choose not to confront the conflict at all. Avoidance may be the wisest course of action if (1) others can better handle the problem, (2) time is needed to let people cool down and regain perspective, or (3) the potential disruption that may occur from confronting the problem is greater than the potential benefit from solving it.

There are likely to be occasions when the other party's issues have priority. If you find out that the position you have been arguing is wrong or you wish to minimize a losing position, you may choose to give in. Perhaps by **accommodating** the other party's desires, you can earn "social credits" for your next interaction ("You have convinced me on this one, but just remember that you owe me one.").

Finally, if both sets of goals are important, but not worth the potential disruption of more aggressive strategies, then a **compromising** strategy may be most effective. If a quick, temporary solution is needed or nothing else seems to be working, then a simple compromise may be what is needed. Compromising—a solution that "splits the difference" between the disputants—is probably the strategy with which we have the most experience. The classic compromise is a strategy used by many families in trying to solve the "last-piece-of-pie-and-two-children-want-it" dilemma. The solution: one child cuts the pie into two pieces, the other child selects the first piece.

Conflict and conflict management represent very broad categories of behavior—so broad that it is often difficult to grasp exactly how to implement a particular strategy. To understand the usefulness of the five strategies we presented, it is important to place them in a specific context. An individual might view conflict resolution in a variety of ways. Given the nature of organizations and western society, negotiation is a particularly fruitful mechanism for resolving conflict.

Negotiation Negotiation is a widely used conflict-management technique. **Negotiation** is the process whereby two or more parties decide what each will give and take in an exchange between them.[9] This definition of negotiation highlights (1) its interpersonal nature, (2) the dependency of the parties, and (3) its allocation of resources.

Negotiation can be distinguished from other conflict-management techniques in that it involves a dispute with or between two or more parties who are in approximately equal power positions. Further, negotiation involves the division of tangible and intangible resources through a sequential evaluation of alternatives. In an attempt to manage conflict through negotiation, both parties (either explicitly or implicitly) prefer to search for a mutually acceptable solution rather than to fight openly, give in, break off interaction, or have their dispute resolved by a higher authority.[10]

---

[9]J. Z. Rubin and B. R. Brown, *The Social Psychology of Bargaining and Negotiation* (New York: Academic Press, 1975).

[10]R. J. Lewicki and J. R. Litterer, *Negotiation* (Homewood, Ill.: R. D. Irwin, 1985).

Negotiation is a process in which parties decide what each will give and take in an exchange. It generally involves parties who are interdependent and of roughly equal power. Negotiating a new contract between workers and management might be best handled by using integrative bargaining techniques, where both can gain.

The next section examines the specific information about the negotiator's and opponent's interests, priorities, and alternatives that are necessary to produce high-quality negotiated agreements.

Negotiating Rationally[11]   The goal of negotiating is to arrive at a *good* agreement. Far too often, individuals may substitute the goal of arriving at *any* agreement. Thus, it is critical that a negotiator know what is a good agreement or contract and what is not. To differentiate between these two outcomes, negotiators need to know what is their *best alternative to a negotiated agreement* (BATNA) as well as their *reservation price*. A BATNA represents the negotiator's best alternative should no agreement be reached. While people typically begin negotiating with some idea of what it is they hope to get, more important is knowing what is the least they will accept—the reservation price—or the point at which they are indifferent between reaching an agreement and settling for an impasse. While BATNAs and reservation prices are similar in many respects, they are also different. If you are trying to negotiate the purchase of a new car, your BATNA may be to continue riding your bicycle to school. Your reservation price may be the price offered to you for a similar car at another dealership.

Specifying the negotiator's BATNA and reservation price is not enough. The rational negotiator will also try to discern an opponent's BATNA and res-

---

[11] This section relies considerably on the book *Negotiating Rationally* by Max H. Bazerman and Margaret A. Neale (New York: Free Press, 1992). Adapted with permission of The Free Press, a division of Macmillan, Inc.

ervation price. While this may be difficult information to obtain, one should make as good an estimate as possible, knowing that the actual negotiation interaction will provide additional opportunities to gather information about the opponent.

Next, a good negotiator will identify, to the extent possible, the true issues in the negotiation and how important each issue is to each of the parties (both the focal negotiator and opponent). The basis for true integrative agreements is that the parties are willing to make trade-offs. That is, they are willing to make concessions on issues that are less important to obtain concessions on issues that are more important.

Regardless of the particular type of negotiating situation, identifying the alternatives, issues, and preferences of both parties is critical to reaching good agreements. This information can facilitate the negotiator's assessment of the two strategic opponents of the negotiation task: integrating or enlarging the available pool of resources and distributing or claiming of as large a share of that pool as possible.

Depending upon the desires of the parties, negotiation can incorporate all of the conflict-management tactics previously described. One may choose to avoid certain issues or provocations, one can give in on certain issues (usually with the expectation that the other party will be accommodating on other issues), or one can state one's position and resist conceding. These strategies are part and parcel of the two dominant types of negotiation—distributive negotiating and integrative negotiating.

Distributive negotiation is the most commonly used negotiation strategy, and it is what most of us imagine negotiation to be. In distributive negotiation, the parties decide how to allocate a fixed amount of resources. The perception of a fixed pie of resources leads negotiators to behave in a competitive, contentious manner. The assumption is that every time one party wins, the other must give up something. As a result, the other party is seen as an adversary and as the origin of the problem—"it's me against you." Both must concede or compromise their initial positions. As such, neither wins completely, but then again, neither loses everything. Of course, splitting the difference or compromising is sometimes a silly strategy as suggested by the cartoon in Figure 6–3.

As suggested by our earlier description of the compromise strategy, distributive negotiation is a style of conflict management best implemented under the following conditions:

1. No ongoing relationship or potential for one exists—the interaction is a one-shot deal.
2. A quick, simple solution to the conflict is needed.
3. The parties have mutually incompatible goals.

What about conflict between supervisors and subordinates, coworkers, spouses, friends, and family groups? Many of these interactions are characterized by the potential for or the existence of long-term relationships, compatible goals, and longer time horizons for discovering solutions. When these conditions exist, distributive negotiation is an inappropriate technique. Rather than an adversarial perspective, one might wish to assume an advocacy, or cooperative, orientation.

Integrative bargaining is different from distributive negotiation in that it assumes that there can be an expanding pot of resources for the parties to

FIGURE 6-3 ▶

Their community property had been
equally divided. Still, neither one of
them was happy with the divorce settlement.

Source: RUBES by Leigh Rubin. By permission of Leigh Rubin and Creator's Syndicate, Inc.

divide. Thus, one can gain without the other having to lose. If the resources can be expanded through creative problem solving, then the parties need not compete with each other. Since, in this case, one is not the enemy or adversary of the other, the disputants may be more willing to share concerns, ideas, and expectations. An example of an integrative division of resources is illustrated in Figure 6–4.

However, integrative bargaining also has its own unique set of demands. For integrative bargaining to succeed, both participants must have high aspirations or goals (for the attainment of the "right" solution), a problem-solving orientation (it's both parties against the problem), and a sufficient level of trust so that information can be shared.[12]

While integrative bargaining is a more difficult process, its benefits are considerable. Agreements reached integratively are more stable and strengthen the relationship between the parties. They also may be the only way to get an agreement between individuals who have high aspirations and resist conceding on these important issues.[13] Figure 6–5 illustrates the differences between distributive and integrative bargaining.

---

[12] D. G. Pruitt, "Integrative Agreements: Nature and Consequences," *Negotiating in Organizations*, eds. M. H. Bazerman and R. J. Lewicki (Beverly Hills, Calif.: Sage Publishing, 1983).

[13] Ibid.

FIGURE 6-4 ▶

Integrative agreements arise when two parties find their needs and resources are *complementary*. In this cartoon, a single ice-cream bar provides dessert for two: the ice cream for the man and the wooden stick for the beaver. Both seem to want the ice-cream bar, but they really want different parts of the treat.

FRANK AND ERNEST ©by Bob Thaves

Source: Frank and Ernest reprinted by permission of NEA, Inc.

Each of us has a great deal of experience with and skill in distributive negotiation. It is easy to envision an opponent as the source of the conflict. It is much more difficult to develop and maintain the level of trust required to view the other party as a collaborator (with whom information should be freely shared) and the dispute as the enemy. An all-too-common response is to view all negotiations as adversarial processes. Thus it is important to learn how to "reframe" negotiations from a distributive to an integrative perspective.

It is difficult to transform a conflict with distributive potential into one with integrative potential. Five suggested tactics are described below:[14]

1. **Superordinate goals.** A primary difference between distributive and integrative bargaining is that, in the latter, the relationship between the parties is important. It is therefore much easier to develop goals that supersede the short-term conflict the parties may be experiencing. Organizational members have an explicit superordinate goal—resolving the conflict in the organization's best interest. Acknowledging such goals can enhance the parties' perception that they are aligned in achieving the superordinate goal—that they are advocates rather than adversaries.

2. **Separate the people from the problem.** It is very difficult not to personalize a problem or conflict. As suggested earlier, one of the critical differences between integrative and distributive negotiation is the perception of the other party. To see the other party as an advocate rather than an adversary is critical to developing the trust needed to achieve integrative agreements.

3. **Focus on interests, not on positions.** Positions are demands the negotiator makes. Interests are what underlie demands or positions. While positions may be one-dimensional, individuals typically have multiple interests. Often shared and different (although not incompatible) interests underlie incompatible positions. Consider the typically distributive, adversarial relationship between landlord and tenant. It is not difficult to identify their common and different interests. Both want stability (a permanent address and a stable tenant); a well-maintained apartment; and a

---
[14]R. Fischer and W. Ury, *Getting to Yes* (New York: Houghton-Mifflin, 1981).

FIGURE 6–5	▶ Types of Bargaining

Integrative agreements—those that seek out complementary needs and resources—can be difficult to find. However, they tend to be more stable and strengthen the long-term relationship between the disputing parties.

	Distributive	**Integrative**
Payoff Structure	Fixed amount of resources to be divided	Variable amount of resources to be divided
Primary Motivation	To gain at the expense of the other	To maximize joint outcomes
Interests	Diametrically opposed	Convergent or congruent
Relationships	Short-term relationship	Long-term relationship

good relationship (a tenant who pays his rent regularly and a landlord responsive to repair requests). Their interests differ in that the landlord values the rent more than living in the apartment, and the tenant values living in the apartment more than the rent.

4. **Invent options for mutual gain.** This is the basis for expanding the resource pie. All too often, however, individuals ignore the opportunity for mutual gain because they assume the resource pie is fixed. To invent options for mutual gain, participants must be willing to think creatively. They must separate the act of creating alternatives (brainstorming) from judging those alternatives. They must go beyond the obvious issues or positions and look for broader solutions. In the search for mutual gain, the task is to get the other side to make the decision you want. Thus, you need to make it as easy as possible for them to agree. Understand their perspective, search for precedents, and develop proposals to which they can respond with a single word: yes.

5. **Use objective criteria.** No matter how integrative each party may be, they are likely to have some incompatible interests. Rather than seeing these disagreements as contests of will, a more productive tactic may be to focus on what is fair. Framing your disagreements as searches for fair standards is likely to be much more fruitful than focusing on who will win. Deciding what is fair requires both parties to understand the criteria for judging fairness. Each party must be reasonable and open. In our landlord-tenant interaction, both parties may wish the apartment repainted. The landlord might prefer that the tenant buy the paint and repaint the apartment in a suitable color. In contrast, the tenant would certainly prefer to have the apartment's owner assume responsibility for the painting of the apartment. In determining what is fair, the parties may agree that the landlord will reimburse the tenant for the purchase of the paint and reduce the rent to compensate the tenant for the work.

Even with the best of intentions, even when the negotiated settlement is in both parties' best interests, it is sometimes difficult to reach agreement. A host of factors can cripple even the most well-intentioned set of negotiators.

The "INTERNATIONAL FOCUS ON: Negotiations" illustrates the impact of two of these factors, inexperience and cultural differences, which resulted in a very poorly negotiated outcome. The next section examines the ways in which the cognitions of negotiators can sabotage potential agreements.

Cognitive Biases and Negotiation   In Chapter 5, we identified a number of heuristics, or cognitive shortcuts, which, when used inappropriately, result in systematically biased decisions. In recent years, considerable research has dem-

INTERNATIONAL FOCUS ON

Negotiations

Negotiating with the Japanese
When the plane landed in Tokyo for the 14-day negotiation, I was the first passenger to trot down the ramp, raring to go. At the bottom of the ramp two Japanese gentlemen awaited me, bowing politely. I liked that.

The two Japanese helped me through customs, then escorted me to a large limousine. I reclined comfortably on the plush seat at the rear of the limousine, and they sat stiffly on two fold-up stools. I said expansively, "Why don't you people join me? There's plenty of room back here."

They replied, "Oh, no. You're an important person. You obviously need your rest." I liked that, too.

As the limousine rolled along, one of my hosts asked, "By the way, do you know the language?"

I replied, "You mean Japanese?"

He said, "Right, that's what we speak in Japan."

I said, "Well, no. But I hope to learn a few expressions. I've brought a dictionary with me."

His companion asked, "Are you concerned about getting back to your plane on time?" (Up until that moment, I had not been concerned.) "We can schedule this limousine to transport you back to the airport."

I thought to myself, "How considerate."

Reaching into my pocket, I handed them my return flight ticket, so the limousine would know when to get me. I didn't realize it then, but they knew my deadline, whereas I didn't know theirs.

Instead of beginning negotiations right away, they first had me experience Japanese hospitality and culture. For more than a week, I toured the country, from the Imperial Palace to the shrines of Kyoto. They even enrolled me in an English-language course in Zen to study their religion.

Every evening for four-and-a-half hours, they had me sit on a cushion on a hardwood floor for a traditional dinner and entertainment. Can you imagine what it's like sitting on a hardwood floor for all those hours? If I didn't get hemorrhoids as a result, I'll probably never get them. Whenever I inquired about the start of negotiations, they'd murmur, "Plenty of time! Plenty of time!"

At last, on the twelfth day we began the negotiations, finishing early so we could play golf. On the thirteenth day we met again, and ended early because of a farewell dinner. Finally, on the morning of the fourteenth day, we resumed our negotiations in earnest. Just as we were getting to the crux of things, the limousine pulled up to take me to the airport. We all piled in and continued hashing out the terms. Just as the limousine's brakes were applied at the terminal, we consummated the deal.

How well do you think I did in that negotiation? For many years, my superiors referred to it as "the first great Japanese victory since Pearl Harbor."

Source: Herb Cohen, *You Can Negotiate Anything* (New York: Bantam Books, 1982), 93–95.

onstrated the impact of some of the cognitive biases—framing, anchoring and adjustment, and availability—on negotiator behavior.[15]

As you may recall, the framing heuristic is associated with the risk inherent in an individual's decisions.[16] That is, when a decision is framed in terms of potential gains, the decision maker is more likely to choose the risk-averse option. When the decision is framed in terms of potential losses, the decision maker is likely to choose the riskier option. In negotiation, this tendency can be translated into an increased willingness to reach agreement in the former case and a resistance to agreement in the latter case.

Any potential agreement can be valued in two different ways: a negotiator can consider what is being gained from the new agreement (how much better it is than the old agreement, for example) or what is being given up to get the new agreement. Researchers have shown that individuals who perceived the outcome of a negotiation in terms of what they had to gain were more willing to reach agreement than those who perceived it in terms of potential losses. For example, individuals who were told to maximize profits (gains) in their negotiation reached agreements more easily than those who were told to minimize expenses (losses).[17] Thus, simply altering how the negotiation is presented can significantly influence how the negotiators behave.

The second bias that has been examined in the context of negotiation is anchoring-and-adjustment effect, which was discussed in Chapter 3 as a building block of the perception process. This heuristic suggests that people will use a piece of information as a basis upon which to make a judgment or decision, but will insufficiently adjust from that informational base to the correct answer.

This is the basis for research suggesting that the level of the initial offer is highly correlated with the level of the final agreement. The more extreme the initial offer, the more extreme the final agreement. For example, when real estate agents were asked to assess a piece of residential property, their estimate of the value of the property was significantly influenced by the seller's listing price. The higher the seller's listing price, the higher the perceived value of the property by the real estate agents.[18] This was true whether the property was listed above or below its actual appraised value. The results of this research suggest that negotiators are influenced by the anchor of the party's initial offer—so much so that it can color the final valuation of the negotiated commodity or product.

The availability heuristic occurs when individuals attempt to judge the likelihood of an event's occurrence. The rule here is "that which is most easily remembered occurs most frequently.[19] While it is true that frequently occurring

[15]M. Neale and M. Bazerman, *Cognition and Rationality in Negotiation* (New York: Free Press, 1991).

[16]D. Kahneman and A. Tversky, "Prospect Theory: An Analysis of Decisions under Risk," *Econometrica* 47 (1979): 263–291.

[17]M. H. Bazerman, T. Magliozzi, and M. A. Neale, "The Acquisition of an Integrative Response in a Competitive Market," *Organizational Behavior and Human Decision Processes* 35 (1985): 294–313.

[18]G. B. Northcraft and M. A. Neale, "Experts, Amateurs, and Real Estate: An Anchoring-and-Adjustment Perspective on Property Pricing Decisions," *Organizational Behavior and Human Decision Processes* 39 (1987): 84–97.

[19]A. Tversky and D. Kahneman, "Availability: A Heuristic for Judging Frequency and Probability," *Cognitive Psychology* 5 (1973): 207–232.

events are familiar to us, it is not always true that familiar events occur frequently. Consider the negotiator who is representing a constituency. The consequences of not meeting the constituency's expectations may be very clear to the negotiator (loss of status or position, evaluation anxiety, and so forth). In determining the strategy to be used in the subsequent interaction, the negotiator is likely to overestimate the probability that those costs will be incurred. The costs are more vivid to the negotiator because they are costs he or she would personally bear. The more overestimated the probability of these costs occurring, the more likely the negotiator is to behave in a competitive manner and to be unwilling to concede on issues for fear of his or her constituency's response.[20]

Many more heuristics can systematically bias a negotiator's behavior and subsequent agreements. However, this sampling illustrates how important it is that negotiators give serious consideration to the ways in which they may be crippling their own attempts to reach high-quality negotiated agreements. The barriers to good negotiated agreements are many, and the organizational and individual costs of reaching poor agreements can be quite high. It is in the best interest of the individual to commit the time to prenegotiation planning and strategy that so serious an interaction warrants.

Organizational Conflict Management

In the previous section, we focused on individual methods for reducing or managing conflict. In this section we will focus on ways in which organizations can be structured to alleviate conflict. Two types will be discussed—formal organizational structures and informal organizational structures. Formal organizational structures include liaisons, organizational slack, and ombudsmen or employee/client/customer representatives, whose task is to resolve conflict at both internal and external organizational boundaries. Informal organizational structures to resolve conflict focus primarily on the manager as a dispute resolver. Within such an arena, a manager's task often requires considerable conflict resolution skill.

Formal Organizational Roles   Since conflict is commonly associated with scarce resources and interdependencies, an organization can reduce the potential for conflict by reducing the interaction among groups and the competition for resources. This can be accomplished through the use of slack resources and buffers. **Slack,** or excess, resources can minimize conflict because they reduce the amount of necessary interaction. For example, if two departments are sequentially interdependent, having excess inventory of A's output (slack) insulates or buffers B from the inconsistencies of A. **Buffers** need not be only excess inventory or product. Individuals or groups of individuals may serve the same function. A liaison or linking pin is an individual assigned to integrate the activities of two interdependent organizational units or groups. Within a matrix organization (a form of organizational structure described in Chapter 16), the project manager often serves this function.

---

[20]M. A. Neale, "The Effects of Negotiation and Arbitration Cost Salience on Bargainer Behavior: The Role of Arbitrator and Constituency on Negotiator Judgment," *Organizational Behavior and Human Performance* 34 (1984): 97–111.

A different form of a linking-pin role is that of the **organizational ombudsman.** While linking pins generally integrate the activities of two interdependent organizational units, the ombudsman may focus on conflict at the employee/organizational boundary. The ombudsman provides a formal mechanism for employee grievances to be aired. In different institutions, the ombudsman may offer a means for clients or customers to make their dissatisfactions known.[21] The duties of an ombudsman usually cover interpreting policy, counseling, resolving disputes, and providing feedback and identifying potential problem areas to senior management.[22] For example, ombudsmen at McDonnell Aircraft in St. Louis, Missouri, and Douglas Aircraft in Long Beach, California, have found that most of their cases concern corporate disputes such as conflicts with supervisors, arguments over promotions and transfers, or misunderstandings over benefits. Most such problems can be sorted out by a direct call to the department head involved, without invoking higher authority. A few cases, however, deal with whistle-blowing on the safety of a product design or the billing of a defense contract. Another example of the corporate ombudsman's work can be found in the "FOCUS ON: Corporate Ombudsmen."

Informal Organizational Roles   The ombudsman has a formal role as dispute resolver. This formal designation does not, however, limit the role that others play in reducing or managing conflict in organizational settings. Because conflict is so common in group and organizational life, formal structures or procedures often do not adequately meet the demand for conflict resolution. As a result, a variety of individuals assume the role of dispute resolver or intervenor. The manager is an excellent organizational example of someone who spends a great deal of time managing conflict, even though conflict resolution is not usually considered a formal aspect of his or her job description. A complete list of potential third-party intervenors is presented in Figure 6–6.

Managers often serve as third parties to a conflict. Being a third party means that the manager is indirectly involved in the conflict. He or she is not one of the disputants. **Third-party intervention** in conflict is not limited to managers acting within organizations. The legal system is a common example of a formal third-party intervention system. Judges resolve conflicts between private parties in civil courts or between representatives of public and private parties in criminal courts. Within the context of industrial relations, third parties may resolve differences between labor and management through mediation, arbitration, or factfinding. Consumer complaints, property-settlement and child-custody issues in divorce proceedings, landlord-tenant disputes, and neighborhood disagreements are often resolved through the use of mediators.

Each of these types of third-party intervention solves disputes in specific ways. **Arbitration** is similar to the American judicial system. An arbitrator is a neutral third party who, after hearing both sides of the dispute, determines a final, binding outcome. **Mediation** occurs when a neutral third party encourages interaction between the disputants but has no authority to force a solution

---

[21]D. M. Kolb, "Who Are Organizational Third Parties and What Do They Do?" in *Research on Negotiation in Organizations,* ed. R. J. Lewicki, B. Sheppard, and M. H. Bazerman (Greenwich, Conn.: JAI Press, 1987).

[22]M. P. Rowe, "The Non-Union Complaint System at MIT: An Upward-Feedback Model," *Alternatives to the High Cost of Litigation* 2 (1984): 10–18.

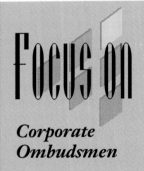

Focus on

Corporate Ombudsmen

Resolving Disputes within Organizations   Making sure that bad news gets passed up the chain of command is a topic receiving a lot of attention in executive suites these days. In the past few years, dozens of major companies have set up formal ombudsman systems in which a senior executive operating outside the normal chain of command is permanently available to deal with employee grievances and alarms on a confidential basis.

Mary Rowe, past president of the Corporate Ombudsman Association, believes that the growing diversity of the work force, while leading to new opportunities in corporate America, will also lead to more friction in the workplace. As education levels fall and the need for skilled workers increases, companies will have to go to greater and greater lengths to keep good employees. Formal grievance procedures are not enough, suggests Rowe. More creative ways of solving problems often bring about better results. Some companies have an individual—in effect, a company judge—who investigates complaints and determines solutions. Others use ombudsmen who can intervene and advise but lack the final authority of the company judges.

Companies that have put these systems into place say that they are worth their modest cost. The sheer number of calls logged—over 3,000 in 1986 at General Dynamics—suggests that workers like and trust ombudsmen. By monitoring the complaints, companies can pinpoint plants, programs, or managers causing serious morale problems. At AT&T's Bell Labs, ombudsman Martha Maselko says that the costs of recruiting and training a skilled engineer are so high that simply keeping three employees a year from quitting is enough to cover the $200,000 yearly cost of her office.

Mary Rowe suggests that a number of elements are necessary for an effective employee grievance program:

1. People's feelings—their hurt, anger, and fear—are dealt with, not just the complaint.
2. Everyone in the organization knows how the procedure works, trusts it, and feels it is a safe channel for complaints.
3. Counseling is used to sort out conflicts and to negotiate solutions.
4. Shuttle diplomats act as go-betweens when needed.
5. The investigation of complaints is fair, prompt, and thorough.
6. Impartial arbitration is available if needed.
7. Complainants have a range of options for how to complain.
8. Complaints are confidential and anyone in the organization may file one.
9. People with special expertise are brought in to handle complaints when appropriate.

Sources: Michael Brody, "Listen to Your Whistle-Blower," *Fortune,* November 24, 1986, pp. 77–78, and D. Goleman, "Managing: Court for Workplace Disputes," *New York Times,* April 8, 1990, section 3, part 2, p. 29.

upon them. **Factfinding** occurs when a neutral third party, based upon the evidence presented by the parties, determines a reasonable solution to the dispute. As in mediation, the parties are not bound to follow the recommendation of the fact finder.

Unlike formal third parties or organizational ombudsmen who have prescribed ways of interacting with the disputants, the manager has considerably more leeway in choosing how to handle a dispute. Managers differ from formal third-party intervenors in many ways. Figure 6–7 describes these differences.

| FIGURE 6–6 | ▶ **Individuals Engaged in Informal Dispute Resolution** |

Many roles in society contain large conflict-resolution components. Managers also spend a lot of their time informally resolving conflict, perhaps without realizing how central conflict-resolving activities are to their role.

Go-betweens (messengers)	Matchmakers
Lawyers	Brokers
Auditors	Agents (insurance agents, real estate agents)
Managerial consultants	
Marriage counselors	Umpires
Psychotherapists	Parents
Special envoys	Dictators
Priests, rabbis	Law enforcement officials
Village elders	International monitors
Elected representatives	Regulatory agencies
Auctioneers	International courts of law

Source: S. Kaufman and G. T. Duncan, "Third-Party Intervention: A Theoretical Framework," in *Managing Conflict: An Interdisciplinary Approach*, ed. M. A. Rahim (New York: Praeger Press, 1988).

Mangerial Dispute Intervention

While formal third parties are usually restricted to acting as mediators, fact finders, or arbitrators, managers have considerably more flexibility and can intervene in organizational disputes as judges (arbitrators), inquisitors, mediators, avoiders, delegators, or providers of impetus. Each of these types of intervention is described below.

1. **Judges** exert high degrees of control over the outcome of the conflict but not the process by which it is resolved. Judges typically allow both sides to present whatever facts, evidence, or arguments they desire, then decide the outcome of the conflict. They have the power to enforce that decision on the disputants.

2. **Inquisitors** exert high degrees of control over both the outcome and the process of conflict resolution. They direct the presentation of evidence, ask questions, act as referees, and call for evidence not willingly offered. As judges do, inquisitors decide the outcome of the conflict and enforce that decision on the disputants.

3. **Mediators** exert high degrees of control over the process of conflict resolution, but not its outcome. A mediator may separate the parties, interview them, and bring them back together. A mediator may also separate the parties and ferry proposals back and forth between them to help them forge their own solution.

4. **Avoiders, delegators,** and the **"providing impetus" tactic** exert low degrees of control over either the process or the outcome. Avoiders prefer to find ways to ignore the conflict or minimize its importance. Delegators recognize that the conflict exists, but try to return responsibility for its solution to the disputants or get someone else to accept it. The "providing impetus" tactic (also known as the kick-in-the-pants style) delegates the conflict back to the parties with a threat—"Either resolve

FIGURE 6-7	▶ Differences between Managerial and Institutional Third-Party Roles

Dimension	Institutional Third Parties	Managers as Third Parties
Dispute Characteristics		
1. Construal of disputes	Disputes exist and involve parties with competing claims. Often with basis in law or prior agreement.	Conflict is a problem of misunderstanding that demands a rational solution.
2. Boundaries of dispute	Dispute well demarcated and isolated from other activities of parties.	Dispute embedded in on-going stream of activity.
3. Point of intervention	Third party sought, often as a last effort at dispute resolution.	Intervention frequently early, at the initiative of the manager.
Third-Party Role		
1. Involvement in dispute	Disinterested third party. Principal concern for resolution.	Frequently a part of the problem with concern, for own and organization's best interests.
2. Authority	Limited authority circum-scribed by role as mediator or arbitrator.	Wide range of authority without clear demarcation of third-party role.
3. Cultural expectations	Expected to act as conflict solver involved in recog-nized conflicts of interest.	Expected to act as decision maker involved in differ-ences of opinions over best direction for organization.
4. Frequency of exposure	Limited exposure to parties, typically only once.	Frequent interaction with parties within many roles. Often dealt with similar problem in past.

this yourselves or the manager will resolve the problem, and nobody will like that solution!"

In working with a variety of disputes, managers were found to use the inquisitorial style most often, followed by the judging and "providing impetus" styles. Managers reported that they use mediation frequently, but in fact seldom give the disputants any real control over the outcome. They were more likely to use strategies that controlled outcomes when (1) there were time pressures, (2) the disputants were not likely to work together in the future, and (3) the settlement had broad implications for the resolution of other disputes.[23]

Researchers may understand what managers do in conflict situations, but they do not suggest that these are the correct or optimal responses. Describing

---

[23] R. J. Lewicki and B. Sheppard, "Choosing How to Intervene: Factors Affecting the Use of Process and Outcome Control in Third-Party Dispute Intervention," *Journal of Occupational Behavior* 6 (1985): 49–64.

managers' behavior does not mean endorsing it as the optimal correct behavior. Lewicki, Sheppard, and their colleagues have proposed and tested a contingency model of managerial intervention. Based upon their research results, they believe that choice of managerial intervention strategy should be based upon what the manager wishes to accomplish in addition to resolving the dispute. Is the objective of the intervention that

1. the conflict be resolved quickly (efficiency)?
2. the optimal solution be chosen (effectiveness)?
3. the disputants be satisfied with the outcome (satisfaction)?
4. the outcome be perceived as just by disputants (fairness)?

Figure 6–8 describes these four outcomes in more detail.

Whether or not the manager attempts to control the outcome of the conflict or the manner in which the conflict is resolved determines which intervention objective will result. Figure 6–9 illustrates the relationship between concern with process or outcome control and the four intervention objectives. If the manager cares most about simply getting a solution, any solution, then the focus on efficiency suggests that the manager should use an inquisitorial style if he or she wishes to have control over how the outcome is reached. If the manager does not want control over either the process or the outcome of the conflict resolution, then the appropriate strategy would be a choice among avoiding, delegating, or providing impetus.

If getting the best or optimal solution to the conflict (effectiveness) is the primary objective of the manager's intervention, then the choice is between using the style of an inquisitor or a judge. If how the solution is determined is at issue, then the inquisitorial style is more appropriate. If a manager has little concern with controlling the conflict-resolving process, then the strategic choice should probably be to act like a judge.

When a manager is most concerned that the disputants are satisfied with the resolution, mediation is the only correct choice of intervention strategy.

| **FIGURE 6–8** | ▶ **Managerial Dispute Intervention Outcomes** |

Efficiency: to solve the problem with a minimum expenditure of resources—third-party time, disputant time, capital outlay, etc. Solving the problem quickly would be an example of procedural efficiency.

Effectiveness: to solve the problem so it is solved well and stays solved. Making sure that the third party listens to all parties who have a relevant perspective on the conflict is an example of procedural effectiveness; brainstorming to invent the best possible solution—one that will *work* or one that will not bring the parties back to the manager with the same dispute—is an example of outcome effectiveness.

Participant satisfaction: to solve the problem so that the parties are satisfied with the solution. Giving all sides an opportunity to present their case or having the disputants play a critical role in the development of the actual solution are examples of procedures that enhance participant satisfaction.

Fairness: to solve the problem so that the parties believe the outcome is fair (by some specific standard—equality, equity, etc.). Hearing both sides, applying rules consistently, and treating both disputants in a similar manner are mechanisms that promote the perception of fairness.

| FIGURE 6–9 | ▶ Strengths of Intervention Strategies |

Conflict intervention strategies differ in the extent to which they exert control over the process and outcomes of the dispute. These differences, in turn, result in maximizing a variety of conflict-resolution goals such as participant satisfaction.

		Third Party Controls the Outcome	
		Yes	No
Third Party Controls the Process	Yes	Efficiency Effectiveness	Satisfaction Fairness
	No	Fairness Effectiveness	Efficiency

Disputant satisfaction may be important when commitment to the solution is critical for its successful implementation.

Finally, if the manager wishes to ensure that the solution is perceived by the disputants as fair, then he or she has a choice of strategies available. If the manager's goal is to control the solution, then intervening as a judge is the best choice. This strategy has the additional benefit of being associated with effective solutions. Alternatively, if the manager is not concerned with the exact nature of the final solution, then a mediating strategy is an appropriate choice. Because mediation promotes both participant satisfaction and perceived fairness, it is the form of intervention most desired by disputants. It allows them the greatest control over the actual solution, while providing them with some incentive to reach agreement (via the involvement of the mediating manager).

Managers seem to understand the attractiveness of this strategy to subordinates, since they report using mediation to a greater extent than they actually do. However, giving up control over the solution is difficult for managers. In fact, a recent study of managers indicated that lower-level managers were more likely to use intervention strategies that stressed control over outcome. The higher the manager was in the organization, the more likely he or she was to use mediation as an intervention strategy.[24]

STRESS IN ORGANIZATIONS ♦♦♦♦♦♦

The Relationship Between Conflict and Stress

Intrapersonal Conflict   When conflict exists at an individual level, it can take the form of intrapersonal conflict (conflict within an individual) or interpersonal conflict (conflict between individuals). In the case of intrapersonal conflict,

---

[24]M. A. Neale and J. W. Brittain, "Managerial Third-Party Dispute Resolution: The Effects of Intervenor Status, Issue Importance, and Level of Conflict," working paper, Northwestern University, Evanston, Ill.

choosing one goal and selecting the appropriate alternative to maximize this goal removes other alternatives from consideration. For example, in deciding to go to graduate school, an applicant must eventually make a choice for one particular program, thus eliminating the other schools from consideration. The amount of conflict that surfaces in these decisions depends upon the attractiveness of each choice. Three common types of intrapersonal goal conflict have been identified, each representing different levels of attractiveness among options.

Approach-approach conflict occurs when an individual must choose between two equally attractive alternatives, such as two outstanding job offers. On first blush, this may seem to be an ideal situation. However, if both alternatives are equally attractive, then the choice between them may be difficult. Fortunately, this type of conflict is not long lasting because often we are able to find reasons why one choice dominates—if only just by a little bit. Once this happens, then the slightly preferred option is chosen.

Unfortunately, approach-approach conflict does not always end there. Often, once the choice is made, "decision regret"[25] may occur. The option not chosen now becomes more attractive, simply because it was not chosen. Decision regret may lead decision makers to reconsider the positive aspects of the chosen option and give them more weight to justify and validate the decision made.

Avoidance-avoidance conflict is created when we are faced with two equally unattractive choices, both with negative outcomes. For example, an employee may be faced with choosing between increased company-related travel time or a demotion. As with approach-approach conflict, this is difficult to resolve because it represents a choice between unattractive outcomes.

Approach-avoidance conflict is the most common type of intrapersonal conflict and is based upon having to choose an option with both good and bad outcomes. For example, one may have to choose between one's current job and a great position in a bad location. The intensity of the approach-avoidance conflict increases as (1) the number of alternatives increase, (2) the attraction/aversion of the outcomes remains about equal, and (3) the issues increase in importance. If the conflict becomes too extreme, individuals may remove themselves from the conflict by refusing to make a decision. This sort of response to conflict probably is not very functional, but is quite common.

Being confronted with these types of choices is difficult. The more such choices we experience, the greater the intrapersonal conflict we may have to manage. One of the primary indicators of intrapersonal conflict is stress. **Stress** has been defined in a number of ways.[26] A common understanding of the term is that stress refers to experiencing something unpleasant. However, more formal definitions of stress are based upon the factors identified as stress originators. The stimulus definitions of stress suggest that stress is an external force, such as imminent deadlines, acting on a person. This suggests that what is stressful to one person is equally stressful to another.

The second perspective on stress suggests that it is a physiological or psychological response of an individual to environmental demands. These demands

---

[25] D. Bell, "Regret in Decision Making under Uncertainty," working paper, Harvard University, Boston, Mass.

[26] J. M. Ivancevich and M. E. Matteson, *Stress and Work: A Managerial Perspective* (Glenview, Ill.: Scott, Foresman, & Co., 1980).

Although work is a major source of stress for many people, some handle it better than others. Factors which influence how an individual handles stress include organizational, social, and family demands and the individual's health and personality.

are known as stressors. Hans Seyle, often referred to as the originator of the concept of stress, suggests that stress is "the rate of all the wear and tear caused by life."[27]

A third point of view attempts to combine both the stimulus and the response view by suggesting that any attempt to partition what is environment and what is an individual's response to the environment is arbitrary. From this perspective, stress is a mismatch between a person's skills, abilities, and job demands and his or her needs. Stress does not exist in isolation in the environment or in the individual, but rather in the interaction of the two. What is stressful for one person may not be stressful for another. Stress then can be seen as the psychological and physiological response to a substantial imbalance between environmental demands and the individual's ability to cope with them.[28] It is important to note that this imbalance can arise from too many environmental demands as well as too few. Figure 6–10 illustrates the consequences of the demand-response imbalance.

Sources of Stress   As suggested by the above definitions, stress can be induced by a variety of factors. They include organizational, social, and family demands and specific predispositions to the stress response, such as an individual's health and personality.

Figure 6–11 specifies sources of stress that are related to an individual's involvement with an organization. It should be noted that the frustration inherent in conflict is not the only source of stress. We can categorize each of these

[27] H. Seyle, *The Stress of Life*, rev. ed. (New York: McGraw-Hill, 1976), 54.

[28] J. E. McGrath, "Stress and Behavior in Organizations," in *Handbook of Industrial and Organizational Psychology*, ed. M. Dunnette (Chicago: Rand McNally, 1976).

| FIGURE 6–10 | ▶ The Demand-Response Imbalance |

Optimal individual performance occurs when there is a balance between the demands placed on an individual and that individual's ability to cope with those demands. Performance deteriorates not only when demands greatly exceed coping skills but also when coping skills greatly exceed the demands placed upon the individual.

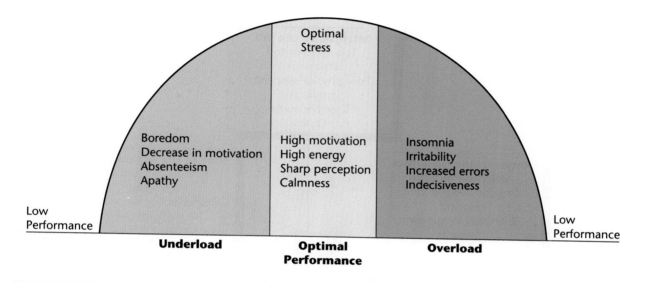

Source: Don Hellriegel, John W. Slocum, and Richard B. Woodman, *Organizational Behavior*, 4th ed. (St. Paul, Minn.: West, 1986), 529.

potential stressors as one of two major forms of frustration—frustration from lack of control and frustration from uncertainty. Thus, the greater an individual's frustration from lack of control and uncertainty, the more potential for stress. Reexamining Figure 6–11 provides support for this point of view. Frustration arising from lack of control (the inability to do what you want to do) can be manifested in lack of consultation, restrictions on behavior, too much or too little work, time pressures, lack of participation in decision making, competing individual and family demands, overpromotion, underpromotion, and poor relations with colleagues, subordinates, and superiors. Frustration from uncertainty centers around the inability to predict future events. The changing nature of office politics, job insecurity, role ambiguity, concerns about delegating (what will happen if . . . ?), downsizing, and reorganization are all potential sources of uncertainty and frustration. Layoffs, for example, are never easy for workers or for the companies that have to lay off their employees. However, layoffs are becoming even more painful, especially in California, because of the way the workers' compensation law is written. Thirty percent of the workers laid off by Security Metal Products Corporation have claimed mental stress and filed claims for as much as $25,000. In 1990 alone, an estimated $380 million was paid out to employed and unemployed workers as a result of stress-related claims.[29] An example of the impact of uncertainty on stress and job performance is highlighted in the "FOCUS ON: Stress."

---

[29] R. Grover, "Say, Does Workers' Comp Cover Wretched Excess?" *Business Week*, July 22, 1991, 2.

FIGURE 6–11 ▶Sources of Work Stress

Conflict is only one source of stress in life. All of the stressors pictured here fit into one of two families: stress from uncertainty or stress from lack of control.

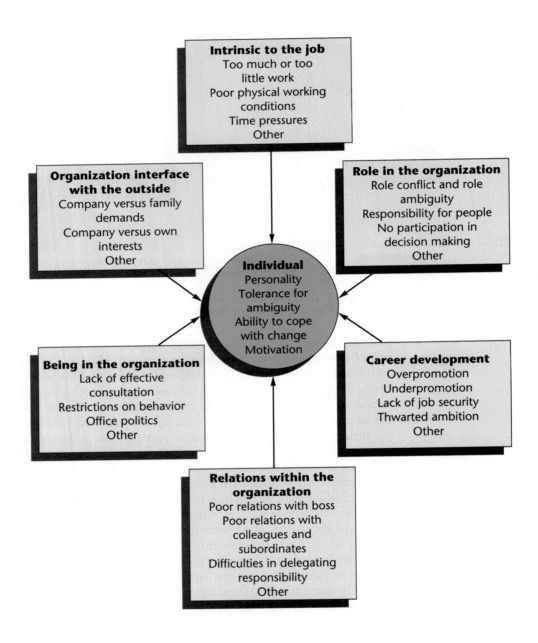

Intrinsic to the job
Too much or too
little work
Poor physical working
conditions
Time pressures
Other

**Organization interface
with the outside**
Company versus family
demands
Company versus own
interests
Other

Role in the organization
Role conflict and role
ambiguity
Responsibility for people
No participation in
decision making
Other

Individual
Personality
Tolerance for
ambiguity
Ability to cope
with change
Motivation

Being in the organization
Lack of effective
consultation
Restrictions on behavior
Office politics
Other

Career development
Overpromotion
Underpromotion
Lack of job security
Thwarted ambition
Other

**Relations within the
organization**
Poor relations with boss
Poor relations with
colleagues and
subordinates
Difficulties in delegating
responsibility
Other

Source: C. L. Cooper and J. Marshall, "The Management of Stress," *Personnel Review* 4, no. 4 (1975): 28. Reprinted with permission of MCB Publications Limited, Bradford, England.

Stress

Stress and Job Security As all employees who depend on a regular paycheck know, job security is paramount when it comes to maintaining financial well-being. What they may not know is that security affects their physical and mental health as well.

Psychologist Karl W. Kuhnert surveyed more than 200 employees in two similar manufacturing companies to see if attitudes toward job satisfaction, job security, and work involvement were predictive of employee health. They were asked to agree or disagree with statements such as "I can keep my job for as long as I want it," "Everything is an effort for me," and "I experience chest pains."

Kuhnert found a strong relationship between perceived job security and health. The more permanent the employees thought their position was, the greater their physical and mental well-being. Surprisingly, perceived job security was found to be a better predictor of employees' health than any other factor.

Further, the study showed that the workers' assessment of their own job performance was tied directly to their belief about how secure their job was. In other words, the higher workers perceived the quality of their work to be, the more permanent they saw their position, regardless of their actual job performance.

It is no secret that organizations suffer financially as a result of employee stress and ill health. With skyrocketing medical costs, rising insurance claims, and worker-compensation laws, it's in employers' best interest to keep their employees happy and healthy, Kuhnert says.

He also suggests that companies can combat the problem of worker insecurity by letting their employees know how well they're doing. "Since employees believe that if they do good work, they'll be able to keep their jobs, and a key feature in job security is knowing where you stand, organizations can help their employees by giving them regular feedback."

Source: Mindy Schanback, "Stress and Job Security," *Psychology Today,* May 1987. Reprinted with permission from *Psychology Today* Magazine. Copyright © 1987 (PT Partners, L.P.).

Stress Moderators Other factors moderate the level of stress an individual will experience within an organization. Remember that, according to the stimulus-response definition of stress, stress results from interaction of the individual and the environment. What is it about some individuals that makes them more prone to the negative effects of stress?

One characteristic found in many stress-prone people is a **Type A personality.**[30] People with the trait are involved in a continuous struggle to accomplish more and more in less and less time. They express a chronic sense of urgency, have very short tempers, and are impatient with any impediments to their successful performance of a task. Figure 6–12 lists the behaviors common to Type A personalities.

In contrast is the **Type B personality.** While Type A personalities seem to be obsessed with the clock, Type B personalities are considerably more relaxed and less agitated. This is not to suggest they are lazy or unproductive. Rather, they are more likely to work at a consistent pace.

---

[30] M. Friedman and R. H. Rosenman, *Type A Behavior and Your Heart* (New York: Fawcett Crest, 1974).

| FIGURE 6–12 | ▶ **Common Type A Behaviors** |

One individual characteristic that has been implicated in stress-prone people is a Type A personality. One clinical study has shown that Type A personalities run twice the risk of premature coronary artery disease.

Explosive, accelerated speech
A heightened pace of living
Impatience with slowness
Concentration on multiple activities
  simultaneously
Preoccupation with personal concerns

Dissatisfaction with life
A tendency to compete, regardless of
  the situation
Free-floating hostility
A tendency to evaluate one's accom-
  plishments in numerical terms

Source: K. A. Matthews, "Psychological Perspectives on the Type A Behavior Pattern," *Psychological Bulletin* 91 (1982): 293–323.

Our current organizational and academic environments appear to reinforce Type A behavior. In general, Type A men and women attain a higher educational level, occupational status, and income. Type A students achieve more academic honors and Type A women are more likely to be employed and less likely to be homemakers.[31] However, in a longitudinal study of several thousand males, those categorized as Type A personalities were found to run at least twice the risk of premature coronary artery disease.[32] Recent research, however, does not suggest that it is the achievement orientation of Type A personalities that makes them more prone to stress; rather it is their high level of hostility, frustration, and depression. Workaholism in itself is not necessarily hazardous to your health as long as you are good at the task involved and enjoy yourself.[33]

The amount of change or upheaval one has experienced may also play a significant role in how one is affected by environmental demands. Figure 6–13 shows the Social Readjustment Rating Scale.[34] The scale points, which range from 11 (minor violations of the law) to 100 (death of a spouse), correlate roughly with the degree of adjustment demanded by the particular change. To determine the point value of recent life changes (both positive and negative), the points associated with each life change were summed. Individuals with more than 200 points in a single year had a 50 percent chance of a serious health problem occurring in the following year. If point totals exceeded 300, then the risk factor rose to over 75 percent. This research suggests that adaptation to positive and negative change is stressful, and takes a physiological toll on the body. Excessive adaptation may drain resources necessary for continued health, thus increasing the body's vulnerability to attack by disease.

[31] O. Behling and A. L. Darrow, "Managing Work-Related Stress," in *Modules in Management*, ed. J. E. Rosenzweig and F. E. Kast (Chicago: Science Research Associates, 1984).

[32] Freidman and Rosenman, *Type A Behavior*.

[33] Laurence Miller, "To Beat Stress, Don't Relax: Get Tough," *Psychology Today*, December 1989, 62–63.

[34] R. H. Holmes and R. H. Rahe, "The Social Readjustment Rating Scale," *Journal of Psychosomatic Medicine* 11 (1967): 213–218.

| FIGURE 6–13 | ▶ **The Social Readjustment Rating Scale** |

Certain events in life can provide shocks to an individual's system that create stress. These shocks can come from major life changes, such as those listed here.

Life Event	Mean Value
1. Death of Spouse	100
2. Divorce	73
3. Marital Separation	65
4. Jail Term	63
5. Death of Close Family Member	63
6. Personal Injury or Illness	53
7. Marriage	50
8. Fired at Work	47
9. Marital Reconciliation	45
10. Retirement	45
11. Change in Health of Family Member	44
12. Pregnancy	40
13. Sex Difficulties	39
14. Gain of New Family Member	39
15. Business Readjustment	39
16. Change in Financial State	38
17. Death of Close Friend	37
18. Change to Different Line of Work	36
19. Change in Number of Arguments with Spouse	35
20. Mortgage over $10,000	31
21. Foreclosure of Mortgage or Loan	30
22. Change in Responsibilities at Work	29
23. Son or Daughter Leaving Home	29
24. Trouble with In-laws	29
25. Outstanding Personal Achievement	28
26. Spouse Begin or Stop Work	26
27. Begin or End School	26
28. Change in Living Conditions	25
29. Revision of Personal Habits	24
30. Trouble with Boss	23
31. Change in Work Hours or Conditions	20
32. Change in Residence	20
33. Change in Schools	20
34. Change in Recreation	19
35. Change in Church Activities	19
36. Change in Social Activities	18
37. Mortgage or Loan Less than $10,000	17
38. Change in Sleeping Habits	16
39. Change in Number of Family Get-togethers	15
40. Change in Eating Habits	15
41. Vacation	13
42. Christmas	12
43. Minor Violations of the Law	11

Source: Reprinted by permission from "The Social Readjustment Rating Scale," by T. H. Holmes and R. H. Rahe, *Journal of Psychosomatic Medicine* 11, pp. 213–218. Copyright © 1967, Pergamon Press.

MANAGING STRESS

While a great deal of attention has been paid to the development of interpersonal and organizational responses to conflict, the success of these strategies depends largely upon the effective functioning of the individual experiencing the conflict. It is important, therefore, that the individual be able to handle the psychological and physiological demands of conflict situations. Because one of the more common consequences of conflict is stress, a major factor in managing intrapersonal conflict is learning to cope successfully with the resulting stress.

Stress Management   Stress and stress-related illnesses are very expensive for American companies. It has been estimated that businesses have lost as much as $15 billion in foregone productivity because of employees' personal problems. The costs of executive stress include $2.9 billion for lost workdays, $.2 billion for hospitalization, $.1 billion for outpatient care, and $16.5 billion for mortality.[35] These numbers represent only the quantifiable costs of stress. We must consider also the cost in human potential of the nonquantifiable costs induced by stress.

An individual or organization can attempt to manage stress in a variety of ways. The following section will describe some of these methods. For a more detailed examination of these topics, consult the references provided at the end of the chapter.

Individual strategies for managing stress are quite varied. Physical exercise (jogging, walking, swimming, bicycling, aerobic exercise, and other such activities) is an excellent way of relieving stress and tension. In fact, many organizations are routinely adding on-site exercise facilities and developing incentive plans to foster their use by organizational members. Other stress-management activities include the use of relaxation techniques such as meditation and biofeedback. Another, rather novel approach to stress management is illustrated in the "FOCUS ON: Managing Stress."

A second way individuals can reduce their vulnerability to potentially stressful situations is through the use of time-management skills. Individuals skilled in time management are able to identify and set daily priorities so that sufficient time is allocated to their more important tasks. The advantage of successful time management is that it returns to the individual a sense of control over his or her life and workday. It can also reduce role overload and role conflict.[36]

The third method for reducing stress at the individual level is to create a strong social support system. Interacting with our social support systems—our spouses, relatives, and friends—enables us to discuss our problems from a different frame of reference, put work into better perspective, and keep from becoming too involved with our day-to-day work activities. In fact, a recent study suggests that persons with few close friends are two to three times more likely to die earlier than those with many close friends, even controlling for preexisting illnesses, smoking, and a number of other factors.[37]

---

[35] Behling and Darrow, "Managing Work-Related Stress."

[36] A. Lakein, *How to Get Control of Your Time and Your Life* (New York: Peter H. Wyden, 1973).

[37] P. J. Rosch, "Stress and Illness," *Journal of the American Medical Association* 242 (1979): 427–428.

Managing Stress

Laughter: The Best Medicine for Burnout? Lighten up a little. You'll feel better. More important, you'll be healthier, more creative and more productive. That's the message 1,000 people paid $200 each to hear at the fifth annual conference on "The Power of Laughter and Play."

Speakers at the three-day conference said there is a growing awareness that workers do best when their jobs are fun and rewarding. Conversely, they burn out and incur higher medical bills when they are thrust into a humorless corporate pressure cooker day after day.

"We've learned that lesson the hard way," said Erin Sommerville, a staff member with the Palo Alto–based Institute for the Advancement of Human Behavior, sponsor of the conference. "Now we're learning that reducing stress really helps employee relations and helps productivity."

Nevertheless, few companies have taken concrete steps to bring any laughter, let alone play, to the workplace, according to several humor consultants who addressed the conference. Matt Weinstein, founder of the Berkeley-based consulting company called Playfair, encouraged those at the conference to help their coworkers take themselves a bit less seriously and to realize "that their lives are more important than their jobs." He recommends, for example, that employees bring a Walkman and a comedy tape to work each day and "force yourself to take at least three or four laugh breaks."

Joel Goodman, director of the Humor Project in Saratoga Springs, N.Y., said he tells his corporate clients to invest in a humor "first-aid kit" containing joke books and tapes, which can be checked out by stressed-out employees.

Most of the speakers said there is a direct connection between playfulness and creativity. If people are intimidated in the office and are afraid to make mistakes, they'll never make the creative leap that really characterizes growth companies," Weinstein said.

In addition to sparking creativity, fun can be just plain healthy, most speakers said. They pointed out that the body releases T-cells, the ones that battle disease, when one indulges in a good, hearty laugh. There's some evidence that endorphins, the body's natural painkillers, are also stimulated through laughter.

"It's not only OK to laugh and have a good time," Sommerville said, "It's beneficial." She added, "If you take yourself too seriously, you're liable to get seriously ill."

Helpful humor does not have to be obvious or wacky. Consider the response of one personnel manager at a high-tech company who had to implement a highly detailed and unpopular new accounting procedure. On the morning the procedure was to be implemented, she got in early and replaced everyone's last name on their nameplates with "Dangerfield," because today they would be getting "no respect!" While this feat probably resulted in no loud laughter, it did effectively convey the message that the manager understood that the day was going to be tough, building solidarity among her employees and reminding them to keep some perspective on the day's activities.

Sources: "Laughter: The Best Medicine for Burnout?" *Arizona Daily Star*, March 22, 1987, A–5; and Anne M. Russell and Lorraine Calvacca, "Should You be Funny at Work?" *Working Woman*, March 1991, 75–76, 128.

Stress also can be managed at the level of organizational activities. Since our definition of stress focuses on an imbalance between the individual and his or her organizational demands, it is important that the person and the position are matched. The correct person-job fit can be attained in two different ways.

First, the person recruited for the position can be carefully screened to ensure a balance between the individual's tolerance for stress and the position's stress level. A second and more promising solution is to alter the position to reduce or increase its **stress quotient,** or the amount of stress the position is likely to generate in the jobholder. Chapter 12 includes an extensive discussion of job design that describes how a position can be enriched. However, it should be noted that too much job enrichment is also stressful.

In decreasing the stress quotient of a position, one should pay special attention to reducing the amount of role ambiguity, role conflict, and role overload. Role ambiguity may be reduced by developing detailed job descriptions, discussing job expectations with subordinates, and promoting a clear understanding of the nature and intent of the performance evaluation system. Role conflict also can be reduced by discussions with superiors and other members of the role set to outline common expectations of performance. Role overload may be monitored through periodic evaluation of the changing capabilities of the employee over time.[38]

A second stress-reduction mechanism that can be instituted at the organizational level is **employee assistance programs.** Many organizations, such as IBM, Equitable Life, and B. F. Goodrich, have programs that diagnose and treat a variety of stress-related problems, such as drug and alcohol abuse and other emotional and psychological problems.

SUMMARY ◆◆◆◆◆◆

Conflict is an organizational reality. Managers and other organizational members are constantly involved in competition for scarce resources. The task of an effective manager is to maintain an optimal level of conflict, given the unique characteristics of the organization and the individuals who compose it.

Ability to cope with conflict is based upon a variety of factors. Of primary concern is a person's ability to deal with stress. Because conflict is stressful, the optimal amount of conflict is a function of the individual's ability to handle it. That ability is influenced by personality and past history. Developing the skills to successfully resolve conflict is an essential aspect of controlling one's environment. Understanding conflict and its impact on individuals and groups increases a

person's ability to predict its outcomes and make interventions when appropriate. Further, once conflict is viewed as a common organizational process rather than an aberration, its presence becomes that much less stressful. The more conflict management is viewed as an appropriate managerial skill, the more structural alternatives will be implemented to address organizational conflict.

Structural forms of conflict management are likely to be found primarily in organizations that exist in constantly changing and unpredictable environments and have high intra-organizational interdependencies. Thus, a typical source of conflict management is the manager. Managers are likely to, on the average, spend one-fifth of each working day on some form of conflict-related activity. Given the

---

[38] Behling and Darrow, "Managing Work-Related Stress."

extensive time crunch all managers experience, increasing their effectiveness in managing conflict can allow more time to be spent on producing the product for which the organization exists. But increasing one's skills means more than simply finding a way (any way) to resolve a dispute for now.

Rather, it requires an understanding of the nature of the conflict and the manager's objective in resolving the conflict. Identifying the objectives or goals of the conflict intervention allows the manager to choose the intervention style that will best achieve those goals.

Key Terms

Accommodating Strategy for interpersonal conflict that maximizes the other party's concerns or outcomes.

Approach-approach conflict Occurs when an individual must choose between two equally attractive options, both with positive outcomes.

Approach-avoidance conflict Occurs when an individual must choose among options with both positive and negative outcomes.

Arbitration Resolution of a conflict by a neutral third party who, after hearing both sides of a dispute, determines a final, binding outcome.

Avoidance-avoidance conflict Occurs when an individual must choose between two equally unattractive options, both with negative outcomes.

Avoiding Strategy for interpersonal conflict that is suitable when the positions of both parties are trivial or when one party is seriously outmatched by the other party.

Buffer Mechanism that reduces the environmental shocks or interdepartmental conflict to allow an organizational unit to complete its task more smoothly.

Collaborating Strategy for interpersonal conflict that is suitable when both your own and the other

party's concerns are equally important, when the issue is too important to compromise, when trying to engender commitment among the parties, or when trying to gain insight.

Competing Strategy for interpersonal conflict that is suitable when the individual is concerned about his or her own needs, issues, or outcomes, such as when in an emergency or critical situation, when the other party is untrustworthy, or when the individual or group is sure of the correct solution.

Compromising Strategy for interpersonal conflict that is suitable when both sets of goals are important but not worth the potential disruption of more aggressive strategies.

Delegator One who returns responsibility for dispute resolution to the involved parties, or passes that responsibility to someone else.

Distributive negotiation Common negotiation strategy in which parties decide only how to allocate a fixed amount of resources.

Employee assistance programs Typically in-house or contractual programs that diagnose and treat a variety of stress-related problems, such as drug and alcohol abuse and other emotional and psychological problems.

Factfinding Form of third-party intervention in which a neutral third party determines a reasonable solution based on evidence presented by the parties, who are not bound to follow the recommendation.

Horizontal conflict Conflict between people at similar organizational levels.

Inquisitor Informal third-party role in a dispute in which a manager exerts a high degree of control over both the outcome and the process of conflict resolution.

Integrative bargaining A more cooperative negotiation strategy that assumes there can be an expanding amount of resources for the parties to divide.

Judge Informal third-party role in a dispute in which a manager exerts a high degree of control over the outcome of a dispute but not the process by which it is resolved.

Line-staff conflict Conflict between employees involved directly in some aspect of producing the organization's product and employees who provide technical and advisory assistance to the line.

Mediation Resolution of a conflict by a neutral third party who can control the interaction between the disputants but has no authority to force a solution on them.

Negotiation The process whereby two or more parties decide what each will give and take in an exchange between them.

Organizational ombudsman An individual whose responsibility it is to interpret policy, counsel disputing parties, resolve disputes, provide feedback, and identify potential problem areas for senior management.

Pooled interdependence Exists when each department or unit contributes to the larger good but is not dependent on the others.

"Providing imptus" tactic Delegating conflict back to the involved parties with the implied threat that if they don't resolve it, someone else will, and the resolution will not be to either parties' liking.

Resource scarcity Not having enough of a particular commodity (for example, food, love, attention, cars, clothes, opportunities, etc.) for all to accomplish their goals.

Reciprocal interdependence Exists when the outputs of one department become the inputs of a second, and the outputs of that second unit become the inputs for the first.

Role conflict Occurs when two or more role-specific activities, or expectations of other organizational members, are incompatible.

Sequential interdependence Exists when the outputs of one unit become the inputs of another unit.

Slack Excess resources that can minimize conflict because they reduce the amount of necessary interaction.

Stress A psychological and physiological response to a substantial imbalance between environmental demands and the individual's ability to cope with them.

Stress quotient The amount of stress a job is likely to generate in the job holder.

Third-party intervention Involvement in a conflict of someone not directly concerned, such as arbitration, mediation, and factfinding.

Type A personality Set of personality characteristics found in many stress-prone people, such as impatience, competitiveness, and the drive to succeed.

Type B personality Classification of behaviors found in less stress-prone people, such as a relaxed, easygoing, noncompetitive attitude toward work and life.

Vertical conflict Conflict between people at different levels in an organization.

Discussion Questions

1. In common usage, the term *conflict* has a negative connotation. Within an organizational setting, however, conflict is a necessary and even critical resource of the successful manager. What is it about conflict that makes it so useful to organizations while being perceived as negative by the general public?

2. What indicators might warn a personnel director in a large organization that excessive, nonfunctional conflict exists?

3. Managers are often required to intervene in conflict within and between their departments and other organizational entities. What specific skills would a manager need to accomplish this role successfully?

4. While managers report using mediation techniques extensively, direct observations of managerial interventions indicate that they rely more upon controlling strategies. What is it about mediation that makes it attractive but not often implemented by managers (except possibly at the higher organizational levels)?

5. How might an organization respond to reduce excessive levels of stress?

6. What effects does intergroup conflict have on the groups themselves?

7. What are some examples of organizational slack? How do these examples "buffer" the organization from conflict?

If You Want to Know More

The study of conflict and conflict management has received a great deal of attention in both the popular and scholarly press in recent years. The most recent book in this area is *Negotiating Rationally*, written by Max H. Bazerman and Margaret A. Neale (Free Press, 1992). Roger Fischer and Bill Ury have written the book *Getting to Yes* (Houghton-Mifflin, 1981), which provides an excellent description of principled, integrative bargaining. Eminently readable, this book is quite popular with practicing managers as well as professional negotiators. A third book, Howard Raiffa's *The Art and Science of Negotiation* (Belknap, 1982), focuses on a prescriptive model for effective negotiating. For a different perspective, those interested in negotiating might also wish to read Herb Cohen's *You Can Negotiate Anything* (Bantam Books, 1980).

Stress and stress management are common topics in the popular press. Many magazines such as *Ms.*, *Inc.*, *Working Woman*, *Time*, *Business Week*, and *Psychology Today* often have articles on this topic. A number of very useful books also have been published on this subject. For example, John Ivancevich and Michael Matteson have written a book called *Stress and Work: A Managerial Perspective* (Scott, Foresman, 1980). Finally, an interesting book entitled *Is It Worth Dying For?* was written by Robert Eliot and Dennis Breo (Bantam Books).

On Your Own

◆◆◆

Conflict Questionnaire *Directions:* Consider situations in which you find your wishes differing from those of another person. For each of the following statements, think how likely you are to respond in that way. Check the rating that best corresponds to your response.

	Very Unlikely	Unlikely	Likely	Very Likely
1. I am usually firm in pursuing my goals.	___	___	___	___
2. I try to make my position win.	___	___	___	___
3. I give up some points in exchange for others.	___	___	___	___
4. I feel that differences are not always worth worrying about.	___	___	___	___
5. I try to find a position that is between the other person's and mine.	___	___	___	___
6. In approaching negotiation, I try to consider the other person's wishes.	___	___	___	___
7. I try to show the logic and benefits of my position.	___	___	___	___
8. I always lean toward a direct discussion of the problem.	___	___	___	___
9. I try to find a fair combination of gains and losses for both of us.	___	___	___	___
10. I attempt to work through our differences immediately.	___	___	___	___
11. I try to avoid creating unpleasantness for myself.	___	___	___	___
12. I might try to soothe the other's feelings and preserve our relationship.	___	___	___	___
13. I attempt to get all concerns and issues immediately out.	___	___	___	___
14. I sometimes avoid taking positions that create controversy.	___	___	___	___
15. I try not to hurt the other's feelings.	___	___	___	___

SCORING: Very Unlikely = 1; Unlikely = 2; Likely = 3; Very Likely = 4.

							TOTAL
Competing:	Item 1 ___	Item 2 ___	Item 7 ___				TOTAL ___
Collaborating:	8 ___	10 ___	13 ___				TOTAL ___
Compromising:	3 ___	5 ___	9 ___				TOTAL ___
Avoiding:	4 ___	11 ___	14 ___				TOTAL ___
Accommodating:	6 ___	12 ___	15 ___				TOTAL ___

Conflict-Handling Modes	Appropriate Situations
Competing	1. When quick, decisive action is vital—emergencies.
	2. On important issues where unpopular actions need implementation—cost cutting, discipline.
	3. On issues vital to organizational welfare when you know you are right.
	4. Against people who take advantage of noncompetitive situations.
Collaborating	1. To find an integrative solution when both sets of concerns are too important to compromise.
	2. When your objective is to learn.
	3. To merge insights from people with different perspectives.
	4. To gain commitment by incorporating concerns into a consensus.
	5. To work through feelings that have interfered with a relationship.
Compromising	1. When goals are important, but not worth the effort or potential disruption of more assertive modes.
	2. When opponents with equal power are committed to mutually exclusive goals.
	3. To achieve temporary settlement of complex issues.
	4. To arrive at expedient solutions under time pressures.
	5. As a backup when collaboration or competition is unsuccessful.
Avoiding	1. When an issue is trivial, or more important issues are pressing.
	2. When you perceive no chance of satisfying your concerns.
	3. When potential disruption outweighs the benefits of resolution.
	4. To let people cool down and regain perspective.
	5. When gathering information supersedes an immediate decision.
	6. When others can resolve the conflict more effectively.
	7. When issues seem tangential or symptomatic of other issues.
Accommodating	1. When you find you are wrong—to allow a better position to be heard, to learn, and to show your reasonableness.
	2. When issues are more important to others than yourself—to satisfy others and maintain cooperation.
	3. To build social credits for later issues.
	4. To minimize a loss when you are outmatched and losing.
	5. When harmony and stability are especially important.
	6. To allow subordinates to develop by learning from mistakes.

Source: Kenneth W. Thomas, "Toward Multi-Dimensional Values in Teaching: The Example of Conflict Behaviors," *Academy of Management Review* 2 (1977): 487, Table 1. Used with permission.

CHAPTER 6

THE MANAGER'S MEMO

FROM: F. Cunningham, Manager, Cookie Sales Force

TO: P. Rodriguez, Vice President, Cookie Division

RE: Problems with Engineering

I think we have a problem with the division's Chief Manufacturing Engineer, Bill Lee. It seems to have started in the meeting where we launched our new novelty-shaped graham crackers, TeleGrahams.

At the meeting, Angela Boskin, who is in charge of sales for this product, was excited about our expectation that we can exceed our initial sales projections by 200 percent. This would involve opening a second production facility in the southeast within three months.

As Angela was explaining the favorable results of our test marketing, Bill said, "When are we going to talk about the bugs in the production process that are causing us to burn 25 percent of the product?" Well, as Angela explained, consumers in the test markets have been satisfied with the product as it is, so we can go ahead with launching the product and work out the bugs later. But Bill just stormed out of the room, shouting something about how we always expect Production to work miracles.

I don't see what his problem is; you'd think he'd be excited about doubling production. I guess he's just a typical engineer—more concerned about his machinery than he is about the big picture.

I tried to call Bill today to smooth things over, but he was out sick. Maybe you can talk to him. Or maybe if we just ignore him, he'll get over his attitude problem. What, if anything, do you think I should do?

Case Discussion Questions

Assume you are the vice-president, and respond to the sales manager's memo. Try to infer the real nature of this conflict, and determine your goals for intervention. Use those goals as the basis for choosing an intervention style and phrasing your response. If you think it will help you achieve your goals for resolving this conflict, also write a memo to Bill Lee, the Chief Manufacturing Engineer.

EXERCISE

PART 2:

Carter Racing (A)

What Should We Do?

John Carter was not sure, but his brother and partner, Fred Carter, was on the phone and needed a decision. Should they run in the race or not? It had been a successful season so far, but the Pocono race was important because of the prize money and TV exposure it promised. This first year had been hard because the team was trying to make a name for itself. They had run a lot of small races to get this shot at the big time. A successful outing could mean more sponsors, a chance to start making some profits for a change, and the luxury of racing only the major events. But if they suffered another engine failure on national television . . .

Just thinking about the team's engine problems made John wince. They had blown the engine seven times in twenty-four outings this season with various degrees of damage to the engine and car. No one could figure out why. It took a lot of sponsor money to replace a $20,000 racing engine, and the wasted entry fees were no small matter either. John and Fred had everything they owned riding on Carter Racing. This season had to be a success.

Paul Edwards, the engine mechanic, was guessing the engine problem was related to ambient air temperature. He argued that when it was cold the different expansion rates for the head and block were damaging the head gasket and causing the engine failures. It was below freezing last night, which meant a cold morning for starting the race.

Tom Burns, the chief mechanic, did not agree with Paul's "gut feeling" and had data to support his position (see Exhibit 1). He pointed out that gasket failures had occurred at all temperatures, which meant temperature was not the issue. Tom has been racing for twenty years and believed that luck was an important element in success. He had argued this view when he and John discussed the problem last week: "In racing, you are pushing the limits of what is known. You cannot expect to have everything under control. If you want to win, you have to take risks. Everybody in racing knows it. The drivers have their lives on the line, I have a career that hangs on every race, and you guys have got every dime tied up in the business. That's the thrill, beating the odds and winning." Last night over dinner he had added to this argument forcefully with what he called Burns' First Law of Racing: "Nobody ever won a race sitting in the pits."

John, Fred, and Tom had discussed Carter Racing's situation the previous evening. This first season was a success from a racing standpoint, with the team's car finishing in the top five in 12 of the 15 races it completed. As a result, the sponsorship offers critical to the team's business success were starting to come in. A big break had come two weeks ago after the Dunham race, where the team scored its fourth first-place finish. Goodstone Tire had finally decided Carter Racing deserved its sponsorship at Pocono—worth a much needed $40,000—and was considering a full season contract for next year if the team's car finished in the top five in this race. The Goodstone sponsorship was for a million a year, plus incentives. John and Fred had gotten a favorable response from Goodstone's racing program director last week when they presented their plans for the next season, but it was clear that his support depended on the visibility they generated in this race.

"John, we only have another hour to decide," Fred said over the phone. "If we withdraw now, we can get back half the $15,000 entry and try to recoup some of our losses next season. We will lose Goodstone, they'll want $25,000 of their money back, and we end up the season $50,000 in the hole. If we run

EXHIBIT 1	▶ Note from Tom Burns

John,

I got the data on the gasket failures from Paul. We have run 24 races this season with temperatures at race time ranging from 53 to 82 degrees. Paul had a good idea in suggesting we look into this, but as you can see, this is not our problem. I tested the data for a correlation between temperature and gasket failures and found no relationship.

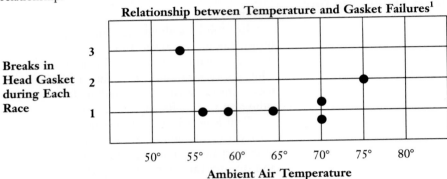

Relationship between Temperature and Gasket Failures[1]

In comparison with some of the other teams, we have done extremely well this season. We have finished 62.5 percent of the races, and when we finished we were in the top five 80 percent of the time. I am not happy with the engine problems, but I will take the four first-place finishes and 50 percent rate of finishing in the money[2] over seven engines any day. If we continue to run like this, we will have our pick of sponsors.

Tom

---

[1]Each point is for a single race. A gasket can have multiple breaks, any of which may produce an engine failure.

[2]The top five finishers in a race are "in the money."

and finish in the top five, we have Goodstone in our pocket and can add another car next season. You know as well as I do, however, that if we run and lose another engine, we are back at square one next season. We will lose the tire sponsorship and a blown engine is going to lose us the oil contract. No oil company wants a national TV audience to see a smoker being dragged off the track with its name plastered all over it. The oil sponsorship is $500,000 that we cannot live without. Think about it—call Paul and Tom if you want—but I need a decision in an hour."

John hung up the phone and looked out the window at the crisp, fall sky. The temperature sign across the street flashed "40 DEGREES AT 9:23 AM."

Carter Racing (B)

"Get Paul Edwards for me." John was calling to get his engine mechanic's opinion on whether they should run. The data Tom put together indicated that temperature was not the problem, but John wanted to get Paul's direct assessment.

Paul Edwards was a classic "gas station mechanic." His fingernails were permanently blackened by grease and his coveralls never stayed clean for more than two minutes on Saturday mornings. He had been knocking around the professional circuit for ten years after dropping out of school at sixteen to follow drag racing. He lacked the sophisticated engineering training that was getting more common in racing, but he did know racing engines.

John had discussed the gasket problem with Paul two days ago. As he waited for Paul to come to the phone, he reflected on their previous conversation. Paul was a man of few words and was not given to overstatement. "The way I see it, the turbo pressure during warmup—in conjunction with the different expansion rates for the head and block—is doing a number on us," was about the extent of what he had to say on the problem. It was his personal opinion on the cause of the engine failures; he would never represent it as anything else.

It was the same story John had heard twenty times, but it did not match Tom's data. "Paul, we have chewed this over before. How do you know this is the problem? When we ran at Riverside the temperature was 75 degrees, and we still lost the gasket and engine."

"I am not sure what happened at Riverside," Paul had replied. "I am not sure that temperature is the problem, but it is the only thing I can figure out. It is definitely the gaskets that are blowing out and causing the engine to go."

Part of Carter Racing's success was due to a unique turbo-charging system that Tom and John had developed. They had come up with a new head design that allowed them to get more turbo pressure to the engine while maintaining fuel consumption at a fairly constant level. By casting the head and turbo bodies in a high-strength aircraft alloy, they had also saved almost fifty pounds of weight. The alloy they were using was not as temperature sensitive as the material in the engine block, but the head gasket should be able to handle the different expansion rates.

John could hear the sounds of race day in the background as Paul approached the phone. "Hello John," he said, obviously excited. "The Goodstone coveralls just got here. We are talking some fine threads. No sew-on patches from these guys. The logo on the back and our names are stitched right into the material. I guess this means we get to keep 'em. Course, I got some grease on mine already, so they probably won't want 'em back anyway."

"I'm glad you like them," John said. "I need to get some information from you. What are we doing about the gasket failure business?"

"The car is set to go. We have been using a different seating procedure since Slippery Rock and had no problems for two races. Tom says the Goodstone deal is set as long as we finish in the money today. The guys in the shop want this bad. Goodstone is a class act. They can make us the number one team on the circuit if they decide to take us on."

CASE

PART 2:

The Case of the Disputed Arches

A complex, technical description of a yieldable arch roof support is not required. Suffice to say that long before Christ, the Greeks knew that the more pressure put on a keystone, the stronger it became. The concept has found numerous applications, including, in this instance, as mine haulage roof supports. I had worked five years as a union miner and acquired a mining engineering degree. Nobody was going to bullshit *me* about yieldable arches.

Joe Bond was a motorman. He was henpecked, cuckolded, and discontented in ways only he could understand. Worst of all he was smarter than his job required. In short, he was a troublemaker. Nobody could bullshit me about Joe Bond either.

I was twenty-four years old and had just become superintendent of the Bunker Mine. The average age of the union employees at Bunker was 46. I had just been left a note that Bond, who worked midnight shift, had complained about the condition of the arches at the 1,200 block on the haulage. He demanded that the arches be replaced. Rumor was that he would "cause trouble" if they were not replaced. Fact was, I was being tested.

James Franklin, the mine foreman of twenty-seven years and a man much respected by the union, looked at the arches. Frank Randall, the federal mine inspector, looked at the arches. I looked at the arches. We all agreed: even though they showed signs of taking pressure, the arches were safe. Furthermore, replacing the arches would require closing the haulage, and therefore the mine, for about four days.

I left a polite note for Joe Bond, to be given him by the midnight shift foreman. I thanked Joe for his suggestion, his attention to matters of safety, and his wisdom in reporting these matters to management. However, the arches in question did appear to be perfectly safe. I would continue to watch them and perhaps change them out at the first convenient opportunity, thank you very much anyway.

The midnight shift foreman called to tell me that Joe had received the note, had promptly gone into the waiting room and announced that management was trying to get him killed. Then he went home. The rest of the shift had followed close behind. The mine was on strike.

I hurriedly phoned the union safety committee and met them at the mine at 2:30 a.m. The safety committee asked me to show them the arches in question. I had a better idea, I said. If these arches were as unsafe as claimed, that fact should be immediately obvious to so well-trained and experienced a group as the safety committee. I would accompany them down the entire length of the haulage, and *they* could tell *me* where the bad arches were.

Two trips up and down the haulage produced half-a-dozen wrong guesses. At the end of the second trip one member of the safety committee told me to cut the crap and just show them the arches in question. Another member suggested that the two of us step into a cross-cut and settle the whole matter man-to-man.

Finally the exact cause of Joe Bond's complaint was pointed out to the committee. They reluctantly admitted that the arches didn't look too bad to them. They indicated they would take the matter under advisement and let me know their recommendation.

Day shift worked, much to the disgust of the men on midnight shift. There was an unwritten union rule that no one could work until the shift that initiated a strike decided to return. Afternoon shift would be the problem. The youngest, most volatile employees were on afternoon shift and I felt that their inclination would be to rekindle the strike. To forestall this, James Franklin and I went into the waiting room to talk to the men on afternoon shift as they arrived. I decided to let James do the talking, relying on his excellent reputation to add weight to his words.

James haltingly explained the situation to the men in terms couched with caution. He refused to definitely disclaim any hazard, saying only that while he didn't believe there was, he couldn't guarantee anything and there was no substitute for a man's own best judgment in these matters. I finally lost patience with him and declared that I could guarantee that there was no hazard, and furthermore, I could see no point in anyone losing a day's pay because of the troublemaker, Joe Bond.

After talking among themselves, the afternoon shift finally decided to continue the strike. This established a two-to-one vote and guaranteed that tomorrow, day shift also would not work.

At this point I had my first consultation with my supervisor, Mike Beanch. Mike was well-known for giving in to union pressure, so much so that the union lacked respect for him. After a lengthy conversation, I convinced Mike that we should "hang tough" and resist the demands to replace the arches.

Thus began what promised to be a long strike. Every day I met with the safety committee in an attempt to prove the safety of the arches and find some way to get the men back to work. Every day I was encouraged and congratulated by the line foremen who worked under me for finally standing up to the union and restoring dignity to management. Every day Mike got more and more nervous.

During one meeting with the safety committee, when Joe Bond was present, I was asked if I had referred to Joe as a troublemaker. I replied that I certainly had, and furthermore, that I had every belief that even Joe didn't think any hazard existed, that he simply did not want to work and chose to penalize everyone else's paycheck along with him.

Halfway through the second week of the strike, Mike called me up. "We have a new wrinkle in the union's demands," he said. "They've backed down. They no longer insist the arches be replaced. I've just finished talking to the safety committee on the phone."

I was a little miffed that the safety committee was talking to Mike directly, bypassing me, but I ignored this for the present.

"They are coming back to work, then," I said.

"No," Mike replied. "Now they won't come back to work until you are fired."

Questions for Discussion

1. How would you characterize the motivations of the case writer? What are Joe Bond's motivations in this case? Do any of these motivations change over the course of the case?

2. What is really in dispute in this case? Does it change from the beginning to the end of the case? How have the case writer's attempts to resolve this conflict made it worse?

3. Are there some important differences in perception in this case? How are they contributing to the problem?

P A R T

THREE

BEHAVIOR IN GROUPS

GROUPS AND COMMUNICATION

A CHAMPION OF COMMUNICATION ◆◆◆◆◆◆

Radical changes have transformed Mattel since John Amerman became CEO of the California-based toy company in 1987. The second day on the job, he told employees that the new watchword at Mattel was going to be "fun." At the time, Mattel was an out-of-control money loser, and morale was low. Amerman assured his work force that they could turn the company around if they worked in teams and tried to enjoy themselves. Part of his agenda was to improve communication with the work force.

The cheerful, white-haired CEO began wandering around the place, eating in the cafeteria, and meeting regularly with employees. The results were gratifying. For example, when he asked for suggestions on how to eliminate some layers in the organization, many employees, to his surprise, recommended that their departments be pruned or scrapped.

Amerman built on the successes of his early communication efforts. In 1989, to announce the company's earning results to the work force, Amerman put together a rap routine, backed by a group of secretaries called the Rappettes. It brought the house down. In 1990, Amerman recruited his top two lieutenants to put on a Las Vegas-style revue. They concluded the show by announcing that all 1,100 headquarters' employees would receive a bonus of two-weeks pay out of senior management's bonus pool—a subtle message that management was trying to work with the employees toward a common goal.

Not all companies handle communication as well as Mattel does. A nationwide survey found that less than 40 percent of the surveyed workers felt that their employer did a good job of seeking workers' views and suggestions. Fewer than one-third of those surveyed said that their employer did a good job of involving workers in decisions that affect the workers, and only one out of four workers felt that their managers did a good job explaining to them the reasons behind decisions.[1]

Robert Lefton, president of Psychological Associates in St. Louis, estimates that only 10 percent of corporate chiefs are effective communicators. The average executive can learn much from skillful counterparts like Mattel's Amerman.

Source: F. Rice, "Champions of Communication," *Fortune*, June 3, 1991, 111–120.

[1] S. Franklin, "Workers Say Bosses Neither Lend Nor Bend an Ear," *Chicago Tribune*, March 27, 1992, Business sec. 1.

INTRODUCTION

Groups and communication in groups are the building blocks of organizations and of social life. Individuals may come into and leave this world alone, but in between they interact with lots of other people. Groups provide the settings in which many of these interactions take place. And when people get together and talk in groups, things happen. The challenge of group dynamics is learning how to manage the energy of groups. Well-managed groups are positive and productive both for their individual members and for the larger organizations and societies in which they exist.

This chapter explores the nature of groups and individual behavior in groups, including the structuring, development, and improvement of group interaction. A model of communication in groups is presented, which highlights the importance of effective communication to successful group functioning.

THE NATURE OF GROUPS

What is a group? A **group** is "an organized system of two or more individuals who are interrelated so that the system performs some function, has a standard set of role relationships among its members, and has a set of norms that regulate the function of the group and each of its members."[2]

There are two important features to this definition. First, groups have a function—they serve a purpose. People do not simply come together to come together. People come together to accomplish something. Second, groups have structure. Groups must be organized to pursue their functions effectively. Some groups, such as task forces, have formal structures. These groups exist as legitimate, documented subunits of larger organizations. Their structures exist on paper in the form of charters or handbooks. Other groups, such as study groups, are informal. These groups exist only in the minds of their members, and their structures may be known only implicitly by the members. In either case, there must be rules that govern the conduct of group members, and each member of the group must have some tasks or duties to perform in the service of the group's function.

Why do people join groups? What are individuals hoping to obtain through groups that they could not obtain alone? The reasons why people join groups fall into two general categories: groups as means and groups as ends.

Means As we noted in the introductory chapter of this book, one important reason why people come together and form groups (and join those groups into organizations) is that groups can be an important means to accomplishing desired outcomes. In particular, groups can enhance individual effectiveness and efficiency. This can be good for each of the individual members of the group, and also for any larger organization of which the group is a part. A neighborhood watch will form because no one individual can police an entire neighborhood alone. A carpool will form because it's more efficient to have only one

[2]J. W. McDavid and M. Harari, *Social Psychology: Individuals, Groups, and Societies* (New York: Harper & Row, 1968), 237.

Rules and roles provide structure for group interaction. Rules and roles help this pit crew work together effectively as a team to achieve more than each member as an individual could. Each crew member can rely on the others to perform the appropriate task in the shortest possible time to maintain the car's position in the race.

person drive to work each day. Groups allow individuals to pool their resources and increase their individual productivities by taking advantage of economies of scale.

Ends   Individuals also join groups because group interactions can be desirable outcomes themselves. Someone may join a carpool because it saves gasoline and time, but that carpool also provides companionship and interesting conversation. A student may join a study group to improve grades, but the interaction of the study group also provides an intimate social circle with whom to commiserate when the demands of the classroom become overwhelming. The processes of group interaction represent more to group members than just the means to accomplishing difficult tasks. Group interaction itself provides important rewards.

College football teams provide a particularly good illustration of the differences between groups as means and groups as ends. Many big-time college athletes play football because football is a *means* to career success. If a college player develops professional-level abilities, a professional team will offer a lucrative professional contract. This in turn could lead to product-promotion contracts and personal-appearance income. Even if the athlete plays football only in college, the scholarship he receives for doing so will underwrite the cost of his education and launch him on a successful career outside of sports. Further, the exposure the player receives while playing and the personal contacts he makes as a player provide valuable networking that also can enhance later career opportunities inside or outside sports.

These are all examples of college athletics as a means to career success. For many college athletes, however, the experience of simply being a member of a successful team offers tremendous benefits; it is an important *end* in itself. Camaraderie develops, lifelong friendships are established, and team members feel a sense of belonging. The successful coordination of team efforts on the playing field, with all members of the team working together like a well-oiled machine, can be tremendously satisfying and rewarding if team efforts lead to achievement.

The Structuring of Group Interaction

Groups are useful only if the interaction of group members produces something greater than the sum of all the individual efforts. Group interaction must be structured so group members will coordinate their actions in the cooperative pursuit of both individual and group objectives. The structure of group interaction is apparent in the rules and roles that define acceptable behavior in the group.

Rules Group rules that define the boundaries of acceptable and expected behavior in the group can be formal or informal. Some groups have formal policies. Formal policies are rules explicitly agreed upon by the group members and even written down—for example, how often or what time of day the group will meet. Many groups structure their meetings according to Robert's Rules of Order. These well-known rules specify in writing who may talk and when, and how disagreements will be settled by discussion and vote.

Informal, unstated rules that govern and regulate group behavior are called **norms.** Groups may have norms about what is appropriate to wear to meetings of the group. Groups often have norms about lateness or absence. It may be the norm, for instance, for group members to call ahead to warn the group if they are going to be more than 10 minutes late for a meeting.

Groups also may have norms prohibiting criticism of group decisions to "outsiders"—people who are not members of the group. This type of norm demonstrates an important difference between norms and explicit group policies. A group might feel uneasy about adopting an explicit rule against airing group dissension outside the group. Nevertheless, an informal rule of this sort may be necessary for group members to feel free to voice dissenting or controversial positions during group discussions, or if it is important for the group to appear united in its opinions to outsiders.

Formal policies and norms also differ in terms of enforcement. Formal policies often specify punishments if rules are breached. For example, a breakfast club may fine members for missing meetings. Because norms are only implicit rules, norms are enforced instead by group disapproval or rejection of the offending group member. This is not to suggest that norms constitute a weaker form of group structure than formal policies. In fact, in some cases norms may have more regulatory power over group members precisely because they are implicit. An explicit policy always can be challenged, reconsidered, and altered through open group discussion. Because norms are unstated agreements about conduct, it may be difficult for group members to question or reconsider a norm's appropriateness or challenge its punishment openly. An unfair norm therefore may be harder to fight than an unfair policy.

Knowing a group's rules for social interaction and playing by them often is critical if a newcomer wants to make good first impressions and establish healthy long-term relationships with members of the group. Nowhere is this more apparent than when managers take their business abroad. As noted in the "INTERNATIONAL FOCUS ON: Rules and Norms," the rules that govern social interaction in other countries often are very different. Managers traveling abroad are well-advised to learn the local rules of social interaction, in order to avoid accidentally insulting their foreign hosts.

The formal and informal rules that structure a group's interaction derive from a variety of sources. Some rules are established by formal consideration

INTERNATIONAL FOCUS ON

Rules and Norms

Strangers in Strange Lands Rules and norms can facilitate smooth and productive social interaction only when individuals are aware of them. Within a country, there may be subtle differences in social conventions among regions, or even among organizations within a region. But these differences pale in comparison to the differences across countries. Consider some of the rules for social interaction in the Arab Middle East.

The Arab concept of privacy is quite different from that held by most Americans. Americans new to the Middle East may schedule a confidential meeting to discuss classified company business, only to find their Arab host's office filled with friends, relatives, and professional associates at the appointed hour. Of course, finding *anything* in the Middle East at the appointed hour is no small triumph because of the Arab sense of time. Arabs view time as a continuous flow of events in which past, present, and future blur together. If unanticipated events prevent an Arab from meeting agreed-upon deadlines, it's the immutable will of Allah. As one frustrated U.S. oil company executive put it, "Arab clocks have no hands."

Hospitality is also an important aspect of Arab social interaction rules. To ancient Bedouins, from whom modern Arabs take many cultural cues, the purpose of hospitality was to strengthen group ties, vital to security in a tenuous nomadic existence in the harsh desert. Today, Arab hospitality is still a two-way street: a show of mutual respect, reciprocity, and delicately balanced obligations between host and guest who will then, in a future situation, become guest and host. Not only do Arabs feel obligated to be generous to their guests, but for a guest to *refuse* such generosity is an insult, a rejection of bonding to the group with which the host is aligned. When the situation is reversed, the former guest is expected to play the host with equal, but not greater, hospitality, so as not to create an imbalance in the relationship.

When you're offered something by an Arab colleague—be it coffee, tea, nuts or dates, an invitation to dinner, even a gift—Arab rules of politeness dictate that you should accept it. Whether or not you want it is irrelevant. It's the symbolic meaning of the offer and your acceptance that matters, not the content of the offer or your desire to receive it. And it's your playing by the rules in a foreign country that matters when it comes to their acceptance of you.

Source: N. Chesanow, "A Thousand and One Arabian Nights," *The World-Class Executive* (New York: Rawson Associates, 1985), 110–147.

and decision. To select a meeting time, for instance, group members might identify potential times and potential conflicts until they finally arrive at a decision. (The process of group decision making of this sort will be discussed in greater detail in Chapter 9.)

Not all rules are arrived at so formally, however. Group members may *import* rules of conduct from other groups. Perhaps a group member has found Robert's Rules of Order to be a useful mechanism for structuring group meetings in the past and suggests that the group adopt them.

What is done first also may determine rules for group interaction. If everyone comes to the first meeting of a group dressed formally (dresses or suits for the women, jacket and tie for the men), that could establish a group norm for being "dressed up" at the group's meetings. This may lead to the establishment of some rather silly norms. For instance, even if it is only by coincidence that everyone comes to the first meeting of a group "dressed up," all group members might conclude that all other group members came dressed that way intentionally. Thus, the norm for being "dressed up" could be established even though everyone in the group would rather be dressed casually at the meetings.

Importation and whatever-is-done-first practices are especially useful for establishing rules of conduct when it is important to have some rule, even though any rule will do. For example, to have free-flowing discussion, it is probably important that all group members be dressed similarly. *How* everyone is dressed (whether dressy or casual) may be less important. Importation or whatever-is-done-first practices may settle this issue without the group devoting time to its resolution.

Critical incidents also establish rules of conduct, either informally or formally. Policies and norms typically do not cover all possible behaviors of group members or the group. New behaviors outside the coverage of the group's policies and norms therefore are always possible. When new behaviors are tried, particularly successful or unsuccessful outcomes—the critical incidents—may lead to the establishment of group policies or norms in order to incorporate a successful behavior or prevent recurrences of past disasters. A group may have no rules regulating romantic attachments among group members, for instance, until two group members become attached romantically. If the romance is successful (in terms of improving or not interfering with group functioning), further such romantic attachments may be encouraged—or at least tolerated or not discouraged—by the group. On the other hand, if the relationship is a disaster from the viewpoint of group functioning, norms may arise or formal policies even may be established to prevent similar disruption of the group in the future.

Roles   While rules delineate the proper behaviors of all members in a group, **roles** define the set of behaviors appropriate to particular *positions* occupied by individuals in a group. Roles also specify the authority relationships within a group, including who has the right to call meetings, set agendas, and assign tasks to group members. Social psychologist Erving Goffman contends that roles (like rules) smooth interaction in groups.[3] Roles allow us to know what we should be doing and what to expect from others. Like rules, the roles that structure the interaction of group members can be formal or informal.

In work organizations, formal roles are specified by job descriptions. **Job descriptions** are written documents that specify what duties individuals must perform, to whom they must report, what goals they must attain—in short, their role in the organization. Job descriptions are very useful because they decrease an individual's uncertainty about what to do to fulfill the group's needs and expectations.

Many groups (especially informal ones) do not have job descriptions. Roles instead evolve or are negotiated informally as the group develops. Some role assignments evolve during group development as particular strengths and talents of group members are revealed. As we shall see in Chapter 10, most groups have at least two leadership roles: a task leader (who focuses on getting the group's goals accomplished) and a socio-emotional (relations-oriented) leader (who focuses on maintaining harmony and good working relationships within the group). While task leadership often is arrived at formally (for example,

---

[3] E. Goffman, *The Presentation of Self in Everyday Life* (New York: Doubleday Anchor, 1959).

by vote of the group members or appointment from a higher source), socio-emotional (relations-oriented) leadership emerges (and even changes) as the group develops and matures. A selection of typical roles occupied by group members is shown in Figure 7–1.

Roles are specific to particular positions within particular groups. The role an individual occupies in one group may be completely different from the role that same individual occupies in other groups. Figure 7–2 identifies a variety of roles that one individual might assume in a variety of different groups and relationships. Because all of us simultaneously occupy different roles, *role conflict* is always a potential problem. Role conflict occurs when the behaviors dictated by one role conflict with the behaviors dictated by another. The coach of a company softball team may find himself in a quandary about how to address his boss if his boss tries out for the softball team. Is the boss still "Ms. Perkins" on the softball field (as she is in the office), or is she "Janet"? And if she's "Janet" on the softball field, is she now "Janet" in the office? This role conflict can become acute if social or even romantic interaction is tolerated or encouraged among softball-team members but discouraged between supervisors and subordinates in the company.

An important component of most roles is status. **Status** refers to the position of a role in a social hierarchy. The amount of status that a role commands is the amount of personal worth, respect, prestige, and deference that the role provides *any* individual occupying that role. Status is a source of power for a role-holder. High-status individuals can influence the behaviors of a group because of their revered positions. High-status individuals also are looked to by other group members as opinion leaders.

These forms of power of high-status individuals over low-status group members are sensible when status reflects ability or expertise. For example, senior students at a university (high-status role holders) are likely to be extremely knowledgeable and thereby worthy of the deference freshman students accord them. The role of university professor carries even more status, though this status may be less deserved if the professor has been on campus only a few days and is therefore ignorant of campus policies, norms, and procedures.

Interestingly, undeserved status may be no less powerful than earned status. In courtroom trials, jurors from high-status occupations disproportionately influence final jury decisions, even though a high-status occupation may make an individual no more capable of rendering a just verdict.[4]

Maintaining Group Adaptability Rules and roles are important for coordinating and regulating group interaction. After all, in their absence there is chaos and a low probability of effective group functioning. This does not mean, however, that rules and roles are universally good for a group. Rules and roles improve the effectiveness of group functioning precisely because they constrain the behaviors of group members, thereby allowing predictability and coordination of group behavior. While a little constraint is not only good but *necessary*, too much constraint can prove disruptive to the effective functioning of a group.

[4]F. L. Strodtbeck, R. M. James, and D. Hawkins, "Social Status in Jury Deliberations," *American Journal of Sociology* 22 (1957): 713–719.

| FIGURE 7–1 | ▶ Typical Roles Occupied by Group Members |

Task-Oriented Roles

The task-oriented role facilitates and coordinates decision-making activities. It can be broken down into the following subroles:

- *Initiators* offer new ideas or modified ways of considering group problems or goals as well as suggest solutions to group difficulties, including new group procedures or a new group organization.
- *Information seekers* try to clarify suggestions and obtain authoritative information and pertinent facts.
- *Information givers* offer facts or generalizations that are authoritative or relate experiences that are pertinent to the group problem.
- *Coordinators* clarify relationships among ideas and suggestions, pull ideas and suggestions together, and try to coordinate activities of members of subgroups.
- *Evaluators* assess the group's functioning; they may evaluate or question the practicality, logic, or facts of suggestions by other members.

Relations-Oriented Roles

The relations-oriented role builds group-centered activities, sentiments, and viewpoints. It may be broken down into the following subroles:

- *Encouragers* praise, agree with, and accept the ideas of others; they indicate warmth and solidarity toward other members.
- *Harmonizers* mediate intragroup conflicts and relieve tension.
- *Gatekeepers* encourage participation of others by using such expressions as, "Let's hear from Sue," "Why not limit the length of contributions so all can react to the problem?" and "Bill, do you agree?"
- *Standard setters* express standards for the group to achieve or apply in evaluating the quality of group processes, raise questions of group goals and purpose, and assess group movement in light of these objectives.
- *Followers* go along passively and serve as friendly members.
- *Group observers* tend to stay out of the group process and give feedback on the group as if they were detached evaluators.

Self-Oriented Roles

The self-oriented role focuses only on members' individual needs, often at the expense of the group. This role may be broken into the following subroles:

- *Blockers* are negative, stubborn, and unreasoningly resistant; for example, they may try to bring back an issue the group intentionally rejected or bypassed.
- *Recognition seekers* try to call attention to themselves; they may boast, report on personal achievements, and, in unusual ways, struggle to avoid being placed in an inferior position.
- *Dominators* try to assert authority by manipulating the group or certain individuals in the group; they may use flattery or assertion of their superior status or right to attention; and they may interrupt contributions of others.
- *Avoiders* maintain distance from others; these passive resisters try to remain insulated from interaction.

Source: Reprinted by permission from *Organizational Behavior*, 5th ed. by Don Hellriegel, John W. Slocum, and Richard W. Woodman, 212–213. Copyright © 1989 by West Publishing Company. All rights reserved.

FIGURE 7–2	▶ One Person = Many Roles

Every person assumes many different roles. At home, an individual might be a parent or spouse, at work a supervisor or subordinate (or both). Each of these roles carries with it prescriptions for behaviors and expectations on the part of others. For example, your boss expects you to obey, while your spouse expects you to be supportive and affectionate. These roles help us know what to do—and help others know what to expect from us.

Source: Lawrence S. Wrightsman, *Social Psychology*, 2d ed. (Monterey, Calif.: Brooks/Cole, 1977), p. 17. Reprinted by permission of Brooks/Cole Publishing Company, Pacific Grove, California 93950, a division of Wadsworth, Inc.

In an article entitled "The Technology of Foolishness," political scientist Jim March has suggested that rules and roles can constrain the creativity and flexibility of a group.[5] This constraint, in turn, can hinder the group's adaptability to changing demands and opportunities. Norms and roles represent prescriptions for behavior—prescriptions that summarize past learning about how the group can best function. For example, a norm previously may have been established for group members to bring food to meetings. The food makes it

[5] J. G. March, "The Technology of Foolishness," *Civil o konomen* 18 (4) (1971).

possible for the group to work during the lunch hour without anyone missing lunch. The food also informalizes the meetings, thereby encouraging open discussion. Having a norm about bringing food to meetings allows these advantages to occur at every meeting without members having to figure out anew how to accomplish them. What the norm also does, however, is to discourage anyone from figuring out a *better* way of accomplishing these same (and admittedly valuable) benefits. This can prove extremely important if circumstances change so that rules that were appropriate for regulating group behavior in the past are no longer appropriate. Once a norm has been established, group members will hesitate to break the norm and risk sanctions by the group.

March suggests that it is important that group members occasionally "act out" and violate group rules and roles. Violating group rules and roles seems foolish. After all, the group's rules and roles summarize past learning about how to structure group interaction appropriately. In most cases, then, violating a group's rules and roles will result in poor outcomes for the group. However, sometimes the violation of group rules and roles will reveal that a norm or policy was ill-advised in the first place, that circumstances have changed, or that there simply is a better way of doing things. Only violation of a rule or role can show why the rule or role is still appropriate, if in fact it still is. Unfortunately, unless one group member is willing to risk sanctions by the group, violations of the group's rules and roles will not occur. Thus, while rules and roles capture past learning about effective group functioning, they also may stand in the way of continual learning and adaptation by the group.

Idiosyncrasy credits provide groups a way to be creative within the necessary constraints of rules and roles. Idiosyncrasy credits are allowances given to group members to violate group rules and roles.[6] If someone has proven to be a good group member—has in the past largely gone along with the behavioral prescriptions of the group's rules and roles—that individual will be *allowed* to violate the group's rules and norms without incurring extreme sanctions. If an individual has been a good group member (that is, played by the rules) for a long period of time, that individual's actions in breaking the group's rules or roles are unlikely to be seen on balance as a threat to the group. In contrast, an individual new to the group or one who has consistently violated rules and roles in the past is likely to be seen by group members as a threat to the rules and roles. Since the rules and roles are important to maintaining the group's coordination and stability, these violations are unlikely to be tolerated. Thus, group members accumulate idiosyncrasy credits by demonstrating their loyalty to the group's rules and roles. This makes later occasional violations less likely to be seen as revolutionary or destructive. Idiosyncrasy credits provide the mechanism by which the continuing appropriateness of group rules and roles can be challenged and reaffirmed by group members.

Rules and roles also can be problematic to group functioning when they define a reality or morality within the group that is inappropriate and inconsistent with reality or morality outside the group. A famous study at Stanford University provided a graphic demonstration of this tyranny of group rules and roles by simulating life in prisons.[7] In the study, the students participating as

---

[6]E. P. Hollander, "Conformity, Status, and Idiosyncrasy Credits," *Psychological Review* 65 (1958): 117–127.

[7]C. Haney, C. Banks, and P. G. Zimbardo, "A Study of Prisoners and Guards in a Simulated Prison," in *Readings about the Social Animal*, ed. E. Aronson (New York: W. H. Freeman, 1984).

guards became extremely brutal and inhumane. There was nothing different about these students that should have led them to commit reprehensible acts. Their own morality simply was swallowed up by the prescriptions of their roles as prison guards.

Any time the rule and role enforcement mechanisms at work in a group lead the group members to engage in behaviors that violate or suspend the larger rules and roles of society, the group's effectiveness and even survival are threatened.

Stages of Group Development

The rules and roles that structure group interaction do not simply exist. Groups must evolve and develop rules and roles over time. Many theories have been offered to explain how groups develop.[8] We will examine two quite different theories: the *five-stages* perspective and the *punctuated-equilibrium* model.

Five-Stages Perspective   The **five-stages perspective** probably is the most popular and best-known theory on how groups develop over time. This perspective proposes five distinct phases that groups pass through as they develop: forming, storming, norming, performing, and adjourning.[9]

Forming   When groups first come together, the members must get acquainted. **Forming** includes learning the traits and strengths of each potential member. If participation in the group is voluntary, potential members might be trying to decide during formation if membership is necessary or whether this group is likely to fulfill their needs. Preliminary identification of a leader usually occurs at this stage as well.

Storming   Once group members have had a chance to assess the human resources available in a group, several battles must be fought within the group. First, the group must decide what its goals and priorities will be. Is a study group there only to study, or does it fulfill an important social function as well? If there is a social function as well, how can these two goals be reconciled? And are there other functions for the group? Can the group fulfill its functions without creating problems for its members? The second battle arises because the group must structure its interaction to ensure effective group functioning. Who will fulfill which roles becomes an important question. Disagreements that are not handled now typically force the group back to this stage again later in its development.

Norming   Once group functions have been (at least tentatively) decided upon and roles have been assigned, the tone of group interaction changes. Group members now identify with a common purpose, and the group has identified the human resources it needs to fulfill that purpose. In norming the group members must define a set of rules and roles to coordinate group interaction and make pursuit of the goals effective.

---

[8]J. P. Wanous, A. E. Reichers, and S. D. Malik, "Organizational Socialization and Group Development: Toward an Integrative Perspective," *Academy of Management Review* 9 (1984): 670–683.

[9]B. W. Tuckman and M. A. C. Jensen, "Stages of Small Group Development Revisited," *Group and Organization Studies* 2 (1977): 419–427.

Performing   Once a group has identified its rules and roles, it has a structure within which to pursue its goals and the group has reached maturity. If further conflicts surface among members, the structure (roles and rules) put in place should lead to nondisruptive resolution of the conflicts.

Adjourning   Some time after a group has reached maturity, it may make sense for the group to disband. **Adjourning** refers to the disbanding of a group. Some groups adjourn because their "time is up." A CEO-advisory group, for instance, would disband when the CEO's term of office expires, or when the CEO quits or is fired. Groups may choose to adjourn because they have outlived their usefulness—for example, if the group has lost critical members or found a solution to the problem it was convened to address (or even has realized that there is no solution). Finally, premature adjournment of a group results when the group fails to develop adequately—for instance, if the group cannot manage the conflict that surfaces during storming.

Two important points should be kept in mind when considering the stages of group development. First, during their development groups may find themselves moving back and forth among these stages. As noted earlier, it is not unusual for a group to find that all of its conflicts were not settled initially. In such cases, a second or even third phase of differentiation may occur, until all conflicts are ironed out. Second, while virtually all groups pass through these stages of development, the transitions may not be obvious to the group members themselves. In fact, much of the negotiation of the group's roles and rules may be quite implicit.

Punctuated Equilibrium   Not all groups develop according to the five-stages model just described. According to one of the newest theories on group development, project teams that have a fixed time frame in which to accomplish a task instead tend to develop through a process known as **punctuated equilibrium.**[10]

According to the punctuated-equilibrium model of group development, the tone for a project team (how it will interact, what approach it will take to the project, what its goals will be) is set in the team's first meeting. The project team stays with these arrangements (regardless of their efficiency or effectiveness) until approximately the mid-point of the time frame for completion of the project. Around the midpoint of the project team's time frame, there is a "revolution" in the team's approach to its project. The team breaks out of its inertia and generates a new set of agreements and arrangements that carry the team through to the project's completion. The team's closing meetings also depart from previous meetings. Typically these last meetings are more focused on preparing the project team's work for external consumption.

The difference between the five-stages and punctuated-equilibrium models of group development is the role of *time* in the punctuated-equilibrium model. Groups without a time deadline for completion of their work and dissolution of the group may progress and develop according to the internal needs of the group or the needs of the group's members. Indeed, such groups may fail precisely because they reach a development stage beyond which they cannot pro-

[10]C. J. G. Gersick, "Time and Transition in Work Teams: Toward a New Model of Group Development," *Academy of Management Journal* 31 (1988): 9–41.

gress. According to the punctuated-equilibrium model, the development of a project team working under a time deadline is not a function of the group's internal needs to develop effective group functioning. Instead, a project team's development is triggered by the deadline imposed on the team and the need for completion of the project by that deadline.

BUILDING EFFECTIVE GROUPS

Groups present tremendous opportunities. Individuals can work harder and smarter together than alone, and group interaction can fulfill the affiliation needs that individuals simply cannot satisfy working in isolation. These are the potential benefits available through the use of groups in organizations. Unfortunately, individuals also can avoid taking responsibility for their actions by hiding behind a group's roles and rules. Also, poor communication within a group can put all the potential benefits of working together out of the group's reach.

The challenge of managing groups in organizations is getting group members to go along with good rules and roles, to communicate openly about the bad ones, and to consider carefully the questions about rules and roles offered by their fellow group members.

The next section of this chapter briefly explores this important challenge in two ways. First, a model that details the characteristics of effective groups will be presented. Second, a technique used in organizations specifically to improve group functioning will be described.

Characteristics of Successful Groups

What makes a group successful? What makes a group able to harness its dark side and put its energies to constructive use? Successful groups typically share five characteristics: group objectives, role differentiation, rule clarity, membership, and communication.

Group Objectives The goals, purposes, and functions that a group is trying to achieve are **group objectives.** For a group to be successful, its goals must be specific. From vague goals are born vague attempts to pursue them. Specific goals get everyone working in the same direction and sharing the same priorities.

Group objectives also should be shared by the entire group membership. It is no help to group functioning if two members of the same group have specific *but different* beliefs about where the group is headed and why. All group members should have in mind the *same* goals for the group, even if some of the members don't completely agree with those publicly stated objectives.

Finally, very successful groups figure out ways to *integrate* individual and group goals. When group and individual goals are integrated, group actions become more than just the price individuals must pay for access to fulfillment of individual goals. Group actions themselves become a path to individual goal fulfillment. As noted by Susan Kare, a Macintosh artist at Apple Computers, "There's nothing like a group effort toward a common goal to unite people."

A demonstration of the importance of individual and group goal integration was provided by the "jigsaw classroom" in Austin, Texas. The jigsaw classroom is a grade-school instructional technique based upon building cooperative student learning teams:

> In a jigsaw classroom, small student-directed groups replace the teacher-dominated lecture method; students serve as the principal sources of information and reinforcement for one another. Students are placed in small groups of five or six for about an hour each day. The day's lesson is divided up into as many segments as there are group members and each student is given a unique part. Each member is then responsible for learning the assigned segment well enough to teach it to the others. Since group members can only learn a lesson in its entirety by pooling all their knowledge, interdependence is established.[11]

The jigsaw classroom was devised to combat racial prejudice during desegregation efforts in Texas. Grading systems in U.S. elementary schools typically reward individual achievement. In a jigsaw classroom, cooperation—and thereby group achievement—is the only effective path to individual achievement. Jigsaw classroom students in Austin learned their classroom lessons better *and* they learned the value of teamwork and coordinated group efforts toward shared goals. The jigsaw classroom also enhanced students' abilities to understand other students' perspectives, leading to decreased racial prejudice and misunderstanding in the schools.

Role Differentiation   Members of successful groups know more than just what the group is trying to accomplish. Each group member also has a role that specifies the individual's contribution. Appropriate **role differentiation** occurs in two ways. First, all group members should have a clear idea of their own roles—their own duties and responsibilities in the organization and how they contribute to the realization of the group's goals. Second, the roles assigned to each member of the organization should reflect individual strengths and interests. It is not enough that each member of the group have a role and know what it is. As much as possible, the roles assigned to group members should maximize each individual's opportunities to contribute to fulfillment of group, organizational, *and individual* objectives.

Rule Clarity   The formal rules and informal norms that structure interactions within the group also should be agreed upon and shared by all members of the group. These rules and norms include authority (task assignment) and reporting relationships. As we discussed earlier in the chapter, rules are critical to the coordination of group member activities. If appropriate rules are not agreed upon or not known, their ability to control and direct group interaction is nonexistent.

Membership   Successful groups strike an appropriate balance among similarities and differences of their members' values and backgrounds. A certain amount of variety in member perspectives is important for providing a healthy background of controversy and conflict in the group. Too much controversy and conflict can lead to hostility and to the eventual breakup of the group. Rules for membership and participation in group activities also should be clear.

---

[11] E. Aronson and S. Yates, "Cooperation in the Classroom: The Impact of the Jigsaw Method on Interethnic Relations, Classroom Performance, and Self-Esteem," in *Small Groups and Social Interaction* 1, ed. H. Blumberg, A. Hare, V. Kent, and M. Davies (New York: John Wiley and Sons, 1983).

Team development activities come in many shapes and forms. At Motorola's headquarters, volleyball games like the one pictured here are used to foster effective cooperation and communication.

Communication   Finally, all successful groups have in place adequate channels of communication. Good communication is any group's first line of defense against threats to its survival, whether from external or internal sources. No matter how well objectives might be selected and shared, rules and roles made clear, and membership constructed, circumstances are bound to change. Good channels of communication in the group are important if the group is to adapt to new challenges and remain successful over time.

This chapter began by noting that groups are essentially collections of individuals whose interactions are structured to fulfill functions. The five characteristics of successful groups we have outlined reflect a group with a good understanding of its functions (objectives) and an appropriate structure (in the form of role differentiation, rule clarity, membership, and communication) for achieving them. How do groups come to possess these five important characteristics? Some groups achieve them through natural evolution. Other groups get a helping hand from team development activities.

Team Development

Team development is defined as "an inward look by the team at its own performance, behavior, and culture for the purposes of dropping out dysfunctional behaviors and strengthening functional ones."[12] The desired outcome of team development is a *team*—a highly effective group of individuals who work well together. Team-development activities teach team members valuable skills in working and getting along with others. These skills become the foundation for team effectiveness. The skills developed for team interaction often have tremendous value beyond the boundaries of the team as well. All team-development (or "team-building") activities share the following important functions:

Diagnosis   Team development always includes activities that focus on identifying functional and dysfunctional aspects of group interaction. Typically, roles

---

[12] W. French and C. Bell, *Organizational Development: Behavioral Science Interventions for Organizational Improvement* (Englewood Cliffs, NJ: Prentice-Hall, 1978).

and rules for group interaction will be examined and their appropriateness openly questioned. Often group members will be asked to complete diagnostic questionnaires. The questionnaire might ask, for instance: How *clear* are the group's goals? How much *consensus* is there about the group's goals? The results of the questionnaire then can be fed back to the group and used to stimulate awareness and discussion of problems concerning any of the five dimensions (group objectives, role differentiation, role clarity, membership, and communication) of effective group interaction.

Change   Once a group has identified its problems, the group must work together to remove impediments to effective group functioning. Naturally, change attempts will prove successful only if diagnosis has been careful and thorough. Many times team development efforts fail because groups accept only surface definitions of group interaction problems. For instance, if a leader is ineffective, changing the leader's behavior may be only part of the solution. Have the behaviors of other group members been reinforcing the previous ineffective behaviors of the group leader? If so, the behaviors of these other group members also must be altered. The immediate identification of obvious behavior problems rarely provides a complete diagnosis of group interaction deficiencies. The "maintaining conditions" that have allowed this problem to persist or grow in the group also must be examined and questioned.

Many groups find it useful to draw up plans in the form of a contract. The contract specifies what is going to be changed and by whom. Just as role clarity is necessary for successful day-to-day group functioning; specifying the role of each group member in the agreed-upon team development changes should help ensure their successful implementation.

Development   Successful group development goes beyond identifying and repairing group interaction dysfunctions. The need for group development activities in the first place suggests that a group is not adequately self-diagnostic. The group's interaction patterns do not include effective problem identification and problem solving. Successful **group development** therefore does more than just solve group interaction problems. It also creates a system for identifying and resolving *future* group interaction problems.

Role therapy is one example of a group-development activity. Role therapy is a training technique in which someone from outside the group (a group process consultant) comes into the group temporarily to act as a catalyst to improve the effectiveness of group interaction. A group engages in role therapy to ensure that role differentiation has been accomplished appropriately. The focus of role therapy is the definition of individual roles in the group. Nevertheless, the process of negotiating any member's role in the group also creates opportunities to clarify the group's overall objectives and rules and to enhance channels of communication within the group.

Role therapy develops a group's self-diagnostic skills through analysis, modeling, and coaching. The process consultant talks with each group member to understand each member's role, how the roles all are meant to function together, and where the problems in the role structure arise. At first, these inquiries by the process consultant are done privately with each group member. Later, the process consultant will convene a meeting of the group and publicly solicit information from group members about role definitions and possible sources of role problems, thereby *modeling* the diagnostic techniques for group members. Finally, the process consultant will encourage group members to take over ownership of the diagnostic process and will only *coach* group members' attempts to engage in appropriate diagnostic behaviors.

Through this intervention cycle of analysis, modeling, and coaching by the process consultant, role therapy achieves two important objectives. First, sources of role problems are identified publicly so that the group can begin to work toward their resolution. Second, group communication processes are improved so that future role problems can be identified, acknowledged, and resolved by the group on its own. Role therapy is one of a variety of techniques that organizations use to develop more effective group functioning. Several more of these techniques will be discussed in Chapter 17.

COMMUNICATION IN GROUPS AND ORGANIZATIONS ◆◆◆◆◆◆

Communication is the transmitting of information and understanding by one group member to another through the use of symbols.[13] Communication is probably the most visible of all group activities, and (as noted in the previous discussion on building effective groups) it is critical to effective group functioning.

Past research has repeatedly shown that enormous amounts of time in groups and organizations is spent communicating. In some occupations, more than half of all time spent on the job is spent communicating.[14] College students spend more than 60 percent of their waking hours engaged in some form of communication activity.[15] There is also evidence that the ability to communicate well is an essential skill that in large measure determines the performance of managers.[16]

The remainder of this chapter addresses this all-important topic of communication in groups and organizations. We begin by describing the basic processes of communication, including nonverbal communication, communication styles, and the important differences between formal and informal communication in organizations. The chapter closes by examining barriers to communication and suggesting some techniques for improving communicator effectiveness.

Basic Communication Processes

As shown in Figure 7–3, effective communication between two individuals (the sender and the receiver) involves many steps. Intended meaning is the thought or idea that the sender would like to convey to the receiver. In order to transmit

---

[13]J. M. Ivancevich and M. T. Matteson, *Organizational Behavior and Management* (Plano, TX: BPI, 1987), 632.

[14]For a summary, see F. Luthans and J. K. Larsen, "How Managers Really Communicate," *Human Relations* 39 (1986): 161–178.

[15]R. Verderber, A. Elder, and E. Weiler, "A Study of Communication Time Usage among College Students," working paper, University of Cincinnati.

[16]L. E. Penley, E. R. Alexander, I. E. Jernigan, and C. I. Henwood, "Communication Abilities of Managers: The Relationship to Performance," *Journal of Management* 17 (1991): 57–76.

FIGURE 7–3 ▶ Communications Model

Communication is essentially a perceptual process. The sender must encode intended meaning to create messages. The receiver then decodes the messages to obtain perceived meaning. Effective communication depends on the sender and receiver sharing an understanding of the rules used to encode meaning into messages.

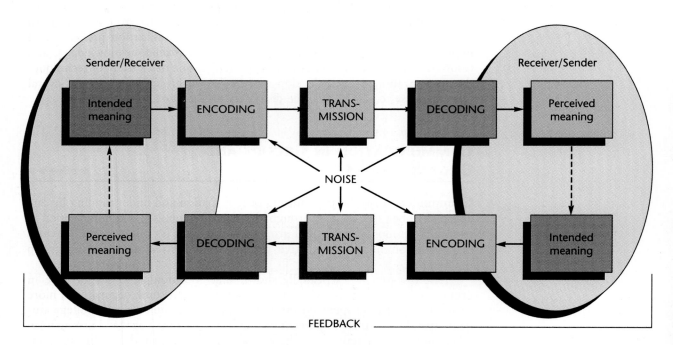

this intended meaning, the sender must encode it. **Encoding** is the process of creating a message for the receiver to receive.

Encoding is a three-part process. First, the sender must select some contents of the intended meaning to transmit. To do this, the sender must decide what the receiver knows, what the receiver will assume, and what else must be conveyed. Second, the sender must select a communication medium and channel (or channels) through which to transmit the intended meaning. For instance, will the communication be verbal or written? If verbal, will other channels (nonverbal gestures or voice inflections, for instance) be used? The importance of communication medium and channel selection was immortalized forever by Marshall McLuhan's pronouncement that "the medium is the message."[17] McLuhan's comment serves as a reminder that medium and channel selections themselves convey information. Sending a memo communicates something different from a personal phone call or a face-to-face discussion, even if the words are the same. Finally, the sender must translate the contents selected for the message into symbols. Communication symbols are agreed-upon representations of meaning in a communication medium. Spoken words, for instance, are appropriate symbols for verbal communication.

---

[17] M. McLuhan, *The Medium Is the Message* (New York: Random House, 1967).

Once the message is transmitted, the receiver must decode it. **Decoding** is an attempt by the receiver to reverse the encoding process and extract meaning from a message. Decoding is a perception process. The receiver must decide what communication medium or channel to attend to and then must select symbols and correctly construct and interpret them. The success of decoding is dependent on the sender and receiver agreeing on the meanings of communication symbols. The perceived meaning that the receiver extracts from a message will not much resemble the sender's intended meaning if the symbols used have different meanings for the sender and receiver.

The sixth stage of communication is feedback. Communication is action taken by the sender, and feedback is the receiver's reaction to the sender's message and the perceived meaning of that message. Feedback is critical to communication effectiveness. Feedback is really nothing more than the receiver becoming the sender and sending return messages. These return messages help the sender know if the intended meaning of the initial message was correctly decoded by the receiver.

As noted in Figure 7–3, effective communication can be disrupted by noise. **Noise** refers to any characteristics in the immediate context or in the communicating individuals that might interfere with the communication process. External noise includes factors external to the communicating individuals, such as the noise level in a crowded room. Physiological noise includes physical properties of the communicating individuals that make successful communication difficult, such as hearing loss in a receiver. Finally, psychological noise refers to forces within the communicating individuals that might lead them to communicate less effectively, such as a sender's dislike for the receiver.[18]

Figure 7–3 probably underestimates the extent to which face-to-face interpersonal communication is a dynamic, *transactional* process.[19] Figure 7–3 suggests that communication is an orderly process in which the sender first sends a message, then the receiver receives and decodes it, and finally the receiver sends a return message (feedback) to the sender. Face-to-face interpersonal communication is much more simultaneous. As the sender sends a message, the receiver is already receiving and reacting—providing feedback to the sender (for instance, via facial gestures or even verbal interruptions). Thus, face-to-face interpersonal communication is not about senders and receivers but about individuals who are simultaneously sending and receiving messages. Face-to-face interpersonal communication is not something one individual does to another but something two (or more) individuals do *with* each other.

Nonverbal Communication

Nowhere is the importance of perception to communication more apparent than in understanding nonverbal communication. **Nonverbal communication** refers to any form of interpersonal communication other than formal verbal language. It typically includes facial cues, hand or arm gestures, and body positioning. Clothing can be used to send nonverbal signals as well—for example, when a male colleague buttons up his shirt and tightens his tie to signal that a meeting is all business. People also surround themselves with objects (such as

[18] R. B. Adler, L. B. Rosenfeld, and N. Towne, *Interplay: The Process of Interpersonal Communication* (Fort Worth, TX: Harcourt Brace Jovanovich College Publishers, 1992).

[19] Adler, Rosenfeld, and Towne, *Interplay*, 8.

Both verbal and nonverbal communication are important in any interaction. The woman and man conversing here convey certain messages to each other and to passersby through their clothing, posture, facial expressions and gestures. Nonverbal communication often supplements verbal communication by emphasizing certain parts of the verbal message.

fancy cars, walnut desks, and corner offices) that communicate who they are—or who they would like to be.

Nonverbal communication channels often are used to supplement verbal communication by highlighting or reinforcing parts of a verbal message. Verbal messages have two advantages over nonverbal messages. First, verbal communication is an accepted and expected channel for transmitting information. Therefore, it is likely to be attended to. Second, verbal communication in the form of language has codified rules of interpretation, so that basic meanings of verbal messages should be readily accessible to perceivers.

Nonverbal communication is generally more uncertain, both in meaning and in likelihood of receipt. Some perceivers may not attend to nonverbal communication attempts or may completely misunderstand them. What is the meaning of a wink at the end of a sentence? What does it mean if a speaker turns away when sending a message? Or, as noted in the "FOCUS ON: Nonverbal Communication," when is a kiss just a kiss?

The meaning of nonverbal communication is particularly ambiguous when it is *inconsistent* with a simultaneously transmitted verbal message. A subordinate may turn away, for instance, while complimenting a superior, thus betraying other (and not so positive!) feelings. The verbal communication channel usually is easy for a sender to control. Nonverbal channels (such as facial expressions) may be less controllable and thereby provide more direct access to a sender's real feelings. But of course, that is only if the receiver knows the "rules" for decoding nonverbal messages.

Communication Styles

People differ in the ways they choose to communicate with others. Consider, for example, the following description of the different communication styles of two U.S. presidents:

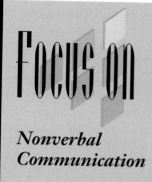

Nonverbal Communication

A Kiss Instead of a Handshake? It happens in a split second: You've been kissed by a business associate. Social kissing—the peck on the cheek—has become so widespread that it's spilling over into the business world. In certain corporate circles, at company parties and even in offices, some people who barely know each other exchange kisses as freely as handshakes.

Yet many people find corporate kissing awkward and confusing. Both men and women say they are often unsure about just whom to kiss, and under what circumstances. And recipients of corporate kisses often are horrified. Indeed, etiquette gurus say corporate kissing is usually a faux pas unless the participants are close friends outside the workplace.

But when two people aren't close friends, the recipient of a corporate smooch often feels uncomfortable. Part of the problem is that those who have been kissed are suspicious of the kisser's motives: are they trying to sell something, ingratiate themselves, or impress others? Many kissers say they do it because it puts people at ease.

As the practice spreads, business-people increasingly face the dilemma of whether to kiss. Steve Hayden, chief creative officer of the advertising agency BBDO/Los Angeles, says deciding can be hard because there are "about 17 variables"—including the city, business, ages, and ranks of the two people—to consider before kissing, while a kiss happens in an instant.

People who move in many different corporate circles may become especially confused. Hayden says he is unsure whether to kiss in business relationships about 10 percent of the time. "We go from a Japanese meeting to a meeting with passionate movie people to a meeting with staid New Yorkers. You start getting your signals mixed up."

He recently met with a female executive from a big Chicago-based company about a new business pitch and gave her a buss on the cheek. "I had just gotten out of a meeting where that was the behavior. I was in a kissing mode," Hayden recalls. But halfway into the kiss he started to regret it, remembering that the woman "had already expressed some concern that we were a bunch of L.A. hot-tub types." The executive wasn't pleased. "Her eyes kind of widened and she drew back. She was a bit shocked. Then she smiled a little bit, as if to say, 'This is how they act in Los Angeles.'" BBDO/Los Angeles didn't get that account. "It was all the wrong kiss," Hayden says with a sigh.

There are also geographical differences. Some Bostonians, for instance, won't even *talk* about kissing. Others just dismiss it. George Lodge, a professor of comparative government–business relations at Harvard, says: "I don't recall any instances of kissing at Harvard Business School."

In Los Angeles, a fear of contagious diseases has boosted the popularity of the "air kiss," in which two people put their cheeks in close proximity without touching. Sometimes they just make kissing sounds, and sometimes they just say, "Kiss, kiss." Still, Los Angeles may well be the nation's kissing capital. "Sometimes people purse their lips and come running at you," says Thomas D. Tannenbaum, president of Viacom Productions, Inc. "If someone puts their face up to be kissed, you can't just let them hang there."

Source: K. A. Hughes, "Kissing in the Workplace Poses Dilemma," *The Wall Street Journal*, July 6, 1988, 27. Reprinted with permission of *The Wall Street Journal* © 1988 Dow Jones and Co., Inc. All rights reserved worldwide.

Soon after President Eisenhower took office, I asked one company's vice-president for governmental affairs to comment on the different communication styles of President Eisenhower and President Truman. She told me that President Eisenhower depended almost completely on all news going through regular channels, with each key man giving him a briefing on what was happening. As a result, he had to see very few people.

President Truman, on the other hand, saw practically everyone. People came and went constantly, until it was almost like having Andrew Jackson back in the White House. To the casual observer, President Truman was the most disorganized person in the world. But through his methods, he was able to personally determine the things that were important. He *really* knew what was going on.[20]

The **Johari Window** has received widespread use by management trainers as a device for assessing and categorizing managers' communication styles. As shown in Figure 7–4, the Johari Window (named after its developers, Drs. Joseph Luft and Harry Ingham) classifies an individual's tendencies to facilitate or hinder interpersonal communication along two dimensions: exposure and feedback.[21] **Exposure** is the extent to which an individual openly and candidly divulges feelings and information when trying to communicate. **Feedback** is the extent to which an individual successfully elicits exposure from others.

These two dimensions of communication—exposure and feedback—give rise to four distinct components of interpersonal communication. As shown in Figure 7–4, the *arena* represents information that is known to the manager and known to others. In the best of all worlds, all communication would be in the arena. A manager would be open and candid in discussions with others, and those others in turn would be open and candid in discussions with the manager. The more information that falls in the arena, the more effective the communication.

The second cell of the Johari Window is the *blindspot*. Information in the blindspot is known to others but not known to the manager. Blindspots occur when a manager doesn't communicate enough, doesn't listen well when communicating, or when a manager antagonizes others so that they don't provide the manager feedback.

The *hidden* components of communication occur when a manager fails (intentionally or unintentionally) to provide information to others. Hidden information can cause problems, particularly if the information isn't communicated to others because the manager incorrectly assumes everyone already knows. Finally, *unknown* information is unknown to both the manager and others. Unknown information is information that is not intentionally being held back but nevertheless remains uncommunicated.

Differences in the extent to which managers' communication skills and abilities result in arena, blindspot, hidden, and unknown information give rise to four distinct communication styles. *Type A* communicators are low in both exposure and feedback. Type A managers would be characterized as uncommunicative, terse, even aloof or impersonal. Type A communication results in both hidden information and blindspots. *Type B* communicators are also low in exposure, but they are high in feedback. Type B managers will constantly seek out information, but they rarely provide information in exchange. Type B communication results in hidden information. Managers low in exposure (Type A or Type B communicators) basically don't trust others with important information. Low exposure communication should be particularly ineffective when paired with high feedback—continual requests for information.

---

[20]H. O. Golightly, "The What, What Not, and How of Internal Communication," *Business Horizons* (December 1973): 49.

[21]J. Hall, "Communication Revisited," *California Management Review* (Spring 1973): 30–48.

FIGURE 7–4	▶ The Johari Window

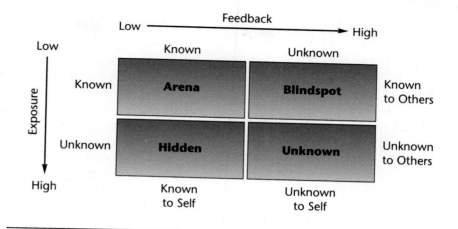

Type C communicators are high in exposure but low in feedback. Type C managers typically would be perceived as autocratic or arrogant. They give lots of information but rarely request the opinions of others. Type C managers would likely be perceived as not valuing others' opinions and perspectives. Type C communication tends to create blindspots.

The final communication style—*Type D*—occurs when a manager is high on both exposure and feedback. In this style, most information becomes arena information and communication is effective.

In addition to these global dimensions of communication style (providing and seeking information), interpersonal communication styles also may differ in the use of physical space, eye contact, and touching. These differences are believed to capture important distinctions between the ways that men and women communicate.[22] As noted in the "FOCUS ON: Communication Styles," men and women also may differ in the most fundamental dimension of communication—*why* they communicate. Of course, whether these differences in communication style really are differences between men and women is less important than the fact that people (even among men and women) differ in their communication styles. And these differences in communication style do interfere with communication effectiveness. An instrument to help you assess your own communication style is provided in the "On Your Own" exercise at the end of this chapter.

Formal Communication in Organizations

A **communication network** is the constellation of communication channels through which information flows in a group or organization—who talks to whom. An organization's *formal* communication network is represented by its organization chart. The organization chart describes the formal reporting relationships in the organization—who is *supposed* to talk to whom.

---

[22] See, for instance, A. Kohn, "Girl Talk, Guy Talk," *Psychology Today*, February 1988, 65–66.

Focus on

Communication Styles

"You Just Don't Understand!" If women speak and hear a language of connection and intimacy, while men speak and hear a language of status and independence, then communication between men and women can be like cross-cultural communication, prey to a clash of conversational styles. Instead of different dialects, it has been said that women and men speak different genderlects.

Women and men are both often frustrated by the other's way of responding to their expression of troubles. And they are further hurt by the other's frustration. If women resent men's tendency to offer solutions to problems, men complain about women's refusal to take action to solve the problem they complain about. Since many men see themselves as problem solvers, a complaint or a trouble is a challenge to their ability to think of a solution; so when a woman presents a man with a broken bicycle or a stalled car, it poses a challenge to his ingenuity to fix it. But whereas many women appreciate help in fixing mechanical equipment, few are inclined to appreciate help in "fixing" emotional troubles.

Trying to solve a problem or fix a trouble focuses on the message level of the conversation. But usually when women habitually report problems at work or in friendships, the message is not the main point they are trying to convey. It is the metamessage that counts: telling about a problem is a bid for an expression of understanding ("I know how you feel") or a similar complaint ("I felt the same way when something similar happened to me"). In other words, troubles talk is intended to reinforce rapport by sending the metamessage, "We're the same; you're not alone." Women are frustrated when they not only don't get this reinforcement but, quite the opposite, feel distanced by the advice, which seems to send the metamessage "We're not the same. You have the problems; I have the solutions."

Furthermore, mutual understanding is symmetrical, and this symmetry contributes to a sense of community. But giving advice is asymmetrical. It frames the advice giver as more knowledgeable, more reasonable, more in control—in a word, one-up. And this contributes to the distancing effect.

Source: D. Tannen, *You Just Don't Understand: Men and Women in Conversation* (New York: Ballantine Books, 1990), 42, 51–53.

As shown in Figure 7–5, formal communication networks in groups and organizations can be classified into several common types.[23] The "*Y*" is typical of highly bureaucratic, hierarchical organizations. In the "Y" network, subordinates report to supervisors, supervisors in turn report to managers, and so on. The only way for information to reach the top of the organization from the bottom is "through channels"—that is, by passing through each and every level of the hierarchy. Typically, *lateral* communication (for instance, among subordinates or supervisors at the same level in the hierarchy) is not part of the formal communication network.

The *wheel*, in contrast, is typical of highly centralized groups and organizations. In the wheel, one individual acts as the conduit for *all* information that passes through the group. Unlike the "Y", wheel communication networks can gather and disseminate information quickly because there are few channels through which information must pass to get from one individual in the network

[23] A. Bavelas and D. Barrett, "An Experimental Approach to Organizational Communication," *Personnel* (March 1951).

FIGURE 7–5 ▶ Formal and Informal Communication Networks

"Y"

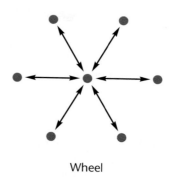

Wheel

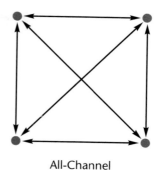

All-Channel

to another. Wheel communication might be typical of a sales force in which all sales personnel report to a "home office" manager, but only rarely see or talk with each other.

The *all-channel* communication network is most typical of participative, egalitarian groups and organizations in which everyone is encouraged to talk with everyone. The biggest distinction between the all-channel and other formal communication networks is the opportunity for lateral communication. For instance, in an all-channel communication network, even supervisors in different departments would be provided opportunities to share information.

As noted in Figure 7–6, which communication network is most appropriate depends upon the goals and objectives of a group or organization. The wheel and all-channel communication networks provide the fastest transmission of information (and also have significantly less conflict[24]) because they reduce the number of channels through which information must pass. However, satisfaction of participants tends to be low in wheel networks, and leadership is slow to emerge when all-channel communication is encouraged.

Organizations use a variety of techniques to enhance the flow of information through the formal network. When General Motors came under fire in the mid-1980s for being too bureaucratic, it embarked on an ambitious campaign to improve communication. General Motors sent employees to public speaking workshops, made available videotapes of top management meetings, improved the more than 350 General Motors publications, and even established satellite links to allow live conversations around the world.[25]

Many organizations enhance their *upward* flow of information from all levels of the organization through organization surveys. An **organization survey** is a questionnaire used to capture and understand what employees think about

[24]R. E. Nelson, "The Strength of Strong Ties: Social Networks and Intergroup Conflict in Organizations," *Academy of Management Journal* 32 (1989): 377–401.

[25]B. H. Goodsite, "General Motors Attacks its Frozen Middle," *IABC Communication World* (October 1987): 20–23.

| FIGURE 7-6 | ▶ Effects of Common Communication Networks | | |

| | | Networks | |
	"Y"	Wheel	All-Channel
Speed	Moderate	Fast	Fast
Accuracy	High	High	Moderate
Emergence of leader	Moderate	High	None
Satisfaction	Moderate	Low	High

Source: Adapted from A. Bavelas and D. Barrett, "An Experimental Approach to Organizational Communication," *Personnel*, March 1951, 370.

a variety of issues. Organization surveys also provide management with a sense of the organization's perceptions of its own strengths and weaknesses. When used correctly, surveys provide top management with anonymous, uncensored feedback about company policies, procedures, and programs. The use of surveys also signals employees that employee ideas and opinions are important to the organization.[26] As noted in the "FOCUS ON: Formal Communication," professionally-conducted, appropriately-utilized organization surveys can be extremely valuable management tools.

Informal Communication in Organizations

In contrast to the formal communication networks represented by reporting relationships and organization charts is the grapevine. The **grapevine** refers a network of channels of communication that are not part of a group or organization's formal communication network.

An example of the difference between a group or organization's formal and informal communication networks is provided in Figure 7–7. Figure 7–7a is the organization chart and represents who is supposed to talk with whom. Figure 7–7b represents the organization's informal communication network—who *in fact* talks with whom in the organization.

The grapevine is represented by communication channels that exist where (according to the formal communication network) there should not be communication channels. For instance, in Figure 7–7b, Supervisor B talks with Subordinate C even though they are in different parts of the organization. Supervisor A then may get the news, after it passes from Subordinate A to Subordinate B.

Formal and informal communication networks also may differ because communication channels *don't* exist where they should. In Figure 7–7b, Supervisor A talks with Subordinate B, but Subordinate A bypasses Supervisor A and talks directly with the Manager. Similarly, Subordinates D and E are isolates, apparently not talking much with anyone except each other.[27]

Grapevines often come into existence because formal channels of communication are inadequate. In Figure 7–7b, extensive lateral communication among subordinates may reflect inadequate supervision, leaving the subordinates to lead and coach each other. Similarly, the existence of direct commu-

[26] S. L. Guinn "Surveys Capture Untold Story," *HRMagazine* (September 1990): 64–66.

[27] R. W. Pace, *Organizational Communication: Foundations for Human Resources Development* (Englewood Cliffs, NJ: Prentice-Hall, 1983).

Formal Communication

Organizational Surveys Managers assume that job security is of paramount importance to employees. In fact, among workers it ranks far below such ethereal-sounding desires as respect, a higher standard of management ethics, increased recognition of employee contributions, and closer, more honest communications between employees and senior management.

When Opinion Research Corp. of Chicago surveyed 100,000 middle managers, supervisors, salespeople, and technical, clerical, and hourly workers of Fortune 500 companies in 1988, it found the lines of communication fraying. With the exception of the sales group, employees believed top management was less willing to listen to their problems than it was five years earlier. The groups also felt top management now accorded them less respect.

A. Foster Higgins and Co., an employee-benefits consulting firm, finds that only 45 percent of large employers make regular use of worker opinion surveys, probably the most obvious means of carrying employee messages upward. Says Richard Knapp, a principal of the firm, "Organizations audit their financial resources regularly but fail to take the temperature of their own employees." Such companies, he says, are "flying blind."

Why don't companies make greater use of surveys? Because, says Bruce Pfau, executive vice-president of Sirota Alper & Pfau, some CEOs still believe that asking underlings questions is tantamount to letting them run the show. "It's a sort of an aristocratic attitude: 'Who are you to tell me what you want? You work for me.'"

Companies that do use surveys sometimes conceal results from employees or fail to explain how policy changes are related to survey findings. Failure to follow through deepens employee cynicism: "Management didn't want my opinion in the first place," employees think. "Now they're sorry they asked." After studying the Fortune 500 companies' use of a wide variety of from-the-bottom-up communications tools—including surveys, telephone hot lines, quality circles, suggestions programs, and exit interviews—Towers Perrin, another big consulting firm, concluded that the "open doors" of many corporations were only "slightly ajar."

LIMRA's Jaci Jarrett Masztal believes that surveys can really open the lines of communication if organizations follow a few simple guidelines. Surveys should be anonymous and confidential; that's how to get at what people are really thinking. It is important to *share the survey results* with the respondents. This will help the employees know if their voice has been heard accurately. Finally, follow-up action must be taken that shows respondents that their opinions are valued. Response rates (the proportion of employees actually completing the survey) average only about 40 percent for organization-wide surveys in large companies. However, when a survey is professionally conducted and employees believe management is sincere in seeking input, response rates can be as high as 90 percent.

Source: Adapted from A. Farnham, "The Trust Gap," *Fortune*, December 4, 1989, 57; and J. J. Masztal, "Survey Says . . ." *Managers Magazine*, May 1991, 8.

nication channels from subordinates to the manager that bypass a supervisor may indicate that the manager distrusts the information being received "through channels." The grapevine provides the manager a check.

Much of the gossip and rumor that is passed through an organization's grapevine—who is dating whom, who is buying a new car, who is being audited by the IRS—may be harmless chitchat that is largely irrelevant to a group or

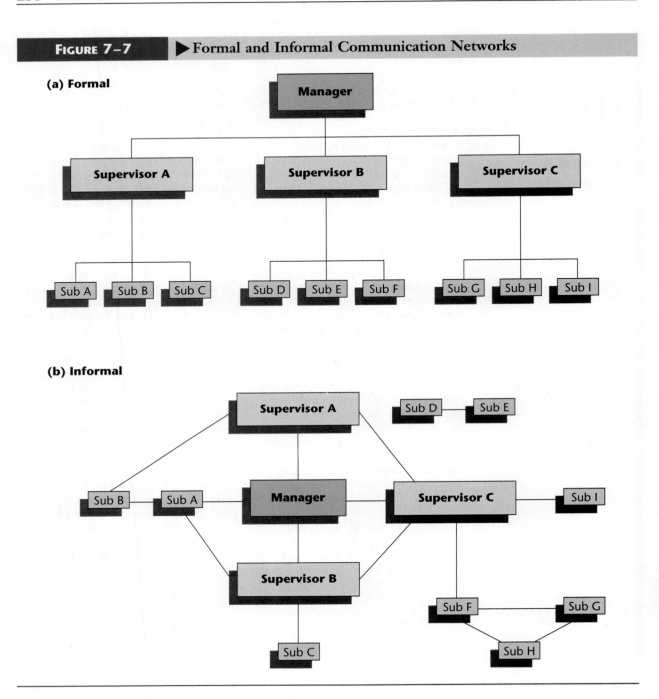

FIGURE 7-7 ▶ Formal and Informal Communication Networks

(a) Formal

(b) Informal

organization's functioning. Nevertheless, managers are well-advised to keep an ear to the grapevine. Employees tend to give the grapevine as much (or even more!) credence than formal communication channels.[28] Inaccurate rumors—such as those about impending but unannounced layoffs, or covered-up product

---

[28] S. J. Modic, "Grapevine Rated Most Believable," *Industry Week*, May 15, 1989, 11, 14.

Tenneco chairman Mike Walsh, shown here at a town meeting, has worked hard to build a corporate culture based on openness and candor. His style exemplifies the all-channel communication network typical of participative organizations, where information is shared freely by employees at all levels.

contaminations[29]—may both reflect and reinforce employees' dissatisfactions or anxieties. Left unchecked, negative rumors circulating through the grapevine can create snowballing negative consequences for an organization.[30] Such rumors, particularly if untrue, necessitate responses (through formal communication channels) that remedy problems, relieve anxieties, and get employees' attention back on the work at hand.

"Old Boy" networks form another informal communication network in organizations. However, while grapevines typically make information available to anyone who is willing to listen, "old boy" networks are *exclusionary*. "Old boy" networks consist of only a select group of individuals in an organization— for instance, only the white males. "Old boy" network members collect information and share it only among themselves. "Old boy" networks create problems for organizations when that exclusionary information sharing provides a competitive advantage for individuals in the "old boy" network at the expense of those not in the network (for instance, blacks or females).[31]

Barriers to Communication

Communication is essentially a perceptual process. Receivers must attend to, construct, and interpret communication symbols to arrive at a meaning for a message. Many communication failures can be explained as problems of perception. We will consider two examples of communication problems here: problems with attention and problems with interpretation.

---

[29] R. Rowan, "Where Did That Rumor Come From?" *Fortune*, August 13, 1979, 130.

[30] D. Krackhardt and L. W. Porter, "The Snowball Effect: Turnover Embedded in Communication Networks," *Journal of Applied Psychology* 71 (1986): 50–55.

[31] P. Watts, "Breaking into the Old-Boy Network," *Executive Female*, November/December 1989, 32+.

Attention and Information Overload   One of the biggest barriers to effective communication is information overload. As noted earlier, information overload occurs when there is more information available than the receiver can decode. In perceptual terms, this is a problem of limited attention. Managers are buried under an avalanche of information transmitted to them daily from a variety of sources: subordinates, superiors, outside mail, and newspapers, to name a few. The problem is deciding what to attend to. As noted in the beginning of this chapter, attention is a scarce resource. Much of the communication directed at a manager may be unimportant or redundant information of little or no value to the manager. No manager can attend to all of the available information in order to decide what is important and what is not. The manager must select which messages to decode. Given that uncertainty is a defining characteristic of organizations, the receiver will not always know which messages are the most important. Therefore, the first barrier to effective communication is that any single message may not even be received.

An individual's frame of reference can influence what gets paid attention to in communication. One study demonstrated that managers' communication activities are dramatically influenced simply by whether a situation is labeled a crisis or a challenge. As shown in Figure 7–8, when managers perceive a situation to be a crisis, they ask fewer questions, listen less carefully to others, and are less interested in hearing what others have to say.[32] Having a crisis orientation apparently constrains a manager's use of communication channels.

Anything that can increase the salience of a message will make it more likely to be received. For instance, unusual formats or colors often are used in resumes to set them apart from the sea of look-alike resumes submitted for job openings. Motivations of the receiver—the individual for whom the communication is intended—also play a role. Communication attempts from above usually are attended to more carefully than those from below.

Interpretation and Decoding   Figure 7–9 suggests that for information to be communicated accurately, the "rules" behind the encoding of the message must be shared by the information decoder. The receiver must share the sender's views about what aspects of the intended message need to be transmitted, and the receiver must share the sender's beliefs about the meanings attached to communication symbols and channels. In the communication failure shown in Figure 7–9, the scientists have attended to and built appropriate constructions of the dolphins' messages. However, the scientists do not know the rules for decoding the message: they have not figured out that the dolphins are speaking Spanish. The scientists have attended to the correct symbols and constructed a correct representation, but they cannot accurately decode the dolphins' communication attempts.

When two communicators literally are not speaking the same language, the importance of shared encoding/decoding rules seems obvious. The importance of sharing rules may be less obvious, however, when two people *seem* to be speaking the same language but really are not. There is a story about a plumber who wrote to the government to find out if it was safe to use hydrochloric acid to unclog drains. The government responded that, "The efficacy of hydro-

[32] D. Tjosvold, "Effects of Crisis Orientation on Managers' Approach to Controversy in Decision Making," *Academy of Management Journal* 27 (1984): 130–138.

| FIGURE 7–8 | ▶ Communication and Frame-of-Reference: Crisis or Challenge? | | |

Number of Questions Asked	Crisis	Challenge
Number of Questions Asked	2.77	3.84
Knowledge of Others' Arguments	2.25	3.30
Interest in Hearing More Arguments	4.64	6.46

Mean responses, measured on a scale of 1 = "few" or "very little" and 7 = "many" or "a great deal."

Source: Adapted from D. Tjosvold, "Effects of Crisis Orientation on Managers' Approach to Controversy in Decision Making," *Academy of Management Journal* 27 (1984): 130–138.

chloric acid is indisputable, but the corrosive residue is incompatible with metallic permanence." What the government meant, of course, was that hydrochloric acid "eats the hell out of pipes"—a message that would have been significantly more understandable to a plumber.[33]

Every occupation or profession—in fact, every group of people—uses special words or attaches special meanings to common words. These special words or common words used with special meanings are called jargon. **Jargon** summarizes a group's common experiences and history and allows the simple communication of complex meanings by group members. Unfortunately, jargon also requires shared understanding and shared experiences to be interpreted correctly.

Improving Communicator Effectiveness

Because communication is essentially a perceptual process, communication can be improved by increasing the probability that the receiver will accurately perceive (that is, attend to and decode) a sender's communication attempt. Three keys to improving the receiver's perceptual accuracy are sender empathy, active listening, and media selection.

Sender Empathy   For communication to be effective, the sender must empathize with the receiver. **Empathy** is the ability of one individual to appreciate another's perspective. Obviously, if the receiver speaks only Spanish, a message in English is unlikely to convey the intended meaning. Even within the same language, however, empathy can help a sender ensure that the intended meaning is the one received. Which channels is the receiver likely to attend to? What meaning will the receiver attach to the choice of a particular communication medium? Will the receiver attach the same meanings to our symbols as we do?

Senders often fail to realize that subtle shades of meaning can be quite group-specific and embedded in personal experience. Does "participative management" have the same meaning for employees at Hewlett-Packard and at General Motors? Since their companies' participative management programs are different, the term will have different meanings for employees of these two companies. Consequently, use of the term *participative management* in a message to an employee of either company will require some clarification. And the clarifications are likely to be different, depending on which company the receiver is from.

---

[33]K. N. Wexley and G. A. Yukl, *Organizational Behavior and Personnel Psychology* (Homewood, Ill.: Irwin, 1977).

FIGURE 7–9	▶Barriers to Communication

In communication, a perceiver can construct a correct representation of incoming sensory inputs but still miss the message by not making the correct interpretation, as the pictured scientists have done. Perceivers often need to "read between the lines"—interpret meaning beyond what is explicitly said, perhaps based on nonverbal cues. A shared set of rules and expectations is essential if this type of communication is to be effective.

"Matthews ... we're getting another one of those strange 'aw blah es span yol' sounds."

Effective communication requires that the sender realize and adjust to how a receiver is likely to decode messages. Effective communication requires that the sender appreciate the receiver's perspective and tailor messages to fit the receiver's ability to decode them.

Active Listening   Active listening is the mirror image of sender empathy. Sender empathy means the sender accepts responsibility for ensuring proper transmission of intended meaning. **Active listening** involves the receiver accepting responsibility for ensuring the proper transmission of the intended meaning by actively assisting the sender in clarifying the meaning of the message.[34]

A receiver's active assistance in clarifying the meaning of a message can take three forms. First, a receiver can improve communication effectiveness simply by working harder at listening. It's easy to think—incorrectly—that when you're listening it's the other person who is supposed to be doing all the work. Some specific suggestions for improving communication by working harder at listening are contained in Figure 7–10. Second, a receiver can use feedback to

[34]C. R. Rogers and R. F. Farson, "Active Listening," in *Organizational Psychology: Readings on Human Behavior in Organizations*, ed. D. Kolb, I. Rubin, and J. McIntyre (Englewood Cliffs, NJ: Prentice-Hall, 1984), 255–267.

FIGURE 7–10   ▶ **10 Keys to Effective Listening**

These keys are a positive guideline to better listening. In fact, they're at the heart of developing better habits that could last a lifetime.

Keys to Effective Listening	The Bad Listener	The Good Listener
1. Find areas of interest	Tunes out dry subjects	Opportunitizes: asks "what's in it for me?"
2. Judge content, not delivery	Tunes out if delivery is poor	Judges content, skips over delivery errors
3. Hold your fire	Tends to enter into arguments	Doesn't judge until comprehension is complete
4. Listen for ideas	Listens for facts	Listens for central themes
5. Be flexible	Takes intensive notes using only one system	Takes fewer notes. Uses 4–5 different systems, depending on speaker
6. Work at listening	Shows no energy output Attention is faked	Works hard, exhibits active body state
7. Resist distractions	Is distracted easily	Fights or avoids distractions, tolerates bad habits, knows how to concentrate
8. Exercise your mind	Resists difficult expository material; seeks light, recreational material	Uses heavier material as exercise for the mind
9. Keep your mind open	Reacts to emotional words	Interprets color words; does not get hung up on them
10. Capitalize on the fact that *thought* is faster than speech	Tends to daydream with slow speakers	Challenges, anticipates, mentally summarizes, weighs the evidence, listens between the lines to tone of voice

Source: L. K. Steil, "How Well Do You Listen?" *Executive Female*, July/August 1986, 37.

check the appropriateness of decoding strategies even as a message is transmitted. For instance, if a sender uses a symbol whose meaning is ambiguous, the receiver can request more information about the sender's use of the term. ("By participative management, did you have in mind something like suggestion boxes or employee committees?") Third, a receiver can help clarify the meaning of a message by reflecting the received meaning back to the sender. ("It seems like you're very angry about what's happened. Is that right?") Feedback about received meaning gives the sender a chance to try again if a message was not received as the sender intended. Of course, feedback is itself another message and therefore also susceptible to lost meaning when the sender (now acting as a receiver) decodes it.

Active listening represents a form of **two-way communication:** communication in which receivers can return messages to senders. Research has shown that one-way communication, in which the receiver cannot return messages to the sender, is more efficient and less threatening for the sender. However, it is

FIGURE 7–11   ▶ The Relationship between Information Medium and Information Richness

Information Medium		Information Richness
Face-to-Face		Highest
Telephone		High
Written, Personal (letters, memos)		Moderate
Written, Formal (bulletins, documents)		Low
Numeric Formal (computer output)		Lowest

Source: R. L. Daft and R. H. Lengel, "Information Richness: A New Approach to Managerial Behavior and Organization Design," in *Research in Organizational Behavior* 6, ed. B. Staw and L. Cummings, (Greenwich, Conn.: JAI Press, 1984), 196.

also less effective and more frustrating for the receiver.[35] Communication is about transmitting meaning, and two-way communication provides the best opportunity for the sender's intended meaning to be the one perceived by the receiver.

Media Selection   An important consideration in sending a message is picking an appropriate communication medium. **Information richness** is the information-carrying capacity of an item of data.[36] When the communication of a single item of data (for instance, a wink) conveys substantial new understanding, that communication is information rich. As shown in Figure 7–11, communication media vary in their information richness. Information richness is determined by such factors as the number of channels utilized in the communication medium and the opportunities for and speed of feedback.

Face-to-face communication is highly information rich because it utilizes multiple channels (words, facial gestures, body language) to reinforce a message. Face-to-face communication also provides opportunities for immediate feedback. Written communication is lower in information richness; written communication lacks the support of multiple, meaning-confirming channels, and feedback is slower.

Organizational researchers Richard Daft and Robert Lengel have proposed that selection of an appropriate communication medium should be determined by the information richness of the medium in conjunction with the complexity of the issue being communicated.[37] As shown in Figure 7–12, effective communication is most likely to occur when the information-richness of the communication medium matches the complexity of the issue. For low-complexity issues, a communication medium low in information-richness will suffice; using

[35] H. J. Leavitt and R. A. H. Mueller, "Some Effects of Feedback on Communications," *Human Relations* (November 1951): 401–410.

[36] R. L. Daft and R. H. Lengel, "Information Richness: A New Approach to Managerial Behavior and Organization Design," in *Research in Organizational Behavior* 6, ed. B. Staw and L. Cummings, (Greenwich, Conn.: JAI Press, 1984), 191–233.

[37] Daft and Lengel, "Information Richness."

FIGURE 7–12	▶Information Richness, Issue Complexity, and Communication Medium Choice

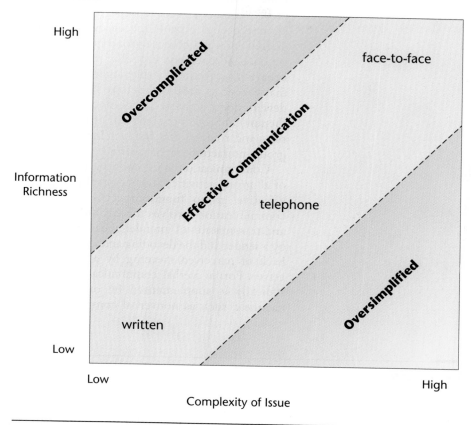

Source: Adapted from R. H. Lengel and R. L. Daft, "The Selection of Communication Media as an Executive Skill," *Academy of Management Executive* 2 (1988): 225–232.

an information-rich medium in this circumstance may waste valuable time and communicate more information than necessary (overload). Thus, it would seem appropriate to simply post (written communication) employees' weekly shift assignments rather than having face-to-face meetings every week to announce the assignments. On the other hand, highly complex issues demand information-rich communication media to help receivers fully understand the meaning of the messages. A corporate reorganization announced through a written memo, for example, would be unlikely to adequately clarify in everyone's minds exactly what was going to happen and why. That would require a face-to-face question-and-answer session, with all the opportunities for clarification that implies. Research has shown that high-performing managers are significantly better at selecting communication media that match the information-richness requirements of their messages.[38]

---

[38]R. H. Lengel and R. L. Daft, "The Selection of Communication Media as an Executive Skill," *Academy of Management Executive* 2 (1988): 225–232.

SUMMARY

◆◆◆◆◆◆

Groups and communication are the building blocks of organizations. People come together and talk in groups because groups provide the means to desired ends and because group interaction is a desired end in itself. Group behavior is governed by rules and roles that evolve as groups develop. Team development activities (such as role therapy) improve the quality of group rules and roles so that the benefits of group interaction can be realized.

Communication is the most visible of all group activities and is critical to effective group functioning. Good communication involves the encoding and transmission of intended meaning by a sender and the decoding and feedback of perceived meaning by a receiver. Formal verbal communication typically is supplemented by other channels, such as nonverbal communication. People differ in the ways they choose to communicate, in how open they are and how much they elicit feedback from others.

An organization's formal communication network is represented by its organization chart. Organizations use a variety of techniques to enhance the flow of information, including organization surveys. Informal communication networks in organizations (such as grapevines and "old boy" networks) arise because of inadequacies in an organization's formal communication network. Communication can be improved in organizations and groups when senders and receivers are more sensitive to the other side's perspective, when receivers practice active listening, and when communicators select communication media appropriate to their message.

Key Terms

Active listening   The receiver accepting responsibility for ensuring the proper transmission of the intended meaning in communication.

Adjourning   The stage of group development in which a group disbands.

Communication   The transmitting of information and understanding through the use of symbols.

Communication network   The constellation of communication channels through which information flows in a group or organization.

Critical incidents   Particularly successful or disastrous new behaviors that lead to the establishment of new group policies or norms.

Decoding   The process by which receivers extract meaning from a message.

Empathy   The ability of one individual to appreciate another's perspective.

Encoding   The process of creating a message.

Exposure   The extent to which an individual openly and candidly divulges feelings and information when communicating.

Feedback   Receiver's reaction to a sender's message.

Five stages perspective   A theory of group development proposing that all groups pass through a predetermined sequence of developmental phases.

Forming Stage of group development in which group members decide whether to join the group, learn the traits and strengths of other members, and identify a leader.

Grapevine An informal communication network in an organization.

Group Organized system of two or more individuals who are interrelated so that the system performs some function, has a standard set of role relationships among its members, and has a set of norms that regulate the function of the group and each of its members.

Group development The process of identifying and resolving present and future group interaction problems.

Group objectives The goals, purposes, and functions that a group is trying to achieve.

Idiosyncrasy credits Leeway given to group members to violate group rules and norms because of consistent past adherence to those rules and norms.

Information richness The information-carrying capacity of an item of data.

Jargon Special words or common words used with special meaning that summarize a group's common experiences and history and allow simple communication of complex meanings.

Job description A written document that specifies an individual's role in the organization.

Johari Window A device for assessing and categorizing managers' communication styles along the dimensions of exposure and feedback.

Noise Any characteristics in the immediate context of communicating individuals that interferes with communication.

Nonverbal communication Interpersonal communication through any channel other than formal verbal communication.

Norm Informal, unstated rules that govern and regulate group behavior.

Norming Stage of group development in which group members define a set of rules and roles to coordinate group interaction and make pursuit of the goals effective.

"Old boy" network An exclusionary informal communication network in an organization.

Organization survey A questionnaire used to capture and understand what employees think about a variety of issues.

Performing Stage of group development in which group members work within the group's structure to pursue the group's and members' goals.

Punctuated equilibrium A theory stating that a project team's development is triggered by the project's deadline.

Role The set of behaviors appropriate to a particular position occupied by individuals in a group or organization.

Role differentiation Establishment of clear concepts for group members of their specific duties and responsibilities to the group, based on their individual strengths and weaknesses, and how these duties and responsibilities contribute to the realization of the group's goals.

Role therapy Training technique in which someone from outside the group comes in temporariliy to act as a catalyst to improve the effectiveness of group interaction by ensuring that role differentiation has been accomplished appropriately.

Status Position of a role in the social hierarchy.

Storming Stage of group development in which the group decides what its goals and priorities will be.

Team development An inward look by the team at its own performance, behavior, and culture for the purposes of correcting dysfunctional behaviors and strengthening functional ones.

Two-way communication Communication in which receivers can return messages to senders.

Discussion Questions

1. What would social interaction be like *without* rules and roles?

2. Think of a group to which you belong. In what ways is your membership in this group a *means*? In what ways is your membership in this group an *end*?

3. If poor ideas and practices in organizations generally are punished to ensure organizational survival, how does an organization *encourage* constructive "foolishness" by its employees? How does the organization know when an employee is acting foolishly for the good of the organization, rather than just acting foolishly?

4. What are the stages of group development outlined in this chapter? How do each of these stages contribute to the effective functioning of the group?

5. In what ways is communication essentially a process of perception?

6. What can *senders* do to improve communication effectiveness? What can *receivers* do?

7. Why is the distinction between formal and informal channels of communication an important distinction for managers? Should the existence of a "grapevine" be troubling?

8. Are "old boy" networks a problem for organizations? How can organizations maintain the benefits they offer (if any) without risking their costs?

If You Want to Know More

A classic overview of the psychology of group processes is provided in an article of the same name by Alvin Zander in *Annual Review of Psychology* 30 (eds. M. Rosensweig and L. Porter, 1979, pp. 417–452). Jonathon Gillette and Marion McCollom offer a contemporary summary of groups and interaction in groups in a collection of essays entitled, *Groups in Context* (Addison-Wesley, 1990).

A good basic review of communication in organizations is provided in *Interplay: The Process of Interpersonal Communication*, by Ron Adler, Lawrence Rosenfeld, and Neil Towne (Dryden Press, 1991). A manager's challenge of tackling defensiveness in communication is discussed by Lyle Sussman in "Managers: On the Defensive" (*Business Horizons*, January/February 1991, pp. 81–87). Deborah Tannen examines communication styles and their impact on the management of relationships in *That's Not What I Meant! How Conversational Style Makes or Breaks Your Relations with Others* (New York: William Morrow, 1986). R. E. Axtell explores the importance of nonverbal gestures to communication across cultures in *Gestures! The Do's and Taboos of Body Language around the World* (Wiley, 1991).

The flip side of "old boy" networks—the communication networks of women and minorities—is examined in Herminia Ibarra's article, "Personal Networks of Women and Minorities in Management: A Conceptual Framework" (*Academy of Management Review* 18, pp. 56–87).

Ralph Rosnow examines the most fascinating of informal organizational communications in his article, "Inside Rumor: A Personal Journey" (*American Psychologist* 46, 1991, pp. 484–496). An interesting questionnaire to help you evaluate your personal listening skill profile is provided in "How Well Do You Listen?" by Dr. Lyman Steil, in *Executive Female* (July/August 1986, pp. 34–37).

On Your Own

Interpersonal Communications Survey This survey is designed to assess your understanding of and behavior in your interpersonal communications practices. There are no right or wrong responses. Rather, the requested response is simply the one that comes closest to representing your practices.

For each item on the survey, you are requested to indicate which of the alternative reactions would be more characteristic of the way *you* would handle the situation described. Some alternatives may be equally characteristic of you or equally uncharacteristic. Although this is a possibility, please choose the alternative that is *relatively* more characteristic of you. For each item, you will have five points that you may *distribute* in any of the following combinations, where 5 = most characteristic and 0 = least characteristic:

	A	*B*
1.	5	0
2.	4	1
3.	3	2
4.	2	3
5.	1	4
6.	0	5

Thus, there are six possible combinations for responding to the pair of alternatives presented to you with each survey item. *Be sure the numbers you assign to each pair sum to 5.*

To the extent possible, please relate each situation in the survey to your own personal experience. As used throughout this survey, the words *he, him,* and *his* include both the masculine and feminine genders unless specifically stated.

1. If a friend of mine had a personality conflict with a mutual acquaintance of ours with whom it was important for him to get along, I would:
   _____ **A.** Tell my friend that I felt he was partially responsible for any problems with this other person and try to let him know how the person was being affected by him.
   _____ **B.** Not get involved because I would not be able to continue to get along with both of them once I had entered into the conflict.

2. If one of my friends and I had a heated argument in the past and I realized that he was ill at ease around me from that time on, I would:
   _____ **A.** Avoid making things worse by discussing his behavior and just let the whole thing drop.
   _____ **B.** Bring up his behavior and ask him how he felt the argument had affected our relationship.

3. If a friend began to avoid me and act in an aloof and withdrawn manner, I would:
   _____ **A.** Tell him about his behavior and suggest he tell me what was on his mind.
   _____ **B.** Follow his lead and keep our contacts brief and aloof since that seems to be what he wants.

4. If two of my friends and I were talking and one of my friends slipped and brought up a personal problem of mine that involved the other friend, and of which he was not yet aware, I would:
   _____ **A.** Change the subject and signal my friend to do the same.
   _____ **B.** Fill my uninformed friend in on what the other friend was talking about and suggest that we go into it later.

5. If a friend were to tell me that, in his opinion, I was doing things that made me less effective than I might be in social situations, I would:
   _____ **A.** Ask him to spell out or describe what he has observed and suggest changes I might make.
   _____ **B.** Resent the criticism and let him know why I behave the way I do.

6. If one of my friends aspired to an office in our student organization for which I felt he was unqualified and if he had been tentatively assigned to that position by the president of the student society, I would:
   _____ **A.** Not mention my misgivings to either my friend or the president and let them handle it in their own way.
   _____ **B.** Tell my friend and the president of my misgivings and then leave the final decision up to them.

7. If I felt that one of my friends was being unfair to me and his other friends, but none of them had mentioned anything about it, I would:
   _____ **A.** Ask several of those people how they perceived the situation to see if they felt he was being unfair.
   _____ **B.** Not ask the others how they perceived our friend but wait for them to bring it up to me.

8. If I were preoccupied with some personal matters and a friend told me that I had become irritated with him and others and that I was jumping on him for unimportant things, I would:
   _____ **A.** Tell him I was preoccupied and would probably be on edge a while and would prefer not to be bothered.
   _____ **B.** Listen to his complaints but not try to explain my actions to him.

9. If I had heard some friends discussing an ugly rumor about a friend of mine that I knew could hurt him and he asked me what I knew about it, if anything, I would:

   _____ **A.** Say I didn't know anything about it and tell him no one would believe a rumor like that anyway.

   _____ **B.** Tell him exactly what I had heard, when I had heard it, and from whom I had heard it.

10. If a friend pointed out the fact that I had a personality conflict with another friend with whom it was important for me to get along, I would:

    _____ **A.** Consider his comments out of line and tell him I didn't want to discuss the matter any further.

    _____ **B.** Talk about it openly with him to find out how my behavior was being affected by this.

11. If my relationship with a friend has been damaged by repeated arguments on an issue of importance to us both, I would:

    _____ **A.** Be cautious in my conversations with him so the issue would not come up again to worsen our relationship.

    _____ **B.** Point to the problems the controversy was causing in our relationship and suggest that we discuss it until we get it resolved.

12. If in a personal discussion with a friend about his problems and behavior, he suddenly suggested we discuss my problems and behavior as well as his own, I would:

    _____ **A.** Try to keep the discussion away from me by suggesting that other, closer friends often talked to me about such matters.

    _____ **B.** Welcome the opportunity to hear what he felt about me and encourage his comments.

13. If a friend of mine began to tell me about his hostile feelings about another friend who he felt was being unkind to others (and I wholeheartedly agreed), I would:

    _____ **A.** Listen and also express my own feelings to him so he would know where I stood.

    _____ **B.** Listen but not express my own negative views and opinions because he might repeat what I said to him in confidence.

14. If I thought an ugly rumor was being spread about me and suspected that one of my friends had quite likely heard it, I would:

    _____ **A.** Avoid mentioning the issue and leave it to him to tell me about it if he wanted to.

    _____ **B.** Risk putting him on the spot by asking him directly what he knew about the whole thing.

15. If I had observed a friend in social situations and thought that he was doing a number of things that hurt his relationships, I would:

    _____ **A.** Risk being seen as a busybody and tell him what I had observed and my reactions to it.

    _____ **B.** Keep my opinions to myself, rather than be seen as interfering in things that are none of my business.

16. If two friends and I were talking and one of them inadvertently mentioned a personal problem that involved me but of which I knew nothing, I would:

    _____ **A.** Press them for information about the problem and their opinions about it.

    _____ **B.** Leave it up to my friends to tell me or not tell me, letting them change the subject if they wished.

17. If a friend seemed to be preoccupied and began to jump on me for seemingly unimportant things and to become irritated with me and others without real cause, I would:
     _____ **A.** Treat him with kid gloves for a while on the assumption that he was having some temporary personal problems that were none of my business.
     _____ **B.** Try to talk to him about it and point out to him how his behavior was affecting people.

18. If I had begun to dislike certain habits of a friend to the point that it was interfering with my enjoying his company, I would:
     _____ **A.** Say nothing to him directly but let him know my feelings by ignoring him whenever his annoying habits were obvious.
     _____ **B.** Get my feelings out in the open and clear the air so that we could continue our friendship comfortably and enjoyably.

19. In discussing social behavior with one of my more sensitive friends, I would:
     _____ **A.** Avoid mentioning his flaws and weaknesses so as not to hurt his feelings.
     _____ **B.** Focus on his flaws and weaknesses so he could improve his interpersonal skills.

20. If I knew I might be assigned to an important position in our group and my friends' attitudes toward me had become rather negative, I would:
     _____ **A.** Discuss my shortcomings with my friends so I could see where to improve.
     _____ **B.** Try to figure out my own shortcomings by myself so I could improve.

Scoring Key In the Interpersonal Communication Survey, there are ten questions that deal with your receptivity to feedback and ten that are concerned with your willingness to self-disclose. Transfer your scores from each item to this scoring key. Add the scores in each column. Now, transfer these scores to the following figure by drawing a vertical line through the feedback score and a horizontal line through the self-disclosure line.

Receptivity to Feedback	Willingness to Self-Disclose
2.B_____	1.A_____
3.A_____	4.B_____
5.A_____	6.B_____
7.A_____	9.B_____
8.B_____	11.B_____
10.B_____	13.A_____
12.B_____	15.A_____
14.B_____	17.B_____
16.A_____	18.B_____
20.A_____	19.B_____
Total:_____	Total:_____

▶ Personal Openness in Interpersonal Communications

As suggested through this figure, higher scores on *receptivity to feedback* and *willingness to self-disclose* indicate a greater willingness to engage in personal openness in interpersonal communications. Of course, we need to be mindful of the situational factors that may influence our natural personal predispositions to be relatively more open or closed in interpersonal communications.

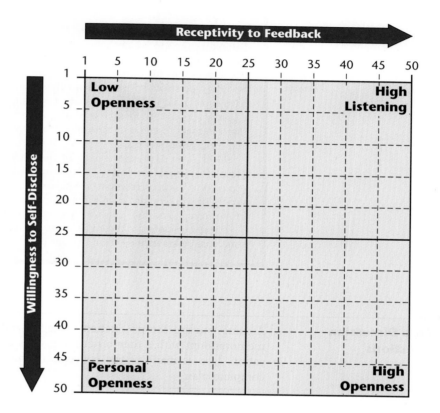

Source: D. Roberts, formerly manager of training, LTV Missiles and Electronics Group, Grand Prairie, TX; and D. Hellriegel, J. W. Slocum, and R. W. Woodman, *Organizational Behavior* 6th ed. (St. Paul, MN: West, 1992) 454–457.

CHAPTER 7

THE MANAGER'S MEMO

FROM: H. Barbieri, Vice President, Consumer Electronics Division

TO: B. Jones, Production Manager

RE: Quality First Program

I think it's time to look at a new approach to our Quality First program. We've had the suggestion box out for a year, and so far we've received only two suggestions for quality improvements, of which only one made any sense. Several supervisors have confidentially informed me that their subordinates have some great ideas. Why aren't we hearing any of these great ideas?

How about a group approach? We can divide the employees into teams that can meet to come up with ideas for improving the quality of our products and production process.

I'd like you to prepare a plan for these groups. How should they operate? How often should they meet? Should we divide the groups into engineers, production workers, maintenance personnel, and so on, or should we put a variety of workers into each group? What problems can we anticipate with the group format, and how can we try to resolve them?

These questions are meant as a starting point. If you have other ideas or concerns, please include them in your plan.

Case Discussion Questions

Assume you are the production manager, and respond to the vice president's memorandum with a memo outlining ways to open up the lines of communication. Use as many of the concepts in the chapter as you can to develop a complete plan.

CHAPTER

POWER, POLITICS, AND INFLUENCE

CEO DISEASE   ♦♦♦♦♦♦

Is egotism a disease? At the seat of corporate power, maybe. Telltale signs include being closed to criticism, acting too much the "statesman," not delegating decisions, getting attached to outward status symbols, and not preparing for successors. Some examples:

The Bank of New England had $1.2 billion in bad real estate loans in 1989, and forced out its CEO Walter J. Connolly Jr. in January 1990. The ex-Marine's management style was dubbed WWW—Whatever Walter Wants. He subjected his managers to relentless grilling in monthly meetings, demonstrating his obsession with details. Competing fiercely with rival Bank of Boston, he made disastrous real estate loans, unbeknownst to lending officers. Only when bank examiners found out was Connolly forced out.

Lone Star Industries Inc. lost $271 million in 1989, but CEO James E. Stewart still had a $2.9 million expense account and commuted to work from Florida to Stamford, Conn. in a corporate jet. To stem the losses, Stewart ordered layoffs, arranged a sell-off of corporate assets, but continued his own perks. Lone Star filed for Chapter 11 reorganization, and Stewart resigned a month later, insisting that the company's failure was a result of a downturn in the cement industry.

The most well-known example of CEO disease is F. Ross Johnson, who kept a fleet of ten planes at RJR Nabisco's corporate hanger in Atlanta. When Johnson's bid to take the public company private did not succeed, he was ousted by the company's new owners. The biggest LBO of all time also included the biggest golden parachute of all time: $53.8 million to make the free-spending Johnson go away.

Vanity and egotism go unchecked in the inner sanctum because CEO's are largely unsupervised and success leads them to "think they are entitled to privilege and royal treatment," said Harry Levinson, a corporate psychologist.

Much of the damage done by CEO disease is insidious. Sometimes it can even lead to a company's bankruptcy, as it did at Bank of New England and Lone Star. But not all CEOs are infected. F. Kenneth Iverson, CEO of Nucor Corp., the nation's seventh largest steel maker, drives his own car to work and flies coach on business trips. When he treats his executives to lunch, they often end up across the highway at Phil's Deli. And it's not that Nucor can't afford the perks. "You won't find any status symbols here," Says Iverson.

What's the cure? Staying close to employees, experts agree, helps CEOs skirt the pitfalls of power. Iverson's philosophy? Reducing differences between management and others at the company.

Source: J. A. Byrne, W. S. Symonds, and J. F. Siler, "CEO Disease," *Business Week*, April 1, 1991, 52–60.

INTRODUCTION

An important part of understanding the role that groups play in organizations is understanding how and why individuals behave differently in groups and organizations than they behave when alone. These differences go beyond the constraints on behavior created by roles and rules in group interaction. In groups and organizations, *other group members* are a potent influence on an individual's thoughts and behaviors. In this chapter, we consider two facets of group influence on individual behaviors: the apparent and direct persuasion that results from the exercise of *power* in groups and organizations and the subtle influence that results from *other group members* as the social context of behavior.

POLITICS AND POWER

Politics is a cornerstone of organizational behavior. As noted in Chapter 1, **political conflict** is a defining characteristic of organizational behavior. Political conflicts occur when different members of an organization use their power to pursue *personal* (rather than organizational) agendas, like the CEOs described in the opening vignette for this chapter. The distribution of power in an organization settles political conflicts. Politics doesn't mean doing what's best for the organization—politics means doing what is favored by the person (or persons) with the most power.

A lot of political behavior is simply part and parcel of working together with others. There are no "right" goals or objectives for groups to pursue; there may not even be a "best" way for groups to pursue their agreed-upon goals. There are only the goals and the means for reaching them that a group's members each prefer. As we saw in Chapter 4, these preferences are quite likely to conflict. Using your power to push a group (or organization) in the direction you prefer—a direction where the group's goals will match your personal goals—is neither right nor wrong; it is just politics. Politics only becomes wrong when it turns into corruption. Corruption is the use of power to pursue personal goals *at the expense* of the organization's goals. "CEO disease" comes dangerously close to the definition of corruption; another example of politics gone bad is provided in the "INTERNATIONAL FOCUS ON: Politics."

Political scientist Robert Dahl has defined power in the following way: "A has power over B to the extent that he can get B to do something B would not otherwise do."[1] There are two parts to this definition. First, power is something between or among people. No one simply has power; an individual (or group) has power *over* another particular individual or group. That means that *power is part of the relationships among people* and therefore exists only as a characteristic of a social system (such as a group or organization). Outside of the social system in which power exists, power relationships may dissolve.

In addition to locating power in the relationships among people, Dahl's definition also emphasizes that power refers to the capacity of one individual to change the attitudes or actions of another individual. Power refers to one individual *influencing* the thoughts of another or *controlling* that other individual's behaviors. Influence and control are outcomes; power is what makes those outcomes occur.

Social Exchange   How does power work? One simple explanation is the **theory of social exchange.** According to this theory:

> Social behavior is an exchange of goods, material goods but also non-material ones, such as symbols of approval or prestige. Persons that give much to others try to get much from them, and persons that get much from others are under pressure to give much to them. The process of influence tends to work out at an equilibrium to a balance of the exchanges.[2]

According to the theory of social exchange, power occurs because of resource dependencies. A **resource dependence** occurs when one individual needs or desperately wants something (the resource) that another individual possesses. The person who wants or needs the resource is dependent upon the person who has it. In the terms of social exchange, power or influence occurs when individuals who need or desire the resource take possession of it *in exchange for* changes in their personal thoughts (influence) or actions (control).

Politics is one obvious demonstration of power, but power also can be exercised in more subtle ways through implicit resource exchanges. Dale Carnegie courses teach sales personnel how to influence and control potential customers by offering them something in addition to the product, something that is valuable to the customer and that the sales force has in unlimited quantities—compliments. In effect, the sales force exchanges compliments for successful sales.[3]

Because power is a form of resource exchange does not mean that these exchanges are fair, or that what the parties exchange is equal. When power is exercised, both sides receive something in the transaction. However, as noted by Aristotle:

> . . . the benefits that one party receives and is entitled to claim from the other are not the same on either side . . . the better of the two parties, for instance, or the more useful or otherwise superior as the case may be, should receive more affection

---

[1] R. Dahl, "The Concept of Power," *Behavioral Science*, (July 1957); 202–203.

[2] G. C. Homans, "Social Behavior as Exchange," *American Journal of Sociology* 63 (1958): 597–606.

[3] Dale Carnegie, *How to Win Friends and Influence People* (New York: Simon Schuster, 1936).

Politics

Korruptsia In most countries, participation in a coup would leave a shadow hanging over an executive's resume. Not so in Russia. Valentin Pavlov, former prime minister and August putschist, was offered a job as consultant to the country's largest commodity exchange and its associated empire of private companies. His answer: yes—as soon as certain "legal and physical aspects" of his situation could be resolved. Pavlov was still in jail.

Pavlov isn't the only former Soviet official to have wormed his way into the new order. When the Soviet central ministries closed down in 1991 in the aftermath of the failed coup, scores of senior managers, with decades of experience and phone books full of contacts, found themselves on the market. Many in effect took their ministries with them, quickly transforming them into independent "corporations" and holding companies.

Not surprisingly, the pioneers of private businesses feel at a disadvantage next to these insiders, and they have been organizing their own lobbying groups to help them compete. With a combination of missionary zeal and the edginess of an embattled minority, these private business leaders use all means at their disposal to push projects past the bureaucracy. Techniques range from the innocent—hiring experts to draft proposed versions of laws and degrees—to the legally dubious—for a fee, many newspapers publish sympathetic interviews with key entrepreneurs or articles pleading their case. Lev Weinberg, president of the Association of Joint Ventures, says, "When I have some sort of weapons, I use them all."

Welcome to the world of *lobbirovaniye*, or as more cynical Muscovites know it, *korruptsia*. As democratic forms interweave with remnants of the Soviet state, a new brand of politics has been emerging in Russia. And newly elected officials are finding that the boundary between legitimate forms of democratic pressure and the pursuit of corrupt advantage is porous indeed. Under the old Communist order, bribes and connections were essential lubricants, providing access to scarce goods. That's still true, but today the stakes are higher, and the rules of play are much more fluid and difficult to divine. Some businessmen speak wistfully of the old days when each official knew his price, commensurate to his level on the administrative scale. Now, with inflation surging and all deals up for renegotiation, prices have gotten out of hand. Registering a business is said to cost 100,000 rubles. And there is no guarantee the bribed official will not have moved on to another post in a month's time.

Source: Adapted from D. Treisman, "Korruptsia," *The New Republic,* May 11, 1992, 14–17. Reprinted by permission of *The New Republic.* © 1992, The New Republic, Inc.

than he bestows; since when the affect rendered is proportional to desert, this produces equality . . .[4]

In effect, the social exchanges of power transactions are governed by supply and demand; the benefit each party receives in the exchange will reflect the relative power of the two parties. More powerful individuals can give less and expect to get back more.

Slack If resource dependence and social exchange explain why and when power works, then slack explains why and when it doesn't. In the book *Equality,*

---

[4]Aristotle, *The Nicomachean Ethic* (Boston: D. Reidel Publishing, 1975).

political philosopher R. H. Tawney notes that to destroy power, "nothing more is required than to be indifferent to its threats and to prefer other goods to those which it promises."[5] Slack (discussed in Chapter 6) refers to any over-abundance of a resource that decreases an individual's or group's dependence for it on any other individual or group. Slack provides an individual the ability to be indifferent to threats and promises. If power represents the capacity of one individual to influence or control a second individual, slack represents the capacity of that second individual to resist.

Slack comes in two forms: **stockpiles** and **alternative sources.** Stockpiles are quantities of a resource set aside for future use; alternative sources are other ways to fulfill a resource dependency, thereby reducing an individual's dependence on any one source. Nest eggs (money put into savings for a "rainy day") are stockpiles that represent a form of slack. If your boss makes an unreasonable request, you could refuse the request and be fired. Or you could go along with the request in order to preserve your job. If you have a nest egg, you have a little slack. You know that the rent will get paid and you will eat (at least for a while) even if you wake up unemployed tomorrow morning. The nest egg reduces your resource dependency on the boss and thereby allows you to resist the boss's attempts to influence or control you.

The other form of slack—alternative sources—also could allow you to refuse your boss's unreasonable request. In this situation, an alternative source would be an alternative source of employment. Another job would be another source of income; knowing another source of income is readily available reduces your dependency on your current boss for income.

A resource dependency in itself does not represent power if the resource dependencies are equal for both parties. The boss may have plenty of applicants to fill your position, while you have only one job. It is the inequality of the resource dependency in a social relationship—you need the boss much more than the boss needs you—that gives the boss power over you. Unfortunately, many times it is easier for us to see how we depend on others than to see how they depend on us. We may have slack and not know it. Once we find out how easy it is to find a new job (if it is easy), no boss will ever again be able to control or influence us with that resource. After the boss has unsuccessfully looked for your replacement for a while, the boss might even try to lure you back to your old job with a higher salary. Perception thus plays a key role in the exercise of power. You must perceive that you are dependent on another individual for that individual to have power over you.

Sources of Power

What kinds of resources do individuals have to exchange? What gives them power? Figure 8–1 presents six sources of power. Five of these, reward power, coercion power, expert power, legitimate power, and referent power, come from a classic article by French and Raven on the social bases of power.[6] The sixth source, task interdependence, was identified later by sociologist Michael Crozier in his studies of European factories. Of these six sources, reward and coercion are the two basic sources of power. Reward and coercion power arise in

[5] R. H. Tawney, *Equality* (New York: Capricorn Books, 1961).

[6] J. R. P. French and B. Raven, "The Bases of Social Power," in *Studies in Social Power,* ed. D. Cartwright (Ann Arbor, Mich.: Institute for Social Research, 1959): 150–167.

FIGURE 8-1	▶ Sources of Power

Individual power in organizations can come from a variety of sources. Structural sources of power refer to power that the organization gives an individual, such as the legitimate authority to give orders to others in the organization. Personal sources of power come from characteristics of individuals, such as charisma or expertise in a field.

Structural Sources

Reward power	→ The capacity to dispense rewards
Coercion power	→ The capacity to dispense punishments
Task interdependence	→ Power that accrues naturally to a particular role in an organization
Legitimate power	→ Authority; the right to give orders

Personal Sources

Expert power	→ Possession of valuable information or status
Referent power	→ Power stemming from the desire of others to imitate an individual

the control of rewards and punishments, respectively. The other four forms of power—expert, legitimate, referent, and task interdependence—refer only to different organizational forms of reward and punishment.

Reward Power **Reward power** occurs when one individual possesses resources that another individual desires and has the ability to *reward* the second person in exchange for the desired behavior.

Reward power is based on the "law of effect" discussed in Chapter 4. In the earlier discussions about motivation, the law of effect was illustrated through the phrase, "People engage in those behaviors that are most likely to be rewarded." If a particular behavior is followed by a reward, the individual will be more likely to engage in that behavior again. A supervisor can encourage subordinates to engage in appropriate work behaviors by making desired rewards contingent upon those behaviors. By making desired rewards contingent on subordinates' appropriate work behaviors, the supervisor exercises power over the subordinates.

Reward power is quite common in organizations. Supervisors can offer subordinates pay raises, promotions, bonuses, favorable work assignments, or even extra training. Reward power doesn't come from just material rewards, though. Supervisors can reward subordinates with praise or recognition. For instance, the owner of a small machine shop in Oakland, California, has a "super employee" ceremony periodically.[7] In these ceremonies, unusually innovative or productive employees are presented cash awards documenting their achievements. The amounts of cash are small; far more important is the praise from the boss and recognition by the group for a job well done.

Reward power is a two-way street. If a supervisor rewards a subordinate for a job well done, the subordinate in turn may work harder, which rewards the supervisor for rewarding the subordinate! This reward cycle makes the subordinate's appropriate work behavior more likely to be repeated and the supervisor more likely to reward subordinate behavior in the future as well.

---

[7] From the PBS video, "In Search of Excellence."

Undermining Intrinsic Motivation   There is danger in using reward power to elicit appropriate work behaviors. **Extrinsic rewards** are rewards (for example, money or praise) provided *in exchange for* appropriate behaviors. An intrinsic reward, on the other hand, occurs naturally as a result of the behavior.

Extrinsic rewards can undermine a worker's intrinsic interest in work. If a worker does a particularly good job and receives a bonus from the boss, the bonus is an extrinsic reward—something provided by the boss in exchange for the appropriate behavior. In contrast, learning from a task is intrinsically rewarding, as are feelings of satisfaction and accomplishment from a job well done. Some work tasks are interesting, challenging, and engrossing. Involvement in tasks of this sort may be rewarding to a worker independent of (or in addition to) any extrinsic rewards provided by the organization. Many health-care professionals, for instance, find that the feeling of helping others is an important *intrinsic* reward in their work.

The secret of using reward power is that supervisors must know their subordinates well enough to know which tasks are most likely to be intrinsically motivating. If the supervisor uses a little reward power to get the subordinate started on an intrinsically rewarding task—and perhaps a little supervision to make sure the subordinate's first experiences with the task are intrinsically rewarding—intrinsic motivation should take over as the driving force behind the subordinate's behavior. Supervisors also need to make sure that subordinates' *inappropriate* behaviors are not maintained by other intrinsic or extrinsic rewards. Inappropriate behaviors perhaps may be encouraged socially as part of the "game" against management. Providing workers with intrinsically interesting work can get them working on a different "game"—the game of being productive. The most important form of reward power, then, is arranging work environments so that appropriate behaviors are intrinsically rewarding for workers, and inappropriate behaviors are neither intrinsically or extrinsically rewarding.

Coercion Power   **Coercion** is the threat of punishment for *not* engaging in appropriate behaviors. Coercion can be based upon material forms of punishment, such as fines or the docking of pay. Coercion also can refer to less material forms of punishment, such as rejection. For instance, an individual may feel coerced into getting along with the group if he or she fears rejection or ridicule for voicing a lone dissenting opinion. In organizations, termination of employment or suspension is a threat used to coerce reluctant employees. Naturally, threats work best when there is no fear of retribution.

As noted in McClelland's comments about the negative face of power and our general discussion in Chapter 4 about the use of punishment in organizations, coercion is effective in only a limited way. An employee who works only to avoid termination is not likely to be an enthusiastic contributor in the workplace. In fact, a coerced employee may even react like a cornered animal by fighting back. Goofing off while the boss isn't looking, taking liberties with office supplies, even sabotaging work are all ways in which subordinates try to give back to the supervisor exactly what the supervisor gave them—trouble. Coercion may be an effective form of power in organizational settings, but only in a very short-sighted sense.

Expert Power   Experts are highly experienced or highly trained in a field. **Expert power** refers to our general willingness to defer to experts and be swayed by their opinions. The two main components of expert power are information and status.

Expert power comes into play when an individual possesses special information, knowledge, or an ability that another individual needs. As we noted in Chapter 1, uncertainty and complexity are defining characteristics of organizations. There is never enough information available for all important decisions to be cut-and-dried. A stockbroker, for instance, may have a dizzying array of financial-analysis information. The information that the stockbroker chooses to share with clients, and the manner in which that information is presented, will have a tremendous impact on the decisions the clients make.

In organizations, power from special information or a special ability is not always reflected on the organizational chart. Certainly the top executives in the organization possess certain knowledge that gives them the power to influence the beliefs and actions of those below them. However, executives often complain that they really don't know what's going on below them in the organization. That information is known by middle managers or first-line supervisors. These managers and supervisors then possess information that gives them power over the top executives in the organization—the ability to sway the top executives' beliefs and actions.

The other form of expert power comes from the status of experts as sources of special information or ability. The title "expert" refers to individuals who have impressive credentials, such as a Ph.D., a medical degree, a law degree, or an equivalent amount of experience or ability. These credentials *imply* the possession of knowledge or ability, which should make the opinions of these experts particularly trustworthy or informative. Expert status thus elicits deference and respect. The result is that expert opinions have a tremendous influence on beliefs and behaviors, even when they are *not* based on sound information or deduction. In fact, the *appearance* of expertise (and the status it conveys) can be more influential than actual knowledge. The opinions of a mature and distinguished, silver-haired professor may be given much more weight than those of a young assistant professor, even though the assistant professor may be more knowledgeable about the latest developments in the field.

Empowering subordinates   There is an important paradox to the idea that information represents power—expert power—in organizations. When a manager withholds information from subordinates that those subordinates *depend* on the manager to provide, then that dependency translates into power for the manager. But is this power over subordinates in the manager's best interests? Managers are rewarded when their subordinates perform well. Subordinates who have less information can do less and they will be less productive. As noted in the "Focus on: Expert Power," a manager who *shares* information transforms the power of that information into the power of subordinates. The manager *empowers* the subordinates to reward the manager with better performance. The point of having power is to accomplish things, to positively influence others. Sometimes giving that power away—empowering others—is the best way to use it productively.

Focus on

Expert Power

The Open-Book Managers There is an ill-conceived idea floating about some management quarters. It states that a company's employees don't need, don't want, and indeed shouldn't have access to the information that is any business's lifeblood. Recognize the mind-set? "If we told our employees how the company's doing, the first thing they'd want is a raise in pay," scoffs one unnamed executive. A middle manager at a manufacturing plant remembers sitting in a conference room with a consultant, reviewing hourly rates and job expectations for blue-collar employees. "Not one word of any of this gets *out there*," admonished the consultant, gesturing toward the shop floor. Everyone nodded, automatically.

All over the country, chief executives have at last begun to see the fundamental contradiction. If you want your employees to work smarter, to take initiative, to act like owners, how are they supposed to do any of that without the nuts-and-bolts information that an owner gets? How can you treat people like serfs and expect them to act like colleagues? So these CEOs are letting their employees into the business by providing them with the information top managers take for granted. And they are reaping the benefits.

At Reflexite Corp. in New Britain, Connecticut, and at Reuther Mold & Manufacturing in Cuyahoga Falls, Ohio, managers prepare annotated financial statements for employees, spelling out what every line means. Hal F. Rosenbluth, CEO of Rosenbluth Travel in Philadelphia, prefers the indirect approach: every employee has an open invitation to tag along after him for a day. "Nothing is kept from them," Rosenbluth says.

John Davis is a vice-president at Re:Member Data's Memphis office. Until 1989, Davis's office was owned by a large corporation that seemed to delight in keeping him in the dark about his own job. And on some occasions, the ignorance proved costly. When Re:Member Data bought the Memphis office in 1989, Davis's frustrating experience of working in the dark stuck with him. He decided to have the computer track each employee's time, daily billing, salary costs, and expenses—and make each employee responsible for his or her own profitability. Every employee would receive a printout. Going out on a job, each employee would know projected revenues and expenses and would be responsible for managing them. At first, employees were nervous. But then two other effects began to emerge. First, employees learned to do their jobs more efficiently, without involving management in every little decision. Then, enlightened about the bottom line, they began coming up with other ways to generate revenue.

Open-book management is hardly a new idea. In the past, it has foundered on mistrust or on the insecurity of middle managers whose claim to authority seems to rest on the fact that they know more about corporate affairs than their subordinates. Today, experimenters like John Davis are learning its power and are preparing to extend their information sharing deeper into their organizations.

Source: J. Case, "The Open-Book Managers," *Inc.,* September 1990, 104–113.

Legitimate Power   One of the most pervasive forms of power in organizations is **legitimate power**—the *right* to give orders. What does it mean to have the right to give orders? It means that a social system (such as an organization or a society) has given an individual the *authority* to exercise control over the behaviors of others for their own good and for the good of the social system. One's role in a social system is the source of legitimate power.

Organization charts detail the formal authority relationships in a typical work organization. The chart explains who is a boss and who is a subordinate. The bosses have the *right* to give orders—to control the behaviors of their subordinates.

Why does legitimate power work? Why would a subordinate obey the orders of the boss? Authority (or legitimate power) is often simply an implicit form of reward, coercion, or expert power. If your boss tells you to make a sales call, you could sit down and decide for yourself if the ordered action is a good idea. However, if you decide against going out on the sales call, you could risk the eventual loss of a valued reward that the boss controls—such as a bonus—or you could face immediate punishment—such as termination for insubordination (failure to follow orders). Or it may be that the boss is the boss because the boss is smarter or more experienced than you, and not following the boss's orders will result in the loss of an important sale. If you truly believe that the sales call is unwarranted but decide to go anyway, you may be reacting to the implicit control the boss exercises over rewards, punishments, and important information.

There are also relatively subtle reasons for being obedient under the watchful eye of the boss, and these have to do with the survival of social systems. People join social systems such as organizations because they offer advantages over going it alone. Failure to obey orders is a challenge not only to the particular order given, but also to the social system that allows the order to be given. If the system has advantages, then challenging the system risks losing the advantages of having a system at all.

While it may be overstating the case, the logical consequences of disobedience are anarchy, the eventual destruction of the system, and the loss of any advantages the system provides. If an organization is to avoid the trap of having all bosses and no subordinates, a little obedience clearly is a good thing.

Unquestioned obedience is just as clearly not a good thing. Decision makers can be wrong, just as rules and norms can be wrong. The dangers of unquestioned obedience to authority—and the strengths of legitimate power—were dramatically demonstrated in a series of studies by Stanley Milgram.

Milgram was particularly interested in why, during wartime conditions such as those in Germany during World War II, individuals often commit atrocities against others that they excuse as simply "following orders." Milgram devised an experimental procedure that allowed him to ask the question: Under what conditions are people willing to obey an instruction to intentionally hurt another person?

The participants in Milgram's experiment were volunteer adult males of various ages and occupations in New Haven, Connecticut. They arrived at Milgram's laboratory and learned that the experiment would examine the effects of punishment on learning. The study would involve two participants working together: a teacher and a learner. The participants drew lots to see who would be the learner and who would be the teacher. In fact, one of the participants was one of Milgram's assistants. The drawing was arranged so that Milgram's assistant always drew the role of learner.

After the drawing for roles, the experimental assistant took the learner into an adjacent room and connected the learner to an electric shock apparatus. The real participant was informed that his job would be to administer a word-pair memory task for the learner to learn. After each incorrect response, the teacher was to punish the learner by administering an electric shock. The teacher was given a sample 45-volt shock. At this point the teacher was seated at a simulated shock generator, with an array of switches and labels corresponding to shocks ranging from 15 volts ("slight shock") to 450 volts ("danger: severe shock"). The teacher was told to give the learner one shock for each incorrect response, and to increase the voltage of the shocks for each succeeding incorrect answer. (In fact, no electric shocks were administered at all.)

The learner's responses had been carefully orchestrated and they were the same for each new teacher. The learner gave many incorrect responses, so the teacher had to administer many shocks. And with the shocks came the apparent painful suffering of the learner:

> Starting with 75 volts, the learner begins to grunt and moan. At 150 volts he demands to be let out of the experiment. At 180 volts he cries out that he can no longer stand the pain. At 300 volts he refuses to provide any more answers to the memory test, insisting that he is no longer a participant in the experiment and must be freed.[8]

The experiment continued until the teacher refused to give the learner another shock.

The Milgram study stands as a testament to the strength (and the danger!) of legitimate power. In the study, the participants were volunteers and could have quit at any time. In fact, many subjects did register complaints during the experimental procedure. Many were obviously tense and anxious during the experiment and demonstrated concern about and sympathy for the learner. These complaints and concerns were met by a simple comment from the experimenter that "the experiment requires that you continue." And that command was enough for 62 percent of the subjects (620 of the 1000 subjects) to remain obedient and administer shocks all the way to the end of the range on the generator to a protesting and eventually ominously silent learner.

Legitimate power is a strong force. We are socialized to believe that if someone in command gives an order, we may have the right to complain but we have a duty to comply.

If legitimate power can have such profound effects in Milgram's laboratory, imagine the power of authority in real, permanent work organizations where the members have a vested interest in both the survival of the organization and their continued membership in it. Even if a lot of obedience is a good thing in organizations, a little *dis*obedience is not only good but necessary. If someone is giving the wrong orders, survival of the organization could just as easily depend on workers disobeying those orders as on their obeying them.

Task Interdependence   Sociologist Michel Crozier has identified a source of power not included in French and Raven's classic list. This source of power

---

[8] D. Katz and R. L. Kahn, *The Social Psychology of Organizations* (New York: Wiley, 1966).

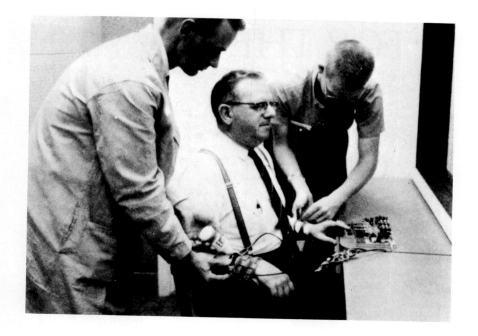

The Milgram studies stand as a testament to the power of formal authority. The subjects in Milgram's study could have walked out at any time. Yet they continued to shock the innocent fellow subject (shown here being connected to the shock apparatus) simply because they were told to do so.

accrues to a particular job (or group of jobs) in an organization because of **task interdependence.** Task interdependence occurs when two or more employees must depend on each other to complete assigned tasks.

The power dynamics between executives and their assistants illustrate power from task interdependence. The executive has legitimate power over the assistant. The organization gives the executive the right (within the limits of the assistant's job description) to give orders to the assistant. The executive's dependence on the assistant in the flow of work, however, gives the assistant some power over the executive. Once the executive has given an order, the executive actually becomes dependent upon the assistant to complete the task correctly and on time. Certainly the executive has the power to replace the assistant if the task is done poorly or late. Unfortunately for the executive, firing the assistant for failing is not equivalent to getting the task done well and on time! Therefore, the executive and assistant have an interdependent work relationship. The assistant depends on the executive for task assignments, resources, and a job, while the executive depends on the assistant for efficient and effective fulfillment of assignments. The organization gives the executive legitimate power over the assistant; the arrangements for getting work done give the assistant task interdependence power over the executive. Legitimate power comes with the job description; task interdependence power comes with the territory.

Crozier studied manufacturing organizations in France and discovered an example of power from task interdependence in a French tobacco factory. The maintenance engineers in the factory occupied only modest positions of authority in the formal organizational hierarchy. Nevertheless, they seemed to have tremendous power in the plant. For instance, they were able to dictate their own work schedules and dress codes, and they seemed always to have management's sympathetic ear. Crozier found that a key source of uncertainty in the plant concerned breakdowns of the manufacturing machinery. Over the years

FOR THE

Every great athlete feels the pressure to perform.

LOVE

But it takes something special inside to be like Mike.

OF THE

Gatorade. For the fluids, minerals, and energy you need.

GAME

IT'S ALL YOU'RE THIRSTING FOR

Chicago Bulls fans adore Michael Jordan and identify with his accomplishments. This makes the fans highly susceptible to the persuasion of referent power, as in product endorsements. In the business world, the results of a junior executive's emulation of and identification with the boss may be more subtle but just as powerful.

the machinery had been modified and customized to fit the facility's needs, so that now it only vaguely resembled the original manufacturer's specifications. Due to these modifications, the maintenance personnel were the only members of the organization capable of coping with breakdowns, so everyone else in the plant was highly dependent upon their goodwill. Thus, their position in the work arrangements gave them great power.[9]

Referent Power Perhaps the most mysterious form of power is **referent power.** Jill has referent power over Jack when Jack willingly imitates or obeys Jill because Jack identifies with or admires her. Identifying with an individual means seeing in that individual traits that you think you have or that you would like to have. For example, many young people dress like the rock star or sports heroes they aspire to be like. The young people communicate their aspirations by imitating their heroes in fashion and behavior.

One form of referent power derives from **charisma.** Charisma is a personal style that captures the attentions, hearts, and imaginations of people. Charisma arises when an individual seems to possess the characteristics that define the model person for many admirers. This means that an individual's charisma will be quite specific to a particular reference group. An individual will have charisma not because of personal characteristics, but because of a *fit* between those characteristics and those desired or admired by others.[10] For instance, T. E.

[9]M. Crozier, *The Bureaucratic Phenomenon* (Chicago: University of Chicago Press, 1964).

[10]J. MacGinnis, *Heroes* (New York: Viking Press, 1976).

Lawrence (better known as the legendary "Lawrence of Arabia") possessed certain characteristics that made him an admired leader of the Arabs during World War I. By contrast, his personal style was unappealing in his home country of England, where his political aspirations failed upon his return.

The personal style of Winston Churchill, on the other hand, became charismatic only when England faced certain defeat during World War II. When the crisis was resolved and the needs of the population changed, Churchill and his government quickly lost favor.[11] People's willingness to identify with another individual—and therefore to be influenced by that person—is highly situationally dependent. If the situation changes, people's needs change, and so do their definitions of a model person. As the definitions of the model person change, so do the people who are perceived as charismatic.

In comparison to other sources of power, referent power is most like expert power. Both are based almost exclusively on *personal* characteristics of the individual. A person is an expert because of background credentials or experience; a person has charisma because that person's personality traits match what the people think they need. In both cases, power derives from the individual. Reward, coercion, task interdependence, and legitimate power, on the other hand, are primarily *structural* sources of potential influence. The ability to dispense rewards and punishments, or the authority to act as if one could, arise from work relationships rather than personal traits.

Using Power: Strategies and Tactics

With many sources of power available, power is actually well distributed in organizations rather than just concentrated at the top. Any member of an organization has access to some sources of power. What may be less clear is how participants in organizations can make effective use of the power they have. This section of the chapter reviews several ways participants in organizations can individually mobilize the powers they do have, then it focuses on one of the very important power tactics in groups and organizations: the coalition. These power tactics are summarized in Figure 8–2.

If you are a newly hired executive assistant in a large industrial corporation, how can you get things rolling your way? There are two answers: (1) identify which valuable resources (information, rewards, punishments) already are at your disposal, or (2) go out and capture some resources that are available for you to control. Once an individual has identified or captured a valued resource, the most obvious power tactic available is exchange. *Exchange* is simply offering to trade what you control (for instance, your vote at a meeting or your expertise using a complex new piece of software) for something you want (like a better office or a cushy job assignment).

The most important and abundant resource often available to lower-level members of an organization is effort. The higher individuals are in an organization, the busier they are and the less time they have to deal with problems below them in the hierarchy. This is an advantage for any lower-level organization member. You can trade your time and effort for things you want. If an issue seems important to you and you continue to bring it up, eventually it will

[11]J. E. Mack, *A Prince of Our Disorder: The Life of T. E. Lawrence* (Boston: Little, Brown, 1976). Cited in D. R. Hampton, C. E. Summer, and R. A. Webber, *Organizational Behavior and the Practice of Management* (Glenview, Ill.: Scott, Foresman, 1987).

FIGURE 8-2	▶ Power Tactics

Exchange	The person makes an explicit or implicit promise that you will receive rewards or tangible benefits if you comply with a request or support a proposal.
Pressure	The person uses demands, threats, or intimidation to convince you to comply.
Ingratiation	The person seeks to get you in a good mood or to think favorably of him or her before asking you to do something.
Rational Persuasion	The person uses logical arguments and factual evidence to persuade you that a proposal or request is viable and likely to result in the attainment of your objectives.
Upward Appeals	The person seeks to persuade you that the request is approved by higher authorities or appeals to higher authorities to gain your compliance.
Inspirational Appeals	The person makes an emotional request that arouses enthusiasm by appealing to your values and ideals or by increasing your confidence that you can do it.
Consultation	The person seeks your participation in making a decision or planning how to implement a proposed policy to provide you ownership and gain your support.
Coalitions	The person seeks the aid of others to persuade you to do something or uses the support of others as an argument for you to comply.

Source: G. Yukl and D. M. Falbe, "Influence Tactics and Objectives in Upward, Downward, and Lateral Influence Attempts," *Journal of Applied Psychology* 75 (1990): 132–140. Copyright 1990 by the American Psychological Association. Reprinted by permission.

become less expensive for those above you to let you have your way than to take the time necessary to dissuade you or even meet with you. Effort thus also provides power when it becomes a form of *pressure*. Persistent effort carries the implicit threat of continuing to be a nuisance until things are changed. On the positive side, if your effort and persistence are valuable to an organization (for example, your persistent hard work) you also can exert pressure by threatening to withdraw your effort.

Lower-level participants in an organization also have available the tactic of **ingratiation**.[12] Ingratiation occurs when an individual does nice things for someone in the hope of creating a sense of obligation in that individual to return the favor. Subordinates can ingratiate themselves with the boss by supporting the boss's ideas in group meetings, going out of their way to do little things for the boss, or even simply playing up to the boss with compliments and gifts.

Ingratiation is a powerful influence tactic because social exchange transactions are governed by the *norm of reciprocity*. The norm of reciprocity states that if someone does something nice for you, you are *obligated* by social convention to return the favor, even if you didn't want it in the first place. Cicero once noted that, "There is no duty more indispensable than returning a kindness ... all men distrust one forgetful of a benefit."[13] Reciprocation is quite

[12] E. E. Jones, *Ingratiation* (New York: Appleton-Century-Crofts, 1964).

[13] A. Gouldner, "The Norm of Reciprocity," *American Sociological Review* 25 (1960): 161–178.

different from compensation—direct payment for services rendered. In fact, any attempt to repay a kindness quickly and directly in order to avoid obligation "is unseemly and conveys distrust."[14] The norm of reciprocity not only entails repayment of a previous kindness, it often suggests an *ongoing exchange relationship* in which favors are traded. If I scratch your back, I expect that at some point you will scratch mine, *and* that exchanges of this sort are part of our ongoing relationship.

Ingratiation represents something of a perversion of the reciprocity norm. The norm of reciprocity allows low-power individuals to give others in the organization things they may not want or need and to expect something in return. Ingratiation creates an obligation of repayment.

Rational persuasion is another power tactic available to influence others. *Rational persuasion* means convincing someone that a particular behavior is "logically" the best course of action because it is the most likely to accomplish that individual's personal objectives. In rational persuasion, you don't even need to personally control the resource another individual wants to influence that individual. You need only convince others that the course of action you prefer is in their best interests. Thus, informing a new coworker that your organization values and rewards cooperation and "team players" can be an effective way to elicit assistance.

Rational persuasion becomes an *upward appeal* when you invoke the reward (and punishment) power of others above you in a hierarchy to rationally persuade a coworker (for example, "Your boss would really appreciate your helping me"). Rational persuasion becomes an *inspirational appeal* when you invoke the rewards and punishments of an individual's self-image and values (for example, "A good friend would help me with this").

The most subtle power tactic in groups and organizations is consultation. **Consultation** occurs when someone gains your support for a course of action by letting you participate in planning it. Participation in planning creates ownership of and commitment to a course of action. When handled skillfully, consultation is really co-opting; it provides an individual the *illusion* of participating in planning a course of action without providing that individual any real opportunities to shape or alter the plan.

In the end, all the sources of power for lower-level organization participants so far discussed share an assumption that the subordinates are not easily replaced. After all, a boss who has lots of fawning subordinates will not be willing to exchange much for flattery, and a boss with an abundance of secretarial help is unlikely to be persuaded to do much by one recalcitrant clerical employee—except maybe to fire that employee! It should not be surprising, then, that the most important source of power for lower-level organization participants is not one source of power at all, but the union of many through the formation of coalitions.

Coalitions   Nowhere is the political nature of organizations more obviously on display than it is in the formation of coalitions. A **coalition** is a collection of individuals who have banded together to combine their individual sources of power. No individual has the power to stand alone against the rest of the organization. The secret to power in organizations is alliances with others. When

---

[14] P. Blau, *Exchange and Power in Social Life* (New York: Wiley, 1964).

you join a coalition, your individual power is increased by the power of the others in the group. If you have one vote in an election, you cannot elect anyone on your own. But if you can gather together a large group of voters (each with one vote), that group of voters can decide who gets elected. Similarly, one disgruntled employee exercising the power to disrupt work by walking off the job may have little or no effect; several thousand employees walking out simultaneously can move mountains.

Coalitions represent a form of power *sharing*, and there are costs to joining a coalition. If you are a middle manager in a large corporation, undoubtedly you have some sources of power at your disposal, but who is going to listen to your one lone voice? You don't have enough power to affect a major change in corporate policy by yourself. Perhaps you could find some other managers who want the same change. Then it would be more than just your one voice–then your voice would have the strength of numbers behind it.

One of the problems with this strategy, of course, is that it may be difficult to find other managers who want *exactly* what you want. As noted in the "FOCUS ON: Coalitions," someone with expertise in finding useful coalition partners could help you here. But if only a few others were interested in your agenda, what other options would you have for increasing your power base?

You could form a **compromise coalition.** In Chapter 6 we defined a compromise decision as one in which two or more parties each give a little to reach an agreement. The parties don't get exactly what they wanted, but they get something better than they would have gotten had they not compromised. In a compromise coalition, all of the members of the coalition are interested in the same issues, but they all don't get exactly what they want. The members of the coalition *compromise* on what each wants to make sure that the coalition gets anything at all.

If the issue is maternity leave, perhaps you think that six weeks of maternity leave at half pay would be appropriate. Someone else thinks that three weeks at full pay would be best. Both of you agree that *anything* is better than the company's current policy of two weeks at half pay. So the two of you compromise on four weeks at three-quarters pay. It is not really what either of you wanted, but you both prefer it to the company's alternative. And by finding a way to agree, you now can *both* put your sources of power behind the one compromise suggestion.

Coalitions don't always form because of shared interests, however. **Logrolling** is a form of coalition in which participants lend each other power so that each can pursue interests *not* shared by other coalition members. If you were the only manager in the company interested in changing the maternity-leave policy, to get others to join your coalition you would have to give them something. And what do you have to give? Your limited sources of power, of course.

Imagine you found an employee (we'll call him Sam) who couldn't care less about maternity leave but cared dearly about getting the company to sponsor a softball league. If you yourself had no strong opinions about softball leagues, the two of you could logroll a coalition. You would support Sam's initiatives on company softball leagues in exchange for Sam's support of your proposed changes to the company's maternity-leave policy. Both proposals would have the strength of two people behind them even though only one employee was interested in each proposal. Logrolls are coalitions that produce strange organizational bedfellows.

Coalitions

Watering the Grass Roots In 1990, American automakers pondered a difficult riddle: How could they quash legislation that improved fuel efficiency, reduced air pollution, and reduced dependence on foreign oil without looking like greedy corporate ghouls? If only The People would rise up and rally to their side—then Congress would listen to them. But how were they to come by this spontaneous popular uprising?

They paid Jack Bonner to find one. Bonner is a corporate "grass-roots lobbyist"—one of a new breed of consultants who influence legislation by stirring up the electorate back home instead of glad-handing members of Congress. Fuel efficiency, Bonner reasoned, would lead to smaller cars. Whom does that hurt? People in wheelchairs! *Contact the handicapped groups.* Smaller cars are also less safe in crashes and could endanger young passengers. *See if the Boy Scouts are interested.* Bonner's sixty operatives telephoned influential groups and within two months had generated thousands of letters and phone calls to key senators. The automakers believe the grass-roots efforts helped kill the amendment. "Call off the dogs," one member of Congress complained.

Washington still has its backroom power lobbyists, but companies are increasingly borrowing from the organizing tactics of environmental and consumer activists. "Some guy in a pinstripe suit telling a senator this bill is going to hurt Pennsylvania doesn't have the impact of someone in Pennsylvania saying it," says Bonner. Watering the grass roots involves more people in politics—but also makes it hard to tell whether democratic outbursts are actually dances choreographed by consultants. The key to any carefully planned effort is to make it look like a natural explosion of raw democracy. Specialized Data Systems peddles a computer program that spews out form letters, each one slightly different from the next. This gives "a strong impression that a grass-roots sentiment is being expressed, rather than an orchestrated letter-writing campaign," says Richard Epstein, founder of the company.

Is this good for democracy? Consumer and environmental groups that have often been outspent by business have compensated with grass-roots organizing, often using volunteers. Corporations can now spend millions to neutralize that tactic. Businesses are also learning what public-interest groups have long known—when you organize you also propagandize, and that affects more than just today's vote.

The cost of joining a compromise coalition is the compromise of your initiative; the cost of joining a logroll coalition is your obligation to support issues in the future in which you have no interest. Both forms of coalitions have costs, although the costs differ.

Consequences of the Use of Power

Two major problems surface when we consider the consequences of using power in organizations. The first has to do with how the use of power affects perceptions of power holders. The second is the addictiveness of power.

Perceptions of Power Users Social scientist D. J. Moberg has noted that it is critical that the objects of power plays not attribute the behaviors of powerholders to self-serving motives.[15] Ingratiation, for instance, is particularly ineffective in evoking feelings of obligation when it is an obvious attempt to do so. Similarly, the relationship between the powerful and the powerless often depends more on the way power is used than on its outcomes.

Toni Falbo explored this problem by asking 141 students each to write an essay entitled, "How I Get My Way."[16] The essays were scored for the use of 16 general power tactics. Each student was rated by other students on six dimensions: consideration, friendliness, quality of self-expression, honesty, desirability as a participant (in another discussion group), and liking. Falbo determined statistically how the use of each power tactic influenced others' perceptions of the user.

Falbo found that her power tactics could be described by two major dimensions: direct/indirect and rational/nonrational tactics. The direct/indirect dimension is concerned with whether the influence attempt is oriented toward changing the individual (direct) or getting the individual to *choose* to change (indirect); the rational-nonrational dimension is concerned with whether the influence attempt entails providing good reasons for the change (rational) or not (nonrational). In general, Falbo found that power users who used rational and indirect tactics such as bargaining and persuasion were perceived much more favorably.

A major limitation of Falbo's work is that it measured only *perceptions* of power users. It is entirely possible that direct and nonrational power tactics may be tremendously effective in the short run. However, if such tactics cause negative perceptions of the powerholder, in the long run they can spell only disaster. Thus, McClelland's negative side of power eventually may have negative consequences for the power user as well.

Addictiveness of Power   The second major problem with the use of power concerns its addictiveness. This problem is described quite well in the observations of two anthropologists in the primitive Indian village of Karimpur:

> If you were to take one of the most harmless men in the village and put him in the watchman's place, he would be a rascal within six months. . . . The sense of power and sudden popularity which a man experiences on finding himself an agent of power is in itself a danger.[17]

This transformation occurs in a series of steps. First, the availability of power leads to its use. Second, the use of power then fuels a perception of control over others, often eclipsing any realization of the *shared* resource dependence of all social exchanges. Third, this perception of control in turn leads power users to view themselves as more worthy and others as less worthy of taking control. Finally, this leads power users to believe that their use of power is justified and appropriate, and that others are incapable of self-control or governance.[18]

---

[15] D. J. Moberg, "Organizational Politics: Perspectives from Attribution Theory" Paper presented at the annual meetings of the American Institute of Decision Sciences, Chicago, 1977.

[16] T. Falbo, "Multidimensional Scaling of Power Strategies," *Journal of Personality and Social Psychology* 35 (1977): 537–547.

[17] W. Wiser and C. Wiser, *Behind Mind Walls* (Berkeley: University of California Press, 1967).

[18] D. Kipnis, *The Powerholders* (Chicago: University of Chicago Press, 1976).

In effect, a power user comes to see the use of power as appropriate and even necessary because others are weak and unworthy, even when the source of the power is in the resource-dependence relationship. Often this distorted belief that others are unworthy encourages the power user to use more direct and nonrational power tactics, such as coercion. These tactics invoke angry reactions from others, and the demise of the power user often follows. Thus, when the addictiveness of power causes the powerholder to lose sight of the symmetry of resource dependencies, the emergence of the dark side of the power user—for instance, the CEO disease with which this chapter began— leads to the loss of power as well. As noted in the "INTERNATIONAL FOCUS ON: The Addictiveness of Power," some Japanese companies have figured out ways to prevent this destructive addiction.

How Japan Vaccinates its CEOs
Japan has its share of personal fiefdoms—companies run by unquestioned rulers such as Akio Morita (Sony), Kazuo Inamori (Kyocera Corp.), and Seiuemon Inaba (Fanuc Ltd.). But on the whole, the Japanese CEO lives in a business environment where groupthink is valued highly. The dean of the business school at Keio University, Noritake Kobayashi, said, "In America, the boss is the boss, and he gives orders. Here, that can be very dangerous."

Example: Chiyoji Misawa, who runs the eponymously named Misawa Homes Co., had ambitious plans to move his company into the U. S. market. He put together an attractive deal to build houses on prime property near San Francisco. Beyond that, his plans included moving into Hawaii. An American CEO would have merely led the way, with subordinates to follow. But Misawa's subordinates nixed the idea. "That's that," he said. "I can decide I want to do something, but if I don't have employee support, it won't work."

Forging consensus is an important role of the CEO in Japan. By the time the usually male executive ascends to the highest post, he has advanced gradually through set salary levels. He has held a predetermined series of jobs designed to increase and showcase his capabilities. By about the age of 45, he might be ready for the top job. Seldom does a whiz kid short-circuit that process.

As a result, Japanese CEOs have less to prove at the outset. Their perks, while generous, don't match those of American CEOs. Their pay is seldom more than 7 to 10 times higher than the salary of a fresh recruit. And Japanese CEOs don't spend a lot of time building up their fame on the outside. Instead they maintain close touch with every rung on the ladder of their companies. They are allowed a thinner profit margin if it is due to expenses incurred in the process of increasing market share. It is assumed that the harmony of the group is more important than personal desires, and that long-term strategy is more important than short-term.

That doesn't mean arrogance is absent from the corner office. But rather than the whole company suffering from it, it's more likely to be the secretary who bears the brunt.

CEOs in such an environment are probably better able to stay in touch with reality, but there is also more danger of mediocrity in a system where so much agreement must be achieved before actions can be taken.

Source: K. L. Miller, "How Japan Vaccinates Its CEOs," *Business Week*, April 1, 1991, 60.

GROUPS AS SOCIAL CONTEXT ◆◆◆◆◆◆

Power and politics concern *intentional* influence in groups and organizations and how individuals deliberately marshall their sources of power to pursue goals and objectives. A second form of influence exists in groups and organizations— what we will call the effects of social context. **Social context** refers to the fact that an individual's behavior in groups and organizations takes place in the context of other individuals. The influence of social context typically is unintended but nevertheless dramatic. Social context exerts two types of influence: influence on judgment and influence on behavior.

Social Context and Judgment

Perhaps the most subtle but powerful form of influence from groups comes under the heading of **social comparison theory.**[19] According to social comparison theory, *the opinions and actions of other people* are a major influence on our perceptions and beliefs about the world around us. When we construct a perception or judgment or belief about the world, we check its accuracy by comparing it to the perceptions and judgments constructed by others around us. If our perceptions and judgments match those of others around us, everything is fine. But what happens when we construct beliefs, perceptions, and judgments that *differ* from those of others? The following fictional account demonstrates the acquisition of a work group norm:

> You are a newly hired worker on the assembly line at Mega Manufacturing. Your supervisor spends the morning introducing you around and explaining your new job to you—how to work the machinery at your work station, where to get raw materials when you run out, when you can take breaks, and so on. She winds up the morning by noting that she would like you to think about shooting for 50 complete units per day as a performance goal. Then she sends you off to lunch with your assembly-line coworkers.
>
> At lunch some of the old hands on the assembly line seem friendly enough and ask if you have any questions about the job. You mention that you are wondering about keeping up with the daily quota of 50 units suggested by your supervisor. At this point the old hands laugh. They reassure you that it's the job of the supervisor to talk about completing 50 units per day, but that no one really *expects* you to do that much. They claim that the supervisor usually seems pleased with 40. One of the old hands even notes that if you did make 50, it would make some of the older workers (for whom even 35 units is a challenge) look bad.
>
> Late in the afternoon, your supervisor stops by to see how you are doing and asks whether, in your judgment, you think you will be able to keep up a 50-units-per-day pace.

As suggested in this story, work group norms often dictate more than just which behaviors are appropriate. Work group norms also may dictate which *thoughts* are appropriate—which perceptions, beliefs, or judgments about possible performance levels are allowed. In the story, what would you say to the supervisor at this point about your ability to keep up a 50-unit-per-day pace? And how would your coworkers' comments at lunch influence your answer?

One possibility is that you might treat the comments of your coworkers as *evidence.* If you have worked the assembly line a couple of hours before the

---

[19]L. Festinger "A Theory of Social Comparison," *Human Relations* 7 (1954): 117–140.

supervisor comes around, you already could have a good idea of what is possible and what is not. Let's say you think 50 units per day is possible. In the back of your mind, of course, are the old hands' comments that 40 is really the normal target for the work group. At this point you might think to yourself, "These coworkers of mine are reasonable people, and while their perceptions may not be entirely accurate, mine may not be entirely accurate either." In the end, you would adjust your own estimate to reflect the old hands' input and report to your supervisor that you will shoot for 46.

What if there is so much uncertainty that individuals have no faith in their own judgment? What if the worker in our example, after several hours on the assembly line, still has no idea of what a reasonable production target would be? What roles do the opinions of others play in that case?

When the perception or judgment process is extremely uncertain, opinions of others can strongly *anchor* judgment, even subconsciously. The **social anchoring** of judgment was convincingly demonstrated by a series of studies concerned with **bystander apathy**—why observers fail to lend assistance in emergency situations. The scenario for a typical bystander apathy study is described below:

> You have been asked to participate in a research study at your university. You report as requested. The experimenter seats you in a small room at a desk, gives you a short background questionnaire to complete, and leaves the room while you fill it out. After working on the questionnaire for about five minutes, you notice that some wisps of smoke seem to be coming out of a vent in the room. What do you do?[20]

It seems obvious if you are alone in the room that you should get up to investigate the smoke. Perhaps you would leave the room to sound the alarm or seek assistance. But what happens if there are *other subjects* in the room with you, also filling out the questionnaire?

The key to understanding human reactions to this situation is that the meaning of the smoke is *highly uncertain*. It could be an emergency, but then maybe it's just dust blowing out of an air-conditioning vent or something equally harmless. The fact is that you really *don't know*, just as when you join a new organization, you really *don't know* what behaviors are regulated by the organization's rules and roles. Under conditions of high uncertainty, we allow others to anchor our judgments, often without even knowing we are doing so! In the study described above, most subjects (75 percent) *when alone in the room* judge the smoke to be a potential emergency and investigate. However, if there are other subjects in the room *who have been told to ignore the smoke*, the real subject gets up to investigate the smoke only 10 percent of the time. The unresponsiveness of the other subjects anchors the uncertain judgment of the real subject.

The difference between evidence and anchoring effects of social comparison is a subtle but important one. When you use someone else as evidence for a judgment, you are aware of your *own* opinion and are attempting to reconcile the differences between your judgments, beliefs, or perceptions and those of others you trust. There is a conscious awareness of the differences in judgment,

---

[20]B. Latane and J. Darley, *The Unresponsive Bystander: Why Doesn't He Help?* (New York: Appleton-Century-Crofts, 1970).

When the world seems too complex or uncertain, we fall back on the actions and opinions of coworkers—often without realizing it—as the basis for forming our own beliefs. Occasionally we will go along with the opinions of others not because we believe those opinions but simply to avoid conflict.

and you feel the need to understand the origins of those differences. In contrast, anchoring effects often catch us unawares. The real subjects in the bystander-apathy study probably didn't realize the extent to which their judgments were being influenced. They experienced a situation that they perceived as *not an emergency.*

Returning to the example of our assembly-line worker, uncertainty would increase the extent to which the production target he provides his supervisor reflects anchoring by the opinions of the old hands. Using their opinions as evidence, he would judge 50 units to be possible but hedge his estimate to 46 in deference to the possibility that they knew something he didn't. If he is really uncertain about what is possible, the opinions of the old hands would anchor his judgment: he would report that 40 units was about right, and honestly believe that it was.

As a final thought on group influences on judgment, remember that evidential and anchoring influences both have important roles in ensuring *appropriate* group functioning. A group's roles and rules summarize the group's past learning. The roles and rules allow newcomers to produce high-quality behaviors and judgments for the group immediately without "reinventing the wheel" through a lot of unnecessary trial-and-error learning. Evidence and anchoring influences both are important mechanisms by which the group teaches the newcomer what the group has learned. If the group has learned well, everyone benefits when newcomers fall in line with the old hands, and a little social influence will be a good thing. If the group has learned poorly, a little "foolishness" (ignoring the old hands) can be a good thing, too.

Social Context and Behavior

Groups also can *directly* influence the behaviors of their members. We will consider several examples of direct group influence: conformity, social facilitation, and social loafing.

Conformity   **Conformity** represents a form of social comparison beyond social anchoring. Conformity occurs when an individual engages in a behavior or admits to a belief encouraged by the group *even though the individual believes that behavior or belief is incorrect or inappropriate.* Conformity occurs *not* because the judgments of others are good evidence and *not* because the individual's own judgment is uncertain, but simply because the individual *wants to go along with the group*. Conformity occurs when an individual is concerned that the course of action selected by the group is inappropriate and fails to say so.

The psychological experiment described below, known as the Asch study, provides a classic example of the effects of conformity:[21]

> You are invited to participate in a research study. You report at the appointed hour and are ushered into a room with six other participants. The seven of you are seated in a row (you occupy the last chair in the row), and you are told that this will be a study of your ability to make visual judgments of size. For each judgment, a machine will project four lines on the wall. One line will be the target line, and you must judge which of the test lines (A, B, or C) best matches the target (see Figure 8–3).
>
> The experiment seems quite boring. For the first six trials, it seems obvious which test line matches the target and there is no disagreement at all among the participants. The seventh target line is just like the one shown in Figure 8–3 and just as easy to match as the others have been, so you are quite surprised when the first subject responds "C"—an *obvious* wrong answer. Before you can even ponder why this has occurred, however, the other five participants each give their responses—*also* "C" and *also* obviously wrong! At this point it is your turn to respond. The other six all have agreed on "C," but you *know* the correct answer is "B." How do you respond?

The key to understanding the importance of the Asch study is to realize that there is *little or no uncertainty* about the right answer in the minds of subjects. Subjects *know* that "B" is the correct answer. When presented the target and test lines in the absence of other respondents, subjects virtually never make mistakes. What that seventh subject in the experiment doesn't know, of course, is that the first six respondents have been told to answer "C" on the seventh trial of the study, even though the correct answer obviously is "B." How does that seventh subject respond in the face of a unanimous but obviously incorrect majority? About *one-third of the time* the seventh subject *goes along with the group* and says that "C" is the correct answer.

Despite its obvious behavioral similarities to evidential and anchoring effects on judgment and behavior, conformity is a different kind of group influence. In using others' opinions as *evidence*, an individual has a good idea of what is correct but is willing to consider and incorporate the opinions of more experienced others. In using others' opinions as *anchors*, an individual really doesn't know what's correct and is open to influence (perhaps without knowing it) from the opinions of more experienced others. In the case of conformity, the individual knows what is correct but doesn't voice that opinion and acts as if in agreement with the group. The individual *conforms* to the group.

What causes conformity? Why do people "go along with the group" when they *know* the group is wrong? In our hypothetical example of the assembly-line worker, why would the new worker report to his or her supervisor that 40 units seems like a reasonable target while knowing full well that 50 units would be more appropriate? There are several possible explanations.

---

[21] S. E. Asch, "Studies of Independence and Conformity: A Minority of One against a Unanimous Majority," *Psychological Monographs* 70 (1956): Whole #16.

| FIGURE 8–3 | ► The Asch Study: Which Test Line Matches the Target? |

The Asch experiment demonstrated the power of group influence. In this figure, it seems obvious that test line B is the best match for the target line. However, if several of your friends all claimed that test line C was the closest match to the target line, what would go through your mind? Would you begin to doubt your judgment? Would you perhaps "go along" with them to avoid looking foolish if they just happened to be right?

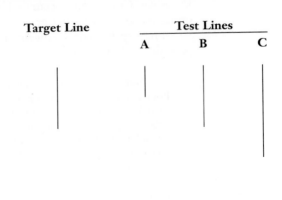

First, the individual may wish to *avoid conflict* with the group. In the case of the new assembly-line worker, it has been made clear to him or her that 40 units is the agreed-upon norm for a production target. Violating this norm by reporting a target of 50 units would risk the wrath of the group members, perhaps by exposing their collusive attempts to keep down management's performance expectations and protect the less able workers. Second, by disagreeing with the majority, the individual risks being *labeled a deviant.* Depending on the individual's reasons for joining the group, being accepted may be more valuable than being right. Disagreement may not be the fastest path to making new friends, especially if it is seen as an attempt to show up the rest of the group. Most of all, disagreement quite simply *risks rejection* by the group—no doubt in part for being a deviant troublemaker.

Normally we think of mistakes in judgment as incurring formal sanctions from the organization. A poor hiring decision, a bad investment, or a sloppy report will be punished formally by the organization. Conformity raises the specter of an *informal,* even *intangible,* set of sanctions within work groups that quietly and implicitly enforce work-group norms. It is worth noting that in the Asch subject group, acceptance or rejection by the group should not have been a big concern for subjects. Nevertheless, the influence of the group over the individual was apparent.

This influence becomes tragic when the norms implicitly enforced by the work group run contrary to the best interests of the organization as a whole and therefore even prove contrary to the long-term interests of the work group. The assembly-line workers who promote the illusion for management that 40 units per day is the maximum possible may one day find that 40 units per day is not enough to justify keeping the plant open. Perhaps more to the point, the silencing effects of conformity beg the question of how many imaginative and useful ideas never are voiced by workers and therefore never taken advantage of either by the organization as a whole or by the work group itself. How many great innovations never have been discovered because workers believed there was only one way to do something—the company's way?

Other individuals' opinions become particularly influential when those individuals are quite similar to us. It is not unusual to find that someone voices different judgments or beliefs if that someone has a different background, makes different assumptions, or entertains different motivations as the basis for perceptual or judgmental construction. In fact, if you can find reasonable explanations for differences between your judgments and those of others, the differences will exert little influence on your conclusions. Thus, when the older workers suggest that 50 isn't possible, you may think that for them 50 really isn't possible, even if it is for you! When an individual can find no obvious basis for differences in opinion, however, these differences can be quite alarming and demand adjustment of judgment, or behavior!

It should be obvious now why idiosyncrasy credits (discussed in Chapter 7) are so critical to organizational growth and survival, and why it is important for organizations to develop a "technology of foolishness." Idiosyncrasy credits allow a way for new ideas to be voiced without risking rejection by the group. Once group members have proven their loyalty to the group, their questioning of the group's roles and rules can be seen as constructive and appropriate by the group. March believes that organizations need to *institutionalize* a process by which norms regularly are challenged or broken—foolishness—and thereby regularly are tested for continuing appropriateness. This ensures that new workers are conforming to appropriate and effective behaviors rather than just conforming to the peer pressures.

Social Facilitation   When the mere presence of other individuals (for instance, other group members) spurs an individual on to greater efforts, **social facilitation** has occurred.[22] Norman Triplett was first credited with exploring social facilitation in 1897. Triplett noticed that world records in sports such as cycling always are set during events when many riders are competing against each other and almost never when athletes are competing only against themselves or the clock. Triplett concluded that world-class athletes derive extra energy from the mere presence of competitors.

Where does this extra energy come from? One possibility is that the mere presence of other individuals arouses fears of failing and then being evaluated negatively by the other group members who are watching.[23] According to this explanation, the extra energy provided by the mere presence of others is a form of arousal that comes from fear or anxiety. Another possibility is that the presence of the others is a distraction for an individual who is working on a task. If the other people are working on the same task, their actions might provide clues for the individual about how to improve performance. If the other people are just observing the individual, their facial expressions provide valuable feedback about how well the individual is doing. The individual feels conflict because on the one hand he wants to concentrate on the task, while on the other

---

[22] T. L. Griffith, M. Fichman, and R. L. Moreland, "Social Loafing and Social Facilitation: An Empirical Test of the Cognitive-Motivational Model of Performance," *Basic and Applied Social Psychology* 10 (1989): 253–271.

[23] N. B. Cottrell, D. L. Wack, G. S. Sekerak, and R. H. Rittle, "Social Facilitation of Dominant Responses by the Presence of an Audience and the Mere Exposure of Others," *Journal of Personality and Social Psychology* 9 (1968): 245–250.

hand he wants to look at the other people. This internal conflict becomes a source of arousal from which the individual derives extra energy.[24]

Social facilitation refers to increases in an individual's supply of *energy*—not necessarily to improvement of performance. Research on social facilitation has shown that the extra arousal derived from the mere presence of others will improve performance only if the behaviors necessary for high-quality performance are well learned or the task is very simple.[25] Arousal increases the probability of dominant responses. If the task is well learned or simple, high-quality responses are likely to be dominant and social facilitation simply will increase their probability, leading to enhanced performance. If the task is difficult or unfamiliar, correct responses are not likely to be dominant. Arousal from social facilitation therefore may only increase the probability of *incorrect* behaviors, thereby leading to worse performance. Social facilitation thus is a "sword that cuts both ways." The presence of others increases an individual's arousal level; whether this arousal level improves or hurts performance depends upon how difficult or unfamiliar the task is.

Social Loafing   **Social loafing** occurs when individuals decrease the amount of effort they put into a task—loaf—while doing that task with other people. The important word here is "with." Social loafing occurs when several people are working on the same task *together* so that it is difficult (if not impossible) to tell who is doing how much of the work. A behavioral scientist named Ringlemann first discovered social loafing. He noticed that in strength tasks like "tug-o-war" the effort exerted by the team never added up to the sum of the amounts of effort that each individual was capable of exerting alone.[26] He later demonstrated the social loafing effect over a variety of tasks. In one study the researchers told a group of subjects each to scream into their own microphones as loud as possible: first one at a time, then together. By hooking sensors up to each of the individual microphones, the researchers were able to show that the subjects each screamed much louder when screaming alone than when screaming as a group.[27]

Social loafing is thought to occur because of **diffusion of responsibility** in groups. When group members work together on a single task and it is difficult to determine who is working hard and who is not, the responsibility for the outcome is diffused—shared—over the entire group. Whether the outcome is a success or a failure, credit is shared relatively equally among group members. This decreases the incentive for any individual to work hard because there is only a loose connection between effort and the outcome for the group or the individual. Extra effort may have little or no effect on the final outcome for the

---

[24] G. G. Sanders, "Driven by Distraction: An Integrative Review of Social Facilitation Theory and Research," *Journal of Experimental Social Psychology* 17 (1981): 227–251; R. S. Baron, "Distraction-Conflict Theory: Progress and Problems," in *Advances in Experimental Social Psychology*, ed. L. Berkowitz (San Francisco: Academic Press, 1985).

[25] R. B. Zajonc, "Social Facilitation," *Science* 149 (1965): 269–274.

[26] From Ringlemann, cited in D. R. Forsyth, *An Introduction to Group Dynamics* (Monterey, Calif.: Brooks-Cole, 1983), 152.

[27] B. Latane, K. Williams, and S. Harkins, "Many Hands Make Light the Work: The Causes and Consequences of Social Loafing," *Journal of Personality and Social Psychology* 37 (1979): 822–832.

The presence of other young people repairing this old house may spur individuals in the group to greater efforts than they would have made on their own. This extra energy, an effect of social facilitation, may enhance or hinder performance, depending on the task at hand.

group and will have *absolutely* no effect on the share of the group outcome received by the individual (as long as the individual *appears* to be trying hard). The result again is the kind of free rider problem noted earlier. Each individual slacks off a little bit and in the end the performance of the entire group suffers.

In extreme cases, diffusion of responsibility can lead to deindividuation. **Deindividuation** occurs when the personal identities of group members—and therefore the responsibility they feel for their actions—are submerged in the identity of the group. Consider an important difference between the "tug-o-war" game mentioned earlier and an infamous incident during the Vietnam War: the My Lai massacre. If someone in the "tug-o-war" game isn't working as hard as possible, no one would know because the collective action is made up of many smaller individual behaviors that cannot be examined separately. There is only one action, the pulling of the rope by the group. In the My Lai massacre of the civilian population of a small village in Vietnam, the collective action (the massacre) was made up of many individual actions. Hypothetically, the death of each My Lai villager was an individual action that could have been attributed to an individual soldier. But in practice this did not happen. In reality, no one knew anything more than that it was American soldiers who massacred the villagers, and to any observer of the incident any soldier would have looked pretty much like any other soldier. There were no individuals involved in the massacre, only group members each acting *not as individuals* but as members of the group.

Anonymity is an important part of the deindividuation process. Mobs often engage in behaviors that no individual alone would ever consider, such as lynching an untried suspect. In a mob, there are no individuals and therefore no individual actions and no individual responsibility for actions. There is only the mob and the mob's actions. If the mob's actions are bad, that is certainly not felt to be the fault of any individual. Similarly, exceedingly cruel, humiliating, and even inhuman treatment of others apparently becomes acceptable behavior when everyone else is doing it under the guise of initiation rites and rituals.[28] Obviously, diffusion of responsibility is an important part of deindividuation.

GROUP CHARACTERISTICS

Not all groups or social settings are equally likely to elicit the social context effects on judgment and behavior discussed in this chapter. We close the chapter by briefly examining two characteristics that dramatically affect the ways that groups function and interact: group cohesiveness and group size.

Group Cohesiveness

Group cohesiveness refers to the desire of a group's members to remain together as a group.[29] Groups are more cohesive when the group's goals are compatible with the individual goals of the group's members, the group members support each other, and the group's leader encourages effective participation by all group members.[30] Cohesiveness increases when group members build personal relationships among each other.[31] Personal relationships promote a sense of closeness among group members and also provide group members with the information necessary to work closely and effectively with each other.

In general, more cohesive groups are more productive,[32] but that does not mean that group cohesiveness is an unqualified asset. The pressure to conform is much more intense in highly cohesive groups,[33] and group members of highly cohesive groups are more likely to trust the opinions of other group members and less willing to risk rejection by the group for disagreeing. Therefore, when a group's goals match those of the organization, cohesiveness will enhance the group's contributions to the organization. However, if a group's goals are out of step with those of the organization, cohesiveness may make that group a formidable and difficult renegade coalition.

Group Size

One of the most important consequences of group size is its effect on communication among group members. With more members in a group, the num-

---

[28] R. Reilly, "What Is the Citadel," *Sports Illustrated*, September 14, 1991, 70–79; and M. Starr, " 'The Night of the Taming': Tales of Hazing and Beatings at a Military Academy," *Newsweek*, May 13, 1991, 37.

[29] R. W. Napier and M. K. Gershenfeld, *Groups: Theory and Experience* (Palo Alto, Calif.: Houghton-Mifflin, 1989), 151.

[30] D. Cartwright and A. Zander, *Group Dynamics: Research and Theory* (New York: Harper & Row, 1968).

[31] R. W. Napier and M. K. Gershenfeld, *Groups: Theory and Experiences* (Palo Alto, Calif.: Houghton-Mifflin, 1989), 197–198.

[32] D. Norris and R. Niebuhr, "Group Variables and Gaming Success," *Simulation and Games* 11 (1980): 301–312.

[33] L. Festinger and J. Thibaut, "Interpersonal Communication in Small Groups," *Journal of Abnormal and Social Psychology* 16 (1951): 92–99.

FIGURE 8–4	▶ Possible Channels of Communication (by group size)

Number of Group Members	Possible Channels of Communication
2	1
3	3
4	6
5	10
6	15
7	21
8	28
9	36
10	45

ber of possible channels of communication between members increases dramatically. As shown in Figure 8–4, doubling the size of a group from 3 to 6 participants increases the number of possible two-person channels of communication from 3 to 15—a five-fold increase! Thus, even if a group of seven or eight individuals is meant to have "all-channel" communication, rarely would all these channels be used in practice.

Smaller groups provide more opportunities for significant contributions by individuals to group activities and discussions among group members, which leads to higher morale.[34] Above a group size of five, group members often will complain that a group is too large, probably because there simply isn't enough "air time" for everyone to participate actively in group discussions.[35] Typically this leads a group to split up into cliques,[36] which can quickly become voting coalitions. As the size of a group increases, the connectedness among members decreases;[37] this can lead to increases in social loafing, bystander apathy, and even deindividuation.[38] Larger groups also promote more conformity, since there are more peers to exert pressure on any individual to conform.[39]

On the other side of the coin, social facilitation effects increase with group size, and more group members means more perspectives and more knowledge in group discussions. The real issue is not group size, but whether a group is managed well enough that its size becomes an asset rather than a liability.

[34] S. Huberman, "Making Jewish Leaders," *Journal of Jewish Communal Service* 64 (1987): 32–41.

[35] G. Gentry, "Group Size and Attitudes toward the Simulation Experience," *Simulation and Games* 11 (1980): 451–460.

[36] C. Mamali and G. Paun, "Group Size and the Genesis of Subgroups: Objective Restrictions." *Revue Roumaine des Sciences Sociales—Serie de Psychologie* 26 (1982): 139–148.

[37] R. W. Napier and M. K. Gershenfeld, *Groups: Theory and Experience* (Palo Alto, Calif.: Houghton-Mifflin, 1989), 38–41.

[38] See, for instance, H. Pantin and C. Carver, "Induced Competence and the Bystander Effect," *Journal of Applied Social Psychology* 12 (1982): 100–111.

[39] H. B. Gerard, R. A. Wilhelmy, and E. S. Conolley, "Conformity and Group Size," *Journal of Personality and Social Psychology* 8 (1968): 79–82.

SUMMARY   ◆◆◆◆◆◆

In groups and organizations, other group members are a potent influence on an individual's thoughts and behaviors. Power and politics are forms of influence in which the resource dependencies of two individuals allow one to change, influence, or control the beliefs or actions of the other. In a power play, both sides receive something. The more powerful person simply receives more for less. Slack refers to the overabundance of a resource, which insulates an individual from power plays by another.

Power arises from the control of a variety of resources. Reward and coercion power are the basic resources. Expert, legitimate, referent, and task-interdependence power all refer to different organizational forms of control over rewards and punishments.

Even the lowliest member of an organization has access to some forms of power. The most important power tactic for upward influence is the coalition. Coalitions represent the gathering and sharing of power in organizations so that relatively powerless individuals can achieve more than they could through their individual power alone.

Certain power tactics—particularly direct and nonrational influence attempts—are poorly received in organizations. Their use may destroy relationships and eventually undermine the power of the powerholder.

Social context refers to the fact that an individual's behavior in groups and organizations takes place in the context of other individuals. According to social comparison theory, the opinions and actions of others have a major—often unintended—influence on our perceptions and beliefs. Groups also can directly influence the behaviors of group members through conformity, social facilitation, and social loafing.

Not all groups or social settings are equally likely to elicit social context effects. Group cohesiveness and group size are characteristics of groups that dramatically affect the ways that groups function and interact.

Key Terms

Alternative sources   Other ways to fulfill a resource dependency, thereby reducing an individual's dependence on any one source; a form of slack.

Bystander apathy   Failure of observers to lend assistance in emergency situations; an example of the results of social anchoring effects on judgment.

Charisma   Persuasiveness derived from personal characteristics desired or admired by a reference group.

Coalition   Collection of individuals who band together to combine their individual sources of power.

Coercion   Threat of punishment for not engaging in appropriate behaviors.

Compromise coalition   Coalition in which all members are interested in the same issues but each is flexible enough about specifics to make sure that the coalition gets its way.

Conformity   Form of social inhibition in which a group member engages in a behavior or professes a belief that is encouraged by the group even though the member believes it is incorrect or inappropriate.

Deindividuation Submersion of personal identities and personal responsibility of group members in the identity group.

Diffusion of responsibility Sharing the credit or blame for the outcomes of a group's actions over the entire group.

Expert power Individual power based on the possession of special information, knowledge, or ability.

Extrinsic rewards Rewards like money or praise provided in exchange for appropriate behaviors.

Group cohesiveness The desire of a group's members to remain together as a group.

Ingratiation Doing nice things for someone in the hope of creating a sense of obligation in the individual to return the favor.

Legitimate power Individual power based on individuals' authority to control the behavior of others for their own good and for the good of a social system.

Logrolling Form of coalition in which participants lend each other power so that each can pursue interests not shared by other coalition members.

Political conflict Occurs when different members of an organization pursue conflicting *personal* (rather than organizational) agendas.

Referent power Individual power based on a high level of identification with, admiration of, or respect for the powerholder.

Resource dependence Individual's need for resources, which exposes the individual to influence.

Reward power Individual power based on the control of resources valued by another; the opposite of coercive power.

Social anchoring Forming perceptions or judgments in an extremely uncertain situation by relying on the opinions of others.

Social comparison Process of having one's perceptions influenced by the comments and perceptions of others.

Social context The individuals in groups and organizations that provide an influential context for all behavior.

Social facilitation Tendency for the presence of others to enhance an individual's energy level.

Social loafing When individuals decrease the amount of effort they put into a task because they are working on that task with other people.

Stockpile Resource set aside for future use, such as money put into savings for a "rainy day"; a form of slack.

Task interdependence Power accruing to a particular job or group of jobs in an organization when two or more employees must depend on each other to complete assigned tasks.

Theory of social exchange Theory suggesting that social behavior is an exchange of material and non-material goods (such as approval and prestige), and that in relationships people continually monitor the rewards and costs to work out balanced exchanges.

Discussion Questions

1. Imagine that the students and the instructor in a university course are unhappy with the way the course is going. What sources of power are available to university students to change things in the classroom? What sources of power are available to the instructor? Are the students or the instructor more powerful in this setting?

2. What does it mean to say that *all* exercises of power are examples of exchanges? When a supervisor gives an order to a subordinate in an organizational setting, what is being exchanged?

3. Why are coalitions such an important way for lower-level participants in organizations to mobilize the power they have?

4. What is meant by the phrase, "those who govern do so at the consent of those governed"? What source of power does this describe?

5. What sources of power depend on the existence of an organization? What sources of power are personal? What does it mean to say that reward power and coercion are the two *basic* forms of power?

6. How do complexity, conflict, and uncertainty as defining characteristics of organizational behavior contribute to group influences on individuals?

7. Are group influences on judgment and group influences on behavior equally likely to occur at each of the different stages of group development as discussed in Chapter 7?

If You Want to Know More

Stanford University Professor Jeff Pfeffer provides a good general discussion of power in his book, *Power in Organizations* (Marshfield, Mass.: Pitman, 1981). Included is a particularly good chapter on the use of coalitions to mobilize power. A good book of readings on power and influence is *Organizational Influence Processes*, by Robert Allen and Lyman Porter (Glenview, Ill.: Scott, Foresman, 1983).

Stanley Milgram's studies on obedience to authority are described in detail in his book, *Obedience to Authority* (New York: Harper & Row, 1974).

The notion of power as a social-exchange process is explained in detail in Peter Blau's book, *Exchange and Power in Social Life* (New York: Wiley, 1964).

Two excellent summaries of the influence of groups on individual thought and action are contained in the books *The Social Animal*, by Elliot Aronson (New York: Freeman & Co., 1984), and *The Individual in a Social World*, by Stanley Milgram (Reading, Mass.: Addison-Wesley, 1977). Aronson's book is accompanied by a collection of readings (entitled *Reading about the Social Animal*) that provides a good selection of papers on the behavior of individuals in groups. Milgram's book in particular focuses on how groups bring out the "dark side" of human nature. The release of the "dark side" of human nature also is considered in some detail in Phil Zimbardo's piece, "The Human Choice: Individuation, Reason, and Order versus Deindividuation, Impulse, and Chaos," in *Nebraska Symposium on Motivation*, ed. W. Arnold and D. Levine (Lincoln: University of Nebraska Press, 1969), 237–307. The issue of deindividuation in college hazing rituals is explored in *Broken Pledges: The Deadly Rite of Hazing*, by H. Nuwer (Longstreet Press, 1990).

Solomon Asch describes conformity and the effects of groups on individuals' thoughts in his classic article, "Effects of Group Pressure on the Modification and Distortion of Judgment," in *Groups, Leadership, and Men: Research in Human Relations*, ed. H. Guetzkow (New York: Russell & Russell, 1963).

Robert Zajonc wrote the seminal article "Social Facilitation" for *Science* (149, 1965, 269–274). Chris Earley provides some insights into social context effects (like social loafing) across cultures in his article, "Social Loafing and Collectivism: A Comparison of the United States and the People's Republic of China" (*Administrative Science Quarterly* 34, 1989, 565–581).

On Your Own

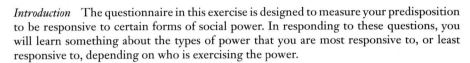

Social Power Inventory

Introduction   The questionnaire in this exercise is designed to measure your predisposition to be responsive to certain forms of social power. In responding to these questions, you will learn something about the types of power that you are most responsive to, or least responsive to, depending on who is exercising the power.

Procedure

Step 1: 5 Minutes   Identify three *different* people who have influence over you. One must be a teacher, a second may be a roommate or spouse, a third may be a boss. Others might include friends, business associates, parents, or people that you negotiate with regularly. Specify the three people you have identified:

▶ Person 1:
▶ Person 2:
▶ Person 3:

Step 2: 20 Minutes   For *each* of the three people work completely through the following questionnaire with that person in mind. For each of the 30 questions, pick A or B depending on which one of the two best describes the way that they affect you. Make sure to *pick one* even if neither is a very good answer.

Step 3: 30 Minutes   Your instructor will hand out a scoring key. Follow the key in order to score your questionnaire.

Person 1	Person 2	Person 3		
_____	_____	_____	1. A.	I sometimes do what that person says in order to get something I want.
			B.	I sometimes have to go along to avoid trouble.
_____	_____	_____	2. A.	That person always convinces me with his/her reasoning.
			B.	I sometimes do things for that person because I admire him/her.
_____	_____	_____	3. A.	That person might do good things for me in return.
			B.	I don't know as much about it as that person does.
_____	_____	_____	4. A.	That person's suggestions always make sense.
			B.	I could receive things I want from that person.
_____	_____	_____	5. A.	I want that person to like me.
			B.	I often feel that it is legitimate for that person to influence my behavior.

——— ——— ———   **6. A.** I take his/her word for things.
                   B. I sometimes try to avoid trouble by doing what is asked.

——— ——— ———   **7. A.** That person has the right to tell me what to do.
                   B. That person is able to harm me in some way.

——— ——— ———   **8. A.** That person knows better.
                   B. I will receive something I want.

——— ——— ———   **9. A.** That person's friendship is important to me.
                   B. That person seems fairly intelligent.

——— ——— ———   **10. A.** The reasoning of the request usually agrees with my way of thinking.
                    B. That person is in a position to legitimately ask things of me.

——— ——— ———   **11. A.** I will receive something I want.
                    B. I sometimes go along with that person to make him/her happy.

——— ——— ———   **12. A.** That person's knowledge usually makes him/her right.
                    B. I feel that person has the right to ask things of me.

——— ——— ———   **13. A.** I want that person to like me.
                    B. I sometimes have to go along to avoid trouble.

——— ——— ———   **14. A.** I would sometimes like to get things from that person.
                    B. Sometimes I feel that person might do something unpleasant to those who do not do what is suggested.

——— ——— ———   **15. A.** That person's suggestions always make sense.
                    B. I do what is asked to keep that person from taking actions which could be unpleasant for me.

——— ——— ———   **16. A.** That person should be listened to.
                    B. That person's friendship is important to me.

——— ——— ———   **17. A.** That person can do things which I would not like.
                    B. That person always knows what he/she is doing.

——— ——— ———   **18. A.** I sometimes have to go along in order to get things I need.
                    B. I often feel that it is legitimate for that person to influence my behavior.

——— ——— ———   **19. A.** The request is sometimes appropriate, considering that person's position.
                    B. At times, that person's suggestions make sense.

———— ———— ———— 20. **A.** I sometimes do so because I feel that person is my friend.
  B. That person's expertise makes him/her more likely to be right.

———— ———— ———— 21. **A.** That person has the right to tell me what to do.
  B. That person could do something unpleasant to me.

———— ———— ———— 22. **A.** That person is able to do things which benefit me.
  B. That person always convinces me with his/her reasoning.

———— ———— ———— 23. **A.** That other person's position permits him/her to require things of me.
  B. That person's knowledge usually makes him/her right.

———— ———— ———— 24. **A.** I trust that person's judgment.
  B. I agree with what that person says.

———— ———— ———— 25. **A.** Sometimes I feel that person might do something which is unpleasant to those who do not do what is suggested.
  B. I always do what is asked because that person's ideas are compelling.

———— ———— ———— 26. **A.** That person might help me get what I want.
  B. It would not be proper sometimes for me to do otherwise.

———— ———— ———— 27. **A.** That person can make things uncomfortable for me if I don't comply.
  B. I do what is asked to make that person happy.

———— ———— ———— 28. **A.** I would like to be his/her friend.
  B. That person can help me.

———— ———— ———— 29. **A.** That person always gives me good reasons for doing it.
  B. I sometimes do what is asked to gain that person's friendship.

———— ———— ———— 30. **A.** What that person says seems to be appropriate.
  B. That person has had a lot of experience and usually knows best.

Discussion Questions

1. What was your score for each of the different forms of power?

Scoring Key

	Expert	Legitimate	Coercive	Reward	Referent	Informational
Person 1						
Person 2						
Person 3						

2. Find others in the class who rated the same *type* of person (teacher, parent, room-mate, and so on). How do your scores compare to theirs in terms of the types that are most and least influential? Why do you suppose that this is so?

3. How do the *situations* that these people are in—for example, their objectives and your objectives, the differences in your ages, the kind of resources they control and you want, and so on—affect the kind of power they are likely to use, and the kind of power that has impact on you? Explain.

4. If you were the powerful party in these situations, would you try to use different forms of power from those now being used? Explain.

5. As a power user yourself, which forms of power are you most comfortable using? Least comfortable? In which situations?

Source: Questionnaire developed by David W. Jamieson, Ph.D., and Kenneth W. Thomas, Ph.D., as appeared in R. J. Lewicki and J. A. Litterer, *Negotiation: Readings, Exercises, and Cases* (Homewood, Ill.: Richard D. Irwin, 1985), 490–493.

CLOSING CASE

CHAPTER 8

THE MANAGER'S MEMO

FROM: E. Grainger, Vice President

TO: F. Blackstone, President

RE: Potentially Damaging Resignation

Pat McDonnell has just given me his resignation, effective in two weeks. Because Pat was responsible for designing the high-powered telescope we sell to the Pentagon, his departure will be a great loss for the company.

I am particularly concerned because the Defense Department has just asked us to submit a bid to produce a miniaturized version of our telescope. In the future, the miniaturized version will be the only version purchased by the military. I believe that two other companies are also bidding on this contract.

As you know, the Defense Department represents over 90 percent of our business. I am afraid that, without Pat, we will be unable to come up with an acceptable design and will therefore lose our major customer.

Pat has hinted that for a substantial raise plus a stock interest in the company, he might be willing to reconsider. To me, this sounds vaguely like blackmail. I find his tactics unpleasantly coercive. Perhaps it's time we ceased being a one-product, one-customer company. What do you advise?

Case Discussion Questions

Assume you are the president, and write a response to the vice president's memorandum. What power does Pat McDonnell have relative to the company? What power does the company have relative to the Pentagon? Use your answers to these questions and your knowledge about power to guide you in considering the alternatives available to the company.

♦♦♦♦♦♦

GROUP DECISION MAKING

GROUP DECISION MAKING WITH SADDAM HUSSEIN IN THE GULF WAR ◆◆◆◆◆◆

Saddam Hussein had a history of miscalculating his opponents. According to Gary Sick, a former national security advisor to President Jimmy Carter, Saddam Hussein invaded Iran in 1979 after consolidating his power. The Iraqi leader thought that victory would only take three months. Instead, the war lasted eight years and there wasn't even a clear winner. In both the war with Iran and the Gulf War in 1991, Iraq fought a defensive war. This military strategy makes it difficult for any attacker to break through in a ground war, but it is an ineffective strategy against an air war. Neither Saddam nor his field commanders fully appreciated the sophistication and power of modern weapons to destroy their defenses, said both Sick and Nadine Goldring, senior defense analyst for the Defense Budget Project, a Washington think tank. And it was not as if Iraq were not warned. In early January 1991, U.S. Secretary of State James Baker told Iraq that if it did not withdraw from Kuwait and there was a war, "it will not parallel your previous experience."

How can such a powerful leader make so many mistakes? One explanation for Saddam's miscalculations may have been his primary weakness as a leader. He brooked no dissent, often eliminating those who chose to disagree with him. If Saddam's commanders had any knowledge of his strategy's deficiency, they were unlikely to have told him. If his advisors were unwilling to provide a different perspective for fear of the consequences, then consensus among his advisory groups was de rigueur. Thus, the advisors and Saddam himself figured that the United States would never challenge his invasion of Kuwait so ferociously and so directly. Even though Saddam was an aficionado of weaponry, he was clearly misinformed on the quality and accuracy of the bombs that would be dropped on his country and his troops. Sick suggests that Saddam and his advisors simply could not or would not believe it.

The Iraqi leader apparently thought that he could withstand the allied air onslaught and then inflict so many casualties in a ground war that the allies would be forced into a stalemate. History has clearly illustrated the error of this belief. Both Saddam Hussein's mistrust of professional military as well as his unflinching demand for loyalty (at the risk of death if the advisors disagreed) and support from advisors may have been the major factors that led to his defeat in the Gulf War. He did not have the benefit of his aides' knowledge and perspective since they were unwilling to counsel their leader when he most needed it—when he was about to make a bad decision.

William Neikirk, "Hussein's Blunders a Boon to the U.S. Military, *Chicago Tribune*, February 27, 1991, 1, 6. All rights reserved. Used with permission.

THE NATURE OF GROUP DECISION MAKING

The allies were clearly the beneficiaries of Saddam Hussein's inability to use his advisory group effectively. Individuals coming together for a common purpose—to solve problems and make decisions—can be more productive and effective than their individual members, on average. What is it about groups that gives rise to such extraordinary levels of performance?

Why Use Groups?

Groups have some obvious advantages over individuals when it comes to making decisions. One is that groups are composed of various individuals with differing perspectives who can contribute ideas and suggestions. Unlike a lone individual, groups have the potential for **resource pooling.** There is obviously more information in the group than there is in any of its members. Even if one member knows much more than anyone else, the unique information of less-skilled individuals can fill in the knowledge gaps of other group members. For example, a worker on an assembly line could tell management how other workers are likely to respond to a new fringe-benefit package.

Group members can stimulate and encourage each other. This mutual influence process is called **synergy.** Individuals working alone on a problem may persist in viewing the problem in a particular way. This mindset may be wrong and, thus, the individual will fail to solve the problem. Individuals in a group have the same tendency, but the number of different approaches may knock group members out of their solution ruts. The information contributed by a member of my group may catalyze my thinking or alter its direction, indirectly aiding my contributions to the group's solution.

Because of the number of different skills found in groups, individual members have the luxury of working on problems or parts of a problem. Groups offer the opportunity for specialization of labor, which is unavailable to individual decision makers.

The benefits of group decision making are not limited solely to the solution-generation stage. Many solutions depend upon the commitment of those involved for their successful implementation. Because more people are involved in group decision making, implementation is easier because a larger number of people feel responsible for making the solution work. It is even possible that a low-quality solution that has good group commitment can be more effective than a high-quality solution that lacks such commitment.[1]

Not only are group decisions more accepted by employees than individual decisions, they are likely to be better understood. Decisions made by an individual must be carried out by others. Thus, individual decisions have an additional step—that of relaying the decision to the implementing parties. Failure to convey the solution effectively (poor communication) can reduce its attractiveness and create greater problems than the one the solution was designed to solve. For example, after attending a seminar on motivating employees, a company CEO may decide to replace the current seniority-based compensation system with a merit-based system. Regardless of the wisdom of this decision, employees may believe that the company is just trying to make them work harder for less money—that the company really does not care about them, only about its bottom line. Further, because it is difficult to implement almost any solution, the solution that is imposed from above does not have the added benefit of "ownership." The only person to whom this particular decision belongs is the CEO of the company. If the decision had resulted from a group interaction, the sense of ownership would be much more widespread. The result of the CEO's decision may be lowered morale and reduced productivity, even though the CEO intended to give the workers more direct rewards for productivity.

If the CEO had included others in the decision-making process, the likelihood of this type of failure would have been reduced. The individuals who would be implementing the system would understand not only why the particular compensation package was chosen, but also why other potential solutions were not chosen. The general assumption that the behavior of the CEO is arbitrary or adversarial would have less impact, because those involved in the decision would know how this particular choice was reached. In the "FOCUS ON: Groups," the benefits of group decision making are illustrated from the perspective of one successful CEO.

Types of Group Decisions

When Are Many Heads Better Than One?   Given the advantages of group decision making suggested above and the number of skilled individuals in a typical organization, perhaps all decisions should be group decisions. Yet many organizational decisions are made by one or two key individuals. Why is there such a wide gap between the benefits of group decision making and its use? Let's examine exactly which types of decisions can benefit from the unique contributions of groups.

Group decision making is usually superior to individual decision making in tasks requiring judgments about uncertain events. These types of decisions are primarily concerned with quality outcomes and usually have the following characteristics:

1.   The potential benefits are substantial, the costs of error are high, and it is difficult to reverse or salvage a poor decision after action has begun.
2.   Information is incomplete or uncertain.
3.   Many feasible alternatives exist.

---

[1]N. R. F. Maier, "Assets and Liabilities in Group Problem Solving: The Need for an Integrative Function," *Psychological Review* 74 (1967): 239–249.

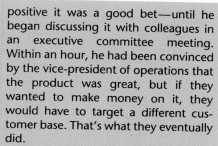

Focus on

Groups

The Importance of Group Meetings Mention committee meetings to a seasoned manager and you are likely to see eyes rolling. The complaints about group meetings often center on the time spent or, more precisely, on what does not come from all the time spent meeting in conference. But meetings can be an efficient way for busy executives to keep up with what is going on in their organization. Ed Houcek, vice-president of sales for Dewar Information SystemCorp, a $10 million supplier of editorial production systems for newspapers, says, "We've found that a group of people working together can come up with smarter decisions than one individual, no matter who he is." Houcek tells about the time he had a terrific idea for a product to be sold to small printing shops. He was positive it was a good bet—until he began discussing it with colleagues in an executive committee meeting. Within an hour, he had been convinced by the vice-president of operations that the product was great, but if they wanted to make money on it, they would have to target a different customer base. That's what they eventually did.

The founder of Dewar Information SystemCorp, president Steuart Dewar relies heavily on groups, but reserves the right to veto any idea. However, he says he has not used the veto. "If I can't persuade three smart people that something makes sense or is at least worth trying, it is probably not a good idea."

"When you leave a meeting, you understand the issues. Even if we have conflicting views going in, we eventually come up with a package that everyone can live with. This process is particularly useful when the issue at hand is controversial or emotional." Earlier in 1989, the executive committee determined that the health benefits package needed to be scaled back. "If I had made the decision on my own or if it had been made by the vice-president of finance," Dewar reports, "we would have been seen as the bad guys." Committee decisions carry more weight with employees, Dewar thinks. Group decisions have become the tool through which the company coordinates every aspect of its growth. "There is a level of coordination here that you rarely see in other businesses."

Bruce Posner, "Death, Taxes, and . . . Meetings," *Inc.,* October 1989, 144–148.

4. Identifying the optimal alternative is difficult.
5. Feedback about results from the chosen alternative will not be available until long after it has been implemented.[2]

When solving a problem involves generating many or unique ideas, recalling information accurately, and evaluating ambiguous or uncertain situations,

---

[2]D. E. Zand, "Collateral Organizations: A New Change Strategy," *Journal of Applied Behavioral Science* 10 (1974): 63–89.

then groups will likely outperform individuals. If group members can perform their jobs relatively independently of each other, individual decision making is probably more appropriate. If, however, group members are interdependent and must cooperate with each other, then effective performance will hinge on their ability to coordinate their decisions.[3]

While groups have been shown to produce judgmental decisions of generally higher quality than individuals,[4] the need for high-quality decisions is not sufficient in and of itself to require group involvement. A second factor to be considered is the need for acceptance of the decision for its successful implementation. As mentioned in the previous section, a major benefit of group decision making is the greater acceptance by organizational members of the decision.

The Participation Controversy

Another way of deciding whether to use groups or individuals to solve problems is to ask a more general question: Should employees participate in decision making, whether it affects them directly or not? The decision to involve others in the decision-making process depends on a number of factors, such as the abilities of the group members, their willingness to search for and share information, and the nature of the decision to be made. In fact, if we ignore these factors, research indicates that in terms of productivity, there is no benefit to participative decision making. That is, participation has no effect on productivity in more than 50 percent of the studies. However, participation does have a positive impact on satisfaction, regardless of the existence of these factors, in more than 60 percent of the studies.[5]

It should be noted that participation can be voluntary or involuntary, direct or indirect, and can vary in degree, content, and scope. For example, participation can be forced through laws, governmental regulation, or decree. Once a union is certified, then both management and labor must participate in contract negotiations. Before creating policies, many governmental regulations require citizen input. Thus, because of the nature of our political system, we must at times participate in its decision making, regardless of our unique desires or preferences.

Participation also may be direct or indirect. As members of a quality circle, individuals have the opportunity to make their views known directly. Alternatively, when each of us votes to elect representatives (who, in turn, participate directly in decision making), we are indirect participants in the decision-making process.

Finally, participation may be formal or informal. If an employee is elected to represent other workers on a work-safety committee, the employee's participation in the decision-making process is formal. However, if the supervisor asks the employee's opinion on a particular work-safety issue, that participation is

---

[3] M. Sashkin, "Changing toward Participative Management Approaches: A Model and Methods," *Academy of Management Review* 1 (1976): 75–86.

[4] J. K. Murnighan, "Group Decision Making: What Strategy Should You Use?" *Management Review* (Spring 1981): 55–62; and P. Laughlin and R. McGlynn, Collective Induction: Mutual Group and Individual Influence by Exchange of Hypotheses and Evidence, *Journal of Experimental Social Psychology* 22 (1986): 567–589.

[5] E. A. Locke and D. M. Schweiger, "Participation in Decision Making: One More Look," in *Research in Organizational Behavior*, vol. 1, ed. B. M. Staw (1979): 265–339.

informal—based not upon the employee's position but rather upon his or her personal relationship with the supervisor.

The complexity of participation may, in part, account for its poor impact on performance in studies. Current research has suggested that participation is very likely *not* to work in some situations. For example, a survey of senior business executives showed that over three-fourths believed that (1) they knew what had to be done and (2) they had the right to make organizational decisions. In such situations, when management sees little benefit in employee participation in decision making, it is unlikely that requiring participation will work.[6]

Employee characteristics also influence the usefulness of participation. If employees have no knowledge of or interest in a decision, their input will probably do little to improve its outcome. Expecting employees to participate in decisions about which they have little knowledge or concern can also increase their sense of frustration. In fact, it seems that too much participation can lead to lower performance, stress, and dissatisfaction.[7]

PROBLEMS WITH GROUP DECISION MAKING

Participative decision making has great potential for improving the decision outcomes of organizations, but it also has a number of inherent pitfalls. One obvious pitfall is that groups take considerably more time to reach a decision than do individuals. The additional time is required because group decision making involves increased information-processing demands and requires decision rules and more complex interpersonal processes.[8]

Greater Complexity

Information-Processing Demands While any decision involves complex processes, the complexity is multiplied when more parties are involved. More decision makers may mean greater opportunities for creative solutions, but they also generate greater cognitive demands on each member of the group.

Decision Rules Individuals in groups must decide on rules concerning how dissenting opinions will be incorporated in a group decision. Decision rules such as requiring consensus, majority rule, and so on, influence the decision-making process.

Groups can make decisions in a number of ways.[9] Groups can make decisions by a lack of response. Alternatives for which no one voices a preference are dropped from consideration. The one idea for which there is support is the

[6]R. Krishnan, "Democratic Participation in Decision Making by Employees in American Corporations," *Academy of Management Journal* 17 (1974): 339–347.

[7]G. Hespe and T. Wall, "The Demand for Participation among Employees," *Human Relations* 29 (1976): 411–429.

[8]M. H. Bazerman, E. A. Mannix, and L. L. Thompson, "Groups as Mixed Motive Negotiations," in *Advances in Group Processes: Theory and Research*, vol. 5, eds. E. J. Lawler and B. Markovsky (Greenwich, Conn.: JAI Press, 1988).

[9]L. L. Thompson, E. A. Mannix, and M. H. Bazerman "Group Negotiation: Effects of Decision Rule, Agenda, and Aspiration," *Journal of Personality and Social Psychology* 54 (1988): 86–95.

one accepted. A second way in which group decisions can be reached is by authority rule. The leader of the group makes a decision based upon the group's discussion. Note that here, the group plays only an advisory role to the decision maker. A third way in which group decisions are made is by the minority. A small subset of the group's membership may be able to convince other group members to accept an alternative it favors. This is also known as "railroading" a particular decision. A common way groups reach decisions is through majority rule. The primary mechanism for majority rule is the vote. The problem here is that there are clear winners and losers. The losers may feel left out and without a say in the direction of the group. Their lack of commitment to a group's decision may lead to difficulties in its implementation. The last two mechanisms by which groups can make decisions are consensus or unanimity. While similar in outcome—all group members accept the final decision—consensus acknowledges that there may be some dissension among members of the group. By contrast, unanimity occurs when all group members agree on the course of action to be taken.

Each of these decision-making rules has its benefits and its costs. If a group member knows that to get a particular solution to a problem all the group member needs do is convince the majority, that member's strategy is likely to be very different than if all members of the group must be convinced (unanimity).[10]

Complex Interpersonal Processes The greater the number of individuals involved in the decision process, the wider the range of skills, abilities, and knowledge available to produce an effective solution. However, the larger the group membership, the greater the potential number of interpersonal relationships. Subgroups and coalitions are more likely to form, and the potential for conflict is greater.[11]

Earlier we indicated that decisions requiring judgments about uncertainty or requiring widespread acceptance are prime candidates for group decision making: the additional complexity involved in getting a group to make the decision is worth the gain in the final decision. However, groups are often required to make a variety of decisions, whether or not the final result merits the group's attention. Consider, for example, the following decision whether or not to go to Abilene.

> The July afternoon in Coleman, Texas, was particularly hot—104 degrees, as measured by the Walgreen's Rexall Ex-Lax temperature gauge. In addition, the wind was blowing fine-grained West Texas topsoil through the house. But the afternoon was still tolerable—even potentially enjoyable. There was a fan going on the back porch; there was cold lemonade; and finally there was entertainment. Dominoes. Perfect for the conditions. The game required little more physical exertion than an occasional mumbled comment, "shuffle 'em," and an unhurried movement of the arm to place the spots in the appropriate perspective on the table. All in all, it had the makings of an agreeable Sunday afternoon in Coleman—that is, until my father-in-law suddenly said, "Let's get in the car and go to Abilene and have dinner in the cafeteria."
>
> I thought: What, go to Abilene? Fifty-three miles? In a dust storm and heat? In an unairconditioned 1958 Buick?

---

[10]Ibid.

[11]D. Goleman, "Why Meetings Sometimes Don't Work," *New York Times*, June 7, 1988.

But my wife chimed in with "Sounds like a great idea. I'd like to go. How about you, Jerry?" Since my own preferences were obviously out of step with the rest I replied, "Sounds good to me," and added, "I just hope your mother wants to go."

"Of course I want to go," said my mother-in-law. "I haven't been to Abilene in a long time."

So into the car and off to Abilene we went. My predictions were fulfilled. The heat was brutal. We were coated with a fine layer of dust that was cemented with perspiration by the time we arrived. The food at the cafeteria provided first-rate testimonial material for antacid commercials.

Some four hours and 106 miles later, we returned to Coleman, hot and exhausted. We sat in front of the fan for a long time in silence. Then, both to be sociable and to break the silence, I said,

"It was a great trip, wasn't it?"

No one spoke.

Finally, my mother-in-law said, with some irritation, "Well, to tell the truth, I really didn't enjoy it much and would rather have stayed here. I just went along because the three of you were so enthusiastic about going. I wouldn't have gone if you all hadn't pressured me into it."

I couldn't believe it. "What do you mean, 'you all'?" I said. "Don't put me in the 'you all' group. I was delighted to be doing what we were doing. I only went to satisfy the rest of you. You're the culprits."

My wife looked shocked. "Don't call me a culprit. You and Daddy and Momma were the ones who wanted to go. I just went along to be sociable and to keep you happy. I would have had to be crazy to go out in heat like that."

Her father entered the conversation abruptly. "Hell!" he said.

He proceeded to expand on what was already absolutely clear. "Listen, I never wanted to go to Abilene. I just thought you might be bored. You visit so seldom I wanted to be sure you enjoyed it. I would have preferred to play another game of dominoes and eat the leftovers in the icebox."

After the outburst of recrimination, we all sat back in silence. Here we were, four reasonably sensible people who, of our own volition, had just taken a 106-mile trip across a godforsaken desert in a furnacelike temperature through a cloudlike dust storm to eat unpalatable food at a hole-in-the-wall cafeteria in Abilene, when none of us had really wanted to go. In fact, to be more accurate, we'd done just the opposite of what we wanted to do. The whole situation simply did not make sense.[12]

Dilemmas such as the one experienced by this family are typical of problems that can derail even the best of work groups. While the foregone resources of taking the trip to Abilene may be minimal, the same factors can work to offset the benefits of groups in making decisions. Two forms of problems associated with group decision making have been identified—groupthink and choice shift effects. Both of these problems result from how groups function. They will be discussed next.

Groupthink

The trip to Abilene is an example of groupthink. First described by Irving Janis, **groupthink** occurs in highly cohesive groups because their members have a tendency to lose their willingness and ability to evaluate one another's ideas

---

[12] Jerry Harvey, "Managing Agreements in Organizations: The Abilene Paradox," *Organizational Dynamics* (Summer 1974): 63–80. Reprinted by permission of publisher. American Management Association, New York. All rights reserved.

Symptoms of groupthink include illusions of invulnerability and a sense of being above the reproach of outsiders. How many of these symptoms, detailed in figure 9-1, apply to Oliver North's conduct during the Iran-Contra affair?

critically.[13] Because of this, there is an overemphasis on agreement and consensus and an unwillingness to critically evaluate alternative courses of action. Consider the following organizational equivalent of a trip to Abilene:[14]

> The Ozyx Corporation is a relatively small industrial company whose managers have embarked on a trip to Abilene. The president of Ozyx has hired a consultant to help discover the reasons for the poor profit picture of the company in general and the low morale and productivity of the R&D division in particular. During the process of investigation, the consultant becomes interested in a research project in which the company has invested a sizable portion of its R&D budget.

> When the consultant asked about the project in the privacy of their respective offices, the president, vice-president for research, and research manager each describe it as an idea that looks great on paper but will ultimately fail because of the unavailability of the technology required to make it work. Each of them acknowledges that continued support of the project will create cash flow problems that will jeopardize the very existence of the organization.

> Furthermore, each has not told the others about these reservations. When asked why, the president says he cannot reveal his true feelings because abandoning the project, which has been widely publicized, would make the company look bad in the press. In addition, it would probably cause the vice-president's ulcer to kick up or cause her to quit "because she has staked her professional reputation on the project's success."

> Similarly, the vice-president for research says she cannot let the president or the research manager know her reservations because the president is so committed to it that "I would probably get fired for insubordination if I questioned the project."

> Finally, the research manager says he cannot let the president or the vice-president know of his doubts about the project because of their extreme commitment to the project's success. All indicate that, in meetings with one another, they try to

---

[13] Irving Janis, *Victims of Groupthink: A Psychological Study of Foreign Policy Decisions and Fiascos* (Boston: Houghton-Mifflin, 1982).

[14] Harvey, "Managing Agreements in Organizations."

maintain an optimistic facade so that the others will not worry unduly about the project. The research director, in particular, admits to writing ambiguous progress reports so the president and the vice-president can "interpret them to suit themselves." In fact, he says he tends to slant them to the positive side, "given how committed the brass are."

The scent of the Abilene trail wafts from a paneled conference room, where the project budget is being considered for the following fiscal year. In the meeting itself, praises are heaped on the questionable project, and a unanimous decision is made to continue it for yet another year. Symbolically, the organization has boarded a bus to Abilene.

The group described above is having difficulty managing its disagreements. It is in cases such as these that greater conflict and disagreement among the members likely would result in a far superior solution. The benefits of confronting differences of opinion are missing. Instead, the organization has made a unanimous decision that *no one* privately supports.

Examples of groupthink are found throughout our history. The lack of preparedness of the U.S. Naval Forces for the Japanese attack on Pearl Harbor, President Kennedy's handling of the Bay of Pigs, and many of the roads paved for our entry into and continued involvement in the Vietnam War are a few very salient examples. From studying these and other examples of groupthink, Irving Janis has identified a number of symptoms that should signal a potential "groupthink situation" to decision makers. Fortunately, Janis provides managers and other decision makers with some guidelines for avoiding groupthink. His lists of symptoms and guidelines appear in Figure 9–1. As suggested in Chapter 7, cohesiveness is often viewed as a critical group trait. It is an extreme emphasis on cohesiveness (and consensus) that produces groupthink. However, note that not all cohesive groups are equally vulnerable to groupthink. When the group is cohesive because it functions well, groupthink is less likely to occur. When cohesiveness is based upon the group's attractive social milieu, then groupthink poses a bigger threat.[15]

Choice Shift Effects

Consider the following situation: You are one of six members of the R&D advisory committee for a large computer manufacturing firm for which you work. During your monthly meeting, your task is to determine which projects are to be funded. One of the decisions that faces your group in tomorrow's meeting is whether or not to fund a $2.2 million request for the development of a 128K memory chip. The product is so far ahead of today's chips that if the company is able to manufacture this chip successfully, there will be a minimum 50 percent return on your investment in the first two years of production. Other projects are also competing for these scarce resource dollars; their expected rate of return runs between 10 percent and 20 percent. What minimum probability for success would you consider necessary to invest the R&D money into the chip-manufacturing project?

Given the advantages of group decision making, should this decision be made by a group or by an individual? That is, which will require a lower probability of success for the computer chip manufacturing project? In such cases,

[15]J. Longley and D. G. Pruitt, "Groupthink: A Critique of Janis's Theory," in *Review of Personality and Social Psychology*, ed. L. Wheeler (Beverly Hills, Calif.: Sage Publishing Company, 1980).

FIGURE 9–1	▶Groupthink

Groupthink occurs when the members of a highly cohesive group lose their willingness to evaluate each other's inputs critically. The symptoms of groupthink listed here can be avoided by following several procedural guidelines for appropriate group discussion and choices.

Symptoms of Groupthink

▶ **Illusions of invulnerability:** Members of the group overemphasize the strength of the group and feel that they are beyond criticism or attack. This symptom leads the group to approve risky actions about which individual members might have serious concerns.

▶ **Illusions of unanimity:** Group members accept consensus prematurely, without testing whether or not all members *really* agree. Silence is often taken for agreement.

▶ **Illusions of group morality:** Members of the group feel that it is "right" and above reproach by outside members. Thus, members feel no need to debate ethical issues.

▶ **Stereotyping of the "enemy" as weak, evil, or stupid:** Members do not realistically examine their competitors and oversimplify their motives. The stated aims of outside groups or anticipated reactions of outsiders are not considered.

▶ **Self-censorship by members:** Members refuse to communicate concerns to others because of fear of disturbing the consensus.

▶ **Mind-guarding:** Some members take responsibility to ensure that negative feedback does not reach influential group members.

▶ **Direct pressure:** In the unlikely event that a note of caution or concern is interjected, other members quickly respond with pressure to bring the deviant back into line.

Guidelines for Avoiding Groupthink

▶ Assign the role of critical evaluator to each group member; encourage the sharing of objections.
▶ Avoid, as the leader, clear statements about your preferred alternative.
▶ Create subgroups or subcommittees, each working on the same problem.
▶ Require that members of the group make use of the information available to them through their subordinates, peers, and networks.
▶ Invite outside experts to observe and evaluate group process and outcome.
▶ Assign a member to play the devil's advocate role at each meeting.
▶ Focus on alternative scenarios for the motivation and intentions of competitors.
▶ Once consensus is reached, reexamine the next (but unchosen) alternative, comparing it to the chosen course of action.

Source: Irving L. Janis, *Groupthink*, 2d ed. (Boston: Houghton-Mifflin, 1982).

research suggests that groups will behave in a more risky manner than the average individual member of the group.[16] Thus, if your individual position is that the probability for success must exceed 25 percent before you are willing to fund this project, it is likely that the group will settle on a lower probability.

[16]J. A. Stoner, "A Comparison of Individual and Group Decisions Involving Risk," unpublished master's thesis (M.I.T., Sloan School of Industrial Management, 1961); and H. Lamm and D. G. Myers, "Group-Induced Polarization of Attitudes and Behavior" in *Advances in Experimental Social Psychology*, vol. 11, ed. L. Berkowitz (New York: Academic Press, 1978).

Were choice-shift effects to blame for the FBI's ill-fated decision in 1993 to raid the Branch Davidian sect's headquarters in Waco? After a 51-day standoff, FBI leaders may have felt they were facing only continued frustration if they did nothing and a chance to "break even" if they gambled, leading them to take an unjustifiably large risk.

This is known as the **risky shift.** In fact, both the group as a whole and each individual will be more willing to accept greater levels of risk after the group discussion than prior to it.

Yet groups do not always make risky shifts. In fact, there is documentation of just the opposite occurring—a **cautious shift.** A cautious shift occurs when group members make less risky decisions than the average of the individual members' decisions.

While many researchers have proposed mechanisms first to explain risky shift and then later to explain the cautious shift (both are now termed choice shifts), they have focused on two primary explanations: information exchange and social comparison. They suggest that individuals shift to more extreme positions following group discussion because members holding the dominant view (either risky or cautious) exchange information during these discussions and are exposed to views they had not previously considered. Further, individuals may also shift their perspectives to be more "in synch" with the group's attitudes. If the group favors risk, then the individual may see the advantages of being perceived as being even more risk seeking than the group, thus gaining idiosyncrasy credits.[17]

However, this notion of choice shift does little to aid managers in predicting whether the group in which they are involved will tend towards a cautious or a risky shift. Recent research, however, has suggested a different explanation for this choice-shift phenomenon that incorporates the decision biases discussed in Chapter 5.[18] It seems that whether groups shift towards risk or towards caution depends upon the type of decision being made. For example, a risky shift occurs in the choice between keeping one's current job and taking a new, potentially more lucrative position (a choice between potential gains). The decisions

---

[17]E. Burnstein, "Persuasion as Argument Processing," in *Group Decision Process*, eds. M. Brandstatter, J. Davis, and G. Stocker-Kreschgauer (London: Academic Press, 1983).

[18]M. A. Neale, M. H. Bazerman, G. B. Northcraft, and C. A. Alperson, "Choice Shift's Effects in Group Decisions: A Decision Bias Perspective," *International Journal of Small Group Research* 2 (1986): 33–42.

that commonly produce a cautious shift involve evaluating a choice among potential losses. A common example is a decision involving protecting the endangered life of an expectant mother.[19] Dichotomizing the choices in this way makes the framing of the issue (described in detail in Chapter 5) very salient. That is, it may be that groups move away from the risk level of individuals, but group decisions may not be affected by the framing bias. When individuals consider risky decisions involving potential gains, they are risk averse rather than risk neutral. Groups may appear to be shifting toward risk in these situations when, in reality, they are simply behaving in a risk-neutral manner.

The same logic can apply to the cautious shift. When individuals are confronted with decisions involving potential losses, they are risk seeking rather than risk neutral. Groups may appear to be less risky when, in fact, they are simply behaving in a risk-neutral manner. While these findings are tentative, they certainly are compatible with the belief that group decision making is often superior to individual decision making. The whole area of whether or not group decision making can reduce the vulnerability of decision makers to cognitive bias is just beginning to receive attention.[20]

SOLUTIONS IN GROUP DECISION MAKING ◆◆◆◆◆◆

When a manager is faced with making a decision, he or she may (1) unilaterally make the decision based solely on the information at hand, (2) unilaterally make the decision but solicit input on the problem from others, or (3) involve others in both providing input and making the actual decision. Because the goal of a manager is making a good decision—one that is timely, acceptable, implementable, and high in quality—it is critical that the manager be able to use these three levels of participative decision making when they are most appropriate and most likely to produce a good decision.

When to Use Group Decision Making	**Levels of Participation in Decision Making** Victor Vroom and Phillip Yetton have developed guidelines for helping managers choose the most appropriate decision-making methods for a variety of situations routinely encountered in daily activities. Initially, they divide the three levels of participative decision making (authoritative, AI or AII; consultative, CI or CII; and group decision making, G) into five levels:

▶ *AI.* In this, the most authoritarian decision-making level, the manager solves the problem or makes the decision based upon information available at that time.

▶ *AII.* The manager obtains the necessary information from subordinates or peers and then makes the decision. The manager may or may not tell those subordinates or peers the nature of the problem. Further, they do not have the option of suggesting or evaluating alternatives.

▶ *CI.* The manager conveys the problem to relevant peers or subordinates, soliciting their ideas and suggestions without bringing them

---

[19] Stoner, "A Comparison of Individual and Group Decisions Involving Risk."

[20] M. A. Neale, et al., "Choice Shift's Effects in Group Decisions."

together as a group. While the other group members have input, the manager makes the decision, which may or may not reflect the others' influence.

▶ *CII.* The manager conveys the problem to subordinates or peers, soliciting their ideas and suggestions as a group. While the group members may collectively make suggestions and provide input, the manager still makes the decision, which may or may not reflect the input of the group.

▶ *G.* The manager conveys the problem to subordinates and peers as a group and the group, through consensus, determines the final solution.

From the manager's perspective, then, the first aspect of making a decision is deciding who will be in the cast of characters that determines the solution. Consider the following problem:

> You are the head of the staff unit reporting to the vice-president of finance. He has asked you to provide a report on the firm's current portfolio to include recommendations for changes in the selection criteria currently employed. Doubts have been raised about the efficiency of the existing system given current market conditions, and there is considerable dissatisfaction with the prevailing rates of return.
>
> You plan to write a report, but at the moment, you are quite perplexed about the approach you should take. Your own specialty is the bond market, and it is quite clear to you that a detailed knowledge of the equity market—which you lack—would greatly enhance the value of the report. Fortunately, four members of your staff are specialists in different segments of the equity market. Together they possess a vast amount of knowledge about the intricacies of investment. However, they seldom agree on the best way to achieve anything when it comes to the stock market. Although they are obviously conscientious as well as knowledgeable, they have major differences when it comes to investment philosophy and strategy.
>
> You have six weeks before the report is due. You have already begun to familiarize yourself with the firm's current portfolio and have been provided by management with a specific set of constraints that any portfolio must satisfy. Your immediate problem is to come up with some alternatives to the firm's present practices and select the most promising for detailed analysis in your report. Given this problem, would you make your decision using AI, AII, CI, CII, or G?[21]

Problem Characteristics   Vroom and Yetton suggest that the correct level of participation in decision making depends upon various characteristics of the problem at hand.[22] They have identified seven characteristics that can be used to diagnose the problem and determine what level of decision making should be used. The seven characteristics and their associated questions are described in Figure 9–2. These characteristics are arranged in the form of questions on a decision tree. The end of each path identifies the optimal level of participation in decision making recommended. The full decision tree is illustrated in Figure 9–3. While each path ends with a specific level of decision participation, Vroom and Yetton suggest that when there is enough time, the manager may choose an option in the feasible set that lends itself to greater subordinate participation. That is, when the decision suggests an autocratic solution is appropriate, the

---

[21] V. H. Vroom and P. Yetton, *Leadership and Decision Making* (Pittsburgh: University of Pittsburgh Press, 1973).

[22] Ibid.

| FIGURE 9–2 | ▶ Problem Characteristics and Diagnostic Questions in the Vroom and Yetton Model |

A. The importance of the quality of the decision

Is there a quality requirement such that one solution is likely to be more rational than another?

B. The extent to which the leader possesses sufficient information or expertise to make a high-quality decision alone

Do I have sufficient information to make a high-quality decision?

C. The extent to which the problem is structured

Is the problem structured? Do I know what information is required and where it is located?

D. The extent to which acceptance or commitment on the part of the subordinates is critical to the effective implementation of the decision

Is acceptance of the decision by subordinates critical to effective implementation? Can I do it without their support?

E. The probability that my autocratic decision will receive acceptance by subordinates

If I were to make the decision by myself, is it reasonably certain that it will be accepted by my subordinates?

F. The extent to which the subordinates are motivated to attain the organizational goals as represented in the objectives explicit in the statement of the problem

Do subordinates share the organizational goals to be obtained in solving this problem? Or do they have personal considerations that might dominate?

G. The extent to which subordinates are likely to be in conflict over preferred solutions

Is conflict among subordinates likely in preferred solutions?

Source: V. H. Vroom, "A New Look at Managerial Decision Making," *Organizational Dynamics* (Spring 1973): 69–70. Reprinted by permission of publisher. American Management Association, New York. All rights reserved.

manager might also use a more participative style—C or G; when a consultative solution is appropriate, the manager might also use a G decision.

Now let's consider the problem facing you, the manager. Examining the problem from the perspective of the Vroom and Yetton decision tree in Figure 9–3, the first question concerns a quality requirement. Is one solution likely to be significantly better than others? In the case of the stock portfolio, the answer is yes. The second question concerns whether you have sufficient information to make the decision on your own. Clearly, you do not. Since the problem of stock portfolio selection criteria is not a structured one, the last question you will have to answer is whether acceptance by subordinates is critical to implementation. Since the decision will be implemented by your superiors, acceptance of the solution by subordinates is irrelevant. This particular path ends after the fourth question and indicates that you should use the CII level of participation. Thus, you should involve the subordinates as a group in offering ideas and suggestions, but make the final decision as to the preferred stock portfolio selection criteria yourself.

This model has been supported by research. Vroom and Yetton found that managers who had been trained to use these problem characteristics to diagnose

| **FIGURE 9–3** | ▶ **Decision Tree for Determining Appropriate Decision Strategy** |

A. Does the problem possess a quality requirement?
B. Do I have sufficient information to make a high-quality decision?
C. Is the problem structured?
D. Is acceptance of the decision by subordinates important for effective implementation?
E. If I were to make the decision by myself, am I reasonably certain that it would be accepted by my subordinates?
F. Do subordinates share the organizational goals to be attained in solving this problem?
G. Is conflict among subordinates likely in preferred solutions?

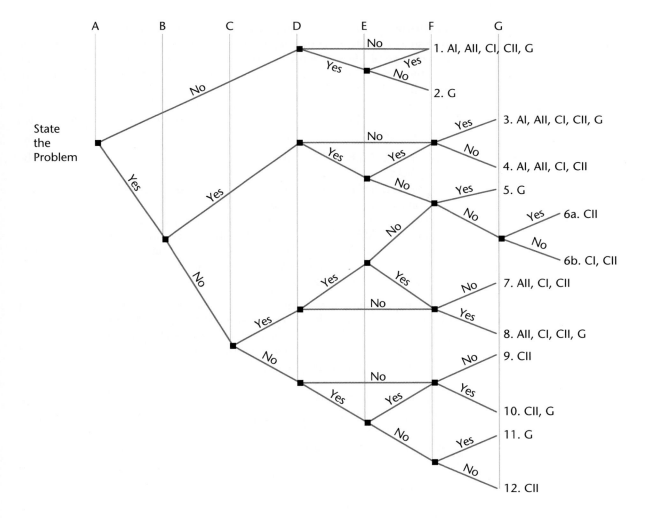

Source: Victor H. Vroom and Philip W. Yetton, *Leadership and Decision Making* (Pittsburgh: University of Pittsburgh Press, 1973). Reprinted by permission of the University of Pittsburgh Press.

the optimal level of participation in decision making were better able to classify decision problems and choose appropriate participation levels than managers without such training.[23] There is also evidence that increased managerial skill in determining the correct level of participation increases the effectiveness of managerial decision making.[24]

How to Use Group Decision Making

Once the number of individuals to be involved in making the decision has been determined, the next step is to determine how the group is to reach a decision. In selecting a particular group decision-making process, the intent is to minimize the liabilities of groups and maximize their benefits. Three different techniques will be described below: brainstorming, nominal group technique, and the Delphi technique.[25]

Brainstorming An advertising executive developed **brainstorming** over 30 years ago as a means of enhancing creativity by encouraging the free discussion and exchange of ideas. Brainstormers are encouraged to produce as many and as creative a set of ideas or alternatives as possible and simultaneously are prohibited from being critical of the ideas generated. When practiced correctly, brainstorming separates the evaluative stage from the idea-generation stage of decision making. The basic structure of a brainstorming session is determined by four rules:[26]

1. *No criticism!* Adverse judgments about your own or others' ideas are to be withheld.
2. *"Freewheeling" is invited.* No idea is too wild or crazy. The more creative or unusual the idea, the better.
3. *Quantity is desired.* Generate as many ideas as possible. The greater the number of ideas, the greater the likelihood that one will work.
4. *"Piggybacking" is encouraged.* Participants should build upon the ideas and suggestions of others. Combining and extending other ideas is a critical aspect of successful brainstorming.

The primary intent of brainstorming is to reduce the participants' fears of criticism and provide multiple sources of stimulation for creative problem solving. In general, brainstorming can work to improve the quantity and quality of ideas or alternatives generated. However, for brainstorming to work, it is critical that evaluation and criticism be suppressed until all ideas are "on the table."[27]

Nominal Group Technique While brainstorming focuses on generating new and creative ideas, the **nominal group technique (NGT)** focuses on gen-

---

[23] V. H. Vroom, "A New Look in Managerial Decision Making," *Organizational Dynamics* (Spring 1973): 66–80.

[24] See V. H. Vroom and A. G. Jago, "On the Validity of the Vroom-Yetton Model," *Journal of Applied Psychology* 63 (1978): 151–162; and R. H. Field, "A Test of the Vroom-Yetton Normative Model of Leadership," *Journal of Applied Psychology* 67 (1982): 523–532.

[25] See A. F. Osborn, *Applied Imagination* (New York: Scribner's, 1957); and A. L. Delbecq, A. L. Van de Ven, and D. H. Gustafson, *Group Techniques for Program Planning: A Guide to Nominal Groups and Delphi Techniques* (Glenview, Ill.: Scott, Foresman, 1975).

[26] Osborn, *Applied Imagination.*

[27] S. J. Parnes, R. B. Noller, and A. M. Biondi, *A Guide to Creative Action* (New York: Scribner's, 1977).

Brainstorming enhances creativity by encouraging the free exchange of ideas among group members. Individuals are encouraged to come up with unusual solutions and to add on to suggestions made by others. No alternatives are evaluated until all ideas are "on the table."

erating alternatives and selecting among them. Conducted within the context of a group meeting, NGT has the following structure:

1. Individuals silently and independently write down their ideas and alternative solutions to a stated problem.
2. All members take turns presenting their ideas, and these ideas are recorded on a chart or chalkboard.
3. The ideas are discussed only in terms of clarification. Evaluative comments are not allowed.
4. A written voting procedure is followed, which results in a ranking of the alternatives.

The exact voting procedure is determined in advance, and the winning alternative becomes the selected alternative. NGT is a very useful process when there is considerable inhibition, hostility, or a dominant individual. An example of the use of NGT is described in the "FOCUS ON: Nominal Group Techniques."

The Delphi Technique For situations in which group members cannot meet face to face, the RAND Corporation developed a group decision-making technique that offers many of the benefits of face-to-face interaction—the **Delphi technique.** Like the NGT, the Delphi technique minimizes the effects of different levels of status and influence on group decision making, but it does not require that the group members convene in the same physical space. Instead of reporting and recording alternatives as in the NGT, participants in the Delphi technique answer a series of questionnaires. A Delphi group might function as follows:

1. The first questionnaire distributed to members identifies the problem and asks for alternative solutions to it.
2. The Delphi coordinator summarizes the solutions, and the summary is returned to participants in the form of a second questionnaire specifically designed to identify areas requiring further clarification and consideration.

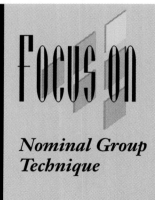

Nominal Group Technique

ARA Services ARA Services used a nominal group technique to identify and resolve a number of the problems encountered during its reorganization from a product-based organizational structure to a geographical-based structure. In particular, the NGT was used to focus on the human problems associated with the change in structure. ARA had initially tried to break up the affected managers into teams to discuss their concerns. Realizing that this technique was not producing the desired outcomes, the company then tried the NGT. Using this technique the company was able to generate alternatives for solving specific problems that had been identified within the groups. Many of the solutions were put into effect, and through the use of NGT the reorganization was completed in one year rather than the proposed two years. In addition, there was no reduction in sales volume, but there was a reduction in managerial turnover.

Along with identifying problems with and developing solutions for the organizational restructuring, NGT was also used at ARA to identify new leaders in the restructured organization. The persons who were selected to lead the new divisions were trained in NGT before meeting the new members of their teams. During the initial meeting with their new subordinates, the new division heads used their skills in NGT to develop group goals, provide direction for achieving these goals, and consider each person's contribution to the group's performance. This became the primary means of establishing new management teams.

Source: Andre L. Delbecq, Andrew H. Van de Ven, and David H. Gustafson, *Group Techniques for Program Planning: A Guide to Nominal Group and Delphi Processes* (Glenview, Ill.: Scott, Foresman, 1975): xii–xiv.

3. The results of the second questionnaire are presented to the participants, who rate the various alternatives presented.
4. The members' ratings are tabulated, and a summary of the data and resulting decision is returned to the participants.

NGT and the Delphi technique are very similar. The primary differences lie in the physical presence or absence of the group. The Delphi technique allows group members to remain anonymous (very helpful for particularly sensitive issues) but requires considerably more time.

Group members who interact often spend much time developing interpersonal relationships, discussing tangential issues, and maintaining pressure for conformity. They also may be unduly influenced by the status, persuasiveness, or seniority of various group members.[28] Thus, when a manager is confronted with a problem in which the generation of creative alternatives is critical and criticism must be held to a minimum, the NGT or Delphi technique may be most appropriate.

The manager, however, should not ignore the potential pitfalls of these methods. In using these two methods of group decision making, managers run three risks. First, because of a lack of discussion and clarification, group members may lack understanding about the problem or the final solution. Second, it is difficult to adopt a truly creative solution through these techniques because the ideas of the minority are usually not clarified. Third, because of the lack of

[28] G. P. Huber, *Managerial Decision Making* (Glenview, Ill.: Scott, Foresman, 1980).

face-to-face interaction, the group members may have developed little commitment to the solution.[29]

Groups do have a great deal to offer management in producing good decisions. However, it is important to remember that there are both advantages and disadvantages to group decision making. The three methods discussed here are based upon the notion that the effectiveness of group decision making is equal to the potential effectiveness of the combined inputs of the members minus the losses in effectiveness that follow from the group processes plus the gains in effectiveness from group processes.[30] In other words:

$$\frac{\text{Actual}}{\text{Effectiveness}} = \frac{\text{Potential}}{\text{Effectiveness}} - \frac{\text{Process}}{\text{Losses}} + \frac{\text{Process}}{\text{Gains}}$$

Process gains include many of the benefits of group decision making outlined early in this chapter, such as synergy, resource pooling, and task specialization. *Process losses* are the costs of group decision making, such as groupthink, undue social influence, or time.

Why Group Decision Making Works[31]

Since the Hawthorne studies described in Chapter 2, managers and organizational scholars have known about the profound influence that groups can have on individual productivity. American managers have even witnessed their own group-oriented technologies being exported to Japan with amazing results. Participative management is a very close relative of work-group activities. Although the nature of group decision making is not novel or unique to American managers, if you examine exactly how decisions are made in organizations and how they are structured, you will likely find individuals—not groups—are primary. Why is it that group decision making has been so consistently eschewed in favor of individual decision making?

A primary reason for this bias towards individual decision making lies in the rationality notion, which assumes that the individual is the elemental unit of organization. This traditional view of organizations is consistent with the assumptions underlying much of American culture. That is, individuals are taught the value and importance of individual achievement. From the individual's perspective, organizations merely represent arenas in which to compete for individual accomplishment, recognition, and satisfaction. This is clearly different from the Japanese emphasis on group performance.

Organizations, however, need to control, or at least direct, this individual achievement along the lines of common organizational objectives. This individual achievement-orientation, coupled with the organization's attempt to mold and direct activity, leads to constant tension between the organization and the individual. Groups first make their appearance in response to this tension,

---

[29]J. Bartunek and K. Murnighan, "Nominal Group Techniques," *Group and Organizational Studies* 9 (1984): 417–432.

[30]J. R. Hackman and C. G. Morris, "Group Tasks, Group Interaction Process, and Group Performance Effectiveness," *Advances in Experimental Social Psychology* vol. 7, ed. L. Berkowitz (New York: Academic Press, 1975).

[31]Much of this discussion is based upon Harold Leavitt's 1975 article "Suppose We Took Groups Seriously . . . ," which appeared in E. L. Cass and F. G. Zimmer, eds., *Man and Work in Society*, Van Nostrand Reinhold.

through the development of worker coalitions to resist the control and influence of the organization.

With the discovery that groups could positively influence individual performance, groups took on an entirely new light. They were used by management to (1) relieve or reduce the tension between the individual and the organization, (2) coordinate individual activities, and (3) discipline and control nonconforming group members. However, organizations were not designed around groups. Rather, groups were tacked on to existing organizational structures—structures that were based on the individual. Thus, the very structure of the groups and the processes that would heighten productivity became a two-edged sword. Groups were too slow and too democratic. They created in-groups that were hard for outsiders to penetrate, and they diffused responsibility for decision making. Although management could never completely remove groups as a source of influence on organizational members, their importance in the structure of the organization has remained ancillary. It is as if "someone had insisted that automobiles be designed to fit the existing terrain rather than build roads to adapt to the automobile."[32]

What might be the advantages of an organization designed around groups? First, the amount of control required would be reduced. Rather than having to supervise every individual directly, the group would supervise its members. Second, individuals have many fewer units with whom they must interact. Rather than interacting with each individual on the traditional organizational chart, the group member would interact with many fewer organizational units or groups, although each unit would be larger. Finally, the increased cohesiveness, motivation, commitment, and higher-quality decisions that flow from group interactions would become a routine benefit for an organization so structured.

What must happen for organizations to take advantage of the potential productivity and decision benefits of groups? Must organizations be restructured to incorporate groups, and if so, what might they resemble? Such organizations would have to select, train, pay, evaluate, and promote groups rather than individuals. Jobs would have to be designed for groups, and an entire group would be at risk for termination or relocation if it did not meet performance expectations.

While these ideas initially go against our embedded ideas about how organizations should function, consider, for a moment, whether managing groups might not be easier than managing individuals. For example, it would probably be easier for upper-level management to evaluate the performance of a work group than to evaluate the contribution of an individual member. Paying groups rather than individuals would increase the collaboration and cooperation among group members.[33] Allocation of rewards to individual members could be delegated to the group. Thus, the likelihood of yoking productivity contributions to rewards may be greater, since group members would have considerable opportunity to observe each other and would be much closer than a supervisor to the activities involved in producing the good or service.

Selecting a group rather than an individual may pose some unique problems. However, an organization could certainly hire individuals not only for

[32] Ibid., p. 3.

[33] M. Deutsch, "Equity, Equality, and Need: What Determines Which Will Be Used as the Basis of Distributive Justice?" *Journal of Social Issues* 31 (1975): 137–149.

their skills and abilities but also for their ability to work together. A step in this direction has been undertaken by the J. L. Kellogg Graduate School of Management at Northwestern University. Unlike most top business schools, Kellogg requires that all applicants—over 5,000 in 1991—be interviewed as part of the admission procedure. The interview is held to ensure that the 480 students admitted to the master's in management program "fit" together—a critical component of an education that relies heavily on classroom experiences structured around the concept of small-group decision making.[34] A slightly different perspective on group selection is illustrated by the hiring practices of the Macintosh group at Apple Computer. The Macintosh group interviewed all candidates for inclusion in the group. To become a member of the Macintosh group, an applicant had to garner group approval. The use of groups as decision-making entities is commonplace in other cultures. The importance of groups in the decision making of Japanese companies is illustrated in the "INTERNATIONAL FOCUS ON: Group Decision Making."

Promoting, transferring, relocating, or terminating an entire group seems considerably more problematic. As one moves up the hierarchy in most organizations, the importance of individual action looms larger, particularly as it relates to leadership. Without individual leaders, the task of directing, coordinating, and controlling the organization may be ignored or poorly orchestrated. Interestingly, however, in a few organizations, such as Hartmarx Corp., a management group, troika, or triumvirate controls the direction of the organization.[35] Further, as we will discuss in Chapter 10, work groups may serve as a substitute for leadership.

Transferring groups seems expensive until one considers the benefits of such transfers. Transferring groups of people and their families may make such a change more bearable. Support groups and networks would remain unbroken, and the need to develop new working relationships would be minimized.

While the hiring of groups is not yet a reality, a number of organizations are now involved in the first steps along such a path. O'Melveny & Myers, one of the nation's largest law firms, has hired several married couples. Martin Marietta, the aerospace and defense contractor, actually has a hire-a-couple policy. Personnel administrator Joseph Weiner notes "eight out of ten times, the recruited person is married to someone with skills we can use."[36] (Interestingly enough, the hiring of couples would require a two-person decision-making process on the part of the applicants. In the case of the group, the decision to accept the offer would entail a group decision-making process!)

Terminating the group is probably the most difficult problem to confront. Wholesale dismissal of work groups may unnecessarily limit the flexibility of management. Of course, the poor performance of a group does not always reflect the poor performance of all individual members. It might well be that a poorly performing group should be dissolved and its members reassigned to other groups.

Some of these notions concerning group-based organizations seem unwieldy at first glance. However, such group-oriented activities are occurring in a variety of modern organizations. The issue seems to be to what extent such

---

[34]"Business Schools: Money Majors," *U.S. News and World Report*, November 2, 1987, 81–83.

[35]S. Weiner, "A New Cut for the Gray Flannel," *Forbes*, December 28, 1987, 61–62.

[36]A. Toufexis, "Dual Careers, Doleful Dilemmas," *Time*, November 16, 1987, 90.

Making Decisions in Japanese Companies An increasing number of Americans are employed by Japanese firms, primarily firms that have plants or factories here or need to have a major presence in the United States. These employees have a unique opportunity to observe in detail the decision-making styles of Japanese managers. Geoffrey Tudor, an employee of Japan Air Lines, reports that the Japanese manager who made a decision unilaterally would quickly be removed from his or her position (in a way that would "save face"). Thomas Cappiello, a public relations officer for Nissho Iwai, a Japanese trading company, believes that the Japanese definition of a good leader is not one who makes decisions; but one who discovers the decisions subordinates have made.

If Japanese managers want to make sure a certain alternative is selected, they must plant the idea of this particular solution with some subordinates. The subordinates will then analyze the suggested solution, among others, and determine how best to solve the problem. According to John Macklin, an executive at Fujitsu, a manager whose preferred solution is accepted will then compliment the subordinates on their good idea and decision.

Source: "Outsiders in Japanese Companies," *Fortune*, July 12, 1982, 114–128.

changes will be institutionalized in future organizations. More detailed comments on the future of organizations and organizational behavior are presented in Chapter 18.

SUMMARY ◆◆◆◆◆◆

Using groups to make decisions is not a new idea. For years, group decision making has been known to foster increased communication, commitment, development, and ownership of the problem and solution among group members. Groups are often able to outperform individuals in making decisions, particularly when the quality and acceptability of the decision are important.

Unfortunately, group decision making is not without its difficulties. Using groups as the basis for a decision increases the complexity of the decision process. The more individuals involved in coming up with a solution, the more information each individual member must process, the more complex the rules governing decision acceptance, and the more complex the interpersonal processes. As a result,

groups require considerably more time and resources to make a decision than do individuals. Groups may also be influenced by factors or processes that do not affect individuals, such as groupthink or choice shift. Groupthink occurs primarily among highly cohesive groups and results in a decision process that emphasizes conformity and suppresses criticism. Choice-shift effects indicate that groups may be either more or less risky than their average individual members.

Deciding when to take advantage of the benefits of group decision making and when to rely on an individual decision-making process is an important component in solving organizational problems. Vroom and Yetton have developed guidelines for determining whether a group or an individual is the most appropriate decision maker. If the decision requires acceptance by subordinates, if one alternative is qualitatively better than another, and if the group possesses information necessary for the selection of an alternative, then group decision making is likely to be the preferred option.

After deciding *who* should make the decision, one must decide *how* the decision is to be made. Three methods of group decision making were described in this chapter—brainstorming, the nominal group technique, and the Delphi technique. All are designed to enhance the benefits and reduce the costs of group decision making. For example, brainstorming, the nominal group technique, and the Delphi technique separate the creative, idea-generation process from the critical, idea-evaluative phase of decision making.

The lack of more group decision-making activities in organizations is puzzling. Groups, it seems, have not been taken seriously in organizations in the United States. Rather, group

and their decision-making processes are often viewed as temporary or Band-Aid measures to reduce the tension between worker and organization, to coordinate individual activities, and to control or discipline group members. They have not been the basis for new organizational structures and, as such, have been doomed to play a tangential role in organizational life.

While converting our individual-oriented organizations to group-oriented structures may take some creative problem solving, a number of organizations are beginning to head in that direction. Groups have been shown to be effective in both manufacturing and service organizations. Group decision making, however, is not without its costs. The decision facing today's manager, then, is how to improve the decision process. Part of the eventual solution will likely be the involvement of groups and group decision making.

Key Terms

Brainstorming Group creativity technique facilitating free discussion and exchange of ideas by withholding criticism of ideas, encouraging unusual ideas, generating as many ideas as possible, and piggybacking ideas.

Cautious shift Tendency of a group as a whole and each member to be less willing to accept risk after a group discussion than prior to it.

Delphi technique Group decision-making technique that minimizes interaction among members; members complete mailed questionnaires and a coordinator summarizes results.

Groupthink Tendency in highly cohesive groups for members to seek consensus so strongly that they lose the willingness and ability to evaluate one another's ideas critically.

Nominal group technique (NGT) Group decision-making technique that focuses on generating alternatives and selecting among them by asking group members to independently write down ideas, present them in turn, clarify them for the group, and rank them by voting privately.

Resource pooling An advantage groups have over individuals by combining the perspectives, ideas, suggestions, and information of all members.

Risky shift Tendency of a group as a whole and each member to be more willing to accept greater levels of risk after a group discussion than prior to it.

Synergy Mutual influence process of stimulation and encouragement among members of a group.

Discussion Questions

1. Consider the decision-making process in a group project you are involved in. What are some benefits you as an individual experienced that directly related to the group and its decision-making process? What are some liabilities you as an individual incurred?

2. When groups convene to make decisions, one of their first acts typically is to determine *how* a decision will be made. What type of decision rule is likely to encourage the greatest amount of information exchange? The most political behavior? Coalition formation among group members? High commitment to the decision? Why?

3. Even when it is in the best interest of a manager to involve subordinates in making a decision, he or she often makes it autocratically. What are some reasons why managers choose an autocratic decision-making process over a group decision-making process, regardless of the quality of the outcome?

4. What are the advantages and disadvantages of brainstorming?

5. Why might a manager choose to collect group members' suggestions and preferences with a Delphi method rather than using a nominal group technique?

6. Groupthink is typically viewed as a group decision-making *error*. In what types of groups or situations might a manager encourage groupthink?

7. What are some of the major advantages and disadvantages to managing by groups?

If You Want to Know More

While the study of group decision making has a rather long history, it has received more practitioner and scholar interest in recent years. Part of this resurgent interest can be traced to two books that illustrated the importance and influence of groups in making decisions. First was Graham T. Allison's book, *Essence of Decision* (Boston: Little Brown, 1971). Second was Irving Janis's initial work, entitled *Victims of Groupthink: A Psychological Study of Foreign Policy Decisions and Fiascos* (Boston: Houghton-Mifflin, 1972), and his subsequent book *Group-think* (Boston: Houghton-Mifflin, 1982).

In attempting to maximize the benefits derived from groups while simultaneously avoiding their liabilities, different group processes were described and tested. A. F. Osborn's *Applied Imagination* (New York: Scribner, 1957) and A. Delbecq, A. Van de Ven, and D. Gustafson's *Group Techniques for Program Planning: A Guide to Nominal Groups and Delphi Techniques* (Glenview, Ill.: Scott, Foresman, 1975) provided three different decision-making processes for groups. The current interest in participation and group decision making is most likely a result of the Japanese experience with quality circles.

Many of the topics presented in this chapter on group decision making are addressed in greater detail in J. McGrath's *Groups: Interaction and Performance* (Englewood Cliffs, N.J.: Prentice-Hall, 1984) as well as in two edited volumes: H. Brandstatter, J. Davis, and G. Stocker-Kreichgauer's *Group Decision Making* (New York: Academic Press, 1982). Another series of articles directed towards the beginning student of group decision making is in the book *Group Decision Making*, edited by W.

Swap and his associates (Beverly Hills: Sage Publishing, 1984).

For a recent review of the participation research to which group decision making is an important contributor, see E. Locke and D. Schweiger's "Participation in Decision Making: One More Look" in B. Staw's *Research in Organizational Behavior* (Greenwich, Conn.: JAI Press, 1979). For a more practical perspective on when to use participative decision making, the interested reader may wish to examine V. Vroom and P. Yetton's *Leadership and Decision Making* (Pittsburgh: University of Pittsburgh Press, 1973).

On Your Own

In the discussion of when to use group decision making, we presented an example of a managerial problem and used the Vroom-Yetton model of decision making to determine who should be involved in the decision-making process. Below are two other problem scenarios. Should the manager in each case use an autocratic (I or II), consultative (I or II), or group decision-making process?

Scenario One   You are on the division manager's staff and work on a wide variety of problems of both an administrative and technical nature. You have been given the assignment of developing a universal method to be used in each of five plants in a division for manually reading equipment registers, recording the readings, and transmitting the scorings to a centralized information system. All plants are located in a relatively small geographic region.

Until now there has been a high error rate in the readings and/or transmittal of the data. Some locations have considerably higher error rates than others, and the methods used to record and transmit the data vary between plants. It is probable, therefore, that part of the error variance is a function of specific local conditions rather than anything else, and this will complicate the establishment of any system common to all plants. You have the information on error rates but no information on local practices that generate these errors or on the local conditions that necessitate the different practices.

Everyone would benefit from an improvement in the quality of the data because they are used in a number of important decisions. Your contacts with the plants are through the quality-control supervisors, who are responsible for collecting the data. They are a conscientious group committed to doing their jobs well, but are highly sensitive to interference on the part of top management in their own operations. Any solution that does not receive the active support of the various plant supervisors is unlikely to reduce the error rate significantly.

Scenario Two   You are supervising the work of twelve engineers. Their formal training and work experience are very similar, permitting you to use them interchangeably on projects. Yesterday, your manager informed you that a request had been received from an overseas affiliate for four engineers to go abroad on extended loan for a period of six to eight months. For a number of reasons, you agreed that this request should be met from your group.

All your engineers are capable of handling this assignment, and from the standpoint of present and future projects, there is no particular reason why any one should be retained over any other. The problem is somewhat complicated by the fact that the overseas assignment is in what is generally regarded in the company as an undesirable location.

Source: Reprinted from *Leadership and Decision Making* by Victor H. Vroom and Philip W. Yetton, by permission of the University of Pittsburgh Press. © 1973 by University of Pittsburgh Press.

CHAPTER 9

THE MANAGER'S MEMO

FROM: P. Dorian, Administrator

TO: J. Sternberg, M.D.

RE: Ethics Task Force

I have been considering your request that the hospital convene an ethics panel whenever we receive a request that some or all treatment be withheld from a patient presumed to be dying. I can't help but be concerned by the idea of tying up the time of a doctor, nurse, social worker, chaplain, family members, and possibly others every time we need to make such a decision. Obviously, this would be costly.

When I started in the business, we took it for granted that doctors made all the decisions about treatment—with the OK of the patient and family members, of course. I'm afraid I don't understand the benefits of the change you are proposing. What do we gain from all the time we would have to invest?

Case Discussion Questions

Assume you are Dr. Sternberg, and respond to the hospital administrator's memo. Support your position with what you have learned about when and how group decision making can be beneficial. Who will benefit most from the group process? Who will bear most of the costs and disadvantages? If you wish, you can assume that you have changed your mind about recommending the formation of a task force. If so, use material from the chapter to support this new viewpoint.

◆◆◆◆◆◆

LEADERSHIP

Focus on the Benefits of Leadership: CEOs' Pay:
Large Differences between the Top and the Bottom

Focus on the Burdens of Leadership:
One Bluff Too Many: Salomon and Gutfreund Get
Snagged in Scandal

International Focus on Leadership:
Literature and Chinese Leadership

Formal and Informal Leadership

Leadership As a Managerial Role

Universal Approaches to Leadership

Trait Approaches

Focus on Transformational Leaders:
WANTED: Leaders Who Can Make a Difference

Behavior Approaches

Focus on Leader Behaviors: Women Executives:
What Makes for Success?

Contingency Approaches to Leadership

Trait Approaches

Focus on Leadership Contingencies:
Successful Leaders, Different Styles

Behavior Approaches

Alternative Theories of Leadership

Leader-Member Exchange Model

Attribution Model of Leadership

Substitutes for Leadership

Focus on Substitutes for Leadership:
Leading without Leaders, Managing without
Managers

WHALES, HUMAN RIGHTS, RAIN FORESTS, AND THE HEADY SMELL OF PROFITS ◆◆◆◆◆◆

At 48, Anita Roddick has made herself one of the richest women in Britain by selling cosmetics, an industry she herself suggests is one that is run by men, creating needs that don't exist. However, in her cosmetics business, she has rewritten the rules and has managed to create a $16 billion global organization with 620 shops worldwide. Rather than sell her products through department stores, she has her own chain of shops; rather than appealing to vanity to market her wares, she emphasizes a concern for the environment and social issues.

As managing director of Body Shops, International, Roddick is responsible for marketing and product development. But her pitch is unique in the belief that businesses can also improve the world. She does not spend any money on advertising, but she does stock literature in her shops for environmental groups, uses recycled containers, supports three orphanages in Romania, and helps out those in third-world countries that help supply her with her products. Of course, in these days of increased environmental awareness, others are trying to play Roddick's game. Estee Lauder, Inc., introduced Origins, a product line that uses natural ingredients and recycled containers and opened its first stand-alone store in Cambridge, Massachusetts. The Limited also opened 42 Bath and Body Works shops that are, at least in appearance, extremely similar to Roddick's Body Shops.

What is concerning her now is that a whole new vocabulary is creeping into her company. Words like three-year plans, net income, and average sales. Then there is the increasing obsession with meetings; and the coffee stains on the new carpeting at headquarters; and the paper that is wasted, and the lights left on after meetings. Her concern is that these behaviors are reflective of a fat-cat mentality sneaking into the organization.

The Body Shops sales and profits have been growing an average of 50 percent per year for the last ten years. And that is without spending any money on advertising. Indeed, there is not even a marketing department—an amazing feat for a company within an industry that is as marketing intensive as any. The reason for this success is that the Body Shop approaches its employees in the same way it approaches its customers. The Body Shop emphasizes information. It teaches with a deluge of videos, brochures, training programs, posters, and newsletters. The company newsletter, for example, is very different from others of its kind. More space is devoted to the company's environmental causes than to the opening of a new store. Roddick is probably the only chief executive who actually invests time and energy into the company newsletter. She is committed to getting across to her employees and customers the aspects of the organization that make business interesting and exciting. In addition, the Body Shops' social action campaigns are aimed primarily at creating excitement and enthusiasm in her shops among the work force. She reports, "I'd never get this kind of motivation if I were just selling shampoo and body lotion. I'd never get the sort of staying late, talking at McDonald's after work, bonding to customers. It is a way for people to bond to the company. They are doing what I am doing. They're learning. It is a process of learning to be a global citizen. And what it produces is a sense of passion you simply won't find in a Bloomingdale's department store."

Even with her obvious success and the increasing attention being paid her by rivals, Roddick has not taken on the typical management strategy of staying in the executive suite plotting strategy. Instead, she leaves the daily administrative activities to her husband and keeps up a frenetic pace: investigating new ingredients for her potions in the rain forests of Brazil, posing for a documentary with the Wodaabe tribe in Niger, or lecturing on one of the causes (such as Amnesty International) that she and the Body Shops support. Roddick has always loved the stage and worked in her mother's pub in Littlehampton. Her delight and success in working the crowd led her to dream of becoming some kind of performer. But after college, she worked for the United Nations and as a teacher. After marrying Gordon Roddick, they ran an inn and then a restaurant. However, when Gordon decided to fulfill a dream and ride horseback across South America in 1976, Roddick opened her first Body Shop to support herself and her children. When her husband returned a year later, she was preparing to open her third shop. Interestingly, pragmatism rather than activism mandated her interest in recycling. She only had 600 bottles and wanted people to return them. As for the unusual color of her stores—green—Roddick reports that the walls of her first shop were green because it was the only color that would hide the damp patches on the walls; now she is not messing with success. Roddick vows that regardless of how competitive the business gets or how successful the business becomes, she expects to remain the banner-waver that she is now.

Sources: Laura Zinn, "Whales, Human Rights, Rain Forest—and the Heady Smell of Success." *Business Week*, July 15, 1991, 114–115; and Bo Burlingham, "This Woman Has Changed Business Forever." *Inc.*, June 1990, 34–47.

INTRODUCTION

In previous chapters, we examined group decision making and the phenomenon of power and influence. The focus of these chapters was on how group behavior influenced the individual or how an individual influenced another individual. In this chapter on leadership, however, we shall focus on how an individual can influence the behavior of groups.

Good leadership may be critical to organizational performance. The success of any venture is often largely attributed to its identified leader. The importance of Anita Roddick to the success of the Body Shops is obvious. She is clearly identified as a necessary component of the success of her company. And leadership roles in the organization can be beneficial to the individual. In the "FOCUS ON: The Benefits of Leadership," we examine the increasing disparity between employee salaries and those of the CEOs of major corporations. At the same time, the responsibility for failure of a venture is often placed squarely on the shoulders of the leader as well. When the Chrysler Corporation performs poorly, the person held responsible is Lee Iacocca. As described in the "FOCUS ON: The Burdens of Leadership," the chairman and president of Salomon Brothers both resigned to try to deflect the U.S. government's pursuit of the company for violations in their purchase of treasury bills.

While all would agree that good leadership is important to the successful organization, agreeing on the definition of leadership is considerably more difficult. Leadership has been defined in terms of individual traits, behavior, influence over other people, interaction patterns, role relationships, and incumbency in administrative positions.[1] For our purposes, however, we will use Katz and Kahn's definition of leadership, which distinguishes it from other forms of influence by suggesting that **leadership** is the influential increment over and above an employee's mechanical compliance with routine directives of the organization.[2]

Leadership is a difficult phenomenon to grasp. How do organizations create leaders? Or is it that leaders are born different, somehow? Does promoting an individual into the president's office make that person a leader? Is there a special font of knowledge that conveys leadership? In the "INTERNATIONAL FOCUS ON: Leadership" it seems that Chinese leaders and managers are schooled in the importance of ancient literature. At best, what we can say about leadership is that it is a complex phenomenon that involves exercising influence in an organization and that involves the interplay of many different organizational actors and issues. Perhaps it is because leadership has been perceived as such an important component of a successful organization that researchers and practitioners over the years have continued to try to understand it. One factor contributing to the confusion is that there are many different kinds of leaders. The next section examines two major types of leaders: formal and informal.

FORMAL AND INFORMAL LEADERSHIP

Formal leadership differs from informal leadership in the organizational legitimacy of the individual in that role. For example, the person occupying the role of executive vice-president of sales has a formal leadership role in the sales division of an organization. However, because that individual is assigned a particular role does not guarantee that the person will be a leader or the only leader

---

[1] G. Yukl, *Leadership in Organizations* 2nd ed. (Englewood Cliffs, N.J.: Prentice-Hall, 1987).

[2] D. Katz and R. L. Kahn, *The Social Psychology of Organizations* (New York: Wiley, 1978).

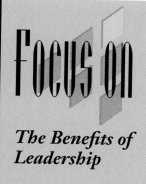

Focus on

The Benefits of Leadership

CEOs' Pay: Large Differences between the Top and the Bottom

The annual paychecks for Paul Fireman are quite impressive: $13.1 million in 1986, $15.4 million in 1987, $11.4 million in 1988, $14.6 million in 1989, and $14.8 million in 1990. Interestingly, the salary for Fireman, the international chairman of Reebok, is not in line with his performance. Once the hottest company in athletic shoes, Reebok's profits rose only 1 percent last year and lost the top sales spot to Nike. Or consider the paycheck of Lee Iacocca. In 1990, Chrysler gave Iacocca a 25 percent increase in total pay, even though earnings dropped 79 percent from the previous year. Employees may have found this raise particularly annoying when Chrysler executives had been vividly demanding cost savings from workers, suppliers, and even stockholders. On the other hand, the CEOs for companies that are doing very well often do not command such exorbitant salaries. Dane Miller is the CEO of Biomet, a producer of orthopedic devices such as artificial hips and knees. Over the last three years, he has received compensation totaling $555,000 in a company that produces $182 million in sales, $34.8 million in net income, and a 22.7 percent return on investment in the last three years.

Besides the lack of any clear relationship between performance and compensation at the highest levels of management, a bigger problem may be the message that is being sent to employees—a message that is being quickly translated into lower productivity and worker morale. For example, the average CEO last year made 85 times the pay of a typical American factory worker (it was 42 times the pay of the average American factory worker in 1980). In Japan, the CEO receives only 17 times the pay of the ordinary worker. In contrast, United Airlines CEO Stephen Wolf collected $18.3 million in salary, bonus, and stock-based incentives at the same time the profitability of United Airlines fell by 71 percent. His salary is over 1,200 times what a new flight attendant earned in each of the last five years: a period when none of them got raises. CEO Eisner of Disney made in one day more than the average Disney employee makes in one year.

There are many places to point fingers, one of which is at the boards of directors, who largely determine the compensation systems of CEOs and who are also taking a lion's share of the company's compensation pool. But, the time of CEO compensation excesses may be at an end. More and more big shareholders are questioning the compensation plans of large corporations such as IBM, ITT, and W. R. Grace. The issue seems to be, in part, that the boards of directors had begun to look more after the interests of the company management and less after the interests of the stockholders.

Source: John Byrne, "The Flap over Executive Pay," *Business Week,* May 6, 1991, 90–96.

of the sales force. Informal leadership is exerted by persons who can influence group members because of factors beyond the formal leader's organizational assignment. The formal leader will often exert influence in one dimension of the task and informal leaders will emerge to fill in the leadership gaps.

Individuals can increase their likelihood of being perceived as informal leaders in several ways. Generally, group members are more likely to be perceived as informal leaders if they provide salient contributions to the attainment of the group's goals and adhere to important group norms.

Contributions to group performance can come in three forms: special expertise or skills, unusually high involvement in activities necessary for group

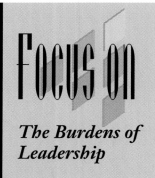

The Burdens of Leadership

One Bluff Too Many: Salomon and Gutfreund Get Snagged in Scandal

Named by *Business Week* as the "King of Wall Street" in 1986, both John Gutfreund, the chairman of Salomon Brothers, and Thomas Strauss, the company's president, resigned on August 26, 1991, in the wake of serious allegations of scandal. In a series of disclosures, the firm said that four brokers violated federal law by buying more than the legal limit of bonds at three Treasury auctions starting in December. Under federal rules, no firm may purchase more than 35 percent of a bond offering at a single auction, but Salomon's traders bought up 57 percent at a February sale and 44 percent at an auction in May. While Salomon admits to the overbuys, it denies that it was deliberately trying to "squeeze" prices by cornering the market. The company asserts that the four traders, who have since quit the firm, connived without the firm's knowledge.

Salomon admitted that Gutfreund as well as the vice-chairman, John Meriwether, and Strauss knew about the February overpurchase in April but did not fire the traders or notify the government until August.

Gutfreund, more than most, exemplified the excess of the 1980s. In fact, some would suggest that Gutfreund and his wife Susan were the inspiration for the nouveau-riche protagonist couple in Tom Wolfe's scathing novel, *The Bonfire of the Vanities*. A gruff, cigar-chomping man, Gutfreund transformed the once staid brokerage house into a machismo-fueled money bazaar, the most profitable on Wall Street. Both his and Strauss's retirement were a move by Salomon Brothers to deflect or ameliorate the government's pursuit of Salomon Brothers on criminal and civil charges that could include fines, suspension, or even disbarment as a primary dealer of Treasury bills.

performance, and active participation in group discussions. Specifically, informal leaders are likely to be those perceived to (1) aid the group's attainment of its goals because of direct knowledge or expertise or indirect influence of those with the necessary knowledge or expertise; (2) volunteer relatively more time in pursuing the group's task; or (3) be more visible in group discussions by contributing ideas and suggestions. It is interesting to note that while contributing high-quality suggestions results in greater perceptions of influence, frequency of participation—independent of quality—significantly increases the perceived influence of the individual by group members.[3]

LEADERSHIP AS A MANAGERIAL ROLE

There is sometimes confusion between the role of a *leader* and the role of a *manager*. The activities of these two roles can differ radically. It is not necessary that the manager of the group also be the group's formal or informal leader. The manager may be the leader or perform functions separate from the tasks

---

[3] R. M. Sorrentino and R. G. Boutillier, "The Effect of Quantity and Quality of Verbal Interaction on Rating of Leadership Ability," *Journal of Experimental Social Psychology* 11 (1975): 403–411.

Literature and Chinese Leadership

The leaders of Chinese companies do not rely on the wisdom of Western thinkers such as Peter Drucker or Tom Peters for their insight. Rather, they have their own set of texts, often books that were published in ancient times. Huo Xinyi is a deputy secretary general of the Society for the Study of China's Ancient Management Thinking. Examples of these texts are Sun Tzu's *The Art of War* (used to direct marketing strategy), Cao Xuequin's *Red Chamber Dream* (which is used as a guide to personnel and financial management), and the sayings of Confucius (to offer insight into a manager's benevolence).

And how do these classics become relevant in practice? Huo tells the tale of the king's horses and the computer in Liangxiang:

There once was a commoner who raced his three horses against three horses belonging to the king. The best was pitted against the best; the middling against the middling; and the slowest against the slowest. Each time, the king won because his horses were a little faster than the commoner's. Afterwards, a clever person told the commoner that he should have raced his slowest horse against the king's fastest; his middling horse against the king's slowest; and his best against the king's middling horse. In this way, he would have won two races out of three. This is why the Liangxiang company sells its medium-range computer in the bottom-of-the-range international market.

Source: "The Chinese Art of Management," *The Economist,* October 26, 1991, 41.

traditionally described as leadership activities. For example, the manager may be involved in developing and securing the necessary budget for the group's activities. While this is clearly not a leadership function, it is critical to the effective functioning of the group.

In addition to ability to accomplish the organization's goals, true leadership has at least two other important characteristics: the situation and the follower. It is interesting to note that early definitions of leadership focused almost exclusively on the identified leader. Students of leadership concerned themselves with the traits and demographic characteristics that differentiated leaders from followers. As leadership theory evolved, so did its emphasis on the situation in which the leader exists. Situational characteristics include the organization, the broader culture, goals, characteristics of the task or project, and the educational, professional, or maturity level of the followers. The most recent development of leadership theory focuses on the reciprocal influence process between leaders and followers. This influence that leaders exert on followers and followers exert on leaders goes beyond mere characteristics of the followers. It extends into the interdependent relationship between followers and leaders.

The primary reason for the continuing evolution of leadership theory has been to identify what separates good leaders from poor leaders. That is, what are the critical components of an *effective* leader? Social scientists and practitioners have approached this question from a number of directions and assumptions about the nature of effective leadership. To bring some order to the various theories and perspectives on leadership presented in this chapter, consider the framework presented in Figure 10–1.

FIGURE 10-1	▶ Framework for Traditional Leadership Theories

Traditional theories of leadership can be categorized into two dimensions. The first dimension focuses on what aspect of the leader is emphasized in the theory: personality traits or behaviors. The second dimension focuses on the type of influence the leader exerts: universal or situation-contingent.

	Leader	
	Trait	**Behavior**
Universal	"Great person" approach Transformational leaders	Socioemotional and task leaders Managerial grid
Situation-Contingent	Fiedler's contingency model of leadership	Path-goal theory of leadership Vroom-Yetton's model of decision making

Traditional theories of leadership may be categorized into two dimensions: traits and behaviors. The first dimension focuses on what aspect of the leader (trait) is emphasized. Leadership has been described in terms of both who the leader is (enduring personality traits) and how the leader behaves (observable behavior). The second dimension focuses on the type of influence the leader's behavior has. Some theories of leadership assume that the traits or behaviors of a leader are consistent, without regard to situational or follower demands. These theories assume that the leader responds consistently or universally to many different situations. Alternatively, other theories assert that the leader may adjust the expression of unique personality traits or behaviors to fit the demands of the situation. From this perspective, then, the leader expresses situation-contingent behavior.

As shown in Figure 10–1, the intersection of these two dimensions yields four theoretical perspectives: the universal-trait approach, the universal-behavioral approach, the situation-contingent trait approach, and the situation-contingent behavioral approach. In this chapter, leadership effectiveness will be considered from each of these four theoretical perspectives.

UNIVERSAL APPROACHES TO LEADERSHIP ◆◆◆◆◆◆

One popular perspective on leadership is that leaders are leaders because of some enduring aspect of their personality or behavior. That is, regardless of the situation in which these individuals find themselves, their leadership abilities will emerge. The primary consideration here, however, is whether such leadership is a function of the individual or the way in which that individual behaves. In the following sections, we will examine (1) theories that leadership is dependent on the person and (2) theories that leadership is dependent on behavior.

Universalist trait or "great person" theories of leadership contend that certain individuals, such as Nelson Mandela, or Martin Luther King, Jr., possess traits that set them apart as leaders regardless of the situations in which they find themselves.

Trait Approaches

The universalist trait approach provided the earliest and also some of the most intuitively appealing of the leadership theories. This approach was also known as the "great man" approach to leadership (or the "great person" approach, to bring this term into modern usage). This theory is based upon the notion that certain individuals are destined to be leaders. It contends that individuals such as Martin Luther King, Jr., Winston Churchill, or Indira Gandhi would have been leaders regardless of the situations in which they found themselves. That is, leaders possess a constellation of personality characteristics that separates them from others—their followers.

The "great person" perspective on leadership makes the implicit assumption that such individuals are **transformational leaders** as opposed to **transactional leaders,** who motivate by providing followers with rewards for their behavior.

Transformational leaders arouse intense feelings and generate turbulent one-to-one relationships with their followers. They are inspirational and concerned with ideas rather than process. They heighten expectations and engender excitement. They are likely to be dramatic and unpredictable.

Transformational leaders rely on such personal sources of power as referent power, discussed in Chapter 8. They motivate their followers to do more than the followers had originally intended by transforming the group's expectations. Such transformations can occur when the leader:

▶ Raises the level of follower awareness, consciousness, and commitment to designated outcomes as well as knowledge of how to achieve these outcomes.

▶ Gets followers to transcend their self-interests for the sake of the organization.

▶ Alters the followers' needs or expands their wants.

Thomas J. Watson transformed IBM; George Patton transformed the Third Army; Adolf Hitler transformed Germany. These types of leaders have an

Transformational leaders like Steven Jobs, founder of Apple Computers, lift their followers to new heights of awareness and accomplishment by articulating common goals and visions. Transformational leaders are likely to be successful in small, entrepreneurial organizations where enthusiasm and excitement are more valuable than rules, routines, and procedures.

almost magical appeal for followers. They identify for their followers a way to achieve a superordinate goal. Through their appeal, they are able to change the organization, its environment, and the organizational participants. Self-confidence and self-esteem, low internal conflict, self-determination, and enthusiasm all contribute to the success of transformational leaders.[4] They have the ability to both conceive and articulate goals that lift people out of their petty preoccupations.[5] Such leaders can unite people to seek goals worthy of their best efforts. As Steven Jobs suggested while the CEO of Apple Computer, "the greatest people are self-managing . . . what they need is a common vision, and that's what leadership is is having a vision, being able to articulate it, and getting a consensus on a common vision." The value of such leadership is discussed in the "FOCUS ON: Transformational Leaders."

In contrast to a transformational leader, a transactional leader motivates followers by exchanging rewards for services. The transactional leader:

▶ Recognizes what subordinates want from their work and tries to see that they get it (if their performance warrants it).

▶ Exchanges rewards and promises of rewards for subordinates' effort.

▶ Is responsive to subordinates' immediate self-interests if they get the job done.[6]

Transactional leadership focuses on situational determinants of leadership. In the terms of Chapter 8, transactional leaders rely on reward and coercive power. Situation-contingent theories will be discussed in greater detail later in this chapter. For now, let us note that this approach fails to explain individuals who emerge as leaders no matter where they find themselves. Such exceptional peo-

[4] See, for example, B. M. Bass, *Leadership and Performance*; R. J. House, "A 1976 Theory of Charismatic Leadership," *Leadership: The Cutting Edge*, ed. J. G. Hunt and L. L. Larson (Carbondale, Ill.: Southern University Press, 1977); W. Keichell III, "Wanted: Corporate Leaders," *Fortune*, May 30, 1983, 135–140; M. Weber, *The Theory of Social and Economic Organization*, trans. and ed. T. Parsons and A. M. Henderson (New York: Oxford University Press, 1947).

[5] W. G. Bennis and B. Nanus, *Leaders: The Strategies for Taking Charge.* (New York: Harper & Row, 1985).

[6] B. M. Bass, *Leadership and Performance beyond Expectations* (New York: Free Press, 1985).

Transformational Leaders

WANTED: Leaders Who Can Make a Difference Say farewell to the classic postwar American manager, the model of rational decision making who coolly piloted us through the prosperity of the fifties and the go-go of the sixties, only to begin stubbing his toe in the seventies. Vanguard corporations are deciding that this generally amiable character—he did get a bit autocratic at times—isn't up to the challenges of today. No, what's required now, the emerging wisdom indicates, are not mere managers, but *leaders*—people like Lee Iacocca of Chrysler, Jack Welch of General Electric, and John Reed of Citicorp. The new paragon is an executive who can envision a future for his or her organization and inspire colleagues to join in building that future. Perhaps the most notable departure from managerial practice is that these new leaders do not fear change—instead they embrace it and create it. They know that their most important job is probably to transform the way the company does business.

Corporate America has always maintained a nodding interest in the subject of leadership, but the exigencies of global competition, deregulation, and accelerating technological change have whipped that interest into an anxious search for new answers to old questions: Can leadership be taught? How do you spot potential leaders? And what, precisely, sets leaders apart from everyday managers?

Much of the current thinking on leadership had its beginnings in a famous 1977 *Harvard Business Review* article entitled "Managers and Leaders: Are They Different?" Yes, concluded the article's author, Abraham Zaleznik, a Harvard Business School professor. Managers do the same things over and over again, but it takes a leader to innovate. While a good leader needs to be a manager, too, a manager is not necessarily a leader. The corporate chief must be able to change things, to make a substantive difference in the organization, in contrast to the merely "transactional" manager who keeps on cutting the same kinds of deals with employees, customers, and society at large.

Corporations do not take kindly to transformational leaders. "The natural state of an organization is conservative, to maintain the status quo," says Walter Ulmer, Jr., president of the Center for Creative Leadership. Which is why, of course, a leader is exactly what's required when only radical change will preserve the organization in the face of new realities. These individuals must possess a "divine discontent with the status quo."

Source: Jeremy Main, "Wanted: Leaders Who Can Make a Difference," *Fortune*, September 28, 1987, 92–102.

ple have the unique ability to go beyond transacting with their subordinates and transform the situation and their followers.

If we reconsider our earlier discussion of the differences between managers and leaders, it seems that transactional leaders are more like managers, making sure tasks get done right, and transformational leaders are what we generally refer to as leaders. David Berlew describes this latter form of leadership as Stage 3, or **charismatic leadership,** and differentiates it from the two other stages (or types) of leadership.[7] Stage 1 leadership is termed **custodial;** custodial leaders are concerned more with improving working conditions, compensation, and fringe benefits. Stage 2 leadership is termed **managerial.** Managerial leaders focus on providing subordinates work that is less routine and more challenging,

---

[7] D. E. Berlew, "Leadership and Organizational Excitement," *Organizational Psychology: A Book of Readings*, ed. D. A. Kolb, I. M. Rubin, and J. M. McIntyre (Englewood Cliffs, N.J.: Prentice-Hall, 1979).

building cohesive work teams, and giving employees more say in decisions that affect them directly. These first two stages of leadership seem much more consistent with what we consider to be transactional leadership. In contrast, Stage 3 (*charismatic*) leaders concern themselves with developing a common vision of what could be, discovering or creating opportunities and strengthening organizational members' control of their own destinies.

Few leaders fall cleanly into this third category. The demands of maintaining the charismatic hold over followers are extreme. For example, leaders of complex organizations must represent and articulate goals for many different groups simultaneously. Only the exceptional leader of a large, complex organization can identify a vision truly common to such diversity. Transformational leaders are more likely to be found in small, entrepreneurial organizations, since they are more concerned with a vision than with maintaining the rules, routines, and procedures necessary for larger organizations to survive. Second, the charismatic leader must give meaning to the organization for followers. Figure 10–2 identifies different opportunities that transformational leaders can provide to organizational participants to help them find meaning in their jobs.

In addition to identifying a common vision and giving meaning to the organization and its related activities, the charismatic leader also must empower followers—make them feel stronger, more confident, more in control of their destinies, and more competent. Berlew suggests that charismatic leaders engender this feeling of power among followers by having high expectations of them, rewarding good performance rather than punishing poor performance, encouraging collaboration among individuals, helping only when asked, and creating success experiences for followers.[8]

Given the attraction and effectiveness of such leaders, it is little wonder that behavioral scientists have searched for ways to identify them. However, the search for specific factors that clearly and consistently predict which individuals will be effective transformational leaders has not been overly successful. Thousands of studies have investigated the impact on leader effectiveness of demographic characteristics (such as height, weight, and age), social characteristics (such as educational level, socioeconomic background, grades, appearance, and popularity), and personality characteristics (such as dominance, introversion-extroversion, initiative, and cooperation). While the transformational perspective has considerable intuitive appeal (especially considering the success of such transformational leaders as John Kennedy and Lenin), research provides only minimal support for the ability to identify charismatic leaders.

After an exhaustive review in 1948 of over 100 review and empirical studies, one researcher reported that leadership is not a matter of possessing some combination of traits.[9] It appeared to emerge instead from a working relationship among members of the group. Thus, an individual who may be a leader in one situation is not necessarily a leader in other situations. A more recent review by this same researcher paints a more positive picture of the importance of personality traits on leader potential.[10] While the appropriateness of specific leader characteristics varies with the situation, there appears to be a constellation of leadership traits that distinguishes leaders from followers, effective from inef-

---

[8] Ibid.

[9] R. M. Stodgill, "Personal Factors Associated with Leadership," *Journal of Psychology* 25 (1948): 35–71.

[10] R. M. Stodgill, *Handbook of Leadership* (New York: Free Press, 1974).

FIGURE 10–2	▶ Sources of Meaning in Organizations

A charismatic leader must provide for followers a sense of meaning in organizational activities. Meaning comes when employees can see their organizational activities in a new light—as a chance to change or contribute something important to society.

Type of Opportunity	Related Need or Value
1. A chance to be tested; to make it on one's own	Self-reliance Self-actualization
2. A social experiment; to combine work, family, and play in some new way	Community Integration of life
3. A chance to do something well; for example, to return to real craftsmanship, to be really creative	Excellence Unique accomplishment
4. A chance to do something good; for example, to run an honest, no-rip-off business or a youth counseling center	Consideration Service
5. A chance to change the way things are; for example, from Republican to Democrat to Socialist, from war to peace, from unjust to just	Activism Social responsibility Citizenship

fective leadership, and higher-status from lower-status leaders. These characteristics include a strong sense of social and personal responsibility for decisions and outcomes, a desire for task completion, originality in problem solving, initiative in social situations, willingness to tolerate frustration and delay, self-confidence and a strong sense of self, and a capacity to structure social situations to achieve specific goals.

If we assume that transactional leaders are managers, one example of a recent application of universal trait perspectives to modern management is the identification of individuals with leadership potential through assessment centers. Assessment centers are testing mechanisms for identifying potential managerial talent. First developed by the Office of Strategic Services in World War II to select spies, assessment centers are now used by many major corporations. Participants in an assessment center undergo a series of role-playing exercises, psychological tests, simulations, and management games that measure their managerial talent. Assessment centers use both trait and situational information, and the accuracy of their selections is quite impressive. For example, the results of AT&T's management progression study showed that of the 422 men originally tested, 78 percent of those who reached middle management were correctly identified by the assessment center.[11] In addition, the assessment center was able to identify 95 percent of those who did not reach middle-management positions within ten years of their evaluation. Additional studies reported in 1983 based on 1,200 male and female employees of AT&T supported the usefulness of combining both individual traits and situational responses in selecting managerial talent.

Traits alone demonstrated very weak predictive power. It seems that trait measures are not sufficiently sturdy to stand alone as predictors of leadership

---

[11] D. W. Bray and D. L. Grant, "The Assessment Center in the Measurement of Potential for Business Management," *Psychological Monographs* 80, no. 17, Whole N. 625 (1966).

talent and success. It should also be noted that, while assessment center results have shown good predictive validity for managerial jobs,[12] these assessment centers were not designed to identify transformational leaders. Because of the potential overlap between what makes a successful manager and a successful leader, however, these findings are certainly intriguing. It seems that although traits are poor predictors of leader effectiveness, they do a fair job of predicting leadership *perceptions*. That is, we all have some ideas about how leaders are, and these traits can predict who we will believe to be leaders.

Behavior Approaches

Although research into the specific traits of leaders is still being conducted, leadership research in the late 1940s began to focus on *behaviors* of leaders rather than their personality and demographic characteristics. Thus, rather than attempt to use personal characteristics to separate leaders from followers, this stream of research attempted to determine exactly which leader behaviors resulted in follower satisfaction and high performance.

The focus on leader behaviors rather than leader traits has a number of advantages. First, examining behaviors rather than traits allows us to consider informal as well as formal leaders. If we focus only on leaders identified by personal traits, then leadership is limited to those individuals in stable positions of leadership. Identifying leaders by their behaviors is more likely to include both stable, formal leaders and more volatile, informal leaders. Second, if critical and effective leader behaviors can be identified, our ability to train leaders will be enhanced. The "Focus on: Leader Behaviors" pursues this line of thinking. Finally, the behaviors of a leader and the reciprocal behaviors of the followers allow us to examine closely the exchange relationship between leaders and followers. Exchange theory (the basis for transactional leadership), described in Chapter 8, contends that all social interactions involve some form of trade-off of benefits or costs. For example, the leader may give the group direction, coordination, legitimacy, and access to valued resources. The followers, then, reciprocate these benefits with resources of their own, such as compliance and deference.[13]

In addition to this ongoing exchange of benefits, leaders can build up reserves, or idiosyncrasy credits (discussed in Chapter 7), with group members. For example, when leaders contribute to the group's performance, they gain idiosyncrasy credits. However, when leaders detract from group performance, they can lose these credits.

The importance of idiosyncrasy credits to leadership can be seen in the difference in initial power and influence between those *elected* and those *appointed* to leadership roles. Research has found that elected leaders are more likely than appointed leaders to make decisions in opposition to group preferences.[14] Election to leadership represents group acceptance and provides the

---

[12] A. Howard, "An Assessment of Assessment Centers," *Academy of Management Journal* 17 (1974): 115–134; R. J. Ritchie and J. L. Moss, "Assessment Center Correlates of Women's Advancement into Middle Management: A Seven Year Longitudinal Study," *Journal of Applied Psychology* 68 (1983): 227–231.

[13] E. P. Hollander, *Leadership Dynamics: A Practical Guide to Effective Relationships* (New York: Free Press/Macmillan, 1978).

[14] E. P. Hollander and J. W. Julian, "Studies in Leader Legitimacy, Influence, and Innovation," *Advances in Experimental Social Psychology*, vol. 5, ed. L. Berkowitz (New York: Academic Press, 1970): 33–69.

Women Executives: What Makes for Success? While executive men and women score similarly on measures of personality, intelligence, and behaviors in problem-solving groups and are just as able to lead, influence, and motivate other group members, women are not making the same progress as men in achieving the executive rank. Among Fortune 500 companies, only 1.7 percent of the corporate officers are women. To try to understand how women's movement up the corporate ladder compares with men's, 76 women at or near the general- management level in Fortune 500 companies were compared with similar male managers. In addition, 22 "savvy insiders" (16 men and 6 women) in ten companies—people responsible for identifying and selecting executives for top positions—were interviewed. These interviews identified the factors contributing to success or derailment among executives.

In this study, the criteria for success included reaching one of the top ten to twenty positions in the corporation and living up to one's full potential in the eyes of the company. Derailment was achieving a very high level in the company but not going as high as the organization had expected. In attempting to distinguish those individuals who had succeeded from those who had derailed, the insiders identified roughly the same number of derailment factors for men and women (on the average, 4 for men and 3.5 for women), but they listed nearly twice as many success factors for women (10.4) as for men (5.7).

The women described as successful and as derailed were put through a number of tests as they progressed up the corporate ladder. They had to show toughness and independence and at the same time depend on others. It was essential that they contradict the stereotypes that their male bosses and co-workers had about women. They had to be seen as different, "better than women" as a group, but they couldn't go too far and forfeit all traces of femininity because that would make them too alien to their superiors and colleagues. In essence, their mission was to do what *wasn't* expected of them while doing enough of what was expected of them as women to gain acceptance. Based upon the results of this study, women must reconcile themselves to four such contradictory expectations to succeed in corporate life:

1. Take risks, but be consistently outstanding.
2. Be tough, but don't be macho.
3. Be ambitious, but don't expect equal treatment.
4. Take responsibility, but follow others' advice.

These demands (which do not exist in such contradictory forms for men) are in response to stereotypic views of women. These unrealistic expectations are a part of the environment in which women must work and live, even though mounting evidence suggests that, when careers are matched, women are remarkably similar to men in their characteristics, abilities, and motives. This qualitatively different environment, then, may be the crucial—and only meaningful—difference between male and female executives.

Source: A. M. Morrison, R. P. White, and E. Van Velsor, "Executive Women: Substance Plus Style," *Psychology Today*, August 1987, 18–26.

flexibility to make decisions in what the leader perceives to be the group's best interest. Appointment to a leadership position does not necessarily include a reserve of idiosyncrasy credit. Thus, such leaders are more likely to gain these credits by maintaining the status quo or proving (by behaving consistently with group preferences) that they have the best interests of the group at heart. Once sufficient credit or acceptance is gained, then the leader must begin to introduce some form of change into the group to improve performance or these idiosyncrasy credits will deteriorate. Because a leader is expected to introduce change or provide some mechanism for improving group performance, ignoring this expectation can seriously erode a leader's influence and acceptance by group members.

From the perspective of exchange theory, leader behavior has the potential to significantly influence both group performance and follower satisfaction. Researchers at the University of Michigan and The Ohio State University were early leaders in determining the critical aspects of leader behavior.

These two research centers conducted independent research programs, yet it is interesting to note that both described two distinct types of leader behavior: **production(task)-oriented leadership** (initiating structure) and **employee (socioemotional)-oriented leadership** (initiating consideration). Production or task-oriented leadership focuses almost exclusively on activities specifically related to the task. Employee-oriented or socioemotional leadership emphasizes the individual worker's needs in managing group performance.

The Ohio State University and University of Michigan Studies   The Ohio State studies sought to identify the basic types of behaviors that all effective leaders use. To identify these behaviors, almost 1,800 descriptions of leader behavior were collected. Through statistical analyses, the 1,800 descriptions were reduced to 150 descriptions of good leader behavior. When these items were transformed into questions, they became the Leader Behavior Description Questionnaire (LBDQ).

These behaviors fell into a variety of categories, the two most important of which were those of initiating structure (task leadership) and consideration (socioemotional leadership). Given that any individual may rank either high or low on initiating structure and high or low on consideration, four different types of leaders were identified, as described in Figure 10–3. The important research question, then, was this: Which of these general categories of leader behavior routinely results in superior group performance?

After large investments of time and energy, the results of this line of research have been disappointing. A recent review of this literature shows that is has yielded very inconsistent and inconclusive results.[15] There does not seem to be any combination of initiating structure and consideration that *consistently* results in superior group performance.

The work conducted at the University of Michigan led to a four-factor theory of leadership.[16] The four factors are as follows:

1. *Support:* Behaviors that enhance group member's feelings of personal worth and importance.
2. *Interaction facilitation:* Behaviors that encourage group members to develop close, mutually satisfying relationships.

---

[15] B. M. Bass, *Stodgill's Handbook of Leadership: A Survey of Theory and Research*, rev. ed. (New York: Free Press, 1981).

[16] D. G. Bowers and S. E. Seashore, "Predicting Organizational Effectiveness with a Four-Factor Theory of Leadership," *Administrative Science Quarterly*, 1966, 238–263.

FIGURE 10–3	▶ Outcomes of The Ohio State University Leadership Studies' Behavior Model

Researchers at the University of Michigan and The Ohio State University were pioneers in the attempt to identify critical aspects of leader behavior. Their studies identified several primary dimensions of leader behavior, but they have been unable to identify consistently effective leader behaviors.

		Manager's Initiating Structure	
		High	**Low**
Manager's Initiating Consideration	**High**	High Performance Low Grievance Rate Low Turnover	Low Performance Low Grievance Rate Low Turnover
	Low	High Performance High Grievance Rate High Turnover	Low Performance High Grievance Rate High Turnover

Source: J. R. Gordon, *Organizational Behavior*, 2d ed. (Boston: Allyn & Bacon, 1987).

3. *Goal emphasis:* Behaviors that stimulate enthusiasm for meeting group goals and achieving high performance.
4. *Work facilitation:* Behaviors that directly aid goal attainment by providing resources such as tools, materials, and technical knowledge.

It should be noted that the first two factors are associated with behaviors common to socioemotional leaders, while the latter two factors are associated with task-oriented leader behaviors. As with the Ohio State two-factor theory of leadership, the Michigan studies also yielded inconsistent results. In his review of this research, Yukl found no support for all four of these categories taken together or individually as predictors of leadership effectiveness.[17]

The Managerial Grid   Even though the research on universal leader behaviors has received mixed support at best, the notion of an ideal leadership style continues to be intuitively appealing. This idea has served as the foundation for many leadership training programs over the years. The most famous of these—called the managerial grid—is conducted by Robert Blake, Jane Mouton, and their associates. The **managerial grid,** described in Figure 10–4, reflects the two dimensions of leader behavior—concern for production (task-oriented leadership) and concern for people (socioemotional leadership). While Blake and Mouton identify five different types of leadership—country club, impoverished, authority, organizational man, and team management—they believe that high production *and* high concern for people (team management) is the only style that will result in superior performance. With a team-management style, the leader is able to elicit high-quality performances from a group of

[17] Yukl, *Leadership in Organizations.*

FIGURE 10-4	▶ The Managerial Grid

The managerial grid is a variation of the two-dimensional perspective of leader behavior. These two dimensions result in five distinct leadership styles.

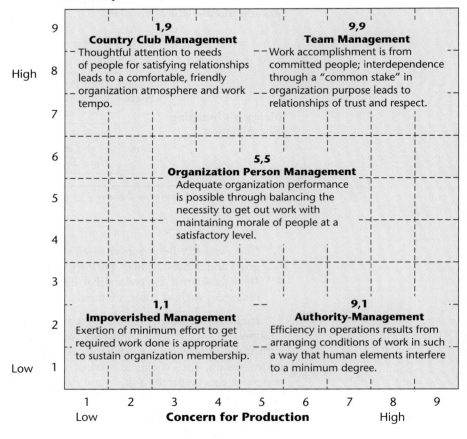

Concern for People

1,9 Country Club Management
Thoughtful attention to needs of people for satisfying relationships leads to a comfortable, friendly organization atmosphere and work tempo.

9,9 Team Management
Work accomplishment is from committed people; interdependence through a "common stake" in organization purpose leads to relationships of trust and respect.

5,5 Organization Person Management
Adequate organization performance is possible through balancing the necessity to get out work with maintaining morale of people at a satisfactory level.

1,1 Impoverished Management
Exertion of minimum effort to get required work done is appropriate to sustain organization membership.

9,1 Authority-Management
Efficiency in operations results from arranging conditions of work in such a way that human elements interfere to a minimum degree.

Concern for Production

Source: R. R. Blake and J. S. Mouton, *The New Managerial Grid* (Houston: Gulf Publishing, 1978).

highly committed followers who share a common purpose. The team leader uses mutual trust and respect to accomplish both individual and organizational goals.[18]

Despite its appeal and the large number of dollars spent training managers to adopt the team-management leadership style identified by Blake and Mouton, again research has revealed little empirical support for any relationship between a style of leadership and such factors as productivity, absenteeism, and turnover.[19] Given the lack of support for this universalistic notion, we now turn to the next set of leadership theories: the contingency theories.

[18] J. R. Gordon, *Organizational Behavior* (Boston: Allyn & Bacon, 1987).

[19] A. K. Korman, " 'Consideration,' 'Initiating Structure,' and Organizational Criteria: A Review," *Personnel Psychology* 19 (1966): 349–361.

CONTINGENCY APPROACHES TO LEADERSHIP

The fruitless search for a universal or trait perspective of leadership has led leadership researchers to reformulate their questions. Rather than search for a Holy Grail of executive leader behaviors, researchers in the last three decades have turned their attention to the situations in which leaders find themselves. Determining which set of leader behaviors is most appropriate for which situation requires an understanding of situational differences, or *contingencies* (such as the nature of the task, subordinate attributes, and group characteristics).

Trait Approaches

Contingency Model of Leadership The earliest theory specifically called a contingency theory was Fred Fiedler's **contingency model of leadership.** The basic assumption of his model was that the nature of the situation determined the effectiveness of the leader's behavior. To determine what style a leader possessed, he developed the **Least-Preferred Coworker (LPC) scale.**

Consistent with previous work on leader behavior, Fiedler's LPC scale measured two basic styles of leader behavior: (1) task-oriented and (2) relationship-oriented behavior. Research conducted by Fiedler and Rice[20] suggests that low-LPC leaders emphasize completing tasks—even at the expense of interpersonal relationships—and gain self-esteem through task completion. In contrast, high-LPC leaders derive satisfaction and a sense of accomplishment from relationships with others. Fiedler argued that the importance of the LPC scale was in ferreting out an individual's ability to overlook negative traits in followers. Individuals unable to overlook such traits because of potential influence on future task accomplishment are more likely to be task oriented. Those who can maintain a strong relationship with an individual, regardless of negative traits, are more likely to be relationship-oriented individuals. The LPC scale, reproduced in Figure 10–5, produces scores between 18 and 144. Low-LPC leaders are usually described as those scoring below 58 points. High-LPC leaders score 64 or more points.

Once an individual's leadership style is ascertained, it is then important to diagnose the particular situation in which the leader works. Because Fiedler believed that leadership style was a trait—a stable personality characteristic—he suggested that organizations assign leaders based on a fit between their LPC and the situation. He felt that it was considerably easier (and more appropriate) for individuals to find situations that required their leadership style than to change their style to fit a situation.

Fiedler identified three situational characteristics that influenced whether a high-LPC or low-LPC leader would be more effective:

1. *Leader-member relations:* The extent to which the group trusts and respects the leader and will follow the leader's directions.
2. *Task structure:* The degree to which a task is clearly specified and defined as opposed to unstructured and ambiguous.

---

[20]F. E. Fiedler, *A Theory of Leadership Effectiveness* (New York: McGraw-Hill, 1967); R. W. Rice, "Construct Validity of the Least Preferred Co-Worker Scale," *Psychological Bulletin* 85 (1978): 106–118.

FIGURE 10–5	▶ Least-Preferred Coworker (LPC) Scale

Fred Fiedler's contingency model of leadership contends that situational characteristics determine which leadership traits or skills are effective. Fiedler developed the LPC scale to measure an individual's leadership skills.

Directions: Think of all the people with whom you have ever worked, and then think of the person with whom you could work *least well.* This person may be someone with whom you work now or with whom you have worked in the past. This does not have to be the person you liked least well, but should be the person with whom you had the most difficulty getting a job done.

Describe this person on the scale that follows by placing an *X* in the appropriate space.

Look at the words at both ends of the line before you mark your *X*. *There are no right or wrong answers.* Work rapidly; your first answer is likely to be the best. Do not omit any items, and mark each item only once.

Now describe the person with whom you can work least well.

Scoring

Left	8/7/6/5/4/3/2/1	Right	Score
Pleasant	8 7 6 5 4 3 2 1	Unpleasant	—
Friendly	8 7 6 5 4 3 2 1	Unfriendly	—
Rejecting	1 2 3 4 5 6 7 8	Accepting	—
Tense	1 2 3 4 5 6 7 8	Relaxed	—
Distant	1 2 3 4 5 6 7 8	Close	—
Cold	1 2 3 4 5 6 7 8	Warm	—
Supportive	8 7 6 5 4 3 2 1	Hostile	—
Boring	1 2 3 4 5 6 7 8	Interesting	—
Quarrelsome	1 2 3 4 5 6 7 8	Harmonious	—
Gloomy	1 2 3 4 5 6 7 8	Cheerful	—
Open	8 7 6 5 4 3 2 1	Guarded	—
Backbiting	1 2 3 4 5 6 7 8	Loyal	—
Untrustworthy	1 2 3 4 5 6 7 8	Trustworthy	—
Considerate	8 7 6 5 4 3 2 1	Inconsiderate	—
Nasty	1 2 3 4 5 6 7 8	Nice	—
Agreeable	8 7 6 5 4 3 2 1	Disagreeable	—
Insincere	1 2 3 4 5 6 7 8	Sincere	—
Kind	8 7 6 5 4 3 2 1	Unkind	—
		Total	—

Source: Fred E. Fiedler, Martin M. Chemers, and Linda Mahar, *Improving Leadership Effectiveness* (New York: Wiley, 1976), 7.

Contingency theories of leadership emphasize the importance of fit between individual characteristics and situational demands. When companies grow beyond their small entrepreneurial beginnings, their need for leadership changes. John Sculley was brought in as the new CEO of Apple Computers in 1976. In 1993, he stepped aside for Michael Spindler to bring Apple into the next generation of PC technology.

3. *Position power:* The extent to which the leader has official power or the potential or actual ability to influence others in a desired direction because of the leader's position in the hierarchy.

Despite their bias that people are better off finding situations that require their leadership style, Fiedler and his colleagues have identified strategies for individuals to fine-tune situations to better fit with their leadership styles. These strategies are described in Figure 10–6.

Figure 10–7 illustrates the style of leadership most appropriate for a particular combination of situational characteristics. These recommendations are based on the amount of control a leader has. In high-control situations, where the group will expect *and* allow the leader to take charge, task-oriented leadership is more effective. Task-oriented leadership is also more effective in low-control situations. In a low-control situation, task-oriented leadership allows the leader to focus the activities of the group on the task rather than on the unfavorable nature of leader-follower interactions. Only in the moderate-control situation does Fiedler recommend a relationship-oriented leadership style. In such conditions, leaders must elicit the cooperation and commitment of their subordinates to accomplish the task.

Research has supported Fiedler's approach to leadership. However, there is controversy over the use of the LPC as a measurement of leadership style. The LPC does not directly measure leader behavior; instead, it measures an individual's *feelings* about a coworker. This concern, coupled with a lack of consistent scores among individuals who complete the scale on different occasions, has called into question the usefulness of the LPC questionnaire. However, Fiedler and his colleagues have provided us with a useful notion: *contingency* leadership. While Fiedler and his colleagues are clearly wedded to a contingency model of leadership and the importance of a situation-style fit, it is obvious that very different styles of leadership can be successful in different organizations. In the "FOCUS ON: Leadership Contingencies," two successful leaders and their very different management styles are highlighted.

| FIGURE 10–6 | ▶Leader Actions to Change Situations |

Contingency theory implies that individuals are better off finding situations that require the leadership skills they possess. Nevertheless, there are some strategies that individuals can use to alter their situations to fit their leadership skills.

Modifying Leader-Member Relations

1.   Spend more—or less—informal time with your subordinates (lunch, leisure activities, and so on).
2.   Request particular people for work in your group.
3.   Volunteer to direct difficult or troublesome subordinates.
4.   Suggest or effect transfers of particular subordinates into or out of your unit.
5.   Raise morale by obtaining positive outcomes for subordinates (special bonuses, time off, attractive assignments, and so on).

Modifying Task Structure

If you wish to work with less-structured tasks, you can:

1.   Ask your boss, whenever possible, to give you the new or unusual problems and let you figure out how to solve them.
2.   Bring the problems and tasks to your group members, and invite them to work with you on the planning and decision-making phases of the tasks.

If you wish to work with more highly structured tasks, you can:

1.   Ask your superior to give you, whenever possible, the tasks that are more structured or to give you more detailed instructions.
2.   Break the job down into smaller subtasks that can be more highly structured.

Modifying Position Power

To raise your position power, you can:

1.   Show your subordinates who's boss by exercising fully the powers that the organization provides.
2.   Make sure that information to your group gets channeled through you.

To lower your position power, you can:

1.   Call on members of your group to participate in planning and decision-making functions.
2.   Let your assistants exercise relatively more power.

Source: F. E. Fiedler, "How Do You Make Leaders More Effective?" *Organizational Dynamics* (Autumn 1972): 3–8.

Behavior Approaches

Path-Goal Theory of Leadership   In contrast to Fiedler's view that specific individuals should be chosen to be leaders based upon the match between their leadership style and the amount of situational control, this notion of contingency suggests that leaders *can and should* adapt their styles to various situational demands. Specifically, the task of a leader is to strengthen subordinates' expectancy links.[21] These expectancy links come from expectancy theory (discussed in Chapter 4) and are the subordinates' perception of the ties between effort, performance, and desired outcomes. An effective leader will (1) encourage sub-

---

[21] R. J. House and T. R. Mitchell, "A Path-Goal Theory of Leadership," *Journal of Contemporary Business* 3 (1974): 81–97.

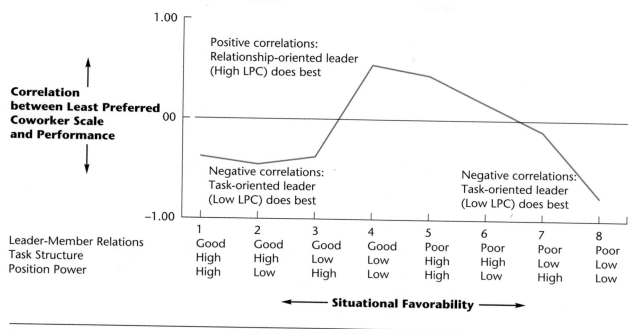

FIGURE 10–7 ▶ **Results from the Contingency Model Research**

Task-oriented leadership fits best with both high-control and low-control situations. Only in moderate-control conditions does contingency theory recommend relationship-oriented leadership.

Source: F. E. Fiedler, *A Theory of Leadership Effectiveness* (New York: McGraw-Hill, 1967).

ordinates' desires for outcomes over which the leader has some control; (2) ensure that performance is rewarded as expected (that the link between performance and expected outcome is strong); (3) coach and direct subordinates along the path of successful performance; (4) help subordinates clarify expectations (set goals, specify organizational expectations, identify the route to successful job performance); (5) ensure that the necessary resources (skills, equipment, training) for successful task performance are available to subordinates; and (6) develop both the extrinsic and *intrinsic* motivational forces of subordinates. To the extent that the leader is able to accomplish these tasks, the path-goal model of leadership suggests that subordinates will

1. *Experience high job satisfaction* as the path to job performance and subsequent rewards is more direct,
2. *Accept the leader* as the leader aids in the attainment of valued rewards, and
3. *Become motivated* (they will come to believe that they are performing the task required of them and that, in doing so, they will receive valued rewards).

Choosing a Leadership Style   The path-goal theory identifies four styles of leader behavior: directive, supportive, achievement-oriented, and participative. The

Focus on

Leadership Contingencies

Successful Leaders, Different Styles Carol Bartz of Autodesk was the Number 2 executive in Sun Microsystems, Inc., where she was responsible for half of the 12,000-member work force. When Scot McNealy tapped her to head his new Federal Systems Division back in 1987, she was worried that military buyers would not take a woman seriously. She was right, as secretaries kept asking when *Mr.* Bartz was arriving. Within a year, she tripled sales and put her career in overdrive. Now chairman and CEO of Autodesk, Bartz is a proponent of yes-and-no decision making. "I am not a dreamer," she says. Called Sun's most capable manager during her tenure there, her commanding presence is built on her no-nonsense style and determination. These characteristics sometimes put her at odds with her old boss.

Elizabeth Perle was named vice-president and publisher of Prentice-Hall Press in 1988. Her first act after being promoted to that position was to dismantle the office hierarchy. The only way she felt she could get the company going was to create an ego-free environment, where she could motivate her staff while remaining sensitive to the needs of her employees' professional and personal interests. To this end, Perle strives to create a safe environment. "I am as insecure as anyone on earth," she says. "I know I respond best in a safe environment where I know I can make a mistake. I don't mean endless job security; you should be expected to do your job. I mean safety predicated on respect. We want people to feel they're in a nonjudgmental environment, to be comfortable admitting they don't know something, to feel there is no hidden agenda." In creating such an environment, she has encouraged group communication and participative decision making. Office morale has improved and business is up. When the results were tallied, new book sales had increased by almost 40 percent in the two years following Perle's promotion.

Sources: Robert Hof, "25 Executives to Watch," *The 1991 Business Week 1000,* 52; and "How I Did It: Creating the Perfect Staff (for Fun and Profit)," *Working Woman,* November 1990, 73–76, 171.

first two styles are similar to the task-oriented and socioemotionally oriented leader behavior of other leadership theories. The third, achievement-oriented style, focuses on performance, goal setting, and other aspects consistent with McClelland's theories of motivating subordinates (discussed in Chapter 4). The fourth leadership style is participative. It focuses on behaviors that enlist the subordinates in the decision-making process of the organization. Examples of these specific leader behaviors are outlined in Figure 10–8.

In determining which leadership style to implement, the path-goal approach suggests that *both* subordinate and situational characteristics are important. Subordinate characteristics to be considered are their level of authoritarianism (rigidity), locus of control, and level of ability. The greater the

FIGURE 10–8	▶ Leader Behavior Dimensions in House and Mitchell's Path-Goal Theory

In the path-goal theory, there are four styles of leader behavior. The path-goal theory suggests that both subordinate and situational characteristics are important determinants of the appropriate leadership style.

Leader Directiveness
Letting subordinates know what is expected.
Providing specific guidance as to what should be done and how.
Making leader's part in the group understood.
Scheduling work to be done.
Maintaining definite standards of performance.

Leader Supportiveness
Showing concern for status and well-being of subordinates.
Doing little things to make work more pleasant.
Treating members as equals.
Being friendly and approachable.

Leader Achievement-Orientedness
Setting challenging goals.
Expecting subordinates to perform at their highest level.
Showing a high degree of confidence in subordinates.
Constantly emphasizing excellence in performance.

Leader Participativeness
Consulting with subordinates.
Soliciting subordinate suggestions.
Taking subordinate suggestions seriously.

Source: R. J. House and T. R. Mitchell, "Path-Goal Theory of Leadership," *Journal of Contemporary Business* (Autumn 1974): 81–94.

subordinates' perception of their ability relative to task demands, the less willing they are to accept a directive style of leadership. The more authoritarian the subordinates, the more likely they are to accept a directive style of leadership. Individuals with an internal locus of control (who believe that rewards are contingent upon their behavior—that they control what happens to them) are more satisfied with a participative style of leadership than are those with an external locus of control (who believe that their behaviors have little to do with the rewards they receive—that fate controls their destinies).

The situational or environmental variables to consider include the nature of the task, the formal authority structure of the organization, and the norms of interpersonal relationships within the organization. The more unstructured or ambiguous the task, the more likely subordinates are to be satisfied with a directive style of leadership. The more structured the task, the more important a supportive leadership style is to subordinate performance and satisfaction.[22]

[22] R. J. House and G. Dessler, "The Path-Goal Theory of Leadership: Some Post Hoc and A Priori Tests," *Contingency Approaches to Leadership*, ed. J. G. Hunt and L. L. Larson (Carbondale, Ill.: Southern Illinois University Press, 1974).

FIGURE 10–9	▶ Effective Leadership Styles under Certain Conditions: Predictions from the Path-Goal Theory of Leadership

According to path-goal theory, subordinate characeristics that determine appropriate leadership style include social and achievement needs; situational determinants include the nature of the task.

Sample Situational Characteristics	Leadership Styles			
	Directive	Supportive	Achievement	Participative
Task				
Structured	No	Yes	Yes	Yes
Unstructured	Yes	No	Yes	No
Clear goals	No	Yes	No	Yes
Ambiguous goals	Yes	No	Yes	No
Subordinates				
Skilled in task	No	Yes	Yes	Yes
Unskilled in task	Yes	No	Yes	No
High achievement needs	No	No	Yes	No
High social needs	No	Yes	No	Yes
Formal Authority				
Extensive	No	Yes	Yes	Yes
Limited	Yes	Yes	Yes	Yes
Work Group				
Strong social network	Yes	No	Yes	Yes
Experienced in collaboration	No	No	No	Yes
Organizational Culture				
Supports participation	No	No	No	Yes
Achievement-oriented	No	No	Yes	No

Source: J. C. Wofford and T. N. Srinivasan, "Experimental Tests of the Leader-Environment-Follower Interaction Theory of Leadership," *Organizational Behavior and Human Performance* 32 (1983): 35–54.

Figure 10–9 illustrates the situations in which each of the leadership styles results in positive outcomes. This figure illustrates, for example, that subordinates with a high need for achievement will respond satisfactorily only to a leader using an achievement-oriented leadership style.[23]

The path-goal theory of leadership provides some specific, testable predictions about leader effectiveness. Unfortunately, a review of the recent research on the path-goal theory of leadership has provided only marginal support for some of these predictions. For example, there is consistent evidence that subordinates will be more satisfied to perform in a structured situation when the leader effects a supportive style of leadership. With a directive style of lead-

---

[23] J. C. Wofford and T. N. Srinivasan, "Experimental Tests of the Leader-Environment-Follower Interaction Theory of Leadership," *Organizational Behavior and Human Performance* 32 (1983): 35–54.

ership in a highly structured task situation, the findings are mixed. Sometimes subordinate satisfaction suffers; sometimes subordinate satisfaction is enhanced.[24]

The evolution of leadership theory from a trait or behavior approach to a contingency perspective is critical to our understanding of this complex phenomenon. Just as the need theorists in Chapter 4 provided us with the insight that people are different and their needs and motivations cannot neatly fit into simple economic models, the contingency theories of leadership have illuminated the association between appropriate leadership style and task characteristics.

ALTERNATIVE THEORIES OF LEADERSHIP

Unfortunately, contingency theories of leadership have not answered all our questions about leadership. In fact, such models are primarily descriptive—that is, they describe which leadership style is best associated with which task or situation. Therefore, they leave gaps in our understanding of leadership. For example, what is the real impact of leader-subordinate interactions? Is it the leader who influences the subordinate, or does the subordinate's behavior subtly influence and shape the leader's behavior? What impact do leaders' perceptions of their subordinates have on their choice of leadership style? What characteristics of the task, the subordinates, or the situation make leaders more or less necessary? Finally, are there substitutes for leadership, such as work arrangements that make leadership less necessary?

Researchers recently have begun to fill in these gaps by examining leadership from different and relatively novel perspectives. For the most part, these new theories do not assume that leadership as an objective and consistent construct exists. Rather, they assume that leadership is a *social construction* of reality—a way that people talk about the relationships among employees in organizations. According to these new theories, leaders and leader behavior cannot exist independently from the task, situational, and subordinate components of the work environment. The final section of this chapter will address these more radical notions of leadership.

Leader-Member Exchange Model	In the behavioral theories of leadership discussed earlier, the leader's behavior was assumed to be consistent across all subordinates. However, the **leader-member exchange model,** which is based on exchange theory, focuses on the differential patterns of leader interaction within the work group. As an extension of exchange theory, it suggests that the leader does not interact with the group as a whole. Rather, the leader has individual relationships with each

---

[24]C. A. Schriecheim and A. Denisi, "Task Dimensions as Moderators of the Effects of Instrumental Leadership: A Two-Sample Replicated Test of Path Goal Leadership Theory," *Journal of Applied Psychology* (October 1981): 589–597; and J. Indvik, "Path-Goal Theory of Leadership: A Meta-Analysis," *Proceedings of the Academy of Management Meetings.* (1984): 189–192.

work-group member, and the nature of these dyadic (two-person) relationships determines the behaviors of subordinates.[25]

The relationships between individual work-group members have been categorized based on each member's association with an in-group or an out-group. Whether or not a person is a member of the in-group depends on that individual's association with the leader. Subordinates are members of the in-group if they share common interests with the leader and are part of the leader's communication and support network. Members of the out-group, then, have less in common with the leader and are less likely to support or associate with the leader.

In-group membership results in a better understanding between the subordinate and the leader. As supervisors become more knowledgeable about the specific strengths and weaknesses of their in-group subordinates, they are likely to express more faith in their performance potential and judgment than in those of out-group members. The competitive advantage of in-group membership is that it is a self-fulfilling prophecy. While differences in the performance potential of in-group and out-group members may be low initially, over time these differences will be magnified. For example, if a task is sufficiently critical or complex, the supervisor is more likely to assign it to an individual in whom that supervisor has more trust. Particularly valued assignments will likely go to someone who deserves to be rewarded—a member of the in-group. Out-group members are likely to be assigned the remaining tasks—tasks that are repetitive, unimportant, and repugnant.

Over time, then, the leader will come to see in-group members (whose abilities have been challenged and rewarded) as better able to handle the responsibilities of important hierarchical positions. The performance of out-group members, on the other hand, will have deteriorated, thus completing the cycle of the self-fulfilling prophecy. Not only will these employees be unchallenged by their assignments, but both the employees' and their leader's perceptions of their capabilities will be seriously eroded. Job satisfaction will be low and turnover high.

Given human nature, the development of in-groups and out-groups is difficult to avoid in organizational settings. Such a split may not be damaging to work-group effectiveness if there are tasks that do not require a great deal of coordination among the groups. Tasks that can be accomplished through the skills of a few exceptional individuals also may not suffer from the existence of in-groups and out-groups. However, overreliance on a small portion of the work force to the exclusion of other members can seriously hamper a work group's overall performance. As suggested in Chapter 9, one of the clear advantages of group decision making lies in the added benefit accruing from the full use of the unique knowledge and skills of group members. Systematically excluding the contributions of some individuals clearly is undesirable. Leaders trying to avoid such a split should examine their patterns of work assignment and reinforcement carefully. In some cases, they might have to behave counter to their instincts by assigning challenging and critical tasks to those about whom they are unsure.

---

[25] G. Graen, F. Dansereau and T. Minami, "Dysfunctional Leadership Styles," *Organizational Behavior and Human Performance* 7 (1972): 216–236; and D. Duchon, S. Green, and T. Taber, "Vertical Dyad Linkage: A Longitudinal Assessment of Antecedents, Measures, and Consequences." *Journal of Applied Psychology* 71 (1986) 56–60.

That the leader's perception of the subordinate influences leader behavior and, in turn, influences subordinate behavior should not be surprising. The mutual influence processes of exchange theory, equity theory, and negotiation have been described in other chapters. The notion that subordinate performance may be more influenced by leader perceptions and subsequent behavior than by innate ability and skill is also critical to the second alternative theory of leadership, the attribution model.

Attribution Model of Leadership

Unlike other leadership models, the attribution model of leadership deals specifically with perceptions and subsequent behaviors of organizational actors. This model has two facets: (1) leader attributions for and reactions to poor performance by subordinates, and (2) observer attributions for and reactions to poor performance by the leader. Similar to the leader-member exchange model, it is based upon the notion that leaders and followers are involved in a mutual influence process.

Leader Attributions In the daily performance of work, a leader obtains information about subordinates and their behaviors. Based upon this information, the leader makes a determination—an attribution—of the cause of each subordinate's behaviors and selects strategies to deal with any poor performers. The leader's attributions as much as the subordinate's behaviors determine how the leader responds to poor performers.

As detailed in Chapter 3, attributions are based upon three dimensions of behavior: distinctiveness (Did the behavior occur on this task but not on other tasks?), consensus (Is this level of performance common to other organizational actors?), and consistency (Is this level of performance common for this employee?). The answers to these three questions identify for the leader either an external (situational) or internal (personal) cause for the employee's poor performance.

This attribution is critical to leader-follower relations. A subordinate whose successes or failures are attributed to personal traits such as skill or natural ability will have very different interactions with the leader than a subordinate whose successes or failures are attributed to environmental factors, such as luck.[26] These attributions can influence many different facets of a leader's behavior. The perceived causes of a subordinate's poor performance have important implications for how a leader rewards or punishes a behavior. Typically, leaders attempt to change a subordinate's behavior only when an internal (personal) attribution is made. These types of changes are most clearly amenable to the influence of rewards and punishments. If the leader attributes a subordinate's performance to an external cause, then the leader likely will focus on changing the environment—what the leader perceives to be the *real* cause of the subordinate's poor performance.

A second aspect of leader behavior affected by a leader's attributions for subordinate performance is the level of supervision. If the leader believes that a subordinate's earlier successes were due to intense supervision, then the leader

[26]T. R. Mitchell, S. G. Green, and R. E. Wood, "An Attribution Model of Leadership and the Poor Performing Subordinate: Development and Validation," *Research in Organization Behavior,* vol. 3, eds L. L. Cummings and B. M. Staw (Greenwich, Conn.: JAI Press, 1981): 197–234.

likely will continue the previous level of supervision. If the subordinate's performance is attributed to an internal cause such as personal skill or effort, then supervision is likely to be less intense.

Finally, a leader's performance *expectations* of subordinates also will be influenced by attributions. If a subordinate's success is attributed to ability or skill, then the leader will be more likely to expect future performance to be consistently high than if success is attributed to an external cause such as luck.[27] Further, the stronger the internal attribution for success, the higher the leader's aspirations for future follower performance. The complete model of the attribution process from the leader's perspective is illustrated in Figure 10–10.

Observer Attributions   As mentioned earlier in this chapter, leaders often are given credit for organizational successes and blamed for organizational failures, regardless of their real causes. Leadership is a concern of organization observers (such as stockholders, employees, or anyone but the leader) who are attempting to understand and subsequently control their world. It is tempting to trace all organizational successes and failures back to individual leaders rather than try to understand the complex web of individual, organizational, and environmental factors involved. People want to believe that individuals can significantly influence organizational performance. One study found that when observers were told that a work group had performed well, they concluded that the leader had been more consistent and provided more task structure than he or she did when the work group performed poorly.[28] Thus, the importance and reliance on leaders as the causal agent for organizational success or failure imbues them with considerable (and possibly undeserved) power.

The belief that leaders are responsible for organizational outcomes may be reinforced by such organizational actions as the investment of critical resources in selecting a leader or the firing of a leader whose work group's performance is inadequate. If there is an elaborate and detailed search and selection process to identify a new leader, followed by formal ceremonies to install that individual in the position, that leader's legitimacy is much greater than it is if chosen by the flip of a coin. In professional team sports, it is unlikely that an owner will fire the entire team when it performs poorly. Instead, the firing of the team's manager or coach as the obvious scapegoat symbolizes management's conviction that steps must be taken to enhance organizational performance.

From this perspective, successful leaders will be those who associate themselves with successes and dissociate themselves from failures—who figure out where the group is heading and arrive there first. When they know that a group or division is about to improve because of economic cycles, successful leaders will visibly and vividly associate themselves with that group and its performance. When failure of a group or division is imminent, then successful leaders will distance themselves from the actions of that group, perhaps going as far as transferring to another group or to a completely different organization.[29]

---

[27] B. Weiner, R. Nierenberg, and M. Goldstein, "Social Learning (Locus of Control) versus Attributional (Causal Stability) Interpretations of Expectancy of Success," *Journal of Personality* 44 (1976): 52–68.

[28] J. R. Larson, J. H. Lingle, and M. M. Scerbo, "The Impact of Performance Cues on Leader-Behavior Ratings: The Role of Selective Information Availability and Probabilistic Response Bias," *Organizational Behavior and Human Performance* 33 (1984): 323–349.

[29] J. Pfeffer, "The Ambiguity of Leadership," *Academy of Management Review* 2 (1977): 104–112.

FIGURE 10–10 ▶An Attribution Model of Leader Behavior

As with the leader-member exchange model, the attribution model of leadership emphasizes the mutual influence of leaders and followers. The core of this model is attributions for and reactions to poor performance by either the leader or followers.

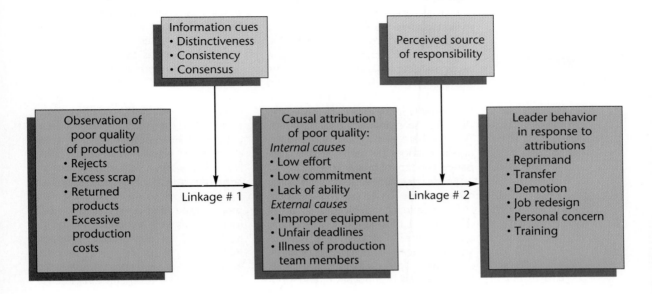

Source: T. R. Mitchell and R. E. Wood, "An Empirical Test of an Attributional Model of Leader's Responses to Poor Performance," in *Academy of Management Proceedings*, ed. R. C. Huseman (Academy of Management, 1979), 94.

Both the attributional model of leadership and the leader-member exchange model assume that the perception of hierarchical leadership and its subsequent influence are important for organizational performance. A third and final perspective on leadership suggests that many individual, organizational, and task characteristics have the capacity to serve as **substitutes for leadership.**

Substitutes for Leadership

Many of the theories introduced in this chapter make the implicit assumption that leadership makes a difference. While it is generally accepted that no one leadership trait is dominant enough to be effective in all situations, the focus in most modern theories of leadership is on determining in which situational contingencies a particular style of leadership will be more effective. Sometimes, however, hierarchical leadership does not have its intended influence. Even some of the more traditional leadership theories such as path-goal theory suggest that when both paths and goals are clear, attempts by the leader to clarify them will be redundant and will be seen by subordinates as imposing unnecessary, close control.[30] Such close control may enhance performance by reduc-

---

[30]House and Mitchell, "A Path-Goal Theory of Leadership."

Focus on

Substitutes for Leadership

Leading without Leaders, Managing without Managers   The SemCo Corporation was close to financial disaster in 1980. It was 27 years old and its 100 employees manufactured hydraulic pumps for ships, generating about $4 million in sales. Now, it is one of Brazil's fastest growing companies with 800 employees, sales of $37 million, and a profit margin of 10 percent. One of the main differences between 1980 and now is that Ricardo Semler joined the family-owned company as president. How did he manage the turnaround? Through hard work, good luck, and the drastic changes he made in the company's concept of management.

Semler has three fundamental values on which he bases his management style: employee involvement, profit sharing, and information. Transforming the bureaucracy of SemCo to encourage employee involvement required overcoming four major obstacles: size, hierarchy, lack of motivation, and ignorance. Semco had too many managers in too many layers holding too many

meetings. So, Semler decided to physically restructure the organization into three separate groups housed in three separate buildings. This separation was not only physical but also organizational. The company separated everything it could: entrances, receiving docks, inventories, telephones, and auxiliary functions such as personnel, management information systems, and internal control. Semco even scrapped the centralized mainframe computer for three independent PC-based systems. In doing so, the company lost the benefit of economies of scale. As such, its restructuring initially increased costs. However, within a year, the company's aggregate sales doubled, inventories fell from 136 days to 46 days, eight new products that had been stalled in R&D for two years were launched, and the rejection rate on one product dropped from 33 percent to less than 1 percent. In addition, the work force was reduced by 32 percent through attrition and retirement incentives.

Second, Semler restructured the or-

Ricardo Semler, "Managing Without Managers," *Harvard Business Review*, September/October 1989, 76–84.

ing goldbricking, but it will reduce participant satisfaction as well. While leader behavior is redundant in such situational, a number of research studies now go further, arguing that, in many situations, leader behavior and hierarchical leadership are irrelevant.

Studies examining the impact of leader behaviors in organizations occasionally find that situational factors can neutralize or substitute for the formal leader's ability to influence work-group satisfaction or performance.[31] A **neutralizer** is a factor that paralyzes, destroys, or counteracts the effectiveness of leader behaviors, making it impossible for them to have an impact. A **substitute** makes leader behaviors not only impossible but also unnecessary. Thus, all substitutes are neutralizers, but all neutralizers are not necessarily substitutes for leadership. For example, a professional orientation (a commitment to a profession rather than to an organization) is more of a substitute for leadership than a neutralizer. Individuals who are seriously committed to their professions care more about horizontal than vertical relationships, give considerable credence to peer reviews and evaluations rather than to hierarchical evaluations, and tend to develop relationships external to the employing organization.[32] Alternatively,

[31] S. Kerr, "Substitutes for Leadership: Some Implications for Organizational Design," *Organizational Administrative Science* 8 (1977): 135–146.

[32] A. C. Filley, R. J. House, and S. Kerr, *Managerial Processes and Organizational Behavior* (Glenview, Ill.: Scott, Foresman, 1976).

ganization into three concentric circles. The small central circle contains five people called counselors (who include the CEO and Semler) who integrate the company's movements. The second concentric circle contains the heads of the eight divisions, called partners. Finally, the third and largest circle holds all the remaining organizational members, most of whom are associates. Some of the associates are permanent or temporary team and task leaders, called coordinators. So, in this organization, there are four titles and three layers of management.

Decision making is collegial and group driven. For example, individuals are not hired or promoted until they have been interviewed and accepted by all their future subordinates. And twice yearly, all employees anonymously fill out a survey on the credibility and competence of top management. Even such important and bid-dollar decisions such as the site of a new plant are made by the employees. For example, after deciding on the new building, the employees designed the layout of the flex-

ible manufacturing system and hired the artist to paint the entire building, including the machinery. Five years after the move, the division's productivity in dollars per year per employee jumped from $14,200 to almost $50,000.

Most of the rules and regulations have also been abolished and replaced with common sense. There is no formal dress code, no rules about travel expenses, no security searches, storeroom padlocks, no audits of petty-cash accounts, and the company has eliminated time clocks. Employees rotate jobs every two to five years to prevent boredom. People come in on their own schedules, even on the factory floor. They coordinate their work hours with their coworkers. In general, employees are treated like adults. As Ricardo Semler reports, "They can paint the walls whatever color they like. They can come to work whenever they decide. They can wear whatever clothing makes them comfortable. They can do whatever they want. It is up to them to see the connection between productivity and profit and to act on it."

hierarchical leadership is neutralized when the work is very standardized, machine-paced, or serially interdependent. In these situations, the employee has little autonomy or ability to be influenced by leader behaviors. Examples of potential substitutes for or neutralizers of leadership are presented in Figure 10–11.

Leadership substitutes or neutralizers are often aspects of the task sought by employees and employers alike. For example, Figure 10–11 identifies task-provided performance feedback as a mechanism that can supplant leader usefulness. Since task-provided feedback is the most immediate, accurate, and intrinsically motivating source of performance information, a leader's ability to influence employee performance through performance evaluation may pale in comparison.[33] Organizations should create mechanisms for including such factors as task-provided feedback or peer evaluation systems or goal setting in their daily activities. If the organization is to benefit from these substitutes, it is essential that such factors be incorporated in the routine of the firm. In the "FOCUS ON: Substitutes for Leadership," one president describes his organizational structure and management philosophy, which serves as a substitute for leadership.

[33] S. Kerr and J. Jermier, "Substitutes for Leadership: Their Meaning and Measurement," *Organizational Behavior and Human Performance* 22 (1978): 375–403.

FIGURE 10–11	▶ Potential Substitutes for and Neutralizers of Hierarchical Leadership

Factors embedded in situations can neutralize or substitute for a leader's influence on group satisfaction and performance. Substitutes and neutralizers include characteristics of the worker, the worker's task, or the organization.

Worker	Worker's Task	Organization
Ability	Repetitiveness and ambiguity	Formalization
Experience	Methodological invariance	Inflexibility
Training	Intrinsic satisfaction	Highly specific, active advisory and staff functions
Knowledge	Task-provided feedback concerning accomplishment	
Professional orientation		Closely knit, cohesive work group
Need for independence		Rewards outside leader's control
Indifference toward organizational rewards		Spatial distance between leader and subordinate

The concept of substitutes for and neutralizers of hierarchical leadership is an interesting one. It is unlikely that any organization will have so many such factors that leadership is rendered totally useless. On the other hand, it is equally unlikely that they will be so rare that followers will be forced to rely exclusively on leaders. Thus, in attempting to better understand the impact of leaders and leader behaviors, it is important that we consider when leadership is useful *as well as* when it is irrelevant or harmful to organizational performance.

SUMMARY

Leadership is a broad and difficult topic within organizational behavior. Researchers and practitioners alike have wrestled with this concept, trying to understand its specific components. Early in its history, leadership research focused on the personalities of those identified as leaders. The basic assumption of this research was that a set of unique personality and demographic characteristics differentiated leaders from followers. As this method proved less than useful, emphasis was placed on specific leader behaviors— whether the leader was concerned with the socioemotional or task aspects of the work group. The universal-trait and universal-behavior approaches both ignore the influence of the particular situation in which the leader works. In contrast, the contingency approach to leadership—that leadership makes a difference and that its effectiveness depends on the specific situation—provides a more complex and interactional view of leader behavior. No longer is the efficacy of leader behaviors thought to be based only on the unique personality or predilections of the designated leader. Rather, the efficacy of leadership may be tied to the favorableness of the situation. However, Fiedler recommends that leaders be chosen to fit the situation in which they will be working rather than situations altered to fit the leadership style of the individual.

The intransigence of leadership style was at odds with the experience of many organizational actors, creating a theoretical and practical vacuum. What was needed was a theory of leadership that incorporated a responsibility for organizational leaders. In the path-goal theory of leadership, the leader's effectiveness is influenced by various situational components. The leader's task is to make the paths to performance and rewards for performance clearly visible to subordinates. While this perspective on leadership provided more flexibility for the leader in responding to organization demands, it (along with its predecessors) implicitly assumed that leadership was real, that it was a construct that could be identified and studied separate from other organizational influences—particularly subordinates.

Alternative views of leadership such as the leader-member exchange model suggest that, while leadership is important, it is by no means one-dimensional. The same leader behavior can influence subordinates in a variety of ways, depending on their in-group or out-group membership. The primary assumption of the leader-member exchange model is that leadership is *interactive*.

An extension of this interactive notion is found in the attribution model of leadership. This model suggests that leadership exists because people (subordinates and leaders alike) have certain expectations about how individuals will behave. Therefore, what people think is more important than what is. If leaders develop attributions about the behavior of subordinates, they will behave consistently with those attributions, regardless of their veracity. Subordinates also make attributions about individuals in the role of leader. Those attributions influence the leader's ability to effectively impact subordinate performance.

The final model of leadership presented here assumes leadership may be more or less useful, depending upon the existence of substitutes for or neutralizers of leadership. That is, the greater the presence of particular task, subordinate, and organizational characteristics (such as intrinsically satisfying work, ability and experience, and inflexibility, respectively) the less relevant or necessary the role of the leader.

Regardless of the particular perspective on leadership, of whether it exists as a unique psychological construct, or of the inability of leadership theories to predict leader effectiveness, the importance of leadership to organizational effectiveness is an intriguing and amorphous topic. It would be premature to suggest either that leadership is a topic that has outlived its usefulness or that all the answers have been found. Most likely, this is an area that will continue to motivate both researchers and practitioners to search for better answers.

Key Terms

Charismatic leadership Process used by transformational leaders to develop a common vision of what could be, discover or create opportunities, and strengthen organizational members' control of their own destinies.

Contingency model of leadership Theory suggesting that leadership effectiveness is determined both by the characteristics of the leader and by the level of situational favorableness that exists.

Custodial leadership Process used by transactional leaders to improve working conditions, compensation, and fringe benefits.

Employee (socioemotional)-oriented leadership Process used by leaders that emphasizes the individual worker's needs in managing group performance; also called *initiating consideration*.

Leader-member exchange model Model based on exchange theory that stresses the importance of individual relationships between leader and subordinates. Each relationship is termed a vertical dyad.

Leadership Increment of influence over and above an employee's mechanical compliance with routine directives of the organization.

Least-preferred coworker (LPC) scale Questionnaire that measures how respondents characterize their feelings about a person with whom they work least effectively. A high LPC score (favoring the least preferred coworker) suggests that the leader derives satisfaction and a sense of accomplishment from relationships with others; a low LPC score suggests that the leader emphasizes completing tasks, even at the expense of interpersonal relationships.

Managerial grid Leadership training program conducted by Robert Blake and Jane Mouton that reflects two dimensions of leader behavior: concern for production (task-oriented leadership) and concern for people (socioemotional leadership).

Managerial leadership Process used by transactional leaders to provide subordinates work that is less routine and more challenging, build cohesive work teams, and give employees more say in decisions that affect them directly.

Neutralizers of leadership Factors that paralyze, destroy, or counteract the effectiveness of leader behaviors, making it difficult for them to have an impact.

Production (task)-oriented leadership Process used by leaders to direct activities related specifically to the task; also called initiating structure.

Substitutes for leadership Individual, organizational, and task characteristics that have the capacity to serve the same purposes as leader behaviors.

Transactional leader Leader who motivates followers by exchanging rewards for services.

Transformational leader Leader who arouses intense feeling and generates turbulent one-to-one relationships with followers and is inspirational and concerned with ideas rather than processes.

Discussion Questions

1. The current wisdom—based on leadership theories—is that effective leaders must be flexible in implementing specific leader behaviors. What, if any, are the potential problems with this perspective?

2. Although they are very different, Fiedler's contingency theory of leadership and House and Mitchell's path-goal model of leadership are categorized as contingency models. What does the term *contingency* really mean in these instances?

3. Based on your knowledge of leadership theory, how would you go about selecting an effective leader from a group of managers? What is an "effective" leader?

4. What is it that the LPC scale *really* measures? What background characteristics would distinguish a person with a high LPC and a low LPC score?

5. While most organizational behavior theorists would support a contingency perspective as the premier model of leader behavior, articles such as the recent *Fortune* article highlighted in this chapter's "FOCUS ON: Transformational Leaders" indicate the increasing attraction of a trait approach to leadership. What is it about transformational leaders that practitioners find so compelling? What are some of the problems with the "great person" notion?

6. Why should managers be sensitive to the existence of substitutes for leadership in their organizations? How might such substitutes enhance or detract from their leadership efforts?

If You Want to Know More

Leadership is a topic for which there is no dearth of material or interest. For a more traditional perspective on leadership research and findings, Gary Yukl's *Leadership in Organizations* (Englewood Cliffs, N.J.: Prentice-Hall, 1989) is a useful starting point. *Stodgill's Handbook of Leadership*, authored after Stodgill's death by Bernard Bass (New York: Free Press, 1981) is a classic in the area of leadership. Stodgill was instrumental in moving the leadership field away from its preoccupation with the trait approach. A recent addition to the leadership literature is an excellent analysis of executive leadership written by Robert G. Lord and Karen J. Maher entitled *Leadership and Information Processing* (Boston: Unwin Hyman, 1991). For a more practitioner-oriented perspective, Edwin P. Hollander's *Leadership Dynamics: A Practical Guide to Effective Relationships* (New York: Free Press/Macmillan, 1978) is helpful.

Examining the latest perspectives on transformational leadership is the purpose of Noel Tichy and Mary Ann Devanna's *The Transformational Leader* (New York: Wiley, 1986). Their book examines the unique kind of leader demanded by organizations and corporations in the 1980s.

From a different perspective, the interested reader may wish to consider Kathy Kram's *Mentoring at Work* (Glenview, Ill.: Scott, Foresman, 1985). This book is based upon Kram's research examining the mentoring process in the development of managerial and leadership talent. Finally, one might also wish to read Jim Wall's *Bosses* (Lexington, Mass.: Lexington Books, 1986). Modeled in part after Studs Terkel's *Working*, this book examines the leadership process, expectations, and behaviors of a variety of individuals, including transients, air controllers, and gangsters.

On Your Own

T–P Leadership Questionnaire: An Assessment of Style Some leaders deal with general directions, leaving details to subordinates. Other leaders focus on specific details with the expectation that subordinates will carry out orders. Depending on the situation, both approaches may be effective. The important issue is the ability to identify relevant dimensions of the situation and behave accordingly. Through this questionnaire, you can identify your relative emphasis on two dimensions of leadership: task orientation and people orientation. These are not opposite approaches, and an individual can rate high or low on either or both.

Directions: The following items describe aspects of leadership behavior. Respond to each item according to the way you would most likely act if you were the leader of a work group. Circle whether you would most likely behave in the described way: always (A), frequently (F), occasionally (O), seldom (S), or never (N).

A F O S N	1. I would most likely act as the spokesperson of the group.
A F O S N	2. I would encourage overtime work.
A F O S N	3. I would allow members complete freedom in their work.
A F O S N	4. I would encourage the use of uniform procedures.
A F O S N	5. I would permit members to use their own judgment in solving problems.
A F O S N	6. I would stress being ahead of competing groups.
A F O S N	7. I would speak as a representative of the group.
A F O S N	8. I would needle members for greater effort.
A F O S N	9. I would try out my ideas in the group.
A F O S N	10. I would let members do their work the way they think best.
A F O S N	11. I would be working hard for a promotion.
A F O S N	12. I would tolerate postponement and uncertainty.
A F O S N	13. I would speak for the group if there were visitors present.
A F O S N	14. I would keep the work moving at a rapid pace.
A F O S N	15. I would turn the members loose on a job and let them go to it.
A F O S N	16. I would settle conflicts when they occur in the group.
A F O S N	17. I would get swamped by details.
A F O S N	18. I would represent the group at outside meetings.
A F O S N	19. I would be reluctant to allow the members any freedom of action.
A F O S N	20. I would decide what should be done and how it should be done.
A F O S N	21. I would push for increased production.
A F O S N	22. I would let some members have authority which I could keep.
A F O S N	23. Things would usually turn out as I had predicted.
A F O S N	24. I would allow the group a high degree of initiative.
A F O S N	25. I would assign group members to particular tasks.
A F O S N	26. I would be willing to make changes.
A F O S N	27. I would ask the members to work harder.
A F O S N	28. I would trust the group members to exercise good judgment.
A F O S N	29. I would schedule the work to be done.
A F O S N	30. I would refuse to explain my actions.
A F O S N	31. I would persuade others that my ideas are to their advantage.
A F O S N	32. I would permit the group to set its own pace.
A F O S N	33. I would urge the group to beat its previous record.
A F O S N	34. I would act without consulting the group.
A F O S N	35. I would ask that group members follow standard rules and regulations.

T——————————————————— P———————————————————

The T–P Leadership Questionnaire is scored as follows:
a. Circle the item number for items 8, 12, 17, 18, 19, 30, 34, and 35.
b. Write the number 1 in front of a *circled item number* if you responded S (seldom) or N (never) to that item.
c. Also write a number 1 in front of *item numbers not circled* if you responded A (always) or F (frequently).
d. Circle the number 1's that you have written in front of the following items: 3, 5, 8, 10, 15, 18, 19, 22, 24, 26, 28, 30, 32, 34, and 35.
e. *Count the circled number 1's.* This is your score for concern for people. Record the score in the blank following the letter P at the end of the questionnaire.
f. *Count uncircled number 1's.* This is your score for concern for task. Record this number in the blank following the letter T.

Source: The T–P Leadership Questionnaire was adapted by J. B. Ritchie and P. Thompson in *Organization and People* (New York: West, 1984). Copyright 1969 by the American Educational Research Association. Adapted by permission of the publisher.

CLOSING CASE

CHAPTER 10

THE MANAGER'S MEMO

FROM: I. Rand, President

TO: T. Meyers, Vice President, Human Resources

RE: Leadership Development Program

To support our plans to open ten new stores over the next five years, I think we need a program to develop future store managers. I would like your support in creating a leadership development program.

This program would have two phases: (1) identifying employees with leadership potential and (2) developing in them the skills that make a person a good leader.

Please submit to me your recommendations for how to carry out each phase of this program. If you would submit these recommendations in the form of a general outline of what the program should include, we can discuss the details in a meeting next week.

Case Discussion Questions

Assume you are the vice-president of the human resources division, and write a response to the president's memo. Use the material in the chapter as a resource for outlining a program you think will most likely succeed in meeting the president's objectives. Consider also the type of leadership most likely to be important in a store manager.

EXERCISE

PART 3:

The Desert Survival Situation

The situation described in this exercise is based on over 2,000 actual cases in which men and women lived or died depending upon the survival decisions they made. Your "life" or "death" will depend upon how well your group can share its present knowledge of a relatively unfamiliar problem so that the team can make decisions that will lead to your survival.

When instructed, read about the situation and do Step 1 without discussing it with the rest of the group.

The Situation

It is approximately 10:00 A.M. in mid-August, and you have just crash landed in the Sonora Desert in the southwestern United States. The light twin-engine plane, containing the bodies of the pilot and the copilot, has completely burned. Only the air frame remains. None of the rest of you has been injured.

The pilot was unable to notify anyone of your position before the crash. However, he had indicated before impact that you were 70 miles south-south-west from a mining camp that is the nearest known habitation and that you were approximately 65 miles off the course that was filed in your VFR Flight Plan.

The immediate area is quite flat and, except for occasional barrel and saguaro cacti, appears to be rather barren. The last weather report indicated the temperature would reach 110° that day, which means that the temperature at ground level will be 130°. You are dressed in lightweight clothing: short-sleeved shirts, pants, socks, and street shoes. Everyone has a handkerchief. Collectively, your pockets contain $2.83 in change, $85.00 in bills, a pack of cigarettes, and a ballpoint pen.

Your Task

Before the plane caught fire your group was able to salvage the 15 items listed in the following table. Your task is to rank these items according to their importance to your survival, starting with "1," the most important, to "15," the least important.

You may assume the following:

1. The number of survivors is the same as the number on your team.
2. You are the actual people in the situation.
3. The team has agreed to stick together.
4. All items are in good condition.

Step 1 Each member of the team is to individually rank each item. Do not discuss the situation or problem until each member has finished the individual ranking.

Step 2 After everyone has finished the individual ranking, rank order the 15 items as a team. Once discussion begins do not change your individual ranking. Your instructor will inform you how much time you have to complete this step.

Items	Step 1: Your Individual Ranking	Step 2: The Team's Ranking	Step 3: Survival Expert's Ranking	Step 4: Difference between Step 1 and Step 3	Step 5: Difference between Step 2 and Step 3
Flashlight (4-battery size)	_____	_____	_____	_____	_____
Jackknife	_____	_____	_____	_____	_____
Sectional air map of the area	_____	_____	_____	_____	_____
Plastic raincoat (large size)	_____	_____	_____	_____	_____
Magnetic compass	_____	_____	_____	_____	_____
Compress kit with gauze	_____	_____	_____	_____	_____
.45 caliber pistol (loaded)	_____	_____	_____	_____	_____
Parachute (red and white)	_____	_____	_____	_____	_____
Bottle of salt tablets (1,000 tablets)	_____	_____	_____	_____	_____
1 quart of water per person	_____	_____	_____	_____	_____
A book entitled *Edible Animals of the Desert*	_____	_____	_____	_____	_____
A pair of sunglasses per person	_____	_____	_____	_____	_____
2 quarts of 180 proof vodka	_____	_____	_____	_____	_____
1 top coat per person	_____	_____	_____	_____	_____
A cosmetic mirror	_____	_____	_____	_____	_____

Totals
(the lower the score, the better) _____ _____

Your Score, Step 4   Team Score, Step 5

Please complete the following steps and insert the scores under your team's number.	Team Number					
	1	2	3	4	5	6

Step 6: Average Individual Score
Add up all the individual scores (Step 4) on the team and divide by the number on the team _____ _____ _____ _____ _____ _____

Step 7: Team Score _____ _____ _____ _____ _____ _____

Step 8: Gain Score
The difference between the Team Score and the Average Individual Score. If the Team Score is lower than Average Individual Score, then gain "+". If Team Score is higher than Average Individual Score, then gain is ">". _____ _____ _____ _____ _____ _____

Step 9: Lowest Individual Score on the Team _____ _____ _____ _____ _____ _____

Step 10: Number of Individual Scores Lower Than the Team Score. _____ _____ _____ _____ _____ _____

Source: J. Clayton Lafferty, Patrick M. Eady, and Alonzo W. Pond, "The Desert Survival Situation: A Group Decision Making Experience for Examining and Increasing Individual and Team Effectiveness," 8th ed. Copyright © 1974 by Experiential Learning Methods, Inc., 15200 E. Jefferson, Suite 107, Grosse Pointe Park, MI 48230, (313) 823-4400. Used with permission.

CASE

PART 3:

The Making of a Bad Cop

What makes a policeman go sour? I can tell you. I was a Denver policeman until not so long ago. Then I quit so I could hold my head up.

Don't get me wrong. I'm not trying to shift the burden of responsibility for the burglaries, break-ins, safe jobs, and that sort of thing. That is bad, very bad. But I will leave it to the big shots and the newspapers and the courts to say and do what needs to be said and done about that.

My concern is about the individual officer, the ordinary, hard-working, basically honest but awfully hard-pressed guy who is really suffering now.

Young fellows don't put on these blue uniforms to be crooks. There are a lot of reasons, but for most of the guys it adds up to the fact they thought it was an honorable, decent way of making a living.

Somewhere along the line a guy's disillusioned. Along the way the pressures mount up. Somewhere along the way he may decide to quit fighting them and make the conscious decision to try to "beat" society instead.

But long before he gets to that point, almost as soon as he dons the uniform, in fact, he is taking the first little steps down the road that does, for some, eventually lead to the penitentiary.

Let me back up a little. I want to talk about how you get to be a policeman, because this is where the trouble really starts.

Almost any able-bodied man can become a policeman in Denver. If he is within the age brackets, if he is a high school graduate, if he has no criminal record, he is a cinch.

There isn't much to getting through the screening, and some bad ones do get through. There are the usual examinations and questionnaires. Then there is the interview. A few command officers ask questions. There is a representative of civil service and a psychiatrist present.

They ask the predictable questions and just about everybody gives the predictable answers: "Why do you want to become a policeman?" "I've always wanted to be a policeman. I want to help people." Five or ten minutes and it is over.

Five or ten minutes to spot the sadist, the psychopath—or the guy with an eye for an easy buck. I guess they weed some out. Some others they get at the Police Academy. But some get through.

Along with those few bad ones, there are more good ones, and a lot of average, ordinary human beings who have this in common: They want to be policemen.

The job has (or had) some glamour for the young man who likes authority, who finds appeal in making a career of public service, who is extroverted or aggressive.

Before you knock those qualities, remember two things: first, they are the same qualities we admire in a business executive. Second, if it weren't for men with these qualities, you wouldn't have any police protection.

The Police Academy is point No. 2 in my bill of particulars. It is a fine thing in a way. You meet the cream of the Police Department. Your expectations soar. You know you are going to make the grade and be a good officer. But how well are you really prepared?

There are six weeks at the academy—four weeks in my time. Six hectic weeks in which to learn all about the criminal laws you have sworn to enforce, to assimilate the rules of evidence, methods of arbitration, use of firearms, mob and riot control, first aid (including, if you please, some basic obstetrics), public relations, and so on.

There is an intangible something else that is not on the formal agenda. You begin to learn that this is a fraternity into which you are not automatically accepted by your fellows. You have to earn your way in; you have to establish that you are "all right."

And even this early there is a slight sour note. You knew, of course, that you had to provide your own uniforms, your own hat, shoes, shirts, pistol, and bullets out of your $393 a month.

You knew the city would generously provide you with the cloth for two pairs of trousers and a uniform blouse.

What you didn't know was that you don't just choose a tailor shop for price and get the job done.

You are sent to a place by the Police Department to get the tailoring done. You pay the price even though the work may be ill-fitting. It seems a little odd to you that this is always the same establishment. But it is a small point, and you have other things on your mind.

So the rookie, full of pride and high spirits, his head full of partly learned information, is turned over to a more experienced man for breaking in. He is on "probation" for six months.

The rookie knows he is being watched by all the older hands around him. He is eager to be accepted. He accepts advice gratefully.

Then he gets little signs that he has been making a good impression. It may happen like this: The older man stops at a bar, comes out with some packages of cigarettes. He does this several times. He explains that this is part of the job, getting cigarettes free from proprietors to resell, and that as a part of the rookie's training it is his turn to "make the butts."

So he goes into a skid-row bar and stands uncomfortably at the end waiting for the bartender to acknowledge his presence and disdainfully toss him two packages of butts.

The feeling of pride slips away and a hint of shame takes hold. But he tells himself this is unusual, that he will say nothing that will upset his probation standing. In six months, after he gets his commission, he will be the upright officer he meant to be.

One thing leads to another for the rookies. After six months they have become conditioned to accept free meals, a few packages of cigarettes, turkeys at Thanksgiving, and liquor at Christmas from the respectable people in their district.

The rule book forbids all this. But it isn't enforced. It is winked at on all levels.

So the rookies say to themselves that this is OK, that this is a far cry from stealing, and they still can be good policemen. Besides, they are becoming accepted as "good guys" by their fellow officers.

This becomes more and more important as the young policeman begins to sense a hostility toward him in the community. This is fostered to a degree by some of the saltier old hands in the department. But the public plays its part.

Americans are funny. They have a resentment for authority. And the policeman is authority in person. The respectable person may soon forget that a policeman found his lost youngster in the park, but he remembers that a policeman gave him a traffic ticket.

The negative aspect of the job builds up. The majority of the people he comes in contact with during his working hours are thieves, con men, narcotics addicts, and out-and-out nuts.

Off the job his associations narrow. Part of the time when he isn't working, he is sleeping. His waking, off-duty hours do not make him much of a neighbor. And then he wants to spend as much time as he can with his family.

Sometimes, when he tries to mix with his neighbors, he senses a kind of strain. When he is introduced to someone, it is not likely to be, "This is John Jones, my friend," or "my neighbor"; it is more likely to be, "This is John Jones. He's a policeman." And the other fellow, he takes it up, too. He is likely to tell you that he has always supported pay increases for policemen, that he likes policemen as a whole, but that there are just a few guys in uniform he hates.

No wonder the officer begins to think of himself as a member of the smallest minority group in the community. The idea gradually sinks into him that the only people who understand him, that he can be close to, are his fellow officers.

It is in this kind of atmosphere that you can find the young policeman trying to make the grade in the fraternity. But that is not the whole story.

A policeman lives with tensions, and with fears.

Part of the tensions come from the incredible monotony. He is cooped up with another man, day after day, doing routine things over and over. The excitement that most people think of as the constant occupation of policemen is so infrequent as to come as a relief.

Part of the tensions come from the manifold fears. I don't mean that these men are cowards. This is no place for cowards. But they are human beings. And fears work on all human beings.

Paramount is the physical fear that he will get hurt to the point where he can't go on working, or the fear that he will be killed. The fear for his family.

There is the fear that he will make a wrong decision in a crucial moment, a life-and-death decision. A man has been in a fight. Should he call the paddy wagon or the ambulance? A man aims a pistol at him. Should he try to talk to him, or shoot him?

But the biggest fear he has is that he will show fear to some of his fellow officers. This is the reason he will rush heedlessly in on a cornered burglar or armed maniac if a couple of officers are present—something he wouldn't do if he were alone. He is tormented by his fears and he doesn't dare show them. He knows he has to present a cool, calm front to the public.

As a group, policemen have a very high rate of ulcers, heart attacks, suicides, and divorces. These things torment him, too. Divorce is a big problem to policemen. A man can't be a policeman for eight hours and then just turn it off and go home and be a loving father and husband—particularly if he has just had somebody die in the back of his police car.

So once again, the pressure is on him to belong, to be accepted and welcomed into the only group that knows what is going on inside him.

If the influences aren't right, he can be hooked.

So he is at the stage where he wants to be one of the guys. And then this kind of thing may happen: One night his car is sent to check on a "Code 16"—a silent burglar alarm.

The officer and his partner go in to investigate. The burglar is gone. They call the proprietor. He comes down to look things over. And maybe he says,

"Boys, this is covered by insurance, so why don't you take a jacket for your wife, or a pair of shoes?" And maybe he does, maybe just because his partner does, and he says to himself, "What the hell; who has been hurt?"

Or maybe the proprietor didn't come down. But after they get back in the car his partner pulls out four $10 bills and hands him two. "Burglar got careless," says the partner.

The young officer who isn't involved soon learns that this kind of thing goes on. He even may find himself checking on a burglary call, say to a drugstore, and see some officer there eyeing him peculiarly.

Maybe at this point the young officer feels the pressure to belong so strongly that he reaches over and picks up something, cigars perhaps. Then he is "in," and the officers can do what they wish.

Mind you, not all officers will do this. Somewhere along the line all of them have to make a decision, and it is at that point where the stuff they are made of shows through. But the past experience of the handouts, the official indifference to them, and the pressures and tensions of the job don't make the decision any easier.

And neither he nor the department has had any advance warning, such as might come from thorough psychiatric screening, as to what his decision will be.

Some men may go this far and no further. They might rationalize that they have not done anything that isn't really accepted by smart people in society.

This is no doubt where the hard-core guy, the one who is a thief already, steps in. A policeman is a trained observer, and he is smart in back-alley psychology. This is especially true of the hard-core guy, and he has been watching the young fellows come along.

When he and his cronies in a burglary ring spot a guy who may have what it takes to be one of them, they may approach him and try him out as a lookout. From then on it is just short steps to the actual participation in and planning of crimes.

Bear in mind that by this stage we have left all but a few policemen behind. But all of them figure in the story at one stage or another. And what has happened to a few could happen to others. I suppose that is the main point I'm trying to make.

Questions for Discussion

1. From what you have read and learned in Part Three, what are decision-making, leader, group, and political influences that contribute to the making of a bad cop?
2. What recommendations would you make to restructure the selection, training, and apprenticeship processes to reduce the likelihood of a police rookie "going bad"?

Source: Reprinted by permission of The Denver Post.

ORGANIZATIONAL ENTRY AND SOCIALIZATION

WORLDS APART: AMERICAN WORKERS IN JAPANESE FIRMS

◆◆◆◆◆◆

Most Japanese companies operating on American soil focus on hiring the best Americans to work in a bicultural environment. However, these same companies are having a hard time retaining top talent. Many of the 300,000 Americans working for Japanese companies fear they will never be considered important players in such firms. For example, consider one bilingual, bicultural MBA who was born and educated through high school in Japan. His Japanese is fluent, and he is married to a Japanese woman. But even he has difficulty navigating his way through his Japanese firm. His Japanese colleagues don't mean to leave him out, but he was on staff for the better part of a year before his boss invited him to lunch. It took even longer before he was asked to join his marketing team for a drink after work.

His experience is not unique. The intensity of the conflict between American and Japanese employees is documented in a survey conducted by the Japan Society in which 30 percent of the Japanese companies surveyed reported complaints of discrimination in hiring and promotion practices. In December of 1990, a federal judge found Matsushita's Quasar subsidiary guilty of bias in 1986 when management layoffs affected only its American staff. Similar charges were filed in the first half of 1991 against advertising giant Dentsu by laid-off American employees of its U.S. subsidiary, DCA.

Several efforts have been made to smooth out the cultural clash. Honda's overseas exchange program offered to both white- and blue-collar employees from the United States and Canada is one such experiment. Other Japanese companies are hiring and conveying significant power to human resource management directors in the hope of improving their relations with state and federal equal opportunity regulators. Many hope that these changes will allow some Japanese companies to emerge as truly autonomous international entities such as Shell, Nestle, or IBM. As Bret Anderson, an American who helped develop Honda's new training program suggests, "We can't go on thinking of one another as strictly American or Japanese. We have to think of ourselves as Honda people."

Source: Richard Phalon, "Worlds Apart," *Business Tokyo*, June 1991, 30–35.

INTRODUCTION

What distinguishes an organizational member from a new hire? How does a new employee learn the organizational ropes? Because it is clear that the development of a committed employee requires more than having him or her simply accept the job, the purpose of this chapter is to examine some of the factors that influence an individual's association with and commitment to an organization. While many of these issues may be discussed in considerably more depth in other management courses, our intent is to give you a beginning point for thinking about how an individual becomes an organizational member. Starting with the selection process, we will examine critical issues in how organizations choose individuals and how individuals choose organizations. However, this is simply the first step in becoming a member of an organization.

Once an individual joins an organization, the next step is to link the organization and the individual—to commit the individual to the goals, expectations, and aspirations of the organization. After focusing on the situational characteristics that lead to commitment—such as the visibility of behaviors, the irreversibility of choices, and the responsibility for making those choices—we will examine how organizational commitment is transmitted from one member to another via the organization's culture.

Next, we will consider the process by which a newcomer learns how work is done in a particular organization. Organizations transmit their cultures by socializing their employees. The ways in which they socialize their employees (such as by providing mentors, role models, and training) are the focus of the final section of this chapter.

ENTRY: ORGANIZATIONAL PERSPECTIVE

Getting the best individuals into the organization is critical to the organization's performance. If all applicants were able to perform the job equally well, then organizational selection would require little more than hiring the right number of "warm bodies." However, in the vast majority of instances, *who* is hired makes a big difference. In fact, research on worker productivity suggests that a high-ability worker will be two to three times as productive as a low-ability worker.[1] Thus, the benefits of identifying and hiring the best-qualified candidate for a job can be considerable.

Finding the right employee is a question of fit—a fit between the person and the job as well as the person and the organization. The importance of such a fit stems from the organization's need for shared outlooks or a common purpose among its members and the individual's need to be comfortable within the working environment. A good fit between the organization and the employee may improve performance, since tasks will be completed more efficiently. This

---

[1]N. H. Mackworth, "High Incentives versus Hot and Humid Atmospheres in a Physical Effort Task," *British Journal of Psychology* 38 (1947): 90–102; and F. L. Schmidt and J. E. Hunter, "Individual Differences in Productivity: An Empirical Test of Estimates Derived from Studies of Selection Procedure Utility," *Journal of Applied Psychology* 68 (1983): 407–414.

efficiency advantage occurs because individuals with similar views are better able to form teams and cooperate with each other.[2]

The lack of such a fit certainly contributes to high levels of turnover among new organizational members as well as first-year college students and transfers.[3] Further, a lack of fit between the person and the organization may also result in lost potential for innovation and cooperation.[4] Lack of fit can occur because the individual selected for the position is underqualified or overqualified. In the 1960s, there were many stories of cab drivers and waiters with PhDs in engineering or chemistry. Their job satisfaction and longevity in their positions were often quite limited. The 1990s equivalent of being underemployed may be fueled by the rising number of two-income couples. When one member of the couple accepts a new position or is transferred, the spouse may have to settle for a less-than-desirable position, depending upon the size, prospects, and economy of the new location.

One of the best ways an organization can enhance the fit between itself and its employees is through the selection process.[5] The next section examines selection from the perspective of the organization.

Selection and Placement

How do people become members of particular organizations? Selection can be viewed as a matching process in which organizations seek out (recruit) specific individuals and individuals select among a variety of organizations. Thus, organizational entry can be examined from the perspective of both the organization and the individual.

For an organization, **selection** is the process of collecting and evaluating information about an individual in order to extend an offer of employment.[6] Selection is typically perceived as occurring at the point when the employee accepts the organization's offer of employment. However, many organizations now realize that the usefulness of the selection decision in creating a person-job fit is known only over time. When the match between the individual's talents and needs and the organization's demands is good, then the organization can reduce the costs associated with rapid turnover, lower performance levels, and the friction between employee and organization that results from such a mismatch.[7] An example of the growing importance of the selection process is illustrated in the "INTERNATIONAL FOCUS ON: Selection."

Three steps are necessary for a good selection process. As illustrated in Figure 11–1, they include job analysis, selection of assessment devices, and the processing of applicants via screening, interviewing, and testing of the applicant pool. The selection process is most likely to succeed in identifying interested, qualified candidates and to be worth its costs when the process itself is valid,

---

[2] S. Keisler, *Interpersonal Processes in Groups and Organizations* (Arlington Heights, Ill.: AHM Publishing Corp., 1978).

[3] J. Wanous, *Organizational Entry* (Reading, Mass.: Addison-Wesley, 1980); and L. Pervin and D. Rubin, "Student Dissatisfaction with College and the College Dropout Rate: A Transactional Approach," *Journal of Social Psychology* 72 (1980): 285–295.

[4] C. A. O'Reilly and J. A. Chatman, "Organizational Commitment and Psychological Attachment: The Effects of Compliance, Identification, and Internalization on Prosocial Behavior," *Journal of Applied Psychology* 71 (1986) 492–499.

[5] J. A. Chatman, Matching People and Organizations. *Administrative Science Quarterly* 36 (1991): 459–484.

[6] R. D. Gatewood and H. S. Feild, *Human Resource Selection* (Hinsdale, Ill.: Dryden Press, 1990), 5.

[7] J. P. Kotter, "The Psychological Contract," *California Management Review* 15 (1973): 91–99.

INTERNATIONAL FOCUS ON

Selection

When in Japan, Recruit As the Japanese Do—Aggressively   When it came to hiring college graduates in Japan, U.S. companies traditionally had to settle for second best. The graduates typically expected foreign companies to offer unstable and not very prestigious positions. Also, U.S. managers did not help their images by wrongly associating English-language fluency with managerial talent. But in the Japanese labor market for college graduates, where there are 143 positions for every 100 applicants, Western companies are now emerging as serious contenders and are attracting the best and the brightest at increasing rates. In a recent survey of students at leading Japanese universities, almost 8 percent reported that foreign companies were their first choice.

Hiring competent Japanese managers is critical to the success of U.S. companies hoping to succeed in the Japanese marketplace, and some U.S. companies are succeeding. Digital Equipment Corp. Japan hired its first Japanese graduate in 1980. In 1990, the company hired 295 new graduates, and in 1991, it hired 400. Additionally, Western firms are beating the Japanese companies in one important demographic category—hiring women. In a recent survey conducted by the American Chamber of Commerce, 35 of the 110 companies surveyed indicated that over half of their 1990 college-graduate hires were women. Japanese women are typically more attracted to Western companies because they are less afraid to use their English and they see a broader set of advancement and responsibility opportunities than are available to them in Japanese firms (although, as the Japanese work force shrinks and grows older, Japanese companies are beginning to realize the importance of recruiting women). U.S. firms doing business in Japan rated successful recruiting as their highest-ranking problem, second only to the high cost of doing business in Japan. However, some American firms are finding ways to be successful at both hiring and surviving in this new international marketplace.

Source: Robert Neff, "When in Japan, Recruit as the Japanese Do—Aggressively," *Business Week,* June 24, 1991, 58.

when there are more qualified applicants than positions to fill, and when a small percentage of applicants is successful.

Job Analysis   The logical way for an organization to ensure a good person-job fit is to begin with a thorough understanding of the position to be filled. **Job analysis** is the gathering of information about a job in an organization. The information collected should describe the tasks and activities, the results (products or services), and the equipment, materials, and working conditions that characterize the job.[8]

The primary purpose of a job analysis is to determine the critical job dimensions and worker characteristics needed in successful job incumbents. Relevant job dimensions are those aspects of the job essential for good performance. For example, promptness, low absenteeism, or participation in an advanced training program may be critical to an individual's success on the job. Worker characteristics include the specific knowledge, skills, and abilities that an individual must possess to qualify for the position. Thus, the job analysis

---

[8] Gatewood and Feild, *Human Resource Selection.*

| FIGURE 11–1 | ▶ Major Steps in the Selection Process |

Selecting the right employee for a job entails three steps. Job analysis catalogs the tasks in a job and the skills required of job incumbents. Assessment procedures that test applicants for these skills must be developed. Finally, the assessment procedures are used to identify qualified applicants.

Job Analysis
(Identification of Tasks Performed, Skills and Abilities Required)
↓
Development and Validation of Assessment Devices to Measure Knowledge, Skills, and Abilities
↓
Use of Assessment Devices in Processing of Applicants

Source: R. D. Gatewood and H. S. Feild, *Human Resource Selection* (Hinsdale, Ill.: Dryden Press, 1990).

conveys not only the important job characteristics, but also the critical worker qualifications.

In addition to specifying who should be recruited, the job analysis aids in the organization's performance appraisal, training, and compensation functions. To evaluate employees effectively, the performance appraisal system must reflect the job's important duties. Selection into training programs also must be related to the position's important dimensions. Only by knowing the skills the position requires can the organization train and promote employees effectively. A job analysis also evaluates the relative worth of a position to the organization. A good job analysis assures that each position is appropriately compensated relative to other positions within the organization.

Identification of Assessment Devices   Assessment devices can include application blanks, references, intelligence tests, special ability tests, personality tests, work simulation exercises, and the selection interview.[9] While not all of these components are used in every selection decision, the use of most is supported by empirical or anecdotal evidence.[10] The critical factor in deciding which selection devices should be used in a particular situation is their ability to differentiate among applicants and, given the litigious environment in which selection takes place, their defensibility in a court setting.[11] Because a particular job requires certain skills, abilities, and knowledge, the process used to screen applicants should be able to identify those who possess those particular traits and abilities.

Identification and Processing of Applicants   Once the organization understands both the position (through the job analysis) and how to measure the needed worker characteristics (through assessment devices), it is ready to iden-

[9]Chatman, *Matching People and Organizations.*

[10]See, for example, R. Guion, "Personnel Assessment, Selection, and Placement," in *Handbook of Industrial and Organizational Psychology*, ed. M. Dunnette and L. Hough (Palo Alto, Calif.: Consulting Psychologists Press, 1991); Andrews, Schmitt, and Schneider, "Current Issues in Personnel Selection," in *Research in Personnel and Human Resource Management*, vol. 1, ed. K. Rowland and G. Ferris (Greenwich, Conn.: JAI Press, 1983), 85–126; and J. Holland, *Making Vocational Choices: A Theory of Careers* (Englewood Cliffs, N.J.: Prentice-Hall, 1973).

[11]Chapter 14 includes an extended discussion of the legal (regulatory) environment and its impact on organizations.

Mazda wants to hire new employees who can work well with others—good team players. Part of Mazda's selection process includes a test of teamwork skills, in which a group of applicants work together on a task, like this one of assembling flashlights.

tify and evaluate applicants. Applicants can be identified through a number of different mechanisms, including the classified sections of newspapers and journals, personal contacts and references, executive-search firms, employment agencies, college and university placement centers, and outplacement services.[12]

Executive search firms, or "headhunters," are under contract to organizations to find candidates for specific jobs. Private employment agencies that charge fees for their services often advertise job openings (so that the actual company remains anonymous), screen applications, and conduct initial interviews. Governmental employment agencies often work with lower-level employees, because their services are often a required aspect of unemployment benefits. In addition to supplying job applicants to organizations, they may assist employers in employee testing, job analysis and evaluation, and community wage surveys, among other activities. Outplacement firms are a recent phenomenon created in response to the "learning" (trimming down) of large American organizations, through either downsizing or mergers and acquisitions. Typical outplacement activities include job counseling and job placement for employees who have been dismissed from firms. They are described in additional detail in Chapter 13.

Recent research suggests that the source of recruitment is an important factor in predicting the future performance of an employee. In general, it seems that candidates who apply directly to organizations or are recruited at professional meetings or conventions are more dependable, are absent less often, and report higher levels of job satisfaction and involvement than those recruited through newspaper ads or college placement offices.[13] One reason for this difference may be that individuals who apply directly to the organization or are

[12] G. Kenny, D. Fisher, L. Katzenstein, and J. A. Sonnenfeld, "Note on Executive Search, Career Counseling, and Other Placement Services (Cambridge, Mass.: Harvard Business School Case 9–482–034, 1981).

[13] J. A. Breaugh, "Relationships between Recruiting Sources and Employee Performance, Absenteeism, and Work Attitudes," *Academy of Management Journal* 24 (1981): 142–147; and S. Rynes, "Recruitment, Job Choice, and Post Hire Consequences," in *Handbook of Industrial and Organizational Psychology*, ed. M. Dunnette and L. Hough (Palo Alto, Calif.: Consulting Psychologists Press, 1991).

| **FIGURE 11–2** | ▶Steps in Processing Applicants: The Organizational Perspective on Entry |

From the organization's perspective, selection of new employees resembles a series of hurdles. When an applicant successfully passes all the qualification screens, the process culminates in a job offer from the organization.

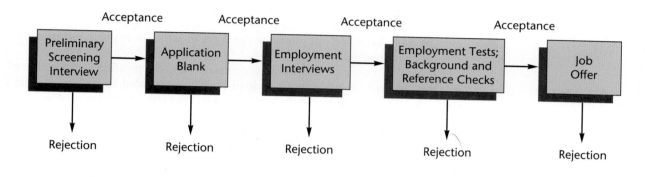

Source: R. D. Gatewood and H. S. Feild, *Human Resource Selection* (Hinsdale, Ill.: Dryden Press, 1990), 16.

recruited at professional meetings and conventions are likely to have more accurate information about the position than do individuals recruited through newspaper advertising or college placement offices. Thus, it seems that having accurate information about the position is significantly associated with success in that particular position.

Once the applicants have been identified, they may complete an application blank, participate in a preliminary screening interview and selection interview, take a variety of employment tests, and provide references to be checked. The culmination of this process occurs when a job offer is made to a candidate. Figure 11–2 graphically represents this process.

ENTRY: INDIVIDUAL PERSPECTIVE

While the organization is processing the applicants, the individual applicants are processing the organization. That is, applicants are simultaneously determining whether or not this is the type of organization they would like to join. Two mechanisms help an individual understand the organization so that such a decision can be made: the realistic job preview and the psychological contract.

The Realistic Job Preview

In seeking a position, job candidates sometimes have unrealistically high expectations about the organization. For one thing, organizations trying to hire a recruit are likely to present their best sides. In addition, if the position is attractive, the applicant is likely to pay more attention to the positive aspects of the job and downplay the negative aspects. However, once the individual has begun the job, then the difference between what the now-incumbent thought the job was going to entail and what it actually entails becomes quite salient. So, early in the employee's tenure with the organization, job satisfaction may be low because of unmet expectations. The implications of these unrealistic expectations are described in the "FOCUS ON: Unrealistic Expectations."

One way to avoid such unrealistic expectations is through the use of a **realistic job preview**.[14] A realistic job preview is a mechanism used by organizations to present both the desirable and undesirable aspects of the job and the organization so that the potential employee has complete and accurate information about the position. Videotapes, work simulations, and interviews with current jobholders are just some of the ways in which a realistic job preview can be accomplished.

Providing a clear picture of the organization and the position is not without its risks. Individuals who are undecided may be persuaded to withdraw their names from consideration as their view of the organization becomes more realistic. However, those who do take the position are likely to be more committed and remain in the position longer.[15] As suggested earlier, candidates who have more complete and accurate information about a position are more likely to succeed in that position.[16] In addition, the organization's candidness in realistically portraying a position may increase the recruit's feeling of being fairly treated by the organization.[17]

Given the costly nature of the selection process (each employee selected is a potential half-million-dollar asset or a half-million-dollar liability to the organization[18]), weeding out the "undecideds" may have considerable long-term benefits for the organization. The experience of such organizations as Texas Instruments, Prudential Insurance Company, and West Point Military Academy suggests that candidates should receive a realistic job preview to assess their own fit with the organization.[19] This increases the likelihood of a good person-job match.

The Psychological Contract

Individuals who decide to accept a position with an organization enter into a **psychological contract** with the employing organization. A psychological contract is a set of unwritten, reciprocal expectations between an employee and an organization.[20] It is the bedrock of the individual-organization link because employment is based upon an implicit exchange of beliefs and expectations

---

[14] Wanous, *Organizational Entry*; and S. Premack and J. Wanous, "A Meta-Analysis of Realistic Job Preview Experiments," *Journal of Applied Psychology* 70 (1986): 706–719.

[15] J. P. Wanous, "Organizational Entry: The Individual's Viewpoint," in *Perspectives on Behavior in Organizations*, ed. J. R. Hackman, E. E. Lawler, and L. W. Porter (New York: McGraw-Hill, 1977).

[16] Breaugh, "Relationships between Recruiting Sources and Employee Performance."

[17] R. J. Bies and J. Moag, "Interactional Justice: Communication Criteria of Fairness," in *Research on Negotiating in Organizations*, vol. 1, ed. R. J. Lewicki, M. H. Bazerman, and B. Sheppard (Greenwich, Conn.: JAI Press, 1986): 43–55.

[18] P. M. Podsakoff, M. L. Williams, and W. E. Scott, "Myths of Employee Selection Systems," in *Readings in Personnel and Human Resource Management*, ed. R. S. Schuler, S. A. Youngblood, and V. L. Huber (New York: West Publishing Co., 1987): 178–192.

[19] J. A. Breaugh, "Realistic Job Previews: A Critical Appraisal and Future Research Directions," *Academy of Management Review* 8 (1983): 612–619.

[20] E. A. Schein, *Organizational Psychology* (Englewood Cliffs, N.J.: Prentice-Hall, 1980).

Focus on

Unrealistic Expectations

When a New Job Proves to Be Different Than Expected To Lynda McDermott, the job offer sounded ideal. So she left her position at an accounting firm and became executive vice-president of a fledgling management consulting company in New York, a job that her new boss said would allow her to play a major role in landing new business. Eleven months later, she quit. Her boss, she says, had immediately relegated her to administrative duties, a far cry from the role she had expected. As McDermott sees it, she was the victim of a job bait-and-switch. Promised the world as an applicant, she eventually realized as a new employee that the job was something quite different. Such realizations often lead to employee disgruntlement, stalled careers, and costly turnover.

New employee disillusionment has several sources. Some companies unduly hype a position to snare a particular person; sometimes the personnel department or manager is unfamiliar with the details of the job or managers cannot deliver on their promises. Alternatively, eager applicants can deceive themselves about a position by minimizing its shortcomings. Both applicants and employers may gloss over the job description, particularly if the applicant believes that such probing behavior will irritate the interviewer or if such information is not what the applicant wants to hear. The employer or recruiter may be at fault if the company is new or the job is difficult to fill.

Avoiding this pitfall is difficult. Consider the speechwriter who will soon leave his job after 15 months. He was promised that he wouldn't have to write speeches on nuts-and-bolts financial instruments for narrow audiences. In fact, that is all he writes. Now he finds himself in the ironic position of having agreed to select his successor. "I see three possibilities," he says. "I could tell the total truth about the job and thereby only have people accept who are not totally qualified. I could say it's a 'real challenging' job and so on, but that's not honest, and ultimately the needs of the corporation and the individual aren't served. Or I could leave the job unfilled." Thus far, he is telling the applicants the truth and the job remains unfilled.

Source: L. Reibstein, "Crushed Hopes: When a New Job Proves to Be Something Different," *Wall Street Journal,* June 10, 1987, Section 2. Reprinted with permission of *Wall Street Journal* © 1987 Dow Jones and Company, Inc. All rights reserved worldwide.

about the actions of the individual vis-à-vis the organization and the organization vis-à-vis the individual. Psychological contracts usually involve expectations about working conditions, work requirements, the level of effort to be expended on the job, and the amount and nature of authority the employer has over the employee in directing work.[21] They differ from other types of contracts in that they may contain thousands of items (although the employee and employer may be aware of only a few); both parties may have different expectations, since some may have been explicitly discussed and others only inferred; and they change as individual and organization expectations change.[22]

The psychological contract is based upon the exchange of **contributions** and **inducements.** Individuals entering into a psychological contract contribute

---

[21] Ibid.

[22] See both Kotter, "The Psychological Contract," 91–99; and D. M. Rousseau, "New Hire Perceptions of Their Own and Employers' Obligations: A Study of Psychological Contracts," *Journal of Organizational Behavior* 17 (1990): 389–400.

Although he may not realize it, this individual's level of commitment to his work is based in large part on the psychological contract he has with his employer, a set of unwritten reciprocal expectations. Contributions on the part of the individual such as effort, loyalty, and skills are offered in exchange for organizational inducements such as job security, pay, and benefits.

their productive capacity towards achieving the organization's purpose. Organizations provide inducements to employees in exchange for their contributions. That is, organizations compensate employees for their contributions. The psychological contract is generally viewed as committing both sides to the relationship, with employees contributing loyalty and the company, steady employment.[23] Figure 11–3 illustrates the contribution-inducement link that is the basis of the psychological contract.

Balanced psychological contracts are necessary for a continuing, harmonious relationship between the employee and the organization. Since psychological contracts are entered into as individuals join the organization, whether or not the individuals' expectations about the contract are met is crucial to their ongoing relationship with the organization. For example, if an individual accepts a position with the expectation of full autonomy in structuring the workday only to find out that the supervisor views planning employees' workdays as his or her prerogative, then the employee is likely to suffer considerable job-related dissatisfaction, based primarily on the perception that the psychological contract has been violated. An employee who had no such expectations prior to starting the job would not experience this level of dissatisfaction. The violation of the psychological contract can signal to the participants that the parties no longer share (or never shared) a common set of values or goals. Once this happens, one can expect a breakdown of communication between the parties, a failure in mutual understanding, and increasing frustration (and emotional responses) in both parties.[24]

Realistic job previews, by implicitly adjusting a recruit's expectations about life as a member of the organization, can have an impact on the psychological contract and, hence, the employee's job satisfaction. In fact, the psychological

---

[23] M. L. Marks, "The Disappearing Company Man," *Psychology Today* (September 1988): 34–39.

[24] Schein, *Organizational Psychology.*

FIGURE 11–3	▶ The Psychological Contract: The Contribution-Inducement Exchange Process

An individual accepting a job enters into a psychological contract with the employer consisting of unwritten expectations on both sides. Balanced, equitable psychological contracts are necessary to harmonious relationships between employees and employers.

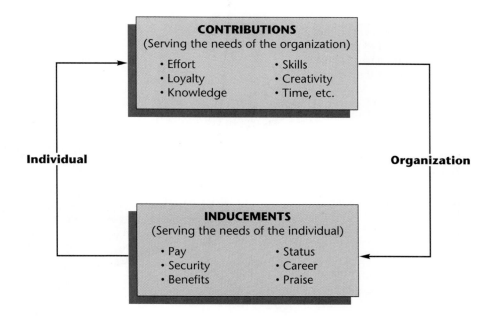

Source: J. R. Schermerhorn, J. G. Hunt, and R. N. Osborn, *Managing Organizational Behavior* (New York: Wiley & Sons, 1988), 38.

contract may be the central determinant in whether a person is working effectively; generating commitment, loyalty, and enthusiasm for the organization and its goals; and obtaining satisfaction from work. The delicate balance of the psychological contract depends to a large measure on two conditions: (1) the degree to which employee expectations of what the organization will provide and what is owed in return match the organization's expectations of what it will give and get; and (2) agreement on what is actually to be exchanged. Examples include money in exchange for time at work; social-need satisfaction and security in exchange for work and loyalty; opportunities for self-enhancement and challenging work in exchange for high productivity, quality work, and creative effort in the service of organizational goals; or various combinations of these and other things.[25] Figure 11–4 illustrates the importance of the match between inducements and contributions for organizational productivity.

---

[25] Ibid.

FIGURE 11-4	▶ The Importance of the Match between Contributions and Inducements in the Psychological Contract

A good match between what an organization gives its employees and the contributions it receives in exchange is critical to work-force morale. Realistic job previews may facilitate equitable psychological contracts by stimulating thoughts and discussion about employee and employer expectations.

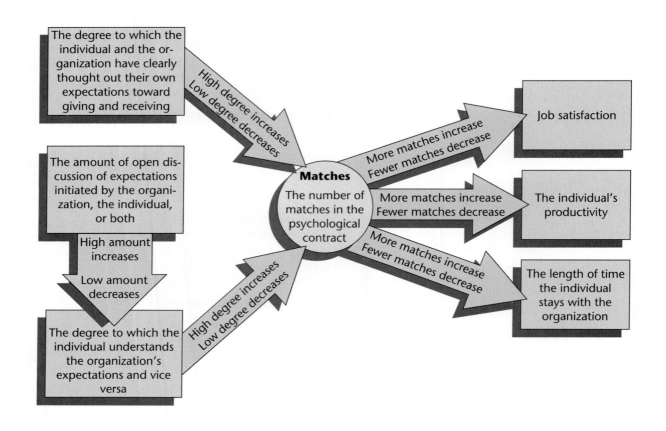

ORGANIZATIONAL COMMITMENT ◆◆◆◆◆◆

Once the organization has extended an offer to an applicant and that individual has decided to enter into a psychological contract by accepting the offer, then the applicant becomes an organizational member. However, the preparation needed to become a functioning part of the organization has just begun. The applicant must now become schooled in and committed to the organization's goals, objectives, and ways of conducting business.

Simply defined, **organizational commitment** is the relative strength of an individual's identification with and involvement in a particular organization.[26] It usually includes three factors: (1) a strong belief in the organization's goals and values; (2) a willingness to exert considerable effort on behalf of the organization; and (3) a strong desire to continue as an organizational member. Organizational commitment, then, is not simply loyalty to an organization. Rather, it is an ongoing process through which organizational actors express their concern for the organization and its continued success and well-being.

There are many reasons why an organization should want to increase the level of organizational commitment among its members. For example, research has found that the more committed the employee is to the organization, the greater the effort he or she expends performing tasks.[27] In addition, highly committed workers are likely to remain with the organization for longer periods of time—that is, there is a positive relationship between the level of organizational commitment and job tenure.[28] Finally, given the contribution of a highly productive, trained employee can make to organizational productivity, keeping such an employee should be a high priority for the organization. Because highly committed employees wish to remain associated with the organization and advance organizational goals, they are less likely to leave. Thus, high levels of organizational commitment are associated with low levels of employee turnover.[29]

Factors Influencing Commitment

Once individuals select membership in an organization, what is it about their early experiences that leads them to be more or less committed to the organization? To answer this question, we must first consider exactly what leads to the phenomenon of commitment. Gerald Salancik suggests that four major factors lead to commitment: visibility, explicitness, irreversibility, and personal volition.[30]

Visibility One major determinant of how committing a particular behavior may be is how observable that behavior is to others. Behaviors that are secret or unobserved do not have a committing force behind them because they cannot be linked to a specific individual. One of the most simple and straightforward ways to commit individuals to an organization is to make their association

---

[26]R. T. Mowday, L. W. Porter, and R. M. Steers, *Employee-Organization Linkages: The Psychology of Commitment, Absenteeism, and Turnover* (New York: Academic Press, 1982).

[27]R. M. Steers, "Antecedents and Outcomes of Organizational Commitments," *Administrative Science Quarterly* 22 (1977): 46–56.

[28]See, for example, R. T. Mowday, R. M. Steers, and L. W. Porter, "The Measurement of Organizational Commitment," *Journal of Vocational Behavior* 14 (1979): 224–247; Steers, "Antecedents and Outcomes of Organizational Commitments"; and J. L. Koch and R. M. Steers, "Job Attachment, Satisfaction, and Turnover among Public Employees," *Journal of Vocational Behavior* 12 (1978): 119–128.

[29]H. Angle and J. Perry, "An Empirical Assessment of Organizational Commitment and Organizational Effectiveness," *Administrative Science Quarterly* 26 (1981): 1–14; Mowday, Steers, and Porter, "The Measurement of Organizational Commitment"; and Steers, "Antecedents and Outcomes of Organizational Commitments."

[30]The following section draws heavily from G. R. Salancik, "Commitment Is Too Easy!," *Organizational Dynamics* (Summer 1977): 207–222.

with the organization public information. If they are part of the organization, they (by association) support that organization and its goals. Many organizations are already taking advantage of this visibility notion by publishing the employee's photograph and a formal announcement in the local newspapers, in-house publications, and other such outlets to inform others of the new arrival. The new employee may even be outfitted in the company's uniform—an obvious and visible sign of organizational membership.

Maintaining **visibility** is not a difficult task. For instance, it takes about the same time for inspectors to write a number after their task is completed as it does to write their names, or for the company to provide a nameplate on a door as to leave it blank. Very little additional effort is required to associate individuals with their work, their accomplishments, and their organization. The more visible individuals and their contributions, the more committed they are likely to be to the organization.

On some occasions, however, an organization does not want its members clearly associated with their acts. For example, there is a conscious attempt through the use of uniforms to reduce the visibility of individual soldiers, prison guards, and police officers so a particular individual is not associated with some of the more unpleasant tasks. Thus, the uniform in this case clearly identifies the individual as a soldier or police officer, but the individual within the uniform is not unique. In addition, organizations may decrease the visibility of individuals performing onerous tasks or tasks with a high likelihood of failure. This reduced visibility is likely to enhance the willingness of an individual to take on a task with negative overtones.

Explicitness and Irreversibility   Visibility alone is not sufficient to commit individuals to their actions. It must be combined with explicitness; the more explicit the behavior, the less deniable it is. Thus, **explicitness** is the extent to which the individual cannot deny that the behavior occurred. How explicit the behavior is depends on two factors: its observability and its unequivocality. When a behavior cannot be observed but only inferred, it is less explicit. For example, if I left a sensitive document on my desk and later heard one of my subordinates talking about the content of that document, I could not know that the subordinate had been in my office and read the document. At best, I might suspect that he or she had, but all I know for sure is that this sensitive information is now public. If I had seen that subordinate reading the document in my office, then I would know which subordinate released the information. Equivocality is the difficulty of pinning down the act or behavior. It can be seen in the way people qualify the statements they make (such as "It sometimes seems to me that . . ." versus "I think . . .").

Irreversibility, on the other hand, means that the behavior is permanent—it cannot easily be revoked or undone. The importance of irreversibility can be observed in the circumstances that committed Great Britain and France to building the Concorde.[31] The Minister of Aviation, James Avery, included a clause in the 1961 agreement with France that made both France's and Britain's decision to produce the Concorde virtually irreversible. The clause required that if either of the two partners withdrew from the collaboration, the entire

---

[31] Ibid.

development cost up to that point would be borne by the withdrawing party. Interestingly, the more rational it became to withdraw (because of escalating costs), the more committed the parties were to continuing. This type of commitment is typically referred to as behavioral commitment or escalation, which was described in detail in Chapter 5.

Organizations also are aware of the committing aspect of irreversible acts. Many organizations develop benefit packages that are not transferable from one firm to another. The irreversible loss of these benefits, should an individual choose to leave the organization, commits the individual to continued employment. Training an employee in a skill that is specific to the organization or developing an employee's abilities to match the unique constellation of an organization's expectations also reduces the likelihood that the person will disengage from the organization.

Consider, for example, the cost a bookkeeper might incur in learning a particular accounting software package. Consider the much greater cost to this individual of relearning if this accounting package is unique to the organization. This is an example of how knowledge that is very useful within a particular organization may be completely irrelevant elsewhere. The time contributed to learning this system has a payoff in the current organization, but may be irreversibly lost if the bookkeeper were to transfer to any other organization.

Other factors influence a person's perceived attachment to the organization. Personal or family-related factors may foster an individual's commitment to an organization. Children in school, the cost of housing in other parts of the country, the circle of friends and acquaintances, and the spouse's job are all personal factors that may bind a person to an organization.

Of course, some employees may be more committed to the status quo than to the organization. Imagine that an organization were to offer its employee a promotion that required relocation of the employee's family. The personal factors that may have initially enhanced the employee's commitment to the organization may now be enhancing a similar commitment to a locality. The unique problems of dual-career couples are a salient example of the factors that tie individuals to an area.

An organization may attempt to compete with the personal factors that tie an individual to a locality by creating a network of relationships at work that become important to the employee. Developing work or project teams or fostering collaborations among specific coworkers are primary ways to connect workers to the organization. Further dependencies upon coworkers are fostered when employees are unable to develop relationships outside the organization because of frequent moves.

All of these are attempts to entangle the individual in organizational relationships. The greater the employee's entanglement with these relationships, the more costly termination would be to the employee. Employees' perceptions of the irreversibility of their positions in an organization develop naturally over time. The longer they are employed by an organization, the more their skills are tailored to the unique demands of that firm. What they know and how they think about a business become, in reality, what they know and how they think about the particular way their organization does business.

In fact, given the committing nature of organization-specific skills, it is probably against the best interests of the organization to encourage employees to develop general skills that would make them more attractive to other organizations. Developing generalized skills reduces the uniqueness of an individual's fit with a particular organization while simultaneously increasing that individual's attractiveness to others. The organization should clearly consider the potential costs and benefits of encouraging such skill development.

The irreversibility of behavior is important because it influences the psychological contract. Consider, for example, the plight of college-student cadets who had joined the Reserve Officers Training Corps (ROTC) in the late 1960s and early 1970s. Some were required to sign two-year contracts and others were not. During the Vietnam War, joining ROTC was viewed as a way to avoid the draft or to control the site and type of war experience one could expect. Because the war and thus the need for military personnel was limited, a lottery based on birth dates was designed to rank the order in which young men were subject to being drafted into the services. If you were assigned a low number through the lottery process, the odds were that you would soon receive a draft notice. If you were assigned a high number in the draft lottery, you were almost assured of not being drafted.

Barry Staw, a researcher with an interest in organizational commitment, examined the impact on ROTC cadets' behaviors of having a birth date with a very low probability of being drafted into the service.[32] Among those who had joined ROTC to avoid the draft, one would expect little reason to continue with the program. This was true, but only for those who had not signed a contract committing them to a specific period of service. While those without a contract began to be openly hostile towards ROTC, those with a contract became increasingly attached to the program. Thus, the irrevocable nature of the contract they had signed now influenced their commitment to the organization, regardless of the fact that the reason for their joining ROTC no longer existed.

These findings suggest that when the instrumental nature of our associations ceases to exist, we justify our continued association with emotional, rational, or socially desirable trappings. Once we have accepted a position, then the perceived attractiveness of that position and our commitment to that position and the organization increase. Of course, this commitment increase also occurs when we accept a marriage proposal, buy a home, or make any choice we perceive to be irrevocable (or revocable only at great cost).

Volition   We have been considering the importance of irreversibility in the commitment process, but there is still a piece of this puzzle missing. For example, if someone makes an irrevocable choice under duress or pressure, does that choice commit the person? Suppose your supervisor assigns you the task of firing several subordinates. How might you feel about the appropriateness of firing the employees if your supervisor applies a great deal of pressure on you to perform this task ("Either fire them or I will fire you!") or applies very little pressure ("Please terminate the following employees.")? It is likely that if you carry out your supervisor's instructions, you will feel more justified in terminating the employees when there is little pressure than you will when there is considerable pressure to comply. If there is very little pressure applied to get you to comply, then you are more likely to believe that the employees deserved

---

[32] B. M. Staw, cited in G. R. Salancik, "Commitment Is Too Easy!" *Organizational Dynamics* (Summer 1977): 207–222.

Irrevocable commitment to an organization can bias our perceptions of it. Some students joined ROTC in the late 1960s only to evade the draft. Many of them came to view the ROTC more favorably if they had signed contracts irrevocably committing them to the program.

to be fired. (After all, you did terminate the individuals; they must have deserved it.) However, if your supervisor applied considerable pressure to you and then you fired the employees, you are more likely to perceive that you had little choice in the matter. That is, you made the choice to act, but it was not of your own volition; you were forced to make that decision.

Volition, then, and its observable equivalent—personal responsibility—is the fourth mechanism that binds us to our actions. Without volition, behaviors are not committing. "Since I have no choice," one might reason, "I really cannot be held responsible for the consequences of my behavior." When trying to separate ourselves from our actions, we might protest that we do not like what we are doing, but the money was too good to refuse. Another way in which we try to distance ourselves from certain behaviors (usually those associated with unpleasant circumstances) is to insist that we have little personal responsibility for the behavior or the outcome. For example, in trying to explain why he did not turn in a paper by the deadline, a graduate student might report that his car had been stolen and the only copy of the paper was in the car at the time. Because he could not control the stealing of his car, he believes that his not meeting the deadline was not volitional.

If we reconsider the ROTC example, volition was certainly a factor. Because many ROTC cadets had avoided signing a contract, those who signed such a contract must have done it of their own volition. Those who signed contracts but had no other reasons for being in ROTC (the lottery indicated they had a low probability of being drafted) must be in ROTC because they enjoyed it. Thus, they became more committed because they were choosing to be cadets.

Enhancing employees' personal responsibility for their actions is critical to establishing and maintaining their commitment to the task and the organization. A number of organizational interventions acknowledge the importance of personal volition. For example, organizations are designing tasks in ways that increase an individual's personal responsibility for performing or scheduling them. In Chapter 12, the importance of volition in task design will be explored in more detail.

A second form of organizational intervention that emphasizes volition or personal responsibility is *participative decision making* (discussed in Chapter 9). If a work group is involved in making a decision or solving a problem, its members will be more committed to the implementation of that decision or solution than if they were simply informed of it. Their reasoning might be that if they chose to participate in the development of a solution, then they must be committed to it. This feeling of personal responsibility in turn increases employees' stake in the solution's successful implementation.

We have established that visibility, explicitness and irreversibility, and volition are important in the creation of commitment. Further, commitment to the organization and its goals is important because individuals adjust their attitudes and expectations in situations to which they are committed. While enhancing organizational commitment is an ongoing process, it is probably most critical early in an employee's association with an organization to assure continued attachment.

Mowday, Porter, and Steers suggest a number of factors that may lead to greater organizational commitment early in an employee's tenure with an employer.[33] Their complete model is pictured in Figure 11–5. According to this model, commitment depends on (1) personal factors, such as the employee's initial level of commitment (deriving from initial job expectations, the psychological contract, and so on); (2) organizational factors, such as an employee's initial work experiences and subsequent sense of responsibility; and (3) nonorganizational factors, such as the availability of alternative jobs. Each of these three factors will be discussed in turn.

Personal Factors   The primary personal factor is the amount of potential attachment an employee brings to work on the first day—the employee's propensity to develop a stable attachment to the organization. Individuals who are highly committed to an organization on their first day are likely to stay with the organization. Individuals who are highly committed at entry are likely to be willing to take on additional responsibilities and contribute more to the organization. This early commitment process may become a self-reinforcing cycle. That is, if individuals, early in their tenure with an organization, put forth extra effort, then they may justify that extra effort by being more committed to the organization.

Organization Factors   Such organizational factors as job scope—the job's feedback, autonomy, challenge, and significance—increase behavioral involvement. The ability to participate actively in task-related decision making will also influence level of commitment. Consistency between work-group and organizational goals will increase commitment to those goals. Finally, organizational characteristics such as concern for employees' best interests or employee ownership are also positively associated with increased commitment to the organization.[34]

---

[33] Mowday, Porter, and Steers, *Employee-Organization Linkages: The Psychology of Commitment, Absenteeism, and Turnover.*

[34] See, for example, R. M. Steers and S. R. Rhodes, "Major Influences on Employee Attendance: A Process Model," *Psychological Bulletin* 63 (1978): 391–407; and Steers, "Antecedents and Outcomes," 46–56.

FIGURE 11–5   ▶ Major Determinants of Organizational Commitment during Early Membership

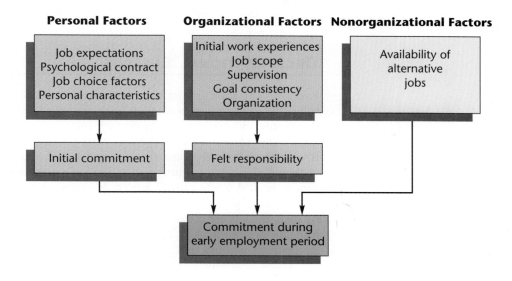

Source: R. T. Mowday, L. M. Porter, and R. M. Steers, *Employee-Organization Linkages: The Psychology of Commitment, Absenteeism, and Turnover* (New York: Academic Press, 1982), 56.

Nonorganizational Factors   The primary nonorganizational factor that enhances commitment is the availability of alternatives after the initial choice has been made. Research has found that Master's in Business Administration (MBA) students who did not take the job with the highest salary (insufficient external justification for the choice) reported significantly higher levels of job commitment six months later when no other job offers had been received than when alternative positions were available. Individuals who had accepted the position offering the highest salary (sufficient external justification for the choice) reported approximately equal levels of job commitment, regardless of whether subsequent alternative offers existed or not. Thus, it seems that the highest level of initial commitment occurs among those who (1) have insufficient external justification for their initial choice and (2) view the choice as relatively irrevocable; that is, believe they have had no subsequent opportunities to change their initial decision.[35]

Commitment to the organization and its goals is a major factor in predicting performance. Thus it is critical that organizations have mechanisms to enhance the development of organizational commitment among new employees. In fact, one way in which organizations with high levels of employee com-

[35]C. A. O'Reilly and D. Caldwell, "Job Choice: The Impact of Intrinsic and Extrinsic Factors on Subsequent Satisfaction and Commitment," *Journal of Applied Psychology* 65 (1980): 559–565.

mitment differ from organizations with low levels of employee commitment is that the former are "strong culture" firms. For employees to be part of a strong culture, they must be educated as to the expectations and practices of the organization. The extent of their commitment to their jobs and the organization may well hinge on their ability to understand, accept, and become a part of the **organizational culture**—"the way we do things around here."[36]

ORGANIZATIONAL CULTURE

Every organization has its own **organizational culture**—a system of shared values about what is important and beliefs about how things work that produce the norms and expectations of performance.[37] Sometimes that culture is very fragmented and difficult to perceive; other times, the culture of an organization is very strong, cohesive, and clear to insiders and outsiders alike. Whether weak or strong, the culture of an organization has a profound influence on how work gets done. It can affect many aspects of organizational life, from who gets promoted and what decisions are made to how people dress, act, and play at work. As such, the culture is the organization; much more so than buildings, five-year plans, or bottom lines.[38] The importance of a culture to the organization and its members is illustrated in "FOCUS ON: Corporate Culture."

There is a widely held notion among managers that organizations with strong cultures will enjoy a number of competitive advantages, such as high commitment among its organizational members and an ability to respond quickly to a changing environment.[39] An organization with a strong culture generally displays five different elements: (1) a widely shared philosophy of norms and values within the organization, (2) a view of people as a critical human resource, (3) charismatic leaders and heroes, (4) ritual and ceremony, and (5) clear expectations about the direction of the organization.[40] To the extent that an organization has a strong culture, the *guiding philosophy* of its leaders will be consistently and widely shared among its employees. Developing the management philosophy of the company and its direction is not a sideline of top management; it is the essence of the company. Individuals in organizations with strong cultures are viewed as *critical organizational resources.* Most of the "rules" of the organization center around its philosophy. Authority is often dispersed.

Charismatic or transformational leadership[41] is common among strong-culture organizations. Myths and stories of heroic employees, leaders, and products, which provide tangible role models for employees, are well integrated into the organization's oral history. Even when organizational members are aware

---

[36]J. S. Ott, *The Organizational Culture Perspective* (Chicago, Ill.: Dorsey Press, 1989).

[37]Stanley Davis, *Managing Corporate Culture* (Cambridge, Mass.: Ballinger Press, 1984).

[38]T. Deal and A. Kennedy, *Corporate Culture: The Rites and Rituals of Corporate Life* (Reading, Mass.: Addison-Wesley, 1982).

[39]T. Peters and R. Waterman, *In Search of Excellence* (New York: Harper and Row, 1982).

[40]Deal and Kennedy, *Corporate Culture.*

[41]Charismatic leadership is discussed in detail in Chapter 10.

Corporate Culture

NCR's Corporate Culture Crosses International Boundaries It was August 1945, and S. C. Allyn, chairman of the board of National Cash Register Corporation (NCR), was one of the first allied civilians to enter Germany at the end of the war. He had gone to find out what had happened to an NCR factory, built just before the war, that had been promptly confiscated by the German military command and put to work on the war effort. He arrived via military plane and traveled through burned-out buildings, rubble, and utter desolation until he reached what was left of the factory. Picking his way through bricks, cement, and fallen timbers, Allyn came upon two NCR employees whom he hadn't seen for six years. Their clothes were torn and their faces grimy and blackened by smoke, but they were busy clearing out the rubble. As he came closer, one of the men looked up and said, "We knew you'd come!" Allyn joined them in their work, and together the three men began cleaning out the debris and rebuilding the factory. The company had even survived the ravages of war.

A few days later, as the cleaning continued, Allyn and his coworkers were startled as an American tank rumbled up to the site. A grinning GI was at its helm. "Hi," he said. "I'm NCR, Omaha. Did you guys make your quota this month?" Allyn and the GI embraced each other. The war may have devastated everything around them, but NCR's hard-driving sales-oriented culture was still intact.

Source: Terence A. Deal and Allen A. Kennedy, *Corporate Cultures: Rites and Rituals of Corporate Life,* (p. 3) © 1982 by Addison-Wesley Publishing Company, Inc. Reprinted by permission.

that the myths they tell are pure fantasy, they often still continue to relate them to new employees. The myths show the newcomer what he or she must do to succeed in the company, and they are so important that their factual accuracy is irrelevant.

Finally, many strong-culture firms have daily, systematic, and programmed routines and rituals that show employees the kind of behavior expected of them. Ceremonies mark vivid and potent examples of what the organization stands for. They give meaning to organizational events. In fact, ceremonies are to culture what movies are to scripts.[42] While ceremonies and rituals may include such things as the annual Christmas party or sales meeting, they can also refer to the complex and expensive process by which a new CEO is chosen in the organization. The ritual of selection conveys to the organizational members the critical nature of the CEO on the organization's performance.

A number of factors facilitate an organization's development of a strong culture. If strong cultures are important to an organization, then the methods of developing such an organizational culture will also be important. But it is not sufficient that there be a strong culture. Rather, what may lead to good organizational performance is the fit between the person and the organization. This thought is not new. In fact, organizations spend considerable time and energy trying to find the "right" people for their organizations because it seems obvious that some people are better suited for an organization than others.[43] A

[42] Deal and Kennedy, *Corporate Culture*, 63.

[43] D. Caldwell and C. O'Reilly, "Measuring Person-Job Fit Using a Profile Comparison Process," *Journal of Applied Psychology* 75 (1990): 648–657.

person-organization fit requires consistency between important organizational values and core individual values. Consider the difficulty faced by a new employee with a long history of individual accomplishments who has joined a firm where all rewards are based on team efforts and no one is recognized for solo contributions. The most likely response of this new employee is to leave the organization as it may be easier for her to find a more consistent organizational culture than it would be to change her basic work values.[44]

There are three major mechanisms through which the organization can enhance the fit between its culture and its employees: selection, socialization, and mentoring. We have already addressed selection as a means of bringing the "right kind" of individuals—those whose values and beliefs are consistent with the organization or those who can be inculcated with the organization's values—into the organization. However, once the individual is an organizational member, then the actual process by which culture is conveyed and commitment is produced—organizational socialization—is initiated.

ORGANIZATIONAL SOCIALIZATION ◆◆◆◆◆◆

Organizational socialization is the process by which the organization's goals, norms, and preferred ways of doing things are conveyed to the new employee. Socialization molds the new employee to fit the organization.

The more intense the socialization, the more similar are the employees and organizational values. Through organizational socialization, the employee comes to appreciate the values, abilities, expected behaviors, and social knowledge that are essential for assuming an organizational role and for participating as an organizational member.[45] As such, organizational socialization conveys the organization's *culture*. How the new employee is socialized into the organization's culture is often unique to particular organizations and strongly influenced by the culture of the organization.

Organizational socialization may be a necessity for organizational effectiveness.[46] Pascale suggests a seven-step approach to successful organizational socialization:

1. *Selection.* The careful selection of entry level candidates is essential.
2. *Humility-inducing experiences.* Such experience encourage a candidate to question prior behaviors, beliefs and values, which may lower the individual's resistance to accepting the organization's norms and values. A common example of this was "hazing" of underclass students or fraternity pledges.

---

[44]J. A. Chatman, "Matching People and Organizations: Selection and Socialization in Public Accounting Firms," *Administrative Science Quarterly* 36 (1991): 459–484.

[45]See M. R. Louis, "Surprise and Sense Making: What Newcomers Experience in Entering Unfamiliar Organizational Settings," *Administrative Science Quarterly* 25 (1980): 226–251; and E. A. Schein and J. Van Maanen, "Toward a Theory of Organizational Socialization," *Research in Organizational Behavior*, ed. B. M. Staw (Greenwich, Conn.: JAI Press, 1979).

[46]R. T. Pascale, "The Paradox of Corporate Culture: Reconciling Ourselves to Socialization," *California Management Review* 27 (1985): 26–27.

3. *Training.* The mastery of one of the core disciplines of the business cements a candidate's orientation to the organization's way of doing things. While training is obviously an important component of organizational socialization, the "FOCUS ON: Training" suggests that American companies are lagging behind other countries in their training efforts.

4. *Results and rewards.* Meticulous attention is given to systems measuring operational results and rewarding individual performance. Such systems are comprehensive, consistent, and focus on those aspects of the business that are tied to competitive success and corporate values.

5. *Careful adherence to the firm's transcendent values.* This step is the most critical, as it establishes the foundation of trust between the organization and the individual.

6. *Reinforcement of folklore.* Folklore emphasizes a code of conduct about "how we do things around here."

7. *Consistent role models.* Consistent traits are associated with successful organizational members.

These seven steps suggest that *how* a person is brought into the organization can have a major impact on that person's future relationship with the organization and his or her subsequent productivity. Figure 11–7 illustrates important details to which organizations should focus their attention on facilitating a newcomer's entry process. Examples of ways to accomplish this include developing a *welcome package* which can ease an individual's transition from outsider to insider. In addition to such useful information as outlined in Figure 11–7, other techniques used to bring a new person into the organization are particularly salient to the maintenance of the organizational culture.

There are times, however, when socialization—even of an older employee—is critical to the maintenance or re-establishment of organizational commitment. With a larger number of employees taking overseas assignments, it is important to remember that the socialization process really never ends. The "FOCUS ON: Socialization" examines the experience of repatriated U.S. managers who find themselves back in their home organizations. Oddly enough, while most organizations see the need to steep their employees and their families in the national culture of their new assignments, few see the importance of developing such activities to prepare their employees for the trip home.

Individuals involved with newcomers to the organization (or repatriated employees) should also consider the impact of mentors or role models, rewards systems, and career paths—all of which reinforce the culture and expectations of the organization vis-à-vis its employees.

While Chapter 13 will focus specifically on compensation and reward systems as mechanisms for identifying and maintaining performance, the following sections describe how these two other socialization mechanisms can be used to reinforce the organization's culture.

It should be kept in mind, however, that many of the factors that make an organization attractive to a newcomer or job applicant may be contingent on what stage in his or her career development the newcomer is. In fact, work by Dalton, Thompson, and Rice found four distinct phases in career development.[47] In the first phase, individuals work under the direction of others, sort

---

[47] G. W. Dalton, P. H. Thompson and R. Rice, "The Four Stages of Professional Careers," *Organizational Dynamics* (Summer 1977): 19–42.

Training

Training, Empowering Employees Pays Off   When Anne Nagy took a job with Donnelly Corp., a small auto-parts manufacturer, she assumed it was just another mindless job where she would work for a few years and then move on. But nine years later, she is still with Donnelly, and during that time she discovered that this was not the typical factory job. Nagy didn't punch in each day because there were no time clocks. Supervisors advised rather than bullied. She didn't have to race to meet stiff production goals because she and her coworkers set their own. The formula for her success—and Donnelly's—is simple: invest in human capital. Donnelly has done just that. Since 1990, Donnelly has doubled its spending on direct training costs. These costs amount to about 2 percent of Donnelly's operating expenses. Donnelly's workers are not let go if they recommend a way to do away with their jobs or if a machine replaces them. The company looks for other jobs for them. If workers are sick, late, or mess up on their jobs, their teammates will make up for them. Company officials meet regularly with workers to explain future decisions. All wages are posted, and company-wide bonuses are given monthly. Donnelly's commitment to its workers has paid off. During the last decade—a very tough time for the auto industry—Donnelly's sales have grown annually by over 20 percent. From 1,000 workers ten years ago, the firm now employs 2,300 workers in the United States and 300 at a facility in Ireland.

Donnelly has learned that boosting workers' skills and freeing them to assume more responsible tasks results in increased productivity; and greater productivity typically leads to greater profits that hike salaries, fatten consumers' wallets, and stir demand. Yet, many U.S. companies ignore this simple prescription. Many organizations retain a mindset that values technical capital over human capital and short-term profits over long-term growth. If the U.S. does not train more workers, and seek the most from them, then the nation is "headed toward an economic cliff," the nonprofit Commission on the Skills of the American Workforce warned in 1990.

Anthony Carnevale, chief economist with the American Society for Training and Development, a professional organization for company-based training, estimated that in 1985, U.S. companies spent about 1.5 percent of their payroll expenses for training. In late 1992, the number fell to about 1 percent. Nor is training very widespread. In a 1991 study, Carnevale discovered that only one-half of one percent of the nation's 3.8 million companies carry out some

of as apprentices. In the second phase, they begin to make independent contributions. In the third phase, they serve as mentors for others in the first phase. In the fourth phase, individuals provide direction for their organizations. For the remaining sections of this chapter, we will focus on factors influencing those in the first phase of their careers—the apprenticeship.

Mentors and Role Models

A **mentor** is a senior employee whose primary role is to instruct a younger, less experienced protégé.[48] Mentoring contributes to the fit between the employee

---

[48] K. E. Kram, *Mentoring at Work: Developmental Relationships in Organizational Life* (Glenview, Ill.: Scott Foresman, 1985).

form of training. In addition, many firms that do train also are not rewarding better trained employees with salary increases, said Carnevale.

Most training seems to be directed toward white-collar workers and managers. However, based on interviews with 2,252 executives at major firms, Robert Ellis, an executive at management consultants Wyatt Company in Chicago, recently concluded that most training is fractured, uncoordinated, and often not even accounted for. "We don't see much overall training strategy," he reports.

FIGURE 11-6 ▶ **A Comparison of Worker Training**

Worker training in the U.S. has traditionally been very limited and has lagged behind Japan and Germany. What follows is a look at various aspects of training and how the U.S. measures up, according to a report by the U.S. Office of Technology Assessment.

	U.S.	GERMANY	JAPAN
School-to-work transition	Only some businesses have ties with schools	Most youth not headed to college have apprenticeships	Employers and local schools have working relationships
Vocational education	Found in most urban areas, but quality varies widely, from poor to excellent	Readily available and quality is generally good	Limited availability, yet quality is fair to good
Employer-provided training	Usually limited to managers and technicians; some training is excellent, but most is weak	Tends to be good and is prevalent at entry level and to qualify for promotions	Tends to be very good and prevalent

Source: *Chicago Tribune*, December 20, 1992, Sec. 7, page 1.

---

and the organization because senior employees can provide information about and historical contexts of the organization. This is another component of the socialization process and one that unites those in the first phase with those in the second phase of their careers.

Mentoring is also a political activity. A mentor-protégé relationship is a form of *vertical coalition*. As we suggested in Chapter 8, developing political relationships and forming coalitions are common organizational activities. Taking advantage of the natural bonds between mentor and protégé is one way to facilitate the development of a coalition. Whether we consider mentor-protégé relationships from a socialization or a political perspective, such relationships with successful, experienced managers are very important to newcomers throughout much of their tenure with an organization. In fact, research on this form of

| FIGURE 11-7 | ▶**A Newcomer's Welcome Package** |

Many employees do not receive a good first impression of their firms. They often must search for information about how to do their jobs—a task that is frequently burdensome and frustrating. To combat this information deficit, some organizations have established a welcome package.

The welcome package is a compilation of useful information that employees need to conduct their routine activities. At the very least such a package should include:

1. *Phone listings:* Because much of the modern employee's work requires telephone contact, having to search for such numbers is very time consuming. To offset this, the welcome package should contain a section of frequently called numbers of organizations, services, and people.
2. *Mailstop listings:* This section contains a complete listing of employee and organizational internal mail locations to expedite routing of critical documentation that the employee will receive and mail.
3. *Forms:* Because of the importance of standard forms to the smooth flow of information on a variety of topics, the package should also contain a listing of all important forms. This listing would provide the name, purpose, destination, and special characteristics of all such forms.
4. *Equipment and facilities listings:* All major equipment such as personal computers, word processors, modems, and copiers should be listed, along with their locations and functions. A separate listing of the locations of any facilities such as a library or recreational and dining facilities and their hours of operation should also be included.
5. *Schedules:* The package may also include a schedule of daily operations such as breaks, lunch hours, and holidays.
6. *Glossary:* An important section, this listing should include common acronyms of projects and organizations and frequently used esoteric terms. This enhances the newcomer's ability to "speak the language" of the firm.
7. *Organizational descriptions:* This section should identify the mission of the organization, the top managers, and other pertinent information.
8. *Project descriptions:* This section should include a compendium of the major projects with which the organization is involved to give an employee a wider view of its direction and functions.
9. *Procedures:* A very important component of the package, this section should include a listing of all policies and procedures of which the new employee must be aware.

Source: R. L. Kliem, "Welcoming New Employees the Right Way," *Administrative Management* (July 1987): 14–15.

intergenerational cooperation suggests that younger managers are more satisfied and progress faster when they have mentors than when they do not.[49] But, the opportunity to have a mentor does not seem to be as accessible to women as men. For example, women may be more reluctant to initiate a mentoring relationship with a man for fear that others will interpret such an approach as a sexual advance. Men may perceive that mentoring women is more difficult because there is the added complication of destructive office gossip. Finally,

[49] W. Whitely, T. Dougherty, and G. Dreher, "Relationship of Career Mentoring and Socioeconomic Origins to Managers and Professionals' Early Career Progress," *Academy of Management Journal* 34 (1991): 331–351; and E. Fagenson, "The Mentor Advantage: Perceived Career/Job Experiences of Proteges and Nonproteges," *Journal of Organizational Behavior* 10 (1989): 309–320.

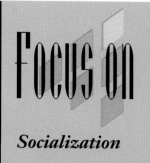

Socialization

Repatriating U.S. Managers More Americans are taking overseas assignments than ever before. Companies typically acknowledge the culture shock of such global assignments and provide training and support for managers and their families making this transition. However, recent research suggests that coming back home to the United States is not that easy for American executives after they have been overseas. In fact, one out of four doesn't make a successful readjustment. The problem is that companies don't consider that returning to the United States after years overseas requires readjustment. Linda Stroh and Arno Haslberger, professors at the Institute of Human Resources and Industrial Relations at Loyola University of Chicago, found that 25 percent of those who return to the corporate home office leave the company because they cannot adjust to being back. "When these people return," says Stroh, "colleagues notice that they have changed a lot. For example, their perspective is more worldly; they don't look at things as ethnocentrically; they see things differently. But their peers in the home office aren't interested in listening to a returning employee talk about the experience abroad."

The survey found that only about one-third of the 24 companies surveyed provided a repatriation program for their returning employees, while two-thirds provided programs for employees and their families to prepare them for the overseas post. If companies continue to ignore this problem, they may find themselves hesitating about sending managers overseas for fear that the managers will not be able to adjust to life in the United States when they return home.

Source: R. E. Yates, "Long Road Home for Expatriates," *Chicago Tribune,* December 30, 1991, section 4, 1–2.

women may have fewer formal and informal opportunities to develop mentor-protégé relationships, especially if mentors select protégés based on their involvement in key or visible projects.[50]

While mentoring is a socialization process, four distinct phases have been identified: initiation, cultivation, separation, and redefinition.[51] The initiation stage usually lasts for about six months to a year, during which time the parties get to know each other. The second stage, cultivation, is the major stage of mentoring. During this stage, the mentor supports, directs, and counsels the protégé. It is this stage in which the "teacher-student" relationship is most evident. The third stage is the separation stage in which there is a significant change in the nature of the relationship. In fact, virtually all mentor-protégé relationships end with some negative emotion, ranging from feelings of ambiguity to outright anger at being rejected. The separation phase is difficult for the parties, but if the mentoring relationship has been successful, then the two parties may be able to recognize and value both the old and the new forms of the relationship. This reconceptualization of the mentor-protégé relationship is accomplished in the last, the redefinition, stage.

---

[50] D. A. Bowen, "Were Men Meant to Mentor Women?" *Training and Development Journal* 39 (1985): 31–34; B. R. Ragins and J. L. Cotton, "Easier Said than Done: Gender Differences in Perceived Barriers to Gaining a Mentor," *Academy of Management Journal* 34 (1991): 939–951.

[51] K. E. Kram, "Phases of the Mentor Relationship," *Academy of Management Journal* 26 (1983): 608–625.

A mentor-protégé relationship is a form of vertical coalition. Such relationships with successful, experienced managers are very important to newcomers throughout much of their tenure with an organization. In fact, younger managers are more satisfied and progress faster when they have this form of intergenerational cooperation than when they do not.

Mentoring relationships are not, however, without their risks. If there is a mismatch between the mentor and protégé, the relationship between these two can be anything but supportive. An individual may feel pressured into a mentoring role, regardless of his or her level of skill or enthusiasm for this assignment. Finally, it is not clear that mentoring is required for organizational success. Some organizational scholars suggest that a newcomer can obtain the information necessary to navigate the corporate system from a variety of people. A newcomer may take advantage of sponsors (strong supporters, but less powerful than mentors), guides (individuals conversant with the policies, procedures, and obstacles in the organization), and peers (equals who can act as sounding boards and information sources).[52]

A mentor-protégé relationship is often a formal or, at least, acknowledged interchange between an inexperienced and an experienced manager. However, the term mentor is often applied to relationships of much shorter duration. For example, a "designated" mentor is a person assigned to an organizational newcomer to facilitate his or her early transition from outsider to organizational member. Unlike the mentoring process we have described above, the designated mentor is a role assigned to a particular individual by the organization. In the same vein as the "welcome package," the designated mentor is an information source—but one with a considerably more personal touch.

Sometimes an experienced manager can facilitate the socialization of a newcomer without ever knowing it—by serving as a role model. A role model is a person whose behavior, attitude, image, or performance sets an example that others wish to imitate. Role models are common components in our understanding of how to respond in new or unfamiliar situations. Parents, teachers, public figures, and friends are common role models for conveying "the way to

---

[52]J. Sheridan, J. Slocum, R. Buda, and R. Thompson, "Effects of Corporate Sponsorship and Departmental Power on Career Tournaments," *Academy of Management Journal* 33 (1990): 578–602; and K. Kram and L. Isabella, "Mentoring Alternatives: The Role of Peer Relationships in Career Development," *Academy of Management Journal* 28 (1985): 110–132.

do things" in different aspects of our lives. In unfamiliar social situations, we commonly defer to role models. When faced with a vast array of silverware at a formal dinner party, a common response is to wait and observe the behavior of others. Using their behavior as a model, we may imitate or adapt what they do. Thus, whether as mentors, designated mentors, or role models, experienced organizational members play a vital role in the socialization of new employees. But, their responsibilities lie primarily in the informational and political arenas. Committing the employee to a long-term relationship with the organization is the function of career paths.

Career Paths and Career Ladders

Career paths are job-progression routes along which employees advance through the organization. While career paths are often designed for a particular employee, they may be drawn up by the organization as common highways for career advancement. Such routes usually consist of a combination of lateral, downward, and upward moves through the organizational hierarchy to gain needed experience. When career paths are formalized, they become career ladders. Thus, a **career ladder** is a specific series of jobs or experiences necessary to advance in the organization. For example, in most airline companies, a clear career ladder must be followed to achieve the command of an aircraft. An individual qualified to be a pilot must first serve as a navigator and then as a second officer before advancing to the rank of captain.

The existence of career paths and career ladders plays a role in socializing the new employee. While much of the benefit that employees will receive from these paths and ladders lies in the future, understanding how one advances in the organization provides critical information to (1) the individual deciding whether to join the company and (2) the newcomer searching for a mentor or role model. In addition to providing information, career paths also play a more symbolic role. They let employees know that the organization is interested in a long-term relationship with them—that it is committed to them not just for

Teams can provide an important source of role models for new employees. Well-managed teams like this quality control team at Pontiac, also quickly establish a sense of belonging in the new employees, a favorable initial work experience that could help develop an early organizational commitment.

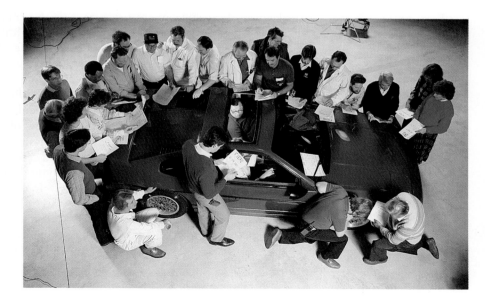

now, but for the future as well. In fact, one major reason for turnover in organizations is the lack of clear opportunities for career advancement.[53]

By now it should be clear that many factors help to socialize newcomers into an organization and its culture. The importance of a strong culture and appropriate socialization to organizational performance is gaining credibility among both practitioners and researchers in the field. Structuring the way in which newcomers are brought into an organization can enhance their level of organizational commitment and, thus, their long-term productivity.

SUMMARY ◆◆◆◆◆◆

This chapter focused on how individuals become organizational members. In recent years, considerable attention has been paid to the processes—such as selection and socialization—that ensure a good person-organization and person-job fit.

The selection process is the first contact with potential organizational members—the applicants. From the organization's perspective, a good selection process can identify the "right kind" of people for the organization. Such individuals may be those with specific skills, values, and expectations, or those who are amenable to the values and expectations of the organization. From the applicant's perspective, selection of an appropriate organization is aided by gathering the "right kind" of information. Knowing both the desirable and undesirable aspects of the job requires a realistic job preview. Clarifying the inducements and the contributions that the organization and the individual will exchange is the basis of the psychological contract between the individual and the employer.

After the individual accepts an offer of employment and becomes an organizational member, then the next task is to commit the individual to the goals and expectations of the organization. Such a commitment is in the organization's best interest, because committed employees are more likely to remain with the organization and expend greater effort in the accomplishment of their tasks.

Commitment to the organization is generated through the visibility of individuals as organizational members, through the explicitness and irreversibility of their choices and behaviors, and through the volition or personal responsibility they feel for their actions. Organizations can enhance the visibility, irreversibility, and volition of behaviors by selecting the appropriate individuals and structuring their tasks and work groups accordingly.

A primary way in which organizations with highly committed employees differ from those with less committed employees is their possession of a strong organizational culture. An organization's culture is composed of five elements: a widely shared philosophy, a view of people as critical resources, charismatic leaders and heroes, rituals and ceremonies, and clear expectations about the organization's direction.

To convey the culture of an organization to newcomers requires organizational socialization—communication of the organization's goals, norms,

---

[53] J. Greenhaus, *Career Management* (Hinsdale, Ill.: Dryden Press (1987); and J. Forbes, "Early Intraorganizational Mobility: Patterns and Influences," *Academy of Management Journal* 30 (1987): 110–125.

and preferred ways of doing things. Specific mechanisms to accomplish this socialization include mentors and role models, welcoming packages, and clearly defined career paths and career ladders. The importance of a strong culture and efficient socialization mechanisms in creating highly productive organizations cannot be ignored.

Key Terms

Career ladder Specific series of jobs or experiences necessary to advance in an organization.

Contributions The productive capacity toward achieving an organization's purpose offered by an individual who is entering into a psychological contract.

Explicitness Extent to which individuals cannot deny that a behavior occurred, serving to commit individuals to their actions.

Inducements The compensations of steady employment and payment offered to an individual by an organization that is entering into a psychological contract.

Irreversibility Extent to which behavior cannot easily be revoked or undone, serving to commit individuals to their actions.

Job analysis Gathering of information about a job in an organization, including a description of tasks and activities, results (products or services), and the equipment, materials, and working conditions that characterize the job.

Mentor A senior employee whose primary role is to instruct a younger, less experienced protégé.

Organizational commitment Relative strength of an individual's identification with and involvement in a particular organization.

Organizational culture Expectations and practices of the organization, including shared philosophy, attitude toward employees, leaders and heroes, rituals and ceremonies, and belief about the direction of the organization.

Organizational socialization Process of conveying the organization's goals, norms, and preferred ways of doing things to new employees.

Psychological contract Set of unwritten, reciprocal expectations between an employee and an organization.

Realistic job preview Mechanism used by organizations to present both the desirable and undesirable aspects of the job and the organization, to provide the potential employee with more complete and accurate information about the position.

Selection Process of collecting and evaluating information about an individual in order to extend an offer of employment.

Visibility The observability of behaviors serving to commit individuals to organizations by making their association with them public knowledge.

Volition Extent to which individuals believe they have a choice in their behaviors, serving to commit them to their actions.

Discussion Questions

1. The selection process in organizations has taken on increasing importance in the last decade. What factors are responsible for this change?

2. Realistic Job Previews (RJPs) are one way organizations can convey their expectations of employee performance to potential organizational members. In what ways do RJPs facilitate the development of an effective psychological contract?

3. One way in which organizations deal with newcomers is to try to humble them early in their tenure with the company. Why might organizations put their employees through such experiences, and why might the newcomers learn from them and find them useful?

4. In recent years, fraternity hazing has become a larger problem on college campuses. In fact, such hazing activities have resulted in a number of highly publicized deaths. What is the purpose of hazing? If you were asked to solve this problem by the president of your university, how would you go about making sure that the practice of hazing would be eliminated?

5. Distinguish between organizational commitment and behavioral commitment.

6. Why are socialization activities so important in bringing employees of newly acquired firms up to speed in productivity?

7. Under what conditions might a firm want to maintain a "weak" culture?

8. Career paths and career ladders are often one way an organization can convey its commitment to its employees. One obvious example of a career path is the promotion and tenure process for faculty at colleges and universities. What are the advantages and disadvantages of such a system for the organization? For the individual?

If You Want to Know More

The new employee is the focus of much recent organizational behavior research. There are a number of interesting readings written from both the organization's perspective and the new employee's perspective. Organizational selection is the topic of Gatewood and Feild's book, *Human Resource Selection*, published in 1990 by Dryden Press. This book presents a detailed description of the selection process and is an excellent reference on this topic.

Realistic job previews are the specific focus of organizational entry, the general focus of a book by John Wanous entitled *Organizational Entry: Recruitment, Selection, and Socialization of Newcomers*, published by Addison-Wesley (Boston, 1980). Probably one of the more detailed descriptions of psychological contracts can be found in

E. H. Schein's book, *Organizational Psychology* (Englewood Cliffs, N.J.: Prentice-Hall, 1980).

To get more information on the general process of commitment, a good article to read is Jerry Salancik's piece "Commitment Is Too Easy," published in *Organizational Dynamics* (Summer 1977). Focusing specifically on organizational commitment is the book by R. T. Mowday, L. W. Porter, and R. M. Steers, *Employee-Organizational Linkages: The Psychology of Commitment, Absenteeism, and Turnover* (New York: Academic Press, 1982).

Organizational culture is the topic of T. Deal and A. Kennedy's book, *Corporate Culture: The Rites and Rituals of Corporate Life* (Boston: Addison-Wesley, 1982). Our understanding of organizational socialization is examined in a review written by E. A. Schein, "Toward a Theory of Organizational Socialization," which appears in volume 1 of *Research in Organizational Behavior* (Greenwich, Conn.: JAI Press, 1979). Those interested in additional reading on mentors and the mentoring process should examine K. E. Kram's book, *Mentoring at Work: Developmental Relationships in Organizational Life* (Glenview, Ill.: Scott-Foresman, 1985). Finally, an excellent sourcebook for information about various aspects of career management is J. Sonnenfeld's *Managing Career Systems: Channeling the Flow of Executive Careers* (Homewood, Ill.: R. D. Irwin, 1984).

On Your Own

Alien Invasion Organizational cultures are so ubiquitous that we often overlook the information they can convey to an observer. The trick to deciphering a culture is learning to read the clues. What do the building style and layout say about the company? What symbols does it use in dealing with the public, and what do those symbols say about how the company wants to be seen? What can we interpret from the activities of employees? Are they energetic or apathetic? Are they friendly or hostile? What stories do they tell about the organization and its major executives? What are the norms of dress? How formal are relationships between people, particularly people of different status levels, such as supervisors and secretaries? It is surprising how much of a feel for an organization one can acquire simply by looking and listening carefully.

Consider an organization to which you belong, such as your family, university, volunteer agency, fraternity or sorority, or church. Now look at your chosen organization through the eyes (and antennae!) of an alien. You have just arrived on the first spaceship to Earth from your planet. Your supervisors have ordered you to learn how Earthlings behave without doing anything to make them aware that you are from another planet. It is vital to the future plans of your superiors that you do nothing to disturb the Earthlings. Unfortunately, your people communicate by electromagnetic waves and are incapable of speech, so you cannot talk to the natives. Even if you could, it is reported by the usually reliable Bureau of Interplanetary Intelligence that Earthlings may become cannibalistic if annoyed. A crash course in Earth languages taught by the bureau has enabled you to read and understand the language.

These instructions limit your ability to interact verbally with the organization you are observing. There are two reasons for this. First, your objective is to learn about what the organization does when it is simply going about its normal business and not responding to specific questions. Second, you are likely to be surprised at how much you can learn by simply observing if you put your mind to it. Many skilled managers employ this ability in sensing what is going on as they walk through their plant or office area. When you have completed your observation of the chosen organization, develop a short description of the culture of the organization, focusing on its ideologies, myths, values, and norms of behavior.

Source: Donald D. Bowen, "Alien Invasion: An Organizational Culture Assignment," in *Experiences in Management and Organizational Behavior*, 3d ed., R. J. Lewicki, D. D. Bowen, D. T. Hall, and F. S. Hall, eds. (New York: Wiley, 1988).

CHAPTER 11

THE MANAGER'S MEMO

FROM: H. Roadruck, Vice President, Pickle Division

TO: T. Phinney, Production Supervisor

RE: High Turnover

It has seemed to me that turnover among the pickle production workers has been high. I obtained some figures from the Personnel Department, and the numbers show my assumption was right. Out of a 135-person work force, we have lost the following numbers during the last 12 months:

Within 5 years of hiring	6
Within 1 year of hiring	23
Within 6 months of hiring	31
Within 1 month of hiring	97

These figures show that we are constantly replacing our production work force. We cannot afford to keep this up. We also cannot afford to pay any more than we do now. Our wages are already above the industry average.

The numbers also tell me that a lot of the people you are hiring either are unqualified or quickly become disillusioned with their jobs. According to the Personnel Department, some of the departing workers have been saying that working here is a lot more boring than they were led to believe it would be. I even heard that one worker said he was on the job for a full week before he was allowed to touch the packaging machine. Another said he was getting embarrassed to tell his friends he makes pickles all day long.

Please provide some ideas on how you can rectify this situation.

Case Discussion Questions

Assume you are the production supervisor, and respond to the vice-president's memorandum. Review the concepts in the chapter, and apply the ones you think would be most effective in selecting and assimilating production workers. Be sure to support your recommendations.

JOB DESIGN

CHANGE ROLES, NOT COMPANIES ◆◆◆◆◆◆

In today's job market, some employee turnover seems inevitable. People want new horizons or more money. Even when a business is growing fast, it can't satisfy everyone. Most managers think some turnover is good because new people bring new ideas to a company. But how often can you afford to see your best people seeking their fortunes elsewhere?

One company, G.S.I. Transcomm Data Systems, Inc., in Pittsburgh, has taken an almost radical position on turnover. Transcomm does not accept employee decisions to move on as ordinary events but views them as management failures. President Philippe Beaurain concedes that some Transcomm employees get bored and frustrated, but few of them quit. Instead, they are encouraged to seek changes within the company by redefining their roles.

The policy works. Last fall, Karen Tedesco, 29, who had been with the company for over four years, was growing weary of her operations job. She had become proficient at managing software installations at customer locations but had reached a point where she was eager to broaden her business experience— either at Transcomm or elsewhere. Beaurain tried to persuade her to stay longer in operations, but she wasn't interested. After consulting with her manager and colleagues, he came up with a solution. After a four- or five-month transition, Tedesco would take her experience and use it in the sales department. "If we hadn't faced this problem," Beaurain believes, "we would have lost her in six months."

Transcomm's success with Tedesco is not an isolated one. Over the past three years, nearly 20 percent of Transcomm's more experienced employees have made substantial role changes—usually lateral moves at the same level of compensation. Many of the shifts (like Tedesco's) were for professional reasons, but sometimes the reasons are more personal. Last winter, Alan Koch, a recently married programmer, found that he could no longer be as flexible about out-of-town assignments. At other companies, says Koch, "I might have been apprehensive about going to my supervisor. But not here." Over the next few weeks, Koch and his supervisor figured out a reasonable way to restructure Koch's responsibilities. Today he provides support to more-established customers who don't require site visits.

In some respects, organizing a business to meet employee's needs for growth is both demanding and costly. But Beaurain is confident that the effort is worth it. "Before people think about leaving, they come in and talk. Employees don't do that at many companies, but to us, that's worth a lot of money."

Source: B. G. Posner, "Role Changes," *Inc.*, February 1990, 95–98.

INTRODUCTION

Philosopher and historian David Hume once wrote, "the richest genius, like the most fertile soil, when uncultivated, shoots up into the rankest weeds: and instead of vines and olives for the pleasure and use of man, produces to its slothful owner the most abundant crop of poisons." Hume's quotation highlights the challenge facing an organization's management. Finding the right personnel and successfully getting them into the organization is only the first step in developing a healthy and productive work force. This chapter addresses the second step in this managerial challenge: designing jobs and roles for workers that take full advantage of each individual's ability to contribute to the organization's efficiency and effectiveness. The chapter presents three perspectives on the design of jobs: (1) the tradition of work simplification, (2) job characteristics approaches to job design, and finally (3) work-group approaches to job design. The chapter concludes by considering several important qualifications to the success of all job design efforts.

JOB DESIGN IN PERSPECTIVE

As noted in Chapter 2, the field of organizational behavior traces its roots to shortcomings of the traditional job design efforts of the early 1900s. Traditional job design—as exemplified by Frederick Taylor's "scientific management" and Henry Ford's assembly line—focused almost exclusively on efficiency. Often this focus on efficiency meant **work simplification**. Managers designed work tasks to be simple and therefore easily mastered and quickly accomplished. Each worker focused on a small number of very simple tasks, such as screwing several nuts onto several bolts. The basic philosophy behind this approach to job design was that each worker could become expert at a few tasks and learn to do them repeatedly, with lightning speed and no mistakes. In the electronics industry, for example, simplified jobs may have a "cycle time"—the amount of time it takes an employee to complete the entire task—as short as 10 seconds.[1] That translates into more than 2,500 cycles per eight-hour workday.

---

[1]E. E. Lawler III, *High-Involvement Management* (London: Jossey-Bass, 1986), 84.

The Work-Simplification Paradox

Whatever simplified, routinized jobs gain in potential efficiency they often more than lose in boredom and alienation. This woman feels like a part of the machine as she keeps the product flowing along the production line. There is virtually no variation or interest in her day.

The philosophy behind a work-simplification strategy is very appealing, and by some estimates as many as 50 percent of all manufacturing jobs today still are designed on the premise that simpler is better.[2] However, work simplification considers only the most efficient way to design a work task *assuming that workers are indifferent* to what they are doing. In truth, workers are *not* indifferent to the design of their work. The Hawthorne studies (discussed in Chapter 2) proved that what workers feel and need can be just as important to efficiency as specialization and simplification of tasks.

In his book *High-Involvement Management*, management theorist Edward Lawler III summarizes the effects of work simplification on worker behaviors:

> . . .the work simplification approach is often associated with (1) low quality because individuals do not care about product quality, (2) low productivity because individuals are not motivated to be productive, and (3) high wages because individuals demand them for repetitive, boring, unsatisfying jobs. In addition, it often leads to high levels of turnover and absenteeism, and therefore overstaffing to replace absentees and people who quit. Further, despite the fact that jobs are relatively simple to learn, training costs may be high because of the high turnover rate. Finally, the social costs are high. Although largely undocumented, it is thought that the dissatisfying nature of simplified, repetitive work causes mental problems, alcohol and substance abuse, and a general alienation from society."[3]

The message here is that a job that is sensibly designed from the viewpoint of the task may not be sensibly designed from the viewpoint of the worker. This is the paradox of work simplification. A job that consists of continuous repetition of several simple tasks may be easy to do in principle. However, when a job is too easy, a worker's attention will wander; the worker will become bored and alienated. Quality and productivity both will suffer.

The literature on job design is filled with managers' horror stories of what happens when workers are assigned tasks that are too simple and repetitive. The comments of one manager of a large microelectronics manufacturer in Holland are revealing. The workers in his plant were required to wear gloves to protect the product from fingerprints and skin oil. When management wasn't looking, the workers would roll their gloves into a ball and play "soccer" in the work bays. Each work bay also was equipped with an air hose for blowing dust off the work surfaces. Somehow the workers figured out how to disconnect the nozzles and use the hoses to shoot rubber drawer-knobs at each other across the work bays. This kind of dysfunctional playfulness on the assembly line represents alienation, lost productivity, and even potential hazards for the worker. Further, it usually means that the organization must spend money to provide more supervisors to keep employees in line. Some further examples of this problem are provided in the "INTERNATIONAL FOCUS ON: Worker Alienation."

In addition to lost productivity, the issue of lost employees is not trivial for organizations. As noted in the opening vignette for this chapter, small amounts

---

[2] Ibid., 86.

[3] Ibid., 86.

*Worker
Alienation*

Shaking Those Blue-Collar Blues

What was it like to work on a Detroit automobile assembly line in the 1970s? Henry Belcher, a 40-year-old welder at a Dodge plant, described it this way: "I am as much a machine as a punch press or a drill motor is." A local UAW president at Cadillac summed it up grimly: "Every single unskilled young man in that plant wants out of there. They can't face it. They hate to go in there." What is it that they hate? Consider the following description of Henry Belcher's job:

Promptly at 5 A.M., the assembly line begins sending cars past his work station, and from then on Belcher is part of the line, like the well-oiled gears and bearings. The noise is deafening; Belcher could not talk to the men at the next stations three feet away even if there were time. There never is. Partially assembled cars move past him at the rate of 62 an hour; in less than one minute he is expected to look over each auto, pound out a dent in a fender, or reweld an improperly joined seam. Cars that cannot be fixed that quickly are taken off the line. In the winter, drafts from ill-caulked windows chill Belcher's chest, while hot air blasts from rust-proofing ovens 30 feet away singe his back. After two hours of standing on the concrete floor his legs ache, but the whistle does not blow for lunch until 10 A.M. . . . Says Belcher . . ." Everything is regulated. No time to stop and think about what you are doing; your life is geared to the assembly line.*"

Belcher's experience was hardly unique. Workers would do anything to

*"The Grueling Life on the Line," *Time,* September 28, 1970, 70.

avoid feeling like part of the machinery—have water fights, paint fights, whatever. Drugs and heavy drinking were common, and so was product sabotage—an ignition key dropped in the gas tank, a lighted glove locked in the trunk, slit upholstery, severed ignition wires. And in the back of everyone's mind was the same slim hope that the line would break down.

Today, Japanese managers and owners are bringing a philosophy to American manufacturing that acknowledges the importance of shaking the "blue-collar blues" by cultivating the minds of the workers. In Georgetown, Kentucky, a generation of Americans is learning that assembly-line workers can be respected, consulted, and given authority. Georgetown's $2 billion Toyota Motor Manufacturing U.S.A. facility started production in July 1988. It still uses Henry Ford's mass production system, but the employees will tell you that every worker is an active member of a team, not a human robot doing the same task again and again. Team members learn each other's tasks and rotate them to stave off boredom and repetitive motion injuries that plague traditional auto workers. Uniforms are voluntary, but almost all employees—executives particularly—wear the blue shirts with their first names embroidered in white. There's no executive parking lot or executive dining room. Nobody, not even the company president, has his own office. Rock music wafts along the assembly line, but Japanese chimes signal breaks in production. The managers and owners of the plant prize dedication, loyalty, and training, and they look for applicants who share those values. The workers are trained, stretched, and challenged; but mostly they are treated as partners.

Sources: "The Luddites in Lordstown," *Harper's* magazine, June 1972, 68–73; "Blue-Collar Blues on the Assembly Line," *Fortune,* July 1970; and M. Mercer, "Reinventing the Factory," *The Arizona Daily Star,* February 18, 1990, G1–G2.

of worker turnover no doubt are healthy for organizations and represent natural renewal of the work force.[4] However, the departure of an organization's potentially valuable and productive but alienated human resources can be extremely costly. Replacing an employee may cost an organization anywhere from 5 to 25 times an employee's monthly salary in lost productivity, search, socialization, and training costs.[5]

The bottom line is that workers have a reservoir of interest and energy. If this reservoir is not tapped by the job itself, it will be wasted or will surface in other forms—such as counterproductive playfulness on the assembly line. The challenge of job design is to harness worker interest and energy and direct it toward the accomplishment of organizational objectives.

In this chapter, we will consider two approaches to redesigning jobs: redesign focused on characteristics of individual jobs and work-group approaches to job redesign.

JOB CHARACTERISTICS

Management attempts to harness worker interest and energy by changing the characteristics of individual jobs generally are of two sorts: job enlargement and job enrichment. **Job enlargement** changes the range of a job—the number of tasks that a worker performs—to make the job more interesting and involving. **Job enrichment** makes jobs more interesting and involving by allowing workers to fulfill higher-order needs—such as achievement and control—through work.

Job Enlargement

Job enlargement is based on the simple premise that a job will be more interesting and involving if the worker has a wide range of skills (rather than just one) to master and perform. Consider the range of tasks required to produce a shirt, as portrayed in Figure 12–1(a). A work-simplification strategy would assign each worker one of these three tasks. Each worker then could master one particular task, providing (in principle at least) the best potential for efficiency through specialization. This specialization approach, however, would run the risk of worker alienation. Job enlargement, on the other hand, decreases the probability of worker alienation or boredom by increasing the variety of skills each worker has to master. In its simplest form, managers increase skill variety in workers' jobs by giving workers more tasks. In Figure 12–1(c), for instance, each worker does *all three* tasks.

A slightly different way to increase the skill variety of a job is job rotation. As shown in Figure 12–1(b), **job rotation** increases skill variety by allowing workers to switch jobs occasionally. The first worker does Task #1 (stitching on collars) only for a while, and then moves on to Task #2 (ironing and folding)

[4]J. R. Hollenbeck and C. R. Williams, "Turnover Functionality versus Turnover Frequency: A Note on Work Attitudes and Organizational Effectiveness," *Journal of Applied Psychology* 71 (1986): 606–611.

[5]P. H. Mirvis and E. E. Lawler III, "Accounting for the Quality of Work Life," *Journal of Occupational Behavior* 5 (1984): 197–212.

| FIGURE 12-1 | ▶Comparison of Job Specialization, Job Rotation, and Job Enlargement Strategies |

Simplifying the tasks assigned to a worker in principle should make a job easy to do, but in practice will make the job boring and alienating. Job rotation and job enlargement make jobs more interesting by increasing the variety of skills a worker uses.

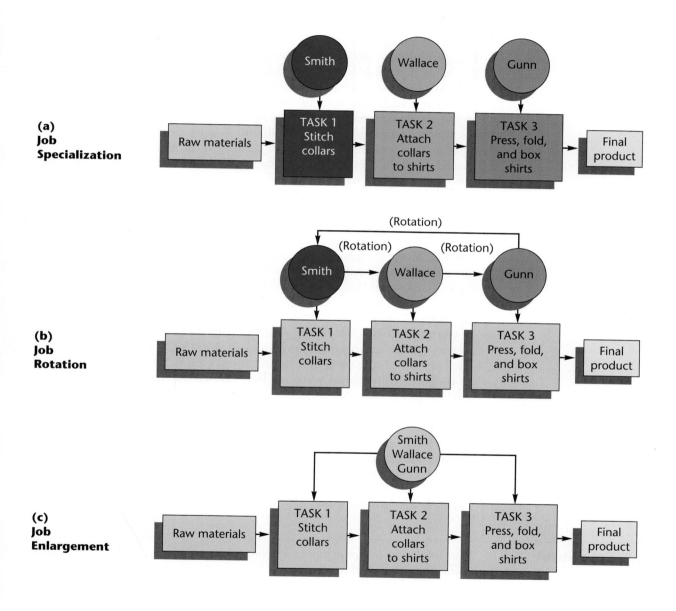

Source: From *Organizational Behavior and Performance*, 4/e by Andrew D. Szilagyi, Jr. and Marc J. Wallace, Jr. Copyright © 1987, 1983 by Scott, Foresman and Company. Reprinted with permission of Harper Collins Publishers.

for a while, and finally on to Task #3 (boxing). Rotation breaks up the monotony of working a single repetitive task by changing a worker's task every once in a while. Rotation might occur every week, every day, or even every few hours.

Skill variety also can be increased through cross-training. **Cross-training** occurs when management encourages employees to learn their coworkers' jobs. Cross-training provides benefits for both the individual and the organization. For the individual, learning new skills increases variety on the job and breaks up the monotony of working on only a small number of tasks. In Shell Oil's Canadian plant in Sarnia, Ontario, it takes workers as long as 9 or 10 years to master all the different tasks.[6] That gives every worker some new challenges to look forward to every day. For management, cross-training provides additional flexibility; if an employee calls in sick or leaves the organization, or if a particular task becomes a temporary bottleneck, work assignments can be shifted around to handle the changes. At a Chrysler plant in New Castle, Indiana, cross-training was used effectively to reduce manufacturing costs by 30 percent, resulting in a savings of over $3 million.[7] Cross-training also allows management to train personnel for supervisory roles. An employee who has been cross-trained on all the jobs in a work group should make a better work-group supervisor than someone who has learned only one task in the work group. Cross-training is seen as such an overall benefit that some companies even use compensation schemes (known as "pay-for-knowledge" plans) that reward employees for each new skill acquired.

Corporations that take skill-enlargement seriously can show eye-popping benefits. Motorola spends about $60 million a year on additional training for more than 100,000 employees worldwide, but Motorola figures that additional training has saved the company no less than $1.5 billion over the past three years. Corning, Inc., is also a skill-enlargement convert. Corning expects every member of its work force to spend 5 percent of the workday learning new skills. At Corning's Erwin (New York) plant, everyone on the production teams knows how to operate and repair the machines, load the kilns, pack and ship the finished product, order parts, and control for quality. Each of these tasks used to be assigned to individual workers. This skill-enlargement has improved *both* product quality *and* work force morale in the plant.[8]

While job enlargement, rotation, and cross-training are certainly improvements over work simplification as ways to design jobs, they also have drawbacks. Perhaps most critically, increases in the range of jobs do not go far enough in tapping the interest and energies of most workers. A 1987 survey found that most workers want more than just enlarged jobs; they want a say in deciding how their work is organized.[9] Workers want a chance to fulfill their "higher-order" needs through work.

Job Enrichment

The origins of job enrichment are found in Herzberg's two-factor theory of motivation (discussed in Chapter 4). Herzberg maintained that workers will be interested and involved in work when their jobs provide opportunities for "pos-

---

[6] Lawler, *High-Involvement Management*, 104.

[7] W. S. Cascio, *Managing Human Resources* (New York: McGraw-Hill, 1986). 130.

[8] "Shaking the Blue-Collar Blues," J. Fierman, *Fortune*, April 22, 1991, 209–218.

[9] "Managers Underrate Employee Values," *Administrative Management*, July 1987, 8.

At the Federal Reserve Bank of Chicago, checks used to be processed assembly-line style— one task per worker. Now check processors handle multiple tasks through the use of high-speed sorters, thereby increasing skill variety and task identity. Productivity and satisfaction have both benefited.

itive, task-related experiences" such as control and achievement.[10] A list of these positive, task-related experiences is shown in Figure 12–2. We will consider four ways to enrich jobs: providing task identity, task significance, decision-making responsibility, and feedback.

Task Identity   When the set of tasks a worker is assigned allows the worker to see a process through from start to finish, **task identity** occurs. Task identity provides the worker with a sense of completion and achievement. Management at Continental Illinois National Bank and Trust learned how important task identity can be. Check processing at the bank used to be done on an "assembly line," where each clerical worker performed one function over and over. The work was boring and the workers were prone to make errors. That changed when the bank went to a "modular" arrangement that allowed workers to handle entire transactions from start to finish. With the modular arrangement, a single worker processed an incoming check, transferred funds in the account by computer, telephoned the customer if necessary, and mailed out a confirmation of the transaction. "I like it," noted one worker, "because you see the package from beginning to end." The bank liked it, too, because error rates went down.[11]

Naturally, task identity is dependent upon skill variety. A job must incorporate a fair number of skills in order to take a process through from start to finish.

Task Significance   Managers also can enrich jobs by increasing **task significance**. A task is significant when a worker can see that good or poor performance makes a difference to someone. Task significance often is tied to contact with the consumer of a product or service. Any chance a worker has to experience a customer's appreciation for a job well done will enhance that worker's feeling that the task is significant.

Task significance is an important component of job design at Chantiers Beneteau, a French custom sailboat manufacturer. When Xavier Fontanet, chief

---

[10]R. W. Griffin, *Task Design: An Integrative Approach* (Glenview, Ill.: Scott, Foresman, 1982), 31.

[11]"You See the Package from Beginning to End," *Business Week*, May 16, 1983, 103.

FIGURE 12–2	▶ **Positive Task-Related Experiences**

1. *Accountability.* Workers should be held responsible for their performance.
2. *Achievement.* Workers should feel that they are accomplishing something worthwhile.
3. *Control over resources.* If possible, workers should have control over their task.
4. *Feedback.* Workers should receive clear and direct information regarding their performance.
5. *Personal growth and development.* Workers should have the opportunity to learn new skills.
6. *Work pace.* Within constraints, workers should be able to set their own work pace.

Source: F. Herzberg, "The Wise Old Turk," *Harvard Business Review*, September/October 1974, 70–80.

executive, took over the small company, he quickly learned that his work force had lost interest and was turning out seaworthy but undistinguished craft. To reverse this trend, Fontanet encouraged the company's customers to send some personal information with their orders—photographs, personal background information, even descriptions of the adventures they were planning with their new boats. Suddenly workers were not just building sailboats, they were building a racer for customer Ted Hall to parade around San Francisco Bay, and a summer sailing vacation for the Schmidt family in Hamburg. Their work had become significant, and within a year their workmanship had improved dramatically.[12]

Task significance occurs when workers can see that their effort and workmanship make a difference in the overall quality of a product, and therefore in its value to someone. A worker on a traditional assembly line doing just one task in an assembly process probably has a hard time believing that quality of workmanship—how well or poorly that worker does the one task—makes much of a contribution to the overall quality of the product. On the other hand, when a job is enlarged, a worker can feel responsible for a significant portion of the overall product. If the enlargement includes task identity, it becomes easy for a worker to imagine that the quality of the overall product makes a significant difference to the final consumer.

Decision-Making Responsibility   Job enrichment often goes beyond job enlargement by allowing workers to take responsibility for decision making on the job. Job enrichment becomes a big step in job design when it represents the first move by management to share control in the workplace. Managers can increase workers' decision-making responsibility either by allowing them to participate in management decision making (perhaps by soliciting worker opinions through problem-solving groups) or by allowing workers limited decision-making autonomy within the scope of their jobs.

Consider again our shirt assembly line. In the Figure 12–3 depiction of job enrichment, each worker not only has responsibility for all the component tasks (collar stitching, folding and ironing, and boxing), but also *controls* the arrangement of these tasks. Should all the collars be stitched on first, then all the folding and ironing done, and finally all the boxing? Perhaps the whole process

---

[12] R. H. Waterman, *The Renewal Factor* (New York: Bantam Books, 1987), 4.

FIGURE 12–3 ▶Comparison of Job Specialization and Job Enrichment

Job enrichment increases the decision-making responsibility of the worker. In this example, the workers' enriched jobs give them responsibility for quality and task arrangement.

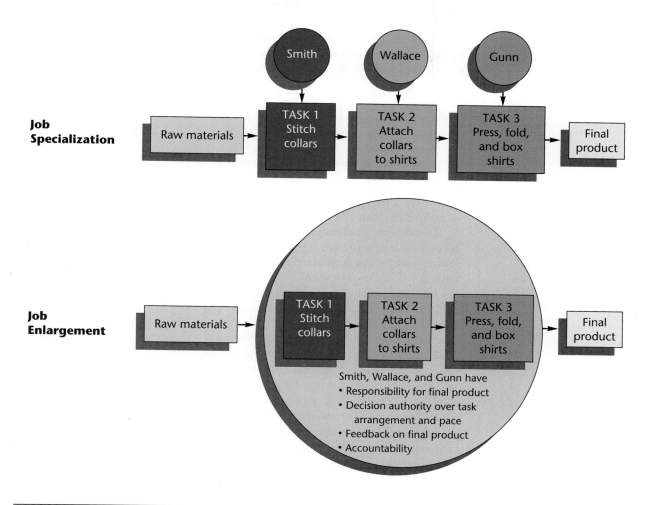

Source: From *Organizational Behavior and Performance*, 4/e by Andrew D. Szilagyi, Jr. and Marc J. Wallace, Jr. Copyright © 1987, 1985 by Scott, Foresman and Company. Reprinted by permission of Harper Collins Publishers.

could be run through in lots of five or ten shirts? Management has delegated these decisions to the worker. The worker controls the immediate work environment and has the option of changing the order of the tasks when the current arrangement gets boring.

The job-enriched workers in Figure 12–3 also now have responsibility for quality-control decisions—checking the work and certifying it to be error free. In a traditionally designed job, quality assurance would be the responsibility of another worker. In an enriched job, the responsibility for quality comes with the job. Management trusts the workers to check their own work.

Worker feelings of control and responsibility also are enhanced when managers consult workers about management decisions, such as how to design a new manufacturing line. Participation in organizational decision making allows workers to feel that management respects their opinions. For the organization, worker participation in decisions opens up a communication channel so that management can access an important source of knowledge and innovation— the workers. A 1986 article entitled "The Golden Nuggets on the Factory Floor" provides some striking examples of the thoughtfulness of factory workers. Consider the insightful comments of one cannery employee:

> We change over an awful lot from 8-oz. to 16-oz. cans. Why can't they drop the size but keep the same diameter for the base as in the 16-oz.? That would save half the amount of changeover time. It would save three to four hours once a week of six to eight expensive people. I am the mechanic, so I know. Now we have to change everything. If we made the change as suggested, all you would have to do is lower all the machines. That's a half hour's work.[13]

Workers on the factory floor like this one are, after all, closest to the work and often have a perspective on the production process that is quite different from —and often clearer than—that of management.

In practice, workers often are unfamiliar with taking responsibility on the job or making innovative suggestions. Time and even training may be required before workers can productively exercise the decision-making control management is willing to give them.[14]

Job enrichment programs that enhance workers' decision-making responsibilities allow workers to experience the psychological benefits of exercising control in the workplace. At the same time, the organization reaps invaluable benefits in improved efficiency and effectiveness. Limited autonomy is designed to accomplish these objectives *within* the well-defined limits of workers' job descriptions. In effect, job enrichment that enhances workers' decision-making responsibility may be a way for management to have its cake and eat it too— to allow the benefits of worker autonomy while retaining the control of an essentially autocratic organizational decision-making structure.

The problem is that allowing workers a taste of control through limited autonomy raises rank-and-file worker expectations in three critical ways. First, limited autonomy allows workers to see that their suggestions can make a difference in the workplace. Good suggestions save the organization money, and the workers come to see themselves as important organizational resources. This sense of power and accomplishment is not easily forgotten, nor surrendered, by workers. It can prove to be a particularly touchy matter if supervisors are threatened by the successes of their subordinates' suggestions.

Second, when limited autonomy works, the workers come to expect the organization to value their opinions. Once management solicits worker opinions, an expectation is created that opinions will be solicited in the future. Nothing kills a participation program faster than management's failure to respond to a suggestion in a timely fashion—except perhaps management's failure to solicit worker opinions about issues when workers expect to be consulted. Finally, limited autonomy raises expectations about compensation. An enriched

---

[13] W. Imberman, "The Golden Nuggets on the Factory Floor," *Business Horizons*, July/August 1986, 64.

[14] R. M. Kanter, "The Dilemmas of Participation," in *The Changemasters* (New York: Simon & Schuster, 1983), 241–278.

job may be more interesting and more involving for the worker, but it also entails more responsibility and therefore deserves more pay.

If management thwarts the expectations that job enrichment engenders in the work force, enthusiasm for participation will wane. This may be why many attempts by American corporations to become more participative end up being only "gimmicks"—short-lived fads whose time in the organization comes and goes.[15] The other choice, of course, is for management to accept and build on workers' expectations for a larger role in their organization. One company's attempts to give its employees this larger role are detailed in the "FOCUS ON: Decision-Making Responsibility."

Context Enrichment   Decision-making responsibility in a job also can be increased by enriching the *context* of work; for example, by giving workers decision-making control over the context of their work. One example of context enrichment is **flextime work scheduling**. In a flextime program, management delegates to each individual worker the responsibility for deciding when to come to work. This does not mean that flextime workers can just come in any time they please. That would create chaos, since no one in a work setting ever could depend on anyone else being there. In fact, flextime represents a good example of the *limited* autonomy management can provide workers in an enriched job. As shown in Figure 12–4, even in flextime scheduling management specifies certain times when *everyone* is expected to be at work. Outside of the required work periods, however, workers can decide for themselves which hours they will be at work in order to fill out their eight hours per day. Schedules then are set up quarterly or yearly so other workers will know when they can count on someone being there, and so that management can be sure that the minimally required work force always is present during business hours.

In the flextime schedule in Figure 12–4(a), for example, all workers are required to be at work between 10 A.M. and 3 P.M., with everyone taking a standard noon to 1 P.M. lunch break. However, that only accounts for four hours of the eight-hour workday. Management leaves the decision of which other four hours to work with the individual employee. Figure 12–4(b) provides a second example of a flextime schedule where the required times are from 9 A.M. to 11 A.M. and 2 P.M. to 4 P.M., allowing for flexible scheduling around the lunch break as well.

Flextime scheduling works best when workers do not need to interact with others to do their work. For a typical assembly line, flextime work scheduling is not appropriate. In our shirt assembly line (Figure 12–1), if the worker who folds and irons the shirts comes in at 6 A.M. to begin work but the collar stitcher doesn't arrive until 9 A.M., that second worker on the line may have nothing to do for three hours! For secretaries in a typing pool, however, flextime may be perfect. Work left the night before (perhaps by someone working till 7 P.M.) will be waiting at 6 A.M. when the first typist arrives.

Flextime allows workers to schedule work around the rest of their lives. Single parents, for instance, may want to start work early in order to be home by 4 P.M. when children return from school. Other workers may want to take classes at a local university. Flextime scheduling allows these workers to fit work

---

[15] T. Peters and R. H. Waterman, *In Search of Excellence*, from the chapter "Productivity through People" (New York: Random House, 1981).

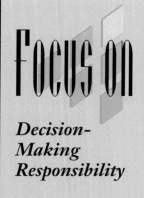

Decision-Making Responsibility

Giving Away the Store One thing for sure, Arthur Friedman, president of Friedman-Jacobs Co., has some pretty strange ideas about how to run a business.

In the early 1970s, he had his most outrageous brainstorm. He allowed his employees to set their own wages, make their own hours, and take their vacations whenever they felt like it, and it worked.

Friedman first unleashed his proposal at one of the regular staff meetings. Decide what you are worth, he told his employees, and tell the bookkeeper to put it in your envelope next week. No questions asked. Work any time, any day, any hours you want. Having a bad day? Go home. Hate working Saturdays? No problem. Aunt Ethel from Chicago has dropped in unexpectedly? Well, take a few days off, show her the town. Want to go to Reno for a week? Need a rest? Go, go, no need to ask. If you need some money for the slot machines, take it out of petty cash. Just come back when you feel ready to work again.

His speech was received in complete silence. No one cheered, no one laughed, no one said a word.

"It was about a month before anyone asked for a raise," recalls Stan Robinson, 55, the payroll clerk. "And when they did, they asked Art first. But he refused to listen and told them to just tell me what they wanted. I kept going back to him to make sure it was all right, but he wouldn't even talk about it. I finally figured out he was serious."

Instead of the all-out raid on the company coffers that some businesspeople might expect, the 15 employees of the Friedman-Jacobs Co. displayed astonishing restraint and maturity. As a result, they developed a strong sense of responsibility and an acute sensitivity that would have been impossible under the traditional system. Furthermore, turnover dropped and net profit increased, while employee malingering and pilferage completely disappeared.

Over the years, other companies have come to understand the wisdom of letting the rank-and-file take charge. When Ralph Stayer's workers at Johnsonville Foods, a Wisconsin sausage company, botched sales orders, mislabeled products and even smashed a forklift into a wall, he changed bosses. Stayer put his workers in charge. Yes, he decided that the same bored people who made careless, costly errors could run his company, make it more profitable, and turn it into a bigger, better business.

And that's exactly what they did. The workers at Johnsonville Foods now hire and fire each other, buy equipment, write budgets. They are their own bosses. This run-it-yourself philosophy has been in place for eight years at Johnsonville Foods, and many Fortune 500 heavy hitters like General Mills are starting to sing the same tune.

"It's not a social experiment. It makes good business sense," says Pat McNulty, who manages a new worker-run General Mills cereal plant. "Nobody knows the job as well as those doing it. If you empower those people to make the decisions, they make good ones."

The payoff is lower costs, better quality, greater efficiency. McNulty expects productivity to be 30 to 40 percent higher than in traditional plants. At Johnsonville Foods, sales have increased more than 20 percent annually since the changes were made, and productivity has increased 50 percent since 1986.

Sources: Martin Koughman: "Arthur Friedman's Outrage," *The Washington Post*, February 23, 1975. © The Washington Post. Used with permission; and Sharon Cohen, "Giving Away the Store," *Atlanta Journal-Constitution*, December 3, 1990, B1.

FIGURE 12–4	▶ Two Sample Flextime Schedules

Flextime scheduling enriches a job by giving workers decision-making responsibility over the *context* in which they work. With a flexible working schedule, workers can decide when to work and can arrange work around nonwork commitments or interests.

(a)

6 a.m.   10 a.m.   3 p.m.   7 p.m.

(b)

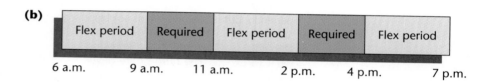

6 a.m. 9 a.m. 11 a.m. 2 p.m. 4 p.m. 7 p.m.

hours around class offerings. In both cases, flextime scheduling allows workers the freedom to fit the rest of life around work.

Flextime enriches jobs by enriching their *context*. Flextime allows workers to fit their obligations at work around their obligations or needs outside the work setting. Another example of enrichment of the job context is provided by the McDonald's "Crew Olympics" competitions. These competitions, described in the "FOCUS ON: Context Enrichment," enrich the job context by providing for fun and rewarding job challenges.

In fact, many companies are finding, like McDonalds has, that a little fun at work can build team spirit, expand creativity, defuse conflict, and increase communication. In short, companies are learning that a little fun at work is good for their people and good for their business.[16]

Feedback   Feedback occurs when management provides workers with information about their performance. Feedback plays an important psychological role by reducing uncertainty in workers. Practically, it makes sense for management to give workers control over decisions only if management also is willing to give them the information necessary to make good decisions. Timely feedback can help alert workers to the existence of problems and also help pinpoint their source. *Any* form of worker participation or autonomy will work only if the workers making the decisions have enough information to make high-quality decisions.

Several years ago, Professor David Garvin of Harvard University conducted a study comparing the defect rates of American and Japanese air-conditioner manufacturing plants. He found 63.5 defects per 100 air-conditioning units produced in the U.S. plants compared to 0.9 defects per 100 units produced in

---

[16]J. Gordon, "Structured Fun," *Training*, September 1992, 23–29.

Focus on

Context Enrichment

Turning Work Into Play at McDonald's All the excellent companies celebrate superior performance. But when it comes to tailoring hoopla to fit its own needs, McDonald's is the master.

In the coming year, about 17 million customers will visit the "golden arches" each day, consuming some 50 billion burgers in the process. In fact, it's safe to say that the vast majority of Americans have at least sampled a Big Mac. Dining at McDonald's is no gourmet experience. But in a world full of unpleasant surprises, what you do get at McDonald's is the comfort of knowing what to expect. The burgers are never burned or raw, the service is sunny, and the restaurants generally are spotless inside and out. McDonald's stays far ahead of its competition in the fast-food industry by maintaining its standards throughout a worldwide system. This is no easy trick since over 75 percent of McDonald's 8,000 restaurants are independently owned franchises, outside the reach of corporate control.

How are the standards so rigidly maintained? By making sure each worker understands McDonald's values and visions and has the requisite pride and purpose to pursue them. And how does McDonald's maintain pride and purpose? Job content does not seem to be the key here; the rules and standards for tasks at McDonald's are rigidly specified in the 700-page operations manual. Working at a McDonald's, from a job-content point of view, is the equivalent of working on a fast-food assembly line. But what McDonald's jobs lack in content they make up for in *context*.

Consider the McDonald's "Crew Olympics." McDonald's management spent six months and $500,000 on a competition *for its workers* prior to the 1984 Olympics in Los Angeles. The competition featured a McDonald's decathlon; counter workers at every McDonald's around the world had the opportunity to compete at each of the tasks McDonald's workers perform on the job every day. "Compete" meant doing a task as fast as possible while still adhering to the rules and standards laid out in the McDonald's operations manual, which includes every attitude and gesture to be used in dealing with McDonald's customers. In-store and local competitions led up to regional competitions. Eventually the finalists—the best McDonald's hamburger flippers in the world—all were flown to Los Angeles for a culminating competition and awards ceremony, not to mention a few visits to the real Olympic games.

This kind of hoopla may sound corny, but it works. To compete successfully, counter workers had to know the operations manual cold. So, by the way, did the judges—the independent owner-operators of individual McDonald's outlets that McDonald's headquarters had referee the local and regional competitions. McDonald's couldn't enrich the contents of assembly-line food preparation, so they enriched the context in which that job takes place. The result was that McDonald's made doing the job right a game—a giant competition that every McDonald's worker in the world could practice for every day at work.

Source: Adapted from the television special, "In Search of Excellence," PBS.

Japan. The study took longer than Garvin had anticipated because the Americans hadn't bothered to calculate defect rates before Garvin asked for them. The numbers had to be reconstructed in the American plants! In the Japanese plants, these numbers were posted publicly for all workers to see and consider.[17] The importance of timely performance feedback is illustrated by the experiences of USAA, which are described in the "FOCUS ON: Feedback."

---

[17] D. A. Garvin, "Quality on the Line," *Harvard Business Review* 61(5), (1983): 65–75.

Focus on

Feedback

Putting Information Where It Matters Most The first step to increasing productivity may be figuring out how to measure it. Traditional indexes of labor efficiency track output (units or dollars) per input (typically, hours worked). But assessing "knowledge work" (for instance, providing service on an insurance policy) in that manner can produce absurd results.

In the early 1980s, productivity was slipping at USAA, a prosperous insurance and investment management company. The problem, concluded CEO Robert McDermott and his managers, wasn't the abilities of the workers but the way they were being measured. The company's efficiency index divided the total number of policies on the books by the number of employees who wrote, sold, and maintained them. The customer was missing from the equation. The quality measurement and improvement director, Gerald Gass, recalls, "If you increased service by adding employees, your productivity would go down."

Working with the American Productivity & Quality Center in Houston, USAA came up with a revolutionary evaluation system called the Family of Measures (FOM). Every month the FOM scores each of USAA's 14,000 employees on dimensions of quantity, quality, timeliness, and customer service. In the telephone sales department, for example, the FOM includes the number of policies each representative sells, the accuracy of his or her price quotes, the

amount of time he or she spends on post-call paperwork, and the pleasantness of the representative's telephone manners. Every salesperson is part of a team, each of which has a collective FOM chart and a competitive team nickname such as Top Guns, Noble Eagles, and Success Express. Teams with the best monthly FOM scores are singled out for public commendations. Supervisors use FOM tallies to determine bonuses and promotions.

USAA also effectively uses computers to handle information. USAA's "image-processing" computer program allows a policy service representative to instantly call up electronic pictures of a customer's entire file on his or her computer terminal. Says McDermott, "The system enriches the job by giving workers information right at their fingertips, so that they can make a decision on the first phone call."

Source: R. Henkoff, "Make Your Office More Productive," *Fortune*, February 25, 1991, 72–84.

Participation also can prove important in the *collection* of feedback. Feedback is most effective when workers participate in the collection and analysis of performance feedback data. Workers place greater trust in feedback they themselves have generated, and being entrusted to collect it seems to have positive effects on worker effort.[18] At Emery Air Freight, for example, management asked dockworkers to collect the container utilization information that became the impetus for dramatic improvements in their performance.[19] Similarly, by

[18]G. B. Northcraft and P. C. Earley, "Technology, Credibility, and Feedback Use," *Organizational Behavior and Human Decision Processes* 44 (1989): 83–96.

[19]"At Emery Air Freight, Positive Reinforcement Boosts Performance," in *The Applied Psychology of Work Behavior*, ed. D. Organ (Plano, Tex.: Business Publications, Inc., 1987), 138–149.

the late 1980s, some major electronics firms in the United States had begun to follow Japan's lead and train their manufacturing workers to collect statistical quality-control data—data that those workers then could use to improve the efficiency and effectiveness of their own jobs.

Feedback works best when it is diagnostic and timely. Feedback is diagnostic to the extent that it reveals problems with performance. A videotape of your public speaking style, for instance, may reveal aspects of your performance that you were not aware needed to be changed. Feedback is timely when it arrives as soon as possible after performance. Feedback about your performance three or four weeks after the fact may not tell you what you're doing wrong *now*—and will have allowed you to continue making mistakes for three or four more weeks!

The context in which feedback is provided also turns out to be important. Individuals will seek feedback less if the feedback threatens their public image—for instance, if they fear the feedback will be negative and others will learn of it.[20] Individuals should be more receptive to feedback when it is provided regularly (so they don't have to decide whether to ask for it) and if they can receive it privately.

The Job Characteristics Model

Job enrichment is a big step for management. It signals a change in management's philosophy about the role of workers. Job enlargement typically doesn't give workers credit for being much more than physical resources for the organization. Job enlargement increases the probability that workers will perform their role as physical resources well (by not becoming bored) and decreases the probability that workers will quit or be absent (by making jobs less alienating). Job enrichment, on the other hand, represents the acceptance by management that workers are a dual resource of the organization—both a physical and mental resource.

Job enrichment programs have proven successful in two different ways. First, job enrichment often leads to improvements in product *quality*. Product defect rates may drop anywhere from 10 to 60 percent when a job enrichment program is instituted. In one review of 21 job enrichment programs, job enrichment improved product quality (as measured by error rates) by an average of 28 percent.[21] Why does job enrichment lead to quality improvement? First, job enrichment increases the responsibility that workers feel for the product. Workers are much more motivated to turn out something they can be proud of. Second, job enrichment invests workers with a broader perspective on their work. In the shirt assembly example, when management entrusts a worker with responsibility for quality control, the worker may begin to think about what quality means in a shirt. This broader perspective may lead the worker to think of innovations that would never occur to a worker who was concentrating just on fulfilling the letter of the tasks. For the workers, job enrichment also improves job satisfaction. The review of job enrichment cited earlier found an

---

[20]G. B. Northcraft and S. J. Ashford, "The Preservation of Self in Everyday Life: The Effects of Performance Expectations and Feedback Context on Feedback Inquiry," *Organizational Behavior and Human Decision Processes* 47, 42–64.

[21]R. E. Kopelman, "Job Redesign and Productivity: A Review of the Evidence," *National Productivity Review* 4(3), (1985): 237–255.

| FIGURE 12–5 | ▶ The Job Characteristics Model of Job Enrichment |

The job characteristics model summarizes the relationships among features that can be designed into jobs (such as skill variety), the psychological effects of these features (such as meaningful work), and the outcomes for workers and organizations (such as productivity and satisfaction).

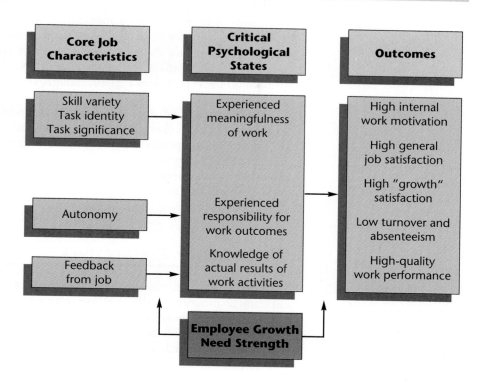

Source: J. R. Hackman and G. R. Oldham, *Work Redesign* (Figure 4.6) © 1980 by Addison-Wesley Publishing Company, Inc. Reprinted by permission.

average decrease of 14.5 percent in employee turnover and absenteeism when job enrichment was instituted. Apparently, workers enjoy the opportunity for achievement and control on the job.

The combined effects of both job enlargement and enrichment are captured in the **job characteristics model,** shown in Figure 12–5. The model proposes three "critical psychological states": meaningfulness of work, responsibility for work outcomes, and knowledge of work activity results. According to the model, a redesigned job must foster these three psychological states in workers to achieve such desired outcomes as worker satisfaction and high-quality performance. The model suggests that these critical psychological states are likely to occur when managers redesign jobs to contain five of the characteristics favored by job enlargement and enrichment strategies: skill variety, task identity, task significance, autonomy, and feedback.

Plenty of anecdotes about job redesign programs support the job characteristics model, and it unquestionably has become the dominant model of job design theory.[22] Research on the effectiveness of actual job redesign programs

[22] M. G. Evans, M. N. Kiggundu, and R. J. House, "A Partial Test and Extension of the Job Characteristic Model of Motivation," *Organizational Behavior and Human Performance* 24 (1979): 354–381.

based on the model has not been so positive, however. One survey of 30 redesign efforts found that successes of the model were as common as failures.[23] Even the researchers who developed the model, J. R. Hackman and G. R. Oldham, stated several years after introducing it, "While there is support in the research literature for the basic Job Characteristics Model, it would be inappropriate to conclude that the model provides a correct and complete picture of the motivational effects of job characteristics."[24] The amount of supportive research on the model does suggest, though, that it contains important insights about job design.

Hackman and Oldham's research on the model also revealed that the relationships among job characteristics, psychological states, and outcomes (such as job satisfaction and productivity) would be stronger for workers high in "growth need strength"—workers who want to grow and develop in their jobs.[25] This and other qualifications concerning the power of job characteristics to enhance job design will be discussed in the final section of this chapter.

WORK-GROUP PERSPECTIVES ◆◆◆◆◆◆

What happens when management takes the successes of limited autonomy job enrichment programs seriously? Successes with job enrichment provide management the refreshing insight that rank-and-file workers are important—if not critical—problem-solving allies of management. This conclusion can lead only to a different approach to the way organizations function. Two of these different approaches will be discussed next: quality circles and semiautonomous work groups. (A third work-group perspective on job design—the socio-technical systems approach—will be discussed in Chapter 15.)

Quality Circles

Quality circles are volunteer employee groups that meet to discuss work-related problems. They have been an extremely popular form of job enrichment and worker decision-making participation in the United States. In the 1980s, most Fortune 500 companies used quality circles at one time or another.

While the format of quality circles (QCs) is a little different in every company, most QC programs share several defining characteristics. First, membership is voluntary. Over time, membership may change as some members become disenchanted and leave the circle while other become curious and join. QCs are made up of individuals who either work side by side—for example, as part of an assembly line—or have the same job in a plant. They meet for a specified period of time (such as an hour) on a very regular basis (such as once every two weeks). Typically there is no extra pay for participating in the QC (though meetings are held during paid work hours), and most QCs are not rewarded for making good suggestions.

---

[23] Kopelman, "Job Redesign and Productivity," 239.

[24] J. R. Hackman and G. R. Oldham, *Work Redesign* (Reading, Mass.: Addison-Wesley, 1980), 97.

[25] E. F. Stone, R. T. Mowday, and L. W. Porter, "Higher-Order Need Strengths as Moderators of the Job Scope–Job Satisfaction Relationship," *Journal of Applied Psychology* 62 (1977): 466–471.

Quality circles can be thought of as a form of job enrichment because they empower workers to make suggestions and some decisions. The agenda of QC meetings is limited to discussing ways to improve quality, reduce costs, or improve productivity in the QC members' immediate jobs. QCs are never given a broad mandate to come up with suggestions to change the overall organization. Further, QCs do not have budgets. They are urged to come up with suggestions that require changes in procedures rather than expenditures. Finally, management typically retains veto power over QC suggestions, especially if expenditures are required. In such cases, the QC will have to present its suggestion formally to management for approval.

Quality circles can be costly for organizations. Naturally, the organization must forego some productivity to allow members the time to participate in circle activities. Further, many QC volunteers are not well prepared to handle the group dynamics in problem-solving meetings. To give a QC a good chance to succeed, training in group problem solving is recommended.[26]

As a form of job enrichment, there are two reasons for having QCs: benefits to the organization and benefits to their members. For the organization, quality circles represent an attempt to take advantage of the greater problem-solving synergy of groups. An article in *Industry Week* touted the "tremendous" savings produced by QC suggestions. One company claims to have reduced production costs by *70 percent* as a result of QC suggestions. The payback for expenditures to support QC activities and to implement their suggestions has been estimated to be as high as 8 to 1.[27]

Membership in quality circles seems to have a positive impact on job satisfaction, which in turn can lead to reduced absenteeism and turnover.[28] QCs provide a forum in which employees can make suggestions and decisions concerning ways to improve efficiency and effectiveness. And many employees enjoy the social interaction and camaraderie of quality circle activities.

Semiautonomous Work Groups

A **semiautonomous work group** is a team of workers assigned full responsibility for a series of tasks. Semiautonomous work groups represent a radical departure from quality circles. Even with quality circles, management retains responsibility for assigning particular tasks to each individual worker. When semiautonomous work groups are used, management assigns groups of tasks to groups of workers; each work group (rather than management) then has responsibility for deciding what tasks are performed by which workers. With quality circles, management retains responsibility for making day-to-day operational decisions; the quality circle acts in an advisory capacity. When semiautonomous work groups are used, management delegates responsibility for day-to-day operational decisions to the work group.

In effect, the semiautonomous work group acts as an independent contractor within the larger organization. Management provides task assignments for the work group, but how those tasks are accomplished is up to the work group itself. Often the work group elects its own leaders, develops its own work

---

[26] Lawler, 48.

[27] P. Pascarella, "Quality Circles," *Industry Week* 213(7), (1982): 50–55.

[28] R. E. Cole and D. S. Takachi, "Forging International Links: Making Quality Circles Work in the U.S.," *National Productivity Review* 3(4), (1984): 407–429.

rules and culture, and makes its own task assignments to individual workers. As long as the work gets done, management may leave well enough alone. In fact, one of the *indirect* benefits of using semiautonomous work groups is that the demands on the organization for supervisory, support, and management personnel may be reduced substantially. For example, in one General Motors plant only 24 white-collar employees were needed to manage a blue-collar manufacturing work force of nearly 500 employees. An electronic service organization found that the need for first-line supervisors was cut in half when the organization moved to work teams. The Scott Paper Company found that supervisory personnel simply weren't needed during off-shifts in one of their plants once work teams had been implemented.[29] These reductions in white-collar manufacturing support personnel represent substantial savings in labor costs. These are savings in addition to those generated by improved worker performance. In one survey of companies using autonomous work groups, 14 of 15 companies reported increased worker productivity.[30]

Semiautonomous work groups first gained widespread notice when they were successfully implemented in one of England's coal mines in the 1940s.[31] However, the best-known (and most-written-about) implementation of semiautonomous work groups in a traditional manufacturing setting occurred at the Topeka, Kansas, plant of General Foods. The Topeka plant is part of the Gaines Pet Food division of General Foods. General Foods management was concerned about the seriousness of productivity problems in other Gaines Pet Food plants when the final plans for the Topeka plant were being drawn up. Gaines Pet Food decided to try out semiautonomous work groups as a potential solution to these productivity problems.[32]

The procedures by which the Topeka work groups functioned became known as the Topeka System. The Topeka System addressed aspects of the plant's supervision structure, reward system, and social system.

Supervision The work force of the Topeka plant was divided into three kinds of teams: processing teams, packaging teams, and an office team. Processing teams (about 8 employees per shift) managed receipt and storage of the raw materials (corn, soya, vitamins, and meat meal delivered to the plant in railroad cars) and mixed the ingredients in predetermined percentages to produce the Gaines dog-food mixture. Their objective was to produce at least 100 tons of dog food per shift so that the packaging teams would never run out of work. The packaging teams (17 employees per shift) coated the dog food, packaged it in bags or boxes, and had responsibility for warehousing the completed product. The office team handled both personnel and distribution paperwork.

These teams were entirely self-managed. It was up to each team to assign tasks to its members. The teams also were given responsibility for controlling quality, maintaining the facility, counseling employees who did not perform

[29] Lawler, 112, 176.

[30] T. G. Cummings and E. S. Molloy, *Improving Productivity and the Quality of Work Life* (New York: Praeger Press, 1977).

[31] E. L. Trist and K. W. Barnforth, "Some Social Psychological Consequences of the Longwall Method of Coal-getting," *Human Relations* 4 (1951): 3–38.

[32] D. A. Whitsett and L. Yorks, "Looking Back at Topeka: General Foods and the Quality of Work Life Experiment," *California Management Review* 24(4), (Summer 1983): 93–109.

well, appointing team members to serve on plant safety and recreation committees, and even screening and selecting new team members. Plant management imposed few rules on the teams and tried to provide them with much of the economic, quantity, and quality information provided only to supervisors or management in most manufacturing settings.

The Reward System   Compensation at the Topeka plant was linked to *skill acquisition*. There were four pay levels: starting rate, single rate (for mastery of a single job), team rate (for mastery of all jobs performed by the team), and plant rate (for mastery of all jobs performed in the plant). Team members also could qualify for supplemental increases if they acquired special skills needed by the team.

Management designed this pay system to encourage team members to learn all jobs within the team, thereby giving the teams additional job assignment flexibility. No limits were placed on the number of workers in the plant who could achieve a given pay rate; it was hoped that this would encourage team members to teach each other. (This turns out to be an important benefit of using teams. Since a productive team member helps everyone else on the team, there is a clear incentive for team members to help each other acquire needed skills.) Further, in keeping with the overall team philosophy of the plant, decisions about compensation (for instance, deciding when a team member had mastered all the team's jobs) also remained with the team.

The Social System   To convey management's commitment to the semiautonomous work group philosophy, many of the status symbols that segregate managers and workers at most plants were eliminated at the Topeka facility. There were no assigned parking places for management in the parking lot, office decor was uniform throughout the plant, and all employees used the same entrance and the same lunchroom.[33] Offices were designed with glass walls facing the plant floor. Further, because the teams were self-managed, workers had a high level of freedom to circulate and socialize on the job.

One thing the Topeka System did *not* include was alteration of the plant's physical design or technology to accommodate the move to semiautonomous work groups. Technologically, Topeka was very much like any other modern processing/packaging facility.

How well did Topeka's radical experiment in job design work? Industrial engineers had estimated that 110 employees would be needed to run the plant; the work force stabilized at something less than 70 employees. After 18 months, the teams at the Topeka plant had lowered fixed overhead 33 percent, were reporting 92 percent fewer quality rejects, had achieved an absenteeism rate 9 percent below industry standards and lower turnover, and had one of the best safety records of any plant in General Foods. Annual savings were estimated to be about $600,000. Visitors to the plant also reported high satisfaction, involvement, and openness and mutual respect among the plant's employees.[34]

General Foods was unable to duplicate the successes of Topeka at any of its other plants. This may be because the Topeka plant was a new plant, so prior values and practices did not have to be overcome or changed. Further, the suc-

[33] Lawler, 173.

[34] R. E. Walton, "How to Counter Alienation in the Plant," *Harvard Business Review* 50(6), (1972): 70–81.

cesses of the Topeka plant were not without problems. The open social system was uncomfortable for some workers, who reverted back to traditional supervisor-subordinate relations with other team members. The pay system also created some tension in the plant. Since pay was tied to task mastery and mastery judgments were made by the teams, questions about the consistency of standards arose. In sum, problems arose at Topeka because the work force was not prepared to deal with the uncertainty and autonomy that self-governance requires. Training personnel to handle the new demands of more participation-oriented jobs often turns out to be a major hurdle in introducing job redesign innovations.

Problems also arose at the level of plant management. Less than six years after the start of the Topeka experiment, virtually all of the key management personnel in the plant had left General Foods. It appears that the delicate alliance of management personnel at Topeka was a key to its success. When Topeka's initial successes led General Foods to promote the alliance's originator and corporate protector, Lyman Ketchum, beyond direct responsibility for the plant, understanding and support for the plant's philosophy waned.

Other companies' attempts to implement autonomous work groups have met with similarly mixed results. An Australian minerals processing company found that autonomous work-group participants had more favorable work attitudes and organizational commitment. However, absenteeism and turnover also were higher among participants. Autonomous work groups also *negatively* affected the morale of nonparticipating coworkers.[35] In retrospect, the successes of the Topeka plant probably stand as a testament to the *potential* of job redesign using semiautonomous work groups and, as shown in the "FOCUS ON: Semiautonomous Work Groups," this potential has attracted a lot of attention.[36] The importance of the problems experienced at Topeka (and the problems reported by other users of autonomous work groups) will be discussed next.

QUALIFICATIONS

The different approaches to job redesign reviewed in this chapter promise tremendous *potential* benefits. However, statistics (such as those presented in Figure 2–8 in Chapter 2) show only mixed successes of employee involvement programs. These statistics stand as a sobering testament to the fact that choosing a good system for redesigning jobs is hardly enough to guarantee success. If job redesign efforts are not properly managed, they are likely to increase only job satisfaction but not productivity.

Many job redesign efforts *have* increased job satisfaction of workers, and job satisfaction plays a role in employee turnover. Nevertheless, realization of the *full* benefits of job design—both work-force satisfaction *and* enhanced productivity—requires an understanding of its limits. Three limits will be addressed in the remainder of this chapter: social information processing, individual differences, and management support.

---

[35] J. L. Cordery, W. S. Mueller, and L. M. Smith, "Attitudinal and Behavioral Effects of Autonomous Group Working: A Longitudinal Field Study," *Academy of Management Journal* 34 (1991): 464–476.

[36] A. D. Szilagyi and M. J. Wallace, *Organizational Behavior and Performance* (Glenview, Ill.: Scott, Foresman, 1987), 170–172.

Focus on

Semiautonomous Work Groups

Who Needs a Boss? Many American companies are discovering what may be *the* productivity breakthrough of the 1990s. Call the still-controversial innovation a self-managed team, a cross-functional team, a high-performance team, or, to coin a phrase, a superteam. Says Texas Instruments CEO Jerry Junkins, "No matter what your business, these teams are the wave of the future." Corning CEO Jamie Houghton, whose company has 3,000 teams, echoes the sentiment: "If you really believe in quality, when you cut through everything, it's empowering your people, and it's empowering your people that leads to teams."

What makes superteams so controversial is that they ultimately force managers to do what they had only imagined in their nightmares: give up control. If superteams are working right, they manage themselves. No boss is required. A superteam arranges schedules, sets profit targets, and—gulp—may even know everyone's salary. Superteams typically consist of between 3 and 30 workers—sometimes blue collar, sometimes white collar, sometimes both. These teams, composed of people with different skills and from different parts of the company, can swoop around bureaucratic obstacles and break through walls separating different functions to get a job done.

Ten years ago, there were practically no superteams among America's industrial giants. However, in a recent survey of Fortune 1000 companies, half the companies questioned said they will be relying significantly more on superteams in the years ahead.

Federal Express has been particularly successful using superteams in its back-office operations. In 1988, as part of a company-wide push to convert to teams, FedEx organized its 1,000 clerical workers into superteams of five to ten people and gave them the training and authority to manage themselves. During one team meeting, a clerk from quality control pointed out a billing problem. The bigger a package, the more FedEx charges to deliver it. But the company's wildly busy delivery people sometimes forgot to check whether customers had properly marked the weight of packages on the air bill. That meant that FedEx, whose policy in such cases is to charge customers the lowest rate, was losing money. The team switched on its turbochargers. One team member found out which field offices were forgetting to check the packages and then explained the problem to the delivery people. Another set up a system to examine the invoices and make sure the solution was working. Last year alone the team's ideas saved the company $2.1 million.

Source: Adapted from B. Dumaine, "Who Needs a Boss?" *Fortune*, May 7, 1990, 52–60.

Social Information Processing

The job characteristics model and work-group approaches to job design discussed in this chapter both make an important assumption. They assume that workers perceive their jobs the way that managers intend those jobs to be perceived. However, as we know from our discussions of perception in Chapter 3, this is an unrealistic assumption. Just because a manager decides to give a subordinate some autonomy on the job does not mean that the subordinate will perceive autonomy in the job. As we noted in Figure 3–6, subordinates' and supervisors' perceptions often differ dramatically.

The **social information processing** framework of job design emphasizes the importance of perception in understanding how workers react to their jobs.[37] According to the social information processing framework, how an employee perceives and reacts to a job will depend on cues provided socially by coworkers[38] and even the jobholder's supervisor.[39] For managers, the role of perception and social cues in worker reactions to jobs underscores the importance of positive attitudes, a positive atmosphere, and open channels of communication in a work group.[40] Workers react to *perceptions* of their jobs rather than to their objective characteristics. A positive work-group climate, which encourages favorable perceptions of job characteristics, may be as important to work outcomes as a good job design.

Individual Differences

One of the important lessons of Chapter 4 was that no two employees are likely to be motivated by quite the same things. This becomes a critical issue in job design. Job design efforts that suit the needs of one employee may be hopelessly inappropriate for another employee.

The approaches to job design outlined in this chapter differ in what they require of the typical worker. Work simplification requires the least of the worker. Tasks are simple and repetitive; there is very little demand that the employee think on the job or take responsibility. Job enlargement assumes that employees at least want some variety in their work. Job enrichment and work-group redesign efforts assume quite a bit more. These approaches assume that the rank-and-file worker is willing to take on the responsibility associated with making consequential decisions on the job, and that workers are interested in more than just being told what to do. This is not always true. In General Foods' highly successful Topeka plant, a small minority of workers resisted management's new philosophy. Researchers have found that there are always some workers who prefer highly repetitive, low-skill jobs, even when there are opportunities to bid for more interesting tasks.[41]

Even if workers are interested in going beyond just earning their paychecks, the particular job design scheme of a company may not match all employees' needs and interests. One researcher of radical job redesign efforts tells a story

---

[37] G. Salancik and J. Pfeffer, "A Social Information Processing Approach to Job Attitudes and Task Design," *Administrative Science Quarterly* 23 (1977): 224–253.

[38] H. M. Weiss and J. B. Shaw, "Social Influences on Judgments about Tasks," *Organizational Behavior and Human Performance* 24 (1979): 126–140.

[39] R. W. Griffin, "Technological and Social Processes in Task Redesign: A Field Experiment," unpublished manuscript, Texas A&M University, 1981.

[40] J. Kelly and C. Kelly, "Them and Us": Social Psychology and the New Industrial Relations. *British Journal of Industrial Relations* 29(1), 1991, 25–48.

[41] M. Fein, "Job Enrichment: A Reevaluation," *Sloan Management Review*, Winter 1974, 69–88.

about a worker who said to him, "I don't care what those turkeys think, I just want to be left alone to do my job." The "turkeys" he was referring to were his coworkers! For this worker at least, programs such as quality circles would seem ill-advised.[42]

Differences among workers must be handled in a couple of ways. First, increases in worker autonomy should be *voluntary*.[43] If a worker is uninterested in playing a larger role in the workplace, forcing that worker to do so is not more freedom for the worker but less—just another aspect of work where the worker has no choice. Further, it seems unlikely that a reluctant participant (for example, in a quality circle) will be a positive contributor.

If management wants to make enriched jobs a permanent part of its management approach, managers should assess employee interest when employees are hired. **Growth need strength** is the interest of the worker in growing and developing on the job. Hackman and Oldham identified growth need strength as an important determinant of worker reaction to job redesign efforts. Responses to a growth need strength questionnaire could be used to identify job applicants who would be more receptive to job enrichment, or to identify job incumbents who are prime candidates for enrichment of their jobs. Honda, Toyota, and Nissan already use this philosophy in selecting employees for their American plants.[44]

Finally, it is important to realize that interest is not the only barrier that might prevent an employee from being receptive to job redesign efforts. As noted in earlier discussions about worker autonomy and participation, many workers are shocked to hear that their input would be valued by management. For these people, expectations developed in the past that management-worker relationships are adversarial could be hard to shed. Often additional training is necessary before these workers can feel comfortable in their new roles as mental as well as physical resources for the organization.

These concerns about the appropriateness of job redesign for some employees should not, however, be used as an excuse to *not* initiate any form of substantial job redesign effort. Consider again the survey results mentioned early on in this chapter. Most managers seriously underestimate the desires of their employees to make positive contributions to the organization and play larger roles in organizational decision making. Ignoring this untapped resource can be costly.

Management Support

Many if not most job redesign efforts are aimed at the rank-and-file workers of an organization. Yet one key to the success of job redesign may not be the rank-and-file workers but the layers of supervisors and management above them. Three major concerns about supervisors and management must be addressed if a job redesign effort is to succeed: their responsiveness, their feelings of being threatened, and how they handle success.

[42] Lawler, 182.

[43] Kanter, "The Dilemmas of Participation."

[44] R. Koenig, "Toyota Takes Pains, and Time, Filling Jobs at Its Kentucky Plant," *Wall Street Journal*, December 1, 1987, 1+.

Responsiveness   A critical issue in ceding limited autonomy to workers in job redesign is that management *must appear sincere*. Sincerity often is a function of responsiveness—how quickly and completely management responds to worker suggestions. Consider the following tale about the demise of a quality circle:

> . . . In one change effort, a quality circle focused on the purchase of new trucks for the organization. After months of study an extensive set of specifications were developed. They promised to save the organization hundreds of thousands of dollars by buying trucks that were both easier to maintain and more effective. There was great resistance from the purchasing agent and the industrial engineer to changing the specifications, even though top management approved the idea. It literally took months to get them to change the specifications. By the time the specifications were changed and the actual trucks were purchased, the group had long since disbanded in discouragement, convinced that management was simply engaged in a sham exercise to keep them quiet.[45]

The sad part of this particular tale is that management really was taking the suggestions of the employee group seriously. However, their lack of feedback to the group unintentionally sent a different message, namely, that no one in management really cared about the suggestions that the group came up with.

Even if an employee-generated suggestion is not a good one—for example, if there are practical, budgetary, or political reasons for not implementing it— a thorough response from management can accomplish two important goals. First, even negative feedback sends the message that management is listening. If employees have the sense that management is just toying with them, they can "dry up" as a source of ideas pretty quickly. Second, if management takes the time to discuss with workers the reasons for rejecting an idea, management is providing invaluable input to workers so that future suggestions have a better probability of being adopted.

Feelings of Being Threatened   If the lowest-level workers in an organization are given more control through limited autonomy job redesign programs, who is losing that control? For most supervisors, the obvious answer seems to be themselves.

At Topeka, the autonomous work group redesign effort achieved a personnel reduction of 33 percent. It was no secret that the savings in personnel came from the fact that semiautonomous work groups don't have supervisors. As noted earlier, a General Motors plant using autonomous work groups uses only 24 white-collar employees for a production work force of almost 500 workers. If limited autonomy job redesign is going to be pursued to its natural conclusions, supervisors may have reason to feel threatened. Obviously, this fear on the part of the supervisors must be dealt with if they are to support rather than obstruct the implementation of job redesign.

Even if elimination of supervisory personnel is not a legitimate concern, an increased role for rank-and-file workers still could seem like a loss to supervisory personnel. After all, the need for control and the desire to make a contribution are felt by workers at *all* levels of an organization. An attempt to

---

[45]Lawler, 55.

enlarge or enrich the scope of jobs at the lowest level of an organization probably needs to be followed up at other levels of the organization as well. If management enlarges or enriches the scope of rank-and-file jobs, supervisors are unlikely to feel that their authority has been usurped if the scope of their own jobs is similarly enlarged or enriched. In short, job redesign efforts should not be used as Band-Aids for productivity, quality, or morale problems. Behind every approach to job design lurks an overall philosophy about the role of workers at all levels of the organization. The most successful job redesign programs will be ones where the philosophy is implemented consistently across all levels of the organization, from rank-and-file workers to supervisors to middle managers and on up.

How Management Handles Success Interestingly, a final major stumbling block to the success of job redesign programs is what to do when they succeed. Many times this turns out to be a problem management is ill-equipped to deal with.

One big problem created by successful job redesign is the spiral of rising employee expectations detailed in Figure 12–5. All successful job redesign efforts develop in employees more self-respect, more self-confidence, and a stronger image of themselves as potentially valuable contributors to the organization's goals and objectives. This suggests that successful job redesign must be a journey, not a destination. Management must be prepared to meet the rising expectations of workers to contribute.

At one southwestern manufacturer, this particular challenge is being met. Intel, a large computer chip manufacturer, decided several years ago to institute quality circles. Management was, however, aware that employee successes in the program would give rise to new demands for further opportunities to contribute. To deal with this new demand, Intel coupled its job redesign efforts with a career counseling program. The counseling program served two extremely useful functions. First, if a rank-and-file worker acquired a new sense of self-worth and wanted to pursue it further, the counseling program could identify possibilities (both within and without Intel's own sphere) for career advancement that would meet the employee's newfound needs and expectations. Second, the counseling program could help the employee understand the additional training that might be needed to bring those career opportunities within reach. At Intel, management was not only prepared to deal with employees' rising expectations but also willing and able to help employees deal with their rising expectations themselves.

As noted earlier, successful job redesign programs can also lead to thorny compensation issues. As workers' jobs are enlarged or enriched, their belief in their ability to contribute is not the only thing that grows. Workers' belief that their work has become more valuable to the organization also can grow. If management does not adjust compensation schemes to reflect the enlarged contributions of the work force, again the well of worker ideas and energy may soon run dry. On the other hand, providing employees opportunities to take control *and* financial incentives for doing it well can really bring out the best in them.[46] Designing effective compensation schemes will be discussed in the next chapter.

[46]B. G. Posner, "Raising the Stakes," *Inc.*, March 1990, 100–102.

SUMMARY

◆◆◆◆◆◆

American industry has come to an important crossroads in job design. The average educational level of the American worker is on the rise. In 1964, only 45 percent of the American work force possessed a high school diploma. For workers in the newest cohort of the American work force the percentage is closer to 86 percent.[47] Furthermore, this better-educated work force has an "entitlement" mentality. Workers now feel that they have a *right* to good wages, interesting work, and a say in management decision making.[48] In short, management in the 1990s must face up to the challenge of providing work for an American work force that has more to offer than ever before and fully expects to have opportunities to offer it.

Traditional approaches to job design focused almost exclusively on work simplification in order to take advantage of efficiency through specialization. Unfortunately, these approaches ignore the message of the Hawthorne studies—that what people think about their work environment makes a difference in how hard and well they work. If the work is uninteresting, the workers are uninterested. Management pays the price.

More enlightened approaches to job design have attempted to take the needs of workers into account by providing more interesting and involving work. Job enlargement and job enrichment are two individual approaches to job design in which management focuses on changing the characteristics of jobs to fit the needs of workers. Job enlargement makes jobs more involving by increasing the range of skills that a job requires. Job enlargement does not, however, satisfy workers' needs to feel control and accomplishment on the job. Job enrichment goes beyond job enlargement by allowing workers to fulfill higher-order needs (such as the need for control) in doing their work.

The successes of enlargement and enrichment job design programs may lead management to mold job design efforts around entirely different approaches to the management of organizations. Autonomous work groups take limited autonomy to its limits by delegating virtually all operational decisions to worker groups. Sociotechnical systems design molds job design efforts to match the needs and limitations of both human workers and technological advances. Both of these approaches have had noteworthy successes.

In the end, the success of management's job design efforts does not depend just on having a good approach to job design. Job design efforts will work only if workers and managers see jobs similarly, if the jobs match the needs of the work force, and if management supports the changes.

Key Terms

Cross-training Encouraging workers to learn their coworkers' jobs; provides challenges for workers and flexibility for management.

Flextime work scheduling Method of context enrichment in which management gives workers

---

[47] Lawler, *High-Involvement Management*, 15.

[48] J. O'Toole, *Making America Work* (New York: Continuum, 1981).

limited discretion in arranging their work hours.

Growth need strength   Interest of a worker in growing and developing on the job.

Job characteristics model   Theory of job enrichment in which the presence of five job characteristics (skill variety, task identity, task significance, autonomy, and feedback) leads to critical psychological states (meaningfulness of work, responsibility for work outcomes, and knowledge of work activity results) that in turn result in positive work-related outcomes such as productivity and worker satisfaction.

Job enlargement   Redesign of work tasks that increases the number of tasks in a job to make it more interesting and involving.

Job enrichment   Redesign of work tasks that makes a job more interesting and involving by allowing workers to fulfill higher-order needs such as achievement and control.

Job rotation   Method of increasing workers' skill variety by allowing them to switch jobs occasionally.

Quality circle (QC)   Voluntary groups of workers who meet periodi-cally to discuss and develop solutions to problems related to quality, productivity, or product cost.

Semiautonomous work group   Team of workers given full responsibility for a series of tasks (including arrangement and assignment of the work).

Social information processing   Framework of job design that emphasizes the importance of perception and social cues from coworkers and supervisors in understanding how workers react to their jobs.

Task identity   The sense of completion and achievement that occurs when the set of assigned tasks allows the worker to see a process through from start to finish.

Task significance   Worker's sense that a good or poor performance on the job makes a difference to someone.

Work simplification   Design of work tasks to be simple and easily mastered so each worker can become expert at some very small number of tasks and learn to do them repeatedly with lightning speed and no mistakes.

Discussion Questions

1. Think of your role as a university student as a job. How could you redesign that job to enhance your performance? To increase your job satisfaction?

2. An acronym used in many organizations—KISS—is supposed to be the key to successful management. KISS stands for "Keep it simple, stupid." Would KISS be a good rule of thumb for designing jobs?

3. How do enrichment approaches to job design differ from enlargement approaches? Are there any dangers for management in moving from job enlargement to job enrichment?

4. What are some of the qualifications or barriers to the success of any job redesign effort? What

steps do these qualifications suggest that management should take to ensure the success of a job design program?

5. When would enriching the *context* of a job be a more effective or appropriate approach to job redesign than enriching the *content* of the job?

6. When might a *group* approach to job design be more appropriate than an *individual* approach?

7. Why should feedback be an important part of any individual job enrichment program?

8. Who is likely to benefit when a company decides to use quality circles? Why do quality circle programs fail?

If You Want to Know More

An excellent description of the horrors of traditional job design in coal mines is available in "Some Social and Psychological Consequences of the Long Wall Method of Coal Getting" (E. L. Trist and K. W. Bamforth, *Human Relations* 4, 1951, 3–38). The depressing realities of life on an automobile assembly line are described in detail in "Luddites in Lordstown" (*Harper's* magazine, June 1972, 68–73) and in "Blue-Collar Blues on the Assembly Line" (J. Gooding, *Fortune*, June 1970, 69–71).

A review and consideration of job enrichment is provided in "Is Job Enrichment Just a Fad?" (J. R. Hackman, *Harvard Business Review* 53(5), 1975, 129–139). A useful discussion of the use of quality circles is provided in "Quality Circles: Panacea or Pandora's Box?" (G. W. Meyer and R. G. Stott, *Organizational Dynamics* 13, Spring 1985, 34–50). R. M. Kanter discusses the dilemmas of managing participative systems in her book *The Changemasters* (New York: Simon & Schuster, 1983).

An excellent summary of the Topeka experiment at General Foods is provided by D. A. Whitsett and L. Yorks in "Looking Back at Topeka: General Foods and the Quality-of-Work-Life Experiment" (*California Management Review* 25, 1983, 93–109). A summary of the job reform efforts in Scandinavia is provided in a book by Volvo's president, Pehr G. Gyllenhammar,

People at Work (Reading, Mass.: Addison-Wesley, 1977).

The best available overall discussion of job design issues is provided in E. E. Lawler III's book, *High Involvement Management* (London: Jossey-Bass, 1986). A good book of edited readings is *The Innovative Organization*, R. Zager and M. P. Rosow, editors (Elmsford, N.Y.: Pergamon Press, 1982). Lawler provides a review of the latest developments in job design in his article, "The New Plant Revolution Revisited" (*Organization Dynamics* 19, Autumn 1990, 4–14).

Eric Sundstrom, Ken DeMeuse, and David Futrell provide an excellent overall review of work teams in their article, "Work Teams: Applications and Effectiveness" (*American Psychologist*, February 1990, 120–133). The pros and cons surrounding the use of teams in organizations are represented in Brian Dumaine's piece, "The Bureaucracy Busters" (*Fortune*, June 17, 1991, 36–50) and Neill Carson's article, "The Trouble with Teams" (*Training*, August 1992, 38–40).

An interesting example of the use of job rotation at the executive-management level is provided in the article, "Building Top Management Muscle in a Slow-Growth Environment" (G. B. Northcraft, T. L. Griffith, and C. E. Shalley, *Academy of Management Executive* 6, 1992, 32–41).

On Your Own

Job Characteristics Instrument Think about a job you have held recently, perhaps last summer. With this job in mind, answer the following questions. The scoring instructions follow the questions. In what design areas was your job deficient? How do you think these deficiencies could be corrected?

The following questions are concerned with the characteristics of your job. Each of the questions should be evaluated according to the following responses:

Very Little	Little	A Moderate Amount	Much	A Great Deal
1	2	3	4	5

Two separate responses are required. In column 1, please mark your response according to how you evaluate the *actual* characteristic of your job. In column 2, please mark your response according to how you would like, or *desire*, that characteristic to be.

Question	Column 1	Column 2
1. To what extent does your job provide the opportunity to do a number of different duties each day?		
2. How much are you left on your own to do your work?		
3. To what extent can you tell how well you are doing on your job without being told by others?		
4. To what extent do you feel like your job is just a small cog in a big machine?		
5. To what extent do you start a job that is finished by another employee?		
6. Does your job require a great deal of skill to perform it effectively?		
7. How much of your job depends upon your ability to work with others?		
8. To what extent does your job limit your opportunity to get to know other employees?		
9. How much variety of tasks is there in your job?		
10. To what extent are you able to act independently of supervisors in doing your work?		
11. Does seeing the results of your work give you a good idea how well you are performing?		
12. How significant is your work to the overall organization?		
13. To what extent do you see projects or jobs through to completion?		
14. To what extent is your job challenging?		
15. To what extent do you work pretty much by yourself?		
16. How much opportunity is there in your job to develop professional friendships?		
17. To what extent does your job require you to do the same thing over and over again each day?		
18. To what extent do you have the freedom to decide how to do your work?		
19. To what extent does doing the job itself provide you with feedback about how well you are performing?		
20. To what extent do you feel like you are contributing something significant to your organization?		
21. To what extent do you complete work that has been started by another employee?		

22. To what extent is your job so simple that virtually anyone   _____   _____
could handle it with little or no training?

23. To what extent is dealing with other people a part of your   _____   _____
job?

24. To what extent can you talk informally with other employ-   _____   _____
ees while at work?

Scoring Instructions   For each of the eight job characteristics (A through H), compute
a total score by summing the responses to the appropriate questions. Note that some
questions are *reversed* (for example, #17), and that the response to these should be subtracted
from 6 to get a response value. Transfer the scores to the *final* scores, where column 1 is
actual scores, column 2 is *desired* scores, and column 3 is *comparative* scores to be provided
by your instructor.

Vari-able	Column 1 Actual			Column 2 Desired			Final Scores		
	Question		*Response*	*Question*		*Response*	1	2	3
	(#1)	=	+ _____	(#1)	=	+ _____			
A	(#9)	=	+ _____	(#9)	=	+ _____			
	(6−#17)	=	+ _____	(6−#17)	=	+ _____			
	(Total ÷ 3) = A_1 = + _____			(Total ÷ 3) = A_2 = + _____			( ) A_1	( ) A_2	( ) A_3
	(#2)	=	+ _____	(#2)	=	+ _____			
B	(#10)	=	+ _____	(#10)	=	+ _____			
	(#18)	=	+ _____	(#18)	=	+ _____			
	(Total ÷ 3) = B_1 = + _____			(Total ÷ 3) = B_2 = + _____			( ) B_1	( ) B_2	( ) B_3
	(#3)	=	+ _____	(#3)	=	+ _____			
C	(#11)	=	+ _____	(#11)	=	+ _____			
	(#19)	=	+ _____	(#19)	=	+ _____			
	(Total ÷ 3) = C_1 = + _____			(Total ÷ 3) = C_2 = + _____			( ) C_1	( ) C_2	( ) C_3
	(6−#4)	=	+ _____	(6−#4)	=	+ _____			
D	(#12)	=	+ _____	(#12)	=	+ _____			
	(#20)	=	+ _____	(#20)	=	+ _____			
	(Total ÷ 3) = D_1 = + _____			(Total ÷ 3) = D_2 = + _____			( ) D_1	( ) D_2	( ) D_3
	(6−#5)	=	+ _____	(6−#5)	=	+ _____			
E	(#13)	=	+ _____	(#13)	=	+ _____			
	(6−#212	=	+ _____	(6−#21)	=	+ _____			
	(Total ÷ 3) = E_1 = + _____			(Total ÷ 3) = E_2 = + _____			( ) E_1	( ) E_2	( ) E_3
	(#6)	=	+ _____	(#6)	=	+ _____			
F	(#14)	=	+ _____	(#14)	=	+ _____			
	(6−#22)	=	+ _____	(6−#22)	=	+ _____			
	(Total ÷ 3) = F_1 = + _____			(Total ÷ 3) = F_2 = + _____			( ) F_1	( ) F_2	( ) F_3

	(#7)	=	+ _____	(#7)	=	+ _____				
G	(6–#15)	=	+ _____	(6–#15)	=	+ _____				
	(#23)	=	+ _____	(#23)	=	+ _____				

$(\text{Total} \div 3) = G_1 = + $_____ $(\text{Total} \div 3) = G_2 = + $_____ $\dfrac{(\ \ )}{G_1}$ $\dfrac{(\ \ )}{G_2}$ $\dfrac{(\ \ )}{G_3}$

	(6–#8)	=	+ _____	(6–#8)	=	+ _____
H	(#16)	=	+ _____	(#16)	=	+ _____
	(#24)	=	+ _____	(#24)	=	+ _____

$(\text{Total} \div 3) = H_1 = + $_____ $(\text{Total} \div 3) = H_2 = + $_____ $\dfrac{(\ \ )}{H_1}$ $\dfrac{(\ \ )}{H_2}$ $\dfrac{(\ \ )}{H_3}$

Source: From *Organizational Behavior and Performance*, 4/e by Andrew D. Szilagyi, Jr. and Marc J. Wallace, Jr. Copyright © 1987, 1983 by Scott, Foresman and Company. Reprinted by permission.

CLOSING CASE

CHAPTER 12

THE MANAGER'S MEMO

FROM: W. Johnson, Office Manager

TO: M. Callahan, Clerical Support Supervisor

RE: Performance of Clerical Staff

With regard to your concern that error rates and absenteeism are rising among the clerical support staff in our law firm, perhaps the problem lies in part with the design of their jobs. It may be that redesigning the work load could increase motivation and satisfaction.

In reviewing the procedures you sent me, I see that their tasks are quite specialized. One worker enters data into standard forms, another types documents, another makes corrections to previously entered work, and so on.

I also note that typically the clericals have no direct contact with the attorneys in the firm, presumably to insulate them from conflicts with the attorneys. You should know, however, that because the attorneys don't know which individuals are doing their work, they tend to criticize all the members of your department as a whole.

My suggestion is that you consider ways to expand and enrich the work of the clerical staff. If you will outline some general ideas, we can then meet to discuss them and how they fit in with the overall needs of the firm.

Case Discussion Question

Assume you are the clerical staff supervisor, and respond to the office manager's memorandum. Select the ideas from the chapter that you think will be most effective, and compile them into an overall redesign of the clerical staff's jobs. Be as specific as you can.

MAINTAINING PERFORMANCE

TAKE THIS JOB AND LOVE IT   ◆◆◆◆◆◆

With profits declining and competition on the rise, IBM wants to make sure that all of its employees are pulling their weight. So, the computer giant is making it easier for its people to get fired. By contrast, Kodak's Eastman Chemical Company has stopped grading employees. To eliminate a tier of managers and push responsibility down the line, Eastman recently did away with the top jobs in marketing, production, and product development. Now decisions in manufacturing and solutions to problems are hammered out in monthly meetings by the heads of the company's three major plants. Because the new team structure makes it difficult to evaluate individual performance, Eastman Chemical is likely to adopt a system of peer review.

Companies as diverse as General Motors and Eastman Kodak are experimenting with a pass/fail approach to performance as a way to replace the traditional star or merit system. According to Edward Deming, often credited with playing a critical role in Japan's postwar rise to economic dominance, "the merit rating [system] nourishes short-term performance, annihilates long-term planning, builds fear, demolishes teamwork, and nourishes rivalry and politics." Walton Burdick, the senior vice-president of personnel at IBM, contends that performance appraisal systems must reflect the ingrained culture of individualism long fostered by American companies. However, in 1989, General Motors abandoned its company-wide ranking scheme that graded its employees on a curve, arbitrarily giving 10 percent of the staff a poor rating. The scheme caused morale to plummet and set off a near revolt among managers. It was gone within a few months.

To replace it, a number of GM units decided to implement a system that reinforced a one-for-all culture. It tied compensation to an individual's seniority, level of expertise, and the overall market for his or her services. Evaluations were based on input from peers, subordinates, and managers. With this new process, people are more confident that it's an even exchange," says Chris Meagher, an employee of Chrysler who oversees 20 engineers. The system is also considered to have been a contributing factor to the turnaround of Cadillac.

Andrea Gabor, "Take This Job and Love It." *New York Times*, January 26, 1992, section 3, 1,3.

INTRODUCTION

As the controversy in the opening vignette illustrates, companies are experimenting with ways to highlight exactly the kind of performance we, as managers, want to reward: individual productivity or group performance. This concern of identifying appropriate behaviors and developing incentive structures to maintain them is central to the topic of this chapter. Managers often would prefer that employees behave a certain way, yet the organization's incentive structures may not reward the behaviors managers want. Throughout this chapter, we will be examining various mechanisms managers may use to promote and maintain effective organizational performance. One of the most obvious ways to maintain employee performance is through the use of compensation systems. However, designing and implementing effective compensation programs requires that employers tell employees what is expected of them and give them feedback about their performance. Thus, setting performance goals and conducting performance appraisals are critical to the success of any compensation system.

Even with all of these factors in place, managers still face the problems of improving the performance of poor performers. In addition, such organizational changes as downsizing will have an impact on the performance and morale of the survivors. Figuring out the causes of and solutions to poor performance is the final component of this chapter.

COMPENSATION SYSTEMS

Compensation systems are the primary mechanism by which organizations endeavor to influence employees' behavior. In fact, most compensation systems are developed with two broad goals in mind: (1) to produce the desired behaviors from employees and (2) to accomplish the first goal within the limitations faced by the organization. The first goal includes motivating employees to join the organization, to remain with it, and to perform well for it. The second goal focuses on the constraints or limitations faced by most organizations, including their ability to pay, legal constraints such as minimum wage regulations, labor unions, and external labor markets (compensation levels for the internal labor pool are greatly influenced by the "market rate" for similar jobs in the external labor market).

Compensation systems include more than just the dollars employers pay to employees for their work. Total compensation can also include base pay, a variety of incentive schemes, cost of living adjustments, various forms of stock options, and an array of benefits. Organizations have to decide what forms of compensation to offer, what aspects of the total compensation system will be contingent on an individual's membership in the organization (that is, entitlements) and what forms of compensation will be based on performance (incentives), the relative importance of each form of compensation, and what employees are eligible for what forms of compensation.[1] In addition, employees often

---

[1] George T. Milkovich, "A Strategic Perspective on Compensation Management," In *Research in Personnel and Human Resources Management*, vol. 6, ed. G. R. Ferris and K. M. Rowland. (Greenwich, Conn.: JAI Press, 1988), 263–288.

derive noneconomic rewards for working (such as a sense of accomplishment or power from one's job and the opportunity to socialize with colleagues and peers). Its compensation system is a major way an organization conveys to its employees what it wants done and how they should behave.

In designing their compensation systems, many organizations unfortunately find that what they want and what they get from their employees are very different. In fact, many compensation systems reward behaviors that employers are trying to *discourage* and do not reinforce the behavior they want. Consider the following examples.[2]

In business organizations where rewards are dispensed for unit performance or for individual goals achieved without regard for overall effectiveness, performance counter to the hopes of management is common. The organization is often in a position where it *hopes* for employee effort in the areas of team building, creativity, and interpersonal relations, but it formally *rewards* none of these activities. In cases where promotions and raises are tied to goal achievement, the system itself contains a paradox in that it "asks employees to set challenging, risky goals, only to face smaller paychecks and possible damaged careers if these goals are not accomplished."[3]

Organizations hope that managers will pay attention to long-run costs and opportunities and will institute programs that will focus on the future. However, many reward systems often pay off for short-run sales and earnings only. Thus, it is personally advantageous for such managers to sacrifice long-term profit and growth for short-term advantages; such a view, unfortunately, is not likely to be in the best interest of the organization.

These two general examples suggest that compensation systems are often put into place without a careful consideration of their impact on employee behavior. In developing a new compensation system or revising an existing system, managers should examine exactly what set of employee behaviors is desired. Second, if there is an existing compensation system, managers should identify exactly what set of employee behaviors *is being rewarded*. Given the way most compensation systems work, it would not be unusual for managers to find that their organization is not rewarding desired or expected behaviors. Setting up a compensation system consistent with the performance expectations of management reduces the likelihood that managers will have to depend upon the telepathic ability of employees to divine their intents. Relying on the good nature or responsibility of workers puts a greater burden on the organization's selection mechanism to find such people than if the organization relies on the compensation system to reward the appropriate type and level of employee performance.

In addition to rewarding the wrong behaviors, a number of other factors are common obstacles to the development and implementation of effective compensation systems. Probably the most crucial is the difficulty of knowing what behavior is desired *and* being able to measure that behavior reliably.[4]

---

[2] This example was taken from S. Kerr, "On the Folly of Rewarding A while Hoping for B," *Academy of Management Journal* 18 (1975): 769–783.

[3] Ibid.

[4] P. M. Podsakoff, C. N. Greene, and J. M. McFillen, "Obstacles to the Effective Use of Reward Systems," in *Readings in Personnel and Human Resource Management*, 3d ed., ed. R. Schuler, S. Youngblood, and V. Huber (New York: West Publishing, 1987), 270–285.

This task is difficult for several reasons. First, the changing nature of work performed by employees (for example, the big shift from manufacturing positions to service positions or the increasing number of managerial or professional jobs) means that work is becoming less quantifiable. It is certainly easier to count the number of widgets produced by an individual than to determine the quality of service provided by a mental-health counselor.

Second, work is becoming more complex and multidimensional. Technological advances and machine-paced performance may reduce the variability in actual job performance, so that differences in evaluation are based upon subjective employee characteristics rather than objective performance.

Third, managers who are required to make distinctions among employees often neither are trained in how to assess performance nor have the desire to evaluate—and defend their assessment of—their employees. Finally, managers have difficulty identifying rewards valued by their employees. As the cartoon in Figure 13–1 suggests, there may be some commonalities among employees. More likely, however, some employees may find certain rewards very reinforcing while others may find those same rewards completely irrelevant.

The preceding discussion highlights only some of the difficulties a manager faces in trying to develop or implement a compensation system. Up until this point, we have been examining the compensation system as a whole. The next sections focus on the specific components of the compensation system—wages and salaries, employee benefits, nonrecurring financial rewards, and noneconomic rewards (see Figure 13–2). As you read the next four sections, consider the impact of each of these factors on motivating employees to perform in concert with management's desires and expectations.

Wages, Salaries, and Nonrecurring Financial Rewards

Most people define compensation systems as how much individuals are paid for the work they perform. Monetary rewards are the most salient of the forms of compensation under the control of organizations. The general notion is that monetary rewards are the primary mechanism for motivating high performance

---

FIGURE 13–1 ▶ The Importance of Incentives

Managers often have difficulty identifying rewards valued by their employees. Some rewards, such as continued employment, appeal to almost all employees.

BLONDIE

Source: Reprinted with special permission of King Features Syndicate, Inc.

FIGURE 13–2	▶ Components of the Compensation System

The company's total compensation package includes a variety of economic rewards and also nonmonetary rewards such as autonomy, recognition, and a sense of achievement.

among employees. As we suggested in Chapter 4, a number of assumptions based upon expectancy theory must be met for monetary rewards to be effective in influencing performance levels. In the following list, we have described in parentheses which component of expectancy theory relates to each assumption:

1. *Employees must be capable of performing at high levels.* Unless the work force has the capability to perform the task, there is no possibility that high-quality task performance can result (E→P).

2. *Employees must believe they can perform at high levels.* Even if individuals have the ability to perform the task, they are unlikely to try unless they believe they can accomplish it. (E→P).

3. *Employees must believe that higher performance will result in more money.* Employees must perceive a relationship between performance and monetary rewards. That is, they must realize that the level of reward varies systematically with the level of performance (P→O).

4. *Employees must value money.* While not all employees value money equally, for money to be motivating, they must value money sufficiently (Valence).

5. *Money must be valued relative to other rewards.* Money must be valued over other incentives, such as peer acceptance. If peer acceptance is valued more highly than money, then the possibility of antagonizing peers because of high performance will restrict the level of performance (Valence).

6. *Jobs must allow for performance variation.* The job must be designed so that individuals may perform at different levels. If the job is machine-paced, then levels of performance (because they are based upon the machine) are not subject to worker control. In this case, the notion of high performance is irrelevant (P→O).

7. *Performance must be measurable.* Employees must be convinced that the level of their performance can be reliably measured. If, for example, an

employee exerts considerable effort during one evaluation period and little effort in a subsequent period and there is no difference in the level of reward, then the "incentive" system has less of an influence on the individual's performance (P→O).

8. *The plan must be compatible with the nature of the work (individual versus group).* Unless the organization can assess who does the work, an incentive plan probably will not work because the organization will not be able to attribute contributions of the individual or the group (P→O).

If these assumptions are met, then it is likely that an incentive system will foster high performance. How the incentive system will be structured, however, is still in question. Consider the types of incentive systems (shown in Figure 13–3) from which one can choose. If one is rewarding individual performance, then employees can be paid on a piece-rate plan or on a standard hour rate. In the **piece-rate plan,** the employee is paid a given rate for each unit produced. Piece-rate incentive plans are based upon objective performance and are oriented toward future productivity. Such an incentive system differs from merit-based pay, or pay-for-performance, in that merit systems reward past performance and usually are based upon a subjective evaluation of performance. Depending upon the nature of the task, such performance-based systems have always been an option in developing a compensation system. However, most organizations shy away from a purely merit-based or piece-rate system. In the "FOCUS ON: Developing a Total Compensation System," we examine the experience of one entrepreneurial CEO in developing a compensation package that

FIGURE 13–3	▶**Types of Incentive Systems**

The company has a variety of options for structuring its compensation system. These options include ways to reward individual performance or the performance of the group as a whole. The choice of an option depends in part on the individual's control over the desired outcome and the degree of cooperation required among group members.

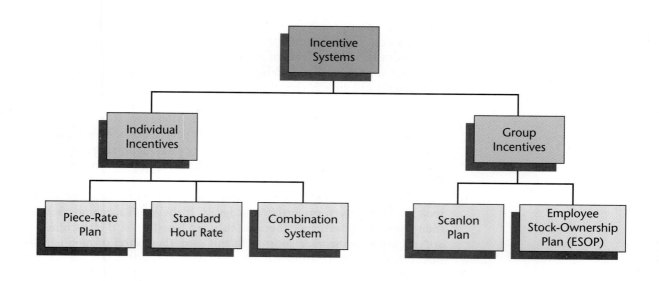

*Developing
a Total
Compensation
System*

Sharing the Company's Success
In 1978, Jeffrey and Karen Banks founded Metropolitan Outdoor Advertising Corporation. By 1990, it had grown to one of the country's largest billboard advertising firms. Jeffrey Banks knew that if he wanted to hold on to the people he was hiring, he would have to share the company's success with them. From his perspective, the best executive compensation plans were those that operated like a jigsaw puzzle with various pieces that could be divided up among the key players in the company.

The first piece was a profit-sharing plan that was instituted in 1980 for the company's 12 employees (which included Jeffrey and Karen Banks). Because it was a particularly good year, Banks allocated a share of the profits to each employee based on his or her salary. The funds were deposited into an individual retirement account in each employee's name. While the company made no guarantee about the level or even frequency of the contributions, they were made in seven of the next eleven years.

By the mid-1980s, Banks felt he had to come up with other ways of binding his top employees to the company. Metropolitan had expanded into billboard markets in southern California, Texas, Idaho, and elsewhere from its original San Francisco location. This meant that Banks needed to rely on his regional managers for much of the company's site selection, marketing de-velopment, and day-to-day office supervision. So in 1985, he divided the company into seven corporations, drawn up according to regional markets, with all stock owned by the holding company: Metropolitan Outdoor Advertising. The next year, he hired a regional manager whose incentive package included the potential to earn a stake based on the region's profitability in his local division. Eventually three other managers were hired and offered the same plan. But now the problem was becoming one of recordkeeping. As the divisions kept growing, it became increasingly difficult to keep track of the value of the different employees' stocks. He then hit on the idea of phantom stocks. In this situation, employees are able to earn exactly the same capital gains profits as they would have received from true stock ownership. Yet no stock actually changed hands; thus, the employees owed no money until payouts actually occurred. Banks then created a pool of 8 percent of his holding company's stock to be handed out on a discretionary basis to Metropolitan's most valuable executives and regional managers. To date, he has awarded about half of the pool.

What is the payoff for all this attention to compensation matters? According to Banks, his work force now "understands that we're a family working toward a common goal, toward rewards we're all going to share."

Source: Jill Andresky Fraser, "State of the Art," *Inc.*, November 1990, 68–76.

evolved to incorporate a number of different components and was effective at motivating employees.

Standard hour rates differ from piece rates in that they are determined not by what the employee actually produces but by the amount of time (determined by industrial engineering standards) that it *should* take to produce each unit. Then the employee is paid a standard rate, regardless of the length of time it took to produce the unit.

Combinations of these two forms exist as well. For example, salespeople who are paid a salary plus commission have parts of a piece-rate and a standard-hour incentive structure. Such employees are guaranteed both a minimum wage (standard-hour plan) and also rewards based directly on the sales they produce.

Rewarding individual performance, regardless of the system, is based on equitable distribution of rewards. This is a common assumption about how rewards should be distributed, but unquestioning acceptance of the equity norm of reward distribution does not exist among all workers. In fact, a recent survey conducted by Towers Perrin found that only 40 percent of the companies with pay-for-performance systems reported being satisfied with the results. Researchers began to examine pay-for-performance systems to determine what lead to more or less favorable reactions. The responses of over 2,000 managers and executives revealed that reactions to pay-for-performance systems were more positive when the distribution of rewards were consistent with policy, when they would fare better under such a system than under more traditional seniority systems, when performance evaluations were based on written standards, and when there were sufficient funds available to create a salient distinction between levels of performance.[5] As illustrated in the "International Focus on: Incentive Systems," Chinese workers are much more comfortable with equal distribution of rewards and may find more equitable systems problematic.

While such combinations reward individual performance, some tasks require group performance. Therefore, incentive structures should have sufficient flexibility to reward groups when appropriate. Group-level incentive plans operate under the same set of assumptions as individual incentive plans. However, they are more effective in situations where productivity is a function of group rather than individual contributions. For example, if a project's success depends upon the contributions of an entire department, then it is important that all of the contributors be rewarded for their combined performance. Rewarding only certain individuals in a department is likely to lead to increased competitiveness among group members rather than the cooperation required for a successful outcome.

There are a variety of group-based incentive plans. These plans can focus on either rewarding groups for successful cost reduction or rewarding groups for gains in productivity. The most well-known example of a cost-reduction group-level incentive plan is the Scanlon plan.[6] Under such a plan, all employees share the benefits of efficiency increases among the work force.

Another, more recent development in group-based incentive plans allows the employees to share in the profits of the firm. Under **Employee Stock Ownership Plans (ESOPs),** companies make tax-deductible contributions of stock or cash to a trust fund to buy stock. The stock is then allocated to employees based upon their seniority. When they retire or leave the company, they receive their stock and can either sell it on the market or sell it back to the company.[7] The financial benefit of stock ownership both to employee attitudes and employee performance is considerable. An ESOP can provide each employee with a considerable nest egg and may also serve as a visible symbol that the company views the employee as a critical and important resource. Fur-

---

[5] M. P. Miceli, I. Jung, J. P. Near, and D. B. Greenberger, "Predictors and Outcomes of Reactions to Pay-for-Performance Plans," *Journal of Applied Psychology* 76 (1991): 508–521.

[6] W. F. Whyte, "The Scanlon Plan," in *Compensation and Reward Perspectives*, ed. T. Maloney (Homewood, Ill.: R. D. Irwin, 1979).

[7] C. Rosen, K. J. Klein, and K. M. Young, "When Employees Share the Profits," *Psychology Today*, January 1986, 30–36.

Incentive Systems

Changing Reward Systems in China In the first quarter of 1978, one of the first companies to reinstate a bonus incentive system in China was the Capital Iron and Steel Company. This attempt to deviate from the path dictated by the "Iron Ricebowl" policy was met with considerable discomfort and debate among the various levels of the organization. The "Iron Ricebowl" describes the absolute egalitarian system under which China's work force operated during the Cultural Revolution. Under the old system, each worker was guaranteed a job, and in most cases that guarantee had little to do with the worker's performance. Under the new system, a series of bonuses based on superior performance would be allocated to the workers. With this bonus system, the factory was organized into 10 units. Each unit was evaluated on completeness and superiority. Completeness meant that all technical and economic indicators such as quantity, quality, and variety of products were evaluated. All workers who did not meet their quotas would forfeit part of their bonus. Under the criterion of superiority, the work unit that met its respective quotas and outperformed others in the same industry (nationwide) would receive a bonus.

However, this program met with considerable ideological differences. Some managers were concerned about the low wages of many workers and believed that their chances of receiving monetary bonuses should be greater than the probability of their forfeiting the bonuses. Some workers, because of the desire to abolish the evaluative criteria, recommended that the superior achievement bonuses be tied to individual quotas. Other workers demanded that the production quotas be lowered and argued that, although people could get more by exceeding the quotas, they should not forfeit their bonuses when they did not meet their quotas.

After two years of adjusting and implementing this bonus system, the Capital Iron and Steel Company has discovered a unique way to introduce such changes in incentive systems to their workers. They integrate ideological and political indoctrination with a rigorous system of personal responsibilities and clearly defined codes of rewards and penalties. To the extent that they did not successfully integrate ideological and political systems into explanations, but rather tried to separate them from the daily functioning of the new incentive system, they were unable to gain the cooperation of the workers.

Whereas American workers do not have to be convinced of the "appropriateness" of equity-based incentive systems, such incentive systems and the assumptions they include are indeed foreign to other cultures such as the Chinese. The Capital Iron and Steel Company is one of a new breed of Chinese organizations that are attempting to re-educate the Chinese worker on the multiple goals of an organization—goals that clearly include efficiency and productivity.

Sources: M. A. Von Gilnow and M. B. Teagarden, "The Transfer of Human Resource Management Technology in Sino–U.S. Cooperative Ventures," *Human Resource Management* 27 (1988): 201–229; and "The Capital Iron and Steel Company, The Reward System in China," *International Studies of Man and Organization* 12 (1982): 77–89.

ther, managers in ESOP firms often see such employee participation and ownership as central to the organization's culture and mission. Such ownership may increase employee influence in decisions affecting the organization, enthusiasm, and commitment to the organization.

An important question, however, is what impact such employee-ownership programs have on a firm's performance. The "FOCUS ON: Employee Ownership" illustrates the often positive performance effect associated with employee ownership plans such as ESOPs.

Focus on

Employee Ownership

The Positive Effects of ESOPs Employee-owned companies such as producer cooperatives have existed since 1791, but the real increase in employee ownership has occurred in the last decade. In 1976, for example, there were approximately 1,000 employee owned organizations in the United States. By 1990, there were more than 10,000. Many well-known companies including Anheuser-Busch, Lockheed, Procter & Gamble, and Polaroid have implemented employee-ownership plans. Avis Corporation, with nearly 13,000 shareholders, is completely owned by its employees.

Considering the heightened interest in this form of organizational compensation, what is the evidence for its success? At first glance, this rush to employee stock ownership plans (ESOPs) looks great; after all, these plans turn employees and managers into owners. Such a transition would align everyone's interests in performance. According to a 1989 article in *Business Week* "ESOPs . . . can deter takeovers, save taxes, and boost productivity," suggesting that ESOPs may help reverse the declining labor productivity that has plagued the United States since 1973. Following a 1983 implementation of an ESOP program, Brunswick Corporation reported a 50 percent increase in sales. The vice-president of finance at Brunswick reported an increase in employee morale as well. At Avis and Weirton Steel, ESOPs have proved a real catalyst for performance.

However, other researchers have reported different results. In a 1987 study (considered one of the largest and most thorough), the General Accounting Office found no correlation between ESOPs and productivity growth. Also, Richard Long of the University of Saskatchewan published a series of studies in the 1980s that were equivocal at best: some of the studies showed evidence of increases in productivity; some showed no changes; and others showed decreases in productivity after conversion from conventional ownership schemes to employee ownership. Thus, it seems that the effect of ESOPs on organizational performance depends on more than the simple existence of ESOPs. The latest research suggests that firms offering ESOPs are more profitable than comparable firms where participative schemes do not exist, especially in firms where workers perceive it is legitimate for them to participate. For ESOPs to be most effective, research suggests that the following conditions be present:

1. Employees should be provided with physical evidence and situational reminders that part of the equity in the company is theirs.
2. ESOPs should be operated so that employees have timely access to information about significant organizational events.
3. The ESOP should be designed so that employee-owners have the continual opportunity to exercise influence over organizational decisions.

As suggested by these three components, participation is the key element; but not just the symbol of participation. Rather, the successful system gives employees power, information, and knowledge of how to participate and some reward for doing so. The successful employee ownership program can have a positive effect on a work group's norms, cohesiveness, and cooperative behavior; on an employee's work-related attitudes, motivation, and behavior; and on the organization's ability to perform. Unfortunately, it is not just ownership per se, but a commitment on the part of management and employees for meaningful ownership.

Source: Jon Pierce and Candace Furo, "Employee Ownership: Implications for Management," *Organizational Dynamics* (Winter 1990): 32–43.

Avis Corporation, one of the nation's largest rental car companies, is wholly owned by its employees. Successful employee stock ownership plans such as Avis' may spur gains in productivity if employees understand their role in making the company successful.

Employee Benefits

Employee benefits are all the indirect economic rewards that employees receive.[8] A lengthy list of potential employee benefits is illustrated in Figure 13–4. While the purpose of a compensation system is to influence an individual's willingness to behave in accordance with the organization's wishes, employee benefits are not likely to influence this process directly. Since the majority of employee benefits are given to all employees, regardless of level of performance, they are not likely to motivate performance. However, they probably do influence individuals in deciding to stay with an organization. This is particularly true of benefits that increase in value with employee seniority. Examples of such benefits are pension plans, vacation time, and sabbatical leaves.

In most organizations, a standard set of benefits is offered to each employee. Recently, some organizations have begun to offer customized benefits packages. In this "cafeteria" approach to benefits, the employee is given a core set of benefits that does not vary across employees, but the employee is also offered the opportunity to select among other benefits. Usually, the employees are given a certain amount of "benefit dollars" to spend and can allocate those dollars across different benefits. For example, a member of a dual-income family with no children may forego additional health-care coverage. An employee with children may choose greater insurance benefits and a prepaid child-care option.

Allowing employees to customize their benefit plans has two major advantages. First, it increases the value of the benefits package to the individual employee while maintaining a set cost per employee. Second, it increases employee awareness of the actual value of the benefits the company is providing. Without such a system, employees often seriously underestimate the value

---

[8] See "Benefits Boosts: Most Firms Expand Health Coverage to Keep Pace with Inflation," *The Wall Street Journal*, February 23, 1982, 1; and S. S. Hills, *Compensation Decision Making* (Hinsdale, IL: Dryden Press, 1987).

FIGURE 13–4	▶ A Menu of Employee Benefits

Employee benefits are all the indirect economic rewards that employees receive. These benefits can represent as much as 40 percent of a company's total compensation costs, but they are rarely valued that highly by employees.

Optional Benefits

Pension plans	Dental insurance
Vacation time	Life and accident insurance
Holiday pay	Long-term disability insurance
Sick leave	Automobile insurance
Jury-duty pay	Liability insurance
Maternity/Paternity leave	Moving expenses
Funeral leave	Severance pay
Military-duty pay	Subsidized employee meals
Health insurance	Discount on goods or services

Legally Required Benefits

Social security	Unemployment compensation
Workers' compensation	

of the benefits the company provides. For example, one group of employees reported that they thought the company made an average monthly contribution of $21.69 per employee for their health-care benefits, when in fact the company contributed $64.07.[9]

Noneconomic Rewards

Managers often focus solely on the economic rewards of employment, ignoring noneconomic rewards as a means of influencing individual performance. These nonpecuniary or noneconomic rewards do not directly affect the employee's wages and benefits. However, many rewards that flow from employment influence employee performance.

To assume the only important rewards are economic is naive. An individual who dislikes the duties of a job may leave it. Other workers may decide to stay in an organization because of the power they have, because they believe their jobs are significant and important, because they like their colleagues, or because they like the geographic area in which their positions are located.

Noneconomic rewards can take many forms. They can include intrinsic job rewards, extrinsic job rewards, and non-job-based rewards. Intrinsic job rewards are those reinforcers that relate directly to performing the task. They include such job-related factors as autonomy, power and control, and a sense of task completion and achievement. An example of a noneconomic, intrinsic job reward is the use of flextime. Extrinsic job rewards are those rewards external to or separate from the job itself, such as supervisory recognition and social interaction. Finally, non-job-based rewards are those which accrue to employees because they are employed by a particular organization, independent of their unique positions within the organization. Two such rewards are organizational

[9]M. G. Wilson, G. B. Northcraft, and M. A. Neale, "The Perceived Value of Fringe Benefits," *Personnel Psychology* 38 (1985): 309–320.

status (status based upon association with the particular organization) and a favorable geographical location.

The rewards we have discussed all contribute to an organization's compensation system. However, as we know from previous chapters, compensation systems are not foolproof in rewarding good performance. In some cases, compensation can systematically discriminate among employees. In the next section we discuss comparable worth as a basis for determining the compensation of a specific class of employees.

Comparable Worth   Among all the forms of compensation, monetary incentives are the most easily divisible and the easiest to allocate. As such, they are most likely to be the basis for discriminating among employees. Discrimination is an ominous term. However, in allocating rewards, organizations must discriminate between good and poor performers. This type of discrimination is vastly different from discrimination based on factors unrelated to job performance.

In fact, we can describe four different types of discrimination: legal and fair, legal and unfair, illegal and fair, and illegal and unfair. An example of legal and fair discrimination is to give the largest pay increases to younger workers if they outperform older workers. Discriminating by giving a friend a higher pay raise than another employee about whom you are indifferent is unfair but not illegal. An example of illegal but fair discrimination is requiring women to contribute more to employee pension plans. It is fair discrimination because women as a group live longer than men and are likely to receive more benefits from a retirement plan. However, recent court rulings have made it illegal to require higher pension contributions from women.[10] Illegal and unfair discrimination is granting a pay raise to a white employee whose performance is only average while not granting one to a black employee with above-average performance.

Currently, when the topic of discrimination is considered, the focus often turns to the comparable worth controversy. **Comparable worth** is based on two factors. The first is that the Equal Pay Act requires equal pay for jobs that are substantially equal in terms of skill, ability, and effort. Second, even though the Equal Pay Act has been around for over 20 years, there is still a significant difference between the average pay of men and women. Although a substantial portion of this difference can be accounted for by occupational gender segregation, the low pay associated with "female" occupations is not just a function of history. Occasionally, a largely segregated occupation (such as bank teller or public-school teacher) has begun to accept members of the opposite gender, and the pay has changed accordingly: increased if the new jobholders were male and decreased if they were female.[11] As we will explore in more detail in Chapter 18 in the discussion of discrimination, there is considerable evidence for gender discrimination: even when men and women have similar educations, work in similar industries, stay in the work force, and accept transfers and relocations equally, they are still paid significantly less. Further, a recent survey illustrated the pay differential for even highly trained women who, on average, are paid

---

[10]Manhart v. City of Los Angeles, Department of Water and Power, 552 F. 2d 581, 13 FEP 1625 (9th Cir. 1976); Norris v. Arizona, Governing Comm., 486 F. Supp. 645, 22 FEP 1059 (D. Ariz. 1980).

[11]J. Pfeffer and J. Ross, "Gender-Based Wage Differences: The Effects of Organizational Contexts," in *Work and Occupations* 17(1) (1990): 55–78; and Monica Roman, "Women, Beware: An MBA Doesn't Mean Equal Pay," *Business Week*, October 29, 1990, 57.

The basis of comparable worth discrimination lies in the differential valuing of occupations because of the dominant gender of the jobholders. Though the Equal Pay Act requires the same pay for jobs that are substantially the same in terms of skill, ability and effort, in most cases courts allow different wage rates for different jobs if based on market demands.

12 percent less than their male counterparts.[12] Figure 13–5 illustrates these differences.

The basis of comparable worth discrimination lies in the differential valuing of occupations based on the dominant gender of the jobholders. In Denver, for example, nurses argued that their jobs required more skill and ability than other jobs for which the employer paid more—tree trimmers and sign painters. In a similar case in Wisconsin, nurses argued that their positions were worth more than those of sanitation workers. In most cases the courts are accepting a market defense—that is, wage rates are based on market wage surveys for these occupations. Thus, to pay different rates for different jobs based on market demands currently is not considered discrimination.[13]

The issue of comparable worth discrimination is still being battled in the courts. Its potential impact on organizations could be incredible. Consider the case of the state of Washington. The state had conducted numerous job evaluations over several years and found that predominately female jobs were paid less than comparable jobs held predominately by males. The state had known this condition existed but failed to implement any changes in its compensation system. If states conduct job evaluations on comparable jobs and find systematic differences, the cost to rectify the inequities all at once would be staggering. It is unlikely that any organization would reduce the wage rate of the higher-paid jobs, such as maintenance engineers or tree trimmers, yet raising the wages of nurses, clerical assistants, and teachers could easily bankrupt a public system. The more likely alternative, if comparable worth discrimination is not recognized by the court, would be an incremental process of bringing the wage rates of predominately female jobs in line with those of comparable male jobs. In addition to assuring that employees are not the subject of discrimination, many other factors must be present to assure good performance. The next section focuses on one of those factors, the setting of performance goals.

[12] Monica Roman, "Women, Beware: An MBA Doesn't Mean Equal Pay."

[13] G. Sape, "Coping with Comparable Worth," *Harvard Business Review* (May 1985) 145–152.

FIGURE 13–5   ▶ **The Pay Gap Between Men and Women**
Annual Salary After Graduation (by school)

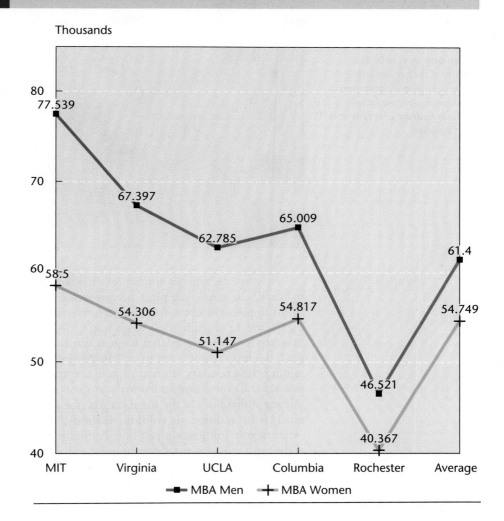

Thousands

GOAL SETTING   ◆◆◆◆◆◆

Another important factor in the employee performance equation is the setting of performance goals. **Goals** specify a direction for action and a specific quantity of work to be accomplished.[14] Considerable research supports the notion that employees who are assigned difficult and specific goals perform at higher levels than those assigned easy goals. Further, those with specific, challenging goals outperform individuals told to "do your best."

[14] E. A. Locke and G. P. Latham, *A Theory of Goal Setting and Task Performance* (Englewood Cliffs, N.J.: Prentice-Hall, 1990).

Goals specify a direction for action and a specific quantity of work to be accomplished. Athletes who set themselves difficult and specific goals perform at higher levels than those with easy goals. The height of the bar can influence this high jumper's commitment to achieving her goal and provide feedback about her own performance.

It is not enough to simply set challenging, specific goals. For these goals to work, the employee must be *committed* to achieving them. **Goal commitment** implies the extension of effort, over time, toward the accomplishment of a goal and an unwillingness to give up or lower the goal.[15] However, goal commitment is inversely related to goal difficulty. That is, the more difficult the goal, the less commitment to it.[16] Increasing the difficulty of a goal while maintaining the necessary amount of goal commitment is an important task for the manager. Committing individuals to goals is, in many ways, similar to committing individuals to the organization (for a detailed discussion, refer to Chapter 11). In addition to volition, visibility, and explicitness and irreversibility, other factors influencing just how committed an individual is to a goal include ability and self-esteem, the complexity of the task, past successes, how involving the job is, and how supportive the supervisor is.[17] Figure 13–6 shows the steps involved in setting performance goals.

Commitment to challenging, specific performance goals provides many benefits to the employee *in addition to* raising productivity. If employees are to perform at high levels, it is critical that they understand exactly what is expected of them. Goals are a primary way in which management can convey performance expectations to employees. In addition, goals can relieve boredom.[18] Specifying a goal that is difficult but attainable adds a measure of challenge to a task, regardless of the job's innate interest level.

[15] M. A. Campion and R. G. Lord, "A Control Systems Conceptualization of Goal Setting and Changing Process," *Organizational Behavior and Human Performance* 30 (1982): 265–287.

[16] E. A. Locke, "Relation of Goal Level to Performance with a Short Work Period and Multiple Goal Levels," *Journal of Applied Psychology* 67 (1982): 512–514.

[17] J. R. Hollenbeck and H. J. Klein, "Goal Commitment and the Goal Setting Process: Problems, Prospects, and Proposals for Future Research," *Journal of Applied Psychology* 72 (1987): 212–220.

[18] E. A. Locke and J. F. Bryan, "Performance Goals as Determinants of Level of Performance and Boredom," *Journal of Applied Psychology* 51 (1978): 120–130.

| FIGURE 13-6 | ▶ Steps in Setting Performance Goals |

Setting effective performance goals not only raises productivity, but also clarifies for employees what is expected of them. The six-step process shown here helps the manager ensure that the goals will be effective.

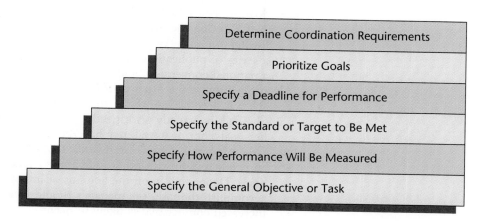

Determine Coordination Requirements

Prioritize Goals

Specify a Deadline for Performance

Specify the Standard or Target to Be Met

Specify How Performance Will Be Measured

Specify the General Objective or Task

Finally, goal attainment provides feedback to employees about their performance. If goals provide a clue to management's expectations about employee performance, then meeting the goals set by management gives employees information about the level of their performance. Thus, goals provide a bench mark for employees to judge their performance. They also increase their pride and confidence in their ability to accomplish the assigned task.

In setting performance goals for employees, a manager should follow the following six steps:[19]

1. *Specify the general objective or task to be accomplished.* What is it you want the employee to do? One way employees' attention can be focused on what they are to do is through job descriptions. As described in Chapter 11, a job description usually conveys a great deal of information to the employee, including what tasks need to be performed, what outcome is expected, and what deadlines are important.

2. *Specify how the performance in question will be measured.* Performance on some tasks is more easily measured than on others. For example, the performance of a salesperson is often evaluated on the dollar value of generated sales; the performance of a secretary may be measured by the number of assignments completed daily.

3. *Specify the standard or target to be met.* In addition to identifying what will be evaluated, a manager should also specify exactly what level of performance is expected. This is the challenging portion of the goal.

[19]Locke and Latham, *A Theory of Goal Setting and Task Performance.*

4. *Specify a deadline for performance.* Generally, as the level of responsibility of a task increases, so does the time allowed for performance. For example, semiskilled or blue-collar workers may be given daily or weekly goals. Upper-level managers may be evaluated yearly or even in three- or five-year cycles.

5. *Prioritize goals.* Employees are likely to have many goals to accomplish, especially as the complexity of their positions increases. Thus, setting goal priorities directs effort in proportion to the importance of the goals. Not knowing the priority of tasks can be dangerous. Consider the following example. An executive was hired by a national association to edit a series of publications. In an emergency, she was asked to take charge of a national convention, and she spent a great deal of time planning the convention at the expense of her editorial work. After the convention, she was fired for not doing the editorial work for which she was hired! She had incorrectly prioritized her goals. If her employer had prioritized her goals, her dismissal may have been avoided.[20]

6. *Determine coordination requirements.* Consider the amount of coordination and cooperation with other individuals needed to accomplish the set goals. Depending upon the amount of interdependence necessary to accomplish the task, the manager should be aware of and account for the increased conflict that is likely to occur.[21]

Goal setting has been shown to be a very effective mechanism for improving performance. However, there are a number of potential pitfalls that should be avoided if goal setting is to be effective. Setting extremely difficult goals may produce greater levels of effort, but it also increases the level of risk managers and employees are willing to take. While risk taking is a component of managing in uncertain environments, excessive risk taking (as we suggested in Chapter 5) clearly can be counterproductive. If goals are too difficult, they may produce unnecessary levels of stress for employees and may reduce their acceptance of and commitment to meeting them. While challenging goals that demand high levels of performance may be inherently stressful for employees, it is important to avoid levels of stress that hamper performance. Further, if goals are too difficult, employees' goal commitment may be lowered, which likely will offset the typical benefits of setting challenging goals.

Other potential pitfalls of goal setting include perceiving goals as *ceilings* on performance. Goals are usually intended to identify the minimum acceptable level of performance, not the maximum. Further, since goals direct employee effort, areas of performance for which goals are not set may be ignored. Along this line, goals set for short time periods may encourage short-term performance. An employee is likely to focus on whatever timeline is contained within the goal. Finally, in a high-pressure, unsupportive atmosphere, demanding and difficult goals can lead employees to take shortcuts, cheat, or misrepresent their actual levels of performance to meet performance demands. Figure 13–7 illustrates some ways in which each of these pitfalls can be avoided.

While setting specific goals can increase performance, it is important that employees have feedback about how they are doing. When employees are told

[20]Ibid.

[21]G. B. Northcraft and P. C. Earley, "Goals Setting, Conflict and Task Interdependence," in *Conflict Management: An Interdisciplinary Approach*, ed. M. A. Rahim (New York: Praeger Publications, 1989).

FIGURE 13–7   ▶ **Goal-Setting Pitfalls and Potential Solutions**

Goal setting can be a very effective mechanism for improving performance in an organization, but only if managed well. There are a number of pitfalls that must be avoided for goal setting to be effective.

Pitfall	Potential Solution
Excessive risk taking	Specify acceptable risk levels for the employee and the organization
Increased stress	Adjust goal difficulty, increase staff as needed, and ensure that employees have the skills necessary to accomplish their goals
View of goals as ceilings rather than floors	Reward those who exceed their goals
Ignoring of nongoal areas	Make sure that goals are comprehensive—developed for all important areas of performance
Encouragement of short-range thinking	Increase the time span of goals
Dishonesty and cheating	Set an example of honesty in actions, give frequent feedback, and be open to negative information to avoid a climate of high pressure and low support

Source: E. A. Locke and G. P. Latham, *Goal Setting: A Motivational Technique That Really Works!* (Englewood Cliffs, N.J.: Prentice-Hall, 1984), 171–172.

how their behaviors measure up to an expected standard of performance, they can then modify their behavior if necessary to reach their set goals. Thus, feedback is necessary if goal setting is to work. While feedback that is timely and self-generated is probably the most useful in modifying work behavior, it is also important that employees receive formal feedback about their performance on a routine basis in the form of a performance appraisal.[22] The next section focuses on the importance of performance appraisals in maintaining employee performance.

PERFORMANCE APPRAISAL SYSTEMS

Performance appraisals serve many purposes in organizations. They provide feedback to the employee and serve as the basis for decisions concerning promotion, salary and wage increases, demotion, transfer, training, and layoffs. The general strengths and weaknesses of the employee population can be evaluated and directions for training identified. Performance evaluations can also aid the individual in determining personal strengths and weaknesses. Finally, information garnered from a performance appraisal system can aid in the maintenance or modification of the current organizational selection process.

[22] G. B. Northcraft, and P. C. Earley, "Technology, Credibility, and Feedback Use," *Organizational Behavior and Human Decision Processes* 44 (1989): 83–96.

Performance appraisals are an important organizational tool. They provide valuable opportunities for performance-enhancing discussions between supervisors and subordinates as well as diagnosing weaknesses in an organization's selection, socialization, and training programs.

Conflicts and Problems

Using performance appraisals for so many diverse purposes can cause problems. If all the reasons for performance appraisal use are categorized, three major functions emerge: (1) to provide feedback, (2) to distribute rewards, and (3) to counsel employees. If we examine these three functions more closely, it is easy to see how they can conflict with one another.

Consider the obvious conflict employees must experience in trying to respond to both the counseling and the reward-distribution functions of performance appraisals. A supervisor trying to understand the obstacles that keep employees from performing their jobs will want to focus on the employees' perceptions of problems, weaknesses, and failures. However, if employees view the performance appraisal as an opportunity to make their case for a substantial promotion or salary increase, then the last thing they will want to do is to focus on the problems, weaknesses, and failures they have experienced in their positions. They want to present their performance in the best possible light. Thus, they are likely to gloss over difficulties and potential problems and present only their successes. It may be that expecting employees to be honest about their shortcomings while simultaneously evaluating them for a salary increase or promotion is asking too much. To answer the questions honestly would probably mean going against what employees see as their best interests.

Conflict engendered by performance appraisals is also responsible for vanishing performance appraisals. This conflict develops not only from the conflicting functions of a performance appraisal system, but also from the difficulty of the lack of incentives for conducting high-quality performance appraisals. The major difficulty with performance appraisals is the inability of supervisors to convey negative feedback in a constructive manner. Supervisors—especially those who must convey negative performance information—are often vague and indirect in conveying this information to their employees. As a result, supervisors may believe that an evaluation has been conducted while employees may be unaware that they have been evaluated.

The second reason for vanishing performance appraisals is the lack of organizational incentives for supervisors to spend the time and effort necessary to conduct good performance-appraisal interviews. In fact, this is probably a good example of the "folly of rewarding A while hoping for B."[23] Most organizations probably hope that their supervisors will spend the necessary time to diagnose the reasons behind poor performance and, together with the employee, implement solutions to address these problems. Yet the reward structures of most organizations actually *reward* supervisors for conducting superficial performance appraisals (they take less time away from "productive" activities) or ignoring them altogether.

Even supervisors who understand the importance of performance appraisals often find themselves in a no-win situation. For example, a supervisor's appraisal of an employee's performance may be very different from the employee's self-appraisal. In fact, because of disparate perceptions, it is difficult even for a supervisor with good interpersonal skills to conduct a positive performance interview. Employees often display considerable levels of discomfort when confronted with a performance evaluation, *regardless of their level of past performance.* Part of this discomfort can be explained by their anxiety about evaluation. However, some of the discomfort is probably based on a perceived lack of control over the outcome: the final evaluation. Recent research suggests that employees generally believe performance appraisals to be arbitrary and capricious, independent of their level of performance.[24] That is, both poorly performing and highly performing employees view performance appraisals as unrelated to their levels of performance.

The reasons for this almost universal dissatisfaction with the process of performance appraisal are numerous. They include dissatisfaction with what is being rated, the performance-appraisal instruments, who conducts the actual ratings, and how often the ratings are conducted. The next section considers each of these concerns.

Improving Performance Appraisal Systems

Creating an effective performance appraisal system is a difficult undertaking. Although 90 percent of organizations report having performance appraisal systems in place, approximately the same percentage report dissatisfaction with their current systems. Even in the military services, which traditionally invest considerable resources in developing accurate and effective performance appraisal systems, a newly implemented performance appraisal system has an expected life of only a few years. The search for an accurate, reliable, and well-received performance appraisal system may be never-ending, but managers could certainly improve the quality of their performance appraisal systems by focusing on the following issues, which are the root of much participant dissatisfaction with the evaluation process.

Measure Behavior, Not Traits One of the most popular formats for evaluating employees is a **trait-rating scale**.[25] The trait approach typically asks the rater to evaluate the ratee on such factors as dependability, cooperation, leadership, obedience, and loyalty. While we often evaluate our acquaintances on

[23] Kerr, "On the Folly of Rewarding A while Hoping for B."

[24] R. Folger and J. Greenberg, "Procedural Justice: An Interpretive Analysis of Personnel Systems," in *Research in Personnel and Human Resource Management*, vol. III, ed. K. Rowland and G. Ferris (Greenwich, Conn.: JAI Press, 1985), 141–183.

[25] H. J. Bernardin and R. W. Beatty, *Performance Appraisal: Assessing Human Behavior at Work* (Boston: Kent Publishing, 1984).

such dimensions, there are serious problems associated with rating employees by traits. If performance appraisals exist to measure past *performance*, then evaluating employees' various personality traits is inconsistent with that purpose. Personality traits are measures of neither performance nor behavior. In fact, considerable research into the relationship between personality and behavior reports little relationship between the two.[26] Even if the correlation between personality and behavior were much higher, traits only *predict* behavior, they do not *measure* it. For example, there is a positive relationship between success in an organization and an individual's height.[27] However, a manager would be hard-pressed to justify using an employee's height as a measure of performance. While an individual's height may indeed predict performance, it does not *measure* performance!

Further, evaluations based upon employee traits or personality characteristics are usually generic in nature, not based upon specific, identifiable (and thus modifiable) behaviors. For example, if you receive a performance evaluation that indicates that you are viewed by the supervisor as being low in leadership, how will you modify your behavior to reduce that deficiency? How will you, specifically, alter your level of "leadership"? On the other hand, if you are told that you "tell new people how to do the job, show them when it is done wrong, but don't explain why or check whether they understand what they are doing and the reason for the method,"[28] then you are likely to be able to alter your behavior to improve performance.

The difficulty of adjusting one's personality traits to meet organizational expectations is not lost on employees. Performance appraisal systems that primarily evaluate traits rather than observable behavior are typically viewed with suspicion by employees. For employees to be more accepting of performance appraisals, organizations must focus on measuring observable behavior. Along this line, then, the performance-appraisal instrument must measure such behaviors.

The Proper Performance-Appraisal Instrument   As we described previously, the most commonly used performance-rating form is the graphic rating scale, an instrument that purports to measure employee traits. On the other end of the performance-appraisal continuum are instruments that measure behaviors. The most common form of "behavioral" instrument is the **behaviorally anchored rating scale (BARS).** In developing a BARS, an organization must first analyze the particular job to determine what types of behavior reflect varying degrees of performance. That is, how does an "outstanding" employee behave? An "average" employee? An "unsatisfactory" employee? Actual descriptions of behaviors are then used to define, or *anchor,* the ratings on the scale. For example, in rating an employee's perseverance, a BARS might offer options from "keeps working on difficult tasks until job is completed" to "likely to stop work at the first sign of difficulty."[29]

While a BARS is often perceived by employees as a major improvement over trait scales, few organizations have implemented this particular form of

---

[26] R. I. Henderson, *Performance Appraisal* (Reston, Va.: Reston Publishing, 1984).

[27] B. M. Bass, *Stodgill's Handbook of Leadership: A Survey of Theory and Research,* rev. ed. (New York: Free Press, 1981).

[28] Henderson, *Performance Appraisal,* 189.

[29] Berkeley Rice, "Performance Review: The Job Nobody Likes," *Psychology Today,* September 1985, 30–36.

appraisal instrument and the research on its superiority is sparse. The development of such scales requires lengthy job analyses and a considerable amount of the organization's resources—particularly money and time. In addition, BARS are designed for a specific job in a specific organization. Thus, one BARS cannot be developed and applied to all positions in an organization. Since they are unique to a position and they require such a large amount of resources to produce, BARS are usually developed only for job categories in which there are many incumbents, such as bank tellers, nurses, grocery clerks, bookkeepers, and secretaries. It is rare that a BARS will be developed for professionals or executives—the cost is just too great. Finally, some research suggests that ratings based upon memory may capture more accurately the essence of an individual's performance than ratings (such as a BARS) conducted immediately after viewing a sample of the employee's performance.[30] Probably the most common reason *for* using a BARS is that it seems to fare much better under judicial scrutiny; that is, it is legally more defensible. In a number of court cases, trait rating scales have been found not to be legally defensible.

While trait scales and BARS represent two ends of the continuum, there are other types of performance-appraisal instruments. They are briefly described and their position along this continuum illustrated in Figure 13–8.

Who Should Rate Employees?

The easy answer to this question is that the supervisor should rate employees. In fact, in the vast majority of organizations, supervisors are the ones who evaluate a subordinate's performance. Unfortunately, the easy answer is not always the correct answer. Deciding who should evaluate an employee's behavior should depend upon certain criteria. The ideal rater should be (1) aware of the objectives of the employee's position, (2) able to determine if the observed behavior is satisfactory, (3) able to observe the employee frequently, and (4) able to ascertain whether the employee is effective. Rather than assuming that the supervisor is most qualified to evaluate a subordinate's performance, let's first examine the cast of organizational—and non-organizational—actors who might serve as raters.

Supervisors Supervisors are often viewed as the only people in the organization who are familiar with the responsibilities and duties of each job within their purview. In addition to knowing the jobs, supervisors should also have a grasp of the various strengths and weaknesses of those individuals they supervise. Further, they are the obvious conduits between the employee and the organization. As the organization's agents, they often are able to influence the allocation of organizational rewards and punishments.

The problems with supervisory appraisals occur when the supervisor does not have adequate opportunity to observe the employee's performance. For example, a supervisor is unlikely to be able to rate a traveling salesperson's performance other than by comparing rates of completed sales. How such a salesperson actually performs the job can only be inferred from sales levels. Further, employee evaluations are often based upon supervisors' beliefs about how they *think* the work should be done rather than how well it is actually being done.[31]

---

[30]K. R. Murphy and W. K. Balzer, "Systematic Distortions in Memory-Based Behavior Ratings and Performance Evaluations: Consequences for Rating Accuracy," *Journal of Applied Psychology* 71 (1986): 39–44.

[31]R. S. Barrett, "Influence of Supervisor's Requirements on Ratings," *Personnel Psychology* 19 (1966): 375–387.

FIGURE 13–8	▶ Types of Performance Appraisal Instruments

Graphic rating scales are the most commonly used performance-rating instruments. On the other end of the range of available techniques for measuring performance are behavior-based instruments such as the behaviorally anchored rating scale (BARS).

MEASUREMENT OF TRAITS ⟶ MEASUREMENT OF BEHAVIORS

Trait Scale	Ranking	Paired Comparison	Forced Distribution	Weighted Checklists	Behaviorally Anchored Rating Scales (BARS)
Evaluates the employee on such factors as commitment, creativity, loyalty, initiative, and so forth. It requires judgment of ratee performance along an unbroken continuum (from excellent to unacceptable) or by discrete categories (superior, satisfactory, unsatisfactory).	The simplest of all comparative techniques, it involves ranking all employees from the best to the worst on the particular dimension being considered.	Every person is rated against every other person; the final ranking depends on how many times a particular employee is ranked better than comparison employees.	The number of individuals who can be assigned certain performance categories is limited. For example, only 10 percent of employees may be rated "very good," 20 percent "good," and so on.	Group of statements that describe types and levels of behavior. Each statement has a weight attached to it. Not only is the actual rating considered in this form of performance appraisal instrument, but also the value of that behavior or level of behavior to the performance of the job or task.	This instrument is a set of rating scales. There is one scale for each important aspect of job performance. Each scale is composed of brief descriptions or critical incidents of effective and ineffective job performance.

Employees   Self-appraisals are becoming an increasingly popular addition to performance reviews. This form of evaluation is consistent with the trend toward increasing employee participation in organizational decision making. In addition, having employees evaluate themselves reduces their level of defensiveness when confronting problem areas or weaknesses. Employees rate an evaluation based on self-appraisal as more satisfying, and they are less defensive. Such evaluations can provide the supervisor with new information about how the employee perceives the job and its associated problems. They can also help to clarify differences between the performance expectations of a supervisor and subordinate. Self-appraisals have been shown to have greater validity when self-raters expect their ratings to be compared to an identified standard, raters have previous experience with self-evaluation, and the evaluation instructions stress the comparison with others.[32]

The disadvantages of self-appraisals focus primarily on the inexperienced employee. Employees who have had little experience in being evaluated by

---

[32] Paul A. Mabe III and Stephen G. West, "Validity of Self-Evaluation of Ability: A Review and Meta-Analysis," *Journal of Applied Psychology* 67 (1982): 280–296.

supervisors often express greater satisfaction with more traditional, supervisory evaluations. Employees who do not have clearly established performance standards or goals by which to measure their performance are likely to use a different yardstick than the supervisor. In addition, few employees believe their performance to be average. Since the very definition of the term *average* indicates that it describes the majority of individuals, the likelihood of consistency among supervisor ratings and self-ratings is low.[33]

Peers   Probability the best evidence of the usefulness of peer appraisals is the reliability and validity of these reviews. In fact, they routinely have higher predictive validity than do supervisory ratings. The differences in validity between peer and supervisory ratings can be accounted for by the opportunity each group has to observe the ratee. Peers often interact with the ratee in many different arenas; thus, they have a large sample of behavior by which to evaluate performance.

The problem with having peers as raters is that they often resist evaluating their coworkers, viewing it as a threat to their relationships with others. In fact, if performance reviews are tied to salary raises or promotions, peer reviews suffer. Rather than evaluate performance accurately, peers may choose to evaluate coworkers strategically—to evaluate others in a way that maximizes their own evaluations.[34]

Subordinates   Subordinates have the unique ability to appraise the leadership and management potential of the rated superior. Superiors can receive useful feedback from this type of appraisal. Accepting such feedback can enhance future cooperation among organizational actors.

However, the greatest disadvantage in using subordinates to rate superiors is their (understandable) concern about the impact of their evaluations on their relationship with the supervisor. Subordinates may be hesitant to rate their supervisors accurately for fear of reprisal. Subordinates also may have different ideas of the important performance criteria for their bosses and may choose to rate their superior on dimensions unrelated to job success.[35]

Outside Individuals   Outside raters are individuals outside the organizational unit, such as members of the human resources management department, external consultants, or clients of the firm. The benefit of having these individuals rate performance is that they rarely have a vested interest in the final outcome. That is, their own promotions, raises, or evaluations are not dependent on or influenced by their evaluation of the ratee. Outside appraisers can also provide information from a completely different perspective. For example, clients or customers may see a very different side of a salesperson than that observed by either the supervisor or coworkers.

The major problem with outside reviews is that they reduce the meaningfulness of the discussions among supervisors and their subordinates. Further,

---

[33] G. C. Thornton, "Psychometric Properties of Self-Appraisals of Job Performance," *Personnel Psychology* 33, (1980): 263–272.

[34] S. J. Carroll and C. E. Schneier, *Performance Appraisal and Review Systems* (Glenview, Ill.: Scott, Foresman, 1982).

[35] Ibid.

employees may find fault with a supervisor who "abdicates" responsibility to review their performance. Finally, the greatest advantage of outsider evaluations—the outsider's perspective—is also their greatest weakness. Because outsiders typically have little opportunity to observe the employee in a variety of settings, their evaluations may be based upon too small a sample of behavior.

While there are clearly both advantages and disadvantages to every type of rater, some generalizations about raters can be made. First, it is important that there be multiple raters, if possible. Having multiple raters increases the probability of obtaining a comprehensive picture of an employee's performance. Second, whoever is chosen to evaluate an employee should have considerable opportunity to observe the employee directly. Finally, the type of rater used should be consistent with the type of evaluation desired. If a manager is being evaluated for promotion to upper management, then subordinate evaluations of performance may be critical. If the supervisor has little opportunity to observe the individual directly, then perhaps peers, clients, or customers may provide the best performance information. All in all, choosing the type and number of raters can have a significant impact on the quality of the performance appraisal process.

The Timing of Performance Appraisals   Most organizations conduct formal performance appraisals annually. As a result, supervisors are expected to remember and evaluate behaviors that have occurred over the last 365 days. In such cases, the most recent behaviors—especially if they differ significantly from the person's usual behavior—will have the greatest impact on an evaluation. It is difficult enough for us to remember what transpired 30 days ago, much less to accurately recall what occurred one year ago.

There are two solutions to this problem. A rater could schedule multiple appraisal interviews—say, four—during the year and have each review cover only the period of time since the last review. One review each year could result in a summary evaluation to be used for salary and promotion decisions. The second solution involves the use of memory aids to help the rater remember a larger sampling of employee behavior. Formally, the rater might keep a **critical incidence file** on each employee. A critical incidence file contains examples of the employee's behaviors—instances that exemplify outstanding, good, and poor behaviors. Informally, the rater might record brief observations of employees in a "little black book."[36] Ratees might also keep such a diary, noting both good and poor examples of their performance.

The suggestions above represent ways in which any performance appraisal system can be adjusted to improve its acceptance by employees. However, improving the structure of a performance appraisal system is only part of the answer to maintaining performance. In fact, it may be that many of the problems associated with formal performance appraisal systems have less to do with their structure than with motivation—how willing managers are to commit the necessary time to producing high-quality evaluations of their employees.[37] Figure 13–9 contains some advice for managers who are motivated to improve the quality of their performance appraisal systems.

[36] Henderson, *Performance Appraisal.*

[37] Rice, "Performance Review: The Job Nobody Likes."

FIGURE 13-9	▶ **Performance-Appraisal Reviews: Advice for Managers**

Many of the problems encountered with performance appraisal systems may be less the fault of the system than of the motivation and skills of the managers using them. Listed here are some recommendations for managers who wish to improve their appraising of employees.

- Know precisely what you want to achieve (and what company policy says you should achieve) with your performance reviews, such as determining raises, evaluation, criticism, training, or morale-building.

- Don't wait until the review itself to let your staff know what you expect. Let them know early on exactly what the job requires, what specific goals, standards, and deadlines you expect them to meet and how you plan to evaluate and reward their performance.

- Keep a record of subordinates' performance so that you can cite specific examples to back up any criticisms or comments.

- Listen. Numerous surveys of employee attitudes reveal the feeling that "management doesn't care what we think." The review is your chance to get valuable feedback from your own subordinates about their jobs or company policy.

- Ask fact-finding questions to get employees to recall instances in which they performed well or poorly. See if they have a realistic estimate of their abilities.

- Go over your written evaluation with each employee. Find out if they feel your ratings are fair. They don't have to agree with you completely, but strong disagreements will lessen their motivation to improve.

- Focus steadily on each individual's performance. Show that you care about that person's career. Otherwise it looks like you're just going through the motions, and employees will get the message that the review, and perhaps their performance, doesn't really matter.

- When critiquing an employee's performance, do some stroking: Reinforce the good habits with praise.

- Be specific and constructive in your criticism. Don't just tell employees they're not "aggressive enough." Point out how they can improve, with specific examples.

- Critique the behavior, not the employee. Keep the discussion on a professional level.

- Be fair, but don't be afraid to give honest criticism when necessary. Most employees don't want a meaningless pat on the back. They want to know where they stand and how they can improve.

- Don't play the role of therapist. If personal problems are affecting an employee's performance, be supportive, but be careful about getting involved. Suggest outside professional help if necessary.

- Explain how the employee's performance in meeting goals contributes to department or corporate objectives. In this way, the review can help build morale and loyalty.

- Don't wait till the next performance review to follow up. Use informal progress reports or mini-reviews to help spot problems before they become serious.

- Use the occasion to get an informal review of your own performance. Encourage your staff to tell you about any of your habits that make their work difficult or to suggest changes you could make that would help them do their jobs better.

Source: Berkeley Rice, "Performance Review: The Job Nobody Likes," *Psychology Today*, November 1985, 35. Reprinted with permission from *Psychology Today* Magazine. Copyright © 1985 (PT Partners, L.P.).

MANAGING FOR IMPROVED PERFORMANCE ◆◆◆◆◆◆

Until now, this chapter has discussed general techniques for maintaining employee performance. In this section, we will focus on identifying the poor performer and developing specific prescriptions for addressing the causes of poor performance. While designing specific incentive systems, setting performance goals, and developing an effective performance appraisal system will improve the performance of both good and poor performers, managing the poor performer demands more of the supervisor's resources and analytical skills.

The Poor Performer

All supervisors hope that all of their employees will perform their respective jobs adequately. When this happens, the job of the supervisor is much easier, and the difficult interpersonal problems associated with negative evaluations and upset employees can be avoided. Unfortunately, this is not always the case. Most managers must face, from time to time, the specter of the poorly performing employee. In addition to identifying such an individual, the supervisor must diagnose the causes of the employee's poor performance *and* develop strategies for improving it.

Diagnosing the Poor Performer Knowing that a person is performing poorly is vastly different from knowing *why* a person is performing poorly. Poor performance can be highlighted by performance-appraisal ratings, behavior (missed deadlines, tardiness, absenteeism, poor work habits, or insubordination), or other such violations of performance expectations. Once poor performance has been observed, then the manager must determine its cause in order to find the appropriate remedy.

Managers usually assign blame for poor performance based on the attribution process. Recall that, in Chapter 3, we identified three principles people use to attribute the causes of behavior to internal or external causes: distinctiveness, consistency, and consensus. Internal causes are associated with the individual performer—that person's skills, abilities, effort, and personality. External causes are associated with the environment—task difficulty, resource availability, interpersonal demands, and information availability.[38] For example, if an employee is consistently absent from work, the employer needs to determine whether the absences are due to factors the employee can or cannot control. The "FOCUS ON: Flexible Work Schedules" describes some solutions to employee absenteeism and turnover.

In addition to the three principles for determining whether poor performance can be attributed to the individual or the environment, the fundamental attribution error will also influence the determination of blame. Supervisors are likely to believe that poor performance is caused by internal (or personal) failings of the subordinate. Alternatively, subordinates are likely to attribute their failure to external (or environmental) factors out of their control. Thus, because of their different perspectives, supervisors and employees rarely agree on the cause of poor performance.

---

[38]G. P. Latham, L. L. Cummings, and T. R. Mitchell, "Behavioral Strategies to Improve Productivity," *Organizational Dynamics* (Winter 1981): 5–23.

Focus on

*Flexible
Work
Schedules*

Pioneers of the New Balance

When most people think about flexible work schedules, they think of flextime: a core of hours during the day or week in which all employees must work and a range of times, or "flexband," in which employees can choose to work. But flexible work schedules can cover more than just this arrangement. They also include unconventional work hours, part-time work, job sharing, leaves of absence, and working at home. Flexible time schedules can, from the company's view, allow employees to have more pliable hours (one mechanism to attract and retain top-caliber people), foster a sense of empowerment among workers and a sense that the companies trust them, and enable dual career parents to integrate work and family concerns more effectively. It turns out that employees with these flexible arrangements are fiercely loyal, and they strive to prove themselves worthy of the company's trust. While they do take on fewer projects and clock less time, flextime managers say their truncated hours force them to be better managers, delegating real responsibility to their subordinates, planning ahead, and setting priorities rather than treating marginal issues like crises.

Job-sharers Joan Girardi and Stephanie Kahn worked together enrolling college students as cardholders. Together they were responsible for 20 percent of American Express's new personal accounts. Kahn worked on Monday, Tuesday, and Thursday; Girardi on Tuesday, Wednesday, and Friday. They split the work by marketing channels. Girardi, who handled direct mail, exceeded her goal by 12 percent; Kahn, who oversaw telemarketing and the "Take-One" displays, beat her goal by 8 percent.

Part-time employment also enables skilled people to keep up with their skills. For example, 23 percent of the women taking maternity leave from Aetna did not return. The director of family services noted that those who were not returning tended to be high performers. They strived to be high performers in everything. They wanted to be good parents and felt they had to make a decision between home and work. When Aetna began offering a six-month unpaid maternity leave, it also offered its leave-taking employees a part-time option after the leave expired. The result: the maternity drop-out figure was cut in half.

In an ideal work world, employees would be compensated for their performance rather than their "face time" (or presence at the job). Anne Brown, a vice-president in the money market group at Goldman Sach, sells fixed income securities to big institutions. She works on Monday, Tuesday, Thursday, and every other Friday. Her salary and bonus are docked by a third to account for the time she spends at home; but her bonus—the largest part of the remuneration of a successful Wall Street employee—is specifically designed to reward performance. At Lotus, the nine teams of job sharers ranked among the company's top performers in the annual merit raise appraisals.

With the changing demographics of the work force, there will be big payoffs for companies that can accommodate workers' needs with flexible schedules. Some of their most prized assets—high performing employees—will stay on the job. Says consultant Margaret Regan of Towers Perrin, "You'll know it's the 21st century when we no longer equate presence with performance."

Source: Alan Deutschman, "Pioneers of the New Balance," *Fortune,* May 20, 1991, 60–68.

Managers can, however, ask themselves a series of questions (listed in Figure 13–10) to develop a systematic understanding of the basis for the poor performance. These questions assume that the poorly performing individual is one who is capable, but for whatever reason (or reasons) is not performing at

| FIGURE 13-10 | ▶ Determining the Cause of Poor Performance |

Ability

Has the individual performed at a higher level in the past?

Is the performance deficiency total, or is it confined to particular tasks?

How well do the individual's capabilities match the job's selection criteria?

Has the individual been properly trained for the current task requirements?

Support

Have clear and challenging task goals been set?

Are other employees having difficulty with the same tasks?

Is the job properly designed to achieve a "best fit" with the individual's capabilities?

Do any policies and/or procedures inhibit task performance?

Is the manager providing adequate feedback?

Is the individual being fairly compensated?

Is the work environment comfortable?

Is the manager providing sufficient empathy and emotional support?

Are the individual's coworkers providing sufficient emotional support?

Has the manager actually encouraged high performance?

Effort

Does the individual lack enthusiasm for work in general? For the assigned task in particular?

Are individuals with similar abilities performing at higher levels?

Has the individual been properly recognized for past accomplishments?

Are rewards and incentives provided on a performance-contingent basis?

Is the individual aware of possible rewards and incentives?

Does the individual have an appropriate role model?

Source: John Schermerhorn, William Gardner, and Thomas Martin, "Management Dialogues: Turning on the Marginal Performer," *Organizational Dynamics* (Spring 1990): 47–59.

expected levels. Because of the theoretical expectations derived from the expectancy theory, marginal performance can arise from lack of ability, effort, support, or some combination of these factors.

To maximize ability, the manager is concerned primarily with ensuring or achieving a match between the skills of the employee and the task. Matches may be created by altering the skills of the employee through training, changing the job so it better fits the individual, or switching employees to create better fit. To maximize support, the manager's task is to ensure that the marginal employee has the resources necessary to accomplish the task and to help remove obstacles to high performance. The manager must create a supportive work environment through the use of clear performance expectations, adaptive job designs, better interpersonal relations, more performance specific feedback, and the elimination of unnecessary job/performance constraints. To maximize effort, the manager must convey to the marginal employee that his or her performance falls below standard and that this substandard performance has adverse consequences on other employees, groups, and the organization as a whole. Finally, the manager can serve both as a positive role model and as a provider of clear, positive, performance-specific rewards.

In motivating the poor performer, managers must:

1. Recognize that marginal performers are a source of productivity gains for organizations.
2. Recognize the need to implement positive turnaround strategies for dealing with marginal performers.
3. Be ready to accept at least partial responsibility for the subordinate's marginal performance.[39]

Many of the strategies needed to transform poor performers into good performers have been described in previous sections of this chapter: appropriately designed incentive systems, goal-setting activities, and effective performance appraisal systems. While these mechanisms are useful to all employees, they are uniquely important to the poorly performing employee.

These are not easy tasks to accomplish in most organizations. Given the cost of replacing poorly performing employees or, even worse, the cost to the organization of lost productivity[40] if the employee remains, these factors are well worth considering and implementing in organizations.

SUMMARY ◆◆◆◆◆◆

This chapter examined how managers and other organizational decision makers can maintain employee performance. The first component of this process is the organization's incentive system. Composed of both economic and noneconomic elements, the incentive system is the most visible way in which an organization can influence employee behavior. Wages, salaries, and nonrecurring economic benefits can influence an employee's behavior if the employee is capable of high performance, believes it is beneficial, sees the relationship between high performance and monetary rewards, values economic rewards, and is involved in tasks where performance can be measured. The incentive structure also must be consistent with the nature of the work performed (individual- or group-based). Examples of individual-based incentive structures are piecerate or standard-hour systems. Group-based incentive structures include the Scanlon plan and employee stock-ownership plans.

Employee benefits are the indirect economic rewards that employees receive. One of the more recent innovations in the benefits area has been the development of cafeteria benefit plans. In such plans, the employees are allowed to customize their benefits package within a prescribed dollar amount per employee. Noneconomic benefits include the inherent interest of the job, the quality of the work life, the status associated with belonging to an organization, and the amount of power and autonomy associated with a position.

Unfortunately, having a well-developed incentive system is not sufficient to ensure high levels of employee performance. In addition, employees need performance goals. Goals specify the direction for action and the quantity of work to be accomplished. For goals to

---

[39] John Schermerhorn, William Gardner, and Thomas Martin, "Management Dialogues: Turning on the Marginal Performer," *Organizational Dynamics* (Spring 1990): 58.

[40] As we suggested in Chapter 11, each employee is a potential half-million-dollar investment or liability for the organization.

be effective, they must (1) specify the task to be accomplished, (2) indicate how performance will be measured, (3) specify the level of performance to be achieved, (4) specify a deadline for performance, (5) be accepted by the employee, and (6) set priorities for performance and coordination.

For an employee to reach a goal, feedback about performance is crucial. Providing employees with feedback is one of the purposes of a performance appraisal system. These systems have three major functions: providing feedback, distributing rewards, and counseling employees. Unfortunately, these three functions are often in conflict with each other. If managers use the same performance-appraisal interview to accomplish all three objectives, employees are likely to experience conflict in their responses. Should they present their accomplishments in the best pos-sible light, or should they identify various problems and weaknesses encountered over the past year? In addition, the anxiety created by the evaluation may be so great that employees are unable to comprehend or even *hear* the information being provided.

To improve the organization's performance appraisal system, evaluations should be (1) based on observable behavior, (2) conducted by raters who have the opportunity to observe the ratee, (3) conducted several times a year, and (4) conducted with instruments that measure behavior, not traits.

Even if all these components are in place, the manager is still likely to face the marginal performer. With the poor performer, the manager must first determine the cause of the employee's poor performance and then develop strategies for improving productivity.

Key Terms

Behaviorally anchored rating scale (BARS) Employee evaluation format in which the organization analyzes a particular job to determine what types of behavior reflect varying degrees of performance, using actual descriptions of behavior to define the ratings.

Comparable worth discrimination Discrimination in which men are paid more than women for jobs that are substantially equal in terms of skill, ability, and effort required.

Compensation system A major way an organization conveys to its employees what it wants done and how they should behave, consisting of wages or salaries, benefits, non-recurring financial rewards, and noneconomic rewards.

Critical incidence file A memory aid containing examples of an employee's behavior to help managers prepare for performance appraisals.

Employee Stock Ownership Plan (ESOP) Group-based incentive plan in which an organization contributes to a trust fund to buy stock, which is allocated to employees based on seniority.

Goal A specific direction for action and a specific quantity of work to be accomplished.

Goal commitment Extension of effort, over time, toward the accomplishment of a goal and an unwillingness to give up or lower the goal.

Piece-rate plan Incentive plan in which employees are paid a given rate for each unit produced.

Standard hour rate Payment rate per hour based on the amount of time, determined by industrial engineering standards, that it should take to produce each unit.

Trait-rating scale Employee evaluation format that asks the rater to evaluate the ratee on such factors as dependability, cooperation, leadership, obedience, and loyalty.

Discussion Questions

1. Which of the major systems for maintaining performance is likely to be most effective among professional employees? Among blue-collar employees? Among white-collar employees? Why?

2. What factors, besides overt and intentional discrimination, might lead to the large difference in wages between the average male and female worker?

3. In early 1989, controversy arose over what was called the "mommy track" in organizations. What are the advantages and disadvantages to working women for organizations to have two career tracks: one for women with children and one for women without children?

4. How might a cafeteria benefits plan ensure that employers do not discriminate *in favor* of employees with families?

5. Even employees who are rated highly believe that performance appraisals are arbitrary and capricious. How might the typical organization respond to this charge? How might the review process be altered to increase its fairness?

6. In evaluating an employee's poor performance, what is likely to be the manager's first impression about the cause of the poor performance? What factors might lead the manager to adjust this evaluation?

7. How might a manager go about structuring an employees' workday to improve his or her performance?

If You Want to Know More

Maintaining employee performance is probably one of the most written-about topics in organizational behavior. Despite the sheer magnitude of the writings, a number of books and articles stand out. In the area of compensation systems, the interested reader might consider Frederick Hill's *Compensation Decision Making*, published in 1987 by Dryden Press. Marc Wallace and Charles Fay have also written an interesting (and shorter) book on compensation systems, *Compensation Theory and Practice*, which was published in 1983 by Kent Publishing Company. Finally, David Balkin and Luis Gomez-Mejia have written a book that addresses many of the issues surrounding organizational compensation systems. Entitled *New Perspectives on Compensation*, it was published by Prentice-Hall in 1987. Readers interested in the financial consequences of poor performance might refer to Wayne Cascio's 1982 book, *Costing Human Resources: The Financial Impact of Behavior in Organizations*, published by Kent Publishing Company.

Performance appraisal is the subject of a large number of books. For a concise view of the current state of the art, the reader is directed towards the following two books: John Bernardin and Richard Beatty's 1984 *Performance Appraisal: Assessing Human Behavior at Work*, published by Kent and Stephen Carroll; and Craig Schneier's *Performance Appraisal and Review Systems*, published in 1982 by Scott, Foresman. For a more detailed review of performance appraisal systems, see Frank Landy and James Farr's *The Measurement of Work Performance*, published in 1983 by Academic Press.

While reams have been published on goal setting, one of the more readable manuscripts is Edwin Locke and Gary Latham's *Goal Setting: A Motivational Technique That Works*, a 1984 book published by Prentice-Hall. An interesting review of the research on goal setting up through 1990 can be found in E. A. Locke and Gary Latham's *A Theory of Goal Setting and Task Performance*, published by Prentice-Hall. Another review of the effects of goal setting can be found in A. J. Mento, R. P. Steel, and R. J. Karren's "A Meta-Analytic Study of the Effects of Goal Setting on Task Perfor-

mance," in *Organizational Behavior and Human Decision Processes* 39 (1987): 52–83.

Finally, to understand more about how to handle the poorly performing employee, the interested reader should consult a review article by T. R. Mitchell, S. G. Green, and R. E. Wood, entitled "An Attributional Model of Leadership and the Poor Performing Employee." It may be found in *Research in Organizational Behavior*, vol. 3, eds. B. Staw and L. Cummings (Greenwich, Conn.: JAI Press, 1981): 197–234, as well as in pp. 5–23 of the 1981 *Organizational Dynamics* publication entitled "Behavioral Strategies for Enhancing Productivity." A more recent article on the topic was published in *Organizational Dynamics* (Spring 1990) by J. R. Schermerhorn, W. L. Gardner, and T. N. Martin entitled "Management Dialogues: Turning on the Poor Performer."

On Your Own

◆◆◆

Developing a Performance Appraisal System for Faculty How would you go about setting up a performance appraisal system to evaluate faculty at your university or college? Think about your instructor for this course. First, consider what you as a student think are the important dimensions of an instructor's behavior. Next, consider what other faculty (your instructor's peers) might identify as important dimensions of behavior. What about the dean of the business school or the president of the university or college? List the major dimensions of behavior that are important to each:

Students	Other Faculty	Dean	President
_____	_____	_____	_____
_____	_____	_____	_____
_____	_____	_____	_____
_____	_____	_____	_____
_____	_____	_____	_____
_____	_____	_____	_____
_____	_____	_____	_____

How are each of these dimensions valued by these four different constituencies? What would be good behavioral indicators of each? How would you choose which dimensions to use in the evaluation of your instructor?

CLOSING CASE

CHAPTER 13

THE MANAGER'S MEMO

FROM: P. Wilcox, President

TO: O. Hansen, Vice President, Human Resources Management

RE: Dissatisfied Former Employees

As you know, within the last six months, three of our most capable divisional vice presidents have left the company to take positions with our major competitor. Clearly, pay was not the problem, as they received a level of salary plus bonuses that was until then unprecedented in the industry.

From recent conversations with them and some of the remaining executive team, all I have been able to learn is that there is some dissatisfaction with our performance appraisal system. One of the departing executives made some comment about there being no incentive to be innovative.

I really don't understand these remarks. We spent a great deal of time trying to develop a performance rating scale that is fair and rewards results, not personality. I cannot think of a better system than our method of assigning points for each product that exceeds expected performance, deducting points for failed ideas, and paying a generous bonus based on accumulated points. The system admittedly penalizes executives for failures, but that encourages them to think carefully before launching into risky ventures. Furthermore, one of the departing executives never had a failing idea. Clearly, the performance-rating system was very good to them.

I would appreciate your letting me know what you learned from your exit interviews with these former executives. If the performance appraisal system really is the reason they left, how can we modify it to avoid losing our key people in the future?

Case Discussion Questions

Assume you are the vice-president of the human resources management division, and respond to the president's memo. Assume that the executives who left were in fact dissatisfied with the performance appraisal system. From the information given in the president's memo, what types of compensation was the company providing generously, and what types were lacking? How can the company modify its performance appraisal system to provide the missing rewards?

EXERCISE

PART 4:

The Hovey and Beard Company

The Hovey and Beard Company manufactured a variety of wooden toys including animals, pull toys, and the like. The toys were manufactured by a transformation process that began in the wood room. There, toys were cut, sanded, and partially assembled. Then the toys were dipped into shellac and sent to the painting room.

In years past, the painting had been done by hand, with each employee working with a given toy until its painting was completed. The toys were predominately two colors, although a few required more than two colors. Now, and in response to increased demand for the toys, the painting operation was changed so that the painters sat in a line by an endless chain of hooks. These hooks moved continuously in front of the painters and passed into a long horizontal oven. Each painter sat in a booth designed to carry away fumes and to backstop excess paint. The painters would take a toy from a nearby tray, position it in a jig inside the painting cubicle, spray on the color according to a pattern, and then hang the toy on a passing hook. The rate at which the hooks moved was calculated by the engineers so that each painter, when fully trained, could hang a painted toy on each hook before it passed beyond reach.

The painters were paid on a group bonus plan. Since the operation was new to them, they received a learning bonus that decreased by regular amounts each month. The learning bonus was scheduled to vanish in six months, by which time it was expected that they would be on their own—that is, able to meet the production standard and to earn a group bonus when they exceeded it.

Questions

1. Assume that the training period for the new job set-up has just begun. What change do you predict in the level of output of the painters? Why?
2. What other predictions regarding the behavior of these painters do you make based upon the situation described so far?

Source: Abridged and adapted from Chapter 10, "Group Dynamics and Intergroup Relations," by George Strauss and Alex Bavelas from *Money and Motivation*, ed. William F. Whyte. Copyright © 1955 by Harper & Row. Published by permission of Harper & Row, Publishers, Inc.

CASE

PART 4:
Perfect Pizzeria

Perfect Pizzeria in Southville, a town in deep southern Illinois, is the second-largest franchise of the chain in the United States. The headquarters is located in Phoenix, Arizona. Although the business is prospering, it has employee and managerial problems.

Each operation has one manager, an assistant manager, and from two to five night managers. The managers of each pizzeria work under an area supervisor. There are no systematic criteria for being a manager or becoming a manager trainee. The franchise has no formalized training period for the manager. No college education is required. The managers for whom the case observer worked during a four-year period were relatively young (ages 24 to 27) and only one had completed college. They came from the ranks of night managers or assistant managers, or both. The night managers were chosen for their ability to perform the duties of the regular employees. The assistant managers worked a two-hour shift during the luncheon period five days a week to gain knowledge about bookkeeping and management. Those becoming managers remained at that level unless they expressed interest in investing in the business.

The employees were mostly college students, with a few high-school students performing the less challenging jobs. Since Perfect Pizzeria was located in an area with few job opportunities, it had a relatively easy task of filling its employee quotas. All the employees, with the exception of the manager, were employed part time. Consequently, they worked for less than the minimum wage.

The Perfect Pizzeria system is devised so that food and beverage costs and profits are set up according to a percentage. If the percentage of food unsold or damaged in any way is very low, the manager gets a bonus. If the percentage is high, the manager does not receive a bonus; rather, he or she receives only his or her normal salary.

There are many ways in which the percentage can fluctuate. Since the manager cannot be in the store 24 hours a day, some employees make up for their paychecks by helping themselves to the food. When a friend comes in to order a pizza, extra ingredients are put on the friend's pizza. Occasional nibbles by 18 to 20 employees throughout the day at the meal table also raise the percentage figure. An occasional bucket of sauce may be spilled or a pizza accidentally burned. Sometimes the wrong size of pizza may be made.

In the event of an employee mistake or a burned pizza by the oven operator, the expense is supposed to come from the individual. Because of peer pressure, the night manager seldom writes up a bill for the erring employee. Instead, the establishment takes the loss and the error goes unnoticed until the end of the month when the inventory is taken. That's when the manager finds out that the percentage is high and that there will be no bonus.

In the present instance, the manager took retaliatory measures. Previously, each employee was entitled to a free pizza, salad, and all the soft drinks he or she could drink for every 6 hours of work. The manager raised this figure from 6 to 12 hours of work. However, the employees had received these 6-hour benefits for a long time. Therefore, they simply took advantage of the situation whenever the manager or the assistant was not in the building. Though the night manager theoretically had complete control of the operation in the evenings, he did not command the respect that the manager or assistant manager did. This was because he received the same pay as the regular employees; he could not reprimand other employees; and he was basically the same age or sometimes even younger than the other employees.

Thus, apathy grew within the pizzeria. There seemed to be a further separation between the manager and his workers, who started out as a closely knit group. The manager made no attempt to alleviate the problem, because he felt it would iron itself out. Either the employees that were dissatisfied would quit or they would be content to put up with the new regulations. As it turned out, there was a rash of employee dismissals. The manager had no problem in filling the vacancies with new workers, but the loss of key personnel was costly to the business.

With the large turnover, the manager found he had to spend more time in the building, supervising and sometimes taking the place of inexperienced workers. This was in direct violation of the franchise regulation, which stated that a manager would act as a supervisor and at no time take part in the actual food preparation. Employees were not placed under strict supervision with the manager working alongside them. The operation no longer worked smoothly because of differences between the remaining experienced workers and the manager concerning the way in which a particular function should be performed.

Within a two-month period, the manager was again free to go back to his office and leave his subordinates in charge of the entire operation. During this two-month period, the percentage had returned to the previous low level and the manager received a bonus each month. The manager felt that his problems had been resolved and that conditions would remain the same, since the new personnel had been properly trained.

It didn't take long for the new employees to become influenced by the other employees. Immediately after the manager had returned to his supervisory role, the percentage began to rise. This time the manager took a bolder step. He cut out any benefits that the employees had—no free pizzas, salads, or drinks. With the job market at an even lower ebb than usual, most employees were forced to stay. The appointment of a new area supervisor made it impossible for the manager to "work behind the counter," since the supervisor was centrally located in Southville.

The manager tried still another approach to alleviate the rising percentage problem and maintain his bonus. He placed a notice on the bulletin board, stating that if the percentage remained at a high level, a lie-detector test would be given to all employees. All those found guilty of taking or purposefully wasting food or drinks would be immediately terminated. This did not have the desired effect on the employees, because they knew if they were all subjected to the test, all would be found guilty and the manager would have to dismiss all of them. This would leave him in a worse situation than ever.

Even before the following month's percentage was calculated, the manager knew it would be high. He had evidently received information from one of the night managers about the employees' feelings toward the notice. What he did not expect was that the percentage would reach an all-time high. That is the state of affairs at the present time.

Questions for Discussion

1. How would you characterize the compensation plan for managers and student workers at Perfect Pizzeria? Would you want to work there?
2. What kinds of group dynamics are at work at Perfect Pizzeria during the case?
3. What do you think of the manager's attempts to solve the problems at Perfect Pizzeria? What would you suggest he do instead?

P A R T

FIVE

THE LARGER CONTEXT
OF ORGANIZATIONAL BEHAVIOR

14 ▶	The Environment
15 ▶	Technology
16 ▶	Organizational Structure and Design
17 ▶	Managing Change
18 ▶	Diversity in the Workplace: Managing in the Twenty-First Century

THE ENVIRONMENT

REAL WORLD HIGH TECH   ◆◆◆◆◆◆◆

On a cold day in Toledo, Northern Ohio's flat terrain offers a remarkably clear view of many of the area's industrial buildings and their apparent idleness. The Toledo companies that serve in the shadow of Detroit's auto industry are learning the harsh lessons of survival in a shrinking market. Some, like Toledo-based Ohio Belting and Transmission (OB&T), face not only Toledo's depressed economy, but also the difficulties of adjusting to an industry-wide transition into high-technology manufacturing. OB&T is a distributor of electrical products—components for the latest wave of high-tech manufacturing miracles. OB&T president and owner Tom Volk, along with other members of the Association of High Tech Distributors, is busy wrestling with what the term "high tech" really means.

"What's high tech today won't be high tech tomorrow," says Volk. He notes that companies who don't stay on top of the latest technology, or who overstock products that may become obsolete, risk putting themselves on the "bleeding edge" of technology. While traditional distributors have much of their assets in inventory, the shelves of OB&T's small warehouse seem barren by comparison.

Volk has a business credo that accepts change as inevitable, emphasizes being proactive rather than reactive, and sticks to a few simple rules. "I wanted to be in a business where there was an opportunity for the distributor to put in value beyond a basic distribution value," says Volk. One of OB&T's most popular customer service programs is its customer education seminars. For a nominal fee, customers get instruction that begins with the basics of electrical engineering and progresses up to the application of some of OB&T's most sophisticated products.

Despite the many strikes against it, OB&T survives, maintains market share, and positions itself for success in a region that Volk believes is destined to rekindle its love affair with industry. "Toledo is a good place to live," says Volk. "We've got water, we've got land. Long-term, Toledo has to be good. This is just a shakeout."

Source: Adapted from L. Ulanoff, "Real World High Tech," *Electrical Wholesaling*, April 1991, 43-47, 73.

INTRODUCTION

Up to this point, this book has focused on the challenge of understanding and managing resources *within* an organization. We have explored how individuals behave, how groups interact, and how managers can use knowledge of individual behavior and group interaction to manage an organization's work force effectively. But the picture is not yet complete. The management of resources within an organization becomes important only if managers have acquired resources from the environment to manage. Managing the acquisition—and retention—of those resources presents another challenge altogether.

The purpose of this chapter is to paint a picture of the environment in which today's organizations must function. This picture will have two parts: first, the form and content of environmental *demands* on behavior in and of organizations; and second, some *strategies* that organizations use to manage those demands. Chapter 15 will discuss one particularly important source of influence in today's business environment: technology. Chapter 16 follows with an examination of the ways in which organizations are designed both to adapt to the demands of the environment and to manage internal conflicts. Chapter 17 details the problems organizations face and the strategies they use when organizations find that they need to change. Finally, Chapter 18 will close Part 5 with some thoughts about what new challenges the environment is likely to present organizations in the future.

THE MYTH OF THE CLOSED SYSTEM

Large work organizations often are talked about as if they were **closed systems**: completely self-contained machines that function apart from and are unaffected by what goes on around them. Nothing could be further from the truth. Consider the convents and abbeys of the Middle Ages—the ultimate attempts to design completely self-contained social systems:

> Needs were kept to a minimum; foods were grown within; and many required utensils, tools, and clothing were made by the abbey's available labor. An attempt was made, consciously, to isolate the organizations as much as possible from the secular world outside. But, abbeys were peopled by people, usually of one sex, and humans are mortal. This meant that new members had to be recruited from the outside, which required the organization to maintain relations with sources of recruits. . . . Moreover, these religious organizations had land, and to maintain their land, it was necessary to ensure a position of social legitimacy and political acceptance so that other groups would not attempt to seize the land for themselves.[1]

The message here is that it is virtually impossible for any organization to be truly isolated or insulated from environmental influence or interaction. The abbeys and convents of the Middle Ages intended to be *totally* apart from the less-than-pure influence of society at large. Yet even these organizations were *required* for survival to interact with their environment.

Many students probably think of the university classroom as a closed system. The professor's management of classroom activities appears to be totally

---

[1]J. Pfeffer and G. Salancik, *The External Control of Organizations* (New York: Harper & Row, 1978), 2–3.

independent of the larger university system. In many universities the *right* of the professor to be independent in managing classroom activities appears to be protected under the doctrine of academic freedom—a doctrine that says that since the professor is an expert, no one has the right to tell the professor what to do in the classroom.

A professor's academic freedom in the classroom is an illusion, however. As depicted in Figure 14–1, the university classroom is hardly immune to influence from the external environment. Behaviors in the university classroom are influenced dramatically by what goes on in the larger university environment. If an instructor is good, word gets around, the number of students interested in taking the course goes up, and the instructor has a larger class to manage. Fluctuations in the number of students desiring to take the course also depend on factors over which the instructor has little or no control, such as the number of students that the university admits for study, and whether the course is required or elective. Social trends may make some areas of study more popular than others. For example, international management and negotiations recently have become hot topics for MBA courses.

What goes on in the classroom also will be influenced by the *quality* of the students (Are they highly intelligent? Are they well prepared for class?) and the

FIGURE 14–1 ▶ **Example of an Open System**

The college classroom may seem to students to be a closed system where the instructor completely controls what goes on. In reality, classroom activities are open to influence from a host of environmental forces including social trends, accrediting agencies, curriculum committees, and even the kinds of jobs that are in demand.

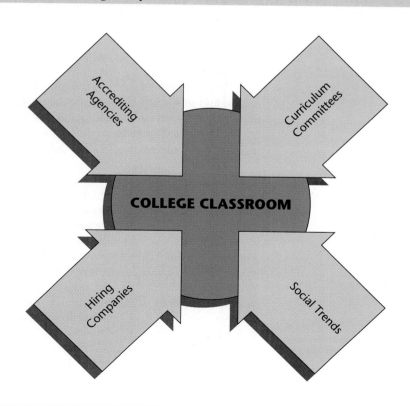

expectations they bring to the course from other courses they have taken at the university. What happens in the classroom will further be influenced by developments in the field that need to be added to the curriculum. When the U.S. tax laws were dramatically changed in 1986, the contents of tax-accounting courses had to be changed as well. Similarly, developments in teaching materials—such as the availability of better texts, videos, or computer programs—also change what happens in the classroom. Finally, what happens in the classroom often is *regulated* by college, university, or departmental curriculum committees, accrediting agencies (such as the American Association of Colleges and Schools of Business), and even licensing boards (such as the graduate college committees that decide who will be awarded Ph.D.s and therefore have the proper credentials for university instruction). Even the "customers" of the university—the companies that employ its graduates—indirectly influence what goes on in the classroom. If companies are interested in hiring business students with some understanding of international business issues, then international business issues are likely to turn up in business course curriculums.

The importance of environmental considerations in understanding behavior of and in organizations is illustrated in two concepts: open systems theory and resource dependence. Their importance to the relationship between organizations and their environments in turn depends upon a third (and familiar) concept: perception.

Open Systems Theory

Both the abbeys and convents of the Middle Ages and the university classrooms of the twentieth century demonstrate that organizations are open systems. An **open system** is an organization whose activities are inescapably influenced by its environment. Open systems share several defining characteristics, as shown in Figure 14–2.[2]

First, all open systems take inputs from the environment. For abbeys, convents, and university classrooms, the most salient input is people. For a manufacturing firm, the input might be raw materials such as iron ore, leather, or grain. However, for most organizations, inputs also include a production technology, the building that houses the organization, and even past learning.

Second, all open systems transform the inputs received. The key here is that the organization does something to the inputs that *adds value* beyond any intrinsic value of the inputs themselves. For instance, leather might be made into shoes, steel might be made into automobiles, paper into books, or a professor's time into learning by students. If nothing else, some organizations (such as distributors like Ohio Belting and Transmission, featured in the opening vignette for this chapter) *organize and store* inputs so that another organization can use them. Typically, the transformation process is *cyclical*, meaning that most organizations don't just take *any* inputs and transform them in *any* way. Organizations maintain some consistency over time; they repeat the same transformation cycle. The organization accepts roughly the same inputs and uses roughly the same transformation processes over and over.

Third, the transformation process creates an *output*. An organization's outputs are its goals: shoes, automobiles, worker satisfaction, profit, perhaps a living wage for the organization's work force. The last two examples are partic-

---

[2] D. Katz and R. L. Kahn, *The Social Psychology of Organizations* (New York: Wiley & Sons, 1978), 23–30.

FIGURE 14–2 ▶ Defining Characteristics of Open Systems

The environment provides inputs such as raw materials and labor. The organization transforms these inputs to add value to them. Clients or customers in the environment then consume the outputs of this transformation process. The process is cyclical; in return for consuming the organization's outputs, the environment provides new inputs for the organization to restart the transformation cycle.

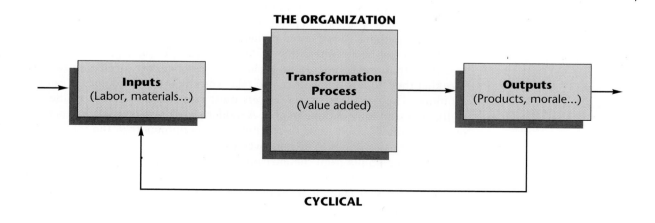

ularly telling, since most organizations have as a goal continued survival over time. In fact, some organization theorists suggest that survival is *the* goal of organizations—that all organizations, from the first cave clans to General Motors, exist primarily to transform inputs into survival.[3] Any other outputs produced by an organization (such as automobiles or shoes) are simply means for ensuring survival.

Finally, the idea that organizations exist as a means for survival has an important implication for the open systems model. The outputs of an organization must do more to enhance the organization's survival than to discourage it; in other words, the net value of the transformation process must be positive. If the net value of the transformation process is more destructive than creative (for instance, if byproducts of the transformation process such as pollutants or worker dissatisfaction are greater than the value of what is created), the organization eventually will lose the ability to take inputs from the environment and transform them.

Resource Dependence

The open systems model of organizations exposes the susceptibility of organizations to environmental influence, and the origin of this influence is *resource dependence* (for a definition of resource dependence, see Chapter 8). In Figure 14–2, the organization represents the transformation process. To do anything, it is *dependent* upon the environment for resources—inputs such as raw materials, labor, and energy. The organization is even dependent upon the environ-

---

[3] Pfeffer and Salancik, *The External Control of Organizations*, 2–3.

ment for a transformation technology. Great money-making inventions often are precisely transformation processes: new ways to turn raw materials and labor into something worth considerably more than the value of the inputs. However an organization rarely develops a transformation process completely from scratch. Prior transformation systems, their parts or components, and even education are resources available in the organization's environment. These resources play a role in the development of innovative transformation technologies, and the organization therefore is dependent on them.

Organizations also are dependent upon the environment to accept or consume their outputs. As we noted earlier, a key characteristic of open systems is that there must be a positive flow of "value added" for an organization to survive. In a traditional agricultural society, for instance, the farmers must make sure that they do not simply take and take from their farmland until it can give no more. Their transformation process must give something back to the land so that the land can continue to give. A modern work organization is dependent upon consumers' willingness to pay more for its outputs than the total cost of transforming those inputs. If not, over time the organization clearly loses its ability to take inputs from the environment. The organization fails to survive.

The resource dependence described here between organizations and their environments is an example of a power relationship, discussed in Chapter 8. As companies like Ohio Belting and Transmission quickly learn during recessionary times, the environment has power over organizations because organizations depend upon the environment for resources. Organizations in turn may gain power over their environment when the environment depends upon the organization's unique transformation skills.

Knowledge of the Environment

Open systems theory and resource dependence depict the organization in a fluid relationship with its environment. Organizations cannot be closed, self-contained entities. Organizations depend upon the environment for inputs to transform, for energy, labor, and ideas to carry out the transformation, and for consumers who desire their outputs.

A key issue here is that the resource dependence between organizations and their environments is not deterministic. Many changes in an organization's environment are not directly and automatically reflected in commensurate changes in the organization. For example, if Congress passes a law about worker safety, one might suspect that an organization would change its behavior to conform to the law. However, managers in the organization might ignore the law if they feel it will not be enforced. Or they might not even be aware of the change in the law—until one of their employees sues them for a violation!

This example highlights the fact that organizations and their environments usually are loosely coupled. What happens in the environment may or may not be reflected by immediate changes in the organization. **Loose coupling** has both advantages and disadvantages. To carry on an orderly transformation process, organizations must be somewhat insensitive to changes in the environment. An organization that reacts to *everything* that happens in its environment would spend more time reacting to the environment than it would transforming inputs into outputs. On the other hand, an organization that reacts too slowly (or not at all) to important changes in the environment will fail in the struggle to survive.

Perception is an important determinant of how changes in the environment translate into reactions by the organization. In Chapter 3, we learned that people's perception of what goes on in their environment is determined by three processes: attention, construction, and interpretation. How individuals react to something that happens around them will depend on (1) whether they realize that it has occurred, (2) what they decide has occurred, and (3) what importance they attach to what has occurred.

The processes of perception are critical to the way organizations relate to their environments as well. If the government passes a new law, an organization should change its behavior to conform to the law. However, whether an organization does in fact conform to a new law depends on (1) whether the organization is aware that the new law has been passed, (2) whether the organization's lawyers think the law applies to their organization, and finally (3) whether the organization thinks the government is serious about enforcing the law. In effect, unless the organization *perceives* a resource dependence (and therefore the need to change), changes in the environment are unlikely to cause changes in the organization.

The critical role of perception in resource dependence means that an organization's environment does not exist objectively for that organization; instead, the organization's environment is a social construction—a set of beliefs that individuals in the organization construct based on their interactions with and perceptions of the environment.

Organizational theorist Karl Weick has coined the phrase **"enacted environment"** to capture the idea that an organization's environment is sensitive to the organization's perception of that environment,[4] in a way reminiscent of the self-fulfilling prophecies discussed in Chapter 3. An organization does not just perceive its environment; an organization *enacts* its environment—it perceives, reacts to, and, *by its reactions*, influences the future perceptions it has of its environment. A top management team's beliefs that the union is untrustworthy and adversarial will dictate how top management treats the union (at best cautiously, at worst aggressively) and what information top management collects or attends to about the union's actions. Since management's treatment of the union will not be lost on the union, management's beliefs that the union is untrustworthy and adversarial may turn out to be the very causes of the union acting that way!

The important point here is that while resource dependencies with the environment determine the fate of an organization, it is the organization's *perceptions* of these resource dependencies that determine what actions it takes. These actions in turn influence the nature of the environment that organization perceives.

Examples of the role of perception of the environment in organizations' actions abound. One interpretation of the December 7, 1941, decimation of the U.S. Pacific fleet in Pearl Harbor was that decision makers in Washington, D.C., felt that Japan had neither the capability nor the gall to attack the United States in Hawaii. This turned out to be a disastrously incorrect perception.

In the 1960s, corporate boards and CEOs generally ignored stockholders because they viewed them as an impotent distraction. One CEO summarized the sentiment of the times with this comment about the annual stockholders'

---

[4]Karl E. Weick, "Enactment Processes in Organizations," in *New Directions in Organizational Behavior*, ed. B. M. Staw and G. R. Salancik (Chicago: St. Clair Press, 1977), 267–300.

Traditionally, organizational shareholders kept their hands off of the day-to-day management of major U.S. corporations, perhaps feeling it was not their place to interfere. Today, that perception has changed. Shareholders now intervene in organizational decision making—for example, by taking legal action against corporate management teams that appear to be mismanaging shareholder equity.

meeting: "I don't give a damn about the annual meeting. I'd like to see the thing abolished. The object of our meeting is to end as fast as possible without making a fool of the chairman."[5] In line with this view, corporations rarely if ever responded to stockholder initiatives. No doubt this view of the stockholders' powerlessness was linked to the stockholders' similar perception. Today, all that has changed, however. As stockholders have realized the power they hold by virtue of the resources they control, the have forced a change in perceptions on corporate boards. The corporate boards in turn have responded by altering their behaviors to keep stockholders content and minimize dissident-sponsored revolutions.

THE FORM OF ENVIRONMENTAL FORCES

The open systems and resource dependence orientations highlight the importance of an organization's environment. In this section we will begin to paint a picture of the environment that faces work organizations. This picture includes four dimensions that determine environmental resource dependencies: uncertainty, instability, complexity, and beneficence. The following section examines the particular sources of environmental resource dependencies.

Uncertainty

In Chapter 1, uncertainty was described as a defining characteristic of life in organizations. Uncertainty refers to a lack of information, an inability to know what exactly is going to happen or when. Much of the uncertainty that plagues organizational planning and action comes from the environment. Environmental uncertainty has three components.[6] First is the *lack of clear information* about the state of critical variables in the environment. If you were an automobile manufacturer, it would be critical for you to know the future price of gasoline

---

[5]J. L. Hysom and W. J. Bolce, *Business and Its Environment* (St. Paul, Minn.: West, 1983), 167.

[6]P. R. Lawrence and J. W. Lorsch, *Organization and Environment* (Homewood, Ill.: Richard Irwin, 1964).

so that you would know whether fuel mileage was going to be an important consideration for American consumers. If you were a university, it would be critical for you to know how social trends would change the popularity of certain subject areas in the foreseeable future. If you were a high-tech distributor like Ohio Belting and Transmission, it would be critical for you to know what new inventions were going to appear in the marketplace in the next few years. All of these pieces of information are critical to decision making, yet none of them can be known, only guessed at or estimated.

A second source of environmental uncertainty is the *cause-and-effect relationships* between organizational actions and environmental responses. If banking customers want greater convenience, will putting in automated teller machines respond to that need? Even if organizational actions are followed by the resolution of identified problems, it can be difficult to know if the actions *caused* the problems to be solved. If a bank puts in automated teller machines and customer satisfaction increases, what does that mean? Did the new automated teller machines increase customer satisfaction, or did it increase for other reasons? These causal relationships often cannot be known ahead of time, and sometimes not even afterwards.

Finally, uncertainty also arises because of the *length of feedback cycles* in the response of the environment to organizational planning and action. It may take years for an organization to understand the effectiveness of its work-force recruiting strategy. By the time it finds out whether a particular approach works or not, one or even two more recruiting seasons may have passed, thereby determining the fate of the organization's short-term performance.

In general, uncertainty means that some amount of what an organization does will be wrong because top management is always guessing. Organizations functioning in uncertain environments must distribute the risk inherent in uncertain plans and decisions (for example, by redundancy or diversification) in the hope of winning on the average.

Instability

Instability reflects the rate of change in an organization's environment. The rate of change in the environment determines the necessity for regular evaluation of environmental cues and reaction by the organization. For a company like Ohio Belting and Transmission, for example, product life cycles are extremely short because the advance of technological innovation and invention is so rapid. This means that customers' needs and desires are changing constantly, and an organization in this environment must be willing and able to adapt to these rapidly changing needs to survive. In a rapidly changing environment, an organization must remain flexible and adaptive—it must be prepared to change quickly in response to changes in the environment.

Environmental instability can come in many forms. The last ten years have seen a major Wall Street stock market crash, several foreign invasions by U.S. troops, the total demise of the U.S. savings-and-loan industry, the destruction of the Berlin Wall, an unprecedented number of mergers and acquisitions, and the emergence of the AIDS epidemic. Each of these developments (and many others!) have dramatically changed the nature of the environment that U.S. organizations face. Some of these developments represent long-term environmental shifts, while others are only short-term blips on the environmental horizon. Some instability is even apparently continual, such as the unbelievably rapid evolution of computer software and hardware. All of these developments present opportunities and dangers for organizations that must be evaluated and (possibly) responded to.

Complexity

Complexity refers to the number of environmental cues that are critical to an organization's functioning and therefore must be monitored. A complex environment is one in which there is a lot going on that is important to the functioning of the organization. The U.S. Congress, for example, exists in a very complex environment. Many different interest groups and cause-and-effect relationships must be considered in every decision that is made. If Congress wants to fund a highway project in Georgia, how will environmental protectionists react? How will the residents of other states who wanted highway projects react? How will other interest groups who wanted the money for other projects react?

There are two costs to operating in a complex environment. First, more inputs require more information collection and evaluation if planning and decision making are to be of high quality. (Alternatively, a decision maker in a highly complex environment simply can choose to ignore some of the inputs, as long as the decision maker is willing to accept outcomes that are on the average lower in quality.) Second, environmental complexity generally means that plans and decisions are more constrained by resource dependencies. For example, if each environmental factor that a manager considers eliminates one possible course of action, the end result may be a very small range of realistic alternatives. This could render decision making easy—but only if the decision maker can recognize the implications of all the constraints.

Beneficence

The final dimension of environmental resource dependencies is beneficence. **Beneficence** refers to the generosity, leniency, and helpfulness the environment shows an organization. To grasp the importance of this concept, consider for a moment the fictional tale of two organizations, both located in a small southwestern town. One of the organizations is the city's only junior high school; the other the city's only pool hall. When both organizations run into financial difficulties, what is the environment's reaction? In this tale, the answer is that city tax dollars come to the rescue of the junior high school while the pool hall is allowed to fade away. The fact is that some organizations are likely to be helped by their environment in times of trouble, and some are likely to be attacked. (In this tale, for instance, the financial difficulties of the pool hall stemmed in part from the picketers outside its door threatening to take pictures of patrons—a clear example of a hostile environment.)

Why would an environment be beneficent (helpful) to some organizations and not others? There are two possibilities. First, the stated *goals or values* of an organization may be consistent with those of important resource holders in the environment. The town leadership, for instance, may feel it is important to have a junior high school in town to attract new residents with children. The presence of the junior high school thus is important for symbolic reasons and therefore is supported by its environment. Significantly, support provided to an organization because of its symbolic value may be enough to ensure the organization's survival but *not* its quality—in this case, the quality of education provided.

The beneficence of a business environment can vary tremendously. In a highly competitive business environment, clients may be unforgiving and one serious mistake may put a company out of business. On the other hand, if your company is the sole supplier of a valued service, the environment may cater to your every need. Maxime Faget, for some time the only private party interested in building an industrial space platform, found his environment very beneficent— to the tune of a $700 million federal subsidy for his project.

Environments also may be helpful to an organization if the transformation process it performs is *unique and highly desirable.* In 1987, the U.S. government guaranteed Maxime Faget, a struggling space-technology entrepreneur, $700 million in leases for his privately funded space station. These guarantees were, at the time, incentive enough for the entrepreneur to continue development of his project. Why did the federal government offer this support? The government's $30 billion funding of its own space development efforts had begun to stir strong public opposition and could not be continued. Nevertheless, many in power felt that somehow, U.S. development efforts needed to continue. Supporting a private effort seemed to be a low-cost compromise. Faget's environment (the government, in this case) came to his rescue because his organization provided a transformation process—low-cost, private-sector space station technology development—that was seen in some circles as both essential and unique.[7]

THE CONTENT OF ENVIRONMENTAL FORCES

◆◆◆◆◆◆

The dimensions of environment we have been discussing—uncertainty, instability, complexity, and beneficence—provide us with an understanding of how the forces in an organization's environment vary. But what are these forces? Where do they come from? As shown in Figure 14–3, the next section of this

---

[7] E. Clark and T. Smart, "A Space Station That's Losing Its Boosters," *Business Week*, March 7, 1988, 116–118.

FIGURE 14–3	▶ Sources of External Dependence

Other Organizations
Suppliers: organizations that provide inputs, including capital, raw materials, and labor.
Consumers: organizations that purchase the organization's outputs.
Competitors: other organizations that produce the same outputs.

The Regulatory Environment
Laws and court rulings that legislate the behavior of organizations, what the outputs look like, and how the transformation process creates those outputs.

The Social Environment
Social adjustment: societal trends to which the organization must adjust.
Social responsibility: the need to make sure corporate actions measure up to society's moral and ethical standards.

Technology
Changes in all the different ways available for an organization to transform its inputs into outputs.

---

chapter examines four important sources of external dependence for organizations: other organizations, the regulatory environment, the social environment, and technology.

Other Organizations

Perhaps the most prominent features of any organization's environment are other organizations. Our definition of organizations as open systems provides a framework for understanding what kinds of other organizations are in an organization's environment. An open system takes inputs from the environment, transforms them into outputs, and then provides the outputs to the environment. This three-stage definition of an open system suggests three types of other organizations, corresponding to the stages of input, output, and transformation: suppliers, consumers, and competitors.

Suppliers Suppliers provide an open system its inputs, such as raw materials. A cotton-garment manufacturer needs to have a source of cotton—perhaps a cotton growers' association or a cotton-cloth weaving company. It is important to realize, however, that an organization's inputs include far more than just its raw materials. Labor and capital also are critical inputs to any organization. Labor (the organization's work force) provides the energy to transform the organization's inputs into outputs. Capital is needed to purchase inputs prior to transforming them. The garment manufacturer must buy raw cotton from the cotton growers or buy cotton cloth from cotton weavers. In service organizations, on the other hand, raw materials often are not purchased at all. A carpet-cleaning organization, for example, doesn't *buy* dirty carpets to clean. The service consumer provides the input (the dirty carpets) to the service organization. The service organization then uses labor and a transformation process (in this case, a carpet-cleaning machine) to transform the dirty carpets into clean ones.

All organizations need capital to get started. Capital (money) is needed to purchase the transformation technology and to hire labor. Usually capital also is needed to make contact with consumers through marketing efforts. Sometimes the need for capital is not large. A computer-software-development organization, for example, may start out with one or two programmers working in their garages in their spare time. However, even an organization this small still needs paper and pencils to write computer codes and floppy disks to get its output to potential consumers.

As an organization gets larger, its need for capital grows as well. Large organizations that need lots of capital will have to get it from the environment. Banks often provide business loans to organizations to get them started or to help them develop beyond the scope of their immediate cash resources. An organization also can get capital from the environment by selling shares in the company or publicly issuing stock. When an organization sells shares or issues stock, it is selling its potential to make money through the value added by its transformation process. The person or company who buys the stock, the share-holder, provides the organization capital in exchange for ownership of a piece of the company.

Shareholders are not necessarily inactive observers of an organization's performance. Shareholders and organizations are mutually dependent; organizations are dependent upon their shareholder for financial support, and shareholders depend on the organization to take good care of their capital. As long as an organization provides its shareholders a good return on their investment (through stock dividend payouts or stock-price appreciation), shareholders are likely to leave well enough alone.

But what happens when things are not going well? As part owners of an organization's assets, shareholders have the right to voice their views about how the company should be run. If shareholders think an organization's top management is doing poorly, they can pressure the board of directors—often through election of board officers—to institute major changes. Shareholder activism can be reflected in corporate policy as well. Executive compensation in organizations with powerful and active shareholders tends to be much more performance based.[8] Responsiveness to shareholders can be a mixed blessing, however. If shareholder interests run in the direction of short-term financial gain, top management may find itself selling out the future in order to look good in the present.[9]

As noted in the "INTERNATIONAL FOCUS ON: Shareholder Activism," moves taken by management to defend its company against hostile takeovers have been known to galvanize shareholders into action. If a takeover effort promises to inflate stock prices but results in major changes in management personnel, the management team has an incentive to fight the takeover to preserve its jobs—even though the takeover might be in the best interests of the shareholders. In 1985, the management team at the St. Regis paper company tried to thwart an attempted takeover by buying out the raider's interest in the company at $52 per share when the stock was trading at only $42.25. An angered shareholder group brought suit against the management team for improper use of shareholder equity.[10]

[8]L. R. Gomez-Majia, H. Tosi, and T. Hinkin, "Managerial Control, Performance, and Executive Compensation," *Academy of Management Journal* 30 (1987): 51–70.

[9]C. W. L. Hill, M. A. Hitt, and R. E. Hoskisson, "Declining U.S. Competitiveness: Reflections on a Crisis," *Academy of Management Executive* 2 (1988): 51–60.

[10]R. Greene, "Greenmail: The Backlash," *Forbes*, December 2, 1985, 86–90.

Shareholder Activism

These Mouses Are Roaring Recession in Europe is forcing shareholders to get tough with management, something they're not accustomed to doing. By tradition, European executives have been well shielded by anti-takeover devices and cozy relationships among families and fortunes. Now, institutional investors such as banks are leading an assault on the status quo. When corporate governance becomes an issue, life changes for top managers. They cannot be so easily bailed out of choppy fiscal waters. Major pension funds and insurance companies lobby for more outside directors and greater control over executive pay, all designed to put CEOs on a shorter leash.

In Germany, the German Shareholders' Protection Association has succeeded in increasing stockholders' voting rights at influential companies. The CEO of Continental, a German tiremaker, was forced out after vainly attempting to rebuff a takeover by Pirelli, an Italian tiremaker. In its bid, the Italian company had simply bypassed the CEO, Horst Urban, taking its bid instead directly to the company's chairman, Ulrich Weiss. Urban reacted with a poison pill strategy that failed, and then discovered that the influential Deutsche Bank was on Pirelli's side of the plan. Failing to marshal the necessary support from the German industrial establishment, he had to stop blocking the merger. The year-long intrigue ended in Urban's resignation.

In France, an insurance company with large holdings helped to oust Michel François-Poncet from the chairmanship of the merchant bank Compagnie Financière de Paribas. François-Poncet's fatal error was leading a stalled takeover attempt of Compagnie Navigation Mixte. He paid $1.3 billion for a 40 percent stake, and the company retaliated by purchasing Paribas shares.

Executives are being forced out of companies that run up unmanageable debt or engage in abortive financial maneuvers. After $250 million in trading losses, British company Allied-Lyons announced the early retirement of Chairman Sir Derrick Holden-Brown and CEO Richard G. Martin, because they had made the firm vulnerable to a takeover bid. Also in Britain, the Granada Group PLC held off on a new $280 million stock issue until their debt-happy CEO Derek Lewis was gone.

Companies with good shareholder relationships are not immune to the trend. The chairman of Britain's Imperial Chemical Industries woke up one morning to find that Hanson PLC held 2.85 percent of its shares. Such investments sometimes lead to takeover attempts, forcing the target company to sell off assets. Like other European executives, chairman Sir Denys Henderson is discovering that European investors are mice no more.

Source: "Those Mousy European Investors Begin to Roar," R. A. Melcher, *Business Week*, May 27, 1991, 60–62.

Shareholders also may act to alter company policies for reasons other than personal financial gain. In the 1980s, many companies found themselves the targets of shareholder revolts not because of poor financial performance but because of their unwillingness to cease dealing with South Africa. Shareholders were not disappointed in their firms' financial performance. They were disappointed in their firms' *morality*.

Like capital, the supply of labor is a critical concern for organizations. Acquiring labor usually means dealing with individuals rather than organizations. Individuals respond to job ads and negotiate deals with organizations to compensate them for their efforts. In some cases, organizations in need of short-term assistance may turn to temporary-help organizations that maintain stables of potential employees. They also may turn to "headhunter" firms— companies that specialize in locating labor with the specific talents an organization needs. In effect, these actions are attempts by an organization to delegate aspects of managing this interaction with the environment.

By far the most prominent example of labor organizations are unions. **Unions** are groups of workers that have banded together to give themselves more bargaining power with their employers. An organization and its labor are mutually dependent. There is no company if there is no work force, and there are no jobs for the work force if there is no company. However, for any individual worker this mutual resource dependence is unlikely to be balanced. With rare exceptions, most individual workers probably need their jobs more than the company needs them. It tends to be easier for a company to find a new worker than for a worker to find a new company.

Unions represent an attempt to balance this mutual resource dependence. When workers band together and speak with one voice (that of the union) they can threaten companies with having to replace an entire work force (for instance, because of a strike or walkout). Unions representing a work force can gain concessions that no individual worker would have the power to gain.

Unions initially arose because labor was being exploited by organizations. Management often took advantage of the imbalanced resource dependence between large organizations and individual workers. So workers banded together to form unions and get a better deal. Over many years, though, government legislation has restricted the power of organizations over their work force. Further, the competitive environment of modern business has forced organizations to acknowledge their dependence on their work force. While in the past fair treatment of workers had to be won in hard-fought negotiations between unions and management, today many organizations recognize the shortsightedness of adversarial relations with their workers. Organizations willingly provide their workers fair treatment in the hope that they will return the favor by being loyal, hardworking, and productive contributors. Not surpris-

Recently, unions have tried to expand their control over organizational resource dependencies through secondary boycotts. In a secondary boycott, employees of an organization try to enlist the support of their own organization's customers or suppliers as a way of putting additional pressure on management to make changes. In the secondary boycott pictured here, workers at the Chicago Tribune *encourage consumers to stop buying the newspapers.*

ingly, these dual trends of more legislation guaranteeing workers' rights and greater appreciation by organizations of their dependence upon their work force have decreased the power of unions in modern American business.

Consumers Like suppliers, consumers are a feature of the environment linked in a resource-dependence relationship with the organization. And like suppliers, consumers may be either groups or organizations. As we have noted earlier in the chapter, organizations are highly dependent upon their consumers for resources. Shareholders provide only seed capital for an organization—money to get the input-transformation-output process underway. After that, consumers must compensate the organization for any value added to inputs by the organization's transformation process. This compensation paid to the organization for value added to the inputs is the profit. Some of the profit is returned to shareholders in the form of dividends, to ensure their future support. Some of the profit becomes working capital for the organization and is used to secure future inputs.

The resource-dependence balance between consumers and organizations often favors the consumer. Because organizations depend upon consumers to reimburse them for value added to the inputs, organizations often are willing to tailor their outputs to meet consumer demands. On the other hand, resource dependence can be balanced in favor of the organization when its transformation process is unique or in short supply.

Competitors In addition to suppliers and consumers, organizations also must deal with the existence of competitor organizations in their environment. Competitors stimulate an organization in two major ways: through financial pressure and modeling.

Financial pressure occurs when a competitor can transform the same inputs better, faster, or at lower cost. These characteristics typically make a competitor's outputs more attractive to consumers, therefore undercutting an organization's continued access to working capital. If consumers can get what they want better, faster, or at a lower price elsewhere they will, and an organization's survival will be threatened. Financial pressure will force the organization to look for ways to innovate and streamline in order to survive.

Not surprisingly, competitors themselves usually present the best model of how to respond to competitive pressures in the environment. For example, if consumers discovered that a sports equipment company was producing a new tennis racket that was much easier to play with, financial pressure would be brought to bear on competitors as consumers flocked to purchase the new racket. A suitable competitor response would be to copy and start producing the new racket. But this may not be possible, or at least not easy. Patents may prevent direct copying.

Even in these cases, the behaviors of organizations in the environment may model solutions for a company feeling competitive financial pressure. If it became known that the new tennis racket design was dreamed up in an employee quality circle, the next day some competitors no doubt would institute quality circles for product development. Even if a competitor's outputs or transformation process cannot be copied directly, the behavioral process that led to its competitive edge—such as quality circles or incentive programs—can be copied to help get an organization back into the competitive picture. Many of the most innovative approaches to employee involvement in U.S. corporations today have come from America's "offshore" competitors. The success of these competitors in American markets has put financial pressure on American producers to become better, faster, and cheaper. In many cases the solutions American firms have adopted to become more competitive are modeled after the successes of their offshore competitors.

The Regulatory Environment

In addition to other organizations, a significant feature of any organization's environment is regulation. **Regulation** refers to any way in which the actions of an organization are restricted. Laws are a primary source of regulation. Consumers often think about regulation in terms of laws that prohibit organizations from producing certain outputs or from producing them in certain ways. Drug companies, for instance, are prohibited from marketing untested substances and toy companies are prohibited from marketing dangerous toys. As shown in the "FOCUS ON: The Regulatory Environment," virtually all manufacturing organizations face regulations about such byproducts of the transformation process as carcinogens or toxic pollutants. Regulations also exist to maintain competitiveness in certain industries. For instance, the U.S. government has imposed quotas and heavy duties on some offshore imports to encourage the survival of stateside competitors.

However, regulation goes far beyond legislating the outputs that organizations can provide. Regulations also restrict the kinds of behaviors that organizations can engage in while transforming inputs into outputs. Laws protect the rights of workers by dictating which behaviors will be allowed in organizations and which will not. Some of these laws even include the appointment of a regulatory body that performs a watchdog function to ensure that organizations comply.

A particularly good example of how legislation regulates behavior in organizations are the Guidelines on Sexual Harassment:

> Unwelcome sexual advances, requests for sexual favors, and other verbal or physical conduct of a sexual nature constitute sexual harassment when (1) submission to such conduct is made either explicitly or implicitly a term or condition of an individual's employment, (2) submission to or rejection of such conduct by an individual is used as the basis of employment decisions affecting such individual, or (3) such conduct has the purpose or effect of unreasonably interfering with an individual's work performance or creating an intimidating, hostile, or offensive working environment.[11]

These guidelines have done more than just regulate the sexual behaviors of employees in organizations. They also have led organizations to establish both (1) training programs to help supervisors identify and manage sexual harassment among subordinates and (2) communication channels to help victims of sexual harassment come forward without fear of retribution.

Other examples of regulatory legislation that impacts behavior in organizations include the Americans with Disabilities Act (which has implications for selection, job design, and even building construction), the Equal Pay Act, the Fair Labor Standards Act (all of which regulate compensation of full-time

---

[11]J. Ledvinka, *Federal Regulation of Personnel and Human Resource Management* (Boston: Kent, 1982), 66–67.

The Regulatory Environment

The Greening of Corporate America

Many companies no longer resist clean-up efforts. Instead, they are adopting a stance of "enlightened self-interest." New laws, increased enforcement of existing laws, and the efforts of grass-roots movements are costing companies billions to clean up past problems. Now big business is looking at prevention of pollution as a potential contributor to the bottom line.

Environmental initiatives have been launched by giant firms such as Monsanto, Du Pont, Westinghouse, Allied-Signal, Procter & Gamble, Texaco, Merck, IBM and AT&T. IBM has planned to stop using chlorofluorocarbons, or CFCs, which attack the ozone layer, while Du Pont has plans to develop CFC substitutes at a cost of $1 billion. The American Paper Institute, a trade organization, announced that recycled paper will double as a percentage of all paper produced from 1988 to 1995.

New hazardous waste clean-up ventures have been launched by both big and small companies. While industry giants such as Rhône-Poulenc and Westinghouse venture into waste cleanup, small firms come up with innovative, earth-friendly products such as bricks made of sludge.

Other signs of corporate greening: business schools are offering courses in environmental management. Corporate compliance officials now report directly to CEOs in many companies. Right down to the shop floor, where hazardous wastes are generated in manufacturing, training programs are restructuring production officials' priorities. At a GE aircraft engine plant in Evendale, Ohio, waste oil was cut 20 percent and a new engine was developed which cut fuel use by 10 percent and noise by 33 percent.

At consumer products companies such as Procter & Gamble, there's an agenda "to make our products environmentally friendly," according to chairman Ed Artzt. That includes the replacement of inks and pigments which eventually leach heavy metals into groundwater. Plastics recycling and reduction of excess packaging show that high profile companies such as Procter & Gamble are ambitious in trying to make up for their past profligacy.

Sometimes companies go too far, calling materials "recyclable" and "biodegradable" when federal investigators can prove they are not. According to Tina Hobson, executive director of Renew America, many corporate "green" moves are "a lot of smoke and mirrors." Government intervention will continue, but it doesn't always come in the form of strict mandates. For example, new regulations allow a market for the trading of pollution rights.

Corporate America has begun a long journey to reverse past mistakes, with the help of government and also the venture-capital industry, which is investing hundreds of millions of dollars in environmental startups. When will it be possible to see results? According to Peter Savage, vice-president for chemical strategies for DeWitt & Co., a Houston consulting firm, "the proof will be five years from now, when we look back and see what has been accomplished."

Source: E. T. Smith and V. Cahan, "The Greening of Corporate America," *Business Week*, April 23, 1990, 96–103.

employees in U.S. firms), the establishment of the Occupational Safety and Health Administration (which regulates working conditions), and the Civil Rights Act of 1991 (which has redefined discrimination in employment practices and established new guidelines for employer financial liability).[12]

For the most part, government regulation provides an important service. Regulatory agencies police the fairness of organizations. Regulations ensure that organizations deal fairly with their employees and with their environments, including consumers and their immediate neighbors. In most cases, regulations impose on organizations standards of behavior that are socially beneficial in the long run. In the short term, however, regulation is a form of environmental constraint that must be managed.

The Social Environment

Another component of the environment arises because all organizations are part of a larger society. Social trends that occur in that larger society influence the behavior of organizations in many ways. We will consider two examples: social adjustment and corporate responsibility.

Social Adjustment   Social trends that are unrelated to an organization's actions but to which the organization must adjust require **social adjustment.** For example, between 1960 and 1980 the proportion of one-earner households in the American economy declined from 49.6 percent to 22.4 percent, the percentage of married women in the American work force rose from 32 percent to 51 percent, and the number of working mothers rose beyond the number of nonworking mothers.[13] All of these statistics convey a strong sense of change in the fabric of American society: specifically, the entry of working mothers into the American work force.

Other major changes have altered the characteristics of the American work force. The age profile also is changing. The average American worker is getting older as a consequence both of the 43 million "baby boomers" born immediately following World War II and legislation repealing mandatory retirement. And, as mentioned earlier, the education profile of the American work force is changing. In 1964, only 45 percent of the American work force had graduated from high school. By 1984, 59.7 percent were high school graduates, and 86 percent of the younger segment of the work force (25 to 29 years of age) had high school diplomas.[14] No one can predict the future directions in which society will move. Whatever they are, as social trends unfold, organizations must adjust to and evolve with them—or be left behind.

Corporate Responsibility   Standards for corporate responsibility are one aspect of the evolving social scene that modern business corporations must face. **Corporate responsibility** has to do with actions taken (or avoided) by an organization and how they measure up to society's moral and ethical standards. By way of example, consider the actions of Warren Beatty as the top executive of

---

[12] See, for example, R. S. Schuler and V. L. Huber, *Personnel and Human Resource Management* (Minneapolis: West Publishing, 1993), 90.

[13] J. Cocks, "How Long till Equality?" *Time*, July 12, 1982, 20–29.

[14] E. E. Lawler III, *High-Involvement Work Strategies* (San Francisco: Jossey-Bass, 1986), 16.

a major conglomerate in the movie, "Heaven Can Wait." In the film, Beatty's character finds his corporation under siege by citizen groups for a variety of transgressions, including the accidental killing of porpoises in its tuna-canning process (a very real problem for tuna fishermen). The problem for Beatty is that harvesting the tuna without killing the porpoises would be more expensive. But in his plea for the corporation to change its thinking, Beatty's character captures the crux of corporate responsibility. Killing the porpoises may be legal, he notes, but it isn't right. Implicit in his argument is a concern that any short-run savings the conglomerate realizes may lead only to long-term costs when the consuming public turns its back on the corporation.

This kind of corporate responsibility goes beyond fulfilling the letter of the law. Corporate responsibility includes such issues as good citizenship and social sensitivity. Good citizenship refers to returning something to the community that is an organization's home. For example, E.B. Industries and Fisher Price Toys contribute substantially to the emergency fire and ambulance services in their communities by releasing employees from work on a regular basis.[15] Such actions cannot directly enhance a corporation's profit picture, but they will contribute to the development and well-being of a community, which in turn enhance a corporation's probability of survival.

Social sensitivity occurs when a corporation selects an alternative that will minimize negative impact on the surrounding social environment. Legislation requires organizations to give their workers 60 days' notice before closing a plant, but it does not require them to help workers find new jobs. Organizations that provide their displaced workers outplacement assistance during tough times will likely find the community more supportive when they later resume operations. In some cases social sensitivity may not cost the company anything. When a company is deciding between two prime locations for a new plant, choosing the one that minimizes damage to wildlife habitats may cost the company no more but make a big difference to the community. In the end, though, corporate responsibility is a bottom-line issue. Organizations are dependent upon their environments for resources. Adhering to the environment's dictates of acceptable corporate behavior—whether through good citizenship or social sensitivity—is one way for an organization to make sure its nest remains feathered.

Technology

A final content of organizations' environments is technology. **Technology** includes all the different ways available to an organization to transform inputs into outputs. Because of the recent rapid advance of technological development, an entire chapter (Chapter 16) will be devoted to an in-depth examination of this powerful environmental force.

MANAGING ENVIRONMENTAL DEPENDENCE ◆◆◆◆◆◆

In the previous two sections of this chapter, we have described the form and the contents of the environment that today's modern business organizations must face. The challenge for today's organizations is managing the resource

---

[15] Hvsom and Bolce, *Business and Its Environment*, 4.

dependence that this environment presents. In this section we will consider three strategies that organizations use for managing environmental resource dependence: anticipation, negotiation, and control. As shown in Figure 14–4, these three approaches to dealing with the environment differ in the extent to which the organization's efforts are internally or externally focused. **Anticipation** focuses on making internal changes in the organization to *respond* to the demands of the environment, while **control** entails molding the environment to fit the organization's needs. **Negotiation,** defined in Chapter 6, falls somewhere in between. Many organizations use a mixture of these strategies.

Anticipation

Anticipation occurs when an organization collects information about what its environment is doing (or is about to do). The organization then can predict and respond appropriately to the environment's demands. Two component processes of anticipation are scanning and forecasting.

Scanning Collecting information from the environment is known as **environmental scanning**. Environmental scanning may involve the creation of new data; for example, information may be gathered through surveys. Scanning also can be accomplished by tapping into existing data sources, such as government labor statistics. As we noted in the last section, government labor statistics suggest that the American work force on the average is becoming older and better educated. An organization that has collected this information may be able to use it to redesign future jobs to be more stimulating and involving for its work force.

FIGURE 14–4 ▶ **Strategies for Managing Environmental Dependence**

Organizations can try to manage resource dependencies in the environment by anticipating the actions of the environment or by negotiating or controlling the environment's demands. Which strategy a firm chooses to pursue may depend on how susceptible to influence it perceives its environment to be.

Anticipation
　Scanning: collecting information about the environment and its possible actions.
　Forecasting: predicting future actions of the environment, often using statistical models.
Negotiation
　Lobbying: having agents plead the organization's case with regulatory bodies.
　Interlocking directorates: having influential suppliers and consumers on the board of directors to provide policy input.
　Public relations activities: attempting to build up the image of the organization in the environment.
Control
　Contracts: obtaining legally enforceable promises from consumers or suppliers.
　Buffers: stockpiling resources.
　Vertical integration: acquiring or merging with a supplier to guarantee resource availability.
　Horizontal integration: entering a different market to diversify risk.
　Joint ventures: sharing resources on a project with another organization to share risk.

The need for environmental scanning can be a function of the instability of an organization's environment. Organizations in rapidly changing fields or markets should scan the environment continually to keep abreast of the latest developments; organizations in mature or defined fields and markets may even find annual scanning unnecessary.

Environmental scanning has become a part of the Total Quality Movement (discussed in Chapter 2) in the form of **"relationship marketing."**[16] Relationship marketing means more than just collecting information about what the customer might want. It means developing long-term relationships with prospective customers via intensive information exchange. At its extreme, relationship marketing means getting the customer to help design the product. This not only ensures that the product is exactly what the customer wants, but it also makes the customer feel some ownership of and loyalty to the product. Federal Express, for instance, has installed its own computers in the offices of its steady customers. The computers are linked to Federal Express's headquarters in Memphis, keep tabs on all shipments, and allow Federal's customers to reassure their own clients about timely deliveries. In turn, Federal Express polls 1,000 of these customers every month for ways to improve its service.[17]

Forecasting An organization's use of information collected from the environment to predict future environmental demands is called **forecasting**. Last year's unemployment figures may provide only limited information about the labor supply in the immediately foreseeable future. However, a company that has collected unemployment figures for the last 20 years, as well as background information concerning the possible factors that drive unemployment statistics, is in a good position to *predict trends* in unemployment for the upcoming years. Forecasting uses statistical models to predict what the environment has in store for an organization in the future.

One example of environmental anticipation by an organization is the social audit.[18] The **social audit** is a mechanism that organizations use to see where they stand with respect to corporate responsibility demands placed on them by their social environments. Social audits have three goals. First, social audits identify and analyze important issues in a firm's social environment. These might include (1) issues affecting the firm, such as changes in community demographics, that could require alterations in a company's recruitment policies; (2) issues that the firm affects, such as plant closures that could have widespread effects on a community's economy. Second, social audits catalogue the scope of socially responsive programs or actions that an organization is undertaking. Finally, social audits assess the effectiveness of a firm's social actions and programs in addressing identified social issues.

Social audits can serve two important functions for an organization. First and foremost, social audits help an organization realize any shortcomings it might have in addressing its social responsibilities. The social audit is the first step an organization takes to prevent or correct any problems it might have in

---

[16] A. L. Stern, " 'Relationship Marketing' Helps Cultivate Loyal Customers," *Arizona Daily Star*, January 24, 1993, 1G.

[17] Stern, 4G.

[18] Hysom and Bolce, *Business and Its Environment*, 47–51.

managing its corporate responsibility demands. In addition, however, social audits provide an important documentation function. An organization that had conducted a social audit will have documented its level of social responsiveness. Assuming it paints a pretty picture, this documentation can be made available to representatives of the social environment as proof of a firm's willingness to fulfill its social obligations. And a firm that conducts periodic social audits— and uses the information appropriately—can be sure the picture painted will be one of a socially responsive and responsible organization.

Negotiation

When practiced by itself, anticipation assumes that the resource dependencies of the environment are a given—something that the organization must face up to and react to. As a strategy for managing environmental demands, negotiation takes a different view—that the environment, in particular the *beneficence* of the environment, is susceptible to influence. An organization can bargain with its environment and negotiate the demands that it places on the organization.

Lobbying   Lobbying is one way that organizations bargain with their environments. **Lobbying** occurs when the representative of an organization tries to convince a source of resource dependence in the environment (such as another firm or the government) of the correctness of the organization's world view. An organization of grain farmers, having a vested interest in the passage of a bill guaranteeing price supports for their products, might lobby Congress. This lobbying effort would include personal visits by grain farmers' representatives. The representatives would present the grain farmers' position, provide information supportive of their views, and generally advocate their viewpoint in the hopes of gaining support. Attempts to persuade Congress of the correctness of constituents' viewpoints are not always just a matter of providing information. Threatened withdrawal of monetary or even voting support also may sway someone's way of thinking.

Interlocking Directorates   A slightly more elegant device that firms use to subtly negotiate their environmental resource dependencies is **interlocking directorates.** A corporation can appoint to its board of directors representatives from a variety of organizations on which it is dependent. A major medical-supplies manufacturer, for instance, will have hospital and banking representation on its board of directors to cover the consumption and financing ends of its enterprise. These representatives typically possess either decision-making power or influence in their own organizations. In addition to any strategic insights or information they might have to offer, these representatives from the environment give the firm an opportunity to promote its views and gain their commitment. This commitment then becomes an invaluable asset when board members return to their own organizations to make decisions that affect the fate of the firm.

Public Relations   Another way organizations negotiate the resource dependencies they face in the environment is through **public relations** activities. **Image advertising** is one form of environmental negotiation. Image advertising is advertising that attempts to influence the public's overall perception of an organization. Is the organization patriotic? Is the organization community-minded? Does it give you a good feeling? An organization also can influence its overall image in the environment by providing community services, such as McDonald's support of the Ronald McDonald Houses for critically ill children.

Why is it important for an organization to maintain a positive image in the environment? A good impression of an organization will influence the environment's beneficence. Consumers will be more willing to try the organization's products. Further, because of the constructive nature of perception, an organization's good public image will even influence consumers' perception of the quality of its outputs. Regulators, for example, will see a corporation's actions in a more favorable light if they have an overall favorable impression of the corporation. Just because an organization's community-service activities are unselfish does not mean that they also have to be unprofitable.

Control

Negotiation as an environment-management strategy assumes that the environment can be influenced, that resource demands placed on an organization can be negotiated. An even more proactive approach to resource demands is to control them. A variety of strategies for controlling environmental resource dependencies are available to organizations, including contracts, buffers, vertical and horizontal integration, and even joint ventures.

Contracts   A contract is one of the simple ways for an organization to control resource dependencies in its environment. A **contract** is a legally binding document that guarantees an organization delivery of and terms for a particular resource. A department store and a clothing manufacturer might have a contract specifying the delivery dates and terms for a line of sportswear. What does having the contract accomplish for either organization? The department store, through the contract, guarantees itself a supply of sportswear for the upcoming season. The clothing manufacturer, through the contract, guarantees itself a distributor for its clothes.

The point of having contracts is to reduce uncertainty about the availability of resources. Both the department store and the clothing manufacturer can rest a little easier knowing they have signed a contract. Naturally, contracts are no real guarantee. The clothing manufacturer might not come through with the clothes. But a contract provides legal recourse if that happens. The department store can sue the clothing manufacturer for lost revenues if the clothing manufacturer fails to deliver according to the terms of the contract. Suing the clothing manufacturer is not the same as getting the clothes delivered as promised, but the contract does provide the department store some protection.

Buffers   Buffers provide an organization with another way to insulate itself from the unpredictability of its environment. If an organization is concerned that its resource supplies might dry up, it can create a buffer against scarcity by stockpiling resources when they are available against the day when they will not be. A concerned department store might buy a warehouse and fill it full of clothes. In the event that a clothing supplier failed to deliver on time, the department store would have a buffer—a safety margin—of clothes in its warehouse to see it through the crisis.

Clothes, unfortunately, are a good example of a product that cannot be stockpiled easily. Because styles change rapidly, clothes that a department store stockpiles against the possibility of future shortages may be out of style when the department store attempts to use them. Grocery stores face a similar problem with fresh fruits and vegetables—they cannot be stockpiled against the possibility of future scarcity because they would not stay fresh. When resources cannot be stockpiled, **resource redundancy** can be used as a form of environmental buffering.

Resource redundancy is accomplished by maintaining relationships with multiple resource suppliers. A department store that has relationships (perhaps even contracts) with multiple clothing suppliers knows that one supplier's failure to deliver on its promises will not be fatal. The other suppliers will be able to step in and deliver on their promises, and may even be able to fill in the gaps left by the undependable supplier.

Vertical Integration Vertical integration is a much more aggressive way for an organization to control resources in its environment than either contracts or resource buffers. Contracts and buffers allow an organization some measure of control over important resources, but those resources still remain at arm's length in the environment. **Vertical integration** involves the *absorption* of important resources so that an organization's control of them becomes absolute.

Consider again our department store and clothing manufacturer. One way for the department store to increase the clothing manufacturer's dependability is to *buy* it. The department store then can control not only availability of the clothing but also styles, sizes, and so on. On the other hand, a clothing manufacturer that is nervous about the dependability of the department stores that are retailing its goods can vertically integrate by acquiring a chain of factory-outlet stores that it completely controls. For the grocery store, vertical integration might include the acquisition of a dairy farm to ensure availability and terms for a variety of dairy products.

As shown in Figure 14–5, vertical integration means *integrating* different functions in the vertical chain of production under the umbrella of one organization. For clothing, the entire vertical chain might include cotton growers, cotton-cloth weavers, clothing manufacturers, and finally retail distributors. Each of the links in this vertical chain represents a source of resource dependencies. By integrating functions, these resource dependencies can be more closely controlled. Vertical integration is no final solution, however. The department store that acquires a clothing manufacturer eliminates one source of resource dependence, but in turn may learn just how undependable cotton-cloth weavers are as suppliers to the newly acquired business.

Horizontal Integration Horizontal integration is a completely different approach to controlling resource dependence. An organization horizontally integrates by getting involved in multiple, often unrelated vertical chains of production, such as those shown in Figure 14–6. The point of vertical integration is to control resource dependencies; the point of **horizontal integration** is to control the *effects* of resource dependencies. A horizontally integrated organization is one that is in many different businesses. That way, the organization can balance the failures of any one of its businesses with the successes of its

| FIGURE 14-5 | ▶ **Example of Vertical Integration** |

Panel (a) shows four component operations in getting clothing to market. Each of these component operations could be accomplished by a separate firm. In Panel (b), Firm C has vertically integrated by merging with or acquiring Firm B. Having acquired a cloth weaver, the clothing manufacturer no longer has to worry about the supply of cloth.

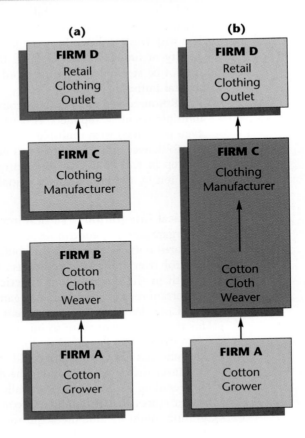

others. Horizontal integration allows an organization to distribute its resource-dependence risks across a variety of activities.

Department stores themselves provide an interesting example of horizontal integration. If a store sold only children's clothes, its success as a business would be highly dependent upon the success of the children's clothing industry as a whole. But what if that store also sold hardware, books, toys, and kitchen supplies? A bad year in children's clothes could be balanced by a particularly good year in kitchen goods. In fact, the term *department store* refers to the fact that department stores have many departments—many little business—all contained under the umbrella of one organization.

Horizontal integration works best when an organization gets into businesses with completely different sources of environmental resource dependence. Imagine, for instance, a corporation that was involved in two businesses: photographic film and silver jewelry. The factors that determine who buys film and who buys jewelry probably are quite different, so that fluctuations in sales in one market would not likely be related to fluctuations in the other. However, both of these industries are highly dependent upon the supply of silver, which is used in the production of photographic film. A scarcity of silver could take both businesses down at the same time. Photographic film and dairy products,

FIGURE 14-6 ▶ Example of Horizontal Integration

In this example, Firm C has horizontally integrated by acquiring a new business in a completely different market, bicycles. If the factors that determine when consumers buy clothing and bicycles are different, this kind of horizontal integration decreases the impact of a problem in either market. Horizontal integration works best when expertise can be pooled across the integrated units. In this case, for example, both units are manufacturing concerns.

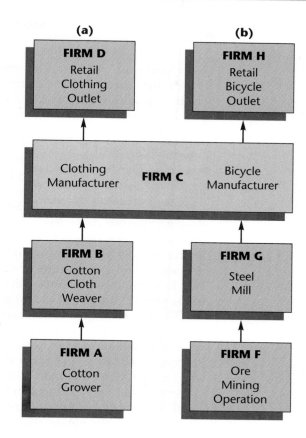

on the other hand, are unlikely to share either supplier or consumer resource dependencies, and therefore might make for effective horizontal integration.

The valuable asset that an organization may lose with horizontal or vertical integration is expertise. A top management team that is very adept at managing a department store might flounder if asked to manage a clothing manufacturer (vertical integration) or a dairy farm (horizontal integration) as well. Horizontal and vertical integration offer the possibility of controlling the stability and uncertainty presented by resource dependencies, but only at the expense of increasing complexity.

One of the complexities that horizontal or vertical integration begs is the marriage of two corporate cultures. While two companies might appear to be a good match on paper, in practice they will each have different ways of doing things, which must be reconciled if the companies are to work together smoothly. Certainly this reconciliation will take time if it can be done at all, and there will be a human toll. For instance, some functions in the newly merged company necessarily will fall under control of a single individual. Where there were previously two heads of production (one for each company), now there can be only one. This individual will come from one of the prior companies or the other (or neither!) but not both. That means one of the previous production heads will disappear or be reassigned; it also means that a good number of subordinates will have to get used to a new boss, and that boss will have to get used to a good number of new subordinates. Not surprisingly, mergers engender enormous stress and a lot of turnover before the smoke all clears.[19] (These issues will be discussed in greater detail in Chapter 17.)

Joint Ventures   An interesting way for organizations to horizontally integrate is the **joint venture**.[20] Joint ventures occur when two or more unrelated organizations pool their resources to collaborate on joint projects. Some well-publicized examples of joint ventures include the Alaska pipeline, which brought several major U.S. corporations together on a massive oil and gas exploration project; a factory in California producing automobiles made jointly by General Motors and Toyota; and McKids clothing, a joint effort by McDonald's and Sears to manufacture and market children's wear.

Why would two organizations—sometimes even competitors—be willing to work together on a project? There are a variety of answers, but they all come down to resource dependence. In the case of the Alaska pipeline, the project was too large and too risky for any one of the companies to underwrite alone. Interestingly, its potential also might have been too great for any of those firms to ignore. Thus, participation of any firm in the project prevented its competitors from gaining an advantage through participation, and also availed the firm of the possible benefits of the project without taking the risks all alone.

The General Motors and Toyota joint venture was slightly different. Both companies were more than capable financially of going it alone, but both also knew that a joint venture could produce huge benefits. Toyota needed to improve its access to American car buyers; having its cars made by American workers in a General Motors plant in the United States was just the ticket. General Motors, on the other hand, knew that its U.S. manufacturing processes could not compete with the effectiveness and efficiency of the Japanese. Joining forces with the competition offered General Motors an opportunity to improve its product, its image, and its expertise in manufacturing automobiles. In effect, both companies had an important resource that the other desperately wanted. A joint venture gave each side control of that valued resource. The reasoning behind the Sears-McDonald's joint venture is similar. Sears has expertise in children's clothing, while McDonald's has the image and visibility that can sell clothes.

In the final analysis, the reasoning behind all joint ventures comes down to managing resource dependence. As shown in the "FOCUS ON: Joint Ventures," such ventures reduce uncertainty by sharing risk, and they also increase the ability of firms to manage environmental complexity by sharing their expertise.

THE BOUNDARY-SPANNING ROLE   ◆◆◆◆◆◆

As a closing comment on the importance of interactions between an organization and its environment, it should be remembered that organizations do not interact with their environments. Instead, *individuals* represent organizations in

---

[19]M. L. Marks and P. H. Mirvis, "The Merger Syndrome," *Psychology Today*, October 1986, 37–42.

[20]J. B. Levine and J. A. Byrne, "Corporate Odd Couples," *Business Week*, July 21, 1986, 100–105.

Joint Ventures

If You Can't Beat Them . . . IBM and Apple Computer are the world's No. 1 and No. 2 PC makers. So why would they agree to share technology? That's one reason their strategic alliance has been met with skepticism. Another reason is that IBM doesn't have a promising track record with such relationships. After acquiring the telecommunications giant Rolm Corp. in 1984, Big Blue was unable to successfully integrate the company's wares into its own product line. In the early 1990s, it stepped up its partnership efforts to develop handwriting-recognition software (Go, July 1990); operating system technology (Metaphor, Sept. 1990); rights to networking software (Novell, February 1991); rights to software development tools (Borland, May 1991); access to imaging and electronic mail technology (Wang and Lotus, June 1991).

The new alliance has impressive goals which may contribute both to increased competitiveness and expanding markets. Part of the plan is to develop software that will increase Apple and IBM networking capabilities. For Apple that means potentially more corporate business. Another part of the plan is to jointly develop operating system software to make Big Blue competitive with Microsoft, a former IBM partner that became a key rival.

Another strategic element of the plan involves IBM's reduced instruction-set computing (RISC) chip. With the IBM technology, Apple may be able to move into workstations. If that happens, the joint venture will have increased muscle to apply against formidable competitor Compaq Computer, which has its own proprietary RISC technology.

The most futuristic aspect of the alliance is joint development of multimedia, now defined as the integration of video and sound with computer text. IBM and Apple working together could throw cold water on Japanese competitors, such as Sony, who are venturing into the same applications of technology.

It's been some time since IBM led the PC industry, and it's no secret that the company would like to be a leader again. Farming out innovation is a different approach from investing in proprietary research and development, and IBM faces a steep learning curve. Past alliances have been sabotaged by Big Blue's own internal structure. Getting back in the driver's seat is going to require a little help from friends, and a lot more listening than IBM has been used to doing in the past.

Source: D. A. Depke, "IBM and Apple: Can Two Loners Learn to Say 'Teamwork'?" *Business Week*, July 22, 1991, 25.

these interactions. These individuals are called **boundary spanners.** Boundary spanners span the boundary between an organization and the forces in the organization's environment.

All members of organizations are boundary spanners to some extent because organizations are open systems. An individual who works on the assembly line for General Motors in Detroit also lives in Michigan and belongs to two worlds: GM's formal work organization and Michigan's social environment. All boundary spanners must learn to move freely between different worlds and to reconcile the differences on opposite sides of the boundary (for instance, differences in goals or ways of doing things).

The formal boundary-spanning role in organizations is both important and difficult. It is important because of the importance of resource dependence. Boundary-spanning individuals who handle their role poorly put their organizations at risk of losing access to important resources. The role is difficult because the boundary spanner must work in two worlds without really belonging to both. Take, for example, the job of liaison for a joint venture between two corporations. To be successful, such liaisons must learn the rules of both corporate cultures and be able to move freely back and forth between the two without forgetting which culture is really "home." If successful, the boundary spanner's loyalties may come to be suspected. Further, because formal boundary spanners must do much of their work in organizations to which they do not belong, they have little legitimate power to fall back on to accomplish their goals. Boundary spanners therefore must be well-schooled in the use of other forms of power. Corporate liaisons cannot order people around; they must rely on less direct tactics, such as ingratiation, to accomplish their mission.

While this discussion provides only a glimpse at the challenge of boundary spanning, it does suggest that individuals formally cast in this role may need different skills than other organizational actors. The selection of such individuals may need to place greater emphasis on flexibility if the boundary spanner is to manage successfully regular transitions between environment and home organization. The boundary spanner will also need to be trained to manage interactions differently when outside the organization—for example, by using other sources of power. For an organization, resource dependence makes the selection and preparation of individuals for boundary-spanning roles at least as important as for any roles internal to the organization.

SUMMARY ◆◆◆◆◆◆

The goal of this chapter has been to paint a picture of the environment in which today's organizations must function. Organizations cannot exist independent of their environment. Organizations are open systems that depend upon the environment for resources and are influenced by their interactions with it. Organizations depend upon the environment for inputs to transform and for customers or clients to consume their outputs.

The environmental forces that influence business organizations have both form and content. Environmental forces vary in their uncertainty, stability, complexity, and beneficence. These environmental forces include other organizations, governmental regulations, social trends, and the current state of technological development.

Successful management of environmental dependence is key to an organization's survival. Three broad strategies for managing environmental forces include anticipation, negotiation, and control. Anticipation requires scanning the environment in order to forecast—and therefore be prepared to respond appropriately to—environmental action. Negotiation is the process of influencing resource dependencies an organization faces in its environment. Organizations can successfully influence environmental resource dependencies through lobbying, the formation of interlocking directorates, and even public relations activities. Finally, organizations can control resource dependencies in their environments through contracting, buffering, vertical and horizontal integration, and even joint ventures.

While any one individual may pale in the face of the enormity and complexity of environmental forces, it is nevertheless individuals that actually manage the boundaries between organizations and their environments. Because of the uniqueness and importance of boundary-spanning roles, organizations need special procedures for selecting and training boundary spanners to ensure successful management of environmental resource dependencies.

Key Terms

Anticipation Making internal changes in the organization to respond to the environment's demands.

Beneficence Generosity, leniency, and helpfulness of the environment concerning needed resources.

Boundary spanners Individuals such as liaisons who represent an organization in interactions with the forces in its environment.

Closed system Completely self-contained organization that functions apart from and is unaffected by what goes on around it.

Contract Control strategy of managing environmental demands using a legally binding document that guarantees an organization delivery of and terms for a particular resource.

Control Molding the environment to fit the organization's needs.

Corporate responsibility Need for an organization to take or avoid actions in order to measure up to society's moral and ethical standards.

Enacted environment The process of perceiving the environment and acting on those perceptions, which in turn changes the environment being perceived.

Environmental scanning Process of anticipation in which the organization collects information from the environment.

Forecasting Process of environmental anticipation in which the organization uses mathematical models to predict future environmental demands.

Horizontal integration Involvement of an organization in several different activities (e.g., product lines) in order to distribute its resource-dependence risks across a variety of activities.

Image advertising Attempts to influence the environment's overall perception of an organization.

Instability Rate of change in an organization's environment.

Interlocking directorates Negotiation strategy for managing environmental demands in which a corporation appoints to its board of directors representatives from a variety of organizations on which it is dependent.

Joint venture Two or more unrelated organizations that pool their resources to collaborate on projects.

Lobbying Negotiation strategy for managing environmental demands in which a representative of an organization convinces source of resource dependence in the environment of the correctness of the organization's perspective.

Loose coupling Relationship of an organization and its environment in which what happens in the environment may or may not be reflected by immediate changes in the organization.

Negotiation A class of strategies for managing environmental resource dependence (see Chapter 6).

Open system Organization whose activities are inescapably influenced by its environment.

Public relations Negotiation strategy for managing environmental demands in which an organization actively controls its interactions with the environment using activities such as image advertising.

Regulation Legal restriction of behaviors in or by organizations.

Relationship marketing The development of a long-term relationship with prospective customers via intensive information exchange.

Resource redundancy Preventing the lack of a particular resource by maintaining relationships with several suppliers.

Social adjustment Changes the organization must make in response to environmental changes that are unrelated to its actions.

Social audit Mechanism organizations use to see where they stand with respect to corporate-responsibility demands by identifying important issues in the social environment, cataloging the actions the organization is presently taking, and assessing their effectiveness.

Technology The knowledge, tools, and techniques available to an organization to transform inputs into outputs.

Union Group of workers who have banded together to give themselves more bargaining power with their employer.

Vertical integration Acquisition of one organization by another with the goal of controlling resource dependencies that are important in its production process.

Discussion Questions

1. What does it mean to say that organizations are open systems? What are the defining characteristics of open systems?

2. In what ways are organizations dependent upon their environments? Explain what might be meant by the phrase, "Organizations are a way of turning the environment into survival."

3. In what dimensions of external dependence do the environments of service and manufacturing organizations differ? Does this have implications for how these two types of organizations might manage their environmental interactions differently?

4. Consider the following prayer: "Grant me the strength to change the things I can change, the patience to endure the things I cannot, and the wisdom to know the difference." Would this make a good corporate policy for managing resource dependencies? Why or why not?

5. What does it mean to say that an organization and its environment are "loosely coupled"? Is loose coupling an advantage or disadvantage?

6. Why is the boundary-spanning role particularly important? Particularly difficult? How could an organization prpare one of its employees for this role?

7. What strategies does an organization have for managing its dependence on the environment?

8. How might mergers, takeovers, and acquisitions be seen as a form of managing environmental dependence?

If You Want to Know More

For anyone interested in learning more about the interaction between organizations and their environments, three classic readings provide the foundation for our current understanding of these topics: Jeff Pfeffer and Gerry Salancik, *The External Control of Organizations* (New York: Harper & Row, 1978); P. R. Lawrence and J. W. Lorsch, *Organization and Environment* (Homewood, Ill.: Richard Irwin, 1964); and F. E. Emergy and E. L. Trist, "The Causal Texture of Organizational Environments" (*Human Relations* 18, 1968, 20–26).

The success of Korean and Japanese companies intensified interest in international management issues during the 1980s. An entire issue of the *Academy of Management Executive* (February 1988) was devoted to managing in the global marketplace, including an article by Richard Steers and Edwin Miller, "Management in the 1990s: The International Challenge." Several articles have looked specifically at the importation of Japanese management techniques into American industry, including James S. Bowan's two-article series entitled, "The Rising Sun in America" (*Personnel Administrator*, September 1986, 63–67 + and October 1986, 81–91); the *Business Week* cover article "The Americaniza-

tion of Honda" (S. Toy, April 25, 1988, 90–96); and L. S. Dillon, "Adopting Japanese Management: Some Cultural Stumbling Blocks" (*Personnel* 32, July 1983, 77–81).

Two interesting books on the issue of organizational stakeholders and their influence on organizations are *Stakeholders of the Organization Mind*, by Ian Mitroff (San Francisco: Jossey-Bass, 1983); and *Strategic Management—A Stakeholder Approach*, by E. Freeman (Boston: Pitman Publishing, 1984).

"State of the Unions," by Keith Atkinson (*Personnel Administrator*, September 1986, 54–59) provides a look at the state of unions in the 1980s in Europe. "U.S. Unions and Foreign Employers: A Clash of Cultures," by Martin and Susan Tolchin (*Management Review*, March 1988, 47–53), discusses the problems foreign employers have experienced in dealing with American unions.

One of the early articles to consider the importance of the boundary-spanning role in organizations was "System Boundaries," by R. L. Kahn, D. Wolfe, R. Quinn, J. D. Snoek, and R. Rosenthal (*Organizational Stress*, New York: Wiley, 1964, 99–124).

On Your Own

The table below provides a framework for analyzing the environmental forces that influence the behaviors of an organization. The table asks you to list different sources of environmental influence and to identify strategies for dealing with them. Using a school club or sports team as an example of an open system, fill in the boxes to complete an audit of the environmental forces influencing the behavior of the club or team. In the first column, list one or two examples of each source of environment dependence listed on the left. Then fill in examples of each of the strategies available to a club or sports team to manage the influence of these environmental dependencies successfully.

		Management Strategies		
	Source	Anticipation	Negotiation	Control
Other Organizations				
Regulatory Environment				
Social Environment				
Technology				

Are any of these boxes harder to fill in than others? Does this suggest anything about what types of strategies might be better for managing different types of environmental forces?

CLOSING CASE

CHAPTER 14

THE MANAGER'S MEMO

FROM: G. Irving, President

TO: P. Rambowski, Vice President

RE: Preparing for Hard Times

These days the antigun fanatics seem to be shooting their mouths off more and more, and I'm getting concerned about the future of Top Gun Shops. If the trend keeps up, our chain of gun and ammunition stores could be under siege, maybe from the government, maybe from community activists. And if the market gets any trickier, you can bet that the competition will be stepping up the pressure.

The successful hunter keeps his eyes open at all times. So how can we do the same in our business? We need a plan for keeping an eye on what's going on, for anticipating changes, for taking action where we can.

I'd like your suggestions. Where should we be watching? How should we watch? And what can we do to head off problems?

Case Discussion Questions

Assume you are the vice-president, and respond to the president's memorandum. Consider as many aspects of the environment as you can apply to this situation. Besides identifying sources of environmental dependence, describe ways in which the company might be able to manage its environmental dependence.

CHAPTER

TECHNOLOGY

Technology and Organizational Behavior
Technological Type
Technological Change

Technology and Automation
International Focus on Robots: It's a Dirty Job, but Something's Gotta Do It
Limitations

Technology and Information
Focus on Information Availability: Keeping an Eye on How the Cookie Crumbles
International Focus on Technology and Information: Japan's Love for High Tech Stops at the Office
Surprising Consequences

Smoothing the Transition
Managing Job Changes
Generating Ownership
Fighting Worker Obsolescence

At These Shouting Matches, No One Says a Word

◆◆◆◆◆◆

At electronic meetings, anonymity breeds boldness. One person in the meeting says, "This company has no leader—and no vision." Another participant asks, "Why are you being so defensive?" Another snaps, "I've had enough—I'm looking for another job."

These candid comments are cloaked in anonymity because they are typed into PC keyboards and flashed on a projection screen in the meeting room. The technique empowers even the shyest participants to say what they feel.

Companies are using the simple techniques of electronic meetings to get better and faster information and consensus. Ancilla Systems Inc., an Elk Grove, Illinois health care company, used one to help put together a five-year plan. Phelps Dodge Mining Co. in Phoenix, Arizona, had an electronic meeting that cut the normal planning process, which usually takes days, down to 12 hours. Greyhound Financial, a division of Greyhound Dial Corp., used an electronic meeting to get staffers to rate their bosses.

The props involve a horseshoe-shaped table, seating up to 50, with a PC for each participant. A local area network acts as a traffic cop while all participants type their comments and responses simultaneously. The fastest thinkers and keyboardists have an advantage. The computers also tally votes and display them, and print out a synopsis for each participant at the end of the meeting.

Boosters of electronic meetings include IBM, which gave the University of Arizona $2 million to perfect the concept in 1986. The company has since built 28 electronic meeting rooms at IBM sites and has planned 22 more. The University of Arizona project spawned the startup of Ventana Corporation, which plans to specialize in consulting and software for electronic meetings.

Anonymity has a negative side: it means a good idea will not be credited to its originator, says Ventana CEO J. F. Nunamaker. And the process is unnatural to those who may not have quick keyboard skills. Critics say it's not as good as face-to-face oral communication, but they said that about the telephone, too.

Source: J. Bartimo, "At These Shouting Matches, No One Says a Word," *Business Week*, June 11, 1990.

INTRODUCTION

What is technology? Broadly defined, technology is what people use to get things done. In the history of management and organizational behavior, the word technology has been used in at least two very different ways. In the terms of Chapter 14, technology is what workers use to transform organizational inputs into organizational outputs. In this use of the word, a technology is a transformation process and can refer to something as abstract as a recipe or formula or something as concrete as a new drill press. More recently, the word technology has been used primarily to describe machinery—particularly *computerized*, or "high-tech" machinery—which is used to enhance or even substitute for human labor in transforming inputs into outputs. The opening vignette for this chapter described one of the space-age technologies (in the latter sense of the word) now available to the modern organization: electronic meeting rooms.

For many managers, new technologies (like the electronic meeting room described in this chapter's opening vignette) represent "the edge." They are supposed to help us do things easier, better, and faster. Like the high-tech gadgets used by James Bond, technology can give us the ability to surprise the competition with an advantage that cannot be overcome.

Not surprisingly, Americans have fallen in love with technology. The speed of technological development in the United States has been staggering. In 1960, no man had traveled in space and computers were just large, boxy adding machines. By 1969, man was on the moon, and by 1990, computer technology was going into its third or fourth generation of development. Through it all, Americans have gobbled up whatever new technologies have come along—even those they didn't understand—perhaps as much to avoid giving the edge to the competition as getting it themselves.

But is the advance of technology a mixed blessing? Are we using technology to take us where we want to go, or are we just going where technology takes us? The U.S. Navy got a quick lesson on this issue in July 1988 when the warship USS *Vincennes* shot down an Iranian commercial airliner in the Persian Gulf, killing 290 civilians. An inquiry revealed that the ship's state-of-the-art technology had performed flawlessly. The problem was that, in doing so, the ship's technology may have provided its decision makers with more information than they could digest and integrate into an appropriate decision in the heat of battle.[1] As the Navy learned, technology is not itself "the edge" after all. Technology only represents potential. Correct *management* of new technology is where the real competitive edge lies.

This chapter explores the nature of the technological challenge: how to manage technological development for competitive advantage. The chapter begins with a review of the concept of "technological determinism"—how different technologies influence behaviors in and of organizations and how the organizations themselves adapt to rapid *changes* in technology within their industry. Next, we explore the effects of two major developments on organizational behavior: automation and information technologies. Finally, the chapter closes with some thoughts about ways that managers can meet the challenge of using technology effectively.

---

[1] D. Griffiths, "When Man Can't Keep Up with the Machines of War," *Business Week*, September 12, 1988, 36.

TECHNOLOGY AND ORGANIZATIONAL
BEHAVIOR

◆◆◆◆◆◆

In Chapter 14, technology was cast as one of the environmental forces that influence behavior of and in organizations. The effects of technology on organizations are captured in theories of technological determinism. **Technological determinism** means that the way that a firm is organized (how the firm makes decisions, or how much training its line workers receive, for instance) is a function of the technology (whether that technology is machinery or not) that the firm uses to transform its inputs into outputs. Researchers have identified two different sources of technological determinism: **technological type** and **technological change**.

Technological Type	The English social scientist Joan Woodward first identified technological type as a determinant of behavior in organizations in the 1960s. Woodward studied 100 manufacturing firms in the South Essex region of England and identified three primary types of technology: (1) unit or small-batch, (2) large-batch, and (3) mass production or process manufacturing.[2] Woodward proposed a theory of technological determinism that involves the amount of **output customization** required of an organization by its customers. Greater demand for output customization means greater uncertainty about the demands of any individual consumer and requires flexibility in the organization's transformation technology.

Woodward's three primary types of transformation technology differ in the extent to which the organization's output is influenced by uncertainty about the customization needs of each customer. Output Type A in Figure 15–1 is customized to meet the needs of each consumer or small numbers of customers (a haircut or dental work, for example). Each output is different and must be produced individually (or in small batches). For Output Type B, some consumers desire similar or identical outputs (such as automobiles or clothing) from the organization so outputs can be produced in larger batches. Finally, Output Type C consists of products that can be produced in mass because needs or desires for the product do not differ from consumer to consumer. Process manufacturing occurs when a good is produced in mass quantities rather than in units (beer, dog food, or medicines, for instance) and then packaged in varying sizes. Mass production occurs when goods (such as pencils or books) that do not need to be altered to fit individuals are produced in mass quantities.

Woodward's technological types illustrate the amount of potential interference that an organization must put up with from its consumers while it transforms inputs into outputs. If an organization produces a Type A output—one customized to the needs of each individual consumer—it needs organizational processes and a production technology that are extremely flexible. Every unit produced may need to be different from all others produced before it. The organization's ability to adapt the production technology swiftly and at low cost is critical to performance, and decision-making authority must be decentralized in the organization so that the organization can respond to output customization needs in a timely fashion. On the other hand, if an organization produced a Type C output—one that requires no consumer customizing—the organi-

---

[2]J. Woodward, *Industrial Organizations: Behavior and Control* (London: Oxford University Press, 1970).

| FIGURE 15-1 | ▶ Technological Determinism |

Woodward's technological determinism deals with the amount of customization required of an organization's outputs. When outputs must be customized to meet individual consumer needs (Output Type A), transformation technology and organizational processes must be flexible. When outputs do not require customization to meet consumer needs (Output Types B and C), transformation technology and organizational processes can be quite inflexible. Intelligent machines may be one way to defeat the trade-off between customization and production volume by making manufacturing systems both highly efficient and highly flexible.

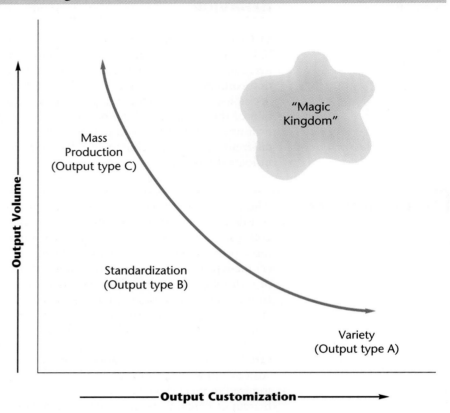

Source: N. Valery, "Factory of the Future," in *Organizations Close-Up: A Book of Readings*, ed. J. Gibson, J. Ivancevich, and J. Donnelly, Jr. (Plano, Tex.: Business Publications Inc., 1988), 274–301.

zation can plan long production runs. The organization can afford a production technology that is inflexible—difficult and costly to change. The organization will not need to change the technology often, and it can write off the costs of changing the technology over many units of output. Further, decision making can be centralized because the lack of customization demanded reduces the number of decisions for which customer responsiveness is an issue.

Woodward's technological determinism contends that uncertainty about customer demand (rather than technology) will determine organizational processes—including what technology the organization uses. If consumer demands necessitate a flexible and responsive transformation technology, the processes of organizational interaction must be flexible and responsive. If consumer requirements allow an inflexible and unresponsive transformation technology, then the processes of organizational interaction also can be rigid and autocratic.

Technological Change

A second aspect of technological determinism arises in the rate of change of transformation technologies in an industry. In some industries, technological developments are quite rapid. In the early 1980s, the life cycle for typical manufactured goods that you might buy in a department store—the time from fad to out-of-fashion—was three to six years. By 1987, the life cycle of consumer electronics in Tokyo was down to about three months.[3] This amount of product turnover in the consumer marketplace puts demands on organizations that are quite similar to the demands for output customization. The uncertainty is not what particular consumers will demand in the output—it is what *all* consumers will demand.

In a market where even products that are not customized have a very short life cycle, an organization cannot afford to be inflexible and unresponsive. Just as an organization copes with the uncertainty of individual consumer demands by adopting a flexible transformation technology, it must cope with uncertainty in its market consumer demands by becoming flexible. Uncertain consumer demand necessitates a flexible and responsive transformation technology. And as we have already seen (in the discussion of Woodward's technological types), a flexible transformation technology in turn requires similarly flexible organizational processes, such as decentralized decision making and skilled labor.

Technology is only one factor that influences the design of organizational processes. Chapter 16 will take a closer look at the important dimensions of organizational processes and structures and the factors—including technology—that influence their design. The remainder of this chapter will focus on current developments in technology and their potential influence on behaviors in organizations. The two major developments we will examine are automation and information technologies.

TECHNOLOGY AND AUTOMATION　◆◆◆◆◆◆

As shown in Figure 15–2, the cost of labor in other industrialized countries—including some of America's commercial competitors—is often only a fraction of U.S. labor costs. In Mexico and Brazil, for example, labor costs are less than 20 percent of those in the United States. To put these figures in perspective, realize that in U.S. manufacturing companies, labor can account for as much as 30 percent of total costs; in service organizations in the United States, labor can account for as much as 80 percent of total costs.[4] Given the high costs of labor in the United States and the significance of these costs to survival in the international marketplace, it is easy to understand why management at many American companies has begun to imagine what corporate life would be like *without* labor costs. Minimal labor costs can mean only one thing: automation.

Automation is the replacement of people with machines. In the service sector, the advent of ATMs (automated teller machines) represented an important step in the automation of banking. Before ATMs, bank tellers handled a variety of tasks that included many simple (and quite "mindless") transactions, such as account withdrawals, deposits, and fund transfers. When ATMs arrived on the banking scene, many banks encouraged their customers to use them for

---

[3]N. Valery, "Factory of the Future," in *Organizations Close-Up: A Book of Readings*, J. Gibson, J. Ivancevich, and J. Donnelly, Jr., ed., (Plano, Tex.: BPI, 1988), 274–301.

[4]R. S. Schuler, *Personnel and Human Resource Management* (St. Paul, Minn.: West Publishing, 1987), 19.

FIGURE 15–2	▶ Labor Costs as a Percentage of U.S. Labor Costs

High labor costs in the United States make it difficult for American companies to compete in the global marketplace. Appropriate use of technology is critical if American companies are to get the most productivity for their labor costs.

West Germany	144%
Japan	87
UK	84
Italy	110
Australia	88
Taiwan	27
Korea	28
Hong Kong	22
Mexico	12
Brazil	19

Source: U.S. Department of Labor, Bureau of Labor Statistics, "International Comparisons of Hourly Compensation Costs for Production Workers in Manufacturing, 1990," April 1991.

simple tasks and to call on the tellers only when human discretion was required—for example, to cash a check or set up a new account. ATMs also provide increased flexibility, such as the opportunity to do banking outside of regular banking hours. ATMs allow customers to do their banking 24 hours per day, 7 days per week—a work schedule no human teller would put up with.

In this chapter, we will consider two levels of automation: mechanization and computer-integrated manufacturing. In **mechanization**, a machine is programmed to execute the component actions of a work task, but to do so faster, more precisely, and more consistently than any human could. Robots are the most visible and direct representation of the mechanization movement to replace people with machines. A **robot** is a machine that acts like a human being. On the manufacturing lines that produce Ford's highly successful Taurus and Sable automobiles, robots perform more than 98 percent of the spot welding. At the General Dynamics plant in Fort Worth, Texas, a robot is used to drill 550 holes into the tail fins of an F-16 jet fighter. The task used to take three workers an entire day (eight hours) to do; the robot does it in three hours.[5] The Japanese are world leaders when it comes to using robots in manufacturing and have been more successful than their Western counterparts at integrating robots into a variety of industrial sectors (as noted in the "INTERNATIONAL FOCUS ON: Robots").

Beyond robots is the realm of **computer-integrated manufacturing (CIM).** As shown in the following passage, CIM represents a world far beyond mere mechanization:

"Imagine, if you will, an engineer sitting at a computer terminal punching in data for the design of a new product and sketching freely with a light pen on the screen before him. Happy with the design, he presses a button and the details are passed electronically to another computer running software that checks to see whether the design's stresses and strains are within prescribed limits. The infor-

[5] G. Bock, "Limping along in Robot Land," *Time*, July 13, 1987.

mation then zips along to a third computer which generates instructions that command the tools in the workshop to machine, assemble, and store the engineer's product ready for distribution—all done automatically, without hassle, delay or hefty manhandling, and all before the morning's coffee break.[6]

What sets CIM apart from mere mechanization is the use of *information* by machines. CIM combines task mechanization with computerized information processing about the task. In the example above, the machines are doing more than just producing a custom part. The machines also are deciding what the part needs to look like, and machines are even telling other machines how to make it.

The value of CIM lies in flexibility. "Unintelligent" mechanization—unthinking robots, for example—can be extremely valuable if an organization's product never changes. But what if customization is the way to the consumer's heart? The intelligent mechanization of CIM systems offers a path to the "magic kingdom" of volume with variety (as shown in Figure 15–1). CIM gets machines not only to produce efficiently, but also to overcome the trade-off between customization and economies-of-scale by changing what they produce efficiently.

Limitations

Despite the obvious promise for improved productivity offered by new technologies, manufacturers' experiences with both mechanization and CIM have been disappointing. General Motors, a pioneer in its efforts to introduce new automotive manufacturing technologies, was fully convinced that automation was the wave of the future. GM invested $500 million in a new factory in Detroit that featured 260 fixed production robots (to do painting, welding, and assembly work) and 50 additional mobile robots to fetch parts. Unfortunately, quality in GM's factory-of-the-future didn't measure up to expectations. In fact, the quality turned out to be much higher at GM's sister plant in Fremont, California—a plant run by Toyota managers using *outdated* manufacturing technology. GM's Buick plant in Flint, Michigan, also received $400 million worth of automation upgrades, but its management has found the benefits to be illusory, leading GM management to cancel $88 million worth of orders for new robots and retreat to the drawing board.[7] Other manufacturers have had similarly discouraging experiences.

Why has automation so far failed to live up to its early promise? One problem is that the new generation of mechanized and "intelligent" systems cannot always be run by a company's traditional work force. As noted by one expert, managers in state-of-the-art plants find themselves needing "experts in computer science, communications and database technology. The number of people in factories with this expertise is probably zero."[8] Thus, while automation offers work-force *reductions*, an unanticipated side effect has been the need for some work-force *additions*—programmers and technicians who understand and can run and maintain the new technologies. By some estimates the advent of serious factory automation means that the proportion of white-collar jobs in U.S.

---

[6] Valery, "Factory of the Future," 274.

[7] Valery, "Factory of the Future," 290.

[8] Bock, "Limping along in Robot Land."

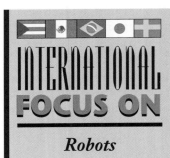

INTERNATIONAL FOCUS ON

Robots

It's a Dirty Job But Something's Gotta Do It   Nuclear waste buried at 31 U.S. sites may cost as much as $100 billion to clean up over the next thirty years. And worse than the cost is its potential to expose humans to lethal doses of radiation.

Enter field robotics, a technology on the verge of major growth. These robots are equipped with wheels, tracks, legs, fins; some even have wings. And the good news is, the technology is largely commercialized, prompting William L. "Red" Whittaker, director of the Robotics Institute's Field Robotics Center at Carnegie Mellon University, to exclaim, "It's the golden age of field robotics."

Field, or service, robots can inspect, repair and clean up commercial nuclear power plants. They can analyze, sample, excavate and clean up hazardous materials and chemical accident sites; they can detect and dispose of bombs. They can also do jobs that are merely inconvenient for humans, such as space station construction and maintenance, and exploration of other planets and deep sea environments.

For a decade field robots have been employed in underwater maintenance

of offshore oil rigs and routine maintenance inside nuclear power plants. The big breakthrough in expanding their usefulness is a fourfold increase in

Source: G. L. Miles and M. Maremont, "It's a Dirty Job but Something's Gotta Do It," *Business Week*, August 20, 1990, 92–97; and N. Gross "Why They Call Japan 'Robot Paradise,'" *Business Week*, August 20, 1990, 93.

manufacturing will rise from 50 percent of the work force in the mid-1980s to 90 percent by the mid-1990s.[9]

If automation leads to drastic changes in the nature of work (from doing the tasks to maintaining machines that do the tasks) and in the nature of the work force (from blue collar to white collar), training will be a key to its successful implementation. The Chrysler Corporation managed to avoid the kind of automation debacle suffered by GM by giving its work force 900,000 hours of training before opening up its intelligent factory. The happy result was a relatively smooth transition to a futuristic factory that produces two new car models per year rather than just one every four years.[10]

The experiences of IBM also suggest that some of the problems with automation have come from a failure to fully appreciate the differences between mechanization and intelligent mechanization. IBM reportedly sunk $350 million into a state-of-the-art typewriter plant in Kentucky. Automation reduced

---

[9]W. S. Cascio, *Managing Human Resources* (New York: McGraw-Hill, 1986), 19.

[10]Valery, "Factory of the Future," 291.

"brain" capacity, which reduces the amount of information that must flow along a tethered line between the robot and its human operator. Unlike factory robots which are neatly bolted to the floor, field robots will need the artificial equivalents of a human's six senses to maneuver safely and contend with the highly unstructured environment in which they will be used.

Field robots in Japan, where they have been in use for years, are indispensable in construction and excavation. Mobile inspection machines, including an Aqua Robot to inspect building sites along the ocean floor, are beneficiaries of Japan's technological infrastructure, which includes the biggest concentration of manufacturing robots in the world: more than 200,000. Twenty Japanese companies have divided the task of developing robot prototypes for cleaning up nuclear power plants, fighting fires, and construction projects under the sea. Beyond the development of functional technology, "the task for each company now is to make its robot smaller, lighter and cheaper," said Takayuki Tsunemi, head of the MITI consortium that has spent $100 million over eight years developing the latest field robot technology.

Besides working in environments where humans are at a disadvantage, field robots also work faster than their human counterparts. In one hour, Westinghouse's 77-inch long Rosa robot can go into a nuclear reactor and complete inspection and repair of steam pipe welds. Formerly the job was done by human "jumpers" who had to rush in and out of an area within 45 seconds to limit their exposure to radiation. Using human workers cost consumers millions in power plant downtime while the required inspections and repairs were completed.

Computer companies are concentrating on vision systems for robots, while Fuji Electric Co. has engineered manipulative devices which possess strength as well as a sense of touch. Other companies have come up with metal skins and artificial sweat glands for firefighting robots, to help them withstand sustained temperatures of over a thousand degrees centigrade.

Once it was science fiction. Now it seems robots will serve man more than we ever imagined.

the work force of the plant from 6,000 to 2,000, while doubling the number of typewriters produced annually. Further, the new typewriters are much more reliable than their predecessors, needing service only once every four years instead of annually, and cost $1,000 less. The plant's automation expert claims that the plant is so flexible that it could handle *several hundred* different product lines. The problem is that IBM never intended to use the plant for several hundred different product lines, and the plant's critics are now saying that the facility is *over*-automated.[11] Automation, especially intelligent automation, is very costly and only makes sense if the additional capacity can be used. A mechanized system will only be worth the price if volume is high. The additional flexibility of a CIM system will pay off only if flexibility is needed to accommodate individual customer needs or quick changes in product lines. American industry's fascination with technology has led to the misguided belief that automated is always better. Management's problem here is not with automation itself but with knowing how to manage it.

---

[11] Ibid., 298.

TECHNOLOGY AND INFORMATION ◆◆◆◆◆◆

According to Warren McFarlan of the Harvard Business School, "We don't change our curriculum very often." Yet 1987 was a year that warranted a major change: information-management classes were added to the list of courses required for earning a Harvard MBA. In explaining the logic behind this move, McFarlan commented that "The general managers of the next 30 years will be unable to do their jobs without a firm grasp of information management."[12]

Harvard's move to provide its business graduates with more education about information management reflects the growing realization in business circles that technology is quickly changing the demands for managing information. On the one hand are claims such as those made in the book, *The Information Edge*, that correctly managed information technology can return a profit as high as 1,000 percent on investment. On the other hand are concerns that incorrectly managed information systems increase job stress and pressures, leading productive workers to the brink of nervous breakdowns.[13]

One of the primary benefits of new developments in information technology is the increased availability of information. Many companies have now turned to electronic record-keeping systems. While an electronic filing system offers obvious advantages by eliminating the need for manual storage of information, the real value of such systems is their *retrieval* capabilities. Using "keyword" access systems, a worker can retrieve information stored on the system instantly. As noted in the "FOCUS ON: Information Availability," such speed can be critical if the information is needed immediately—say as part of the sales pitch to a valued customer or as evidence to back up an important point in a meeting. Portable computers even allow instant information access to be portable as well. Critical information can be loaded into computer memory and literally carried to the point of sale or into meetings.

In one in-house study conducted by Hewlett-Packard, 135 sales representatives were given laptop computers to help handle information storage and retrieval for their sales jobs. After six months, HP found that time spent in staff meetings had been cut by 46 percent and time spent traveling between customers and the office by 13 percent. The result: time spent with customers increased 27 percent and sales went up 10 percent.[14]

Unfortunately, the experiences of the USS *Vincennes* remind us that information availability can prove to be a sword that cuts both ways. The phrase **paralysis of analysis** describes what happens when information systems make too much information readily available. Much of the information available to us is irrelevant, too detailed, too general, obsolete, or poorly organized, and therefore is not only useless but even potentially detrimental to decisive decision making. Information systems cannot simply be passive collectors of data. Information systems must *manage* information, including its presentation, updating, and organization.

---

[12]R. Farmanfarmaian, "Why Managers Are Asking: Is the Computer Stealing *My* Job?" *Working Women*, November 1987, 70–76.

[13]J. Hoerr and M. A. Pollock, "Management Discovers the Human Side of Automation," *Business Week*, September 29, 1986, 70–75.

[14]Ibid., 73.

Focus on

*Information
Availability*

Keeping an Eye on How the Cookie Crumbles "If someone comes into my office without their laptop computer," says Randy Fields, "I tell them, 'I don't think I can talk to you now. Get your laptop.'" Few executives are as committed to information technology as Fields, who is chairman of Mrs. Fields, Inc., the world's largest retailer of cookies and specialty bakery products. To Randy Fields, computers are as vital to operations as the chocolate chips.

Fields sees the computer as the most powerful tool there is for managing people. It is used for keeping the corporate staff lean, for organizing ideas, for enabling employees to communicate directly with Debbi Fields, the company's president and CEO, and for automating most routine paperwork and decision making. "I want to transform the workplace, what people do, and how they do it," he says.

How has technology changed Mrs. Fields, Inc.? Gone are the days when Randy Fields and his team jotted down ideas on bits of paper or entered them into date books. Now, all top managers have laptop computers that help them manage their time and tasks. A computer in each cookie store also tells the store manager how much business is expected that day, based on historical data. It tells the manager, for example, how much batter to mix and at what time. Later, the computer updates the projections based on that day's experience; at the end of each day, sales data

from each store streams into headquarters for analysis. Mrs. Fields, Inc., also has used the computer to flatten its organizational chart. Employees send ideas to CEO Debbi Fields via electronic mail and receive a reply within 48 hours.

At Mrs. Fields Cookies, computers have become much more than a tool for typing reports and working spreadsheets. "If you have a business like retailing," says Randy Fields, "the change is daily, and information has to be managed daily." Wise use of technology, he believes, is one of the reasons for Mrs. Fields' growth into an international retailer with annual sales of over $180 million.

Source: Adapted from S. D. Solomon, "Use Technology to Manage People," *Inc.*, May 1990, 124–126.

New technological developments also have dramatically reduced the time required to *transmit* information from one place to another. Facsimile (fax) machines allow documents to cross the country not in days (as regular mail would require) or overnight (as express delivery services provide) but literally in seconds; cellular car phones provide individuals continuous contact with their places of work, even while traveling from one customer to another; and electronic mail systems allow users to flash their messages worldwide in a matter of seconds to as many people as need access. All three of these innovations get information where it needs to be when it needs to be there, often instantly. The value of timely information transmission is so high that the use of electronic mail systems is expected to double annually between now and the year 2000.[15]

One of the unexpected developments to result from the advancement of information technology is a change in the definition of the office. Home computers—doubling as information storage and retrieval systems *and* electronic mail receipt and transmission stations—have created new opportunities for many employees to complete their duties just about anywhere outside the office.[16] What remains to be seen is whether the growth of "telecommuting" will dramatically alter work outcomes (both personal and organizational) by reducing face-to-face contacts among organizational members.

Even without telecommuting, new information systems already have altered the social interaction patterns of workers within organizations. At banks, for instance, technological advancements have developed information systems that allow clerical workers to complete entire operations at individual work stations. The new work stations give individuals fewer reasons to interact with their coworkers, resulting in fragmentation of *social* relationships at work. Given the importance of social context on worker satisfaction, this potential disruption of the social community leaves many workers feeling at odds with the new technology.[17] As discussed in the "INTERNATIONAL FOCUS ON: Technology and Information," it is interesting to note that the usually innovative Japanese have resisted some of the most recent technological office innovations.

One development in electronic information systems that has changed the way people think about and use information are expert systems. An **expert system** is a computer program that mimics the thought processes of an expert decision maker or problem solver. At Midwest Metal Products, a small midwestern manufacturer, president William Wendt developed an expert system on his personal computer that has saved the company about $100,000 a year. Special fabrication shops like Midwest Metal Products live or die by their price estimates. If the estimate is too high, they lose the order to a competitor; if it is too low, the work doesn't turn a profit; and if they are too slow, the customer loses interest. Without the expert system, a careful estimate might have taken 15 to 20 minutes. With the system estimation time is closer to 15 to 20 *seconds*. Wendt figures the system has allowed him to reduce his estimation staff from 10 or 12 to 6, and it has given him "the edge" in his industry.[18]

The greatest benefits of expert systems, unfortunately, turn out to be their biggest problems. Expert systems are intended to render the decision that an expert would have rendered. They allow nonexperts to trust the answer the system generates. Unfortunately, all expert systems necessarily mirror some of the decision-making frailties of their creators. Worse yet, expert systems suffer from implementation problems such as input information that is outdated, invalid, or even just entered incorrectly. The result can be "expert" judgments that are catastrophically amateurish. And the poor quality of these judgments may

[15] E. Mortensen, "Adapting Electronic Mail to Management's Needs," *Administrative Management*, August 1987, 26.

[16] R. Perez-Pena, "Office for Weary Commuters is a Long Way from the Office," *New York Times*, January 7, 1992.

[17] S. Zuboff, "New Worlds of Computer-Mediated Work," *Harvard Business Review* 60 (September/October 1982): 142–152.

[18] C. L. Harris, "Office Automation: Making It Pay Off," *Business Week*, October 12, 1987.

INTERNATIONAL FOCUS ON

Technology and Information

Japan's Love for High Tech Stops at the Office It's rather puzzling. Japan's cities are some of the most congested and expensive in the world. Commuters in Tokyo are shoehorned into rush-hour trains, sometimes six days a week. Inner-city apartments can run $6,000 a month. The miracle products of the electronic age, many of them made in Japan, could be used to help offset these problems. But by and large, they aren't.

Take cellular phones: Japanese manufacturers have been selling them to Americans for years. But until recently, government regulation meant high prices and low volumes at home. Only 56,000 car phones were installed in Japan in 1987 compared to 1.1 million in the United States. Japan hasn't shown much gusto, either, for its laptop computers, which dominate the world market. Then there are desktop personal computers. The workhorse of American telecommuters, they're hard to find in Tokyo—even in large offices. Overall, personal computers are used in only 20 percent of Japan's offices. Even high-technology companies average 11 workers for each machine versus 4 in typical U.S. offices.

Why? Unlike in America, where IBM and Apple Computers have set strong personal-computer standards, the Japanese PC market is splintered among numerous, incompatible machines. That, some argue, has limited the availability of useful software and the ability to share data over networks.

Japanese writing also is a factor. It includes 2,000 commonly used Chinese characters and two phonetic scripts. As a result, there's never been an easily used Japanese typewriter—and few people take quickly to computer keyboards. Lately, Japanese word processors have caught on, but mainly among young people, not managers.

On the other hand, keyboarditis has made facsimile machines popular in Japan. "Americans like to sign their letters by hand. Japanese feel that way toward all personal communication," says Toru Maekawa, deputy director in the Ministry of International Trade & Industry. "If you get something printed, you assume the same thing has been sent to lots of other people." In technically advanced offices, there's one fax for every 22 workers.

Still, the national culture seems antithetical to telecommuting. "Japanese don't trust electronic information," says Takao Ogiya, planning section chief of the government's Small & Medium Enterprise Agency. A suburban merchant, he says, would much rather go to Tokyo to acquire business information than tap into a remote computer from his shop. "Business is built on interaction," Ogiya says. "Businessmen want to read each other's expressions." Moreover, he adds, Japanese prefer to make decisions in groups. "If one man decides, he's liable to get stuck with all the blame."

The government is trying to encourage more widespread use of new technology. One effort, called *zuno nitchi*, or "brain location," seeks to entice information industries to outlying communities. But success appears far off. "Electronic data is all in the past tense," says Yotaro Suzuki, vice-president of the Japanese Institute of Office Automation. People get the most valuable information, he says, face to face.

Source: N. Gross, "Tokyo's Love Affair with High Tech Stops at the Office," *Business Week*, October 10, 1988, 112.

go unrecognized. In one study of computer-generated judgments, researchers found that the trust in technology-generated computations is so high that answers that were off by as much as 50 percent routinely were not questioned.[19]

---

[19]L. Timnick, "Electronic Bullies," *Psychology Today*, February 1982, 10–15.

While this may be unusual, it does suggest that a little suspicion of technology is healthy. Again this reveals the importance of viewing information systems as *complements* to rather than substitutes for human judgment.

Surprising Consequences

One of the interesting benefits of new-age information systems is their ability to collect and compile information on an ongoing basis. For example, a computer can tabulate the length and destinations of all phone calls made by a sales force. The organization in turn can use this information to analyze and possibly redirect the sales force's efforts. One of the important unintended consequences for organizations of having this monitoring capability is that some employees now may feel that the new information systems are another way for management to watch over them.

Most employers rank improvement of job performance as the top reason for putting in an electronic monitoring system. At American Express, an elaborate telephone monitoring system produces daily reports for supervisors that summarize the frequency and length of calls made by employees, as well as how quickly incoming calls are answered.[20] The ability to identify abuses by employees has proven to be an attractive incidental benefit of computer monitoring systems. For phone systems alone, the cost of abuses to a big employer can run as high as $1 million annually. To discourage misuse of resources, companies use computer monitoring to generate and post usage reports that publicly identify heavy users. Public exposure often is sufficient to stop abuse. Unfortunately, computerized performance monitoring also generates negative feelings among employees. Computer performance monitoring systems have been credited with increases in formal grievances against management, increased union organizing, high work force absenteeism and turnover, and reports of low morale.[21]

In the final analysis, performance monitoring and the availability of instant feedback for employees is an important benefit provided by new-age information systems.[22] Technological advances decrease the psychological involvement of employees in their work, for example by making the tasks more abstract. Some bank-statement processing no longer involves statements at all but only images on a computer screen; some manufacturing jobs no longer involve assembling products but only monitoring a computer console while the computer-controlled robots perform the assembly. In these cases, performance feedback can play a critical role in keeping workers psychologically involved in their work. How this can be accomplished without risking some of the negatives of over-surveillance may simply be a function of how the feedback is managed. Allowing employees *direct* access to the information should minimize the impression that it might be used to punish or prod them. In turn, this should decrease negative feelings about computer monitoring and allow its potential benefits for performance to be realized.[23]

---

[20]J. Rothfeder, "Memo to Workers: Don't Phone Home," *Business Week*, January 25, 1988, 88–90.

[21]Office of Technology Assessment, *The Electronic Supervisor: New Technology, New Tensions* (OTA-CIT-33) (Washington, D.C.: U.S. Government Printing Office, 1987).

[22]T. L. Griffith, "Monitoring and Performance: A Comparison of Computer and Supervisory Monitoring," *Journal of Applied Social Psychology* 23(7) (1993): 549–572.

[23]J. J. Laabs, "Surveillance: Tool or Trap," *Personnel Journal* (June 1992): 96–104.

SMOOTHING THE TRANSITION

There is no question that advancing technology holds considerable promise for increasing worker productivity. Technology can even improve quality-of-work-life for employees by eliminating routine or mindless tasks, thereby freeing up workers to spend their time on more interesting tasks. There is also no question, unfortunately, that managing the introduction of technological changes is a delicate and difficult enterprise. When handled poorly, the advantages of new technology can evaporate in the face of a poor implementation plan.[24] In this final section of this chapter, we will examine several examples of technological innovations in an attempt to discern what practices can influence the success of changes in technology.

Managing Job Changes

An important consideration in making automation work concerns the fit between people and machines. The first Industrial Revolution laid the foundation for a terrible misunderstanding—that the point of automation is to *replace* people. As Japanese industrialist Haruo Shimada puts it, however, "Only people give wisdom to the machines."[25] Automation works best when people and machines are considered *complementary* rather than *competing* inputs.

If people and machines are to work together, what shall be the role of the people? Technology presents a danger for job design: alienation. As an example of this problem, consider what happened when a museum put in a closed-circuit TV system monitored by one security guard to replace a staff of guards patrolling the grounds. The obvious advantage was a reduction in personnel. But at the same time, the task became totally different. Instead of several guards walking and watching as before, one guard now sits and observes a bank of TV monitors. The task—monitoring instead of patrolling—is more passive and less social, and the guard becomes more detached. What is the outcome? A Federal agency did an 18-month test and found that only *5 percent* of several thousand experimental covert intrusions were detected.[26] The technology seems better, but the results certainly are not.

The nature of this paradox is portrayed in Figure 15–3. As automation is introduced, the immediate short-term effect often is simplification of the task for the worker. In a factory, automation may change the job of a low-level worker from assembling a product to monitoring the machines that do the assembly for him. The task is much more passive and much less involving. The worker is more likely to become bored and alienated, and (as in the museum example) the quality of work will reflect it. In the worst of all possible circumstances, the resulting decreases in worker efficiency may even lead management to automate further—thereby further decreasing the worker's active role and further increasing the boredom and alienation problem.

Does automation inevitably lead to work simplification? Not necessarily. The introduction of ATMs in banks in fact had the *opposite* effect. Automation

---

[24] P. S. Goodman and T. L. Griffith, "A Process Approach to the Implementation of New Technology," *Journal of Engineering Technology Management* 8, (1991): 261–285.

[25] R. Neff, "Getting Man and Machine to Live Happily Ever After," *Business Week*, April 20, 1987, 61–63.

[26] Cascio, *Managing Human Resources*, 104.

| FIGURE 15–3 | ▶ The Cycle of Automation and Job Oversimplification |

Automation can be a problem if it oversimplifies the work that remains for the work force. If mechanization of routine tasks leaves workers merely monitoring the machines, alienation may result. This alienation can lead to poor quality and low productivity, which in turn could encourage management to increase automation.

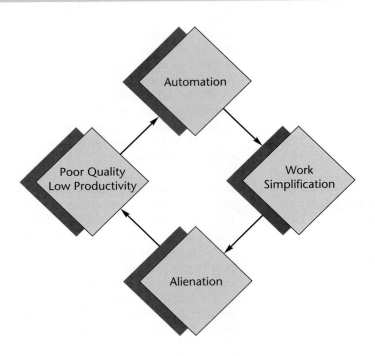

took the most routine tasks (deposits and withdrawals) away from the tellers and left them with the more complicated tasks. Unfortunately, automation in service industries (like banking) usually means a reduction in customer contact by employees—and a consequent loss in task significance for workers.

All this means that the implementation of a new technology must be preceded by an understanding of the effects that new technology will have on the jobs that remain. A new transformation technology is not always better if it means a reduction in employee involvement in tasks. Enlightened automation is automation with an eye toward the effects of technology on job design. **Socio-technical systems** is an approach to managing an organization's work force that makes technology a central concern in redesigning jobs to be more interesting, involving, and motivating for workers.

Figure 15–4 summarizes the major components of sociotechnical-systems design principles. They are the social system, moderators, and the technological system. The "social system" refers to all the human elements (including needs and desires) that are part of the work context and that can influence worker productivity dramatically. The "technological system" refers to the transformation technology—the type of production technology required, the complexity of the assembly tasks, work interdependence issues, and even the nature of the final product. Worker roles, goals, skills, and abilities all act as moderators. The moderators help define an optimal balance among what the workers want or need, what they are capable of, what kinds of tasks need to be done, and how they can get done. In effect, socio-technical systems design asks and

| FIGURE 15–4 | ▶ Sociotechnical Systems Model of Job Design |

Sociotechnical systems theory deals with designing jobs to find a fit between the social system of an organization (including such social needs of workers as affiliation needs) and the technical requirements or limits of an organization's production system.

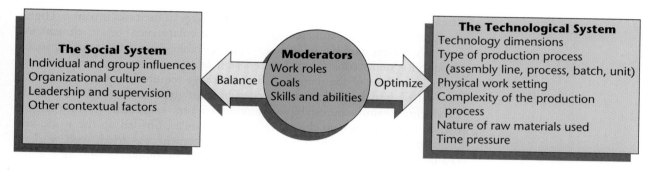

The Social System
Individual and group influences
Organizational culture
Leadership and supervision
Other contextual factors

Balance

Moderators
Work roles
Goals
Skills and abilities

Optimize

The Technological System
Technology dimensions
Type of production process
(assembly line, process, batch, unit)
Physical work setting
Complexity of the production
process
Nature of raw materials used
Time pressure

Source: T. Cummings, "Self-Regulating Work Groups: A Socio-Technical Synthesis," *Academy of Management Review* 3, 1978, 625–634; and Don Hellriegel, John W. Slocum, and Richard W. Woodman, *Organizational Behavior* (St. Paul, Minn.: West, 1986), 382.

answers the questions: How can we adapt our transformation technology to meet the needs of our workers, and how can we adapt our workers to optimize our transformation technology potential? How can we strike a *balance* between what our workers want and what the manufacturing of our product requires?

The origins of sociotechnical systems design efforts of U.S. corporations are found in the pioneering job redesign efforts in Scandinavia in the late 1960s and early 1970s. At the time, the Swedish automotive industry used traditional assembly lines and was having serious problems. Annual turnover among assembly-line workers was more than 50 percent and absenteeism ran as high as 35 percent. Further, a national survey indicated that fewer than 5 percent of high school graduates in Sweden were willing to work on the factory floors.[27]

Both Saab and Volvo first decided to experiment with autonomous work groups to address these problems. At Saab, the assembly lines were reorganized into work groups. The groups in turn were assigned overall production goals (470 engines every two workweeks) and given responsibility for organizing their own work. Under traditional assembly-line production methods, the average assembly operation for each worker lasted only 2 minutes. The semiautonomous work groups instead could combine tasks and assemble half of each engine at once (about 10 minutes) or even follow an engine completely through the assembly process (about a half hour). Work pace and timing and length of breaks also were left up to the work groups, just as long as their production goals were met.

The results of Saab's efforts were mixed. Production flexibility increased, some costs decreased, turnover was cut in half, and product quality improved. On the negative side, production speed decreased and absenteeism remained

[27]Ibid., III; and Szilagyi and Wallace, *Organizational Behavior and Performance*, (Glenview, Ill.: Scott, Foresman, 1987), 148.

essentially unchanged. Saab learned some important lessons from these efforts about the limits of job enlargement and enrichment. In one factory, a work group had been assigned the assembly of truck diesel engines. This turned out to be too much—1,500 parts and six hours—for a single group to handle, so assembly was returned to a more traditional assembly line. Eventually management at Saab realized that the success of its enlargement and enrichment attempts was highly dependent upon the *technology* of the tasks involved. Highly complex tasks offered sufficient challenge that enlargement or enrichment was not only unnecessary but in some cases undesirable. This led to a typical sociotechnical systems conclusion: Job redesign efforts at Saab became dependent upon an analysis of the manufacturing *technology* required for assembly.

Volvo's initial attempts at job redesign were quite similar to those at Saab. Production teams were established among workers with common work assignments; the teams set up their own work schedules, divided up the work, and handled their own quality control. Job enlargement was tried, with workers changing jobs sometimes several times per day, or following the same automobile through a number of consecutive work stations on the assembly line. Unlike at Saab, however, initial mixed results convinced management at Volvo that something different was necessary.

The something different turned out to be radical changes in the technical design of Volvo's Kalmar automobile assembly plant. At the Kalmar plant, traditional automotive assembly *line* technology was abandoned. In its place instead appeared an assembly technology that was suited perfectly to the use of semiautonomous work groups.

The Kalmar plant was not designed like a typical automotive assembly plant. There is no endless assembly line. Instead there are compartmentalized workshops with large windows. The workshops are designed to accommodate the use of separate semiautonomous work teams. Each work team has its own discrete space on the shop floor and can make its own decisions about timing and length of breaks. Computer screens beam production rates out to employees every hour, providing instant feedback. The automobiles being assembled are mounted on trolleys that track from workshop to workshop by following a computer tape affixed to the floor.

Kalmar represents the ultimate in sociotechnical systems design—the redesigning of a factory to accommodate and even enhance job enrichment efforts. Kalmar has its detractors, however. The plant cost $25 million to build, which is between 10 percent and 30 percent more than comparable traditional plants. The plant has limited capacity (only up to 60,000 autos per year, compared to as many as 400,000 per year at similar U.S. facilities), leading to questions about the generalizability of Volvo's successes to higher-volume operations. Finally, production costs at Kalmar are *higher* than at comparable plants, though management claims that productivity is high and absenteeism quite low compared to other facilities.[28]

The experiences of Saab, however, suggest that sociotechnical design principles need not necessitate such a radical redesign plan. At Saab, designing jobs with sociotechnical principles in mind meant tailoring job enrichment programs to address the distinguishing characteristics of a production technology.

---

[28] Szilagyi and Wallace, *Organizational Behavior and Performance*, 450.

Many companies are reluctant to publicize their sociotechnical job redesign efforts. Certainly many Fortune 500 companies, including AT&T and General Motors, have tried sociotechnical systems approaches at one time or another, and reliable sources estimate that probably several hundred U.S. manufacturing facilities have been completely redesigned along the lines of sociotechnical systems principles.[29] Procter & Gamble is a leading advocate of sociotechnical systems, having used these principles to design or redesign 20 plants by the late 1980s.[30]

Generating Ownership

Perhaps the most critical component of the sociotechnical systems approach to successful new technology implementation is increased worker participation in decision making. Sometimes a company can more easily realize benefits of technological changes when workers are brought on board early in the implementation process. Increased participation can compensate for the decreased job involvement brought on by a better transformation technology. Consider the following example:

> Sophisticated computer technology allows the central office of a large company to begin monitoring electronic telecommunications switching equipment in remote locations. This may eventually allow for fewer and less-skilled employees at local sites. But the local technicians resist the central monitoring centers. They fear forced relocation, job loss, the inability to keep up with their skills, and loss of control over their work while they nevertheless remain accountable for the local operation. When a central monitoring center is implemented by management fiat, it fails. Technicians resist working in the center and taking orders from it. . . .
>
> [The] conflict between the center and local technicians led the general manager to shut down the center for one year to explore alternatives. After much consideration, he asked the local technicians to volunteer to be covered by the center. Local technicians could choose the shifts the center would cover. Because they now retained some control over their switches, the local technicians accepted this compromise. The monitoring center was reopened and put into successful operation.[31]

The technological innovation in this case did not necessarily have to diminish the most desirable aspect (autonomy) of the local technicians' jobs. By involving the local technicians in the implementation phase of the change, the general manager was able to enlist their assistance in finding the best way to realize the full benefits of the new technology without undermining the positive aspects of their jobs. Through this kind of employee involvement, management helps the target work force better understand and prepare for a new technology by enlisting its assistance in planning implementation.

At Westinghouse's automated Grand Rapids furniture plant, about 65 percent of the 830 employees are involved in an elaborate system of committees and task forces that discuss anything from business strategy to the redesign of

---

[29] R. E. Walton, "From Control to Commitment in the Workplace," *Harvard Business Review* 63(2), (1985): 76–84.

[30] E. E. Lawler III, *High-Involvement Management* (London: Jossey-Bass, 1986), 84.

[31] M. London and J. P. MacDuffie, "Technological Innovations: Case Examples and Guidelines," *Personnel*, November 1987, 26; and R. Neff, "Getting Man and Machine to Live Happily Ever After," *Business Week*, April 20, 1987, 61–63.

Employee involvement in planning and implementing automated systems is critical to the success of such an endeavor. An employee planning group at Westinghouse's Grand Rapids furniture plant was responsible for the installation of a CAD/ CAM system similar to the one pictured here, which is credited with increasing worker productivity by 70 percent.

work areas for product innovation. This employee-involvement program helped Westinghouse realize a 75 percent improvement in productivity per employee when it brought in a computer-aided design and computer-aided manufacturing (CAD/CAM) system in the mid-1980s.[32]

The importance of worker involvement in automation planning and implementation is explained best by the past masters of successful automation, Hewlett-Packard. HP's William Bowler found that "there were a lot of informal procedures which were not supposed to be there. There's a lot of 'fixing' done by people on the line which never gets shown on any organizational chart." Fixing means using human discretion—the judgment that something subtle is wrong and needs to be altered. If this function performed by the humans cannot be programmed into the machines, the machines cannot compete with the people.[33]

For HP there are several messages here. The company now preaches that a very detailed understanding of a task must precede its automation. Management needs to find out how work in its organization is *really* done—not just how it is supposed to be done—before trying to automate the work. HP also

---

[32] Neff, "Getting Man and Machine," 1987.

[33] OTA, *The Electronic Supervisor.*

preaches slow transition into automation. It does not attempt wholesale automation of entire lines but instead begins with "islands of automation" within a line. As bugs gradually are worked out within the islands (including, no doubt, further learning about how the work *really* gets done), the islands can be expanded.

The larger message of HP's approach to automation is that the correct view of automation is *assistance* rather than *replacement* of human workers. The experiences of Shenandoah Life Insurance reinforce this belief. Shenandoah thought it could dramatically reduce policy processing time by automating its processing and claims operations in Roanoke, Virginia. After installing a $2 million "automated" system, the company found that it still took 27 working days—and 32 clerks—to process a typical policy conversion request. Once Shenandoah realized its new automated system could never *replace* its employees, the company formed semi-autonomous work teams to decide how to best put the technology to use. By having people working *with* the technology, application-handling times dropped to *2 days*. In six years, Shenandoah was processing 50 percent more applications, despite having trimmed its work force by 10 percent.[34]

At the Harvard Business School, they call the newest generation of technology-savvy business school graduates "gold-collar" MBAs who combine business know-how with technical expertise.[35] For these **"gold-collar" managers** to be worth their weight, their technical expertise must go beyond knowledge about technology. As the experiences of other companies have proved, "gold-collar" expertise also must include an understanding of how to get people and machines to fit rather than fight each other in the workplace. Only then will America's newest generation of corporate leaders be able to meet the challenge of managing new technologies for maximum organizational benefit.

Fighting Worker Obsolescence

The optimistic party line now is that the newest generation of machines is intended to complement rather than replace workers. Nevertheless, concerns remain that the increases in productivity achieved through mechanization must result in fewer jobs. In particular, employees are concerned that increasing automation may render their current skills obsolete, necessitating their replacement (either the skills or the workers!), or "de-skilling" jobs. (A de-skilled job can be done by a lower-paid worker with less training.) A related fear is that automation simply will do away with jobs.

Certainly workers do have legitimate cause for concern. In high-technology manufacturing, output per worker is expected to rise by almost 50 percent between 1981 and 1993, which is nearly double the projected increases for traditional manufacturing and service industries. The dollar output of high-tech companies during this period will virtually double, but the work force will increase only by about 30 percent.[36] Thus, even in expanding industries, automation does not seem to promise equal expansion of job opportunities.

---

[34]J. Hoerr and M. A. Pollock, "Management Discovers the Human Side of Automation," *Business Week*, September 29, 1986, 70–75.

[35]Farmanfarmaian, "Why Managers Are Asking."

[36]"America Rushes to High Tech for Growth," *Business Week*, March 28, 1983, 84–90.

The most likely casualties of increasing automation are jobs in small- and medium-size companies. In the lumber industry, for example, high technology has taken over in the last decade and is driving out small operators. In the modern versions of a traditional "Paul Bunyan" sawmill, the mill hands rarely touch wood. An operator at Lakeland Mills, Ltd., sits at a console in a glass-walled booth, flipping switches to position logs; video monitors display the mill's operations. Computers use electronic scanners to measure each log and decide how to cut it up into the largest amount of usable lumber. The computer chooses from among 100,000 cutting patterns. "I have to do a little physical labor," notes the operator, "but not very often. I have to pick up a log if it falls off the conveyor." At the operator's side, a radio plays music all day to relieve the boredom.[37] These new computer-driven sawmills are pictures of precision and efficiency. But for better or worse, they need very few workers to operate them and, through the wonders of computer programming, waste far less wood than manually operated systems. In some of the most modern mills, work-force reductions can run as high as 80 percent.

Consequently, many small lumber mills were forced to close their doors in the 1980s. From 1977 to 1984, the amount of lumber produced in the United States remained constant. At the same time, however, the size of the work force in U.S. lumber mills fell 25 percent and the number of mills decreased 18 percent. The fact is that some of the smaller mills cannot afford the up-front price tag of modernization—often $15 million or more. Further, some of the smaller mills are small precisely because they are located in small or low-volume forests that cannot provide enough work for a large, automated mill to break even. The smaller mills nevertheless must match prices with the larger mills in the lumber market, where the production efficiency of larger, automated operations makes it impossible for the smaller mills to compete.

The possibility that technological advances will result in substantial work-force reductions has not been lost on labor organizers. Unions have adopted two strategies: protectionist and forward-looking. Protectionist actions include writing into labor contracts clauses that protect work-force employment in spite of technological innovation and that prohibit management from lowering wages when job functions are de-skilled. On the forward-looking side, the International Association of Machinists at Boeing requires the company to hold briefings at least annually concerning potential technological innovations on the horizon, and the Graphic Arts International Union has gotten its employers to contribute a fixed amount per worker per month into a fund for retraining technologically displaced workers.[38]

It is interesting to note that the worker-displacement dilemma posed by technological advances may have technological solutions as well. Technological advances have altered more than just the way work is done. Technology also is changing *training methods* for jobs of the future. New methods for training and retraining displaced workers provide considerably more flexibility than before. Computerized courses allow students to work at their own pace. These courses also change the nature of the learning process to make it less threatening.[39]

[37] A. Bayless, "Technology Reshapes North America's Lumber Plants," *The Wall Street Journal*, October 16, 1986, 6.

[38] J. S. Solomon, "Union Responses to Technological Change: Protecting the Past or Looking to the Future?" *Labor Studies Journal*, Fall 1987, 51–65.

[39] M. Ivey, "Long-Distance Learning Gets an "A" At Last," *Business Week*, May 9, 1988, 108–110.

SUMMARY   ◆◆◆◆◆

Technology, broadly defined, is anything the workers of an organization use (including recipes, formulas, tools, and machinery) to transform the organization's inputs into outputs. Technology also represents "the edge"—the way for management to increase the productivity of its work force and increase profits, or at least maintain competitiveness. But in reality, technology by itself is no edge at all. The competitive edge comes when managers achieve a harmonious integration of their human and technological resources.

Technological determinism refers to the influence technology has on behaviors of and in organizations. The extent to which an organization must tailor its outputs to the needs of particular customers will determine what type of production technology the organization can use. The technology in turn affects the behaviors and design of the organization. The rate of change of technology within an industry also will influence an organization's actions. Technology is an important source of environmental uncertainty that organizations must manage.

Two major sources of technological innovation are automation and information technology. Automation occurs when a task performed by a human worker is mechanized to be performed by a machine. Intelligent automation occurs when the design of automated technology includes the ability to adapt or make decisions. Automation works best when designed to complement the skills of, rather than replace, human workers. Information technology is rapidly changing the availability and use of information in organizations. New information technologies have made it possible to find almost any piece of information and send it anywhere instantly. Some of these technological changes are even altering the definition of the "office" by making it possible for employees to be in constant contact with coworkers regardless of their location. Expert systems also are changing the efficiency and effectiveness of human decision-making powers. New information technologies are allowing managers to continuously monitor worker performance. When managed appropriately, this new ability can put more useful feedback in the hands of workers when they need it most. If managed poorly, this monitoring capability can negatively affect work-force morale.

Implementation of new transformation technologies must entail some awareness of the potential of worker alienation if automation oversimplifies work. Employers also must be aware of and plan for worker displacement, replacement, or retraining required when a new technology is brought in. Socio-technical systems is an approach to job redesign that makes technology a central concern in making work more interesting, involving, and motivating for workers. The term "gold collar" refers to a new generation of workers who have both business skills and technology expertise. Because of the rapid advance of technological developments, technological expertise needs to mean more than just understanding how to use new technologies. It also must include an awareness of how to correctly integrate the benefits of that new technology with the organization's human resources. "Gold-collar" managers must understand the effects of new technologies on the nature of work for employees, and they must work hard to encourage a sense of partnership and ownership of new technologies by their workers. For the current generation of managers, an understanding of technology is a plus; for the next generation of managers it will be a necessity.

Key Terms

Automation   Using machines to replace or assist workers.

Computer-integrated manufacturing (CIM)   Manufacturing technologies that combine task mechanization with computerized information processing about the task.

Expert systems   Computer programs that mimic the thought processes of an expert decision maker or problem solver.

Gold-collar managers   Managers who combine business know-how with technical expertise in how to get people and machines to work together (rather than fight each other) in the workplace.

Mechanization   Programming a machine to execute the component actions of a work task faster, more precisely, and more consistently than any human.

Output customization   Extent to which an organization's products or services are influenced by customer needs.

Paralysis of analysis   When timely and decisive decision making fails to occur because too much irrelevant, detailed, obsolete, or poorly organized information is readily available.

Robot   Machine guided by automatic controls to perform various complex functions like a human being.

Socio-technical systems   An approach to managing that makes technology a central concern in redesigning jobs.

Technological change   The rate at which transformation technologies change and develop within an industry.

Technological determinism   Perspective that the way a firm is organized (how it makes decisions or how much training its line workers receive, for example) depends on the technology the firm uses to transform its inputs into outputs.

Technological type   Joan Woodward's classifications of ways an organization can transform inputs into outputs, which determine behavior in the organization: (A) unit or small-batch production, (B) large-batch production, and (C) mass production or process manufacturing.

Discussion Questions

1. There is an old saying that "a little knowledge is a dangerous thing." With the advent of new information technologies, the reverse problem may be true. How might a lot of information be a dangerous thing, too?

2. What are some of the ways that the arrival of a new technology can threaten the jobs of current employees? What can a manager do to minimize the negative impact on work-force morale of a new technology?

3. What is the role of expert systems in organizational decision making? Does the use of expert systems guarantee that managers will make better decisions?

4. Describe the two forms of technological determinism discussed in this chapter. How do both of these reflect the powerful influence of uncertainty on behavior of and in organizations?

5. What does it mean to be a "gold-collar" manager? What specific skills will the "gold-collar" managers of the future need to have?

6. Why is work-force involvement critical to the successful implementation of a new technology?

7. As new information technologies allow the dissolution of the traditional office, how is the nature of work likely to change? Are these changes likely to alter organizational outcomes, such as the quality of organizational decision making?

8. Are advances and developments in information technology (such as high-speed computers and fax machines) making the concept of bounded rationality obsolete?

If You Want to Know More

An entire issue of *Organizational Dynamics* (Autumn 1985) was devoted to the issue of advancing technology and its effects on organizational behavior. The special issue includes three particularly insightful pieces. An article by Shoshana Zuboff entitled "Automate/Informate: The Two Faces of Intelligent Technology" explores the differences between using technology for automation and information functions. An article by Karl Weick entitled "Cosmos vs. Chaos: Sense and Nonsense in Electronic Contexts" discusses how electronic media may alter the meaning of information. Finally, Peter Keen's article, "Computers and Managerial Choice," discusses the role of new technologies in helping managers make better decisions.

An article by Donald Gerwin, "Relationships between Structure and Technology" (in the 1981 Oxford University Press *Handbook of Organizational Design*, edited by P. Nystrom and W. H. Starbuck), discusses some of the issues raised in the beginning of the chapter concerning technology's influence on the design of organizations.

One important issue raised by advancing technology and not discussed in this chapter is information privacy in an age of electronic record-keeping. This issue is addressed in an article entitled "Don't Tread on My Data: Protecting Individual Privacy in the Information Age," by Philip Elmer-DeWitt, in the July 6, 1987, issue of *Time*.

The issue of worker displacement by technological innovation is discussed in "Worker Obsolescence: The Human Resource Dilemma of the '80s," by Jeffrey Bracker and John Pearson, in the December 1986 issue of *Personnel Administrator*. Smoothing the introduction of new technology under these circumstances is discussed by Lisa Mainiero and Robert De-Michiell in their article, "Minimizing Employee Resistance to Technological Change," in the July 1986 issue of *Personnel*. Technology implementation issues also are discussed in "The Electronic Office: How to Make it User Friendly," by Wilbert O. Galitz and David J. Cirillo, in the April 1983 *Management Review*.

Finally, the ways in which information technologies may alter interactions between workers are explored in "Social Psychological Aspects of Computer-Mediated Communication," by Sara Kiesler, Jane Siegel, and Tim McGuire, in the October 1984 issue of *American Psychologist*.

On Your Own

Attitudes toward Computer Usage Are you ready to move into the age of information technology? Your responses to the following questions will provide you an indication of your own receptiveness to the introduction of new technologies in organizations. Answer the following questions using this scale:

Strongly 1 . . . . 2 . . . . 3 . . . . 4 . . . . 5 Strongly
Agree   Disagree

_____ 1. I would prefer to type a paper on a word processor rather than on a typewriter.

_____ 2. Whenever I use something that is computerized, I am afraid I will break it.

_____ 3. I like to keep up with technological advances.

_____ 4. I know that I will not understand how to use computers.

_____ 5. Using a computer is too time consuming.

_____ 6. I feel that having a computer at work would help me with my job.

_____ 7. I prefer not to learn how to use a computer.

_____ 8. I would like to own, or I do own, a computer.

_____ 9. I like to play video games.

_____ 10. I feel that the use of computers in schools will help children learn mathematics.

_____ 11. I prefer to use an automatic teller for most of my banking.

_____ 12. If I had children, I would not buy them computerized toys.

_____ 13. I have had bad experiences with computers.

_____ 14. I would prefer to order items in a store through a computer rather than wait for a store clerk.

_____ 15. I feel that the use of computers in schools will negatively affect children's reading and writing abilities.

_____ 16. I do not like using computers because I cannot see how work is being done.

_____ 17. I would prefer to go to a store that uses computerized price-scanners rather than go where the clerks enter each price into a cash register.

_____ 18. I do not feel I have control over what I do when I use a computer.

_____ 19. I think that computers and other technological advances have helped to improve our lives.

_____ 20. I do not like to program computerized items such as VCRs and micro-wave ovens.

Your instructor will supply you with directions for scoring your responses.

Source: P. M. Popovich, K. R. Hyde, I. Zakrajsek, and C. Blumer, "The Development of the Attitudes Toward Computer Usage Scale," *Educational & Psychological Measurement*, 1987, vol. 47, 261–269.

CLOSING CASE

CHAPTER 15

THE MANAGER'S MEMO

FROM: P. Briggs, Purchasing Manager

TO: T. Han, Sales Manager

RE: Car Phones

I have just received literature on a product that you might be interested in: deluxe car phones. According to the manufacturer, this product could greatly increase the productivity of the sales department.

   If you install a car phone in each salesperson's car, you can be in virtually continuous contact with the sales force. Whenever you want to talk to one of the sales reps, you simply call. Furthermore, each salesperson can use a portable computer to transmit orders and reports through the car phone to the office. With this communication power, the sales reps will seldom have to come into the office and can spend more time on the road making sales calls.

   This means we can also lower overhead costs. Because the salespeople will be on the road most of the time, they will not each need an office. Instead, we can consolidate their offices into one bulpen, and use the extra space for other activities.

   A special benefit of this particular car phone is that it has a long-range beeper. The beeper sends back a signal, so you can use an electronic map to track where each salesperson goes. This information will enable you to review and improve the efficiency of their call patterns.

   Would you like to pursue this idea? Please let me know what you think about it.

Case Discussion Questions

Assume you are the sales manager, and write a response to the purchasing manager's memorandum. Do you think the purchasing manager has thought out the impact of this technological innovation carefully? How is this innovation likely to alter the nature of work for the sales force? How are the salespeople likely to react? What can the sales manager do to improve the likelihood that the new phone will enhance the productivity of the sales force?

◆◆◆◆◆◆

ORGANIZATIONAL STRUCTURE AND DESIGN

HEWLETT-PACKARD RETHINKS ITSELF:
UNDOING THE HP BUREAUCRACY ◆◆◆◆◆◆◆

A management model for all America, the HP Way was based on respect and rapport among executives. But as the 1980's drew to a close, something new was needed. Sluggish decision making was crippling the company's competitive edge in its key product areas. A burdensome bureaucracy caused completion of key projects, such as its high-speed workstations, to slip beyond deadlines.

CEO John A. Young had to do something about it. Management committees had been useful until they began multiplying like a virus. So the company flattened its organization, cutting costs with an early retirement program and revamping the sales and marketing functions. Profits rebounded and new product introductions got back on track. US West ordered $25 million of HP products, and the company won some other highly competitive and lucrative minicomputer contracts.

To model the organizational change, Young and founder David Packard had only to look to HP's successful laser-printer operation, which had become highly competitive while operating outside the entrenched system of management by committee. Without overlapping committees, decisions came fast and furious. One was to incorporate printer hardware from Canon Inc. in Japan. Another was to aim the laser printer marketing effort at the entire universe of PC users, rather than just existing HP markets. Another was to strategically sign hundreds of dealers to stock the printers, which were compatible with all IBM PC clones.

This group could work outside the corporate organization because its products were outside the corporate strategy per se. With its success, the company's executives saw that HP had alternatives to its existing ways of doing business. The unit had figured out how to bring out new models and make money even while the market drove prices down. Managers in other HP units were inspired by what VP Richard A. Hackborn and his team of engineers accomplished. They had decided themselves that there was a huge market for inexpensive printers. They broke all the rules and succeeded, paving the way for innovation to join collegiality and consensus in the HP Way.

Source: Barbara Buell with Robert Hof and Gary McWilliams, "Hewlett Packard Rethinks Itself," *Business Week*, April 1, 1991, 76–79.

INTRODUCTION

The structure of an organization is the formal means by which it coordinates the activities of its work force to accomplish its goals and objects. As suggested in the restructuring effort of Hewlett-Packard, however, putting a structure into place does not mean that it will work. John Young needed to adjust the structure of Hewlett-Packard to remain competitive in the rapidly changing computer industry. In fact, if we examine the history of most successful organizations, we will find that they have restructured several times to improve the coordination of the work and their employees.

Virtually all organized human activity requires two forms of organizational structure: the division of labor into various component tasks to be performed, and the coordination of these tasks to produce the organization's outputs. As

---

FIGURE 16–1 ▶ **A Hospital: An Organization Structured by Knowledge and Skills**

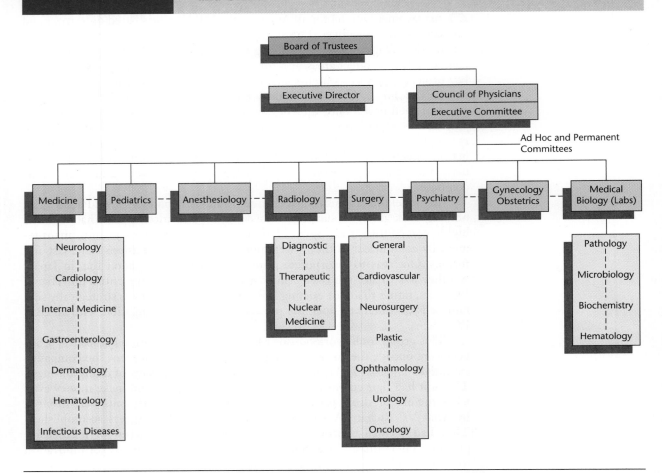

Source: Henry Mintzberg, *The Structuring of Organizations,* © 1979, p. 109. Adapted by permission of Prentice Hall, Englewood Cliffs, New Jersey.

noted in Chapter 1, organizations typically form because some goal or mission entails a variety of component tasks, more than any one individual could hope to accomplish alone. In an organization, different members of the work force are assigned component tasks of the organization's mission, known as their roles.[1] The different roles and behaviors of the organization's work force then must be coordinated. This is where structure emerges. **Organizational structure** is the skeleton of an organization that captures the relationships among different roles in the organization. **Organization design,** on the other hand, is the process of *creating* structure: grouping roles and activities to coordinate the interdependencies among organizational actors effectively.

A common way to represent the organization's structure to employees (and outsiders as well) is through an organizational chart, such as the one shown in Figure 16–1. An organizational chart is a representation of the formal lines of authority in an organization. Each box on the chart represents a position. Boxes are connected to each other with vertical solid lines (indicating a direct reporting relationship). Horizontal solid lines represent communication (but not authority) relationships. Broken lines represent informal or infrequent relationships.

In this chapter, we will describe the most common organizational structures and examine the ways they influence the relationships and interactions among members of an organization. Then we will identify the factors that influence the effectiveness of a particular organizational structure and examine what happens to organizational performance when there is a fit between the organizational structure and the various factors that influence it. We conclude the chapter by examining some symptoms of inappropriate organizational structures.

ELEMENTS OF ORGANIZATIONAL STRUCTURE

An organization's structure reflects the way the organization divides up and coordinates work. An appropriate structure (the division and coordination of tasks) is essential to the efficient attainment of an organization's goals. In this section, we will consider four design features that organizations use to divide up and coordinate work: job specialization, departmentalization, centralization, and span of control.

Job Specialization

The overall task of any organization can be divided into various component tasks. At Hewlett-Packard, the overall task is selling computers and peripherals. The component tasks include production and sales; production itself requires developing new technologies, manufacturing the devices, and creating and exploiting the market for these products. The major benefit of **job specialization**—assigning each member of the work force a limited number of component tasks—is that employees can become very skilled and productive at a limited number of assigned tasks. Further, when workers' roles are limited in

---

[1]James D. Thompson, *Organizations in Action* (New York: McGraw-Hill, 1967).

scope, the skills for a particular role are easily taught to another employee, such as a newcomer.

Jobs can be specialized along two dimensions: the number of tasks assigned to a role (horizontal specialization) and the amount of responsibility for organizing tasks assigned to a role (vertical specialization). Jobs are specialized horizontally to increase productivity and to match employees with tasks. Horizontal specialization increases productivity by using repetition and standardization and by making the task easier to perform. As noted in Chapter 12, however, the increases in productivity achieved by horizontal specialization may be short-lived if they lead to worker boredom or alienation.

While horizontal specialization limits the number of component tasks assigned to a particular role, vertical specialization separates those who perform tasks from those who administer or organize them. Vertical specialization is useful because it takes different skills or perspectives to organize tasks than to perform them.[2] Often jobs that are horizontally specialized also must be vertically specialized. With horizontal specialization, the job incumbent sees only a small piece of the task. This may make it difficult for job incumbents to relate or integrate their work into the larger picture that includes the work of others. The need to see the larger picture was one of the motivations behind HP's committee structure. Unfortunately, other checks and balances needed to be put into place.

Departmentalization

Departmentalization, the grouping of organizational roles by determining which jobs fit together, is another feature used to structure organizations. Related tasks can be assigned to the same subunit (a department, for instance) because of similarities in the required knowledge and skills members bring to the job. For example, universities divide faculty into colleges, schools, and departments; the members of each group become more similar as we move down the list of categories or divisions.

In addition to similarity of skills and knowledge, departmentalization can be based on similar levels of skills and abilities. For example, traditional hospitals and health maintenance organizations (HMOs) have somewhat different structures. The skills required in each setting are similar, but the goals of the two types of organizations are different (curing illness in hospitals versus preventing illness in HMOs). The HMO is focused on efficiently handling patients. The task of seeing patients at an HMO is more specialized, and each member of the medical team has a task to complete. Physicians see patients in both hospitals and HMOs, but in an HMO the patient typically is first screened by another health-care professional, such as a nurse's assistant. The time the physician spends with a patient is limited to make the most efficient use of the physician's time. In contrast, the hospital is more focused on effectiveness. Consequently, hospitals are structured by skills. There is a cardiology unit, a trauma unit, and so on. The physicians in each unit spend more time with each patient and the goal is to cure the illness. Hospitals place less emphasis on efficiency, which is reflected in their organizational structures.

---

[2] H. Mintzberg, *The Structuring of Organizations* (Englewood Cliffs, N.J.: Prentice-Hall, 1979).

An organization's component tasks also can be grouped by the functions of the component tasks. In functional departmentalization, typical organizational functions include production, marketing, finance, personnel, and accounting. The major advantage of functional departmentalization is that experts in an area are concentrated and can share their expertise to accomplish their tasks. A disadvantage of this method of organizational design is the creation of barriers between departments. These barriers limit communication, decrease the salience of organizational goals, and create unnecessary competition for resources among groups.

An organization's component tasks can also be departmentalized by the types of outputs or products they produce. In a diversified organization, all the jobs required to produce and sell a product or group of related products are under the direction of one individual. The firm grows by increasing the number and types of products it produces. In fact, as firms grow, it becomes increasingly more difficult to coordinate the functional areas. A common response to organizational success in the form of growth is to reorganize from functional to diversified (product) departmentalization.

An organization's tasks can also be organized by the type of client they serve (for example, retail versus wholesale) or by geographic region. Banks, for example, have different departments for consumer loans, business loans, mortgage loans, and the like. If an organization is geographically dispersed, then it may be necessary to divide groups based on their geographic relationship. It is very difficult to manage an organization over large distances, and diverse social and cultural expectations add to the problems. Examples of product, function, client, and geographic departmentalization are illustrated in Figure 16–2.

The advantage of these forms of departmentalization is that they allow quick responses to changes in the product, in the client base, or in a geographic region. These structures also encourage departmental loyalty by focusing employees' attention on the attainment of a common goal (such as the success of a particular product line, satisfying the customer, or serving a geographic region). The disadvantage of these forms of structure is redundancy. An organization with a product, client, or geographic orientation must assign people in all functional areas (such as sales and personnel) to each product, customer, or geographic area. In addition, the attention of these functional area specialists will not be focused on their area of expertise, so they may be less likely to keep pace with changes in their profession.

Centralization

Centralization of organizational structure is based on the dual needs of division and coordination of labor. An organization is centralized to the extent that its decision-making power rests with one or a few individuals. In a highly centralized organization, all decisions are made by one person and implemented through formal authority channels. While centralization typically improves the coordination of an organization's activities, it does have problems. Centralized decision makers often do not have all the information necessary to make good decisions, or cannot make decisions and send them back down the organization's formal authority channels quickly enough to be effective. In the past 30 years, the trend among companies in the United States has been to decentralize. Decision-making authority is being pushed lower and lower in American orga-

FIGURE 16–2 ▶Four Types of Departmental Structure

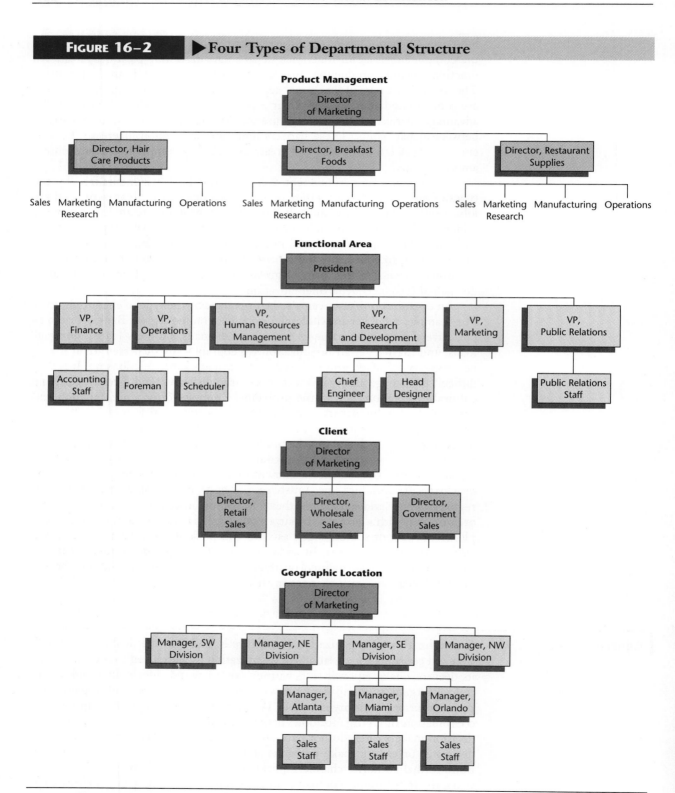

Source: J. R. Gordon, *A Diagnostic Approach to Organizational Behavior* (Boston: Allyn & Bacon, 1987).

nizations so that decisions can be made quickly and at the point where the most diagnostic information is available.

In the "Focus on: Centralization," we examine the impact of decentralization on the structure of an organization. An organization should consider a number of factors before deciding whether or not to decentralize:

1. The more change an organization faces and the more quickly decisions must be made, the more likely that decentralization will prove beneficial. Decentralization allows a work group (for instance, a product division) to respond quickly to changes, rather than having to request instructions through the organization's formal authority channels.

2. As organizations increase in size, centralized decision makers get further and further from the information they need to make high-quality decisions, and it takes longer and longer for information and their decisions to travel up and down the organization's formal channels of authority. Thus, growth inevitably leads to decentralization of decision making.

3. Risk often tends to centralize decision making. Where the consequences of making poor decisions are great, top management will be unlikely to give up control.

4. Finally, centralization may be a function of the quality of an organization's channels of communication. If an organization's channels of communication are highly efficient, centralized decision makers may be able to gather information and return decisions quickly enough to remain effective.[3]

Span of Control

A fourth element of organizational structure is the span of control. **Span of control** is the number of people reporting to a manager. The size of an organization's work groups is determined by its managerial span of control. Span of control is directly related both to the closeness of supervision and the "depth" of the organization. With fewer subordinates, a manager can supervise more closely. Such a narrow span of control is important in an organization or work unit with a task in which close interpersonal control of subordinates is desired. If the task requires machine-paced, well-learned, or easily monitored behaviors, there is less need for a narrow span of control.[4] In fact, to assess the appropriate span of control, a manager must consider both the routineness of the task and the time required to monitor and coordinate subordinates' activities.[5]

Span of control is also directly related to the number of levels in (or "depth" of) an organization. Typically, the greater the span of control in an organization, the fewer the number of hierarchical levels. An organization with few hierarchical levels appears "flat" in its organizational chart. An organization with many hierarchical levels (and typically a narrow span of control) appears

---

[3] E. Dale, *Organization* (New York: American Management Association, 1967).

[4] P. M. Blau and W. R. Scott, *Formal Organizations* (San Francisco: Chandler, 1962).

[5] K. D. Mackenzie, *Organization Structures* (Arlington Heights, Ill.: AHM Publishing, 1978).

Centralization

The Bureaucracy Busters If you were to ask a CEO in the year 2000 to draw the company's organizational chart, what emerged would probably bear little resemblance to even the trendiest flattened pyramid structures around today. While the corporations of the future will still retain some vestiges of the old hierarchy and maybe a few traditional departments to take care of the rote tasks, future organizations will consist of a pattern of constantly changing teams, task forces, partnerships, and other informal structures. Like dancers, tomorrow's corporation teams, variously composed of shop-floor workers, managers, technical experts, suppliers, and customers, will join together to do a job and then disband, with everyone going off to the next assignment.

Call this new model the adaptive organization. It will bust through bureaucracy to serve customers better and make the company more competitive.

Instead of looking to the boss for direction, tomorrow's employee will be trained to look closely at the work process and to devise ways to improve on it, even if this means temporarily leaving her regular job to join an ad hoc team attacking the problem. So far, this adaptive organization exists more as an ideal than as a reality, but aspects of it are taking shape at companies such as Apple Computer, Levi Strauss, Xerox, and Cypress Semiconductor. Last year, for instance, an information Xerox team made up of people from accounting, sales, distribution, and administration saved the company $200 million in inventory costs. Cypress, a maker of specialty computer chips based in San Jose, California, has developed a computer system that keeps track of all of its 1,500 employees as they crisscross between different functions, teams, and projects. Apple is developing a computer network called Spider that instantly tells a manager whether an employee is available to join his project, what the employee's skills are, and where she or he is located in the corporation.

The adaptive organization incorporates the informal organization—one that operates alongside the formal organization composed of alliances between people and the power relationships that actually get work done—and draws its power from the same fund of energy. It provides opportunities for creativity and initiative too often found only in small, entrepreneurial companies. It works by aligning what the corporation wants—innovation and improvement—with what turns people on: namely a chance to use their heads

Sources: Brian Dumaine, "The Bureaucracy Busters," *Fortune,* June 17, 1991, 35–50; and "Xerox Is Rewriting the Book on Organization 'Architecture'," *Chicago Tribune,* section 3, (1), December 29, 1992.

"tall" in its organizational chart. Figure 16–3 illustrates both a flat and a tall organizational structure.

Are tall or flat organizations more effective? In terms of overall performance of organizations with the same tasks, it seems that flat organizations have a slight edge over tall organizations. In a study of Sears, Roebuck and Company, those Sears stores with flat structures had relatively better sales, profitability,

and expand their skills. Traditional hierarchies have often had the opposite effect.

Xerox CEO Paul Allaire explains, "We're never going to outdiscipline the Japanese on quality. To win, we need to find ways to capture the creative and innovative spirit of the American worker." To do so, new managers at Xerox are no longer one-dimensional engineers. They now know about marketing, finance, management and how to concentrate on customer needs—not engineering marvels (a cherished trait at the old Xerox). It seems to be working. Just ten years ago, Xerox was near collapse, mired in bureaucracy, slow to market its ideas, and overwhelmed by its Japanese competitors. Now, Xerox's new divisions resemble independent businesses, incorporating nearly all functions. The company no longer has a president or chief operating officer; instead there is a six-person corporate office headed by Allaire. Instead of four gigantic divisions, now nine divisions with a total of 23 business units make most of the decisions about what machines to build and how to build them. As a result, Xerox's U.S. copier market share rose to 18 percent from 10 percent in 1991. The copiers earned Xerox $454 million in 1991, compared to $87 million in 1990.

With this kind of constantly evolving structure, how does management prevent employees from heading in the wrong direction? Who decides which person ends up on which team and for how long? How do you judge the performance of an employee who is constantly rotating from team to team? In 1990, Becton Dickinson, a manufacturer of high-tech diagnostic systems, launched a new product—the Bacteck 860—in 25 percent less time than its previous best record. However, there was still too much time wasted as marketing and engineering debated over product specifications. Marketing argued that the 860 needed more features to please the customers; engineering countered that the features would take too long to design and be too costly. Further inquiry led management to the real problem: because the team leader reported to the head of engineering, he did not have sufficient clout to resolve the conflict between the two sides. Today the company makes sure all its team leaders have access to a division head, which gives them the authority to settle disputes between different functions.

When people move from one team to another, they and their companies have to think about careers and pay in new ways. Instead of slowly climbing the ladder, it is likely that tomorrow's workers and managers will make more lateral moves, picking up expertise in different functions like marketing and manufacturing. For those who do well on the team, Becton Dickinson is trying out "lateral promotions,"—rotating a financial person into a marketing or manufacturing job. In one division last year, the company rotated ten out of fifty managers. These people got a raise and change of title, just as with any regular promotion, but they weren't necessarily put in charge of any more people. While this perspective requires a real change in our definitions of success and career progress, this type of structure may give the organizations the ability and flexibility to respond to the challenges of a rapidly changing future.

and employee job satisfaction than stores with taller structures.[6] While the performance of flat organizations may exceed that of tall organizations in companies with a constellation of tasks such as Sears, a review of the research in this area suggests that there is no one best number of subordinates for a

---

[6]J. C. Worthy, "Organizational Structure and Employee Morale," *American Sociological Review* 15 (1950): 169–179.

FIGURE 16-3 ▶ Tall and Flat Organizations Compared

Span of control is a major determinant of the number of administrative levels in an organization: the more subordinates managed by each supervisor, the flatter the organization's administrative structure.

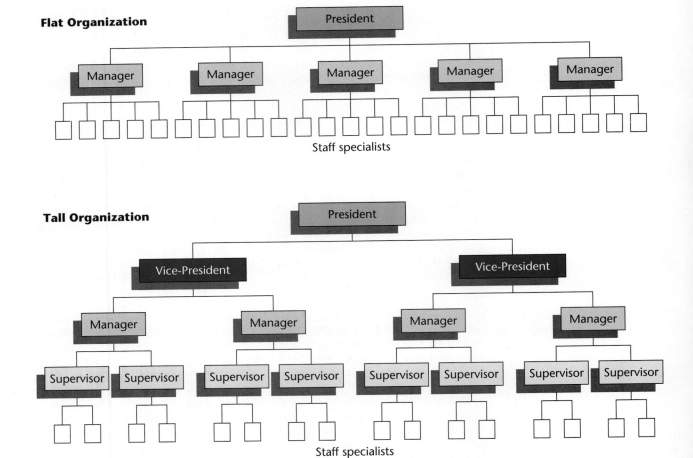

manager's span of control or best number of hierarchical levels.[7] Rather, the optimal span of control depends on the degree of job specialization, the members' need for autonomy and direct access to the supervisor, and the similarity of jobs in the unit.[8]

[7] D. R. Dalton et al., "Organizational Structure and Performance: A Critical Review," *Academy of Management Review* 5 (1980): 49–64.

[8] Mintzberg, *The Structuring of Organizations.*

Related to span of control is **administrative intensity,** the proportion of administrators and managers in an organization's total work force. In recent years, administrative intensity has become a proxy for productivity. Since managers and administrators do not directly produce an organization's outputs, the more administrators or managers an organization has, the higher the number of employees required to transform the raw materials into the organization's output. The differences in administrative intensity between Japanese and American companies is touted as one of the reasons for Japan's lower production costs.

COMMON ORGANIZATIONAL STRUCTURES   ◆◆◆◆◆◆

These four elements of organizational structure—job specialization, departmentalization, centralization, and span of control—all provide ways for organizations to coordinate their employees to create outputs. Using these features to divide up and coordinate the component tasks of an organization's mission, three primary forms of organizational structure emerge: the simple structure, the bureaucracy, and the organic structure.[9] Figure 16–4 provides an overview of these three types of structure and the types of task coordination and control used in each.

Simple Structure

Simple structure most often occurs in young or small organizations. Coordination is largely a function of direct supervision, and the top manager has significant control. In fact, it is common for all employees to report directly to the top manager. Employees have very little discretionary decision-making power, although there is rarely a formal policies and procedures statement. The best illustration of this type of firm is the entrepreneurial firm. Such a firm is aggressive and often innovative, although it is usually careful to remain in the market niche best understood by the founding entrepreneur. Inside the firm, all revolves around the entrepreneur. Its goals are the entrepreneur's goals; its strategy, the entrepreneur's visions. Entrepreneurial firms are often founded by individuals who resist the type of control imposed by bureaucratic organization and who view more formal structure as constraints on their flexibility.

One of the critical problems among today's managers is how to release and sustain the thrust, initiative, and adaptability of the entrepreneur in organizations that employ large numbers of people while preserving the ability to hold individuals accountable for what they do. Bureaucracies are a primary mechanism to structure a unified working system with hundreds (or more) employees. Hierarchies are particularly useful in such a situation because the tasks that organizations must accomplish become more complex as one moves higher in the organization and requires longer time spans of consideration.[10]

---

[9] Ibid.

[10] Elliot Jaques, "In Praise of Hierarchy," *Harvard Business Review* (January/February, 1990): 127–133.

| FIGURE 16–4 | ▶ Overview of Organizational Structures |

The amount of control needed to coordinate interdependence among employees yields one of three types of organizational structure: simple, bureaucracy, or organic.

Coordinating and Control Mechanism

Simple Structure	Direct supervision
Bureaucracy	Standardization of work process or skills
Organic Structure	Mutual adjustment

Source: H. Mintzberg, *The Structuring of Organizations* (Englewood Cliffs, N.J.: Prentice-Hall, 1979).

Bureaucracy

In their classic study of electronics firms in Scotland, two organizational researchers, Tom Burns and G. M. Stalker, classified all the firms they studied into two categories: mechanistic and organic.[11] Mechanistic organizations embody Max Weber's bureaucratic organizational form, described in Chapter 2. The major goal of bureaucratic organizations is predictability. In a bureaucracy, tasks are carefully planned in advance and the quantity and quality of performance is closely monitored. In addition, roles tend to be narrow in scope with extremely well-defined responsibilities. A detailed formal authority hierarchy exists to control and coordinate task performance. Rewards are allocated on the basis of following instructions, and compensation and selection are tied to ability to perform within narrow job functions.

Bureaucracies may be either machine or professional, depending on whether the organization's transformation technology is machines or people. A **machine bureaucracy** has highly specialized and routine tasks, formalized procedures for the transformation process, a proliferation of rules, regulations, and communication channels, a functional departmentalization structure, a large span of control, and an elaborate administrative and technical structure. The technical support staff's primary role is to develop formalized work policies and procedures for other units in the organization. Even though there is considerable formalization of policies and procedures, machine bureaucracies are often criticized for their alienated work forces and lack of innovation. Their large size makes them more suited to efficiency than to creativity. Examples of these organizations include the U.S. Postal Service, steel companies, and automobile manufacturing firms.

Professional bureaucracies differ from machine bureaucracies in that the production technology of a professional bureaucracy is composed of professionals who also control most of the organizational power. However, rather than standardizing policies and procedures as a machine bureaucracy would, the professional bureaucracy seeks to standardize skills. A professional bureaucracy's major mechanism for coordination is training and indoctrination designed to internalize a set of performance and professional standards. These types of organizations often provide services rather than products. Examples of professional bureaucracies are hospitals, universities, social work agencies, and public accounting firms.

---

[11] T. Burns and G. M. Stalker, *The Management of Innovation* (London: Tavistock, 1961).

Organic Structures

A matrix organizational structure has helped Tenneco Inc.'s Newport News, Virginia, shipyard tackle big projects like the construction of the attack submarine Newport News, *pictured here. The matrix structure facilitates coordination of efforts along both functional and project lines.*

The organic organizational structures identified by Burns and Stalker were more flexible; they could adapt more easily to new demands placed on them. In fact, the defining feature of an **organic structure** is being able to respond efficiently and effectively to new demands. Organic organizations emphasize the following characteristics:

1. Knowledge and ability rather than job descriptions or position titles determine who will participate in solving a particular problem. People are valued for their abilities rather than their organizational status.
2. Organizational status and expertise are not assumed to be related. Decision making is decentralized, and the responsibility for decisions is pushed as low as possible in the organization, to take advantage of the "hands-on" expertise of even the lowest-level members of the organization.
3. Communication flows freely in a lateral direction. The use of project teams and task forces is common (as are liaisons between departments or work groups) in order to encourage information sharing across diverse areas of expertise.[12]

The most complex and formal form of organic structure is the matrix. Unlike other organizational structures, in which employees usually report to only one supervisor, the matrix structure has a dual reporting structure. That is, the head of the functional area *and* the project or matrix manager have authority over members of the staff.

The matrix structure is particularly useful when an organization wishes to focus its attention on the development of a particular product. Texas Instruments is a typical example of a matrix organization. The use of the matrix structure to build different types of computers for different markets allows specialization of skills and attention to both the product and its market to develop.[13] Of course, high-technology organizations are not the only ones for which matrix structures are effective. The "INTERNATIONAL FOCUS ON: Matrix Organizations," describes the reorganization of a German multinational corporation. As one would expect, matrix organizations are difficult to manage. Because each employee has two supervisors, the potential for conflict is great. Only when the information and geographical and technological demands are so great that they require the full-time attention of a subgroup of the organization should a matrix structure be considered. The strengths and weaknesses of a matrix organization are listed in Figure 16–5.

But this is not to say that all organizations with routine technologies should be machine bureaucracies or that all nonroutine technologies should have organic structures. Consider, for example, two organizations: Hewlett-Packard, which we described in the opening vignette, and British Petroleum. While HP's technology is nonroutine, BP can be easily categorized within an industry employing routine technology. Yet, as we have seen, HP is moving to more of a hierarchical structure and as evidenced in the "FOCUS ON: Organizational

---

[12]C. R. Gullett, "Mechanistic versus Organic Organizations: What Does the Future Hold?" *Personnel Administrator* 20 (1975): 17–19.

[13]R. Duncan, "What Is the Right Organizational Structure? Decision Tree Analysis Provides the Answer," *Organizational Dynamics* (Winter 1979): 59–80.

INTERNATIONAL FOCUS ON

Matrix Organizations

Reorganization for Growth and Flexibility   With a total of 175,000 employees, Bayer Aktiengesellschaft of Leverkusen, Germany, is one of the largest chemical and health-care products companies in the world. Since its founding in 1863, the company has diversified considerably in both geographic and product activities. On January 1, 1984, Bayer announced that it would restructure the organization to respond to tripled sales and the increasingly important role of its foreign activities, subsidiaries, and foreign companies. Specifically, the changes included adjusting the organizational structure to

1. Shift management emphasis from the parent company to Bayer World by integrating Bayer's foreign activities and those of the subsidiaries more closely into the organization.
2. Regroup and restructure the various business areas and clearly define their responsibilities.
3. Delegate certain duties and decisions to lower levels of management so that the Board of Management could concentrate on the development of corporate strategy and policy.

Bayer implemented these changes by creating a quasi-matrix structure from the organization's initial functional and departmentalized structure. The matrix structure was formed by grouping all business activities of Bayer World into six Business Sectors, each of which consisted of several Business Groups, such as organic chemicals, dyestuffs, rubber, fibers, etc. The central and staff functions were combined into a corporate staff division, which serves the company worldwide. The remaining service functions, such as human resources, administrative services, and plant administration were regrouped into service divisions. In addition, each member of the Board of Management was given responsibility for a geographic region rather than a functional area as in the previous structure.

In analyzing the impact of the restructured organization one year after its implementation, the Chairman of the Board of Management, Hermann J. Strenger, reported the following effects:

1. The Board of Management was able to devote more of its time to developing corporate policy.
2. The sector heads established their roles as connecting link pins between Business Groups and the Board of Management.
3. By regrouping the 9 departments into 19 Business Groups, the company became more flexible and responsive to environmental changes.
4. Each national organization was strengthened at its respective location, and interaction with Bayer World improved.
5. The plant administration and service divisions were streamlined.

Because of the cooperation and commitment of Bayer's employees, the implementation of a matrix structure enabled Bayer World to be more responsive to global influences and environmental shocks.

Source: H. Vossverg, "Bayer Reorganizes in Response to Growth," *Long Range Planning* 18 (1985): 13–20.

Structures," Robert Horton, chairman of BP, is very concerned about the bureaucratic structure of the fourth largest private oil company in the world.

So, in addition to the impact of technology, other factors must come into play to determine the best fit of structure for organizations. In the next section, we will consider other factors—such as internal and external environments, technology, and age and size—that influence the appropriateness of particular organizational structures.

FIGURE 16-5	▶ Weaknesses and Strengths of Matrix Organizations

In a matrix organization, staff members report to *both* functional and product (or project) managers. A matrix organizational structure presents both advantages and disadvantages.

Weaknesses

It is costly to maintain the personnel pool to staff the matrix.

Participants experience dual authority of the matrix manager and functional area manager.

There is little interchange with functional groups outside the matrix, so that duplication of effort—"reinvention of the wheel"—may occur.

Participants in the matrix need to have good interpersonal skills in order for this structure to work.

Strengths

Personnel are able to focus full time on the project of the particular matrix.

The matrix manager is coordinator of functions for a single project.

The matrix structure reduces information requirements, as the focus is on a single product and/or market.

The matrix structure focuses specialized skills on the product and/or market.

Source: R. Duncan, "What Is the Right Organizational Structure? Decision Tree Analysis Provides the Answer," *Organizational Dynamics* (Winter 1979): 59–80.

FACTORS INFLUENCING ORGANIZATIONAL STRUCTURE CHOICE

Examples of each of these common organizational forms—simple, machine and professional bureaucracies, and organic structures—can be observed among successful *and* unsuccessful organizations. What determines whether a particular structural form will prove successful for an organization? The open systems view of organizations described in Chapter 14 emphasizes the fact that an organization must manage its dependence on the environment. The strategies an organization uses to manage its environment are reflected in the structure of the organization. As noted in Chapter 15, the design of the organization's structure also is influenced by the technology necessary to produce the organization's outputs. Other factors besides technology and environment have an impact on the appropriateness of organizational structure. For example, the size and age of the organization play an important role in the interdependencies within an organization and, as such, in the optimal organizational structure. In the following sections, we will examine each of these factors in detail.

Internal Organizational Environments

The organization's internal or task environment has a major impact on the kind of interdependencies it must coordinate. The internal or task environment is whatever managers define as relevant to organizational decision making. It can be subdivided into three components: the organization's personnel, its functional and staff units, and its organizational levels. Figure 16–6 provides a master list of internal environmental factors. It is unlikely that any one organization would have to address all of these components in evaluating its internal environment. The list serves as a guide for managers by highlighting the environ-

*Organizational
Structures*

British Petroleum When Iraq invaded Kuwait in 1989, the value of British Petroleum's five billion barrel oil reserve increased by $100 billion. Yet, over 80 percent of BP's oil production is concentrated in two giant but aging oil fields: Prudhoe Bay in Alaska and the Forties field in the North Sea. Finding and exploring opportunities for replacement fields requires a flexible, fast-moving organization, which BP never was. In fact, by some accounts BP is a multi-tiered, old, sclerotic bureaucracy that stifles speed and imagination. In 1990, Robert Horton, the chairman of BP, began to implement a sweeping strategy designed to rejuvenate BP by combining a wildcat exploration with a thorough dismantling of the company's bureaucracy. Corporate staff, which numbered over 2,500 in 1989, was cut to less than 380 by the end of 1990.

Horton appointed a team of seven young executives (in their 30s and 40s) to redesign the way the company works. While the results won't be evident until 1995, these reorganization efforts have already abolished 80 standing committees and six of the eleven managerial layers that used to stand between Horton and his front-line supervisors. Horton increased the amount of money that managers can spend without authorization by 2.5 times. Spending authorizations that had required up to 12 or 13 signatures now need only two or three. The corporate staff has been reorganized entirely into teams, and information services has been broken up and put into the hands of the four operating divisions: exploration and production, refining and marketing, chemicals, and nutrition.

Peter Nulty, "Batman Shakes BP to Bedrock," *Fortune*, November 19, 1990, 155–162.

mental elements they should consider when deciding the type and intensity of coordination demanded by the organizational task. Examples of the internal environment at the personnel level include the selection and socialization process of employees, their level of job-relevant and interpersonal skills, and their commitment to the organization's goals and objectives. Other examples of the internal environment at the functional- and staff-unit level include the amount of conflict and interdependence between line and staff employees. Organizational-level characteristics focus primarily on the mechanisms the organization uses to direct its employee's efforts to achieve its goals.

External Organizational Environments

Once the internal environment has been specified, the external environment must be classified next. Typically, external environments have been categorized into four groups along two dimensions: the simple-complex dimension and the stable-dynamic dimension. The simple-complex dimension focuses on the number of different environments in which the organization or its units must function. A simple environment might be one faced by a lower-level manufacturing group that is dependent only on its suppliers for raw materials and on the market for sales. A complex environment is one faced by a strategic planning unit. For a successful product to be produced, the planning unit must gather inputs from many different departments in the organization; similarly, its output (the strategic plan) is consumed by many different organizational subunits. Because the planning unit must consider many different factors in the different environments it faces, it has a complex environment.

The stable-dynamic dimension is concerned with the amount of change in environmental factors that the organization must face. A stable environment is

FIGURE 16–6	▶ Characteristics of an Organization's Internal Environment

An organization's internal (or task) environment also provides interdependencies that the organization must coordinate. The internal environment of an organization includes personnel, functional and staff unit, and organizational level components.

Organizational Personnel Component
Educational and technological background and skills
Previous technological and managerial skills
Individual members' commitment to attaining system's goals
Interpersonal behavior styles
Availability of manpower for use in the system

Organizational Functional and Staff Units Component
Technological characteristics of organizational units
Interdependence of units in carrying out their objectives
Intraunit conflict among functional and staff units

Organizational Level Component
Organizational goals and objectives
Process of integrating individuals and groups into contributing maximally to attain organizational goals
Nature of organization's product or service

Source: R. Duncan, "What Is the Right Organizational Structure? Decision Tree Analysis Provides the Answer," *Organizational Dynamics* (Winter 1979): 59–80.

one in which there is little uncertainty. In the past, banks operated in a stable environment. However, since the deregulation of the banking industry, banks have had to face a dynamic environment. That is, banks today must confront a rapidly changing environment to be successful. Figure 16–7 illustrates the classification of organizational environments based on these two dimensions.

Technology

Chapter 15 was devoted exclusively to technology, but it is important here to reconsider the impact of technology on organizational or unit structure. As defined in Chapter 15, technology is the transformation process, the mechanism by which an organization accomplishes its tasks.[14] An important issue in technology is the demand for output customization by an organization's clients or customers. Related to this is the rapidity with which products must be altered. When there is a high demand for output customization or product change, stable organizational structures (for instance, a machine bureaucracy) will be ill-suited for coordinating and controlling the production process. To respond efficiently and effectively to output customization and change demands, an adaptive structure (for instance, organic) will be most effective. Alternatively, if outputs are standardized, customer exceptions are few, and product life-cycles are long, more bureaucratic or mechanistic structures will suffice. In fact, it seems that organizations with relatively fixed transformation technologies ("routine" technologies) are more concerned with efficient performance, and those facing

---

[14]Jeffrey Pfeffer, *Organizational Design* (Arlington Heights, IL: AHM Publishing, 1978).

FIGURE 16-7 ▶ Classification of Organizational Environments

The stability and complexity of the external environment also influences an organization's structure. Environmental stability leads to bureaucracy; environmental complexity leads to decentralization.

	Stable	**Dynamic**
Complex	Decentralized Bureaucratic (standardization of skills)	Decentralized Organic (mutual adjustment)
Simple	Centralized Bureaucratic (standardization of work processes)	Centralized Organic (direct supervision)

Source: C. Perrow, *Organizational Analysis: A Sociological Review* (New York: Wadsworth, 1970).

high demands for output customization or change ("nonroutine" technologies) are more concerned with effective problem solving.[15]

In addition to the mechanistic-organic dimension, we can also examine other structural issues. Employees in organizations with routine technologies require less education and training because their work is standardized. In organizations with nonroutine technologies, employees are more likely to be professionals with considerable training and on-the-job experience.

Span of control also differs with type of technology. The more complex the technology, the more that problems requiring a supervisor's involvement are likely to occur. This increased level of involvement requires a smaller span of control because of the amount of subordinate-supervisor interaction. However, in nonroutine technologies that rely on professional employees, the span of control can be larger: professionals have expert knowledge and personal performance expectations that reduce the need for close supervision. The resulting span of control with professional employees in organizations with nonroutine technologies is smaller than with comparable groups in organizations with routine technologies.[16] Thus, as one would expect, the largest span of control occurs within organizations with routine technologies.

Centralization of decision making is another characteristic of organizations with routine technologies. Coordination and control are also under the purview of a centralized management structure. When the organization's task is analyzable, communication is frequent and tends to be in the form of memos, reports, and rules and procedures.[17] When tasks are less analyzable (more nonroutine), information is usually transmitted through interpersonal communication such as face-to-face or telephone conversations and group meetings. In organizations with nonroutine technologies, decision-making authority is pushed far down the organization, as are coordination and control activities.

---

[15] R. G. Hunt, "Technology and Organization," *Academy of Management Journal* 13 (1970): 235–252.

[16] P. M. Blau and R. A. Schoenherr, *The Structure of Organizations* (New York: Basic Books, 1971).

[17] R. L. Daft and R. H. Lengel, "Information Richness: A New Approach to Managerial Behavior and Organizational Design," in *Research in Organizational Behavior*, vol. 6, ed. B. Staw and L. Cummings (Greenwich, Conn.: JAI Press, 1984).

The production technology available to an organization dramatically influences span of control. Complex technologies (like the one used at the Genetic Systems division of Bristol-Myers) require more attention, so supervisory span of control must be smaller.

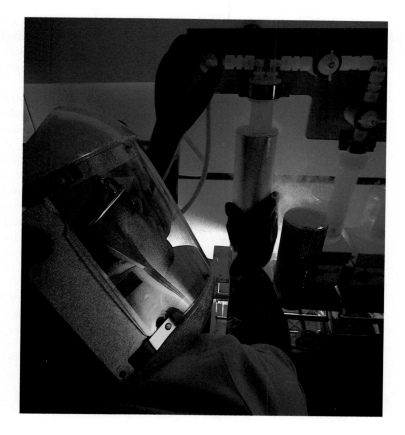

Finally, organizations with routine technologies typically have very clear, standardized performance expectations: their efficiency and output-quantity goals are identifiable and measurable. In firms with nonroutine technologies, the goals are not nearly so obvious. Rather than aiming for efficiency and quantity, such firms are more concerned with the reliability and quality of their products.

From this discussion on technology, we can make some predictions about which organizational structures work best with which forms of technology. For example, machine bureaucracies provide a good fit *only* for organizations with routine technologies. Organic structures are appropriate for other types of technologies, although the fit is probably best with nonroutine technologies.

Age and Size

In the previous sections, we have largely examined factors external to the organization: the environment and technology. Now we will examine the influence of organizational demographic characteristics on structure. In the following discussion, we will assume that the technology and the environment remain constant. This will allow us to observe the impact of age and size on organizational structure.[18]

---

[18] The following discussion is based in large part on the 1979 edition of Mintzberg's *The Structuring of Organizations.*

Age   In general, it seems that the older an organization, the more formal its structure. As organizations age, they are likely to repeat the cycle of tasks they accomplish. Thus, as the task is better understood and the likely complications are more predictable, rules and procedures for performing the task are more likely to be promulgated.

Not only does the age of an organization seem to be related to its level of formalization, but when that particular industry was founded seems to have a big impact on its structure, too. In fact, one researcher found that the age of an industry was inversely related to its use of professionals in staff positions and of job specialization.[19] He also found that industries founded in each of four periods were vastly different. For example, organizations founded in the "pre-factory" period (such as farms, construction firms, and retail stores) relied more on unpaid family members and self-employed owners than organizations founded in any other period. In the second period—during the rise of factories—industries such as apparel, textiles, and banking used virtually no unpaid family members. They relied instead on many paid clerks, indicating the birth of the bureaucracy. Much control during this period, however, remained with the self-employed owners.

The next period, "bureaucratization of industry," marks a time when professional managers took control of railroads and related industries. The final period, the "modern age," includes the founding of the automobile, chemical, and utility industries. These industries introduced the use of professional employees and the development of staff support units. Since 1965, when this particular study was reported, it is likely that a fifth period of industry foundings has occurred. With the development of the aerospace and electronics industries as well as consulting firms, we may well have witnessed a fifth organizational form.[20]

Size   The size of an organization may be measured in a variety of ways, such as the amount of its sales, the size of its capital investment, the size of its budget, or its number of employees. For the purposes of our discussion here, we will use the number of employees as our measure of organizational size.

Research into the relationship between organization size and structure is convincing. It seems that the larger the organization, the more specialized are its tasks, the larger is its administrative component, and the more differentiated are its organizational units.[21]

As organizations grow, they must add new workers. These workers can be assigned to existing departments or units or put into newly created units. As organizations grow in size, they also seem to increase the average span of control for their managers. In fact, it seems that as organizations grow, they

---

[19] A. L. Stinchcombe, "Social Structure and Organizations," in *Handbook of Organizations*, ed. J. G. March (Chicago: Rand McNally, 1965).

[20] Mintzberg, *The Structuring of Organizations*.

[21] See, for example, P. N. Khandwalla, *The Design of Organizations* (New York: Harcourt Brace Jovanovich, 1977); P. M. Blau, C. M. Falbe, W. McKinley, and D. K. Tracey, "Technology and Organization in Manufacturing," *Administrative Science Quarterly* 21 (1976): 20–40; and D. S. Pugh, D. J. Hickson, C. R. Hinings, and C. Turner, "Dimensions of Organizational Structure," *Administrative Quarterly* 13 (1968): 65–105.

increase the size of each unit *and* increase the average span of control at all levels.[22]

Just as older organizations become more structured, larger organizations are more formalized than smaller organizations. The larger the organization, the more the task can be broken down (the more people there are to do parts of the task), and the more predictable the task becomes. The more predictable the task, the more it can be controlled and coordinated through rules, policies, and procedures.

In general, the following organizational characteristics are associated with increased organizational size:

1. Increased number of management levels
2. Greater number of jobs and departments
3. Increased specialization of skills and functions
4. Greater formalization
5. Greater decentralization
6. Smaller percentage of top administrators
7. Larger percentage of technical, professional, clerical, and maintenance support staff
8. Greater levels of written communication and documentation.[23]

Having a large, well-run organization makes it possible for relatively few managers to manage large numbers of people and resources. From this ability comes the orientation towards efficiency. However, sometimes the organization becomes too large to be managed efficiently. The notion that there is some economies of scale has been one of the driving forces behind the development of large corporations. However, in recent years, the controversy over the relative benefits of big versus small have moved to the forefront of organizational structure discussions. Small companies, for example, have fueled much of the job creation and technological innovation in the United States, accounting for more than 20 million jobs added to the economy between 1977 and 1989. These small companies—or, as is suggested in the "FOCUS ON: Size," these small companies within large companies—provide one way to combine the ability to compete in a global economy with the agility and response speed of smaller organizations.

ORGANIZATIONAL LIFE CYCLES

The story of Hewlett-Packard, which began this chapter, suggests a final influence on organizational structure. Organizations change over time, and as they do the forces that influence their structure change with them. In fact, organizations (like the people that compose them) go through predictable life cycles, and organizational structure is determined in part by the particular stage of

---

[22] Blau and Schoenherr, *The Structure of Organizations.*

[23] R. L. Daft, *Organizational Theory and Design* (St. Paul, Minn.: West, 1983).

Focus on

Size

Is the Organization Too Large?
When foreign business executives visited the United States years ago, their trips focused on corporate giants such as those in the automobile and steel industries. Today, they are more likely to visit much smaller, more entrepreneurial types of organizations, even if those organizations are housed within the shell of larger organizations such as Apple Computers or General Electric. Many such minicompanies can be found in the steel industry. In 1984, for example, LT Corp. merged with Republic Steel Corp. in a move that was expected to increase market share and dramatically increase cost efficiencies in production. Further south in Alabama, James Toad, the head of Birmingham Steel, started buying up inefficient small steel plants in 1985. His goal was to build more productive minimills that would convert scrap into finished steel products for small niche uses.

In this case, size only heightened the troubles faced by LT and Republic. As the two companies struggled to integrate their different cultures and bloated operations, the market conditions sent LT into bankruptcy in 1986. Birmingham thrived, reporting some $40 million in net income on $400 million in sales during that same time. Behind Birmingham's success was its entrepreneur boss, flexible work rules, cost efficient facilities, and narrow product lines. Birmingham could make a ton of steel with only a third of the workers required at the large producers.

These obvious benefits have not been lost on LT as it struggles to become a leaner, market-driven company. By the year 2000, steel experts expect that Birmingham and other minis will capture 36 percent of the steel market, up from just over 20 percent in 1989.

Source: John Byrne, "Why a Big Steelmaker Is Mimicking the Minimills," *Business Week*, March 27, 1989, 92.

development in which the organization finds itself.[24] During each stage in the **organizational life cycle,** the structure, leadership style, and administrative systems follow a predictable pattern of evolution. Recently, some researchers have suggested that organizations evolve through four different phases or

---

[24]J. R. Kimberly and R. H. Miles, *The Organizational Life Cycle* (San Francisco: Jossey-Bass, 1980).

cycles.[25] The four phases are the entrepreneurial stage, the collectivity stage, the formalization stage, and the elaboration stage. Each of these stages has its own unique problems or concerns.

Entrepreneurial Stage

When an organization comes into existence, the primary concerns of the founders are to create the product or service and to survive as an organization. There is little formal control in the **entrepreneurial stage;** what control there is comes from the commitment and supervision of the owner-entrepreneur. The working hours are long, and the entire focus of the organization is on the development and marketing of the product or service.

As the organization becomes successful, it grows. Growth, with its demands for more employees, requires the entrepreneur to address management issues. Because entrepreneurs would rather deal with the interesting and creative components of the business, such as creating and selling the product or service, they are not likely to be skilled or interested in management issues. A crisis of leadership often develops. Either the owner restricts the growth of the organization, or it will begin to falter. What is needed at this juncture is the introduction of a strong manager who can inject managerial control processes into the organization. If such a manager is available or the entrepreneur can provide the necessary structure and control, then the organization progresses into the second stage of its life cycle. The "FOCUS ON: The Entrepreneurial Stage" examines the successful restructuring and leadership transition of CMP Publishing.

Collectivity Stage

In the adolescence of an organization, it is typically most concerned with human resource issues such as cooperation, employee commitment, morale, cohesion, and personalized leadership. Employees feel a part of the organization in the **collectivity stage** and value its goals and objectives. During this stage of an organization's existence, we see the beginnings of such formal systems as structured departments, job assignments, and a hierarchy of authority.

The beginning of the formal structure also leads to the major problem at this stage: the simultaneous need for delegation and desire to maintain control. Solving the leadership crisis was the first step; now that very solution catalyzes a second problem. The strong management presence—so successful in the past—now restricts the activities of low-level managers. Because of the development of competent lower-level managers, management must learn to delegate authority and control down the hierarchy—to overcome its fear of losing control of the organization. To survive this crisis, the organization needs to develop formal mechanisms to manage organizational interdependence without direct intervention by top management.

Formalization Stage

In the midlife of the organization, corresponding to the adult years of a person, the organization values stability, efficiency, rules and procedures, and other bureaucratic trends. New employees, particularly specialists, are hired.

---

[25] R. E. Quinn and K. Cameron, "Organizational Life Cycles and Some Shifting Criteria of Effectiveness: Some Preliminary Evidence," *Management Service* 29 (1983): 33–51.

The Entrepreneurial Phase

Reorganizing for Growth In 1971, Gerry and Lilo Leeds founded CMP Publications and did just about everything right. The ten business newspapers and magazines CMP produced were tops in their respective markets and each market offered plenty of room for growth. But the problems CMP began running into had little to do with the publishing business per se. They were problems that every young, successful entrepreneurial firm eventually has to face. First came the vague awareness that it was just harder to get things done. The Leeds became harder to see, it became harder for staff decision makers to move requests through operational departments, and it took longer to get action on ideas for new publications. Entrepreneurs handle such trials in a variety of ways: they work harder; they decide that entrepreneurs don't make very good CEOs and bring in professional replacements; they nag and harangue managers and then fire the ones who don't quit; or they ignore the real problem as best they can.

Instead, the Leeds decided to reorganize and restructure. First they broke the company into two manageable, expandable companies within CMP and placed a manager in charge of each. These managers had the authority to run their divisions in ways that would encourage growth. Then the Leeds created a publications committee composed of vice-presidents who could act on their own within the corporate strategic objectives.

The results of the reorganization are already coming in. Restructuring CMP allowed it to grow again; in 1990, publications numbered 14 and sales climbed by 11 percent to $174 million. As a side benefit, their son, Michael Leeds' experience as a vice-president on the publishing committee allowed Gerry and Lilo to pass on control of CMP to him.

Tom Richman, "Reorganizing for Growth," *Inc.*, January 1991, 110–111.

Communication among employees is less frequent and more formal. Effectiveness in such organizations is typically measured quantitatively through efficiency ratios and productivity measures. Although goal attainment and productivity are important concerns throughout the life of an organization, they are more salient as measures of organizational effectiveness during the **formalization stage**.

During this stage of the organization's life cycle, a crisis of increased bureaucratization occurs. The development of various mechanisms, rules, policies, and procedures to coordinate and control the increasingly large organization now begins to suffocate middle management. Because of this stranglehold, creativity is stifled by the demands of standard operating procedures. Conflict develops between line and staff employees, and the overall impression is that the organization is too large to be managed effectively solely through formal rules, regulations, policies, and procedures.

Elaboration Stage

As the organization matures, it enters the final portion of the cycle. The **elaboration stage** redirects the organization's emphasis from bureaucracy to a renewed interest in cooperation and teamwork. Decentralization of the organization occurs to balance the conflicting demands for differentiation and integration. Rather than rules and standard operating procedures, social control and self-discipline limit the need for direct, hierarchical supervision. More than in other stages, the firm's reputation and stature are important. Innovation and creativity are once again valued. The managerial process is adjusted to augment rather than impede the flow of new ideas. Formal systems are simplified, and integrating mechanisms such as project teams or task forces are created to improve communication across the organization.

The major concern for an organization in the elaboration stage is to monitor its product cycles, paying attention to changes in the environment and technology in order to revitalize itself.[26] Top management is often replaced during this part of the organization's life; the intent is to bring new blood into the organization. Organizations that fail in this revitalization process may become stagnant or enter into a period of organizational decline. The "FOCUS ON: Elaboration" is an example of the continuing evolution of the Toyota company.

SYMPTOMS OF DESIGN DEFICIENCIES

What happens when the organizational structure does not fit neatly with the demands of the environment, organizational task, age, and size of the organization? In the final sections of this chapter, we will examine the potential problems that may arise in an organization when the "right" organizational structure is not in place: organizational conflict and organizational decline.

Organizational Conflict

Much of what we learned about individual conflict in Chapter 6 also applies to conflict at the organizational level. Organizational conflict occurs because of poorly managed division and coordination of tasks among interdependent organizational units. Conflicts can arise from problems in task clarity (the degree to which daily task requirements are known), task complexity (the number of elements to be considered when completing the task), the rapidity of technological change, feedback cycles (how quickly a manager can know the results of a decision), and the goals of the organization.[27] Thus, the more interdependence required to complete the task, the greater the potential for organizational conflict.

While interdependence alone may be sufficient to produce some organizational conflict, the way in which organizational members must interact can exacerbate its level. The appropriate organizational structures can moderate such conflict. If we examine the following prescriptions for managing organizational conflict, the common thread running through them is for managers to reduce the interdependencies among organizational units.

Bureaucratic Authority This form of conflict management is based on the acceptance by organizational members of the right of top management to

---

[26]D. A. Whetten, "Sources, Responses and Effects of Organizational Decline," in *The Organizational Life Cycle*, eds. J. Kimberly and R. Miles (San Francisco: Jossey-Bass, 1980).

[27]J. M. Brett, "Managing Organizational Conflict," *Professional Psychology: Research and Practice* 15 (1984): 664–678.

Focus on

Elaboration

Why Toyota Keeps Getting Better and Better The key slogan that makes up the Toyota culture is *kaizen* or continuous improvement. One consultant calls Toyota's strategy "rapid inchup"—take enough tiny steps and pretty soon you outdistance the competition. By introducing six all-new models within 14 months, Toyota grabbed a 43 percent share of car sales in Japan. In the 1990 model year, it sold over one million cars and trucks in the United States, strengthening its Number 4 position in U.S. sales. Another half dozen new models were introduced in 1991 in the United States, including a sporty two-door and a V-8 coupe. In fact, Toyota may be the best automaker in the world. The company turns out a wide range of cars built with precision, including a luxury sedan of Mercedes-like quality using one-sixth of the labor Mercedes does.

This success requires constant vigilance. At 65, the president of Toyota, Shoichiro Toyoda, has ripped out two layers of middle management, stripped 1,000 executives of their staffs, and reorganized product development, putting himself in charge. "We felt we suffered from large corporation disease. It had become extremely difficult for top executives to convey their feelings to our workers. So we embarked on a cure. We wanted to recertify that customer satisfaction is our first priority," he explained.

While Toyota was Japan's most conservative automaker, it has recently begun to make some changes there. Long housed in Toyota City, some 300 miles from Tokyo, this past year the company opened a design center in Tokyo to feed back fashion trends, and a five-story high-tech display where office workers can kick tires as well as eat lunch. Toyota also appears more open to outsiders and has tripled its R&D spending from $750 million to $2.2 billion between 1984 and 1989.

Like all employers in Japan, Toyota faces a stringent labor shortage because of the slowing population growth and a national reluctance to import workers. Across Japan, there are 1.37 jobs available for every worker; in Toyota City, there 2.13 jobs available per worker. Because a Toyota worker spends an estimated 2,300 hours per year on the job, the company is trying to enrich assembly-line jobs by making work more creative and eliminating what it calls the three Ds; the dangerous, dirty, and demanding aspects of factory work. Toyota is also investing nearly $770 million over the next four years to improve worker housing, add dining halls, and build new recreational facilities. Additionally, the company hopes to be able to hire more women, who presently only account for 9 percent of all employees (and they do not work in the plants).

The next step in Toyota's evolution is likely to be the loosening of its ties to corporate headquarters. With five separate subsidiaries reporting back to Japan, Toyota's North American operation has some top executives make the 24-hour round trip between Los Angeles and Japan as often as nine times per year, frequently to discuss product plans. With its expansion into Europe and the Pacific Rim groups coming on line, Toyota may well be on its way to turning the world into a giant Toyota City and establishing operations wherever they make economic sense.

Alex Taylor III, "Why Toyota Keeps Getting Better and Better and Better," *Fortune,* November 19, 1990, 66–79.

invoke rules, regulations, and procedures to structure how groups and individuals interact within the organization. Within such a system of conflict management, the response to conflict across and within groups is to pass the issues to be resolved to the next higher authority level.

Limited Interaction   When the bureaucratic structure gets overloaded with demands, an alternative way to manage conflict is to limit interaction among conflicting groups. Interaction between conflicting groups is often limited to controversial issues, which does not allow the participants to focus on a common goal. Instead, these two groups can be given a superordinate goal that requires them to coordinate their activities. This strategy works best when the rules and procedures necessary to complete the task or meet the goal are well known and well understood.

Integrating Devices   The previous strategies focus on managing conflict that is not a permanent experience because of the amount of environmental and technological uncertainty. What happens when the interdependence and uncertainty inherent in performing the organizational task is so great that conflict is unavoidable? In this case, perhaps the organization should implement more formal conflict management devices. These devices include liaisons, integrators, task forces, and project teams. The goal of such **integrating devices** is to enhance communication across groups and maintain an appropriate level of interaction.

Liaisons are boundary spanning individuals who facilitate coordination and communication between interdependent organizational units (for instance, production and sales departments). Liaisons typically are located in one department or organizational unit but have responsibilities for working with both units. When coordination of different organizational units becomes more complex, an organization may choose to establish an integrator role. The more different organizational units are in structure, goals, and orientation, the greater the opportunity for conflict. The role of the integrator is to manage (coordinate and moderate) relationships among diverse organizational units. Integrators need (1) a wide set of contacts within various organizational units, (2) some understanding of each unit's goals, orientations, and organization, (3) the ability to talk the language of each unit, (4) some trust of the members of the units, (5) some expertise that members of the units respect, and (6) skills in conflict management and resolution.[28]

While liaisons and integrators are individuals, coordination also may be enhanced by the use of task forces. The task force is a group of people brought together to accomplish a specific assignment. Typically, task forces are disbanded when their assignment is completed. Each member of the task force represents the interests of one organizational unit (a department, for instance) and communicates the task force's decisions or recommendations back to that constituency. Task forces are created by upper-level management to solve problems that require horizontal coordination, thereby taking pressure off the organization's formal structure to create solutions.

When long-term interdepartmental activities demand strong coordination efforts, a project team is likely to be formed. A project team is a permanent task force. It is often composed of mid-level organizational members or those at the executive level (often referred to as an administrative committee or an operations review committee). For example, when the Florida Power and Light Company built a nuclear power plant, the coordination achieved through the

---

[28]Duncan, "What Is the Right Organizational Structure?"

use of project teams was critical in reducing construction time in half, from an industry average of 12 years to just 6. The construction manager assigned critical personnel to 15 different project teams. One team orchestrated the completion of 25,000 tasks needed to finish the plant.[29]

Organizational conflict is only one problem that can arise when organizations are not structured to handle their unique sets of problems and opportunities. In addition to excessive conflict, an organization may experience a performance decline resulting from a poor fit between an organization, its demands, and its structure.

Organizational Decline

The term **organizational decline** has at least two meanings: The first describes a cutback in the size of an organization's work force, budget, resources, clients, and the like. The second definition refers to the view that mature organizations become stagnant, bureaucratic, and passive. These conditions may herald an organization's increasing inability to stay in touch with changing markets, technologies, and client preferences. Rather than lead to a reduction in revenues, the latter form of decline may simply reflect a reduction in the rate of growth.[30] In fact, some authors have made the argument that decline-as-cutbacks occurs in times of resource scarcity, and decline-as-stagnation occurs in times of resource abundance.[31]

Researchers in this area have identified four causes or sources of organizational decline: organizational atrophy, vulnerability, loss of legitimacy, and reduced environmental support.[32] **Organizational atrophy** occurs when an organization continues to use a particular response to a situation long after the situation has changed. In this form of perseverance, successful organizations may continue to behave in ways that were once successful and, as a result, be increasingly vulnerable to failure in the future.

Both slow- and fast-growing organizations are vulnerable to organizational atrophy. Fast-growing organizations are at risk when they fail to identify sagging performance as a problem, as opposed to not trying hard enough. Alternatively, slow-growing organizations are more responsive to changes in their vital signs, but they err in the amount of their response to a problem. Such organizations have so little slack that they may not be able to survive long enough to respond to the problem.

Vulnerability is the second source of organizational decline. At some point in the organization's life, it is more susceptible to decline. Most organizations experience a "liability of newness."[33] The difficulty that new organizations have clearing such barriers as the inefficiency of the inexperienced, the lack of a stable set of suppliers and customers, and their more frequent interpersonal con-

---

[29]Ron Winslow, "Utility Cuts Red Tape, Builds Nuclear Plant Almost on Schedule," *The Wall Street Journal*, February 22, 1984, 1, 18.

[30]K. S. Cameron, R. I. Sutton, and D. A. Whetten, *Readings in Organizational Decline: Frameworks, Research and Prescriptions* (Cambridge, Mass.: Ballinger, 1988).

[31]Whetten, "Sources, Responses and Effects of Organizational Decline."

[32]Ibid.

[33]Stinchcombe, "Social Structure and Organizations."

flict is reflected in their higher death rate, compared to that of older organizations.

Loss of legitimacy occurs when an organization focuses its energy on economic gains and ignores the cultivation of its political acceptance. This issue of legitimacy is probably more salient in public rather than private organizations. The test of legitimacy commonly revolves around the development of a powerful constituency that resists the efforts of other groups to dismantle the organization. Of the four sources of decline, it seems that organizations are most capable of combating this one.

The fourth source of decline is reduced environmental support. The environment in which the organization exists can no longer support the organization. Organizations faced with this situation can either find another niche, product, or service (a new environment) or downsize. The first option suggests that the decline can be reversed if management makes appropriate strategic choices. The second option assumes that the set of circumstances in which the organization is mired is beyond the control of management. As such, management's only option is to scale down the operation.[34]

Managing Decline

After managers have figured out the source of the decline, the next step is to develop an organizational response to the problem. Much of what is known about how organizations respond to decline has been taken from the organizational change literature. While there are four general categories of responses to decline, they can be placed on the continuum illustrated in Figure 16–8. The two reactive responses are defending and responding. The two proactive responses are generating and preventing.

The organization using a defending response is usually a large, bureaucratic organization. A common example of this response occurs when adhering to the organization's rules and policies becomes more important than addressing the goals behind them. A second, reactive way in which organizations respond to decline is retrenchment. Retrenchment is commonly characterized by cutting back: layoffs based on seniority or performance or across-the-board cuts in funding and resources. The focus here is on solving the "problem." Unfortunately, management may respond to the decline by either attaching the wrong solution to the right problem (such as responding to a lack of innovation by cutting the research and development budget) or finding a solution to the wrong problem (laying off production workers when the problem is with research and development). In either case, attaching a solution to a problem will allay management's concerns, as it will believe it has done something to resolve the problem.

The next two responses to organizational decline, preventing and generating, differ from the reacting and defending responses in that they are proactive; that is, they take steps to remove hazards that may cause the organization to decline in the future. Preventing is used when an organization attempts to increase its competitive advantage and remove potential threats. Such tactics

---

[34] R. M. Cyert, "The Management of Universities of Constant or Decreasing Size," *Public Administration Review* 38 (1978): 344–349.

| FIGURE 16–8 | ▶ Management's Responses to Organizational Decline |

There are four categories of organizational responses to decline. Defending and responding are reactive responses, and generating and preventing are proactive responses.

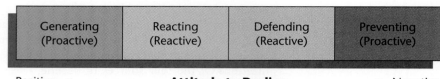

| Generating (Proactive) | Reacting (Reactive) | Defending (Reactive) | Preventing (Proactive) |

Positive ◀——— **Attitude to Decline** ———▶ Negative

Source: D. A. Whetten, "Sources, Responses and Effects of Organizational Decline," in *The Organizational Life Cycle*, eds. J. Kimberly and R. Miles (San Francisco: Jossey-Bass, 1980).

include participating in mergers and acquisitions, changing public opinion and influencing consumer preferences, and shaping economic and social policy.[35] These actions by management are based on the notion that organizations must act to reduce uncertainty by circumventing the need to respond reactively to the environment.

The intent of the fourth response to organizational decline—generating—is to develop "self-designing" organizations. Such organizations are characterized by informal lines of communication, loose criteria for performance evaluation, slack resources, experimentation, tolerance for occasional failure, frequent movement of personnel within the organization, and a high regard for innovation.[36] Interestingly, such organizations would have a high reliance on the integrating structures of liaisons, task forces, project teams, and matrix structures. While this generating point of view has been promoted by organizational scholars, it remains to be seen if organizations can, in fact, achieve this self-designing status when facing a crisis in the form of decline.

The following effects of organizational decline can be felt throughout the organization:

1. Increasing levels of stress among organizational actors as the importance of making good decisions and the penalties for bad decisions increase.
2. Increasing levels of interpersonal conflict as the organization's resource base dwindles.
3. Layoffs and cutbacks directed at the most vulnerable organizational members—the low-skilled, low-income, and minority employees—coupled with attrition among the most mobile and best qualified employees, resulting in a reduction in the variability of employees and the ability of the organization to respond creatively to the decline.

---

[35] See, for example, C. Perrow, *Complex Organizations: A Critical Essay* (Glenview, Ill.: Scott, Foresman, 1979); J. Pfeffer, "Merger as a Response to Organizational Interdependence," *Administrative Science Quarterly* 17 (1972): 382–394; and J. E. Post, *Corporate Behavior and Social Change* (Reston, Va.: Reston Press, 1978).

[36] For example, see K. E. Weick, "Organizational Design: Organizations as Self-Designing Systems," *Organizational Dynamics* 6 (1977): 30–46; B. M. Staw, "The Experimenting Organization," *Organizational Dynamics* 6 (1977): 2–18; and B. L. Hedberg, P. C. Nystrom, and W. H. Starbuck, "Designing Organizations to Match Tomorrow," in *Perspective Models of Organizations*, ed. P. C. Nystrom and W. H. Starbuck, North-Holland/TIMS Studies in the Management Sciences, vol. 5 (Amsterdam: North-Holland, 1977).

4. Death of the organization, either through failure of management to adapt to changes in the environment, political vulnerability, decision demands, or through a transformation (such as a merger or acquisition).

SUMMARY   ◆◆◆◆◆◆

The purpose of this chapter was to examine the components of an organization that determine its structure, the factors that determine which organizational structure should be put into place, and the problems organizations face when their structures do not meet the demands placed on them.

The four elements of organizational structure include job specialization (how the organizational task is divided into jobs), departmentalization (how jobs fit together), centralization (the degree to which decision making in an organization is handled by a small central group of decision makers), and span of control (how many employees report to a manager). These elements of organizational structure differ depending on how an organization coordinates and controls its employees to create organizational outputs.

Typically, organizations are structured in one of three ways. A simple structure is most common in young or small organizations. In a simple structure, employees typically report to one person, usually an entrepreneur who views a more formal organizational structure as restrictive. When greater structure is required and tasks are specialized and routine, an organization may become bureaucratic, with an elaborate administrative structure.

When an organization must remain flexible, the appropriate organizational form is organic. Within this structure, an organization can respond quickly to changes in the market, technology, and product mix. Integrating mechanisms such as liaisons, integrator roles, task forces, project teams, and matrix structures are the markers of an organic structure.

An organization's structure will be influenced by demands from its internal and external environments, the technology required to produce its product or service, and its age and size. A machine bureaucracy is more appropriate for an older, larger organization with a routine technology and a predictable, stable environment. An organic structure is best suited for a smaller, younger organization with a turbulent, unpredictable environment and a nonroutine technology.

The structure of an organization is not stable; rather, organizations like people follow a well-ordered evolution of structure (a life cycle). This life cycle includes the entrepreneurial stage, the collectivity stage, the formalization stage, and the elaboration stage. At each stage of its life, an organization will face a major problem associated with its transformation into the next stage.

Finally, two major problems may occur if an organization has a poor fit between its structure and the demands placed on it, or if its structure cannot successfully handle the problems associated with its stage in the life cycle. Organizational conflict and organizational decline are both related to deficiencies in organizational design.

Key Terms

Administrative intensity   Proportion of administrators and managers in an organization's total work force.

Centralization   Resting decision-making power with one or a few individuals, based on the competing needs of coordination and division of labor.

Collectivity stage   Second phase of the organizational life cycle, in which management concentrates on human resource issues such as cooperation, employee commitment, and morale, and in which the beginnings of formal systems such as structured departments, job assignments, and a hierarchy of authority are seen.

Departmentalization   Grouping tasks into organizational units according to the knowledge and skills required or based on similar levels of skills and abilities.

Elaboration stage   Fourth and last phase of the organizational life cycle, in which management redirects the organization's emphasis from bureaucracy to a renewed interest in cooperation and teamwork, and in which decentralization often occurs and innovation and creativity are once again valued.

Entrepreneurial stage   First phase of the organizational life cycle in which the organization comes into existence and the founders concentrate on creating the product or service and surviving as an organization.

Formalization stage   Third phase of the organizational life cycle, in which management values stability, efficiency, rules and procedures, and other bureaucratic trends.

Integrating device   Strategy of conflict management aimed at enhancing communication across groups and maintaining appropriate levels of interaction.

Job specialization   Division of the overall mission of an organization into various smaller tasks.

Machine bureaucracy   Organizational structure using highly specialized and routine tasks, formalized procedures for the transformation process, a proliferation of rules and communication channels, a functional departmentalization structure, a large span of control, and an elaborate administrative and technical structure.

Organic structure   Flexible organizational structure that can respond efficiently and effectively to new demands placed on it.

Organizational atrophy   Organization's use of a particular response to a situation long after the situation has changed.

Organizational decline   (1) Cutback in the size of an organization's work force, budget, resources, clients, and so on. (2) Mature organization's inability to stay in touch with changing markets, technologies, and client preferences, leading to stagnation, bureaucracy, and passivity.

Organizational life cycle   Predictable pattern of evolution of organizations' structure, leadership style, and administrative systems.

Organizational structure   Skeleton of an organization based on the relationship among its positions or roles.

Organization design   Process of actively creating a structure composed of groups of activities, roles, or positions to coordinate the interdependencies among organizational actors effectively.

Simple structure   Organizational structure common in young or small organizations in which coordination is largely a function of direct supervision, the top manager or entrepreneur has significant control, employees have very little discretionary decision-making power, and there is little formal policy or procedure.

Span of control   Number of people reporting to a manager.

Discussion Questions

1. How does organizational design differ from organizational structure?

2. If organizations face considerable task interdependence, uncertainty, and a dynamic environment, what structural mechanisms can they use to manage these factors more effectively?

3. In a matrix organization, how does the role of a functional manager differ from that of a project manager?

4. What two prime factors might cause an organization to decline? How would management respond to these two factors?

5. What are the costs and benefits of a machine bureaucracy? An organically structured organization?

6. What is the basis for the crisis of leadership in young, entrepreneurial firms?

7. What is the importance of creativity and innovation in older organizations?

8. Why must increased interaction among organizational units be managed to avoid excessive amounts of conflict?

If You Want to Know More

To really understand the issues behind organizational structure, it is important to consider the original work on bureaucracy by Max Weber, *The Theory of Social and Economic Organizations*, translated by Henderson and Parsons and published by Free Press in 1947. In the same vein, one of the first examinations of the relationship of structure to factors unique to an organization is Alfred Chandler's 1966 book entitled *Strategy and Structure*, published by Anchor Press. He developed his perspective on this subject by interviewing managers at General Motors, DuPont, Standard Oil of New Jersey, and Sears, Roebuck and Company.

While Chandler's notion was that the organization's strategy drove the development of structure, other authors have proposed different contingency models. Jay Galbraith (*Designing Complex Organizations*, Addison-Wesley, 1973) and J. D. Thompson (*Organizations in Action*, McGraw-Hill, 1967) both propose such models. Interdependence of the task is what drives Thompson's model, while task uncertainty and the demand to process information drive Galbraith's. While much material has been written about the factors that influence organizational design, one of the better overviews of the contingency notion of organizational structure can be found in Robert Duncan's article, "What Is the Right Organizational Structure?" in the Winter 1979 issue of *Organizational Dynamics*.

A more detailed description of different organizational structures and the factors that influence their fit or lack of fit can be found in Henry Mintzberg's 1979 *The*

Structuring of Organizations, published by Prentice-Hall. Focusing particularly on matrix organizations is a book entitled *Matrix*, written in 1977 by Stanley Davis and Paul Lawrence and published by Addison-Wesley.

Issues of organizational structure and conflict are addressed in R. David Brown's 1983 book, *Managing Conflict at Organizational Interfaces*, published by Addison-Wesley. The idea that organizational structure is a strategy for resolving or preventing conflict is the focus of an article, "Intergroup Relations in Organizations," by Jeanne Brett and Jorn Rogness that appeared in the 1986 volume of *Designing Effective Work Groups*, edited by Paul Good-

man and associates and published by Jossey-Bass.

The area of this chapter probably receiving the most attention these days is organizational decline. An excellent overview of the research and prescriptions in this area can be found in a book edited by Kim Cameron, Robert Sutton, and David Whetten. Entitled *Readings in Organizational Decline*, it was published by Ballinger in 1988. The interest in organizational decline was probably sparked by earlier work elucidating organizational life cycles. In 1980, John Kimberly and Robert Miles authored *The Organizational Life Cycle*, which was published by Jossey-Bass.

On Your Own

Analysis of an Organization's Structure   For this exercise, you should select an organization with which you are familiar. Such an organization may be your family, church, fraternity or sorority, your class, or a firm with which you have been associated through a summer job or part-time employment. Answer the following questions about that organization:

Description   Draw the firm's organizational chart, showing lines of authority, influence, and communication.

Diagnosis   Describe and evaluate the organization's departmentalization, span of control, and job specialization.
   Describe and evaluate the coordinating mechanisms.
   Describe and evaluate the internal environment and the technology, age, and size of the organization.
   Is the organizational structure appropriate, given the answers to the questions above?

Prescription   What changes could be made in the organization's structure to enhance its fit *and* its performance?

Source: J. R. Gordon, *A Diagnostic Approach to Organizational Behavior* (Boston: Allyn & Bacon, 1987).

CLOSING CASE

CHAPTER 16

THE MANAGER'S MEMO

FROM: W. Hightower, Manager, Support Services

TO: J. Weintraub, President

RE: Conflicts and Confusion

Ever since we added the Tax Preparation Division with its staff of 12 people, I have been swamped with complaints from my people. They don't know how to stay in control of their work. This was never a problem when we just had the Consumer Lending business.

In the Copy Room, my people are bombarded with "priority" requests. First someone from the Consumer Lending Division comes in with a major job. Then someone from Tax Prep brings in a stack of tax returns that are supposed to be photocopied immediately. We call both division heads, and both say their job must be done first. We try to call you, but you're often away from the office or in a meeting.

In the Mail Room, it's the same thing. Someone from each division comes in with a mailing that must go out the same day. We can't do it all at once, and the division heads won't agree on what we should do first. The Mail Room is constantly full of people coming in to pick up their mail and look for deliveries. Also, we sometimes have to call the recipient when an overnight delivery comes in, just to find out where that person's office is. It was easier when we knew everybody.

I could go on and on. The Supply Room can't keep up with supplies, because people forget to sign out what they've taken from the shelves. The Word-Processing Pool gets caught in arguments about which division's jobs to do first. I try to call you when I have a problem, like you suggested, but to tell the truth, if I reached you every time, we'd be on the phone all day long.

What can you do about this?

Case Discussion Questions

Assume you are the president, and respond to the memo of the manager of support services. What appears to be the source of the problems? Should the company president be handling these day-to-day matters? How can changes in the company's structure and design improve the situation?

MANAGING CHANGE

STAYING FOREVER YOUNG? ◆◆◆◆◆◆

The scenario is a familiar one. A small company becomes astonishingly successful. The success leads to growth and the growth forces the company to change. Soon, what made the company great when it was young and small threatens to disappear.

The company is Ben & Jerry's Homemade, Inc., Vermont's super-premium ice-cream maker. Throughout its growth, the culture of Ben & Jerry's has emphasized fun, charity, and goodwill within the company and throughout its corporate reach. In 1985, the Ben & Jerry's Foundation was established. It receives 7.5 percent of the company's pretax income to spend on a broad mission of social responsibility. Internally, the company hires the handicapped, provides free therapy and counseling for employees, takes workers on company outings, and even brings in masseurs during high-stress production periods. More to the point, these characteristics of social responsibility and a feeling of family are not just add-ons. They are at the core of Ben & Jerry's corporate mission.

Yet it is these core characteristics of the Ben & Jerry's culture which have been under attack. When the company was small, everyone knew everyone, everyone bought into the mission, and Ben & Jerry's really did feel like family. But rapid growth brought with it a disturbing malaise. There are now departments and memorandums, and suits and ties and MBAs have begun to appear. Several times communication within the company has broken down. At one monthly meeting, the head of retail operations announced plans to open 50 new stores—plans that came as a complete shock to the disbelieving head of production. Employees also claim to have found out about the new Springfield, Vermont, plant through newspaper accounts.

Ben & Jerry's has fought back. The compromise struck by the board of directors was that growth would continue but with more effort devoted to development of the internal organization. Even Jerry admits they can't go home again: "The idea, I think, is to maintain the values of your culture, and yet bring it along with you." How well has Ben & Jerry's survived this storm of change? Well enough that in 1992 the company received one of the ten Optimas Awards given annually for outstanding human resource management.

Sources: "Forever Young," *Inc.*, July 1988, 50–62; "Ben & Jerry Save the World," *Fortune*, June 3, 1991, 247–248; J. M. Wexler, "Videoconferences Give Life to Team Approach," *Computerworld*, September 14, 1992, 67–68; and "1992 Optimas Awards," *Personnel Journal* 71 (January 1992): 51–61.

INTRODUCTION

Even when top management gets an organization off to a good start, there are no guarantees that the organization's initial successes will continue. In fact, there are no guarantees—as Ben & Jerry's of Vermont has learned—that management techniques that have worked in the past will continue to work in the future. There are no guarantees because organizations exist in uncertain business and social environments that are constantly changing. Therefore, organizations must be prepared to change constantly as well as to respond effectively to the ever-changing demands around them. For companies like Ben & Jerry's, success in business is a journey—a continuing battle to adapt—not a destination. In a constantly changing environment, the management challenge is not only to *reach* a successful level of organizational performance but to *maintain* that successful level of performance over time by meeting the demands for change.

This chapter examines how management can meet the demands for change in organizations. It begins with a discussion of the forces that clash in organizations—forces for change and sources of resistance to change—then describes the characteristics of an organization that is ready for change. Next, a four-stage model of change in organizations is presented, followed by a discussion of organizational development as an alternative approach to managing the change process. The chapter concludes with a discussion of an important example of change in contemporary American business—corporate reorganizations.

THE DYNAMICS OF CHANGE

Organizations, like people, are creatures of habit. **Habit** is the tendency of a person or an organization to do things the same way, over and over again. People take comfort in doing things in familiar ways. And as we discussed in Chapter 7, habits in the form of group rules or norms for behavior often represent accumulated organizational experience and learning. It should not be surprising, then, that change is resisted. In fact, it would be surprising if it weren't.

In physical terms, the equivalent of habit is inertia. **Inertia** is the tendency of an object to continue in the same direction with the same velocity or intensity unless influenced by some force of change. A billiard ball on a pool table, for instance, will continue in the same direction until it encounters something—another ball, a side rail, a human hand. According to the laws of physics, inertia must be altered when the object encounters a force of change. This is an important difference between people and physical objects: People can decide whether to alter their path when they encounter a force for change. At Ben & Jerry's, for instance, management resisted changes in the organization's structure and procedures to accommodate growth. Continued growth, and the corporate malaise it brought with it, eventually forced some of these changes to occur.

The challenge for top executives trying to keep an organization afloat in an uncertain, constantly changing environment is how to manage the delicate tension between two forces: forces for change and sources of resistance to change. When managed correctly, the outcome should not be only a financially profitable organization, but one that is healthy from an organizational behavior point of view.

Forces for Change

In 1976, Atari Corporation introduced a new product—the VCS–2600. The VCS–2600 was the first programmable home video player, and its success was astonishing, with over 10 million sold between 1979 and 1982. Atari's star rose with the VCS–2600. It controlled 75 percent of the market for video games and employed more than 7,000 workers.

Then, in 1983, things changed. Seemingly overnight, Atari sales dropped 30 percent. The company lost more than half a million dollars. New management proved unable to stem the tide of Atari's collapse, and in 1984 the company was sold. Atari's work force by that time had dwindled to only 1,000 employees.[1]

Atari's rise and fall in the early 1980s stands as a testament to the power of the forces of change. In the late 1970s, consumers built Atari up into an economic powerhouse; in 1983 those same consumers tore that house down. Perhaps if Atari executives had better understood the forces of change surrounding them, they could have built on their early successes instead of swooning. Similarly, Emery Air Freight enjoyed success because of its innovative and effective use of employee-performance feedback in the late 1970s, but fell on hard times in the 1980s. The message here is that the power of the forces of change can make and break companies. If an organization ever hopes to be more than just a leaf blowing in the winds of capricious environmental forces, it must learn to recognize the forces of change and meet their demands.

In the early 1980s, futurologist John Naisbitt wrote *Megatrends*, a book about the future of American business and society. *Megatrends* turned out to be a best-seller, and throughout the 1980s it played a major role in shaping managers' views about the coming forces of change in America. To students who plan to be practicing managers in the 1990s and beyond, however, what is important are not just the currently "hot" forces for change. Those "hot" forces are constantly changing. Equally important is knowing *where* to look for the forces for change as they develop. For managers in organizations, there are two kinds of forces for change: internal forces and external forces.

Internal Forces   Internal forces for change are signals coming from *inside* an organization that change is necessary. Sometimes the signs are quite direct, such as inexplicably skyrocketing costs for operations. When employees go on strike, the clear message is that they are dissatisfied. The strike leads to negotiations that correct major problems concerning compensation arrangements or working conditions. Other times, the signals may be more subtle. High levels of absenteeism or turnover may indicate smoldering dissatisfaction among the work force. The challenge for management is to realize when the numbers are getting out of hand so that more serious—even catastrophic—problems (such

---

[1]R. I. Sutton, K. M. Eisenhardt, and J. V. Jucker, "Managing Organizational Decline: Lessons from Atari," *Organizational Dynamics* 14 (Spring 1986): 17–29.

as a walkout, work slowdown, or wholesale work-force desertion) can be avoided further down the road.

Internal problems also can be reflected indirectly. Increasing numbers of employee grievances may indicate a high level of tension between supervisors and the rank-and-file work force. Internal squabbling that is out of proportion to the nature of the problem—for instance, two managers arguing for days in a department head's office about which direction a secretary's desk should face—is often symptomatic of deeper problems that need to be brought to the surface and addressed. Tasks that don't get done on time, messages not received or returned (like the expansion plans at Ben & Jerry's), workers who don't seem to understand their roles, meetings that go on and on and on without resolution—all of these are indirect indications that an organization's management habits are not working and need to be overhauled.

Internal forces for change often reflect an organization's failure to accomplish its mission. For all organizations, survival is the primary mission. Problems such as excessive turnover and dwindling market share threaten an organization's survival, and so it must respond. For many organizations, however, monetary survival is only one aspect of the corporate mission. At Ben & Jerry's, the effectiveness of the organization also is measured by fulfillment of its social responsibilities. Whatever the organization's goals, its success in managing the forces of change will be measured by its attainment of those goals—or their abandonment in the face of external pressures.

External Forces The impact of the external environment on behavior of and in organizations was considered in detail in Chapter 14. At this time, it is worth reviewing several environmental forces that act as major catalysts for organizational change.

Social forces are a major force for change in organizations. For instance, in 1964 only 45 percent of the American work force had a full high school education. By 1984, U.S. Labor Department statistics indicated that almost 60 percent of the work force had high school diplomas, and in the young segment of the work force—those 25 to 29 years old—the percentage was closer to 85 percent.[2] What does this rise in general levels of education mean for American corporations? It may mean that workers will be better able to contribute ideas on the job. As noted in Chapter 12, surveys have shown that workers indeed *want* to play a greater role in organizational decision making. This suggests that managers need to rethink selection criteria and design jobs to meet the needs of a changing work force. (Some other aspects of the changing American work force will be discussed in Chapter 18.) Social forces might also include sweeping changes in ways of thinking, such as the demise of communism in Eastern Europe.

Political forces also have a tremendous impact on behavior of and in organizations. Certain political actions—for example, the Affirmative Action policies of the 1970s and the comparable worth debates of the 1980s—change the internal management habits of organizations. Comparable worth in particular probably led many organizations to reexamine their compensation schemes,

---

[2] E. E. Lawler III, *High-Involvement Management* (San Francisco: Jossey-Bass, 1986), 16.

Legislation such as the "plant closing" bill sponsored by Senator Edward Kennedy's Labor and Human Resources Committee provides a major force for change in organizations. While the bill requires only that employers inform their work force of facility shutdowns in advance, this change in notification requirements no doubt will encourage employers to manage the transition process more responsibly.

giving rise to an entire generation of merit-based compensation plans. Other political winds, such as movements to encourage or discourage mergers and acquisitions or the antitrust rulings that broke up AT&T, more directly affect the climate in which an organization exists by regulating the behaviors of other companies in the environment.

The effects of legislation can be subtle as well. The deregulation of banks in the United States altered the business of banking. Opportunities to develop new products or new markets became available, but many banks were not positioned to take advantage of them because banking traditionally had not been an opportunistic business.[3]

The rapid advance of technology constitutes a major force for change external to organizations. The Industrial Revolution forever changed the face of manufacturing, and it has been followed by a variety of smaller revolts, including the birth of interchangeable parts and the modern assembly line. The advent of computerized typesetting and word processors similarly revolutionized newspaper production techniques, while automated teller machines changed bank access from "banker's hours" (typically 10 A.M. to 4 P.M., five days per week) to 24 hours every day of the week.

Finally, market factors provide an important impetus for change in organizations. A decreasing market share should tell any company that some changes need to be made. As noted in the "INTERNATIONAL FOCUS ON: External Forces for Change," new competitors may mean that a company has to slash its own prices, or that internal cost-savings programs must be implemented to maintain profit margins. New products on the market and changes in the tastes and preferences of consumers are market forces that also demand responses from companies. Market forces that influence the behaviors of an organization's *suppliers* need to be watched carefully as well.

[3] R. B. Chase, G. B. Northcraft, and G. Wolf, "Designing High-Contact Service Systems: Application to Branches of a Savings and Loan," *Decision Sciences* 15 (1984): 542–556.

External Forces for Change

Endangered Species, European-Style   Management layoffs are hitting old-line European companies such as Michelin, Renault, Hoechst, Groupe Bull and Philips. Blue-collar ranks have been steadily pared for years. Now it's top-paid managers, sales executives and professionals who are seeing their ranks thinned. Formerly paternalistic employers have become companies fighting for survival in a new competitive game. Not only are jobs being slashed, but salaries for existing $50,000-a-year and up employees are being cut up to 10 percent.

What's different here from America's approach to downsizing? Much of the cost-cutting is the result of reorganizing management to better align with the lifting of international barriers in 1992. Groupe Bull, for example, is installing a single structure to replace its former maintenance, sales, and marketing structure organized on a nation-by-nation basis.

Other factors are very similar to those in America: the increasing spread of personal computers and retrenchments resulting from the leveraged buyout era of the 1980's. Competition is a factor, too. American computer makers are slashing their prices and Europeans must follow suit. Price competition results in slimmer staffs, an inevitability to which even Europe's powerful white-collar unions are resigned.

At British Telecommunications PLC, newly privatized, 5,000 workers were cut in six months. Said Barry D. Romeril, group finance director, ''There's no reason we can't get the same productivity improvements from managers as we've been demanding from the men in yellow vans and the operators.''

The financial services industry has been particularly hard-hit. In England and France, brokerage and securities firms are shrinking. U.S. and European banks are cutting thousands of jobs.

Germany's economy was one of the last to be hit. German companies are now overstaffed with managers. Accountants and administrators may see their jobs replaced by computers in the not-too-distant future.

What's a manager to do? The ones who keep their jobs will have to be willing to take on broader responsibilities. They will need experience in more than one country. Specialists in manufacturing and finance may find fewer opportunities than before. The traditional job-for-life is virtually extinct. And this evolution of the new Europe's work force, punctuated by retrenching and reorganization, is only just beginning.

Source: R. A. Melcher, ''Fired! Now, Europe Is Singing the White-Collar Blues,'' *Business Week,* November 26, 1990, 70–71.

| **Sources of Resistance to Change** | Even with all these internal and external forces pushing organizations to change, some individuals and organizations resist the need to change. For these individuals and organizations, the signals to change never get translated into appropriate responses or actions. Sometimes resistance takes the form of ignoring the signals. Sometimes top management heeds the signals and plans appropriate actions, but those actions never happen—at least not the way they were planned. Several sources of resistance to change are habit, resource limitations, threats to power and influence, fear of the unknown, and defensive perception. |

Habit   Inertia is the tendency for objects to keep doing the things they already are doing—their habits. Inertia is a primary cause of resistance to change. Even with the proliferation of word processors in the 1980s, many people continued to use typewriters. Did they not realize just how much more efficient a word processor would be? Unlikely. Did they not have access to training? Even more unlikely. Probably the typewriter had become a familiar and comfortable companion, and they didn't want to learn the whole new set of habits required to use a word processor.

In many cases, inertial resistance to change stems from an individual's realization that changing a habit will entail some short-term costs. Figure 17–1 shows three typical patterns of individual performance when a change occurs. Pattern A is what top management hopes for. In Pattern A, the change occurs at Time 0. There is no immediate decrease in performance level and, over time, performance gradually increases, reaching a stable new level. Patterns B and C are what usually happens instead. Pattern B represents a classic "Hawthorne effect." (The "Hawthorne effect" and the Hawthorne studies were discussed in Chapter 2.) Top management hears of or reads about something that it thinks is a great idea—quality circles, for instance. The idea is implemented and workforce performance immediately improves. Unfortunately, the improvement in performance is not really because the idea is a good one, but rather because the idea is a *new* one and people are enthusiastic about trying something new. When the enthusiasm for the new idea disappears, so do the improvements in performance.

Pattern C demonstrates a short-term loss from a change that has long-term value. Imagine that you own a small chain of hardware stores and for years your

FIGURE 17–1	▶Three Patterns of Change

Changes in organizations can affect organizational performance in many different ways. Most organizations hope that changes (a) will immediately and permanently improve organizational functioning. In some cases changes (b) cause immediate improvements that unfortunately do not last. Most of the time, though, changes (c) result in short-run losses that are eventually recouped when the changes are fully institutionalized.

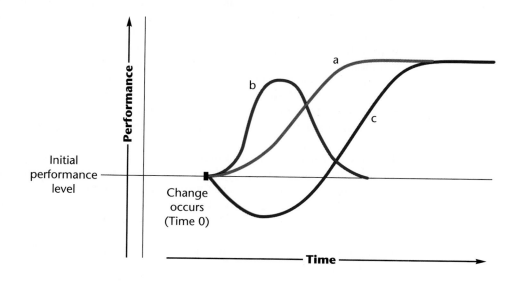

Source: James R. Gibson, John M. Ivancevich, and James H. Donnelly, Jr., *Organizations*, 6th ed. (Plano, Tex.: Business Publications Inc., 1988).

staff has kept the inventory manually, using large paper-and-pencil inventory registers. You are convinced by a computer salesperson that putting your entire inventory system on a desktop computer will save you both time and money in the long run. Further, you can use the computer for other functions such as payroll. This computerized inventory system clearly is your ticket into the twentieth century. There is only one problem: No one on your staff knows how to use a computer.

In such cases, some short-term costs have to be absorbed to get to the long-term benefits. Everyone will have to be trained to use the new computerized inventory system. That may mean closing your store for a couple hours per week for a few weeks, which means lost sales. Or it may mean having your staff come in evenings or weekends, which means overtime pay. Perhaps you will need to add some temporary employees to run the new system while your regulars observe and learn the ropes. You may even need to let some workers go and hire some others with different qualifications. Further, during the training period people are bound to make mistakes, which undoubtedly will translate into lost sales and maybe even lost customers. Some of your staff may even get discouraged and quit. Finally, when you announce the upcoming change to the new computerized system, some of your staff may stop recording inventory in the registers, creating further chaos when the new system is installed.

Knowing ahead of time that many of these costs are unavoidable can create a substantial psychological barrier to change. Any lost revenues and lost goodwill likely to occur as a result of the changeover *should be* recouped eventually. But those short-term costs can be painful, while the old managerial habits are probably familiar, comfortable, and workable, even if not spectacularly efficient.

Resource Limitations   Sometimes obvious changes are avoided because the costs are prohibitive. If a manager faces probable initial losses (Pattern C change), those short-term losses may represent more than just a psychological roadblock. In our previous example, the owner of the hardware-store chain had no one else to answer to for that short-term loss. What if instead that short-term loss was going to show up as red ink on a CEO's annual report to the shareholders, or as a quarterly loss on a division manager's performance appraisal? Even if the long-term benefits look pretty good, the long term is only potential. The short-term bad news may cost the CEO or division manager any opportunity to find out what the long term looks like—especially if the company or division is making a profit *without* the benefit of any changes. In these cases, inertia may be traced to a manager's short-run need to survive.

Threats to Power and Influence   One of the effects of many changes in organizations is the rearrangement of power relationships. In particular, changes often undermine power arising from expertise. Consider again the example of the hardware-store chain. If one or two people in the chain have become influential because of their in-depth understanding of the traditional inventory system, the adoption of a new system about which they know nothing would be quite threatening. Their power in the organization would evaporate, and they would have to start all over on an equal footing with every other computer novice in the company. Worse yet, a brand-new employee who was knowledgeable about computers would suddenly become quite powerful, even though computer experience previously was irrelevant as a condition of employment.

Fear of the Unknown   The sources of resistance that we have discussed so far all arise from an understanding of the probable consequences of a change in managerial habits. Some consequences, of course, cannot be foreseen, and the uncertainty that is part of any organizational change presents another source of resistance.

New employment opportunities provide a classic example of resistance that arises from uncertainty about the actual consequences of a change. If you are offered a transfer to another part of your company, should you go? Salary and job assignments, even housing costs and climate, can be known prior to making the decision. But what about the friendliness of your new coworkers? What about the quality of the new schools for your children? What about the quality of your life-style in a different town? These are all big question marks. If your current situation is good or even just OK, is a transfer worth the risk of losing the nice parts of your life as it is now? In the terms of Figure 17–1, maybe those short-term losses will never be recouped.

For organizationwide changes, similar uncertainties arise. Will I still be able to perform well under the new management? Will I ever be able to work the new computer inventory system? Will I still be respected as a typist when all the others have a word processor on their desk? These fears breed resistance to any changes to the old, familiar, and comfortable.

Defensive Perception   Managers who understand their own resistance to change—due to habit, resource limitations, loss of power or influence, fear of the unknown—may correctly perceive the need for change and act on that need *despite* their reservations or trepidations. A larger fear is that these sources of resistance will *bias* a manager's ability to construct an accurate perception of the need for change.

In Chapter 3 we noted that perception is a constructive process, and one that can be biased. Managers who sense trouble on the horizon if a particular change occurs may be less likely to perceive the need for that change. The signals may be there; managers just may be unwilling to see them or interpret them for what they are. An old-timer who has mastered the hardware chain's traditional inventory registers may have a hard time understanding the need for computers. A supervisor who fears the consequences of any short-term productivity losses may fight tooth and nail against the introduction of new machinery, if for no other reason than to be absolved of any personal responsibility for the outcome.

Defensive perception is really a result of resistance to change—a reflection of an individual's or organization's wish to maintain the status quo. When managers engage in defensive perception, the opportunity to change is missed. Resistance also can surface *after* the wheels of change have been put in motion. An organization's work force may voice its resistance to change by sabotaging implementation of management's new plans, perhaps in the hope of changing management's mind. The craftsmen who wrecked the textile mills in the early days of the Industrial Revolution were demonstrating their fears about the possible consequences of such a major change and hoping to reverse the trend.

The manager must be able to face opposition and balance it against the need for change. Our attention turns next to how these changes occur.

A MODEL FOR CHANGE IN ORGANIZATIONS

While there are many ways of conceptualizing the process of change in organizations, the model devised by psychologist Kurt Lewin is probably the best known and provides the simplest framework for understanding change processes. Lewin's model proposes three phases for change: unfreezing, movement, and refreezing.[4] Over the years, researchers have revised Lewin's model in a variety of ways and identified other phases of the change process.[5] In our discussion, we will consider one additional phase: diagnosis. The relationships among these four phases of change are depicted in Figure 17–2.

Diagnosis

Realizing that change is needed, or even having systems for meeting the demands of change, is not equivalent to knowing exactly what to change. The forces for change will signal the need to alter managerial habits; the next challenge for management is figuring out what actions to take in response to the signals. **Diagnosis** involves three separate tasks: identifying the problem, isolating its primary causes, and coming up with an appropriate and effective solution. Figure 17–3 shows one framework for thinking about where to find appropriate responses to the need for change. This framework includes six places to search for problems, their causes, and solutions when a change is needed: purposes, structure, relationships, rewards, support systems, and leadership.[6]

Purposes Purpose is what an organization is supposed to be doing—its charge, or mission. In 1987, a small home-movie videotape distributor called Vestron watched as the videotape-distribution market became saturated and its revenues plummeted. The response? Vestron's management decided that to remain financially healthy Vestron could no longer be just a videotape distributor. It had to become a *movie* company in a much larger sense of the word. So Vestron made a movie, "Dirty Dancing," that netted the company over $50 million.[7] Enlarging an organization's mission, for instance, through vertical or horizontal integration, is a common way to respond to the need for change.

Structure Organizational structure (which was the focus of Chapter 16) consists of an organization's reporting relationships. These reporting relationships

[4]K. Lewin, *Field Theory in Social Science* (New York: Harper & Row, 1951).

[5]R. Lippitt, J. Watson, and B. Westley, *Dynamics of Planned Change* (New York: Harcourt Brace, 1958).

[6]M. R. Weisbord, *Organization Diagnosis: A Workbook of Theory and Practice* (Reading, Mass.: Addison-Wesley, 1978).

[7]R. King, "Is There More Where *Dirty Dancing* Came From?" *Business Week*, February 15, 1988, 110.

FIGURE 17–2 ▶ Four Phases of Change

There are four distinct phases to organizational change efforts. Diagnosis identifies what needs to be changed; unfreezing prepares the organization for change; in movement, the change actually occurs; and refreezing ensures that the change had its intended effects and no unintended ones.

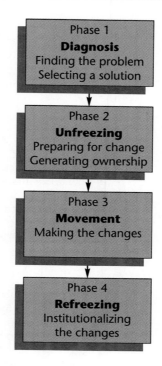

Phase 1
Diagnosis
Finding the problem
Selecting a solution

Phase 2
Unfreezing
Preparing for change
Generating ownership

Phase 3
Movement
Making the changes

Phase 4
Refreezing
Institutionalizing
the changes

in turn reflect how work is divided up in the organization. Organizational structure usually is reflected in a company's organizational chart.

Centralization is an aspect of organizational structure often tinkered with in response to signals for change. In a decentralized conglomerate, each division will act as a virtually independent company with its own marketing and purchasing operations. In a centralized organization, the marketing and purchasing operations for separate product divisions might be handled by central marketing and purchasing units. Marketing and purchasing in a centralized organization might even be divisions themselves. Centralization affords opportunities to avoid duplication of effort and consequently to achieve substantial economies of scale—for example, by having only one person order all the clerical supplies for the whole company. Decentralization, on the other hand, can increase understanding and responsiveness. Purchasing and marketing units that are part of a product division are in a position to be more in touch with that particular division's unique needs and therefore can respond better and more quickly to the division's concerns.

Relationships   Relationships have to do with the ways in which people in an organization get along—the group dynamics. Are there obvious conflicts, and if so, what are their origins? Are communication channels in place to ensure that work groups or individuals who need to share information have a way to do so?

FIGURE 17–3   ▶ A Framework for Diagnosis

Weisbord's "six-box" organizational model provides a road map for identifying problem areas in an organization. Each of Weisbord's six boxes represents one aspect of the organization that may be inhibiting its effective response to environmental forces for change.

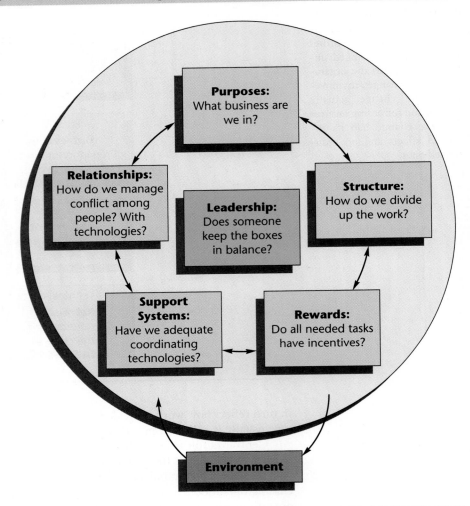

Source: M. R. Weisbord, "Organizational Diagnosis: Six Places to Look for Trouble With or Without a Theory," *Group and Organization Studies* 1 (1976): 430–447; W. Warner Burke, *Organizational Development: A Normative View* (Reading, Mass.: Addison-Wesley, 1987).

Relationships also may involve the roles that different workers are assigned. If someone is not doing the job, perhaps that person's role expectations are unclear. If two people are in conflict, perhaps their roles define their jobs so that conflict is inevitable. A supervisor who is rewarded for production quantity and a quality-control engineer who is rewarded for quality are bound to find their daily agendas in conflict. These kinds of relationship problems dictate a hard look at the roles of workers as one possibility for change.

Rewards   As we noted in Chapter 4, the law of effect suggests that the behaviors that get rewarded are the behaviors that occur. If an organization wants quality, it needs to reward quality; if it wants quantity, it needs to reward quantity. Too often compensation schemes are busy rewarding one set of behaviors (say, individual achievement) when another set of behaviors altogether (such as cooperative collaboration) is really desired.

Profit-sharing compensation programs make individual compensation contingent upon such factors as market reception of a firm's products and general economic climate, which workers clearly cannot control. This can be discouraging—and sometimes confusing—for rank-and-file workers. A production team that performs brilliantly but is not rewarded because the company didn't show a profit is unlikely to perform brilliantly again. Merit-pay programs in which the rules for judging merit are unclear to workers also miss the opportunity to motivate workers by making pay contingent upon work accomplishments.

Finally, it should be remembered that the term *rewards* refers to more than just money. As we discussed in Chapter 12, the design of jobs substantially influences the nonmonetary rewards that accrue to workers, such as job satisfaction and feelings of belonging or accomplishment on the job. A dissatisfied staff might be unhappy about wages, but could just as easily be dissatisfied with a shortage of opportunities to express opinions and exercise independence on the job.

Support Systems Elements in an organization that assist personnel in accomplishing their work tasks effectively are called **support systems**. AT&T ran a series of advertisements in 1987 emphasizing the importance of having a flexible and easy-to-use phone system, both for getting calls through and for projecting the correct corporate image. The phone system is one example of a support system that can dramatically help or hinder the efforts of a work force.

If projects are not getting finished on time or poor decisions are being made, problems may be traced to the support systems. An inadequate, outdated, or overloaded computer system can make life miserable for a production staff that depends upon computer output. An understaffed or poorly equipped maintenance department can turn minor problems into major roadblocks. If projects are continually being completed late, the clerical staff may be woefully undersupported. A shortage of information also can hinder performance. Putting in place performance feedback systems can improve performance by giving workers the information they need to know when their performance is off.

Leadership The leadership role means coordinating and initiating action. Someone must monitor signals, decide when the change is required, and move the organization forward to accomplish the change effectively. Without adequate leadership, important signals may be missed, diagnosis may be poor, inappropriate actions may be planned, and even appropriate actions may never get implemented effectively. Someone has to run the show.

These six components of organizations—purpose, structure, relationships, rewards, support systems, and leadership—hardly comprise an exhaustive list of places to look for problems or solutions in organizations. They do, however, provide a framework for formulating plans for possible organizational change. There are also several ways to approach the *collection* of information about an organization during the diagnosis phase. The advantages and disadvantages of several common information collection procedures are summarized in Figure 17–4. Each of these techniques has particular strengths and weaknesses. Interviewing, for instance, provides opportunities to collect rich, probing informa-

FIGURE 17–4	▶ A Comparison of Different Methods of Data Collection

Each of these four methods of data collection has both strengths and weaknesses. Questionnaires, for example, are easy to administer to large numbers of employees, but their predetermined format can bias the information that respondents supply. The best way to collect information is to use some combination of these different techniques.

Method	Major Advantages	Major Potential Problems
Interviews	1. Adaptive—allow data collection on a range of possible subjects	1. Expense
		2. Bias in interviewer responses
	2. Source of "rich" data	3. Coding and interpretation difficulties
	3. Empathic	4. Self-report bias
	4. Process of interviewing can build rapport	
Questionnaires	1. Responses can be quantified and easily summarized	1. Nonempathic
	2. Easy to use with large samples	2. Predetermined questions miss issues
	3. Relatively inexpensive	3. Overinterpretation of data
	4. Can obtain large volume of data	4. Response bias
Observations	1. Collect data on behavior rather than report behavior	1. Coding and interpretation difficulties
	2. Real time, not retrospective	2. Sampling inconsistencies
	3. Adaptive	3. Observer bias and questionable reliability
		4. Expense
Unobtrusive measures	1. Nonreactive—no response bias	1. Access and retrieval difficulties
	2. High face validity	2. Validity concerns
	3. Easily quantified	3. Coding and interpretation difficulties

Source: David A. Nadler, *Feedback and Organization Development: Using Data-Based Methods* (Table 7.1), © 1977 by Addison Wesley Publishing Co., Inc. Reprinted by permission.

tion. Its value, however, is highly dependent upon the interviewer's skills and the awareness and forthrightness of the interviewee. Trustworthy diagnosis generally comes at the cost of combining multiple collection techniques. Once a problem has been diagnosed and a potential solution identified, the real business of change begins with unfreezing.

Unfreezing

Unfreezing is the process of getting an organization ready for change. Unfreezing is something akin to the pregame warm-ups for a major sporting event. Even if the coaches have a terrific game plan, it will never work if the players aren't told what the plan is and how to execute it. In the pregame warm-ups, the coaching staff has a chance to *prepare* everyone for the game, to get all the players loosened up and make sure they understand their role in the game. The pregame warm-up is also a great time to put any conflicts on the table and get them settled.

Harkening back to the model of organizations presented in Chapter 1, uncertainty, complexity, and politics all present barriers to change efforts in organizations. The time to lower these barriers is during the unfreezing stage. It is the preparation phase, in which resistance can be broken down. The unfreezing phase has three objectives: selling the diagnosis, understanding the implementation, and preparing for the consequences.

Selling the Diagnosis It is easy to assume once you see why a change is necessary or even inevitable that everyone else will see it, too. Unfortunately, that is a dangerous assumption. In fact, the only more dangerous assumption is that workers won't care about changes.

Unfreezing is the time to get everyone up to speed about an upcoming change. Once management has chosen a course of action, sharing with other organizational members insights about the problem, its probable causes, and the identified solution will help them understand the need for the change. This diagnosis sharing promotes ownership of the problem by the rest of the work force. Generating ownership even at the level of rank-and-file workers is critical if the conversion is to go smoothly, without hostility, resentment, or sabotage.

The importance of selling a diagnosis to the work force is illustrated by a story about a posh hotel resort in the Colorado Rockies. To cut costs, hotel management decided to install a video-surveillance security system rather than hire security guards to patrol the hotel. Unfortunately, top management failed to share its thoughts with any members of the hotel work force. When the first surveillance cameras appeared in the hotel kitchen, the kitchen staff was outraged. They assumed the cameras had been installed to police their behaviors. Their reaction was sabotage; the cameras were covered up with dish towels, and a minor blowup between the kitchen staff and hotel management quickly followed. Hostilities subsided as soon as management informed the staff of its real intent in installing the cameras. However, the entire conflict could have been avoided if management simply had shared its diagnosis with the hotel staff at the outset.[8]

Work-force participation in the diagnosis process provides a foundation of worker understanding of the necessity for change. As noted in our earlier discussions about participative management in Chapters 9 and 12, participation is two-way education. Participating workers provide management with a fresh and different perspective on problems, probable causes, and potential solutions. The participation process also allows workers to see more of the facts about a problem, to gain a broader, organizational perspective, and to learn management's thoughts and beliefs. As shown in the "FOCUS ON: Selling the Diagnosis," work-force participation in diagnosis can mean a much stronger sense of diagnosis ownership and consequently a stronger commitment to the changes when they occur.

---

[8]Taken from a personal experience of one of the authors.

Focus on

Selling the Diagnosis

Sharing the Bad News In 1985, Jim Ebright was coming off a high. His Software Results Corp., based in Columbus, Ohio, had made the *Inc.* 500 list of top companies in 1983 and 1984, and sales had reached $4.2 million. Over the next four years, however, Ebright's company fell off a cliff; revenues shrunk to $500,000 and the payroll dwindled from 65 to 10.

Software Results went through three waves of layoffs. The first was relatively easy; the second and third were excruciating. They also took an odd turn. After Ebright called the affected workers in and gave them the bad news, he says, "I'd find some of them consoling *me*." Ebright believes he got that kind of response because his employees knew what the score was. He had decided early on to let his workers know what was happening at the company.

Ebright understands why some managers might be hesitant about keeping employees abreast of everything going on in the company. "There's an obvious downside. Even if you think this is a temporary problem, your best people may leave," he says. But Ebright thinks keeping employees in the dark is short-sighted. Sharing the bad news yields long-term dividends, in the form of employee trust, sacrifice, and a heightened awareness for future trouble.

Trans-Matic Manufacturing Co. of Holland, Michigan, employs 150 people with sales of $15 million annually. Trans-Matic makes stamped metal parts, 50 percent of which go to the automotive industry. The financial reality at Trans-Matic has been grim of late, but that hasn't stopped management from disclosing the situation to workers. Every month, management distributes a sheet of paper: one side displays detailed financial data comparing actual performance with target numbers, the other side provides comments on the numbers. The recent numbers, and comments, have not been pleasant. President Pat Thompson thinks the information has fostered a collegial atmosphere. "There's empathy for a company that's willing to share that information in advance. By identifying the problem, you have not done something *to* those employees. Instead, you've done something *with* them."

Sharing the news inevitably points to a core concern of both workers and managers: credibility. Fragile even when the going is good, credibility in bad times often becomes the first workplace casualty. "In the long run, it's absolutely vital there be a degree of credibility," says Ebright. "Once you start telling white lies, no one will believe you anymore."

Source: Adapted from E. O. Welles, "Bad News," *Inc.*, April 1991, 45–49.

Understanding the Movement Even if all workers accept the need for a change, it is important that they realize their own role in the process. Unfreezing presents an opportunity to communicate the "game plan" to all relevant players in the upcoming conversion. Details should be provided about what will happen—for example, what days new equipment will arrive, what performance expectations are going to be during the conversion, and how business is going to continue (if it is) in the midst of the chaos.

Unfreezing is also the time to train workers to use new equipment or lay the foundations for new managerial habits. If a new compensation plan or a different phone system is going to be used, for instance, management will need to arrange information or training meetings so that everyone knows what to expect and what to do.

Preparing for Consequences   Unfreezing is also the time to prepare the work force for any foreseeable consequences of the change. Particularly sweeping changes in work-force size or organizational climate and culture may lead to the departures of some members. The offer of early-retirement programs or outplacement services may be appropriate to smooth the transition process. Overtime policies and extra temporary staff also may be desirable to get an organization through a particularly large changeover.

Management should make sure that one objective of the unfreezing phase is to reassure workers (if possible) that their jobs are not on the line. The uncertainty that arises in the work force concerning job security does more than distract employees and hurt short-term performance. Psychological studies have demonstrated that perceptions of job security are the number-one predictor of workers' *physical* health. The more permanent that employees perceive their jobs to be, the better their physical and mental well-being.[9] Since it is no secret that an organization suffers financially when the health of its employees suffers, both in lost productivity from sick days and rising health-care costs and insurance claims, it makes sense for management to use the unfreezing phase of organizational change to calm the fears of its work force about what is to come.

Unfreezing is also the time to put in place feedback systems to track the unforeseeable consequences of organizational changes. Management may find it advisable to set up temporary monitoring systems and employee counseling programs. These procedures can not only help deal with unforeseen problems that arise as the implementation occurs, but also provide management with a watchful eye on the progress and problems of their change efforts.

Movement

If the foundation for change has been laid effectively during unfreezing, the actual **movement**—implementation of the change plan—should be trivial. In fact, the ease of implementation should be a good gauge of how well the unfreezing process has broken down any potential pockets of resistance to the change. If unfreezing has been handled well, all employees will understand why the change is necessary and what their own role is in the change. However, it is important during movement that management make sure the channels of communication in the organization remain open and active. If implementation of the change plan creates confusion or unforeseen problems, early detection may be critical to the prevention of a groundswell of work-force resistance.

An important decision for management during the movement phase of an organizational change is whether to use external change agents. **External change agents** are expert consultants from outside an organization that management brings in specifically to execute a change. Their value lies in their experience and objectivity. Because they will have supervised similar changes in other organizations, change specialists will have the experience necessary to identify subtle sources of resistance to change and know what strategies will best deal with them. Because they are not part of the social fabric of the organization, the objectivity of external change agents puts them in a better position to act upon sources of resistance to change.

---

[9] M. Schanback, "Stress and Job Security," *Psychology Today,* May 1987, 16.

Refreezing

Finally, once the change has been fully implemented, **refreezing** is the process of institutionalizing the new changes—making the new changes into organizational habits. Institutionalization means monitoring the systems that have been put in place to track the consequences of implementing the change. Have any unforeseen problems developed? Have any members of the organization become disenfranchised or lost power or status? If so, how should these problems be handled? Did the change solve the problem it was intended to address? If not, should the change be scrapped and something different tried? Refreezing is a time to reflect on what has occurred in the change and get the work force settled into a new routine.

ORGANIZATIONAL DEVELOPMENT

The four-phase model of change we have been discussing in this chapter epitomizes traditional approaches to managing change in organizations: Managers diagnose organizational problems, unfreeze the work force, implement the changes, and then refreeze the work force by institutionalizing the changes. **Organizational development (OD)** represents a different approach to managing the process of change in organizations. Organizational development can be formally defined as "a system-wide application of behavioral science knowledge to the planned development and reinforcement of organizational strategies, structures, and processes for improving an organization's effectiveness."[10] As shown in Figure 17–5, organizational development differs from traditional approaches to organizational change in several important ways.

Behavioral Health

First, traditional organizational change efforts typically are *problem focused*. This means management identifies a problem that needs to be solved, and the focus of the change effort is on resolving the problem. A defining feature of organizational development, on the other hand, is its **process focus.** Organizational development efforts seek to install adaptive behavior patterns, which will be better able to cope with any problems that arise. As demonstrated in the "FOCUS ON: Organizational Development," some organizational development activities are oriented toward the encouragement of *individual* potential. Typically, however, its final objective is to develop a group's or *organization's* potential. Organizational development activities focus on the behavioral (interaction) patterns in an organization that produce or sustain problems. Organizational development assumes that an organization or group that is behaviorally healthy will anticipate and therefore prevent (or quickly resolve) problems.

A behaviorally healthy organization is more than just financially sound. A **behaviorally healthy organization** is one whose internal interaction patterns put the organization in a position to become and remain financially sound. This kind of behavioral health arises from four other characteristics of organizations: communication, adaptation, innovation, and succession. Financial soundness is a partial reflection of these other sources of organizational health.

---

[10]E. F. Huse and T. G. Cummings, *Organizational Development and Change* (St. Paul, Minn.: West, 1985), 2.

FIGURE 17–5	▶ Thirteen Major "Families" of Organizational Development (OD) Interventions

Organizational development activities come in a variety of forms. All share the organizational development focus on improving the effectiveness of an organization's self-diagnosis and problem-solving abilities, rather than solving any particular organizational problem.

1. *Diagnostic Activities:* Fact-finding activities designed to ascertain the state of the system, the status of a problem, the "way things are." Traditional data-collection methods—including interviews, questionnaires, and meetings—are commonly used.
2. *Team-Building Activities:* Activities designed to enhance the effective operation of system teams.
3. *Intergroup Activities:* Activities designed to improve effectiveness of interdependent groups. The focus is on joint activities.
4. *Survey Feedback Activities:* Activities involving analyzing data produced by a survey and designing action plans on these data. Survey feedback activities are a major component of the diagnostic activities category, but they are important enough to be considered a separate category as well.
5. *Education and Training Activities:* Activities designed to improve skills, abilities, and knowledge of individuals. There is a wide range of possible approaches, from T-group and sensitivity training, to structured experiential exercises, to lecturing, and concentrating on technical, interpersonal, or other competencies.
6. *Technostructural or Structural Activities:* Activities designed to improve the effectiveness of the technical or structural inputs and constraints affecting individuals or groups. Examples would include job enrichment, matrix structures, management by objectives, and physical settings interventions.
7. *Process Consultation Activities:* Activities on the part of the consultant that help managers understand and act on human processes in organizations. This includes teaching skills in diagnosing and managing communications, leadership, cooperation and conflict, and other aspects of interpersonal functioning.
8. *Grid Organization Development Activities:* Activities developed by Robert Blake and Jane Mouton, constituting a six-phase change model involving the entire organization. The phases include upgrading individual managers' leadership abilities, team improvement activities, intergroup relations, corporate planning, development of implementation tactics, and evaluation of change and future directions.
9. *Third-Party Peacemaking Activities:* Activities designed to manage conflict between two parties, and conducted by some third party, typically a skilled consultant.
10. *Coaching and Counseling Activities:* Activities that entail working with individuals to better enable them to define learning goals, learn how others see their behavior, explore alternative behaviors, and learn new behaviors.
11. *Life- and Career-Planning Activities:* Activities that help individuals identify life and career objectives, capabilities, areas of strength and deficiency, and strategies for achieving objectives.
12. *Planning and Goal-Setting Activities:* Activities that include theory and experience in planning and goal setting. They may be conducted at the level of the individual, group, and total organization.
13. *Strategic Management Activities:* Activities that help key policymakers identify their organization's basic mission and goals; ascertain environmental demands, threats, and opportunities; and engage in long-range action planning.

Source: W. French and C. Bell, *Organization Development: Behavioral Science Interventions for Organization Improvement* 3/e, © 1983, 126–128. Adapted by permission of Prentice-Hall, Inc., Englewood Cliffs, N.J.

Focus on

Organizational Development

Operation Executive Teamwork?
Not long ago, 160 sales executives from Goal Systems International, a Columbus, Ohio, computer software firm, stepped down from their air-conditioned buses and squinted into the glare of the Tubac, Arizona, sun. When they left their hotel that afternoon, they didn't know where they were headed. All they knew for sure was that what they'd do that day was somehow meant to help them grab a bigger slice of the American economic pie that had been shrunk by the recession. Ladders, tires, and ropes had been strung up in a small forest of telephone poles; rows of mountain bikes lay nearby; and hidden challenges involving logs, hanging ropes, and wooden walls awaited them in the trees.

Welcome to Venture Up, a highly visible entry in a fast-growing national industry that provides wilderness and outdoor training programs for individual executives, management teams, and company groups. More than 100 companies across the United States and many foreign firms now offer some kind of outdoor training. Designed to promote such qualities as leadership, self-reliance, teamwork, and effective thinking, the programs have surged in popularity in the last decade.

Meredith Pennington, first vice-president and regional manager for Security Pacific Bank's central Phoenix region, went through a Venture one-day program with her 13 regional managers. "I had changed management within the last year, and they weren't mixing well as a group together," she noted. The Venture Up program was divided into a half-day session devoted to solving map-and-compass problems and another half-day completing the challenge course. All the problems were set up so that her managers had to work together to solve them. "The most meaningful exercise was a 14-foot wall, and you had to figure out how to get all 14 people over it," she said.

According to Pennington, the business benefits of the program were immediate. "Before this event, there was very little interaction among my managers at our sales meetings. Now they tend to break off and work much better as a team in order to achieve regional goals as opposed to individual branch goals."

It isn't hard to find satisfied customers. Venture Up's co-owner, Dave Lengyel, believes that one of the major benefits in dealing with outdoor problems is that the challenges they present, and the teamwork they promote, are not artificial. "It's not like you're in a conference room acting out a river-rafting scenario, when somebody suddenly goes overboard, and then the participants get up and go to the bathroom or get another Coke."

Source: Adapted from E. Severson, "Outdoor Training," *Arizona Daily Star,* June 16, 1991, E1,E7.

Communication   Andy Pearson, former president of corporate megaconglomerate Pepsico, Inc., once noted, "We have 120,000 employees stashed in various places around the world, and I frankly have no idea what the hell they're doing."[11] If you were a stockholder of Pepsico, Inc., would you find this comment encouraging? Probably not. Certainly the complexity and uncertainty of organizational life make it difficult for any executive to stay in touch with all levels of a major organization. However, for an organization to be healthy, people must know what's going on. This means a lot more than creating the potential for communication. All organizations have reporting relationships; subordinates report to supervisors, supervisors report to managers, and so on, so communication is always possible. In a healthy organization, communication actually occurs.

In the face of forces for change, communication also has to work to help evaluate an organization's past habits. Ben & Jerry's corporate malaise got people asking hard questions: Should we keep doing things the way we always have? Which management habits should be changed? Habits will never be broken if no one communicates the need for change. Management never should find itself in the position of Pepsico's president, who didn't know "what the hell" was going on below him in his own organization. If things are fine, then organizational communication channels should be saying so. If things are not fine, then organization communication channels should signal a need for change. Without active channels of communication, it's impossible for anyone to know what's working and what isn't, and whether there are even any forces for change in the organization.

Adaptation   Activating communication channels is a futile exercise if an organization is not prepared to change when the need is signaled. Organizations must be able to adapt, to alter their plans to fit new constraints. Flexibility must be built into an organization if it intends to weather any significant storms it may encounter on the business horizon. The job-rotation and cross-training arrangements mentioned in Chapter 12 are examples of planned flexibility. Job-sharing schemes like these increase training costs since workers are trained to do multiple tasks, but provide additional options for management.

Imagine that a bank decided to expand by creating semiautomated branch offices of automated teller machines with only a skeleton crew of one or two human workers. If workers in the bank previously had been given highly specialized jobs, none would be in a position to assume all the skeleton-crew functions. Cross-training and job rotation put that flexibility into the bank's work force.

Flexibility also can be maintained by searching out additional ways to accomplish the same task. Many large Japanese firms add temporary employees to the work force when demand increases are first encountered. This avoids the need for terminations or lay-offs if the demand increases prove not to be permanent. Internally, adaptability can be promoted by having problem-solving groups such as quality circles meeting on a regular basis to address operational issues. Then, when problems arise, a system to identify solutions already will be in place.

---

[11] R. H. Waterman, Jr., *The Renewal Factor* (New York: Bantam Books, 1987), 71.

Innovation   A healthy organization should be constantly moving ahead, preventing crises by improving on its old habits before they have a chance to become obsolete. A healthy organization must be innovative.

Like adaptability, innovativeness means having in place active systems for generating new ideas. Research and development arms of organizations are charged with the responsibility for generating product innovations. A healthy organization also should have in place systems for creating innovative managerial practices such as innovative incentive systems, innovative work-sharing systems, even innovative arrangements of production equipment. Employee-involvement programs (such as those discussed in Chapter 12) can be sources of both product and managerial practice innovations.

Succession   Just as organizations must plan ahead and anticipate the eventual obsolescence of their managerial habits, so must they plan ahead to anticipate the eventual **succession** (turnover, retirement, even promotion) of their work force. All of an organization's best-laid plans can be stopped cold when unanticipated shifts in the work force occur. Key personnel can unexpectedly leave an organization for a variety of personal reasons (such as spousal relocation) or financial reasons (a better offer elsewhere).

A healthy organization is constantly cultivating replacements for key personnel to ensure that it is never left in the lurch. This cultivation may include the kinds of mentor-apprentice arrangements mentioned in Chapter 11 or the task cross-training discussed in Chapter 12. These arrangements accomplish two important components of any succession plan: they expose subordinates to the duties and responsibilities of their supervisors, and they allow supervisors to evaluate the potential of their subordinates to handle promotions.

In-house training programs also can cover this dual purpose of simultaneously enhancing and evaluating employee potential. Many large corporations maintain extensive in-house programs to renew and review management potential, such as NCR's management college in Dayton, Ohio. Other companies (such as IBM) participate in tuition-sharing and release-time programs to encourage employees to further their education at local colleges and universities. Finally, many corporations now have early retirement programs. Travelers Insurance has established a program to rehire its own retirees for up to 960 hours per year (almost half time).[12] At Siemens AG in Germany, older employees can reduce their work time to 20 hours per week at 75 percent of full-time pay.[13] If successfully managed, these early retirement programs dramatically increase the flexibility of a work force by retaining the expertise of the "old hands" while simultaneously unblocking promotion opportunities for an ambitious new generation of workers.

The behaviorally healthy organization represented by these four characteristics—communication, adaptation, innovation, and succession—can correctly identify the need for change through effective and active communication systems and has a way to change (adapt, innovate, or graduate) when the need

---

[12] "Retirees Work as 'Temps' at Travelers Insurance," *World of Work Report* 6 (8), (1981): 57.

[13] "Easing into Retirement," *World of Work Report* 8 (9), (1983): 72.

arises. Organizational development assumes that if a problem—anything from deteriorating market share to increasing numbers of employee grievances—does occur, some of these four aspects of an organization's behavioral health are not working effectively. In essence, organizational development assumes that all problems are symptoms of process problems. Not surprisingly, then, organizational development interventions are designed specifically to improve one or more aspects of the behavioral health of an organization.

In addition to its focus on behavioral health, organizational development frames change more dynamically than traditional approaches to change. Organizational development sees the organization as constantly evolving; any change management undertakes is simply one small step in a continuous loop. Traditionally management has viewed change in organizations as a static process; management identifies a problem, and the time horizon for change extends only as far as the resolution of the problem. In the terms of the four-phase model of change we have been discussing up to now, organizational development really has no refreezing phase. The feedback phase from one movement is simply the beginning of a new diagnosis.

Finally, in traditional approaches to change, diagnosis is a management activity. This is known as **"top-down" problem solving.** The diagnosis (identification of the problem, probable causes, and potential solutions) is done by management—the top of the organization. The rest of the work force is informed about the change only when unfreezing begins. Organizational development instead is built on the assumption that work-force involvement is essential in all phases of change, especially diagnosis. This is known as **"bottom-up" problem solving:** the problem diagnosis comes up from the bottom of the organization.

Not surprisingly, there are not really two distinct approaches to change (the traditional approach and the organizational development approach). Rather, there is a spectrum of approaches to managing change in organizations. The process-focused, evolutionary, "bottom-up" orientation at the organizational development end of the spectrum represents a drastic departure from tradition for some managers. However, organizational development is an approach to change in organizations that is clearly in sync with the job design needs and desires of the current American work force, as discussed in Chapter 12.

Several organizational development techniques have been discussed in this book. Team building was discussed in Chapter 7, and quality circles were discussed in Chapters 9 and 12. Both are process-focused change efforts. The object of these activities is not to solve a particular problem. Team building and quality circles are both group processes that handle organizational problem solving naturally, by making the organization more communicative, adaptive, and innovative. Similarly, the time horizon for team building and quality circles is long term and dynamic. The object of these activities is not to solve one problem, but to create an organization that is behaviorally healthy for problem solving over the long haul. Finally, through both team building and quality circles, management puts in place "bottom-up" problem-solving processes that foster work-force participation in organizational problem diagnosis. In effect, organizational development is an approach to the diagnosis and unfreezing phases of organizational change that should make movement and refreezing considerably more effective.

The particular orientation of organizational development can be seen further by examining two other intervention techniques: survey-guided development and quality-of-work-life programs.

Survey-Guided Development

Survey-guided development (or survey feedback) is one of the most popular techniques of organizational development. It has been used in a wide variety of organizational settings including businesses, schools, hospitals, government operations, and even the military. The U.S. Navy alone has used this technique more than 500 times, collecting more than 150,000 individual survey responses.[14] The results of survey-guided development have been mixed. However, evidence suggests that it is the OD intervention technique most likely to produce both process and outcome benefits if only one OD technique is going to be used.[15]

Survey-guided development uses questionnaires to construct a picture of an organization's internal processes and problems. Many organizations use employee surveys to assess the organization's climate and to identify sources of problems in organizational functioning. Survey-guided development differs from these traditional survey efforts in the amount of involvement it requires from rank-and-file workers. In a typical organization's employee survey, rank-and-file workers participate only by filling out the questionnaires. In survey-guided development, employees at all levels of the organization also play a role in *interpreting* the results. In some cases, survey-guided development techniques may even ask employees to identify issues that need to be addressed in the questionnaire.

The rationale behind encouraging employee participation in the development of the questionnaire is simple: The questions asked in a survey and the way they are worded play a large role in the picture of the organization painted by responses to the questionnaire. When management encourages employee participation from all levels of an organization in the design of an employee survey, the discussions about which questions should be included and what issues should be addressed become as revealing as the questionnaire results. Participation in development of the survey itself becomes a forum for employees at all levels to discuss problems in the organization.

Employee participation in the interpretation of survey results is accomplished through a process called **"data handback."** Once a completed survey-guided development questionnaire has been filled out by all employees and the results tabulated, these results are handed back to the employees. In keeping with the spirit of organizational development, top management may see the results first, but in the end *all* members of the organization are encouraged to attend data handback sessions.

Data handback sessions have two purposes. Naturally, management can use these sessions to solicit suggestions from employees at all levels of the organization about implications of the survey results for organizational problem diagnosis. However, in survey-guided development, data handback also serves

---

[14]Huse and Cummings, *Organizational Development and Change*, 133.

[15]J. Porras and P. O. Berg, "The Impact of Organizational Development," *Academy of Management Review* 3 (1978): 249–266.

a more basic function. Employees also are asked to assess whether the picture of the organization painted by the survey results is accurate. The benefit of survey-guided development, then, is that it gives top management *three* opportunities to solicit employee input about problems and processes in the organization—through their participation in survey design, survey completion, and survey results interpretation. Traditional organization survey attempts take advantage of only one of these opportunities.

In its ideal form, survey-guided development is not a one-shot attempt to understand organizational processes. When used on a regular basis (such as annually or semiannually), survey-guided development provides an ongoing set of processes through which top management can track the development of the organization.

Because the intended output of survey-guided development is an accurate picture of the workings of the organization, it is primarily a form of diagnosis. It is not surprising, then, that research has found survey-guided development to work best when combined with other techniques to form broader-scope OD programs.[16]

Quality-of-Work-Life Programs

Quality-of-work-life (QWL) programs are examples of broader-scope organizational development programs. QWL programs are best characterized as systemwide attempts to simultaneously enhance organizational effectiveness (usually defined in terms of productivity) and employee well-being through a commitment to participative organizational decision making. Unlike survey-guided development, QWL does not refer to a particular OD technique. Rather, QWL provides a framework for pursuing organizational development goals, and it may incorporate any number of specific OD techniques.

QWL programs aim to enhance the work experience of the individual worker. They typically have a strong flavor of worker rights and industrial democracy, and many QWL programs have been designed as cooperative ventures between unions and firm management. The typical objectives of a QWL program would include fair compensation, a conducive work environment, development of individual capacities, social integration of the work force, protection of the dignity and rights of each individual worker, and social relevance of the organization and its activities for the organization's work force.[17]

The philosophy of the QWL framework is illustrated in Figure 17–6. In virtually all QWL programs, joint management-union quality-of-work committees are established to oversee QWL program development and planning. QWL programs then may additionally include a team-building or survey-guided development component. In the case of Shell Canada, one component was management-union cooperation in the design of a new plant and its jobs.[18] The General Foods experiment in Topeka, Kansas (described in detail in Chapter 12), is considered to have been one of the pioneer QWL projects.

---

[16] Porras and Berg, "The Impact of Organizational Development"; also J. Nicholas, "The Comparative Impact of Organizational Development Interventions on Hard Criteria Measures," *Academy of Management Review* 7 (1982): 531–542.

[17] Huse and Cummings, *Organizational Development and Change*, Chapter 9.

[18] Ibid., 209.

FIGURE 17–6 ▶ **How Quality of Work Life Affects Productivity**

A quality-of-work-life program will typically include a combination of different organizational-development techniques, and no two programs are ever quite the same. However, all QWL programs share the organizational development focus on improving the quality and effectiveness of employee interactions, on the assumption that improved organizational outcomes such as increased productivity will no doubt follow.

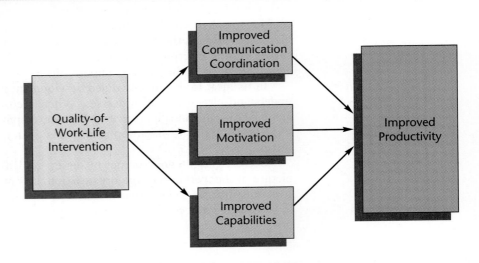

Source: E. Lawler III and G. Ledford, "Productivity and the Quality of Work Life," *National Productivity Review* 2 (Winter 1981–1982): 29.

In keeping with the overall philosophy of organizational development, the immediate focus of a QWL intervention is improving such organizational processes as communication, coordination, motivation, and personal development. The implicit assumption here is that improving these processes will enhance attainment of the individual objectives described above. Improved productivity and organizational effectiveness should follow.

QWL programs have had mixed success. The Ford Motor Company's QWL program at its Sharonville plant has claimed some dramatic successes. Customer complaints dropped by *70 percent* after QWL was instituted, and the proportion of employees in the plant rating quality as excellent rose from 54 to 72 percent. Ford also claimed annual cost improvements of almost 7.5 percent during the QWL program at Sharonville—*three times* the average of other Ford plants during the same time period. Furthermore, 90 percent of Ford's surveyed employees said that Ford's QWL program was a good idea and should be continued.

General Motors has had similar successes with QWL. A QWL program at GM's Tarrytown facility helped take them from sixteenth (out of 18 plants) to first, according to GM's internal measures. And GM management has directly attributed its success in negotiating union contracts to the presence of QWL programs in GM plants. On the other hand, only one of the eight QWL programs studied in depth by the University of Michigan QWL center lasted more than five years. Apparently QWL is not for everyone, and some important organizational factors—such as top management's commitment to QWL and the effectiveness of the labor-management steering committee—play a major role in determining the success of an organization's QWL effort.[19]

---

[19]Lawler, *High-Involvement Management*, 136.

GM's car assembly plant in Tarrytown, New York, was the scene of a major turnaround in work-force morale and productivity through organizational development. Serious problems in the plant led management and union representatives to work together to formulate a participative problem-solving program for the work force. The benefits realized from this initial program encouraged management to initiate a highly successful plant-wide quality-of-working-life effort.

CHANGE IN CORPORATE AMERICA ◆◆◆◆◆◆

The American business environment in the 1980s could be charitably characterized as turbulent. Successful major assaults were made on American product markets by international business competitors, especially the Japanese. Closer to home, a staggering 138 U.S. banks failed during 1986, compared with only 10 in 1981. During all this, 30 million members of the American work force were dislocated by corporate restructuring efforts as Fortune 500 companies eliminated about 3 million jobs.[20] As described in the "FOCUS ON: Change in Corporate America," some U.S. firms learned the hard way that bigger is not better.

Perhaps in response to the chaos—perhaps as *part* of the chaos—mergers, acquisitions, hostile takeovers, plant closings, and severe cutbacks in personnel all became commonplace during the 1980s. In effect, the 1980s provided more than just new heights of turbulence in the American business environment. The 1980s also set new standards for the severity of organizations' responses to the uncertainty and chaos around them. In one remarkable six-year stretch, General Electric alone acquired 325 businesses and sold off more than 225.[21] And at least one business analyst—Tom Peters, coauthor of the business best-seller, *In Search of Excellence*—thinks American companies had better start thinking in terms of even more change if they want to survive.[22] In the final few pages of this chapter, we will use the framework for change developed in the chapter to examine a few of the problems involved in managing major corporate reorganizations.

Corporate Reorganizations

Mergers and acquisitions present very complete pictures of the spectrum of problems that major corporate change creates. As we discussed in Chapter 14, on paper many mergers and acquisitions look like good ways for organizations

---

[20]T. Peters, *Thriving on Chaos* (New York: Knopf, 1987), 3.

[21]Ibid.

[22]T. Peters, "There Are No Excellent Companies," *Fortune*, April 27, 1987, 341–352.

Focus on

*Change in
Corporate
America*

Managing Ungrowth Tony Bykerk had grown up poor, and when he set out to build a telecommunications company, he wanted to build it big. Before long, his fledgling K&B Engineering had 450 employees and 16 offices nationwide. K&B's growth had allowed Bykerk to buy a $2 million house, a 53-foot yacht, and a stable of expensive cars. But it had also brought a troubled marriage, a drinking problem, and a mess at the office. While sales rose, profit mar-

gins shrank, and thievery and foul-ups mounted. Bykerk solved his problems—both personal and professional—by shrinking his business from 450 employees to 85, from 16 offices to 4, and from nationwide to serving just California. His profit margins doubled. Growth, he concluded, was a narcotic. He had been hooked, and he had shaken the addiction just in time.

Experts say that a business that isn't growing is dying. But there is—pardon the pun—a growing group of entrepreneurs who believe that they can build better, stronger, and more durable companies by avoiding growth. Tony Bykerk learned the hard way.

Carl Schmitt, on the other hand, began his company—University National Bank & Trust (UNBT) in Palo Alto, California—with the intention of keeping it small. While California's superintendent of banks in the 1970s, Schmitt (pictured at left) had noted that small banks consistently outperformed their larger competitors. He believed that by being smaller, a bank would have lower

Sources: J. Case and E. Conlin, "Second Thoughts on Growth," *Inc.*, March 1991, 47–57; and E. Conlin, "Small Business," *Inc.*, March 1991, 60–66.

to combine complementary resources in the fight against a hostile and competitive business environment. Unfortunately, the combining of two companies' resources is not done just on paper. The marriage can go sour when one or more of a variety of behavioral problems occur.

While mergers and acquisitions represent the marriage of complementary resources, merging companies undoubtedly have some redundant functions. For example, the payroll offices of two merging companies each may be almost large enough to handle the entire payroll function for the new merged entity. This could necessitate cutbacks or transfers of staff to new functions where both companies previously were short in personnel. **Downsizing**—reducing the size of an organization's work force—also can occur as a reaction to a downturn in product demand. Finally, some mergers and acquisitions are quickly followed by a general "house cleaning"—replacement of key employees with newcomers not wedded to the old managerial habits of either company, or even the selling off or closing down of less profitable or outdated facilities and operations.

Such turmoil can prove extremely damaging to the morale of an organization's work force. Workers may become less productive because of uncertainty about life in the new organization (including job responsibilities and relationships with supervisors and coworkers), legitimate concerns about job security, and even feelings of betrayal if management was not particularly communicative

overhead and could provide more efficient service to a specific market. From the time it opened its doors, Schmitt wanted customers to know that this bank was different. The side of the bank building depicts an alien in a spaceship crashing through the wall; the strange beast also adorns the bank's credit card. The bank's courier trucks have the license plate UN-BANK to spread the message; one truck is painted to show Schmitt cheating at poker while dressed in a prison uniform behind bars.

"One thing I can't do is manage a much bigger company," Schmitt acknowledges. But intentionally avoiding growth isn't easy either. For instance, how do you motivate your employees when opportunities for advancement aren't growing? Schmitt does so by giving his employees an enjoyable workplace—keeping things fun. That means lavish lunchrooms, Un-bank awards, the painted courier trucks, good pay, and an employee stock ownership plan. It also means ensuring that UNBT employees feel free to make day-to-day decisions with customers. At most banks, tellers work from long lists of do's and don'ts. At UNBT, tellers make their own decisions about whether to accept a check, based on their own criteria. While teller turnover at most banks is about 50 percent, at UNBT it is zero, and managers spend less time and money supervising the tellers. UNBT also has a "bank within a bank" program, in which teams of three or four employees have their own list of customers, their own portfolio of loans, even their own letterhead for correspondence. "It provides a sense of ownership without diluting our strategy of limiting growth," says Schmitt.

Schmitt certainly has his critics. Roger Smith, founder of competitor Silicon Valley Bancshares, insists that "Growth helps build the corporate culture. It provides a mission, a sense of purpose." But as Schmitt notes, "We don't intend to be dead in the water. It's really a matter of focus; our focus isn't growth: it's efficiency and return on equity."

about impending possibilities. Undesired turnover among key employees also can occur if they perceive the new corporate entity as too unstable or perceive an erosion of their influence or power, or if early retirement programs designed to thin the ranks are not managed properly. Maybe it is not surprising, then, that the success rate of mergers and acquisitions (as measured by appreciation in shareholder value) has been estimated to be only about 23 percent.[23] What can top management do to make sure its efforts become part of that successful 23 percent?

In the process of unfreezing for a merger or acquisition, it is critical that an organization's channels of communication be extremely open and active. Naturally, workers will want to know what's going on—who is buying whom, what the new name will be, who will be in charge now, and so on—even if their jobs are not going to change much. Federal legislation now requires employers to provide their work force advance notification of major plant closings. Meetings and memorandums can help diffuse a lot of hostility or concern that takes root in uncertainty. Many employees in the face of little or no information are likely to imagine the worst and react accordingly. Employees also

---

[23] Peters, *Thriving on Chaos*, 3.

should be provided opportunities to ask questions. The strategic concerns at the forefront of top management's minds during a major organizational change may have nothing to do with what is on the minds of the employees (their benefits package, for instance).

Included in the unfreezing stage for a major corporate reorganization should be an **outplacement program** to find new jobs for displaced employees, or those who choose not to stay on under a new regime. Good outplacement programs can do a lot more than just soothe a guilty corporate conscience. They also send the message to the *remaining* members of the work force that the organization is not going to abandon them. This message can play an important role in minimizing the psychological damage done to their feelings of job security. Some remaining workers are even likely to feel "survivor guilt"—guilt because they were allowed to remain while some of their coworkers were not.[24] Even though survivors are, in some sense, the winners of reorganization, they often experience a sense of loss of control. It is demoralizing for survivors to discover that they are working for managers who have been demoted three grades. At Exxon, for example, so many young managers have been demoted that there is a layer of them in their early forties: a group that aspiring "up-and-comers" will never be able to penetrate. Those who get demoted may not take a salary cut, but they don't expect any salary increases for a long, long time.[25]

What can management do to maintain productivity of survivors? As survivors, they are likely to have two overriding concerns: "Why was I allowed to remain?" and "Will I be the next to go?" While management may never be able to answer the first question satisfactorily for the survivors, it can respond to the job-security issue. Of the four factors often identified as concerns by survivors, job security and related items such as pay and benefit issues and performance feedback ("How well am I doing?") are often uppermost in their minds.[26] Successful outplacement programs will help these workers turn their attention to the new work at hand, rather than becoming obsessed about their future in the new company. Good outplacement programs also help with community relations.

SUMMARY

To respond effectively to the ever-changing demands around them, organizations must be prepared to change constantly. A key challenge for managers is maintaining a delicate balance between forces that encourage or demand change and forces within organizations that resist it. Managers must be able to recognize the need for change and identify and manage sources of resistance to change.

The change process entails four stages. During diagnosis, information that helps identify an organization's

---

[24]J. Brockner et al., "Layoffs, Equity Theory, and Work Performance: Further Evidence of the Impact of Survivor Guilt," *Academy of Management Journal* 29 (2) (1986): 373–384.

[25]B. Nassbaur et al., "The End of Corporate Culture," *Business Week*, August 4, 1986, 42–49.

[26]D. M. Schweiger, J. M. Ivancevich, and F. R. Power, "Executive Actions for Managing Human Resources Before and After Acquisition," *Academy of Management Executive* 1 (1987): 127–138.

problems and isolate their causes is collected. Unfreezing lays the foundation for a change, and movement executes the change itself. Refreezing institutionalizes the change and checks to make sure the identified problem has been solved and no new problems created.

Organizational development is a different approach to change in organizations. Organizational development assumes that problems occur in organizations because they are not behaviorally healthy. All organizational development change efforts therefore are aimed at improving organizational health—communication, adaptation, innovation, and succession. Survey-guided development uses work-force participation to develop, complete, and interpret questionnaires that construct a picture of an organization's internal processes and problems. Quality-of-work-life (QWL) programs are systemwide attempts to improve work-force effectiveness and morale through a commitment to formal work-force participation in organizational decision making.

The 1980s were an exceptionally turbulent time for businesses in America. Bankruptcies, hostile takeovers, mergers, and major reorganizations and work-force reductions all became commonplace. So much uncertainty plays havoc with an organization's ability to remain efficient and effective. Being able to manage the changes necessitated by such a turbulent business environment has become a key managerial challenge.

Key Terms

Behaviorally healthy organization One whose internal interaction patterns put it in a position to become and remain financially sound; arises from successful communication, adaptation, innovation, and succession.

Bottom-up problem solving Involving workers in all phases of the change process, beginning with diagnosis.

Data handback Providing employees with the results of the questionnaires used in survey-guided development in order to assess whether the picture of the organization painted by the survey is accurate, and to solicit their suggestions about the implications of the survey results for problem diagnosis.

Diagnosis First stage in the process of change; figuring out what actions to take in response to signals that change is needed; includes identifying the problem, causes, and an appropriate and effective solution.

Downsizing Reducing the size of an organization's work force.

External change agents Expert consultants from outside an organization that management brings in specifically to facilitate a change.

Habit Tendency of a person or an organization to do things the same way, over and over again.

Inertia Tendency of an object to continue in the same direction with the same velocity or intensity unless impacted by some force of change.

Movement Third stage in the process of change; implementation of the change plan.

Organizational development (OD) Systemwide application of behavior science knowledge to the planned development and reinforcement of organizational strategies, structures, and processes for improving an organization's effectiveness.

Outplacement program   Finding new jobs for displaced employees or those who choose not to stay on after a major corporate reorganization.

Process focus   Concentration of organizational development on the behavioral (interaction) patterns in an organization that produce or sustain problems.

Quality-of-work-life (QWL) programs   Systemwide attempts to simultaneously enhance organizational effectiveness (usually defined in terms of productivity) and employee well-being through a commitment to participative organizational decision making.

Refreezing   Final stage in the process of change; institutionalizing the change and monitoring the systems

that have been put in place to track the consequences of implementing the change.

Succession   Turnover, retirement, or promotion of personnel.

Support systems   Elements in an organization that assist personnel in accomplishing their work tasks effectively, such as production technology.

Survey-guided development   Use of questionnaires to construct a picture of an organization's internal processes and problems; also called *survey feedback*.

Top-down problem solving   Diagnosis of a problem by management, with the rest of the work force being informed only during unfreezing.

Unfreezing   Second stage in the process of change; lowering barriers to change by selling the diagnosis, understanding the implementation, and preparing for the consequences.

Discussion Questions

1. Considering what you have learned about participative approaches to managerial decision making, are there any circumstances in which "top-down" change efforts might be more appropriate than organizational development?

2. How does the progress of traditional change efforts and organizational development through the four phases of organizational change (diagnosis, unfreezing, movement, and refreezing) differ?

3. Why would survey-guided development probably be a useful first step in *any* organizational change or development program?

4. Refreezing is often a forgotten and neglected phase of organizational change efforts. Does this help explain why apparently successful change efforts often do not have lasting effects? Why is refreezing so important? What is likely to happen if it is *not* done?

5. What skills are likely to be required of a manager in a turbulent industry or during turbulent times?

6. Why is change likely to be easier to manage in a behaviorally healthy organization? Is change likely to be easier in a company like Ben & Jerry's because of its interest in the employees' welfare?

7. Are some sources of resistance to change more "rational" (that is, more justifiable) than others? Why might a little inertia (or even a lot) be a good thing?

8. Organizational development is a vehicle for change in organiza-tions. For many organizations, however, organizational develop-ment itself represents a change. What kind of unfreezing might be needed to ensure success when an organization changes to the use of organizational development?

If You Want to Know More

Two recent popular-press books concern-ing the importance of managing change to corporate survival in today's turbulent busi-ness environment are by the authors of *In Search of Excellence:* Robert H. Waterman's *The Renewal Factor* (New York: Bantam Books, 1987) and Tom Peters's *Thriving on Chaos* (New York: Alfred Knopf, 1987). Rosabeth Moss Kanter's book, *The Change-masters: Innovation for Productivity in the American Corporation* (New York: Simon & Schuster, 1983) also examines the impor-tance of managing change to remaining in-novative on an ongoing basis. Kanter's book includes a particularly good chapter concerning the problems often encoun-tered when organizations attempt to use participative approaches to weather the storms of major change.

A more theoretical treatment of the or-ganizational change process is provided in Noel Tichy's *Managing Strategic Change: Technical, Political, and Cultural Dynamics* (New York: Wiley, 1983).

A classic article on sources of resistance to change in organizations is Coch and French's piece, "Overcoming Resistance to Change," in *Human Relations* (Winter 1948): pp. 512–532. Even today this article remains the foundation of our understand-ing of individual sources of resistance to change.

A classic article on organization diag-nosis processes is William Pound's piece, "The Process of Problem-Finding," an *In-dustrial Management Review* 11 (1969): pp. 1–19. Marvin Weisbord's article, "Organi-zational Diagnosis: Six Places to Look for Trouble with or without a Theory," also provides some important insights into the diagnosis phase of change efforts.

An excellent sourcebook on organiza-tional development is Huse and Cum-mings' text, *Organizational Development and Change* (St. Paul, Minn.: West, 1985). This book explains the theoretical underpin-nings of the organizational development orientation and provides detailed descrip-tions of all major OD intervention strategies.

The February 1987 and January 1988 issues of *Personnel Administrator* have ad-dressed the issue of managing corporate re-structuring and its effects on an organiza-tion's work force. Included in these issues are articles on "Downsizing Strategies" (by J. Franzem, February 1987) and "When the Dust Settles" (by R. Korn, January 1988), which examine the effects of corporate re-structuring on the survivors.

On Your Own

Likert's Profile of Organizational Characteristics: Short Form Are you in a work group that is ready for change? Keeping that group in mind, fill out the questionnaire below. For each question on the left-hand page, circle the phrase on the right-hand page that best describes your work group. Your instructor will give you scoring instructions that will tell you where your group stands, and if it might be ready for some changes.

Leadership

1. How much confidence is shown in subordinates?
2. How free do they feel to talk to superiors about job?
3. Are subordinates' ideas sought and used, if worthy?

Motivation

1. Is predominant use made of (1) fear, (2) threats, (3) punishment, (4) rewards, (5) involvement?
2. Where is responsibility felt for achieving organization's goals?

Communication

1. How much communication is aimed at achieving organization's objectives?
2. What is the direction of information flow?
3. How is downward communication accepted?
4. How well do superiors know problems faced by subordinates?

Decisions

1. At what level are decisions formally made?

2. What is the origin of technical and professional knowledge used in decision making?

3. Are subordinates involved in decisions related to their work?
4. What does decision-making process contribute to motivation?

Goals

1. How are organizational goals established?

2. How much covert resistance to goals is present?

Control

1. How concentrated are review and control functions?

2. Is there an informal organization resisting the formal one?

3. What are cost, productivity, and other control data used for?

System 1	System 2	System 3	System 4
None	Condescending	Substantial	Complete
Not at all	Not very	Rather free	Fully free
Seldom	Sometimes	Usually	Always
1, 2, 3 occasionally	4, some 3	4, some 3 and 5	5, 4, based on group-set goals
Mostly at top	Top and middle	Fairly general	At all levels
Very little	Little	Quite a bit	A great deal
Downward	Mostly downward	Down and up	Down, up, and sideways
With suspicion	Possibly with suspicion	With caution	With an open mind
Know little	Some knowledge	Quite well	Very well
Mostly at top	Policy at top	Broad policy at top, more delegation	Throughout but well integrated
Top management	Upper and middle	To a certain extent, throughout	To a great extent throughout
Not at all	Occasionally consulted	Generally consulted	Fully involved
Nothing, often weakens it	Relatively little	Some contribution	Substantial contribution
Orders issued	Orders, some comment invited	After discussion, by order	By group action (except in crisis)
Strong resistance	Moderate resistance	Some resistance at times	Little or none
Highly at top	Relatively highly at top	Moderate delegation to lower levels	Quite widely shared
Yes	Usually	Sometimes	No—same goals as formal
Policing, punishment	Reward and punishment	Reward—some self-guidance	Self-guidance problem solving

Source: Rensis Likert, *The Human Organization* (New York: McGraw-Hill, 1975). Reprinted with permission.

CLOSING CASE

CHAPTER 17

THE MANAGER'S MEMO

FROM: J. Quigley, Vice-President

TO: P. Winograd, Production Manager

RE: Planning for Greater Productivity

As you know, our profits have suffered during the past year because our production facility has one of the lowest productivity levels in the industry. The Executive Committee has been exploring solutions to this problem, and we have come to the conclusion that we have a major need for greater automation and use of technology.

Therefore, we plan to introduce computer-aided design and manufacturing (CAD/CAM) to our production process. We intend to install the system next year.

CAD/CAM will enable us to offer greater service to our customers and will permit us to cut costs dramatically by eliminating 35 jobs. The remaining workers will have to learn to operate the computerized system, or we will need replacement workers who already have these skills.

I would like to meet with you on Tuesday to begin discussing the particulars of the CAD/CAM system. In the meantime, please send me suggestions for how we can introduce this system to the production work force. We would like to keep morale as high as possible, introducing the change as a positive move for the future of the company.

Case Discussion Questions

Assume you are the production manager, and respond to the vice-president's memorandum. What sources of resistance to this change must you prepare for? What actions can the company take to make the change as beneficial as possible? What, if anything, should the company do for the workers whose positions will be eliminated?

CHAPTER

DIVERSITY IN THE WORKPLACE: MANAGING IN THE TWENTY-FIRST CENTURY

RE-CREATING CORNING   ◆◆◆◆◆◆

Corning, the family-controlled manufacturer of Pyrex, Corning Ware, and Steuben crystal, was trying to make affirmative action work better. The company was able to hire women and African Americans relatively easily, but these employees left Corning at a rate two to three times that of white males. Blaming subtle, but entrenched discrimination as the reason for the departure of women and minorities, Corning, like many other large corporations, has embarked on a campaign to create true cultural diversity within the organization.

Management believed that one reason for the high turnover among African Americans and women was the company's location. Corning, New York, is a small company town located an hour's drive from Ithaca. But, interviews with departing employees revealed that their biggest gripe with the company centered around the inability of blacks and women to break into the upper ranks of management. James Houghton, the CEO of Corning, found these exit interviews disturbing, particularly because of Corning's reliance on scientific workers. With the competition for scientists and engineers heating up over the next decade, those organizations that could successfully attract and retain such employees were at a distinct advantage.

Houghton set one goal for Corning: that there be a better mix of women and blacks in the management and professional ranks. He said he wanted a salad (that is, a place where individual differences remain intact), not a puree in the company work force. He sought blacks who were proud to be African Americans and women who were proud to be mothers and engineers. In the past, women and blacks had adopted not only professional values such as integrity, hard work, and a commitment to profits but also had tried to adopt the social and cultural values of the dominant group of white males. Women, in fact, tried to dress like men, wearing flannel suits and neckties. But the women and blacks who tried to act as the white males acted couldn't do it, were denied promotional opportunities, and eventually left the company.

Now, Corning is very different. When a black job applicant is interviewed, managers have a real incentive to hire him or her—the managers' raises and bonuses depend, in part, on their ability to recruit and retain qualified women and men of color. Corning more readily offers undergraduate internships to women and men of color than it does to white males. Also, more than most companies, Corning goes the extra distance to find jobs for employees' spouses or significant others. Several hundred couples work for the company, the only constraint being that they do not work for one another.

Corning has begun to show some real strides as a result of the programs. Fifty-two percent of the salaried employees it has hired since 1987 are women and sixteen percent are African American. Of salaried personnel, women now comprise 33.6 percent and blacks 5.5 percent. Attrition is down sharply. In 1987, the percentage of turnover for female employees was 16.2 percent; in 1990, it was down to 7.6 percent. For African Americans, the 1987 figures were 15.3 percent, compared to the 1990 attrition rate of 11.3 percent. Additionally, Houghton reports that the cost of these programs is far less than the $4 million Corning used to spend to recruit and train African Americans and women to replace those who were quitting.

Source: "Corning's Class Act," *Business Week*, May 13, 1991, 68–74; and Peter Kilborn, "A Company Recasts Itself to Erase Years of Job Bias," *The New York Times*, October 4, 1990, 1, C21.

INTRODUCTION

Corning realized that to be successful in the coming decade, it had to change the way it recruited and developed its employees. The intensity with which Corning and other large corporations have begun to search for enhanced creativity, productivity, and commitment in their employees is indicative of the enormous problem facing managers who must deal with the new work force. This chapter focuses on the track records of organizations who have attempted to integrate women and men, whites and minorities, young and old, straight and gay employees into an effective, functioning work force.

THE CHANGING DEMOGRAPHICS OF THE WORK FORCE

A great deal of media and organizational attention has been paid in recent years to diversity in the work force. Diversity is often used as a buzzword for racial, ethnic, and gender differences among employees. Organizations are committing major resources to attract diversity in the work force, manage that diversity successfully, and promote a diverse set of employees to positions of power and influence within the organization. Most of the discussions have focused on what we call primary diversity—immutable differences such as age, race, gender, ethnicity, or sexual orientation. Other types of diversity are those aspects of the employee that he or she has some control over, such as educational background, marital or family status, geographic location, work experience or socioeconomic status. Most organizations have the greatest experience with these latter types of diversity, but it is the former type that is making the news today.

In 1956, William Whyte coined the term "organizational man" to refer to the typical employee of that era. According to Whyte, organizational men

> felt confident about their company's paternalistic benevolence. They believed they had jobs in perpetuity. They relished the rigid corporate hierarchy; and like medieval churchmen, they had the security that came from knowing their assigned place and the privileges and responsibilities that came from that place. For many "organizational men," the organization became their fiefdom, a social system with its own customs, habits, feelings, understandings, cliques, and cabals.[1]

During this period of American corporate history, most organizations found themselves operating in relatively stable, predictable environments. The factors that were responsible for corporate success in 1952 were likely to be the same factors that resulted in success in 1959. In a stable, predictable environment, a homogeneous set of employees may be the most effective.

However, as we have shown in Chapter 14, the environment that organizations are facing in the 1990s is clearly not the one that existed during the reign of the organizational man. Organizations must be able to respond successfully to a rapidly changing environment. To do so effectively requires that different people with different experiences, perspectives, and orientations monitor the environment to identify necessary corrections in an organization's course. Part of this changing environment was the changing demographic base of customers and clients. Beginning in the 1970s, the U.S. organizational demographics on age, sex, education, and race began to change dramatically. This change was also reflected in the types of individuals entering the work force. No longer do organizational demographics mirror the composition of the top management team. Instead it is more likely that the top management team will be almost exclusively white and male, while the work force the team manages will be increasingly composed of women and men of color. In fact, by the year 2000, the U.S. work force will be significantly older, with a higher percentage of female and educationally disadvantaged workers. Only 30 percent of the new entrants to the labor force over the next ten years will be white males, compared to 47 percent of the new entrants to the work force in 1987. Almost two-thirds of the new entrants will be women and 61 percent of all women of working age will be working. Nonwhites will make up 29 percent of the new entrants, twice their share of the work force in 1987.[2]

The primary task before managers is to create an environment in which each employee, regardless of race, age, ethnicity, or other factors irrelevant to level of performance, is motivated to perform. Consider the options available to companies who, for example, only wanted to hire and retain white males (ignore, for a moment Equal Employment Opportunity Commission regulations). In the past, when most of the business students in the United States were white males, companies simply had to attract the top candidates and these top candidates would be almost exclusively white males. Now consider the top ten percent of your graduating class. In that group there are likely to be a significant number of females of all races, men of color, and international students. If our

---

[1] William Whyte, Jr., *The Organizational Man* (New York: Simon & Schuster, 1956); and Amanda Bennett, *The Death of the Organizational Man* (New York: Murrow and Company, 1990).

[2] *Workforce 2000: Work and Workers in the 21st Century*, (New York: Hudson Institute, 1987).

Demographic trends indicate that the work force of the future will be a complex mix of sexes, ages and ethnicities. Managers will be increasingly challenged to find ways to motivate this diverse group to perform.

hypothetical organization wanted to restrict its hiring to native white males, then it would have to, on average, recruit students of lower overall quality. While such a strategy is illegal in today's organizational environment, it is unclear why any company would knowingly implement a strategy that would objectively result in a lower overall quality of its new hires.

A second reason for organizations to attract and retain women and men of color is based on the findings of recent research on demographics. For example, people who share experiences, attitudes, and are similar to one another are more likely to interact with each other, like each other, and share a common bond.[3] People who are similar demographically (such as age, race, and sex) are also more likely to have had common experiences, share similar values, and understand one another better. Similarity increases interpersonal attraction and social integration, and perceptions of similarity enhance the quality of interaction.[4] Organizations experienced greater turnover (both voluntary and involuntary) where there were large gaps in rank, and departments showed greater turnover where there were larger age differences among employees. Thus, to the extent that there are large age differences in the organization and the groups of employees entering the work force, those most likely to leave (voluntary and involuntary turnover) were employees who are most different in age.[5]

Men of color or females may face barriers such as negative racial or gender stereotypes, the pressure of the solo role (the only person of color or female employee), or the stereotype of incompetency stemming from the perception

[3] J. Pfeffer, "Organizational Demography: Implications for Management," *California Management Review* 28 (1985): 67–81.

[4] D. Byrne, "Attitudes and Attraction," in L. Berkowitz, ed., *Advances in Experimental and Social Psychology*, vol. 4 (New York: Academic Press, 1971).

[5] B. McCain, C. O'Reilly, and J. Pfeffer, "The Effects of Departmental Demography on Turnover: The Case of a University," *Academy of Management Journal* 26 (1986): 626–641; and G. Wagner, J. Pfeffer, and C. O'Reilly, "Organizational Demography and Turnover in Top Management Groups," *Administrative Science Quarterly* 29 (1984): 74–92.

that they received their jobs because of affirmative action. Men of color or female employees may also find themselves barred from promotion at higher rates than white males. Those who are married, especially those in dual-career marriages, may find that their advancement options are limited since any geographical change requires two new jobs. Finally, those who are parents also face considerable transaction costs in making moves because of the difficulty in finding successful child care, the multiple constituencies to be satisfied, or the desire to maintain family stability.[6] In Figure 18–1, the relationships between various demographic characteristics and the amount of integration and cohesion are presented.

If social interaction, cohesion, and communication frequency are critical for organizational success, then perhaps to be successful, organizations should select individuals who are as similar to one another as possible. But similarity here can as easily refer to similarity in experience, hire date, or education level as to gender, race, or ethnicity.

However, research on creativity and innovation in organizations—a factor that may be increasingly important in the twenty-first century—requires diversity. In fact, researchers of the creative process suggest that the most productive and creative individuals are those who have had a broad range of contacts and have interacted with a variety of individuals of diverse backgrounds. Creativity may occur, then, only when basic beliefs or expectations are challenged. Over time, individuals working closely together tend to become more alike in their values, views, and perspectives. As such, creativity is stifled and people become insensitive to opportunities.[7] In the FOCUS ON: Managing Diversity for Competitive Advantage," six arguments are presented for competitive advantage.

The increasing heterogeneity of the work force, then, has its advantages and disadvantages, and organizations will have to develop strategies for coping with this new work force. As an example, consider the ten ways corporations are adapting to the demands of dual-career couples.[8]

1. *Recruiting.* Recruiters are becoming increasingly sensitive to the role of the spouse in career decisions.
2. *Scheduling.* The need for flexibility has made scheduling more of a problem. Scheduling vacation time and work hours is also affected as more employees seek "off time" to coincide with children's school schedules and day-care center hours.
3. *Transfers and relocation.* This is probably the area of greatest impact and poses the biggest problem for large companies. An employee's refusal to relocate may mean the company must dip into the pool and send less-qualified people into a new assignment. Those who refuse to relocate may be fired or quit, entailing high replacement and training costs.

[6] Linda Stroh, Jeanne Brett, and Anne Reilly, "A Decade of Change: The Impact of Demographics and Corporate Turbulence on Managers' Career Patterns and Work Attitudes," Working paper, Loyola University, Chicago, Ill.

[7] R.M. Kanter, "When a Thousand Flowers Bloom: Structural, Collective, and Social Conditions for Innovation in Organizations," in L.L. Cummings, and B.M. Staw, eds, *Research in Organizational Behavior*, vol. 10 (Greenwich, Conn.: JAI Press 1988), 169–211.

[8] F.S. Hall, and D.T. Hall, "Dual Careers—How Do Couples and Companies Cope with the Problems?," *Organizational Dynamics* (Spring 1978): 57–77. The quote is from page 71.

| FIGURE 18-1 | ▶ Similarity and the Integration and Cohesion of Cohorts |

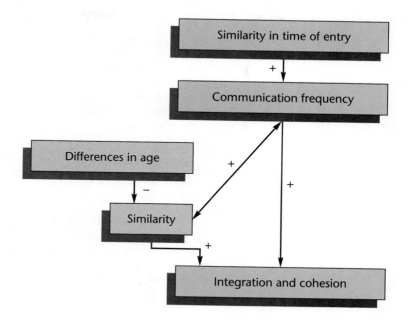

Source: J. Pfeffer, "Organizational Demography: Implications for Management," *California Management Review* 28 (1985): 67–81.

4. *Promotions.* Many couples are less eager for promotion opportunities, regardless of whether they involve a geographic move or not. Many two-career couples have aspirations for more free time, less work pressure, and fewer responsibilities. With two incomes, the pay differentials may not compensate sufficiently to make promotions worthwhile.

5. *Travel.* People are less willing or able to travel in two-career couples where family demands are high. People seem to "burn out" faster in high-travel occupations such as public accounting, sales, and consulting.

6. *Benefits.* The need to revise benefit programs is growing. Both men and women are seeking maternity/paternity leaves or leaves without pay to accommodate spouse and family demands. Life insurance has become more important as people adapt to a standard of living based on two incomes. "Personal days" are another benefit that couples seek and use with greater frequency.

7. *Conflict of interest.* Employees with spouses in the same professions or working for competing firms may represent a potential liability or security risk. In the same firm, one spouse may have information that is not normally available to the part of the organization in which the other spouse works.

8. *Career development.* The most significant change that couples have had on career programs is in "career pathing" or the design of career ladders.

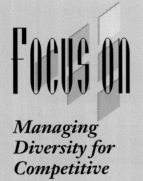

*Managing
Diversity for
Competitive
Advantage*

Arguments for Cultural Diversity

1. Cost Argument
As organizations become more diverse, costs of poor integration will increase. Companies who are able to integrate a culturally diverse work force will realize considerable cost savings over those companies that cannot or do not do so.

2. Resource-Acquisition Argument
Companies develop reputations as good places for women and minorities to work. Those with the best reputations will be able to attract the best people. As the labor pool shrinks and changes in composition, this advantage will be more important.

3. Marketing Argument
For multinational organizations, the insight and cultural sensitivity that employees with roots in other countries bring to marketing efforts should improve the effectiveness of such efforts. This reasoning also applies to the representation of ethnic groups within the United States.

4. Creativity Argument
Diversity of perspectives and less emphasis on conformity and adherence to past practices should improve the level of innovation and creativity among employees.

5. Problem-solving Argument
Heterogenous decision-making and problem-solving groups can produce potentially better solutions because they allow critical analysis from multiple perspectives.

6. System-Flexibility Argument
Organizations that are able to manage multicultural diversity effectively will necessarily become less determinant, less standardized, and more fluid. This fluidity should create greater flexibility to react to environmental changes more effectively.

Source: Taylor Cox and Stacy Blake, "Managing Cultural Diversity: Implications for Organizational Competitiveness," *Academy of Management Executive* 5(3) (1991):45–56.

Many firms are finding the need to redesign training programs with limited geographic mobility in mind.

9. *Deadwood.* The combination of resistance to relocation, lower aspirations, unwillingness to travel, and other drawbacks of this kind presents a potential problem of deadwood among high-potential recruits who would otherwise develop and advance.

10. *Career bargaining.* A newly emerging trend is for couples to bargain for considerations that result directly from the career of a spouse. For example, these couples may bargain for a particular location, assistance in finding a new position for the spouse, and subsidies until the spouse obtains a position.

Thus, organizations will have to plan for new ways to recruit an increasingly scarce resource and one with increasing demands.

Not only will the race, gender, and spousal limitations of the typical worker change, so will the age and educational level. In the 1970s, about 3 million people entered the work force each year at age 18; by 1990, the number had dropped to 1.3 million, and by 1995, there will be 7.5 million fewer workers in the 18- to 24-year-old age group.[9] The proportion of the labor force that has

---

[9]G.S. Odiorne, "The Crystal Ball of HR Strategy," *Personnel Administrator* (December 1986): 103–106.

completed four years of college grew from 14.7 percent to 24.2 percent between 1970 and 1983. While the number of college-educated workers grows, so does the number of entry-level applicants who lack basic skills in reading and arithmetic.

One reason for this swing in demographics is the "baby boom" and the "baby bust." As the large group of individuals born in the late forties and early fifties age, they produce the "bulge" illustrated in Figure 18–2. Notice that the bulge of "under 35" was greatest in the 1980's and then, twenty years later, the

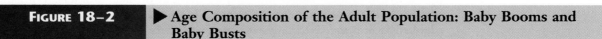

FIGURE 18–2 ▶ **Age Composition of the Adult Population: Baby Booms and Baby Busts**

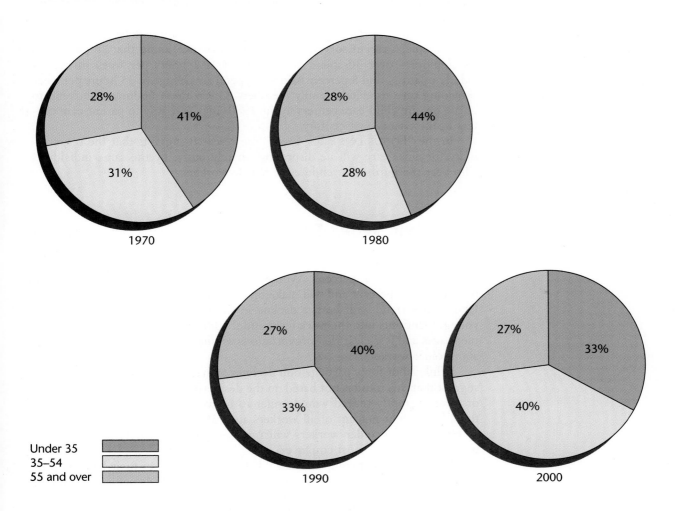

Under 35
35–54
55 and over

Source: Dennis A. Ahlburg and Lucinda Kimmel, "Human Resource Management Implications of the Changing Age Structure of the U.S. Labor Force," Working paper, Industrial Relations Center, University of Minnesota, Minneapolis, Minn.

greatest bulge will be in the 35- to 54-year-old age group. The baby bust of the late sixties was the product of the decision made by many working women to postpone childbearing and the introduction of effective birth-control methods. The results of the baby bust were first felt in the declining enrollment in elementary education and are currently being experienced at the university and college level. One indicator of this is the proliferation of "marketing directors" hired by institutions of higher education to raise their visibility and "sell" slots to the decreasing number of potential consumers.

One major result of the baby boom–baby bust pattern is that younger workers (those just outside the prime baby-boom years) will find their progress up the organizational ladder impeded by the glut of older workers. With the increase in life expectancy and the removal of mandatory retirement laws, a real problem is brewing. Not only will young workers find their climb impeded, there will also be fewer of them to support the increasingly large population receiving social security benefits. Second, as older workers become a larger and more politically powerful group, it is likely that they will demand more job security, employee rights, and programs designed to meet their specific needs. For example, a recent survey by Travelers Insurance found that 28 percent of its employees over 30 spend an average of 10.2 hours per week caring for elderly relatives, and 8 percent said they spend an average of 35 hours per week providing care to elderly family members. Given these findings, the trend to create on-site child-care centers in the 1980s may give way to parent-care centers in the twenty-first century.

In the "FOCUS ON: Elder Care," the research suggests that the responsibility for elder care will be disproportionately borne by the same individuals who bear the burden for child care: female workers.

THE AGING WORK FORCE   ◆◆◆◆◆◆

Between 1988 and 2000, the younger portion of the workforce (25–34 years) will decrease by 11 percent. Workers between the ages of 45 and 54 will increase by 61 percent and will make up 22 percent of the work force by 2000. Couple this trend with both a decline in the quality of the education of the youngest entrants into the work force and the lifting of legally mandated retirement ages and it is clear that organizations will have to rethink traditional ideas about older workers.

While labor force participation declines with increasing age, recent surveys suggest that this trend is not based on the desires of older employees. One third of those currently retired would prefer to be working either part time or full time. Sixty-eight percent of all workers aged 50 or older say they never want to retire. In fact, older workers will represent an increasingly larger pool of untapped talent for most employers.

One change that companies are likely to institute is in their benefits programs. For example, Aetna has recently overhauled its benefits program to include a graduated retirement plan that allows employees to cut back from full time to part time in the two or three years preceding retirement. Benefits are maintained, the company gains because the employee will have time to train his or her replacement, and the employee gains because he or she has more free

Elder Care

The Canadian Experience Dorothy Bell of Rockingham, Nova Scotia, is part of the "sandwich generation." Her adopted son was diagnosed as hyperactive and requires extra attention. But the crunch came two years ago when her elderly father moved in with Bell and her family. Nine months later, Bell left her job as a bookkeeper.

Bell's story is not unique. It is estimated that 200,000 Canadians are caught in the middle of rearing their children and looking after their elderly parents. In fact, a recent study commissioned by the Ontario government last year indicated that more than 80 percent of elderly Canadians are being cared for, to some extent, by family members—and overwhelmingly those family members are women.

In Canada, men are expected to live an average of 75.9 years and women are expected to live 83 years (compared to 63 years and 66.3 years, respectively, in 1941). By 2036, estimates are that almost 29 percent of Canadians will be over 65. In 1990, 11.5 percent of Canadians were over the age of 65. While this situation will get considerably worse in the coming years, many experts already acknowledge that it is a pressing problem. Women, according to Susan McDaniel, a University of Alberta sociologist, tend to do the looking-after for free, whether or not they also work outside the home.

Couple this fact with other trends (women are having children at much later ages as they postpone child bearing until their careers are well under way, the increasing divorce rates that have resulted in growing numbers of single mothers, and the increase in the number of two-income families) and the picture becomes painfully clear—there is no one left at home to care for the elderly. Contrast this with the situation that existed in the mid-1960s when few women worked outside the home, and families were larger, with more children available to share the burden of care. In Canada as in the United States, devising strategies to meet commitments to work, children, and parents will be a priority for more and more of the members of this generation.

Nora Underwood, "Mid-life Panic: Thousands of Canadians Are Caught between Children and Elderly Parents," *Maclean's*, August 19, 1991, 30–34.

time. After retirement, Aetna also has a "return to work" program that hires retirees for temporary work assignments. Retirees get to decide how long they want to work and if they want to be retrained for job re-entry if necessary. Aetna's flexible benefits plan even has a long-term care element to help pay for home health care and long-term or custodial care. The plan also includes a fitness program designed for seniors and a redesigned pension plan to take advantage of the unique retirement interests of older workers. The same changes are occurring at Kentucky Fried Chicken and McDonald's, two other organizations that are adjusting their benefits for a new group of potential employees: the retired.

New technologies, however, require new skills. In the past, employers might have simply laid off workers whose skills were not current. As the baby-bust generation begins work, employers may no longer have that luxury. Luring former employees out of retirement to take new advantage of their knowledge, Travelers Insurance has begun retraining its retirees. People who were knowledgeable clerks, formerly working in a paper-processing environment, have been trained to use computers to fulfill the same function in new ways. In a related vein, Chrysler and the United Auto Workers have created a Joint Skill

As the American population continues to age, organizations may find retired and older workers a source of the skills they will need to stay competitive.

Talent Program that provides a full range of education and training options to workers facing potential displacement.

George Duychak, an official of White Hen Pantry, Inc., a convenience-store chain in Chicago, said his firm's experience has been that older workers are more dependable, polite, stable, efficient, and often become valued confidantes of the company's younger franchise holders.[10] While companies such as these may be leaders in using an older work force, the changing demographics will mandate that organizations more effectively use this particular talent pool.

DISCRIMINATION

It is probably not surprising to most readers that discrimination is included in a chapter on work-force diversity. However, one might expect that overt discrimination in corporate settings is a thing of the past. Legislation in the United States that has made discrimination illegal includes the 1963 Equal Pay Act, which prohibits unequal pay for males and females with equal skills, effort and responsibility working under similar working conditions. The 1964 Civil Rights Act prevents discrimination based upon color, race, religion, sex, or national origin. The 1972 Equal Employment Opportunity Act extends the jurisdiction of these antidiscrimination laws to include government and educational institutions. In 1973, the Vocational Rehabilitation Act prohibited discrimination

---

[10] Stephen Franklin, "Job Fair's Motto: The More Gray Hair, All the More Able," *Chicago Tribune*, November 11, 1991.

against persons with physical or mental handicaps and created the Office of Affirmative Action. Put into force in 1992, the Americans with Disabilities Act will require reasonable accommodations in existing structures (and all new structures) for job applicants with disabilities who request them, thus ensuring that a worker's disability is not a barrier to effective job performance. Examples of federal guidelines for wheelchair access are illustrated in Figure 18–3.

Changes have occurred as a result of these legislations—but the changes primarily have focused on the opportunities that such groups have to be *hired* by organizations. While many more women and men of color have found positions in organizations, they have experienced considerable difficulty in advancing to executive management.

The regulation of organizations centers, for the most part, on attempts to prevent discrimination. Organizations must confront two forms of discrimination.[11] First-generation discrimination is that which occurs at the time one is hired. Much of the previous legislation is directed toward ensuring that any individual (regardless of race, sex, religion, disability, and so forth) has an equal access to employment as any other equally qualified individual. Second-generation discrimination occurs when a company is deciding whom to promote. This is the type of discrimination that managers and employees now and in the future will have to confront. In 1979, for example, Fortune 1000 companies were surveyed. Within a sample of 1,708 senior executives, only three were African-American, two were Asian, two were Hispanic, and eight were female. The 1985 survey of 1,362 senior executives found four African Americans, six Asians, three Hispanics, and twenty-nine women.[12]

In the wake of this legislation, overt (first-generation) discrimination against men of color, women, and the mentally and physically challenged has been replaced by a more covert and insidious form of discrimination (second-generation discrimination). For African Americans in corporate America, this second-generation discrimination may take the form of **colorism:** a predisposition to act in a certain manner because of a person's skin color.[13] While approximately 15 percent of white Americans may be overtly racist, 60 percent are more or less neutral about African Americans. Those managers and executives in this group are not overtly racist, but they are the people who for a number of reasons either see discrimination take place and do nothing about it or inhibit the advancement of African-American managers to avoid conflict within the organization. But what about other, more legal but increasingly unacceptable forms of discrimination? An example of such discrimination is that often invoked by private clubs to limit the types of people to whom membership is offered. This means that many groups, such as ethnic minorities, women, Jews, or Catholics, are denied membership. In the "FOCUS ON: Discrimination in Private Clubs," we consider such discrimination in light of recent legal and regulatory changes at the federal, state, and city levels. Such discrimination may have a big impact on an individual's ability to get ahead if much of the organization's business is conducted in such informal settings.

---

[11] J. Feagin, "Organizational Culture and Conflict: Issues of Gender and Race," Paper presented at the *Theory and Practice in Organizational Conflict: Making the Connection* at the University of Minnesota.

[12] E.W. Jones, Jr., "Black Managers: The Dream Deferred," *Harvard Business Review* (May/June 1986): 84–93.

[13] Jones, "Black Managers."

FIGURE 18–3 ▶ **Wheelchair access**

The Americans with Disabilities Act requires compliance by all government and many public facilities to a wide variety of technical standards. Below are some of the general guidelines for wheelchair access and use in public buildings and places of employment.

a) Clear doorway width and depth

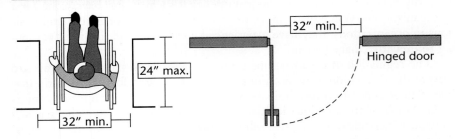

b) High forward reach limit

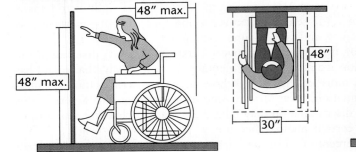

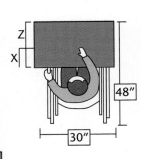

If X is less than or equal to 25", Z shall be greater than X. If X is less than 20", Y shall be 48" maximum. When X is 20 to 25" then Y shall be 44".

c) Clear floor space

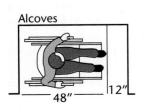

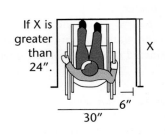

Clear floor space dimensions

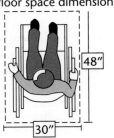

Source: Federal Register

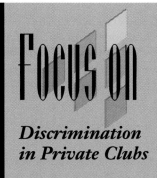

Focus on

Discrimination in Private Clubs

City Clubs and Country Clubs— Discrimination Is Still a Reality In the United States, private clubs are becoming much more popular than they have been for years. Until recently, even very exclusive clubs such as the New York's Knickerbocker had to recruit members, but now there are waiting lists, and the wait can be a long one (as long as 33 years at the Bohemian Club of San Francisco).

Antidiscrimination suits have opened the doors of membership to all but a few of these clubs, at least theoretically. The New York Athletic Club began admitting women in July 1990 and the Olympic Club of San Francisco (which has some of its facilities on public land) is being threatened by the city supervisors to admit women or lose its lease. While most of the clubs have embraced a wider range of potential members, these changes are so new that few women, Jews, and minorities have actually been admitted. Even when they are admitted, they may not gain access to the various clubs-within-the-club. Gloria Allred, a Los Angeles attorney, discovered this when she became the first female member of the Los Angeles Friars Club. Once in, it was clear that she was not welcome to attend the club's foul-mouthed celebrity roasts. She asserted her right as a member to see Arnold Schwarzenegger roasted despite the protests of other members. When she tried to use her reciprocal privileges at the then all-male Friars Club in New York, she was denied entry and Henny

Youngman came out the front door to heckle her. After filing sex discrimination charges, she gained access to that club as well. Back in Los Angeles, Allred found she was excluded from the Friar's gym. She again filed legal charges and the club buckled—sort of. She informed the members that she would be using the gym and told them to "gird up their loins." They ignored her and continued their practice of using the gym nude. She then announced that she would be coming into the gym with a tape measure. The men then cleared out.

Discrimination is not just part of these city clubs. While a recent *Golf Digest* survey found that fewer than one percent of the nation's golf clubs bar women entirely, less obvious discrimination is all too common. Trish Watson, a director at Nynex Corp, was told by several New York–area clubs that since she was married, her application would have to be filed in her husband's name. Others bar women from playing during prime times on Saturday and Sunday. Jan Bradshaw, an interior designer, filed suit against the Yorba Linda Country Club in Orange County. It seems that she purchased a full-price membership at the club but was not allowed to tee off before 11 a.m. on Saturdays and 1 p.m. on Sundays. In addition, she was barred from voting for officers. Because members of clubs deemed exclusionary cannot write off club expenses as business deductions, Yorba Linda agreed to change its policies.

Sources: William Symonds, "Is Sex Discrimination Still Par for the Course?" *Business Week,* December 24, 1990, 56; and Andrew Erdman, "The Mystique of Private Clubs," *Fortune,* June 4, 1990, 170–176.

Sexual Harassment

For women in corporate circles, discrimination can exist either as sexual harassment or as the more subtle "glass ceiling." The problems associated with sexual harassment received considerable attention in late 1991 during the hearings to confirm Clarence Thomas as a Supreme Court justice. Sexual harassment is a fact in the American workplace. A *Newsweek* poll taken in October of 1991 indicated that 21 percent of women surveyed had been harassed at work and that 42 percent of working women knew someone who had been harassed. Fifty-three percent of the 1,300 members of the National Association for Female Executives indicate they were sexually harassed or knew someone who had been. The situation is worse in male-dominated organizations and positions. A 1986 survey by the Association of American Colleges reported that 32 percent of tenured women at Harvard University and 49 percent of untenured women had reported some form of sexual harassment. (If you are wondering about female college students, 40 percent of undergraduate women and 28 percent of graduate students report they have been harassed.)[14] A Defense Department study conducted in 1990 found that 64 percent of military women had faced abuse ranging from obscene jokes to outright assault.

Consider the experience of Francis Conley, a neurosurgeon at Stanford Medical Center who quit, but only after putting up with 25 years of insults and abuse. The Stanford Medical School, amid considerable publicity, responded by setting up a committee to investigate the charges. But Conley, who was rehired, said that the four months after returning to her job were the worst ever.[15]

Sexual harassment is not a unique American experience. About 70 percent of working women in Japan have experienced sexual harassment at work according to a survey of 6,500 working women. Thirty percent of them report that they have been fondled or hugged by male bosses or colleagues. Over half of the women report that their male colleagues displayed nude photos of women, told sexual jokes, or changed clothes in front of female workers. While the Japanese constitution prohibits sexual discrimination and guarantees basic labor rights, there is currently no legal enforcement to punish sexual harassment.[16]

The definition of **sexual harassment** in the United States is fairly broad. According to the 1980 Equal Employment Opportunity Commission (EEOC) guidelines, conduct is sexual harassment if it is verbal or physical and of a sexual nature or if any of the following apply:

▶ Submission to such conduct is made either explicitly or implicitly a term or condition of an individual's employment.

▶ Submission to or rejection of such conduct by an individual is used as the basis for employment decisions affecting such individuals.

▶ Such conduct has the purpose or effect of substantially interfering with an individual's work performance or creating an intimidating, hostile, or offensive work environment.

The last form of sexual harassment, that which creates a hostile work environment, is the most subtle type of harassment. In a 1986 decision, the Supreme Court indicated that sexual harassment does not have to be linked to promises or threats about job advancement or loss for an employer to be liable. For employers, one of the best defenses against a "hostile environment" charge is a clearly stated and strongly enforced policy that has, as its basis, an effective procedure through which sexual harassment complaints may be lodged. If such a policy and set of procedures exists, then it is reasonable to assume that the

---

[14] M. McCarthy and R. Christensen, *Sexual Harassment* (Harvard Business School Publishing Division) No. 9-387-209.

[15] B. Kantrowitz with T. Barrett, K. Springen, M. Hager, L. Wright, G. Carroll, and D. Rosenberg, "Striking a Nerve," *Newsweek*, October 21, 1991, 34–40.

[16] Chieko Kuriki, "Sexual Harassment Mars Workplace in Japan," *Chicago Tribune*, February 9, 1992.

harassing work environment is neither authorized nor condoned by an employer.[17]

Sexual harassment does not just affect the victim. A ruling by the courts indicated that employers are responsible for the sexual harassment committed on or by their employees.[18] Sexual harassment also costs the companies in both lost productivity and legal fees—an average of $7 million a year for a typical Fortune 500 company. At AT&T, where 47 percent of the work force is female, managers are required to attend an annual training session that includes discussions of sexual harassment. Nonmanagers also get a primer on company policy and a code of conduct as well as the opportunity to view training tapes on the subject.

But even with all the recent media attention, the number of sexual harassment complaints filed with the EEOC increased from 3,661 in 1981 to 5,694 in 1990. Some experts suggest that these numbers represent only the tip of the iceberg, claiming that only 6 percent of victims file formal complaints. While most of the widely publicized cases occur in large companies, sexual harassment is reported to be a much bigger problem in smaller companies. Small businesses are less likely to have the resources available to train their employees and the power of business owners is often unchallenged. Also, in small companies, it is more difficult for victims to find avenues for their grievances. The harasser may be the president of the company, one of his relatives, or the general manager.[19]

Employers need to develop strategies to prevent sexual harassment. The EEOC has suggested the following guidelines to help organizations with this problem:

1. Develop a formal policy on sexual harassment and distribute a copy of the policy to all employees.
2. Identify mechanisms for those individuals who feel they have been or are harassed to report those behaviors without fear of incrimination *and* to ensure that such reports are thoroughly investigated.
3. Communicate to all employees (especially to those in supervisory positions) the importance of creating and maintaining an environment free of sexual harassment.
4. Discipline guilty parties with organizational sanctions that include terminating the employee for cause.
5. Train all employees about what constitutes sexual harassment, thereby alerting them to the issues and behaviors at the heart of this matter.

Glass Ceilings

This **"glass ceiling"** is a barrier that keeps women from advancing not because of an inability to succeed at executive management but rather simply because they are women.[20] Women have made strides in the business world—for

---

[17] EEOC Policy Guidelines for Field Personnel; *CPC Spotlight* 13 (12) February 1, 1991.

[18] M.S. Novit, "Employer Liability for Employee Misconduct: Two Common Law Doctrines," *Personnel* (January–February 1982): 11–18.

[19] "In Many Small Businesses, Harassment Is Big Worry," *Wall Street Journal*, October 18, 1991.

[20] A.M. Morrison, R. P. White, E. Van Velsor and the Center for Creative Leadership, *Breaking the Glass Ceiling: Can Women Reach the Top of America's Largest Corporations?* (Reading, Mass.: Addison-Wesley, 1987).

example, women make up 33 percent of corporate mid-level management (as compared with only 19 percent in 1972). However, the story is quite different in executive management positions where this glass ceiling may exist. Only 1.7 percent of corporate officers are women. In addition, only 500 of the 6,700 managers at IBM are women; at AT&T, only 26 of the top 880 executives are women; and at Bank of America, only 20 percent of the top 3,000 executives are women—even though women account for 64 percent of the company's officials and managers.[21] In 1980, there were only two female CEOs of Fortune 500 industrial or service companies and there were three in 1990: Marion Sandler, co-chief executive of Golden West Financial Corporation; Katherine Graham, chief executive of the Washington Post; and Linda Wachner of the Warnaco Group.

While it may be difficult to prove that the glass ceiling and sexual harassment exist, some forms of discrimination are clearly identifiable. Women still earn significantly less than men (only 71 percent of men's earnings). While this figure represents the smallest gap ever in earnings by gender, it is hardly likely that the narrowing was because of rising earnings on the part of women. Rather, the narrowing gap is probably the result of a decline in men's earnings, adjusted for inflation. It should be noted that these pay differentials exist between job categories as well as across categories. Full-time working women who were between the ages of 35–44 (prime earning capacity) were only earning 69 percent of what males in comparable jobs earned.[22] Figure 18–4 provides the comparisons for women's salaries across a number of industries or levels.

Why is it that women are earning so much less than men? Studies of managerial women have ruled out explanations as women having poorer skills, abilities, or motivations. In fact, a recent survey of 25,000 workers in 15 major U.S. corporations, conducted by Charles Rodger of Work/Family Directions, found that before children are born, women work an average of 44 hours per week at their jobs and men work an average of 41 hours per week. After children are born, women still average 44 hours per week, but the average time a male spends at the office increases to 47 hours per week.[23]

Nevertheless, it is a popular belief that women typically earn less than men because they (1) leave the work force intermittently for family reasons, (2) have preferred styles of interacting (or leading) that are suited to lower levels of management, (3) select careers in lower-paying industries, or (4) are less committed to their positions and their companies.[24] To investigate this, Linda Stroh, Jeanne Brett, and Anne Reilly compared female managers and professionals who were as well-educated, had relocated within the previous two years for their company (a measure of their commitment to their organization), were as powerful in their families (that is, earned more money than their spouses), and

---

[21] See, for example, M. McComas, "Atop the Fortune 500: A Survey of the CEOs," *Fortune*, April 23, 1986, 31; K. Blumenthal, "Room at the Top," *Wall Street Journal*, March 24, 1986, 7d; and D.D. Bowen and R.D. Hisrich, "The Female Entrepreneur: A Career Development Perspective," *Academy of Management Review* 11, 393.

[22] Karen Pennar, "Commentary: Women Are Still Paid the Wages of Discrimination," *Business Week*, October 28, 1991, 35.

[23] Carol Kleiman, "Taking Men to Task on Housework," *Chicago Tribune*, February 10, 1992.

[24] Linda Stroh, Jeanne Brett, and Anne Reilly, "All the Right Stuff: A Comparison of Female and Male Managers' Career Progression," *Journal of Applied Psychology*, 1993 (in press).

FIGURE 18–8	▶ Wages of Discrimination		
		Women's Earnings	Percent of Men's Earnings
Sales		$16,986	57%
Executive and managerial		$25,861	64%
Transportation		$16,003	65%
Machine operators, assemblers, and inspectors		$14,655	66%
Service workers		$12,136	66%
All occupations		$19,816	71%

Data: Census Bureau, based on median earnings for year-round, full-time workers, 1990.

were as often employed in higher paying industries as a matched sample of male employees. With this sample of women, one might expect that there would be no difference in earnings between men and women doing comparable work. Yet, the results provide clear evidence that there was still a significant difference (of eleven percent) between the average salaries of women and men in this sample. Even these women, who did "all the right stuff," were only making 89 percent of what a male counterpart earned.

Both colorism and the glass ceiling are insidious primarily because they are not obvious. Managers and organizations who fall prey to these tendencies may not even be aware that they are erecting and maintaining these barriers for women and men of color.[25] In a study commissioned by the U.S. Department of Labor in 1990, nine Fortune 500 companies were randomly selected for review of their personnel policies and practices, specifically regarding the promotion of women and men of color. The results were disturbing, but not unexpected. While none of these nine companies had ever been cited for discrimination, a number of them did not show good faith efforts in meeting affirmative action requirements. Several findings applied to all the companies:

1. If there were not a glass ceiling, there is certainly a point beyond which men of color and women did not advance in some companies.
2. Men of color plateaued at lower levels of the work force than women.
3. Monitoring for equal access and opportunity, especially as managers moved up the corporate ladder to senior levels, was almost never

---

[25] In a recent training program for executives in the transportation industry conducted by one of the authors, a man from the audience commented that while women might be discriminated against in other industries, he believed that such discrimination was a thing of the past in the transportation industry. He remained unconvinced of the ongoing nature of the problem even after seeing the industry-specific comparison data.

considered a corporate responsibility in terms of planning for developmental programs and policies.

4. Appraisal and total compensation systems that determine salaries, bonuses, incentives, and perquisites for employees were not monitored. This is especially problematic because of research that suggests that raters evaluate the job performance of African Americans less favorably than the job performance of whites, especially when those doing the rating are white.[26]

The policies and practices that limit the recruitment and advancement of qualified women and men of color can clearly hamper the success of an organization. In fact, 79 percent of Fortune 500 CEOs agreed that there were identifiable barriers to women getting to the top. These barriers do not seem to be removed by legislation alone. Consider the impact of the rulings and regulations that govern many of the personnel activities of corporate America:

Pregnancy Discrimination Act (1978)   Employers may no longer refuse to hire a women because of her pregnancy, and pregnant employees must be treated just as any other employee for the purpose of benefits. Thus, pregnancy leaves are subject to the same conditions as medical or personal leaves.

Comparable Worth (*American Federation of State, County, and Municipal Employees* v. *State of Washington*, 1983)   The two parties to this case ultimately negotiated a settlement that transferred $482 million over six years to employees such as nurses, word-processing operators, library technicians, and clerk typists in response to a consultant's finding that employees in female-dominated jobs were paid about 20 percent less than those male-dominated jobs that required comparable knowledge, skills, and abilities.

Unisex Pension Coverage (*Arizona Governing Committee* v. *Norris*, 1983)   The court rejected the notion that because women on average live longer than men they should receive a lower monthly pension. Men and women contributed equally to the plan.

Discrimination against the Handicapped/Disabled   Although the initial legislation on this issue was passed in 1973, the current controversy stems from the definition of handicap. According to U.S. law, individuals with "physical or mental impairment that substantially limits one or more major life activities, or has a record of, or is regarded as having such an impairment[27] are handicapped. However, in recent years, the definition has been expanded. Often included are those with contagious diseases (such as tuberculosis and acquired immune deficiency syndrome) and those with severe allergies and color blindness. Finally, the passing of the 1992 Americans with Disabilities Act is likely to have a profound impact on the way in which organizations treat and accommodate indi-

---

[26]J. Greenhouse, S. Parasuraman, and W. Wormley, "Effects of Race on Organizational Experiences, Job Performance Evaluations, and Career Outcomes," *Academy of Management Journal* 33 (1990): 64–86.

[27]U.S. Code 24, Section 706 (7)(B)(Supp. IV, 1980).

The Americans with Disabilities Act, enacted in 1992, requires that employers make reasonable accommodations for workers with disabilities. Such accommodations may range from providing wheelchair access to an office to lightening the work load of an employee with AIDS.

viduals with disabilities. However, the legislation is sufficiently new that the long term impact on companies as they hire and attempt to integrate people with a variety of disabilities is still unclear.

As for employees with AIDS or other contagious diseases, the Supreme Court has ruled that the fear of contracting a disease is not sufficient justification for terminating an employee. Because the victims of such diseases are protected under the law as handicapped individuals, employers have the burden of proof for justifying their actions against infected employees.

Discrimination and Appearance

The most well-known case of this genre is that of Christina Craft and KMBC, a television station in Kansas City, where she worked as an anchor woman. In a lawsuit, Craft charged that she was fired when she refused to meet with clothing and cosmetic consultants—a demand not imposed upon her male co-anchor. In the first trial (which was overturned by the judge), the jury awarded Craft $500,000. In a second trial Craft won again and was awarded $325,000. The decision was appealed and overturned at a higher court.

Other individuals who have brought similar cases to trial have fared better. A woman weighing over three hundred pounds was rejected for employment as a clerical worker for an electric utility, and an airline attendant was fired for being too unattractive and overweight. In both of these cases, the employers lost because they failed to prove that weight or attractiveness were "bona fide occupational requirements" (BFOC)—an aspect of the employee that limits his or her ability to perform at the job. In 1985, Xerox Corporation had to offer a position, some back pay, and accumulated pension to Catherine McDermott, who was refused a job because of her weight. Xerox claimed that if she were hired, it would have to pay higher disability and life insurance costs. That argument did not persuade the court, which held that under state law obesity was a handicap.

Discrimination and Sexual Orientation[28]

In the previous sections, the targets of discrimination have been individuals with clearly visible traits or attributes, such as race or gender, level of attractiveness, or physical disability. In this section, the focus will shift to a basis of discrimination that is not discernible by physical appearance—sexual orientation. Homosexuals make up 10 percent of the U.S. adult population and, regardless of stereotypes, they do not tend to work in certain industries. For example, a survey of over 4,000 gay men and lesbian women conducted by Overlooked Opinions, a Chicago market-research firm, reported that 40 percent more homosexuals are employed in the finance and insurance industries than in the entertainment and arts industries; and ten times as many homosexuals work in the computer industry as in the fashion industry. There are also more homosexuals working in science and engineering than in social services.

The acceptance of gay men and lesbian women in the workplace is not by any means universal. But some organizations do actively encourage support groups of gay men and lesbian women in the same way they encourage other employee-based support groups. Workers on their way to the elevators at Levi Strauss's San Francisco headquarters recently passed under a banner reading "Lesbian and Gay Employee Association Celebrates Pride Week." Similar groups exist with the support of management at AT&T, Boeing, Coors, DuPont, Hewlitt-Packard, Sun Microsystems, US West, Digital Equipment Corporation, Lotus, and Xerox, while other companies such as Hughes and TRW have groups that are not publicly supported. In the "FOCUS ON: Sexual Orientation: Benefits for Gay Partners," the status of benefits policies for gay partners of employees is examined. While few organizations typically have benefits that include life partners, recently there have been changes. Lotus Corporation, Stanford University, and the University of Chicago have recently extended benefits to same-sex life partners.

One of the biggest concerns that gays and lesbians have within the workplace is the freedom to be themselves. In the Overlooked Opinions survey, about 67 percent reported that they had witnessed some form of hostility toward gays on the job; and discrimination based on sexual orientation is still legal in most of the United States. Jeffrey Collins was second in command at a Shell Oil subsidiary when an "incriminating document" concerning his personal life was accidentally left at the copy machine. Shell not only fired him but also concocted records that showed he was fired for reasons unassociated with his sex life. A California judge ordered the company to pay Collins $5.3 million in damages (that verdict is being appealed by Shell).

Ann Quenin had been working for a high-tech company for a few months and had received glowing performance reviews. She was called into the boss's office. He asked about her volunteer activities for an AIDS organization, saying it was taking too much of her time and asked her to resign from her job. Quenin is now working at Lotus and was honored company-wide for that same volunteer work.

With increasing visibility, will gay employees be subject to a glass ceiling of their own? In a 1987 survey by the *Wall Street Journal*, sixty-six CEOs of major companies reported they would be reluctant to put a homosexual on their

---

[28]This section draws heavily from T. A. Stewart, "Gay in Corporate America," *Fortune*, December 6, 1991, 43–56.

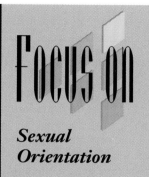

Focus on

Sexual Orientation

Benefits for Gay Partners In September of 1991, Lotus Development Corporation became the first major company to provide the same insurance and other benefits to homosexual partners that it accorded to heterosexual spouses. But the workplace environment is not always benevolent for many homosexuals, as activists battle with Cracker Barrel Old Country Stores, Inc., for firing gay restaurant workers, and with General Motors Corporation over an internal marketing video in which a customer describes Japanese pickups as "little faggot trucks."

Nevertheless, most companies are concerned about the rising cost of health care, especially for this subgroup of the population. So far, only a small number of Lotus's estimated 310 gay employees have signed up for the benefit. This limited demand mirrors the experience of other nonprofit or service companies with similar benefits. When the city of Seattle instituted health coverage for unmarried partners, both homosexual and heterosexual in 1990, it budgeted $430,000, assuming 300 workers would sign up for the benefit. As of the end of 1991, less than 200 had signed up, costing the city $225,000. Some workers still opt not to identify themselves as gay, even confidentially, and many have partners who are insured elsewhere.

To be eligible for the benefits, a couple must live together and share financial responsibilities. If they break up, the employee must wait one year before registering a new partner. Besides health insurance, the new benefits include life insurance, relocation expenses, bereavement leave, and a death benefit. Interestingly, Lotus chose not to offer the same benefits to unmarried partners of heterosexual couples, indicating that straight couples have the option of getting married while homosexual partners don't.

Keith Hammonds, "Lotus Opens a Door for Gay Partners," *Business Week,* November 4, 1991, 80–81.

management committees. While many organizations such as Bank of America have a policy of indifference on employees' sexual orientation, some gay employees suggest that "at top levels, the standards by which you're promoted become incredibly subjective." A gay executive at Marshall Field's was convinced that he hit the glass ceiling when he ran a $60 million a year division. He was not made a vice-president, although others with comparable responsibility were promoted.

Alienating 10 percent of the work force is not an effective strategy for any organization. An environment that is not conducive to productivity and performance harms both the company and its employees. As with organizations that are known to be good places for women or men of color, gay students at top business schools are paying attention to the reputation of potential employers. Students with sought-after training and experience are actually turning down higher salaries to work for companies that are not homophobic. Companies such as Xerox and AT&T are becoming much more attractive because of their reputation for openness.

Sexual orientation is simply another form of diversity. Having this perspective can also open up new venues for customer and client services and products. Since 10 percent of the population is gay, and since they have few children and relatively large amounts of disposable income, they are clearly an untapped and potentially lucrative market for services and products.

DISCRIMINATION AND POTENTIAL REMEDIES

♦♦♦♦♦♦

Up to now, our focus has been on describing the state of the work force and corporate successes and failures in fully integrating diversity within the organization. It is not a particularly positive record, and there is a real question of whether the increasing diversity of the work force will make discrimination more or less of a problem than it has been in the past.

In the remainder of this chapter, we will consider some organizational, governmental, and evaluation remedies that may enhance management's ability to take advantage of the diversity of the work force: affirmative action, changing employer's expectations, social and cultural changes, and technological changes.

Affirmative Action

In 1941, President Franklin D. Roosevelt encouraged minority employment by ordering defense contractors to cease discriminatory hiring practices. In fifty years since this first presidential order was issued, affirmative action is still the subject of the public's attention. In 1961, President John F. Kennedy created a commission to investigate the hiring practices of government contractors, impose sanctions, and collect statistics. In 1964, just after the 1964 Civil Rights Act became law, President Lyndon Johnson issued Executive Order 11246, which required any organization that had a contract with the federal government to take affirmative action to ensure just treatment of employees and potential employees of all races, religions, or national origins; it was amended in 1967 to prohibit sex discrimination. In 1969, President Richard Nixon mandated hiring quotas for construction companies in Philadelphia. In 1978, the Supreme Court struck down the University of California's affirmative action plan (also known as the Bakke case), and in the late 1980s and early 1990s, the Supreme Court and the Republican administration made it more difficult to win discrimination suits.

Affirmative action has had its successes. The percentage of African Americans in the work force has risen 50 percent in the past 25 years. In 1989, almost 5 percent of managers in the U.S. were African American, an increase of almost one-third since 1978. But nearly 97 percent of senior executives in the largest domestic companies are white and only five percent of all professionals are African American.[29] There is considerable evidence that an affirmative-action policy is much better than a policy that simply offers "equal opportunity." The latter type of policy relies too heavily on the person being discriminated against to identify and end the discrimination. Further, the notion of "equal opportunity" can lull us into the false belief that all citizens are given equal access to the same opportunities for education and employment, and it can easily result in blaming the victim: if "they" worked harder or had better skills, then "they" would have succeeded.

Affirmative action acknowledges that individuals with the same set of talents will be more likely to succeed in some circumstances than in others. Simply saying that race and gender do not matter relies too much on good intentions

---

[29]Howard Gleckman, Tim Smart, Paula Dwyer, Troy Segal, and Joseph Weber, "Race in the Workplace: Is Affirmative Action Working?" *Business Week*, July 8, 1991, 50–62.

and systemic blindness to stereotypes. Affirmative action, with its requirements for record-keeping and system monitoring, can make explicit where the problems are and, even if unintentional, who the problems are.

Beginning in the 1990s, the climate for affirmative action also changed dramatically. In better economic times, companies were growing and could, simultaneously, give hiring preferences to women and men of color without affecting the hiring of majority males. There is also the complaint that the advancement of minorities at a too rapid pace hurts the chances of future women and men of color employees. Other critics cite the insidious stigma attached to being the beneficiary of affirmative action. However, the attribution of affirmative action as the reason for hiring women and men of color is too easily made. Colleagues do not know whether an individual was hired because of his or her racial or ethnic group or because of his or her qualifications.

Some critics of affirmative action suggest the most damning aspect of this program may be the feelings it engenders in its recipients. It is one thing for colleagues to think that a person's promotions were unearned, but for the person being promoted to believe that he or she did not earn the promotion can be demoralizing and lead to increased self-doubt. Even when promotions are given to women and men of color, they run the risk of being seen as token, rather than deserved.

Finally, others suggest that with affirmative action guidelines, the focus of many companies is to meet hiring goals, but interest in the continued progression of the candidate once he or she is a member of the organization is quickly lost. Then there is the problem with quotas. It should be clearly noted that quotas are not typically a part of affirmative action programs, although many critics of affirmative action have assumed they are one and the same. The existence of quotas is also one of the primary reasons for resistance to affirmative action. If an organization wants its affirmative action policy to be legitimate, it must explicitly rely on qualifications, not quotas. The worst outcome of an affirmative action plan is to bring unqualified employees into the organization, thus perpetuating negative stereotypes.[30]

What affirmative action was meant to do and what is actually done in organizations can be very different. While affirmative action is not about quotas, many companies doing business with the government set up annual plans, and these plans often include numbers and deadlines for increasing the presence of women and men of color. Quotas can also set a ceiling on hiring women and men of color. Consider the case of Larson Foundries in Grafton, Ohio. Larson's percentage of women and men of color in the work force (14 percent) is higher than the percentage of women and men of color in Grafton, so the company has little impetus to continue bringing women and men of color into its work force.[31] As a result, the 1991 Civil Rights bill had, as a provision, a proposal that would make quotas illegal.

Affirmative action was supposed to bring women and men of color into the organization. The assumption was that once they were there, everything would

---

[30] S. D. Clayton and F. J. Crosby (in press), *Justice, Gender, and Affirmative Action* (Ann Arbor, Mich.: University of Michigan Press).

[31] Gleckman et al., "Race in the Workplace."

be equal. Unfortunately, such a program gave little recognition to the difficulty of ending discrimination by fiat. Companies that will be successful in the next decade will be those that do more than just open their doors to women and men of color. Rather, successful companies will be the ones that make sure the structural barriers to performance and promotion are also removed. In the next section, we will consider how some companies are trying to ensure that employees with ability are able to do their jobs successfully.

Changing Employer Expectations

The days of the "organizational man," when employers could expect lifetime commitment and long hours of "face-time" at the office, are gone. No longer can the vast majority of employees—male or female—be expected to be free for early-morning or late-night meetings. The increasing demands of families and dual career spouses make the employee's ability (and willingness) to move less likely. However, it should be noted that there is little evidence that women are less willing to relocate than their white male counterparts.[32]

As such, organizations will have to adapt by increasing the routineness and predictability of the employee's work responsibilities or provide alternatives such as on-site child and elder day care, greater flexibility in hours worked, job-sharing, and similar structural changes that explicitly acknowledge the importance of family demands in the employee's life. While these types of structural changes are important, another critical facet of employer responses is to increase the ability of current employees to communicate within and between diverse groups.

As companies increase the number of women and men of color in the work place, it becomes critical for those companies to provide a scenario in which these employees can be as productive as possible. Many companies are investing in specific training designed to improve the ability of their employees to be sensitive to and understand the impact of their expectations, assumptions, and communication patterns within a diverse group. Companies often begin this training with sensitivity sessions designed to show employees how subtle biases can have big impacts on the success of women and men of color. Consider, as we describe in the "FOCUS ON: Sensitivity Training," the impact of labels on people's interactions with each other. What is especially important to note about this type of training is that it not only can improve the way a group of *domestic* employees interacts, but it also sets up the potential for successful international performance. After all, what is really being emphasized is understanding the perspectives and views of people from different cultures and with different backgrounds, expectations, and interaction patterns.

Social and Cultural Change

The three components to the category of social and cultural change that may increase the participation and integration of women and men of color in the work force are the increasing use of networks, women and men of color entrepreneurs, and the "daddy" or "family track."

---

[32] J. M. Brett, L. K. Stroh, and A. H. Reilly, "Pulling Up Roots in the 1990s: Who's Willing to Relocate?" Working paper, Northwestern University, Evanston, Ill.

Focus on

Sensitivity Training

Pin a Label on a Manager and Watch What Happens An Asian executive for a multinational company, transferred from Taiwan to the Midwest, appears aloof and autocratic to his peers. A West Coast bank embarks on a "friendly teller" campaign, but its Filipino female tellers won't cooperate. A white manager criticizes an African-American male employee's work. Instead of getting an explanation, the manager is met with silence and a firm stare.

Sounds like the transplanted executive is arrogant, the Filipino women are unfriendly, and the African American is hostile, right? Not so fast. As it turns out, Asian culture encourages a more distant managing style, Filipinos associate overly friendly behavior in women with prostitution, and African-American males as a group act more deliberately, studying visual cues, than most white men do.

These generalizations are not just stereotypes. They are part of the education—or reeducation—that goes on in diversity management seminars. To show how everything from race to gender to political affiliation can affect how a worker is treated, seminar leaders play a game called "labeling." A piece of paper with a characteristic written on it is placed on the manager's forehead, but the manager can't see it. If the label ("CEO," for example) causes others in the seminar to react with respect, the manager soon becomes confident and outgoing. If the words ("militant femi-

nist," for example) elicits negative responses, the manager often grows hostile and silent.

Most diversity experts stress that what passes for "corporate culture" is really white male culture. "The Anglo male model is the standard," says Thomas Kochman. Action is valued more than deliberation; reason more than intuition; leading more than asking. The boardroom is treated like a battlefield, says Madeline Swain, "but combatants aren't supposed to take conflict personally."

For many women and minorities, following these rules does not come easily. Yet, when they try to conform, they can run up against other preconceptions. "If a black man is highly competitive, he is counseled not to be so aggressive," says consultant Elsie Cross. "If a woman is seen as aggressive, she's considered to be bitchy." Experts say managers should draw on a variety of skills. In a sales meeting, for instance, African Americans and women are often good judges of a client's nonverbal cues, watching how things are said, not what is said.

These seminars can get tense. Yet the point is not to place blame. "In most cases, white male managers don't mean to discriminate," says Dianne La Mountain. "Their actions do have a negative impact, only nobody tells them." While no one believes that a day-long seminar can automatically produce greater harmony in the office, yet alone greater productivity, it can be a start.

Special Interest Networks One of the more important changes that favor women and men of color may be the rise of specific special interest groups and networks. Having access to the "old boy" networks, power cliques of male executives at the top of organizations was usually cited as one of the main ways that women and men of color were discriminated against. While there are still very few top-level executives who are female or men of color, an increasing number of networks or special groups serve very similar functions. Around the country, women are now able to join groups such as the Executive Women's Council of

Greater Baltimore or Houston's River Oaks Business Women's Exchange Club. The Clairol Mentor Program for women was inaugurated in 1988, pairing leading women executives with aspiring women in their fields. Within organizations, women can turn to Corning's Women's Issues Quality Improvement Team. For gay and lesbian executives in New York alone, there are advertising and communications networks, a bankers' group, a publishing triangle, and a Wall Street lunch club. There are also support groups associated with particular organizations such as the US West Eagles ("We are going to soar high at US West") or DECplus (*people like us*) at Digital. For Hispanics, options for involvement in large networks include the National Society of Hispanic MBAs, support groups such as AllState's Hispanic Forum or US West's Hispanic employees' organization SOMOS, Avon's Hispanic Network, or AT&T's Hispanic Association of AT&T Employees. For African Americans, there are Corning's Black Progress Quality Improvement Team, National Black MBA Association, and Avon's Black Professional Association, to name a few.

The second way that the culture has changed is that women and men of color who hit the glass ceiling are finding that one way around the barrier is starting their own organizations. It is certainly less likely that employees and managers will discriminate against women and men of color when women or men of color occupy critical decision-making positions in the company. In the last decade, three times as many women as men took over or started up businesses on their own; the number of self-employed women increased by 75 percent—about twice the rate that women were entering the work force. In 1989, for example, nearly one-third of all small businesses in the United States were owned by women, as compared with less than 5 percent in 1972. By the year 2000, it is expected that women will own as many as 50 percent of all small businesses. Women and men of color are also making strides in areas that have typically been viewed as the bastions of white males—such as finance. Between 1986 and 1989, companies owned and managed by women and men of color increased their share of municipal bond underwriting from $700 million to $11.2 billion (an increase from 0.4 percent to more than 11 percent)[33]

The "Daddy Track" In 1989, Felice Schwartz, President of Catalyst, Inc., created quite a maelstrom by publishing an article called "Management Women and the New Facts of Life."[34] While she never actually used the term "mommy track," an instant response by the popular press identified her article as a call for a two-tier system of management progression: one for career women and another for women who were equally interested in their careers and their families. Her opponents expressed grave concern that such a system would legitimize the tracking of women of childbearing age or women with children to staff or support positions.

At the same time, an increasing number of "daddy track" articles appeared. Articles in the latter group described the experience of male executives who had slowed down their careers to devote greater attention to their families. This increased commitment to child rearing by fathers would ostensibly allow women more freedom to focus on the career aspects of their lives.

---

[33] L. J. Nathan, "What Do Women Want? A Piece of the Muni Business," *Business Week*, February 12, 1990, 66.

[34] *Harvard Business Review*, January/February, 1989, 65–76.

The 1990s have brought about a change in level of commitment to the organization, with more executives slowing down their careers to spend time with their families. Changes like flextime and telecommuting will enable both men and women to meet the often contradictory challenges of their professional and personal lives.

Organizational changes are occurring that can improve the ability of individuals to balance their professional and personal lives successfully. First, as we suggested in Chapter 13, more and more corporations are offering flextime scheduling to their employees. The ability of workers to have more latitude in scheduling their work means that they can more easily fit other obligations around working hours. In the 1980s, the number of U.S. corporations using some type of flextime doubled; on average about 1.5 percent more companies adopt flextime scheduling every year.[35]

The second major change that improves the opportunity for women to work is the increased use of technology, in the form of telecommuting, by the U.S. work force. Telecommuting involves the use of technologies such as electronic mail, computers, modems, and faxes to keep in informational, if not personal, contact with the workplace. These and other technological changes are described in the next section.

Technological Change

The position of many types of workers who find it difficult to be away from home for extended periods of time has been significantly enhanced by the increasing use of telecommuting. Between 1982 and 1987, the number of corporate employees working at home and dialing into the office tripled from 20,000 to 60,000. In the 1990s, the number of professionals working at home is expected to reach 13 million—more than 11 percent of the work force. Annual projections see the telecommuting work force growing from 7 percent to 9 percent per year.[36]

As we suggested in Chapter 15, this type of technological change can have significant impact on the way work is done. In a survey of firms that had ongoing telecommuting activities, researchers Terri Griffith and Paul Goodman

[35] E. G. Thomas, "Workers Who Set Their Own Time Clocks," *Business and Society Review*, Spring 1987, 49–51.

[36] D. C. Bacon, "Look Who Is Working at Home," *Nation's Business*, October 1989, 20–31.

reported that 94 percent of those surveyed believed that telecommuting had increased the productivity of telecommuting managers and professionals. Three reasons were given for this increased productivity: (1) telecommuters who were working "after hours" did so for no additional pay, (2) telecommuters typically had not used a computer before they began telecommuting, but now they were bringing this greater analytical ability to their jobs, and (3) telecommuting was increasing the flexibility of and reducing the stress on many workers. For many organizations, telecommuting is often a logical extension of computer-oriented jobs: it allows the company to get extra work from employees (they would now have 24-hour-a-day access to the office); it provides a way to hold on to valuable employees who cannot or will not come into work every day; and finally, managers and professionals can make better use of their time, such as by avoiding the "down time" usually associated with travel or commuting.[37]

The importance of work-force flexibility to the competitiveness of U.S. corporations will become increasingly critical by the twenty-first century. But it is just one problem, or "opportunity," that the next generation of managers will have to face. The ability to foster creativity and innovation among employees, meet the new needs of the changing work force, and create organizations in which the rights of the employee and employer are maintained are the managerial challenges that lie ahead. These and other issues will determine whether managers can meet such challenges in tomorrow's business world.

SUMMARY ◆◆◆◆◆◆

The purpose of this chapter was to examine the notion of work-force diversity from a variety of perspectives. The changing demographics of the work force and how managers and organizations will need to adapt their various incentive systems is a critical component to successful individual and organizational performance. The aging of the work force, the increasing participation of women and men of color, and the concerns of dual-career couples are all issues that demand new approaches. Changing the composition of the work force so dramatically will require a radical rethinking of benefits, recruiting strategies, and incentive structures for these new groups of employees. Not only will there be fewer entrants into the job market of the future, but those who do enter will be overwhelmingly female and minority.

While the government continues to reduce its regulation of industries, it is stepping up its control of the organization/employee relationship. As recent legislature illustrates (for example, the Pregnancy Discrimination Act, the Americans with Disabilities Act, comparable worth legislation, unisex pension coverage, and various discrimination rulings), government has made an attempt to ensure the fair treatment of employees.

Unfortunately, even with past legislation, discrimination is one issue that will continue to haunt current management. While the discrimination of the present and the near-future is generally not based on the radically racist

[37] Terri Hughson (Griffith) and Paul Goodman, "Telecommuting: Corporate Practices and Benefits," *National Productivity Review*, Autumn 1986, 315–322.

or sexist perspectives of the past, women and men of color are still subjected to pervasive and pernicious discrimination. This discrimination deprives women and men of color of opportunities to move up the corporate ladder into executive management. It represents a much more insidious form of discrimination since those who are purveyors of this perspective may be unaware of its existence. Employees have the right to cooperative acceptance. Cooperative acceptance refers to the expectation that employees will be treated with respect, regardless of their race, sex, age, religion, or other demographic characteristics. The issue of sexual harassment in the workplace is probably the most salient of the "cooperative acceptance" doctrines in action.

We have also identified four potential remedies that may influence the amount of discrimination employees face: affirmative action, changing employer expectations, social and cultural changes, and technological changes. While organizations are still struggling with how to take advantage of the natural diversity that currently does (and increasingly will) exist in the work force, the transition from the melting pot (an analogy in which all of our differences are eventually fired away) to the salad (in which we are all able to keep our individual differences and perspectives intact) is very difficult. Making this transition is a primary challenge facing managers in the coming decade.

Key Terms

Colorism Predisposition to act in a certain manner because of a person's skin color.

Glass ceiling Barrier that keeps women as a group from advancing to executive management simply because they are women and not because of their individual ability.

Sexual harassment Verbal or physical conduct of a sexual nature when submission to such conduct is made either explicitly or implicitly a term or condition of an individual's employment, influences employment decisions affecting the individual, or substantially interferes with the individual's work performance or work environment.

Discussion Questions

1. Why is a heterogenous work force critical for maintaining high levels of organizational creativity and innovation? What problems are likely to result from having great variety (different genders, races, cultures, and so on) in a work force?

2. Affirmative action legislation is primarily directed at getting women and other protected minorities into the workplace. Why might such a focus be a factor in the development and strengthening of corporate "glass ceilings"?

3. What is the basic intent of government's increasing regulation of the workplace? How has it succeeded in that intent? How has it failed? What are some of the indicators of the failure and success of its goals?

4. How do female and minority networks get around the problems we identified in our discussion of mentoring in Chapter 11?

5. What are the major implications for managers in organizational staffing during the "baby-bust" years? What are some strategies management might implement to be more successful in future recruiting?

6. Numerous popular press articles suggest that corporations and their managers are making precious few adjustments in preparation for the changing nature of the educational level, age, gender, racial, and ethnic mix of the work force. What are some of the reasons for this apparent nonresponsiveness on the part of managers?

If You Want to Know More

The topic of work-force diversity has received a lot of public attention recently. A number of articles and books have been written on various aspects of this topic. It all seemed to start with the Hudson Institute's report *Workforce 2000: Work and Workers in the 21st Century* (1987, Hudson Institute). For more in-depth information, one might consider reading Rita Mae Kelly's *The Gendered Economy: Work, Careers, and Success* (London: Sage Publications, 1991), Marilyn Loden and Judy B. Rosener's *Workforce America: Managing Employee Diversity as a Vital Resource* (Homewood, Ill.: Dow Jones-Irwin, 1991), or Claudia Goldin's *Understanding the Gender Gap* (New York: Oxford University Press, 1990). Amanda Bennett has done an excellent job of exploring the organizational man myth in *The Death of the Organizational Man* (New York: William Morrow and Company, 1990). Felice Schwartz has focused on the interaction of women and organizations in *Breaking with Tradition: Women, Management and the New Facts of Life* (New York: Warner Books, 1992), which extends the controversial article that she published in January 1989 in the *Harvard Business Review*. Susan Faludi's *Backlash: The Undeclared War Against American Women* (New York: Crown, 1991) focuses on the response in society and the work world to the recent successes of women.

Roosevelt Thomas, Jr., writes "From Affirmative Action to Affirming Diversity" in the March/April 1990 issue of the *Harvard Business Review*, identifying ways that corporations can address diversity in the workplace. Susan Clayton and Faye Crosby examine justice and affirmative action in *Justice, Gender, Affirmative Action* (New York: Free Press, 1992).

An interesting article that chronicles the incidence of sexual harassment on the college campus was written by Marina McCarthy and Roland Christensen and published by the Harvard Business School Publishing Division (1987, No. 9-387-209). Insights on the glass ceiling and colorism can be found in the newly published *Breaking the Glass Ceiling: Can Women Reach the Top in America's Largest Corporations?* by A. Morrison, R. White, E. Van Velsor, and the Center for Creative Leadership. An older, but more general, book on the topic is the John Fernandez text, *Racism and Sexism in Corporate Life* (Lexington, MA: Lexington Books, 1981) The invisible ceiling for African Americans is highlighted in Anne B. Fisher's article, "Good News, Bad News, and an Invisible Ceiling" in *Fortune* (September 16, 1985). In the June 22, 1987, issue of *Business Week*, there is an excellent article on corporate women entitled "Corporate Women: They're about to Break through to the Top." Also see the companion article by Cathy Trost, "Women Managers Quit Not for Family but to Advance Their Corporate Climb" in the *Wall Street Journal* (May 2, 1990). Taylor Cox and Stella Nkomo explore the impact of race and gender on the work experience of

MBAs in "A Race and Gender Group Analysis of the Early Career Experience of MBA's" in *Work and Occupations* 18(4) (1991): 431–446.

To explore further the issues facing women with careers and families, Faye J. Crosby has written *Juggling* (New York: Free Press, 1991). Another possibility in this area is Helen Axel's *Corporations and Families: Changing Practices and Perspectives* published by The Conference Board (1985). Commuter marriages are the subject of Fairlee Winfield's *Commuter Marriages* (New York: Columbia University, 1985). Additional information on the male response to dual career families may be found in L. A. Gilbert's book, *Men in Dual-Career Families* (Hillsdale, NJ: Erlbaum Associates, 1985).

On Your Own

Balancing Roles: Managing Multiple Perspectives On a sheet of paper, draw a large circle. After reflecting on how you have spent your time in the preceding week, divide the circle as if it were a pie into sections representing the different roles you played in that week (include roles that relate to work, family, home, and all other roles). The size of each section should be proportional to the amount of time and energy you invest in that particular activity. Labels for these sections might include student, employee, friend, spouse, and so on.

Now consider what sections of your role pie are most important to your sense of identity. Number the sections from most important (1) to least important (this number will be determined by how many sections you have in your pie). Note that the numbers frequently do not correspond to the size of the sections. Consider which of the sections in your role pie tend to contribute to role overload—that is, what activities and roles infringe upon other important activities and roles? Identify those sections of your role pie.

In light of the conflict and issues you have identified above, complete the "Role Management Inventory." When you have answered all the questions, score the inventory according to the instructions that follow the questionnaire. Which is the most important coping style(s)? Is this optimal for you?

Role Management Inventory How do you deal with these conflicts or issues? How often do you do each of the following?

	Nearly All the Time 5	Often 4	Sometimes 3	Rarely 2	Never 1
1. Decide not to do certain activities that conflict with other activities.	____	____	____	____	____
2. Get help from someone outside the family (e.g., home maintenance help or child care).	____	____	____	____	____
3. Get help from a member of the family.	____	____	____	____	____
4. Get help from someone at work.	____	____	____	____	____
5. Engage in problem solving with family members to resolve conflicts.	____	____	____	____	____
6. Engage in problem solving with someone at work.	____	____	____	____	____
7. Get moral support from a member of the family.	____	____	____	____	____
8. Get moral support from someone at work.	____	____	____	____	____
9. Integrate or combine roles (for example, involve family members in work activity or combine work and family in same way).	____	____	____	____	____
10. Attempt to change societal definition of sex roles, work roles, or family roles.	____	____	____	____	____

11. Negotiate or plan with someone at work, so their expectations of you are more in line with your own needs or requirements. ___ ___ ___ ___ ___

12. Negotiate or plan with members of your family, so their expectations of you are more in line with your own needs or requirements. ___ ___ ___ ___ ___

13. Establish priorities among your different roles, so that you are sure the most important activities are done. ___ ___ ___ ___ ___

14. Partition and separate your roles. Devote full attention to each role when you are in it. ___ ___ ___ ___ ___

15. Overlook or relax certain standards for how you do certain activities. (Let less important things slide a bit sometimes, such as dusting and lawn care.) ___ ___ ___ ___ ___

16. Modify your attitudes toward certain roles or activities (e.g., coming to the conclusion that the *quality* of time spent with spouse or children is more important than the *quantity* of time spent). ___ ___ ___ ___ ___

17. Eliminate certain roles (e.g., deciding to stop working). ___ ___ ___ ___ ___

18. Rotate attention from one role to another. Handle each role in turn as it comes up. ___ ___ ___ ___ ___

19. Develop self and own interests (e.g., spend time on leisure or self-development). ___ ___ ___ ___ ___

20. Plan, schedule, and organize carefully. ___ ___ ___ ___ ___

21. Work hard to meet all role demands. Devote more time and energy, so you can do everything that is expected of you. ___ ___ ___ ___ ___

22. Do not attempt to cope with role demands and conflicts. Let role conflicts take care of themselves. ___ ___ ___ ___ ___

Scoring

▶ Add up the values you entered for items 1 to 12. Divide by 12. This is your *role-redefinition score:* ___

▶ Add up the values you entered for 13 to 17. Divide by 5. This is your *personal-reorientation score:* ___

▶ Add up the values you entered for 18 to 22. Divide by 5. This is your *reactive coping score:* ___

Interpreting Your Scores These three scores give you some indication of the extent to which you use each of the three strategies. The scores can range from a *high* of 5 to a *low* of 1. If you score *over 3* on a scale, you score relatively high, meaning that you make frequent use of this coping strategy. A score of *less than 3* indicates relatively infrequent use of this coping strategy. Here are some problems that may be indicated by your scores on the three scales:

Low Role-Redefinition Scores You often let others place demands on you, often unrealistic demands. You need to negotiate with these people, your role senders, to make certain that the roles they impose on you are compatible with other responsibilities and interests. Some ways of doing this include:

▶ Simply agree with role senders that you will not be able to engage in certain activities. (For example, in our community, a hotbed of volunteerism, we are both known as "spot-jobbers." We will accept specific one-shot volunteer jobs, but we will not accept continuing positioning.)

▶ Enlist assistance in role activities from other family members or from people outside the family (for example, cleaning or babysitting help).

▶ Sit down with role senders (boss, spouse, children) and discuss the problem. Together, work out an acceptable solution.

▶ Integrate conflicting careers by working with your spouse or working in related fields (so that the two careers become more like one). This method of coping has been described as "linking up."

If you can successfully reduce role conflicts by practicing some of these proactive negotiations, you will be stopping them at the source, and chances are you'll be very happy with the results—*you* will be managing the situation.

Low Personal-Reorientation Scores Your problem is that you don't distinguish between the roles assigned to you; you lack a clear vision of what roles are truly important. You need to reevaluate your attitudes about various roles and take on only those heading the list. Some hints to help you achieve this are:

▶ Establish priorities ("A child with a high fever takes precedence over school obligations. A child with sniffles does not. A very important social engagement—especially one that is business related—precedes tennis.")

▶ Divide and separate roles. Devote full attention to a given role when in it, and don't think about other roles. ("I leave my work at the office. Home is for the family and their needs.")

▶ Try to ignore or overlook less important role expectations. ("The dusting can wait.")

▶ Rotate attention from one role to another as demands arise. Let one role slide a bit if another needs more attention at the time. ("Susan needs help now. I'll pay those bills later.")

▶ Remember that self-fulfillment and personal interests are a valid source of role demands. ("Piano and organ playing are a release for me while the children are small and need me at home.")

This style of coping means changing yourself rather than the family or work environment, although personal reorientation may be a necessary step to take before you can accomplish real role redefinition. Before you can change other people's expectations of you, you have to be clear about what you expect of yourself. Personal reorientation alone is not significantly related to satisfaction and happiness.

High Reactive Coping Scores You try to take on every role that happens your way. You cope with conflict by working harder and sleeping less. Your style of coping includes:

▶ Planning, scheduling, and organizing better.

▶ Working harder to meet all role demands. (As one expert on women's roles and role conflict said in frustration, "After years of research, I've concluded that the only answer to a career and a family is to learn to get by on less sleep!")

▶ Using no conscious strategy. Let problems take care of themselves. This reactive behavior, in contrast to role redefinition, is a passive response to role conflict. Not surprisingly, people who use this style report very low levels of satisfaction and happiness (passive coping).

Reactive coping is not a very effective way of dealing with your roles. Rather than managing them, you are letting them manage you. If your goal is to eliminate conflict, then you need to reorient your own perceptions as a first step toward negotiating with others to restructure the roles in your life.

Developed by Francine S. Hall. "Role pie" based on activity originally developed in Barbara L. Forisha, *Sex Roles and Personal Awareness* (Morristown, N.J.: General Learning Press, 1978), pp. 198–199 and adapted by Donald D. Bowen. Parts of this exercise were adapted from Francine S. Hall and Douglas T. Hall, *The Two-Career Couple*, copyright © 1979, Addison-Wesley Publishing Co., Reading, Mass. Adaptation of Chapter 3, pages 75–79 and 104–106.

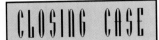

CHAPTER 18

THE MANAGER'S MEMO

FROM: J. Reynolds, Manager, Human Resources

TO: P. Copeland, President

RE: Staffing the European Sales Office

With the opening up of the European market as those countries lower their trade barriers, we will need a creative and energetic team for our new European sales office. Because we'll want to be ready with the best people possible, I have spent considerable time reviewing the resumés we have on file. I recommend that you consider making your selections from the following people:

- David J. McDonald is the top salesperson at our major competitor, Biggs Consumer Products. I think he feels he has reached his potential there and would bite at an offer that would open new opportunities.
- Dan Peachtree has been a reliable member of our sales force for ten years, often among the company's top five sellers. He has already relocated for us six times.
- Thomas Dodd received his MBA from State University three years ago and has been selling for us ever since. His performance appraisals consistently rate him Outstanding.
- Bill Phillips started with us when he received his engineering degree two years ago and he switched to sales one year later. He hasn't been selling long, but with his engineering background, he'll know the product inside and out.
- Robert Peterson will be receiving his bachelors degree in marketing this May. He has a remarkable track record as an Amway salesperson while in school. Last year he sold $1 million of their products.

A few other names have come up. There's Marybeth Peters, our top-performing salesperson of the past two years, and Felicia Jones, who has been on the sales force for four years and who was mentioned because she received her degree in German language and culture. I doubt either would want to move and disrupt her family. Paul Yamamoto developed the new selling system that seems to be increasing our sales so much this year, but I can't imagine he'd feel very comfortable in our Frankfurt office.

I hope I have given you enough ideas for selecting a sales manager and two other representatives. Please let me know who you'd like to interview.

Case Discussion Questions

Assume you are the president, and respond to the memo from the manager of the human resources division. Select who you would like to interview to staff a new, three-person sales office that will launch an important company expansion overseas. Drawing on the considerations raised in the chapter, briefly state your reasons for your selections.

EXERCISE

PART 5:

Sears vs. Kmart

Here is a field exercise you can do the next time you go shopping. It is designed to help you explore the significance of various aspects of organization structure on effectiveness and goal accomplishments.

You will be asked to analyze two different establishments in the same line of business. You will compare and contrast these firms as carefully as you can to see what makes them really work. Since you've probably visited one or both of these stores, you already know something about them. But try to place yourself in a position of seeing them for the first time. Then try to integrate what you have learned in this chapter and from other experiences in this book about how firms are managed.

Form into groups of about four and read your assignment. As a group, visit each store (preferably in the same general location). You might want to evaluate service, quality, price, and so on.

Your Assignment

Your group, Fastalk Consultants, is known as the shrewdest, most insightful, and most overpaid management consulting firm in the country. You have been hired by the president of Sears to make recommendations for improving the motivation and performance of personnel in their operations. Let us assume that the key job activity in store operations is dealing with customers.

Recently, the president of Sears has come to suspect that his company's competitor, Kmart, is making heavy inroads into Sears's market. He has also hired a market research firm to investigate and compare the relative merits of products and prices in the two establishments, and has asked the market research firm to assess the advertising campaigns of the two organizations. Hence, you will not need to be concerned with marketing issues, except as they may have an impact on employee behavior. The president wants you to look into the organization of the two stores to determine the strengths and weaknesses of each.

The president has established an unusual contract with you. He wants you to make your recommendations based upon your observations *as a customer.* He does not want you to do a complete diagnosis with interviews, surveys, or behind-the-scenes observations. He wants your report in two parts.

1. Given his organization's goals of profitability, sales volume, and fast and courteous service, he wants an analysis that will compare and contrast Sears and Kmart in terms of the following concepts:

▶ **Organizational Goals**
Conflict?
Clarity?

▶ **Environment**
Stable/changing?
Simple/complex?
Certain/uncertain?

▶ **Size**
Large?
Medium?
Small?

▶ **Personnel**
Knowledgeable?
Well-trained?

▶ **Horizontal Division of Labor**
Formalized policies?
Departmentalization?
Standardization of rules?

▶ **Vertical Division of Labor**
Number of levels?
Span of control?
Centralization?

▶ **Communication**
Direction?
Openness?

▶ **Leadership Style**
Task oriented?
People oriented?

▶ **Jobs**
Variety?
Wholeness?
Interaction?
Freedom?
Time of work?
Location of work?

▶ **Employee Motivation**
Type?
Intrinsic/extrinsic?
Rewards?
Support?
Coordination?
Decision making?

How do Sears and Kmart differ in these aspects? Which company has the best approach?

2. Given the corporate goals listed under point 1, what specific actions might Sears's management take in the following areas to achieve these goals (profitability, sales volume, fast and courteous service)?

▶ Job design and work flow
▶ Organization structure (at the individual store level)
▶ Employee incentives
▶ Leadership
▶ Employee selection

3. Having completed your contract with the president of Sears, prepare a report for presentation to the class. This should include:
a. Specific recommendations you have considered in 2 above.
b. Reasons for these suggestions based on your knowledge of leadership, motivation, job design, organization, and so on.

Source: Lawrence R. Jauch, Sally A. Coltrin, Arthur G. Bedeian, and William F. Glueck, *The Managerial Experience: Cases, Exercises, and Readings*, 5th ed. (Hinsdale, Ill.: Dryden, 1989), 165–166.

CASE

PART 5:

Dashman Company

The Dashman Company was a large concern making many types of equipment for the armed forces of the United States. It had over 20 plants, located in the central part of the country, whose purchasing procedures had never been completely coordinated. In fact, the head office of the company had encouraged each of the plant managers to operate with their staffs as separate independent units in most matters. Late in 1940, when it began to appear that the company would face increasing difficulty in securing certain essential raw materials, Mr. Manson, the company's president, appointed an experienced purchasing executive, Mr. Post, as vice-president in charge of purchasing, a position especially created for him. Mr. Manson gave Mr. Post wide latitude in organizing his job, and he assigned Mr. Larson as Mr. Post's assistant. Mr. Larson had served the company in a variety of capacities for many years, and knew most of the plant executives personally. Mr. Post's appointment was announced through the formal channels usual in the company, including a notice in the house newsletter published by the company.

One of Mr. Post's first decisions was to begin immediately to centralize the company's purchasing procedure. As a first step he decided that he would require each of the executives who handled purchasing in the individual plants to clear with the head office all purchase contracts which they made in excess of $10,000. He felt that if the head office was to do any coordinating in a way that would be helpful to each plant and to the company as a whole, he must be notified that the contracts were being prepared at least a week before they were to be signed. He talked his proposal over with Mr. Manson, who presented it to his board of directors. They approved the plan.

Although the company made purchases throughout the year, the beginning of its peak buying season was only three weeks away at the time this new plan was adopted. Mr. Post prepared a letter to be sent to the 20 purchasing executives of the company. The letter follows:

> Dear _____,
>
> The board of directors of our company has recently authorized a change in our purchasing procedures. Hereafter, each of the purchasing executives in the several plants of the company will notify the vice president in charge of purchasing of all contracts in excess of $10,000 which they are negotiating at least a week in advance of the date on which they are to be signed.
>
> I am sure that you will understand that this step is necessary to coordinate the purchasing requirements of the company in these times when we are facing increasing difficulty in securing essential supplies. This procedure should give us in the central office the information we need to see that each plant secures the optimum supply of materials. In this way the interests of each plant and of the company as a whole will best be served.
>
> Yours very truly,

Mr. Post showed the letter to Mr. Larson and invited his comments. Mr. Larson thought the letter an excellent one, but suggested that, since Mr. Post had not met more than a few of the purchasing executives, he might like to visit all of them and take the matter up with each of them personally. Mr. Post dismissed the idea at once because, as he said, he had so many things to do at the head office that he could not get away for a trip. Consequently he had the letters sent out over his signature.

During the two following weeks replies came in from all except a few plants. Although a few executives wrote at great length, the following reply was typical:

> Dear Mr. Post,
>
> Your recent communication in regard to notifying the head office a week in advance of our intention to sign contracts has been received. This suggestion seems a most practical one. We want to assure you that you can count on our cooperation.
>
> Yours very truly,

During the next six weeks the head office received no notices from any plant that contracts were being negotiated. Executives in other departments who made frequent trips to the plants reported that the plants were busy, and the usual routines for that time of year were being followed.

Questions for Discussion

1. Was the centralization of purchasing at Dashman necessary?
2. Was the letter from Mr. Post sufficient to implement the new procedure?
3. Why did the head office not receive any notices of contracts being negotiated?

APPENDICES

Appendix A:
The Scientific Method

INTRODUCTION

The study of organizational behavior is aimed at explaining, understanding, and predicting how people behave in organizations. To do this, information that is collected about behavior in organizations must be accurate and trustworthy. How can that be ensured? The best way to collect accurate and trustworthy information is by using the **scientific method.** As shown in Figure A–1, the scientific method is a systematic set of procedures for objectively collecting and evaluating information.

If a consultant offered you a "highly successful" new training program, how would you know whether to trust the consultant's claim? The consultant's belief that the program is highly successful could be a function of the high quality of the program. But the program also could only appear to be "highly successful" because of the way success was measured, the person who did the measuring, or the group of people who were trained. To trust information, you need to be able to evaluate its quality and meaning.

The scientific method allows you to evaluate the quality and meaning of information. As noted in Figure A–1, the scientific method requires that the procedures for information collection be *public* and *precise*. If the consultant told you that the training program was evaluated by participants through an attitude questionnaire (rather than by an objective measurement of participants' learning or subsequent performance) and showed you the questionnaire, you would have a better understanding of the label "highly successful." Therefore you would better understand the limits of the information.

It is also the aim of scientific information collection to be *objective*, so that collected information reflects reality rather than the opinions of the information collector. Public and precise methods for information collection help ensure that personal opinions do not significantly influence information collection processes. The scientific requirement that results be *replicated*—reproduced by other scientists—before being accepted as fact also helps. You should feel better about a training program that has been successfully implemented by a variety of trainers in several different companies. It is then unlikely that the program's success was a function of any single trainer or company setting.

Finally, scientific information collection is *systematic* and *cumulative*. If this training program is successful, what features does it share with other successful programs? Are there common threads that differentiate among many successful and unsuccessful programs? The systematic accumulation of knowledge demanded by the scientific method provides another check on the trustworthiness of information. Trustworthy information should be consistent with past scientific findings.

These characteristics of the scientific method do not suggest that there is only one correct way to gather information or acquire knowledge. In fact, the scientific method encompasses many acceptable ways of gathering information about behavior in organizations. These various approaches differ in the extent

FIGURE A-1	▶ **The Scientific Method**

1. *The procedures are public.* A scientific report includes a complete description of the procedures used to collect information, so that readers could attempt to reproduce the findings or decide for themselves the limitations of the information collection procedures.

2. *The definitions are precise.* When describing the procedures used, it is critical that the wording be clear, with all terms defined. If performance is the outcome of interest, how was performance measured?

3. *The information collection is objective.* The information collection procedures should not allow the information collector to inject his or her subjective opinions into the information. The scientific observer should be collecting or recording information, *not* interpreting it.

4. *The findings must be replicable.* Despite a scientist's best intentions to maintain objectivity, personal feelings can influence scientific findings. Scientific findings become truly trustworthy only when they have been reproduced by other scientists.

5. *The approach is systematic and cumulative.* The object of scientific inquiry is not to produce isolated findings but to combine those findings progressively into more and more complete theories of human behavior.

6. *The purposes of scientific inquiry are explanation, understanding, and prediction.* The reason for having theories in organizational behavior is to use those theories to improve and enhance life in organizations. For this to occur, our theories must do a good job of explaining why behavior occurs, thereby allowing us to predict and control it.

Source: B. Berelson and G. Steiner, *Human Behavior: An Inventory of Scientific Findings* (New York: Harcourt Brace Jovanovich, 1964), pp. 16–18.

to which they trade off control and realism in collecting information. Think back to the new training program. You are considering using the program, but first you need to know: Will the program improve employee performance? How could you answer this question *scientifically*?

THE CASE STUDY

One way of assessing the value of a proposed training program is to do a **case study.** The case study is the method of scientific information collection most like the way we typically learn from experience. A case study would involve collecting information about the experiences of one organization that had used the training program. The scientific observer would look at how well the program had worked in that organization, then try to figure out what characteristics of the training program or the organization might have predicted success or failure.

Several important differences exist between a scientific case study and more informal ways of learning from experience in organizations. First, in a scientific case study information collection is systematic. All employees are asked the same questions. This ensures that different employees do not report different impressions of the training program just because they were asked different questions.

Second, a case study differs from informal observation in terms of the depth of inquiry. You might informally notice that the new training program worked out when it was tried. In a scientific case study, the scientific observer would look harder and deeper. In what ways was the training program successful? For how many of the trained employees was the training helpful? Were there any characteristics shared by all the employees who profited from the training? These questions go beyond simply knowing whether the program succeeded or failed and help generate an understanding of *why* success or failure occurred.

Finally, a scientific case study differs from informal "learning from experience" because the information collected is carefully recorded. Often learning from experience is unreliable because our memory for past experiences is poor. We may completely forget important aspects of past experiences or remember events that never occurred. The scientific case study includes careful recording of information so that all aspects of an experience (and only those which in fact occurred) are retained for later consideration.

In a case study, observations and speculations often occur "after the fact": in this example, after the training program already has been tried. The hallmark of a scientific case study is that the scientific observer of the experience is only that, an observer. The scientific observer makes no attempt to control important factors, such as characteristics of the training program or which employees are selected to be trained.

FIELD RESEARCH ◆◆◆◆◆◆

If you wanted to exercise more control in collecting information about the effects of the training program, you might conduct some **field research.** Typically, in field research the scientific observer carefully measures what workers are thinking and doing (sometimes even *while* they are thinking and doing!) through the use of questionnaires, surveys, and observational techniques. The scientific observer also *controls* which organization (or which part of it) tries the training program and when. In a case study, this control is beyond the reach of the scientific observer.

Often it is difficult to pinpoint the cause of an effect. Did the training program succeed because it is a good program? Or was the trainer particularly good? Or were the trainees particularly motivated? Sorting out the answers to these questions is crucial to understanding whether the training program *or something else* is improving worker performance. To address this problem, researchers use multiple groups of subjects in a study. In our example, some of the groups could be trained by one trainer and others by a different trainer, both using the same training program. Some groups might not receive training or be given a different training program. This would give us lots of useful comparisons that would help us *isolate* the effects of our training program. If performance for the trained groups improved and performance for the untrained groups did not, that would be good evidence that training improves performance. What if performance for both trained and untrained groups improved equally? That would be good evidence that something *other than* training improves performance.

Notice that without the multiple groups (called *control* groups), there would be no way to know whether performance would have improved even without the training program. The control groups help us separate the effects on performance of factors that we are not interested in (such as rumors about layoffs that may make everyone's performance improve) from the effects of factors we are interested in (the training program).

LABORATORY RESEARCH

If you wanted to exercise even more control in assessing the effects of the proposed training program, you might conduct some **laboratory research.** In laboratory research, the employees to be trained would be taken out of the organizational context for training and observation. Many laboratory studies are not really done in scientific laboratories, merely away from the normal organizational setting. This is desirable because the information collected through case studies and field studies suffers from a certain amount of "noise"—things going on in the work setting that have nothing to do with the training program and cannot be controlled but which do influence performance. The laboratory study offers the best opportunity to isolate the effects of the training program on performance from the effects of other factors that we are not interested in. Thus, the laboratory study offers the clearest view of the effects of the training program.

On the other hand, the "noise" factors in work settings (such as the relationships between workers, the culture of a particular organization, and even production crises that arise) are part and parcel of the work setting. They will influence the effects of the training program when it is used in an actual organizational setting. Therefore, while the controlled environment of the laboratory might be best for finding out how the training program works in some ideal sense, only field and case studies will reveal how the training program works in an actual organizational setting.

THE SCIENTIFIC METHOD IN PRACTICE

All three of these methods for collecting information about behavior in organizations—case studies, field research, and laboratory research—share the central scientific orientation noted in Figure A–1 of careful, controlled, objective collection of information. The scientific orientation toward information collection is what differentiates organizational behavior as a scientific endeavor from other, more informal ways of learning about behavior in organizations, such as casual observation or intuition. In practice, these different techniques for collecting information scientifically would be used together. A case study could be used to generate potential insights about what makes a training program a success or failure. These insights then could be refined through the use of laboratory studies. Finally, the successfully refined training program could be put to the test using a field study. The field study would demonstrate whether the successes of the training program in the laboratory (that is, isolated from many of the realities of organizations) could be reproduced in actual organizational settings. The field study results may suggest more fine-tuning of the training program (through more laboratory studies) or may push the researcher back to observing organizations (case studies) for new insights.

Research on group decision making (which was discussed in Chapter 9) provides a good example of the complementary nature of case studies and laboratory and field research. Case studies have documented both good and bad group decision making at the White House prior to the "Bay of Pigs" invasion of Cuba and the Cuban Missile Crisis. These case studies raised important concerns about influence processes in group decision making and also demonstrated their consequences.[1] No doubt these concerns also will be raised in trying to explain and understand the Challenger disaster.

These same influence processes also have been examined in the laboratory, where a variety of studies have identified social comparison processes (discussed in Chapter 7) as an important source of influence in group decision making.[2] Finally, the importance of social comparison processes in decision making has been validated with field experiments examining bystander apathy in emergency situations.[3] In group decision-making research, case studies have stimulated systematic and controlled research in the field and the laboratory. Laboratory research has isolated important cause-and-effect relationships, and field research has verified the importance of these cause-and-effect relationships in real-world settings.

SUMMARY

The scientific method is used to ensure that information collected about behavior in organizations is trustworthy and accurate. The scientific method is a systematic set of procedures for objectively collecting and evaluating information. The scientific method encompasses several different approaches to collecting information, including case studies, field research, and laboratory research. These approaches differ in the extent to which they trade off control and realism in collecting information. In practice, these different approaches would be used in combination, in order to construct an accurate representation of the realities of organizational behavior.

Key Terms

Case study Careful and systematic observation and recording of the experiences of a single organization.

Field research Using questionnaires, surveys, and observational techniques in controlled study of actual organizations.

---

[1] G. T. Allison, *Essence of Decision* (Boston: Little, Brown, 1971).

[2] S. E. Asch, "Effects of Group Pressure on the Modification and Distortion of Judgments," in *Groups, Leadership, and Men*, ed. H. Guetzkow (Pittsburgh: Carnegie Press, 1951), 177–190.

[3] J. M. Darley and B. Latane, "When Will People Help in a Crisis?" *Psychology Today 2* (1968): 54–57, 70–71.

Laboratory research Carefully controlled experimentation and observation outside of traditional organizational settings in order to identify and isolate important cause-and-effect relationships.

Scientific method Systematic set of procedures for objectively collecting and evaluating information.

If You Want to Know More

A general discussion of the process of scientific inquiry is provided in Thomas Kuhn's *The Structure of Scientific Revolutions* (Chicago: University of Chicago Press, 1962). Specific methods and techniques for conducting scientific research studies in organizational behavior can be found in *Research Methods in Organizational Behavior*, by Eugene Stone (Glenview, Ill.: Scott-Foresman, 1978) and *Methods of Social Research*, by K. E. Bailey (New York: Free Press, 1978).

Appendix B:
Continuing On

Continuing On

By the second month of the training period, trouble developed. The painters learned more slowly than had been anticipated, and it began to look as though their production would stabilize far below what was planned. Many of the hooks were going by empty. The painters complained that the hooks moved too fast, and that the engineer had set the rates wrong. A few painters quit and had to be replaced with new ones. This further aggravated the learning problem. The team spirit that the management had expected to develop through the group bonus was not in evidence except as an expression of what the engineers called "resistance." One painter, whom the group regarded as its leader (and the management regarded as the ringleader), was outspoken in taking the complaints of the group to the supervisor. These complaints were that the job was messy, the hooks moved too fast, the incentive pay was not correctly calculated, and it was too hot working so close to the drying oven.

Question

1. What would you recommend that the responsible manager do now? Why?

Continuing On

A consultant was hired to work with the supervisor. She recommended that the painters be brought together for a general discussion of the working conditions. Although hesitant, the supervisor agreed to this plan.

The first meeting was held immediately after the shift was over at 4:00 in the afternoon. It was attended by all eight painters. They voiced the same complaints again: the hooks went by too fast, the job was too dirty, and the room was hot and poorly ventilated. For some reason, it was this last item that seemed to bother them most. The supervisor promised to discuss the problems of ventilation and temperature with the engineers, and a second meeting was scheduled. In the next few days the supervisor had several talks with the engineers. They, along with the plant superintendent, felt that this was really a trumped-up complaint, and that the expense of corrective measures would be prohibitively high.

The supervisor came to the second meeting with some apprehensions. The painters, however, did not seem to be much put out. Rather, they had a proposal of their own to make. They felt that if several large fans were set up to circulate the air around their feet, they would be much more comfortable. After some discussion, the supervisor agreed to pursue the idea. The supervisor and the consultant discussed the idea of fans with the superintendent. Three large propeller-type fans were purchased and installed.

The painters were jubilant. For several days the fans were moved about in various positions until they were placed to the satisfaction of the group. The painters seemed completely satisfied with the results, and the relations between them and the supervisor improved visibly.

The supervisor, after this encouraging episode, decided that further meetings might also prove profitable. The painters were asked if they would like to meet and discuss other aspects of the work situation. They were eager to do this. Another meeting was held, and the discussion quickly centered on the speed of the hooks. The painters maintained that the engineer had set them at an unreasonably fast speed and that they would never be able to fill enough of them to make a bonus.

The discussion reached a turning point when the group's leader explained that it wasn't that the painters couldn't work fast enough to keep up with the hooks, but that they couldn't work at that pace all day long. The supervisor explored the point. The painters were unanimous in their opinion that they could keep up with the belt for short periods if they wanted to. But they didn't want to because if they showed they could do this for short periods then they would be expected to do it all day long. The meeting ended with an unprecedented request by the painters: "Let us adjust the speed of the belt faster or slower depending on how we feel." The supervisor agreed to discuss this with the superintendent and the engineers.

The engineers reacted negatively to the suggestion. However, after several meetings it was granted that there was some latitude within which variations in the speed of the hooks would not affect the finished product. After considerable argument with the engineers, it was agreed to try out the painters' idea.

With misgivings, the supervisor had a control with a dial marked "low, medium, fast" installed at the booth of the group leader. The speed of the belt could now be adjusted anywhere between the lower and upper limits that the engineers had set.

Questions

1. What changes do you now expect in the level of output of the painters? Why?
2. What changes do you expect in the feelings of the painters toward their work situation? Why?
3. Why other predictions do you make about the behavior of the painters?

Continuing On

The painters were delighted, and spent many lunch hours deciding how the speed of the belt should be varied from hour to hour throughout the day. Within a week the pattern had settled down to one in which the first half hour of the shift was run on a medium speed (a dial setting slightly above the point marked "medium"). The next two-and-a-half hours were run at high speed, and the half hour before lunch and the half hour after lunch were run at low speed. The rest of the afternoon was run at high speed with the exception of the last 45 minutes of the shift, which was run at medium.

The constant speed at which the engineers had originally set the belt was actually slightly below the "medium" mark on the control dial. The average speed at which the painters were running the belt was on the high side of the dial. Few, if any, empty hooks entered the oven, and inspection showed no increase of rejects from the paint room.

Production increased, and within three weeks (some two months before the scheduled ending of the learning bonus) the painters were operating at 30 to 50 percent above the level that had been expected under the original arrangement. Naturally, their earnings were correspondingly higher than anticipated. They were collecting their base pay, earning a considerable piece-rate bonus, and still benefiting from the learning bonus. They were earning more now than many skilled workers in other parts of the plant.

Questions

1. How do you feel about the situation at this point?
2. Suppose you were the supervisor. What would you expect to happen next? Why?

Continuing On

Management was besieged by demands that the inequity between the earnings of the painters and those of other workers in the plant be taken care of. With growing irritation between the superintendent and the supervisor, the engineers and supervisor, and the superintendent and engineers, the situation came to a head when the superintendent revoked the learning bonus and returned the painting operation to its original status: the hooks moved again at their constant, time-studied, designated speed. Production dropped again, and within a month all but two of the eight painters had quit. The supervisor stayed on for several months, but feeling aggrieved, then left for another job.

GLOSSARY

Accommodating   Strategy for interpersonal conflict that maximizes the other party's concerns or outcomes.

Active listening   The receiver accepting responsibility for ensuring the proper transmission of the intended meaning in communication.

Adjourning   The stage of group development in which a group disbands.

Administrative intensity   Proportion of administrators and managers in an organization's total work force.

Alternative sources   Other ways to fulfill a resource dependency, thereby reducing an individual's dependence on any one source; a form of slack.

Anchoring-and-adjustment effect   Tendency of individual perceptions or judgments to be similar to a reference point even when the reference point is arbitrary or irrelevant.

Anticipation   Making internal changes in the organization to respond to the environment's demands.

Approach-approach conflict   Occurs when an individual must choose between two equally attractive options, both with positive outcomes.

Approach-avoidance conflict   Occurs when an individual must choose among options with both positive and negative outcomes.

Arbitration   Resolution of a conflict by a neutral third party who, after hearing both sides of a dispute, determines a final, binding outcome.

Attention   Individuals' choice of where to direct and how to ration their limited sensory input system.

Attitudes   Beliefs and feelings that lead an individual to respond consistently to people, ideas, and situations.

Attribution   Process of perceiving the causes of actions and outcomes; provides models of how other people function, what their motives are, and what determines their behaviors.

Automation   Using machines to replace or assist workers.

Availability bias   Assessing the frequency or likelihood of an event's occurrence by how easily it is remembered, even though memory recall is influenced by factors unrelated to the frequency of an event.

Avoidance-avoidance conflict   Occurs when an individual must choose between two equally unattractive options, both with negative outcomes.

Avoiding   Strategy for interpersonal conflict that is suitable when the positions of both parties are trivial or when one party is seriously outmatched by the other party.

Behaviorally anchored rating scale (BARS)   Employee evaluation format in which the organization analyzes a particular job to determine what types of behavior reflect varying degrees of performance, using actual descriptions of behavior to define the ratings.

Behaviorally healthy organization One whose internal interaction patterns put it in a position to become and remain financially sound; arises from successful communication, adaptation, innovation, and succession.

Behaviorism View of human motivation that all behavior can be understood by examining only contingencies and consequences.

Belief system Stored set of theories and expectations about how and why the world works.

Beneficence Generosity, leniency, and helpfulness of the environment concerning needed resources.

Bottom-up problem solving Involving workers in all phases of the change process, beginning with diagnosis.

Boundary spanners Individuals such as liaisons who represent an organization in interactions with the forces in its environment.

Bounded rationality A model of individual decision making that diverges from the rational ideal in being based on a limited perspective, the sequential evaluation of alternatives, satisficing, and the use of judgmental heuristics.

Brainstorming Group creativity technique facilitating free discussion and exchange of ideas by withholding criticism of ideas, encouraging unusual ideas, generating as many ideas as possible, and piggybacking ideas.

Buffer Mechanism that reduces the environmental shocks or interdepartmental conflict to allow an organizational unit to complete its task more smoothly.

Bureaucracy Form of organization in which there are clearly defined lines of authority and responsibility for members, and behavior is tightly controlled by rules, policies, and job assignments.

Bystander apathy Failure of observers to lend assistance in emergency situations; an example of the results of social anchoring effects on judgment.

Career ladder Specific series of jobs or experiences necessary to advance in an organization.

Cautious shift Tendency of a group as a whole and each member to be less willing to accept risk after a group discussion than prior to it.

Centralization Resting decision-making power with one or a few individuals, based on the competing needs of coordination and division of labor.

Charisma Persuasiveness derived from personal characteristics desired or admired by a reference group.

Charismatic leadership Process used by transformational leaders to develop a common vision of what could be, discover or create opportunities, and strengthen organizational members' control of their own destinies.

Closed system Completely self-contained organization that functions apart from and is unaffected by what goes on around it.

Coalition Collection of individuals who band together to combine their individual sources of power.

Code of ethics Mechanism for institutionalizing ethics within an organization that describes the general value system of the organization, its purpose, and guidelines for decision making consistent with these principles.

Codetermination Policy of allowing workers a say in major organizational decisions, not just minor operational decisions.

Coercion Threat of punishment for not engaging in appropriate behaviors.

Cognitions Beliefs and thoughts: the information processing that goes on inside an individual's head.

Collaborating Strategy for interpersonal conflict that is suitable when both your own and the other party's concerns are equally important, when the issue is too important to compromise, when trying to engender commitment among the parties, or when trying to gain insight.

Collectivity stage Second phase of the organizational life cycle, in which management concentrates on human resource issues such as cooperation, employee commitment, and morale, and in which the beginnings of formal systems such as structured departments, job assignments, and a hierarchy of authority are seen.

Colorism Predisposition to act in a certain manner because of a person's skin color.

Commanding Management function of directing and motivating the work force, often by generating direction and enthusiasm for work through leadership.

Communication The transmitting of information and understanding through the use of symbols.

Communication network The constellation of communication channels through which information flows in a group or organization.

Comparable worth discrimination Discrimination in which men are paid more than women for jobs that are substantially equal in terms of skill, ability, and effort required.

Compensation system A major way an organization conveys to its employees what it wants done and how they should behave, consisting of wages or salaries, benefits, nonre-curring financial rewards, and noneconomic rewards.

Competing Strategy for interpersonal conflict that is suitable when the individual is concerned about his or her own needs, issues, or outcomes, such as when in an emergency or critical situation, when the other party is untrustworthy, or when the individual or group is sure of the correct solution.

Complex learning Form of learning requiring acquisition of new behaviors not yet available in a worker's behavioral repertoire.

Complexity Overabundance of inputs that managers must keep track of, consider, and manage.

Compromise coalition Coalition in which all members are interested in the same issues but each is flexible enough about specifics to make sure that the coalition gets its way.

Compromising Strategy for interpersonal conflict that is suitable when both sets of goals are important but not worth the potential disruption of more aggressive strategies.

Computer-integrated manufacturing (CIM) Manufacturing technologies that combine task mechanization with computerized information processing about the task.

Conditioning The use of reinforcement and punishment to create habits.

Conflict Differences among the perceptions, beliefs, and goals of organization members.

Conformity Form of social inhibition in which a group member engages in a behavior or professes a belief that is encouraged by the group even though the member believes it is incorrect or inappropriate.

Consequences A central concept of the law of effect: the good or bad results following from a behavior.

Construction Process of perceiver organizing and editing sensory inputs in a way that makes them potentially meaningful; subject to both input source and perceiver influences.

Content theories of motivation Theories that focus on the factors within people that motivate them to perform; for example, the theories of Maslow, Herzberg, and McClelland.

Contingency A central concept of the law of effect: the relationships between actions and their outcomes.

Contingency model of leadership Theory suggesting that leadership effectiveness is determined both by the characteristics of the leader and by the level of situational favorableness that exists.

Contingency theory Approach to organizational behavior stating that choice of appropriate management technique is dependent on the particular situation.

Contract Control strategy of managing environmental demands using a legally binding document that guarantees an organization delivery of and terms for a particular resource.

Contrast effect Tendency of individual perceptions or judgments to be seen as very different from an extreme reference point.

Contributions The productive capacity toward achieving an organization's purpose offered by an individual who is entering into a psychological contract.

Control Molding the environment to fit the organization's needs.

Controlling Monitoring and correcting the progress of an organization toward its goals.

Coordinating Management function of creating a structure through which members can produce the organization's central goods or services.

Corporate responsibility Need for an organization to take or avoid actions in order to measure up to society's moral and ethical standards.

Covariation Central principle of attribution theory, stating that behaviors are attributed to causes that are present when the behaviors are present and absent when the behaviors are absent; covariation is judged by distinctiveness, consensus, and consistency.

Creativity Individualistic, novel, idea-generating process.

Critical incidence file A memory aid containing examples of an employee's behavior to help managers prepare for performance appraisals.

Critical incidents Particularly successful or disastrous new behaviors that lead to the establishment of new group policies or norms.

Cross-training Encouraging workers to learn their coworkers' jobs; provides challenges for workers and flexibility for management.

Custodial leadership Process used by transactional leaders to improve working conditions, compensation, and fringe benefits.

Data handback Providing employees with the results of the questionnaires used in survey-guided development in order to assess whether the picture of the organization painted by the survey is accurate, and to solicit their suggestions about the implications of the survey results for problem diagnosis.

Decision tree A common type of decision aid using four types of information: possible courses of action, events that might follow from these actions, likelihood of each event, and value of each event.

Decoding The process by which receivers extract meaning from a message.

Deindividuation Submersion of personal identities and personal responsibility of group members in the identity group.

Delegator One who returns responsibility for dispute resolution to the involved parties, or passes that responsibility to someone else.

Delphi technique Group decision-making technique that minimizes interaction among members; members complete mailed questionnaires and a coordinator summarizes results.

Departmentalization Grouping tasks into organizational units according to the knowledge and skills required or based on similar levels of skills and abilities.

Diagnosis First stage in the process of change; figuring out what actions to take in response to signals that change is needed; includes identifying the problem, causes, and an appropriate and effective solution.

Diffusion of responsibility Sharing the credit or blame for the outcomes of a group's actions over the entire group.

Distributive justice Fair treatment of employees in awarding organizational rewards or in administering organizational punishment.

Distributive negotiation Common negotiation strategy in which parties decide only how to allocate a fixed amount of resources.

Downsizing Reducing the size of an organization's work force.

Effectiveness Ability of an organization to accomplish an important goal, purpose, or mission.

Efficiency Amount of effort required to deliver a promised good or service; can be increased through specialization and economies of scale.

Elaboration stage Fourth and last phase of the organizational life cycle, in which management redirects the organization's emphasis from bureaucracy to a renewed interest in cooperation and teamwork, and in which decentralization often occurs and innovation and creativity are once again valued.

Empathy The ability of one individual to appreciate another's perspective.

Employee assistance programs Typically in-house or contractual programs that diagnose and treat a variety of stress-related problems, such as drug and alcohol abuse and other emotional and psychological problems.

Employee (socioemotional)-oriented leadership Process used by leaders that emphasizes the individual worker's needs in managing group performance; also called *initiating consideration*.

Employee Stock Ownership Plan (ESOP) Group-based incentive plan in which an organization contributes to a trust fund to buy stock, which is allocated to employees based on seniority.

Enacted environment The process of perceiving the environment and acting on those perceptions, which in turn changes the environment being perceived.

Encoding The process of creating a message.

Enhancement Attempt to augment the positive consequences of one's behavior to increase the perception of fairness among employees; the opposite of justification.

Entitling tactic Attempt to gain responsibility for positive events and their consequences in order to increase the perception of fairness among employees; the opposite of excuse.

Entrepreneurial stage First phase of the organizational life cycle in which the organization comes into existence and the founders concentrate on creating the product or service and surviving as an organization.

Environmental scanning Process of anticipation in which the organization collects information from the environment.

Equity Workers' judgments of fairness based on the ratio of work outcomes to work inputs.

Escalation Committing additional resources to failing causes based on the slim hope that there will be a dramatic change.

Expectancies Workers' cognitions concerning the likely consequence of their actions.

Expectancy theory Theory stating that worker behaviors are a function of workers' *beliefs* about consequences and contingencies.

Expected value Value of an option, determined by summing the values assigned to each possible consequence of an action, multiplied by the probabilities that each of these possible consequences will occur.

Expert power Individual power based on the possession of special information, knowledge, or ability.

Expert systems Computer programs that mimic the thought processes of an expert decision maker or problem solver.

Explicitness Extent to which individuals cannot deny that a behavior occurred, serving to commit individuals to their actions.

Exposure The extent to which an individual openly and candidly divulges feelings and information when communicating.

External change agents Expert consultants from outside an organization that management brings in specifically to facilitate a change.

Externalities Causes of a worker's behaviors or the consequences of those behaviors that are beyond the worker's control.

Extrinsic rewards Rewards like money or praise provided in exchange for appropriate behaviors.

Factfinding Form of third-party intervention in which a neutral third party determines a reasonable solution based on evidence presented by the parties, who are not bound to follow the recommendation.

Feedback Receiver's reaction to a sender's message.

Five stages perspective A theory of group development proposing that all groups pass through a predetermined sequence of developmental phases.

Flextime work scheduling Method of context enrichment in which management gives workers limited discretion in arranging their work hours.

Forecasting Process of environmental anticipation in which the organization uses mathematical models to predict future environmental demands.

Formalization stage Third phase of the organizational life cycle, in which management values stability, efficiency, rules and procedures, and other bureaucratic trends.

Forming   Stage of group development in which group members decide whether to join the group, learn the traits and strengths of other members, and identify a leader.

Framing   Judgmental heuristic that decision makers use to deal with risk in which they become increasingly likely to take risks when confronting potential losses and increasingly likely to avoid risks when confronting possible gains.

Free rider   Person who accepts the benefits of being a member of a group but is unwilling to contribute to the good of the group.

Fundamental attribution error   Tendency of individuals to perceive others' behaviors as caused primarily by stable, internal characteristics (such as personality) and to perceive their own behavior as primarily a response to environmental characteristics.

Glass ceiling   Barrier that keeps women as a group from advancing to executive management simply because they are women and not because of their individual ability.

Goal   A specific direction for action and a specific quantity of work to be accomplished.

Goal commitment   Extension of effort, over time, toward the accomplishment of a goal and an unwillingness to give up or lower the goal.

Gold-collar managers   Managers who combine business know-how with technical expertise in how to get people and machines to work together (rather than fight each other) in the workplace.

Grapevine   An informal communication network in an organization.

Group   Organized system of two or more individuals who are interrelated so that the system performs some function, has a standard set of role relationships among its members, and has a set of norms that regulate the function of the group and each of its members.

Group cohesiveness   The desire of a group's members to remain together as a group.

Group development   The process of identifying and resolving present and future group interaction problems.

Group objectives   Goals, purposes, and functions that a group is trying to achieve.

Groupthink   Tendency in highly cohesive groups for members to seek consensus so strongly that they lose the willingness and ability to evaluate one another's ideas critically.

Growth need strength   Interest of a worker in growing and developing on the job.

Habit   Tendency of a person or an organization to do things the same way, over and over again.

Halo effect   Tendency for an individual's perception of an input on one dimension to influence his or her perceptions of that input on other dimensions.

Horizontal conflict   Conflict between people at similar organizational levels.

Horizontal integration   Involvement of an organization in several different activities (e.g., product lines) in order to distribute its resource-dependence risks across a variety of activities.

Human resources   View of workers' mental capabilities as key resources in organizational efficiency and effectiveness; emphasizes worker participation for more informed organizational planning and decision making.

Hygiene factors In two-factor theory, workers' basic needs of pay, safety on the job, quality of supervision, and social environment, fulfillment of which prevents dissatisfaction.

Idiosyncrasy credits Leeway given to group members to violate group rules and norms because of consistent past adherence to those rules and norms.

Image advertising Attempts to influence the environment's overall perception of an organization.

Individualistic decision making Each member of the group independently selects his or her most preferred alternative without interacting with other group members.

Inducements The compensations of steady employment and payment offered to an individual by an organization that is entering into a psychological contract.

Inertia Tendency of an object to continue in the same direction with the same velocity or intensity unless impacted by some force of change.

Informal organization Interpersonal realities of an organization, such as employees' personal goals, perceptions, and beliefs, that are not part of the organization's formal goals and plans but that must be taken into account to achieve organizational efficiency and effectiveness.

Information overload State of perceivers when their sensory input systems are overwhelmed with new, unusual, attention-grabbing inputs.

Information richness The information-carrying capacity of an item of data.

Ingratiation Doing nice things for someone in the hope of creating a sense of obligation in the individual to return the favor.

Input source influences Characteristics of a source object or event that affect perceivers' attempts to direct their attention, including motion, distinctiveness, novelty, vividness, contrast effect, anchoring-and-adjustment effect, and halo effect.

Inquisitor Informal third-party role in a dispute in which a manager exerts a high degree of control over both the outcome and the process of conflict resolution.

Instability Rate of change in an organization's environment.

Instrumentality Workers' belief that attaining the required levels of performance will produce desired personal outcomes.

Integrating device Strategy of conflict management aimed at enhancing communication across groups and maintaining appropriate levels of interaction.

Integration Role of management defined by D. McGregor as the creation of conditions such that members of the organization can best achieve their own goals by directing their efforts toward the success of the enterprise.

Integrative bargaining A more cooperative negotiation strategy that assumes there can be an expanding amount of resources for the parties to divide.

Interactive justice Equitable treatment of employees in interpersonal treatment by managers.

Interlocking directorates Negotiation strategy for managing environmental demands in which a corporation appoints to its board of directors representatives from a variety of organizations on which it is dependent.

Interpretation In perception, the process of assigning meaning to a constructed representation of an object or event.

Intrinsic rewards Rewards that occur naturally as the product of engaging in a behavior.

Irreversibility Extent to which behavior cannot easily be revoked or undone, serving to commit individuals to their actions.

Jargon Special words or common words used with special meaning that summarize a group's common experiences and history and allow simple communication of complex meanings.

Job analysis Gathering of information about a job in an organization, including a description of tasks and activities, results (products or services), and the equipment, materials, and working conditions that characterize the job.

Job characteristics model Theory of job enrichment in which the presence of five job characteristics (skill variety, task identity, task significance, autonomy, and feedback) leads to critical psychological states (meaningfulness of work, responsibility for work outcomes, and knowledge of work activity results) that in turn result in positive work-related outcomes such as productivity and worker satisfaction.

Job description A written document that specifies an individual's role in the organization.

Job enlargement Redesign of work tasks that increases the number of tasks in a job to make it more interesting and involving.

Job enrichment Redesign of work tasks that makes a job more interesting and involving by allowing workers to fulfill higher-order needs such as achievement and control.

Job rotation Method of increasing workers' skill variety by allowing them to switch jobs occasionally.

Job specialization Division of the overall mission of an organization into various smaller tasks.

Johari Window A device for assessing and categorizing managers' communication styles along the dimensions of exposure and feedback.

Joint venture Two or more unrelated organizations that pool their resources to collaborate on projects.

Judge Informal third-party role in a dispute in which a manager exerts a high degree of control over the outcome of a dispute but not the process by which it is resolved.

Judgmental heuristics Rules of thumb, or shortcuts, that reduce the information-processing demands on decision makers.

Laboratory research Carefully controlled experimentation and observation outside of traditional organizational settings in order to identify and isolate important cause-and-effect relationships.

Leader-member exchange model Model based on exchange theory that stresses the importance of individual relationships between leader and subordinates. Each relationship is termed a vertical dyad.

Leadership Increment of influence over and above an employee's mechanical compliance with routine directives of the organization.

Learned helplessness Workers' beliefs that they are incapable of producing a required performance or that the required performance, even if produced, would not lead to desired consequences; causes the worker to stop trying.

Learned needs Content theory of motivation proposing that three categories of needs—affiliation, power, and achievement—are learned, not innate, desires.

Least-preferred coworker (LPC) scale Questionnaire that measures how respondents characterize their feelings about a person with whom they work least effectively. A high LPC score (favoring the least preferred coworker) suggests that the leader derives satisfaction and a sense of accomplishment from relationships with others; a low LPC score suggests that the leader emphasizes completing tasks, even at the expense of interpersonal relationships.

Legitimate power Individual power based on individuals' authority to control the behavior of others for their own good and for the good of a social system.

Line-staff conflict Conflict between employees involved directly in some aspect of producing the organization's product and employees who provide technical and advisory assistance to the line.

Lobbying Negotiation strategy for managing environmental demands in which a representative of an organization convinces source of resource dependence in the environment of the correctness of the organization's perspective.

Locus of control A trait which represents the extent to which people think they can control the consequential events in their lives.

Logrolling Form of coalition in which participants lend each other power so that each can pursue interests not shared by other coalition members.

Loose coupling Relationship of an organization and its environment in which what happens in the environment may or may not be reflected by immediate changes in the organization.

Machine bureaucracy Organizational structure using highly specialized and routine tasks, formalized procedures for the transformation process, a proliferation of rules and communication channels, a functional departmentalization structure, a large span of control, and an elaborate administrative and technical structure.

Management A prescriptive view of what organizations are supposed to accomplish and how they are supposed to accomplish it, including planning, organizing, coordinating, commanding, and controlling.

Managerial functions Activities that must be performed for organizations to outperform individuals, including planning, organizing, staffing, and controlling.

Managerial grid Leadership training program conducted by Robert Blake and Jane Mouton that reflects two dimensions of leader behavior: concern for production (task-oriented leadership) and concern for people (socio-emotional leadership).

Managerial leadership Process used by transactional leaders to provide subordinates work that is less routine and more challenging, build cohesive work teams, and give employees more say in decisions that affect them directly.

Mechanization Programming a machine to execute the component actions of a work task faster, more precisely, and more consistently than any human.

Mediation Resolution of a conflict by a neutral third party who can control the interaction between the disputants but has no authority to force a solution on them.

Mentor A senior employee whose primary role is to instruct younger, less experienced protégés.

Moderating variable A variable which influences the effects of another variable on behavior.

Motivators In two-factor theory, factors that provide worker satisfaction, such as the opportunity for achievement, responsibility, and recognition through work.

Movement Third stage in the process of change; implementation of the change plan.

Negotiation The process whereby two or more parties decide what each will give and take in an exchange between them.

Neutralizers of leadership Factors that paralyze, destroy, or counteract the effectiveness of leader behaviors, making it difficult for them to have an impact.

Noise Any characteristics in the immediate context of communicating individuals that interferes with communication.

Nominal group technique (NGT) Group decision-making technique that focuses on generating alternatives and selecting among them by asking group members to independently write down ideas, present them in turn, clarify them for the group, and rank them by voting privately.

Nonverbal communication Interpersonal communication through any channel other than formal verbal communication.

Norm Informal, unstated rules that govern and regulate group behavior.

Norming Stage of group development in which group members define a set of rules and roles to coordinate group interaction and make pursuit of the goals effective.

Objective self-awareness Individuals' perceptions of their own roles in causing behaviors and their consequences.

"Old boy" network An exclusionary informal communication network in an organization.

Open system Organization whose activities are inescapably influenced by its environment.

Open systems theory Management theory proposed by D. Katz and R. Kahn, which focuses on the assumptions that organizations are (1) social systems in which changes in one part are reflected by changes in other parts, and (2) open to influence from the environment.

Organic structure Flexible organizational structure that can respond efficiently and effectively to new demands placed on it.

Organization Form of human association for the attainment of a common purpose by combining the talents and efforts of its members.

Organization design Process of actively creating a structure composed of groups of activities, roles, or positions to coordinate the interdependencies among organizational actors effectively.

Organization survey A questionnaire used to capture and understand what employees think about a variety of issues.

Organizational atrophy Organization's use of a particular response to a situation long after the situation has changed.

Organizational behavior The description and explanation of how people behave in organizations.

Organizational behavior modification (OB–Mod) Systematic application of simple conditioning and reinforcement theory principles to the management of organizational behavior.

Organizational commitment Relative strength of an individual's identification with and involvement in a particular organization.

Organizational culture Expectations and practices of the organization, including shared philosophy, attitude toward employees, leaders and heroes, rituals and ceremonies, and belief about the direction of the organization.

Organizational decline (1) Cutback in the size of an organization's work force, budget, resources, clients, and so on. (2) Mature organization's inability to stay in touch with changing markets, technologies, and client preferences, leading to stagnation, bureaucracy, and passivity.

Organizational development (OD) Systemwide application of behavior science knowledge to the planned development and reinforcement of organizational strategies, structures, and processes for improving an organization's effectiveness.

Organizational life cycle Predictable pattern of evolution of organizations' structure, leadership style, and administrative systems.

Organizational ombudsman An individual whose responsibility it is to interpret policy, counsel disputing parties, resolve disputes, provide feedback, and identify potential problem areas for senior management.

Organizational socialization Process of conveying the organization's goals, norms, and preferred ways of doing things to new employees.

Organizational structure Skeleton of an organization based on the relationship among its positions or roles.

Organizing In Fayol's management functions, arranging for an organization's material and personnel resources.

Outplacement program Finding new jobs for displaced employees or those who choose not to stay on after a major corporate reorganization.

Output customization Extent to which an organization's products or services are influenced by customer needs.

Paralysis of analysis When timely and decisive decision making fails to occur because too much irrelevant, detailed, obsolete, or poorly organized information is readily available.

Partial reinforcement Rewarding an appropriate behavior in a noncontinuous or variable manner, serving to develop desirable work habits that are more resistant to extinction than those acquired under continuous reinforcement.

Perception Process by which individuals receive and interpret sensations from the environment so they may act upon it.

Perceptual set Expectations that a perceiver brings to the perception task, based on suggestions, beliefs, or previous experiences.

Performing Stage of group development in which group members work within the group's structure to pursue the group's and members' goals.

Personality The characteristics that lead an individual to behave in consistent ways over time.

Piece-rate plan Incentive plan in which employees are paid a given rate for each unit produced.

Planning Management thought processes that precede action in an organization.

Political conflict Occurs when different members of an organization pursue conflicting *personal* (rather than organizational) agendas.

Political system Collection of individuals or groups that must work together and speak with one voice even though each has a private agenda to pursue.

Pooled interdependence Exists when each department or unit contributes to the larger good but is not dependent on the others.

Power Ability to influence the attitudes or behavior of others, usually through the control of resources.

Procedural justice Equitable treatment of employees in the processes by which organizational rewards are allocated and punishments are administered.

Process focus Concentration of organizational development on the behavioral (interaction) patterns in an organization that produce or sustain problems.

Process theories of motivation Theories that focus on the process by which rewards direct behavior; for example, expectancy, equity, and reinforcement theories.

Production (task)-oriented leadership Process used by leaders to direct activities related specifically to the task; also called initiating structure.

"Providing impetus" tactic Delegating conflict back to the involved parties with the implied threat that if they don't resolve it, someone else will, and the resolution will not be to either parties' liking.

Psychological contract Set of unwritten, reciprocal expectations between an employee and an organization.

Public relations Negotiation strategy for managing environmental demands in which an organization actively controls its interactions with the environment using activities such as image advertising.

Punctuated equilibrium A theory stating that a project team's development is triggered by the project's deadline.

Punishment Administering an unpleasant consequence (for example, docking a worker's pay) in response to inappropriate work behaviors.

Quality circle (QC) Voluntary groups of workers who meet periodically to discuss and develop solutions to problems related to quality, productivity, or product cost.

Quality-of-work-life (QWL) programs Systemwide attempts to simultaneously enhance organizational effectiveness (usually defined in terms of productivity) and employee well-being through a commitment to participative organizational decision making.

Rationality Basing a decision on careful and calculated action alternatives and their consequences.

Realistic job preview Mechanism used by organizations to present both the desirable and undesirable aspects of the job and the organization, to provide the potential employee with more complete and accurate information about the position.

Reciprocal interdependence Exists when the outputs of one department become the inputs of a second, and the outputs of that second unit become the inputs for the first.

Referent power Individual power based on a high level of identification with, admiration of, or respect for the powerholder.

Refreezing Final stage in the process of change; institutionalizing the change and monitoring the systems that have been put in place to track the consequences of implementing the change.

Regulation Legal restriction of behaviors in or by organizations.

Reinforcement Reward for a behavior that increases the probability that the behavior will be repeated.

Relationship marketing The development of a long-term relationship with prospective customers via intensive information exchange.

Representativeness Decision heuristic based on the belief that an outcome should resemble its cause.

Resource dependence Individual's need for resources, which exposes the individual to influence.

Resource pooling An advantage groups have over individuals by combining the perspectives, ideas, suggestions, and information of all members.

Resource redundancy Preventing the lack of a particular resource by maintaining relationships with several suppliers.

Resource scarcity Not having enough of a particular commodity (for example, food, love, attention, cars, clothes, opportunities, etc.) for all to accomplish their goals.

Reward power Individual power based on the control of resources valued by another; the opposite of coercive power.

Risk Amount of uncertainty associated with a particular decision alternative or choice.

Risk averse Willingness of a decision maker to pay a premium to avoid risk, ignoring the expected-value solution.

Risk neutral Indifference of a decision maker between risky and certain outcomes if they have the same expected value.

Risk seeking Willingness of a decision maker to pay a premium to experience risk.

Risky shift Tendency of a group as a whole and each member to be more willing to accept greater levels of risk after a group discussion than prior to it.

Robot Machine guided by automatic controls to perform various complex functions like a human being.

Role The set of behaviors appropriate to a particular position occupied by individuals in a group or organization.

Role conflict Occurs when two or more role-specific activities, or expectations of other organizational members, are incompatible.

Role differentiation Establishment of clear concepts for group members of their specific duties and responsibilities to the group, based on their individual strengths and weaknesses, and how these duties and responsibilities contribute to the realization of the group's goals.

Role therapy Training technique in which someone from outside the group comes in temporarily to act as a catalyst to improve the effectiveness of group interaction by ensuring that role differentiation has been accomplished appropriately.

Satisficing Foregoing the optimal solution in favor of one that is acceptable or reasonable in order to save the time and effort needed for extended comparisons.

Scientific management Frederick Taylor's theory of careful and systematic observations and prescriptive techniques for designing jobs and incentive pay schemes for rank-and-file factory workers.

Scientific method   Systematic set of procedures for objectively collecting and evaluating information.

Selection   Process of collecting and evaluating information about an individual in order to extend an offer of employment.

Self-efficacy   Workers' beliefs that they can produce required levels of performance by engaging in appropriate work behaviors.

Self esteem   A trait which represents the amount of self-respect an individual has.

Self-fulfilling prophecy   Expectation about how someone is likely to act that actually causes the person to meet the expectation.

Self-perception   Examination of own actions to decide attitudes.

Self-serving bias   Tendency of perceivers to attribute the causes of actions or their outcomes in a way that reflects well on the perceivers or absolves the perceivers from responsibility for poor outcomes.

Semiautonomous work group   Team of workers given full responsibility for a series of tasks (including arrangement and assignment of the work).

Sensation   Process of nerve endings sending inputs to the brain with no meaning attached.

Sequential interdependence   Exists when the outputs of one unit become the inputs of another unit.

Sexual harassment   Verbal or physical conduct of a sexual nature when submission to such conduct is made either explicitly or implicitly a term or condition of an individual's employment, influences employment decisions affecting the individual, or substantially interferes with the individual's work performance or work environment.

Similar-to-me bias   Rating bias in which raters tend to rate more positively those individuals whose background and experience are similar to their own.

Simple structure   Organizational structure common in young or small organizations in which coordination is largely a function of direct supervision, the top manager or entrepreneur has significant control, employees have very little discretionary decision-making power, and there is little formal policy or procedure.

Slack   Excess resources that can minimize conflict because they reduce the amount of necessary interaction.

Social adjustment   Changes the organization must make in response to environmental changes that are unrelated to its actions.

Social anchoring   Forming perceptions or judgments in an extremely uncertain situation by relying on the opinions of others.

Social audit   Mechanism organizations use to see where they stand with respect to corporate-responsibility demands by identifying important issues in the social environment, cataloging the actions the organization is presently taking, and assessing their effectiveness.

Social comparison   Process of having one's perceptions influenced by the comments and perceptions of others.

Social context   The individuals in groups and organizations that provide an influential context for all behavior.

Social facilitation   Tendency for the presence of others to enhance an individual's energy level.

Social information processing Framework of job design that emphasizes the importance of perception and social cues from coworkers and supervisors in understanding how workers react to their jobs.

Social loafing When individuals decrease the amount of effort they put into a task because they are working on that task with other people.

Socio-technical systems An approach to managing that makes technology a central concern in redesigning jobs.

Span of control Number of people reporting to a manager.

Staffing Management function of supplying a work force (people) to fill the organization's designed structures.

Standard hour rate Payment rate per hour based on the amount of time, determined by industrial engineering standards, that it should take to produce each unit.

Status Position of a role in the social hierarchy.

Stereotype Complex set of expectations and beliefs associated with specific personal characteristics, such as sex, race, or occupation.

Stockpile Resource set aside for future use, such as money put into savings for a "rainy day"; a form of slack.

Storming Stage of group development in which the group decides what its goals and priorities will be.

Stress A psychological and physiological response to a substantial imbalance between environmental demands and the individual's ability to cope with them.

Stress quotient The amount of stress a job is likely to generate in the job holder.

Strong situation A situation in which contextual demands are likely to cause everyone to behave the same.

Substitutes for leadership Individual, organizational, and task characteristics that have the capacity to serve the same purposes as leader behaviors.

Succession Turnover, retirement, or promotion of personnel.

Successive approximation Reinforcing increasingly better attempts at a final desired behavior; may include shaping or chaining.

Superstitious behavior Belief that a behavior will be rewarded even though the behavior is in fact irrelevant.

Support systems Elements in an organization that assist personnel in accomplishing their work tasks effectively, such as production technology.

Survey-guided development Use of questionnaires to construct a picture of an organization's internal processes and problems; also called *survey feedback*.

Synergy Mutual influence process of stimulation and encouragement among members of a group.

System 4 Management theory of Rensis Likert proposing that in superior work units management has an optimistic, supportive, and humanistic view of workers, and every worker belongs to a highly cohesive and participative work group with high performance goals and expectations.

Task identity The sense of completion and achievement that occurs when the set of assigned tasks allows the worker to see a process through from start to finish.

Task interdependence Power accruing to a particular job or group of jobs in an organization when two or more employees must depend on each other to complete assigned tasks.

Task significance Worker's sense that a good or poor performance on the job makes a difference to someone.

Team development An inward look by the team at its own performance, behavior, and culture for the purposes of correcting dysfunctional behaviors and strengthening functional ones.

Technological change The rate at which transformation technologies change and develop within an industry.

Technological determinism Perspective that the way a firm is organized (how it makes decisions or how much training its line workers receive, for example) depends on the technology the firm uses to transform its inputs into outputs.

Technological type Joan Woodward's classifications of ways an organization can transform inputs into outputs, which determine behavior in the organization: (A) unit or small-batch production, (B) large-batch production, and (C) mass production or process manufacturing.

Technology The knowledge, tools, and techniques available to an organization to transform inputs into outputs.

Theory of social exchange Theory suggesting that social behavior is an exchange of material and non-material goods (such as approval and prestige), and that in relationships people continually monitor the rewards and costs to work out balanced exchanges.

Theory X Management's traditional view of workers, including the assumptions that workers are naturally lazy, self-centered, and resistant to change and will avoid responsibility, and management must direct, motivate, and control them.

Theory Y View of workers as naturally motivated to work as much as to rest or play; workers will exercise self-direction and self-control in the service of objectives to which they are committed.

Third-party intervention Involvement in a conflict of someone not directly concerned, such as arbitration, mediation, and factfinding.

Time-and-motion studies Scientific management technique of timed observations and experiments to identify the most efficient means for accomplishing a task.

Top-down problem solving Diagnosis of a problem by management, with the rest of the work force being informed only during unfreezing.

Total job situation Seven characteristics of a job derived by C. R. Walker and R. H. Guest, including the worker's immediate job, relation to fellow workers, relation to supervisors, relation to the union, pay and job security, promotion and transfer prospects, and working conditions in the plant.

Total quality management A philosophy about production that emphasizes "building" quality, and that makes quality the responsibility of all workers.

Trait A characteristic, usually expressed as a dimension on which every person can be measured.

Trait-rating scale Employee evaluation format that asks the rater to evaluate the ratee on such factors as dependability, cooperation, leadership, obedience, and loyalty.

Transactional leader   Leader who motivates followers by exchanging rewards for services.

Transformational leader   Leader who arouses intense feeling and generates turbulent one-to-one relationships with followers and is inspirational and concerned with ideas rather than processes.

Two-factor theory   Content theory of motivation framed in terms of factors that affect work dissatisfaction and satisfaction: hygiene factors and motivators.

Two-way communication   Communication in which receivers can return messages to senders.

Type A personality   Set of personality characteristics found in many stress-prone people, such as impatience, competitiveness, and the drive to succeed.

Type B personality   Classification of behaviors found in less stress-prone people, such as a relaxed, easy-going, noncompetitive attitude toward work and life.

Uncertainty   Not knowing for sure; may include future actions or events, or relationships between actions and consequences.

Unfreezing   Second stage in the process of change; lowering barriers to change by selling the diagnosis, understanding the implementation, and preparing for the consequences.

Union   Group of workers who have banded together to give themselves more bargaining power with their employer.

Valence   The perceived value of a behavior's consequences.

Values   An individual's core understanding of what is important to himself or herself.

Vertical conflict   Conflict between people at different levels in an organization.

Vertical integration   Acquisition of one organization by another with the goal of controlling resource dependencies that are important in its production process.

Vicarious learning   Acquiring desirable behaviors by observing the behaviors of other people; also called *social learning*.

Visibility   The observability of behaviors serving to commit individuals to organizations by making their association with them public knowledge.

Volition   Extent to which individuals believe they have a choice in their behaviors, serving to commit them to their actions.

Weak situation   A situation in which the appropriate behavior is not at all obvious and in which people therefore are pretty much free to decide for themselves what to do.

Work simplification   Design of work tasks to be simple and easily mastered so each worker can become expert at some very small number of tasks and learn to do them repeatedly with lightning speed and no mistakes.

Work standards   Scientific management technique of providing specific instructions to workers for doing a task, including expected time for completion and expected volume of output.

◆◆◆◆◆

PHOTO CREDITS

NAME INDEX

Subject index